Get the eBooks FREE!

(PDF, ePub, Kindle, and liveBook all included)

We believe that once you buy a book from us, you should be able to read it in any format we have available. To get electronic versions of this book at no additional cost to you, purchase and then register this book at the Manning website.

Go to https://www.manning.com/freebook and follow the instructions to complete your pBook registration.

That's it!
Thanks from Manning!

D1209284

Praise for the First Edition

The authors blaze through many of the classics of both functional programming and industry programming in a whirlwind tour of Clojure that feels at times more like a class-five tropical storm. You'll learn fast!
> —From the Foreword by Steve Yegge, Google

The Joy of Clojure *wants to make you a better programmer, not just a better Clojure programmer. I would absolutely recommend this to anyone I know who had an interest in Clojure and/or functional programming.*
> —Rob Friesel
> Dealer.com Websystems

Teaches the Tao of Clojure and, oh boy, it's such a joy! Simply unputdownable!
> —Baishampayan Ghose (BG)
> Cofounder & CTO, Qotd, Inc.

The Clojure community, present and future, will be grateful for this book.
> —Andrew Oswald
> Chariot Solutions

Discover the why *not just the* how *of Clojure*
> —Federico Tomassetti
> Politecnico di Torino

The Joy of Clojure *really lives up to its name! Every page oozes with the excitement @fogus and @chrishouser have for the language and its community. This is exactly what makes this book such an enjoyable read, it's hard not to get drawn into the beauty of Clojure when you have two convinced developers sharing their passion with you.*
> —Amazon Reader M.K.

What Irma Rombauer did for cooking, Fogus and Houser have done for Clojure! By going beyond the basics, this book equips the reader to think like a native speaker in Clojure-land.
> —Phil Hagelberg
> Creator of the Leiningen build tool, Heroku

A fun exploration of functional programming and Lisp.
> —Matt Revelle
> Cofounder, Woven, Inc.

The Joy of Clojure

SECOND EDITION

MICHAEL FOGUS
CHRIS HOUSER

MANNING

SHELTER ISLAND

For online information and ordering of this and other Manning books, please visit
www.manning.com. The publisher offers discounts on this book when ordered in quantity.
For more information, please contact

> Special Sales Department
> Manning Publications Co.
> 20 Baldwin Road
> PO Box 261
> Shelter Island, NY 11964
> Email: orders@manning.com

Manning Publications Co.
20 Baldwin Road
PO Box 261
Shelter Island, NY 11964

Development editor: Nermina Miller
Copyeditor: Benjamin Berg
Proofreader: Tiffany Taylor
Typesetter: Dottie Marsico
Cover designer: Marija Tudor

ISBN 9781617291418
Printed in the United States of America
3 4 5 6 7 8 9 10 – DP – 19 18

To Timothy Hart—a hacker of the highest order.
Rest in peace.

brief contents

            12 ▪ Java.next   277
            13 ▪ Why ClojureScript?   310

PART 6   TANGENTIAL CONSIDERATIONS 331

            14 ▪ Data-oriented programming   333
            15 ▪ Performance   363
            16 ▪ Thinking programs   393
            17 ▪ Clojure changes the way you think   423

contents

PART 3   FUNCTIONAL PROGRAMMING 115

foreword to the second edition

In this second edition of *The Joy of Clojure*, Michael Fogus and Chris Houser present a cornucopia of programming concepts, including many of the topics from the programming languages course we taught together for many years. Fundamental programming languages concepts close to our hearts that appear in this book include higher-order functions, lexical scope, closures, tail recursion, mutual recursion, continuations and continuation-passing style, trampolining, lazy sequences, macros, and relational programming. Most important, Fogus and Houser teach you how to define your own *little languages*.

Alan J. Perlis, brilliant language designer and inaugural Turing Award recipient, famously wrote, "There will always be things we wish to say in our programs that in all known languages can only be said poorly." No existing programming language can express precisely those concepts and abstractions needed for your specific application. The only person who can design a language to solve your exact problem is you.

Creating a *little language* to solve a specific problem is the most effective technique yet devised for reducing complexity in software.[1] Two well-known examples are database query languages and the formula languages of spreadsheet applications. These examples are as notable for what they exclude as for what they include, illustrating another of Perlis's epigrams: "A programming language is low level when its programs require attention to the irrelevant." By only including features relevant to the problem, a well-designed little language is inherently high level.

Database query languages illustrate another fundamental aspect of little languages: writing a complete application requires addressing problems in more than

---

[1] Jon Bentley popularized the concept of *little languages* in his article "Programming Pearls: Little Languages," *Communications of the ACM* 29, no. 8 (1986):711-21.

one domain. An application that performs database queries will also make use of other languages. A single little language can't address the exact needs of a nontrivial application any more than can a single general-purpose language.

For this reason, little languages work best in concert. The ideal technique for writing a complex program is to slice it into multiple problem-specific pieces and then define a language for each problem slice. If we slice the program vertically, the result is a "tower" of languages, layered atop one another. Regardless of how we slice the overall problem, we can use the right language, and the right paradigm, for each subproblem.

As with recursion, the art of defining little languages encourages—and rewards—wishful thinking. You might think to yourself, "If only I had a language for expressing the rules for legal passwords for my login system." A more involved example—a story, really—started several years ago, when we thought to ourselves, "If only we had the right relational language, we could write a Lisp interpreter that runs backward."[2] What does this mean?

An interpreter can be thought of as a function that maps an input expression, such as (+ 5 1), onto a value—in this case, 6. We wanted to write an interpreter in the style of a relational database, in which either the expression being interpreted or the value of that expression, or both, can be treated as unknown variables. We can run the interpreter *forward* using the query (interpret ' (+ 5 1) x), which associates the query variable x with the value 6. Better yet, we can run the interpreter *backward* with the query (interpret x 6), which associates x with an infinite stream of expressions that evaluate to 6, including (+ 5 1) and ((lambda (n) (* n 2)) 3). (Brainteaser: determine the behavior of the query (interpret x x).)

Implementing a relational interpreter is tricky, but doing so can be made easier by using a little language specifically designed for relational programming. In the end, our wishful thinking led us to build a tower of languages: a relational Lisp interpreter, on top of a rich relational language, on top of a minimal relational language, on top of a rich functional language, on top of a minimal functional language.[3] (The Lisp interpreter accepts a minimal functional language, turning the tower of languages into a circle!) Given the power of this approach, it isn't surprising that many Lisp implementations—including the Clojure compiler—are built as layers of languages.

Using what you'll learn from Fogus and Houser in *The Joy of Clojure*, you can begin building your own towers of languages, each with its own syntactic forms and evaluation rules, tailored to your specific problem domains. No technique for software development is more expressive or more joyful.

WILLIAM E. BYRD AND DANIEL P. FRIEDMAN
Authors of *The Reasoned Schemer* (MIT Press, 2005)

---

[2] We use *Lisp* to refer to any member of a large family of languages that includes Scheme, Racket, Common Lisp, Dylan, and, of course, Clojure. To us, a Lisp must be homoiconic, have first-class functions, and have some form of macros. (All three concepts are described in this book.)

[3] By *relational language*, we mean a pure logic programming language; or, as in this example, a pure constraint logic programming language.

foreword to the first edition

The authors of this book have taken an ambitious and aggressive approach to teaching Clojure. You know how everyone loves to say they teach using the "drinking from a fire hydrant" method? Well, at times it feels like these guys are trying to shove that fire hydrant right up ... let's just say it's a place where you don't normally put a fire hydrant. This isn't intended as a first book on programming, and it may not be an ideal first book on Clojure either. The authors assume you're fearless and, importantly, equipped with a search engine. You'll want to have Google handy as you go through the examples. The authors blaze through many of the classics of both functional programming and industry programming in a whirlwind tour of Clojure that feels at times more like a class-five tropical storm. You'll learn fast!

Our industry, the global programming community, is fashion-driven to a degree that would embarrass haute couture designers from New York to Paris. We're slaves to fashion. Fashion dictates the programming languages people study in school, the languages employers hire for, the languages that get to be in books on shelves. A naive outsider might wonder if the quality of a language matters a little, just a teeny bit at least, but in the real world fashion trumps all.

So nobody could be more surprised than I that a Lisp dialect has suddenly become fashionable again. Clojure has only been out for three years, but it's gaining momentum at a rate that we haven't seen in a new language in decades. And it doesn't even have a "killer app" yet, in the way that browsers pushed JavaScript into the spotlight, or Rails propelled Ruby. Or maybe the killer app for Clojure is the JVM itself. Everyone's fed up with the Java language, but understandably we don't want to abandon our investment in the Java Virtual Machine and its capabilities: the libraries, the configuration, the monitoring, and all the other entirely valid reasons we still use it.

For those of us using the JVM or .NET, Clojure feels like a minor miracle. It's an astoundingly high-quality language, sure—in fact, I'm beginning to think it's the best I've ever seen—yet somehow it has still managed to be fashionable. That's quite a trick. It gives me renewed hope for the overall future of productivity in our industry. We might just dig ourselves out of this hole we're in and get back to where every project feels like a legacy-free startup, just like it was in the early days of Java.

There are still open questions about Clojure's suitability for production shops, especially around the toolchain. That's normal and expected for a new language. But Clojure shows so much promise, such beautiful and practical design principles, that everyone seems to be jumping in with both feet anyway. I certainly am. I haven't had this much fun with a new language since Java arrived on the scene 15 years ago. There have been plenty of pretenders to the JVM throne, languages that promised to take the Java platform to unprecedented new levels. But until now, none of them had the right mix of expressiveness, industrial strength, performance, and just plain fun.

I think maybe it's the "fun" part that's helped make Clojure fashionable.

In some sense, all this was inevitable, I think. Lisp—the notion of writing your code directly in tree form—is an idea that's discovered time and again. People have tried all sorts of crazy alternatives, writing code in XML or in opaque binary formats or using cumbersome code generators. But their artificial Byzantine empires always fall into disrepair or crush themselves into collapse, while Lisp, the road that wanders through time, remains simple, elegant, and pure. All we needed to get back on that road was a modern approach, and Rich Hickey has given it to us in Clojure.

The Joy of Clojure just might help make Clojure as fun for you as it is for us.

STEVE YEGGE
Google
steve-yegge.blogspot.com

This book is about the programming language Clojure. Specifically, this book is about how to write Clojure code "The Clojure Way." Even more specifically, this book is about how experienced, successful Clojure programmers write Clojure code, and how the language itself influences the way they create software.

You may be asking yourself, "Who are these guys, and why should I listen to them?" Rather than simply appealing to an authority that you know nothing about, allow us to take a few moments to explain how this book came about, who we are, and why we wrote this book in the first place.

Both of us discovered Clojure early on in its life. It's safe to say that there were times when the Clojure IRC channel #clojure (on Freenode) contained only ourselves along with Clojure's designer—Rich Hickey—and a handful of other people. Our story in finding the language is similar to the story of many of its early adopters. That is, our path runs from modern object-oriented languages[4] like Java and C++, through (seemingly) simpler languages like JavaScript and Python, and then into more powerful languages like Scala and Common Lisp before finding Clojure. The precise details of how we found Clojure are unimportant; the point is that we were both searching for something that none of the other languages provided.

What does Clojure provide that none of the other languages can or do? In a nutshell, we think that when you understand Clojure's nature and write code harmonious to this nature, a new perspective on the art of programming and systems construction is revealed. Therefore, the answer to what Clojure provides that those other languages

---

[4] And indeed the younger versions of ourselves were both deeply influenced by the public ponderings of Steve Yegge and Paul Graham.

don't is *enlightenment* (so to speak). We're not the only ones who feel this way; there are projects being developed right now that are deeply influenced by Clojure's nature. From Datomic to Om[5] to Avout to Pedestal, Clojure's influence is apparent. The Clojure Way is starting to spread to other programming languages, including (but not limited to) Scala, Elixir, and Haskell.

In addition to Clojure's influence in the language design arena, many programmers are using the language every day in their work. The use of Clojure and systems written in Clojure to solve hard business problems is growing every day. Since we wrote the first edition, we too have spent our work lives using and learning from Clojure, and naturally this learning prompted a desire to update this book. Although the first edition is still relevant from a factual perspective, we felt that a second edition should include the lessons of our professional use of this amazing language. Nothing in this book is speculative. Instead, we've used every technique and library, from reducibles to core.logic to data-oriented design, to solve real systems problems.

This book is about the Way of Clojure, written by two programmers who use the language on a daily basis and have thought long and hard about its nature. We hope that by thoughtfully reading this book, you can come to an appreciation of Clojure's power and importance.

---

[5] Om is also deeply influenced by the works and ideas of Alan Kay and Bret Victor.

acknowledgments

The authors would like to jointly thank Rich Hickey, the creator of Clojure, for his thoughtful creation, and for furthering the state of the art in programming language design. Without his hard work, devotion, and vision, this book would never have been, and our professional lives would be much the poorer.

We'd also like to thank the brilliant members of the young Clojure community, including but not limited to: Stuart Halloway, Chas Emerick, David Edgar Liebke, Christophe Grand, Meikel Brandmeyer, Brian Carper, Carin Meier, Mark Engelberg, Bradford Cross, Aria Haghighi, Sean Devlin, Luke Vanderhart, Nada Amin, Tom Faulhaber, Stephen Gilardi, Phil Hagelberg, Konrad Hinsen, Tim Baldridge, George Jahad, David Miller, Bodil Stokke, Laurent Petit, Bridget Hillyer, and Stuart Sierra. We'd like to give special thanks to David Nolen and Sam Aaron for rocking our worlds with their wonderful software. And finally, our heartfelt appreciation goes to Daniel Friedman and William Byrd for writing the foreword to the second edition, for their input into chapter 16, and for inspiring many programmers through the years.

Thanks to the following reviewers, who read the manuscript at various stages of its development and provided invaluable feedback: Alejandro Cabrera, Anders Jacob Jørgensen, Cristofer Weber, Heather Campbell, Jasper Lievisse Adriaanse, Patrick Regan, Sam De Backer, and Tom Geudens.

Thanks also to the team at Manning for their guidance and support, starting with publisher Marjan Bace, associate publisher Michael Stephens, our development editor Nermina Miller, and the production team of Kevin Sullivan, Benjamin Berg, Tiffany Taylor, and Dottie Marsico. And thanks again to Christophe Grand and Ernest Friedman-Hill (the primary designer and developer of one of our favorite programming languages, Jess) for their technical reviewing prowess for the first and second editions, respectively.

MICHAEL FOGUS

I'd like to thank my beautiful wife Yuki for her unwavering patience during the writing of this book. Without her, I would never have made it through either iteration. I also owe a great debt to Chris Houser, my coauthor and friend, for teaching me more about Clojure than I ever would've thought possible. I'd also like to thank Dr. Larry Albright for introducing me to Lisp. Additionally, the late Dr. Russel E. Kacher was an early inspiration and instilled in me a passion for learning, curiosity, and reflection. Likewise, the late Tim Good, a colleague and friend, inspired me to work hard and never let a bug rest. Finally, I'd like to thank my boys Keita and Shota for teaching me the true meaning of love and that it's not always about me.

CHRIS HOUSER

My most grateful thanks go to God, the source of all good things. To my parents, thanks for your love and support—your spirit of exploration launched me on a life of wonderful adventure. To my brother Bill, thanks for my earliest introduction to computers and the joys and challenges of programming. To my wife Heather, thanks for your constant encouragement from the very first moments of this book project to the last. To my friend and coauthor Michael Fogus, thanks for the brilliant inspiration and stunning breadth of knowledge you've brought to these pages.

about this book

The only difference between Shakespeare and you was the size of his idiom list—not the size of his vocabulary.

—Alan Perlis[6]

Why learn Clojure?

When this book was conceived, our first instinct was to create a comprehensive comparison between Clojure and its host language, Java. After further reflection, we reached the conclusion that such an approach would be disingenuous at best and disastrous at worst. Granted, some points of comparison can't be avoided, as you'll see occasionally in this book; but Java is very different from Clojure, and to try to distort one to explain the other would respect neither. Therefore, we decided a better approach would be to focus on "The Clojure Way" of writing code.

When we become familiar with a programming language, the idioms and constructs of that language serve to define the way we think about and solve programming tasks. It's therefore natural that when faced with an entirely new language, we find comfort in mentally mapping the new language onto the familiar old. But we plead with you to leave all your baggage behind; whether you're from Java, Common Lisp, Scheme, Lua, C#, or Befunge, we ask you to bear in mind that Clojure is its own language and begs an adherence to its own set of idioms. You'll discover concepts that you can connect between Clojure and languages you already know, but don't assume that similar things are entirely the same.

---

[6] "Epigrams in Programming," ACM *SIGPLAN Notices* 17, no. 9 (September 1982).

We'll work hard to guide you through the features and semantics of Clojure to help you build the mental model needed to use the language effectively. Most of the samples in this book are designed to be run in Clojure's interactive programming environment, commonly known as the Read-Eval-Print Loop (REPL), an extremely powerful environment for experimentation and rapid prototyping.

By the time you're done with this book, the Clojure Way of thinking about and solving problems will be another comfortable tool in your toolbox. If we succeed, then not only will you be a better Clojure programmer, but you'll also start seeing your programming language of choice—be it Java, JavaScript, Elixir, Ruby, J, or Python—in an entirely different light. This reassessment of topics that we often take for granted is essential for personal growth.

Who should read this book?

This book isn't a beginner's guide to Clojure. We start fast and don't devote much space to establishing a running Clojure environment, although we do provide some guidance. Additionally, this isn't a book about Clojure's implementation details,[7] but instead one about its semantic details. This is also not a "cookbook" for Clojure, but rather a thorough investigation into the ingredients that Clojure provides for creating beautiful software. Often we'll explain how these ingredients mix and why they make a great match, but you won't find complete recipes for systems. Our examples directly address the discussion at hand and at times leave exposed wiring for you to extend and thus further your own knowledge. It wouldn't serve us, you, or Clojure to try to awkwardly mold a comprehensive lesson into the guise of a book-length project. Often, language books spend valuable time halfheartedly explaining "real-world" matters totally unrelated to the language itself, and we wish to avoid this trap. We strongly feel that if we show you the "why" of the language, then you'll be better prepared to take that knowledge and apply it to your real-world problems. In short, if you're looking for a book amenable to neophytes that will also show you how to migrate Clojure into existing codebases, connect to NoSQL databases, and explore other "real-world" topics, then we recommend the book *Clojure in Action* by Amit Rathore (Manning, 2011).

Having said all that, we do provide a short introduction to the language and feel that for those of you willing to work hard to understand Clojure, this is indeed the book for you. Further, if you already have a background in Lisp programming, then much of the introductory material will be familiar, thus making this book ideal for you. Additionally, this book is very much a guide on how to write idiomatic Clojure code. We won't highlight every idiom used, but you can assume that if it's in this book, it's the Clojure Way of expressing programs. Although it's by no means perfect, Clojure has a nice combination of features that fit together into a coherent system for solving programming problems. The way Clojure encourages you to think about problems may be

---

[7] Although such a book would be an amazing thing. If you're interested in such a book, then drop a line to Manning asking us to write one.

different than you're used to, requiring a bit of work to "get." But once you cross that threshold, you too may experience a kind of euphoria, and in this book we'll help you get there. These are exciting times, and Clojure is the language we hope you'll agree is an essential tool for navigating into the future.

Roadmap

We're going to take you on a journey. Perhaps you've started on this journey yourself by exploring Clojure beforehand. Perhaps you're a seasoned Java or Lisp veteran and are coming to Clojure for the first time. Perhaps you're coming into this book from an entirely different background. In any case, we're talking to you. This is a self-styled book for the adventurous and will require that you leave your baggage behind and approach the enclosed topics with an open mind. In many ways, Clojure will change the way you view programming, and in other ways it will obliterate your preconceived notions. The language has a lot to say about how software should be designed and implemented, and we'll touch on these topics one by one throughout this book.

Foundations

Every so often, a programming language comes along that can be considered foundational. Occasionally a language is invented that shakes the foundations of the software industry and dispels the collective preconceived notions of "good software practices." These foundational programming languages always introduce a novel approach to software development, alleviating if not eliminating the difficult problems of their time. Any list of foundational languages inevitably raises the ire of language proponents who feel their preferences shouldn't be ignored. But we're willing to take this risk, and therefore table 1 lists programming languages in this category.

Table 1 Foundational programming languages

Year	Language	Inventor(s)	Interesting reading
1957	Fortran	John Backus	John Backus, "The History of Fortran I, II, and III," IEEE *Annals of the History of Computing* 20, no. 4 (1998).
1958	Lisp	John McCarthy	Richard P. Gabriel and Guy L. Steele Jr., "The Evolution of Lisp" (1992), www.dreamsongs.com/Files/HOPL2-Uncut.pdf.
1959	COBOL	Design by committee	Edsger Dijkstra, "EWD 498: How Do We Tell Truths That Might Hurt?" in *Selected Writings on Computing: A Personal Perspective* (New York: Springer-Verlag, 1982).
1968	Smalltalk	Alan Kay	Adele Goldberg, *Smalltalk-80: The Language and Its Implementation* (Reading, MA: Addison-Wesley, 1983).

Table 1 Foundational programming languages *(continued)*

1972	C	Dennis Ritchie	Brian W. Kernighan and Dennis M. Ritchie, *The C Programming Language* (Englewood Cliffs, NJ: Prentice Hall, 1988).
1972	Prolog	Alain Colmerauer	Ivan Bratko, *PROLOG: Programming for Artificial Intelligence* (New York: Addison-Wesley, 2000).
1975	Scheme	Guy Steele and Gerald Sussman	Guy Steele and Gerald Sussman, "The Lambda Papers," http://mng.bz/sU33.
1983	C++	Bjarne Stroustrup	Bjarne Stroustrup, *The Design and Evolution of C++* (Reading, MA: Addison-Wesley, 1994).
1986	Erlang	Telefonaktiebolaget L. M. Ericsson	Joe Armstrong, "A History of Erlang," *Proceedings of the Third ACM SIGPLAN Conference on History of Programming Languages* (2007).
1987	Perl	Larry Wall	Larry Wall, Tom Christiansen, and Jon Orwant, *Programming Perl* (Cambridge, MA: O'Reilly, 2000).
1990	Haskell	Simon Peyton Jones	Miran Lipovača, "Learn You a Haskell for Great Good!" http://learnyouahaskell.com/.
1995	Java	Sun Microsystems	David Bank, "The Java Saga," *Wired* 3.12 (1995).
2007	Clojure?	Rich Hickey	You're reading it.

Like them or not, there's little dispute that the listed programming languages have greatly influenced the way software is constructed. Whether Clojure should be included in this category remains to be seen, but Clojure does borrow heavily from many of the foundational languages and from other influential programming languages to boot.

Chapter 1 starts our journey and provides some of the core concepts embraced by Clojure. These concepts should be well understood by the time you've finished the chapter. Along the way, we'll show illustrative code samples highlighting the concepts at hand (and sometimes even pretty pictures). Much of what's contained in chapter 1 can be considered "The Clojure Philosophy," so if you've ever wondered what inspired and constitutes Clojure, we'll tell you.

Chapter 2 provides a fast introduction to specific features and syntax of Clojure.

Chapter 3 addresses general Clojure programming idioms that aren't easily categorized. From matters of truthiness and style to considerations of packaging and nil, chapter 3 is a mixed bag but important in its own right.

Data types

The discussion of scalar data types in chapter 4 will be relatively familiar to most programmers, but some important points beg our attention, arising from Clojure's interesting nature as a functional programming language hosted on the Java Virtual Machine. Java programmers reading this book will recognize the points made concerning numerical precision (section 4.1), and Lisp programmers will recognize the discussion on Lisp-1 versus Lisp-2 (section 4.4). Programmers will appreciate the practical inclusion of regular expressions as first-class syntactical elements (section 4.5). Finally, longtime Clojure programmers may find that the discussion of rationals and keywords (sections 4.2 and 4.3, respectively) sheds new light on these seemingly innocent types. Regardless of your background, chapter 4 provides crucial information for understanding the nature of Clojure's under-appreciated scalar types.

Clojure's novel persistent data structures are covered in chapter 5; this should be enlightening to anyone wishing to look more deeply into them. Persistent data structures lie at the heart of Clojure's programming philosophy and must be understood to fully grasp the implications of Clojure's design decisions. We'll only touch briefly on the implementation details of these persistent structures, because they're less important than understanding why and how to use them.

Functional programming

Chapter 6 deals with the nebulous notions of immutability, persistence, and laziness. We'll explore Clojure's use of immutability as the key element in supporting concurrent programming. We'll likewise show how, in the presence of immutability, many of the problems associated with coordinated state change disappear. Regarding laziness, we'll explore the ways Clojure uses it to reduce the memory footprint and speed execution times. Finally, we'll cover the interplay between immutability and laziness. For programmers coming from languages that allow unconstrained mutation and strict evaluation of expressions, chapter 6 may prove to be an initially mind-bending experience. But with this mind-bending comes enlightenment, and you'll likely never view your preferred programming languages in the same light.

Chapter 7 tackles Clojure's approach to functional programming full-on. For those of you coming from a functional programming background, much of the chapter will be familiar, although Clojure presents its own unique blend. But like every programming language dubbed "functional," Clojure's implementation provides a different lens by which to view your previous experience. For those of you wholly unfamiliar with functional programming techniques, chapter 7 will likely be astonishing. Coming from a language that centers on object hierarchies and imperative programming techniques, the notion of functional programming seems alien. But we believe Clojure's decision to base its programming model in the functional paradigm to be the correct one, and we hope you'll agree.

Large-scale design

Clojure can be used as the primary language for any application scale, and the discussion of macros in chapter 8 may change your ideas regarding how to develop software. Clojure as a Lisp embraces macros, and we'll lead you through the process of understanding them and realizing that with great power comes great responsibility.

In chapter 9, we'll guide you through the use of Clojure's built-in mechanisms for combining and relating code and data. From namespaces to multimethods to types and protocols, we'll explain how Clojure fosters the design and implementation of large-scale applications.

Clojure is built to foster the sane management of program state, which in turn facilitates concurrent programming, as you'll see in chapter 10. Clojure's simple yet powerful state model alleviates most of the headaches involved in such complicated tasks, and we'll show you how and why to use each. Additionally, we'll address the matters not directly solved by Clojure, such as how to identify and reduce those elements that should be protected using Clojure's reference types.

Finally, this part of the book concludes with a discussion of Clojure's support for in-process parallelism in chapter 11.

Host symbiosis

Clojure is a symbiotic programming language, meaning it's intended to run atop a host environment. For now, the most widely used host is the Java Virtual Machine (JVM), but the future bodes well for ClojureScript, a Clojure implementation targeting JavaScript environments. In any case, Clojure provides top-notch functions and macros for interacting directly with its host platforms. In chapter 12, we'll discuss the ways Clojure interoperates with the JVM, and in chapter 13 we'll focus on Clojure-Script interop. Chapter 13 also discusses how ClojureScript was implemented in the Clojure Way and is a nice example of sound program design and implementation.

Tangential considerations

The final part of this book discusses topics that are equally important: the design and development of your application viewed through the lens of the Clojure philosophy. In chapter 14, we'll discuss how Clojure fosters and motivates a data-oriented approach to program design and how such an approach simplifies implementation and testing. After that, we'll show you ways to improve your application's performance in single-threaded applications. Clojure provides many mechanisms for improving performance, and we'll delve into each, including their usage and caveats where applicable, in Chapter 15.

Chapter 16 is a fun chapter in which we explore the growing trend in the Clojure ecosystem to use logic programming techniques to supplement and extend functional programming. This chapter uses the core.logic library to explore "post-functional programming."

To wrap up the book, in chapter 17, we'll address the ways that Clojure changes the ways you look at tangential development activities, such as the definition of your application domain language, testing, error-handling, and debugging.

Code conventions

The source code used throughout this book is formatted in a straightforward and pragmatic fashion. Any source code listings inlined within the text—for example,

(:lemonade :fugu)—are formatted using a fixed-width font. Source code snippets outlined as blocks of code are offset from the left margin and formatted in a fixed-width font:

```
(def population {::zombies 2700 ::humans 9})
(def per-capita (/ (population ::zombies) (population ::humans)))
(println per-capita "zombies for every human!")
```

Whenever a source code snippet indicates the result of an expression, the result is prefixed by the characters ;=>. If the code was added specifically for the second edition of the book, we generally use ;;=> to help you recognize newer code topics. This particular result comment serves a threefold purpose:

- It helps the result stand out from the code expressions.
- It indicates a Clojure comment.
- Because of this, entire code blocks can be easily copied from an E-book or PDF version of this book and pasted into a running Clojure REPL:

```
(def population {::zombies 2700 ::humans 9})
(/ (population ::zombies) (population ::humans))
;=> 300
```

Additionally, any expected display in the REPL that's not a returned value (such as exceptions or printouts) is denoted with a leading ; prior to the actual return value:

```
(println population)
; {:user/zombies 2700, :user/humans 9}
;=> nil
```

In the previous example, the map displayed as {:user/zombies 2700, :user/humans 9} is the printed value, whereas nil denotes the returned value from the println function. If no return value is shown after an expression, you can assume that it's either nil or negligible to the example at hand.

Reading Clojure code

When you're reading Clojure code, skim it while reading left to right, paying just enough attention to note important bits of context (defn, binding, let, and so on). When reading from the inside out, pay careful attention to what each expression returns to be passed to the next outer function. This is much easier than trying to remember the entire outer context when reading the innermost expressions.

All code formatted as either inline or block-level is intended to be typed or pasted exactly as written into Clojure source files or a REPL. We generally don't show the Clojure prompt user> because it will cause copy/paste to fail. Finally, we at times use the ellipsis . . . to indicate an elided result or printout.

Code annotations accompany many of the listings, highlighting important concepts. In some cases, numbered bullets link to explanations that follow the listing.

Getting Clojure

If you don't currently have Clojure, then we recommend you retrieve the Leiningen project-automation tool created by Phil Hagelberg, located at http://leiningen.org/, and install it via the instructions at http://leiningen.org/#install.

The Leiningen REPL

After downloading and installing Leiningen, run the following from your operating system's console:

```
lein repl
```

You may see output from Leiningen indicating installation progress for required libraries, but this is a bootstrapping step needed to run `lein` for the first time. Once it has completed, you'll see something like the following:

```
nREPL server started on port 53337 on host 127.0.0.1
REPL-y 0.2.1
Clojure 1.5.1
    Docs: (doc function-name-here)
          (find-doc "part-of-name-here")
  Source: (source function-name-here)
 Javadoc: (javadoc java-object-or-class-here)
    Exit: Control+D or (exit) or (quit)

user=>
```

There is a point to note about the Clojure REPL provided by Leiningen. First, the REPL that `lein repl` executes is an enhanced version of the base Clojure REPL. In addition to greater error display, the Leiningen REPL provides a fairly nice command-history feature, autocomplete, parenthesis and bracket matching, and command suggestion. For example, if you know the command you wish to use is "update ... something," you can type `update` into the REPL and press the Tab key, whereupon you'll see the following:

```
user=> (update-
update-in       update-proxy
user=> (update-
```

The Leiningen REPL shows all functions and named values starting with the text update currently available in the active (in this case, `user`) namespace.

Now that Leiningen is installed and running, you can start typing code, perhaps from this book. For now, you can try this:

```
(+ 1 2 3 4 5)
```

Pressing the Enter key will cause the REPL to evaluate the call to the + function, displaying the result like so:

```
15
user=>
```

The REPL is a powerful environment in which to actively test and develop code. Most Lisp and Clojure programmers use a REPL of some sort to develop their code, either directly as shown here or indirectly via another development tool such as Emacs, Eclipse, Vim, Light Table, and so on. If you see a developer writing Lisp code, you better believe that a REPL is close at hand.

A Leiningen project file

The beauty of Leiningen is in the simplicity it provides in creating and managing Clojure project dependencies. It does this by taking a project specification file, usually named project.cl; resolving the dependencies listed in the file; and running any extra tasks, such as compilation, testing, or the like. For example, the project.clj file for the source code in this book is shown and explained in the following listing.

Listing 1 project.clj file for *The Joy of Clojure* source code

```
(defproject second-edition "1.0.0"
  :description "Example sources for the second edition of JoC"
  :dependencies [[org.clojure/clojure "1.5.1"]
                 [org.clojure/clojurescript "0.0-2138"]      ← Each project has a
                 [org.clojure/core.unify "0.5.3"]              name and version
                 [org.clojure/core.logic "0.8.5"]]
```
Project runtime dependencies
```
  :source-paths ["src/clj"]
  :aot [joy.gui.DynaFrame]                    ← Namespaces to precompile
  :plugins [[lein-cljsbuild "0.3.2"]]            to JVM bytecode
  :cljsbuild
  {:builds
   [{:source-paths ["src/cljs"]
     :compiler
     {:output-to "dev-target/all.js"
      :optimizations :whitespace
      :pretty-print true}}
    {:source-paths ["src/cljs"]
     :compiler
     {:output-to "prod-target/all.js"
      :optimizations :advanced
      :externs ["externs.js"]
      :pretty-print false}}]})
```
Where the source files are located

lein-cljsbuild requires specific configuration parameters, keyed with the special keyword :cljsbuild

Leiningen is extended via plug-ins, and we use a great ClojureScript build tool

The book won't proceed under the assumption that you're an expert in Leiningen, but we'll mention it from time to time. We recommend reading up on its capabilities, especially if you plan to write Clojure code on a regular basis, because it's the ubiquitous choice.

Downloading code examples

Source code for all working examples in this book is available for download from the publisher's website at www.manning.com/TheJoyofClojureSecondEdition. We also maintain an external version at https://github.com/joyofclojure/book-source that we update occasionally.

Author Online

Purchase of *The Joy of Clojure, Second Edition* includes free access to a private web forum run by Manning Publications where you can make comments about the book, ask technical questions, and receive help from the authors and from other users. To access the forum and subscribe to it, point your web browser to www.manning.com/TheJoyofClojureSecondEdition. This page provides information on how to get on the forum once you are registered, what kind of help is available, and the rules of conduct on the forum.

Manning's commitment to our readers is to provide a venue where a meaningful dialogue between individual readers and between readers and the authors can take place. It is not a commitment to any specific amount of participation on the part of the authors, whose contribution to the AO remains voluntary (and unpaid). We suggest you try asking the authors some challenging questions lest their interest stray!

The Author Online forum and the archives of previous discussions will be accessible from the publisher's website as long as the book is in print.

About the authors

MICHAEL FOGUS is a core contributor to Clojure and ClojureScript with experience in distributed simulation, machine vision, and expert system construction.

CHRIS HOUSER is a key contributor to Clojure and ClojureScript who has implemented many of their features.

about clojure

To fully appreciate Clojure, we hearken back to Paul Graham's essay "Beating the Averages," an interesting look at the inner workings of his company Viaweb during the years before it was bought by Yahoo! Inc. in 1998.[8] Although the essay is interesting as a survey of startup culture, the truly memorable part is the description of how Viaweb used the programming language Lisp as an advantage over its competition. How could a programming language more than 50 years old provide any market advantage versus Viaweb's competitors, which were surely using modern enterprise technologies? We won't repeat the exact terms of the essay, but Graham makes a compelling case for the capability of Lisp to facilitate a more agile programming environment.

As it turns out, Clojure has gained amazing inroads into industry use since its creation and release in 2007. Many developers use Clojure and/or ClojureScript every day to create their software systems and products. Working software developers have discovered, as Graham describes in his essay, the joy and power of using Lisp. Although there is little doubt that Clojure's slice of the proverbial pie for industry programming language use is humble, it's growing from month to month. These are exciting times for the Clojure programming language.

Clojure is a member of the Lisp family of languages and is particularly suited for concurrent software development and supporting functional programming techniques. Like the Lisp described in "Beating the Averages," Clojure provides an environment conducive to agility. Clojure fosters agility in ways that many popular

---

8 April 2001, rev. April 2003, http://paulgraham.com/avg.html.

programming languages can't. Many programming languages are bewitched by most or all of the following:

- Verbosity
- Unavoidable boilerplate
- A long thought-code-feedback loop
- Incidental complexity
- Difficulties in extension
- Deficiencies in supporting crucial or undiscovered programming paradigms

In contrast, Clojure provides a mixture of power and practicality that fosters rapid development cycles. But the benefits of Clojure don't stop with its agile nature—as the clarion call declares, "Multicore is the new hot topic."[9] Although the idea of multicore processors isn't in itself new, its importance is becoming increasingly focused. Until recently, you could avoid concurrent and parallel programming techniques and instead ride the ever-quickening processor wave to better performance. Well, that ride is slowing to a stop, and Clojure is here to help.

Clojure provides a unique mix of functional programming and host symbiosis—an embrace of and direct support for its platforms, in this case the Java Virtual Machine and JavaScript hosts. Additionally, the simplification and often elimination of the complexities involved in coordinated state change have positioned Clojure as an important language moving forward. All software developers must eventually address these problems as a matter of course, and the study, understanding, and eventual utilization of Clojure is an essential path toward conquering them. From topics such as software transactional memory to laziness to immutability, this book will guide you on your way to understanding the "why" of Clojure, in addition to the "how."

We'll be your guides into a thoughtful understanding of the joyfulness in Clojure, for we believe its art is prelude to a new age of software development.

---

[9] Mache Creeger, *ACM Queue 3*, no. 7 (2005).

about the cover illustration

The figure on the cover of *The Joy of Clojure, Second Edition* is captioned "A Janissary in Full Dress." Janissaries were elite infantry units that formed the household troops and bodyguards of the Emperor of the Ottoman Empire. The illustration is taken from Thomas Jefferys' *A Collection of the Dresses of Different Nations, Ancient and Modern* (4 volumes), London, published between 1757 and 1772. The title page states that these are hand-colored copperplate engravings, heightened with gum arabic. Thomas Jefferys (1719–1771), was called "Geographer to King George III." He was an English cartographer who was the leading map supplier of his day. He engraved and printed maps for government and other official bodies and produced a wide range of commercial maps and atlases, especially of North America. His work as a map maker sparked an interest in local dress customs of the lands he surveyed and mapped, and which are brilliantly displayed in this four-volume collection.

Fascination with faraway lands and travel for pleasure were relatively new phenomena in the late 18th century and collections such as this one were popular, introducing both the tourist as well as the armchair traveler to the inhabitants of other countries. The diversity of the drawings in Jeffreys' volumes speaks vividly of the uniqueness and individuality of the world's nations some 200 years ago. Dress codes have changed since then and the diversity by region and country, so rich at the time, has faded away. It is now often hard to tell the inhabitant of one continent from another. Perhaps, trying to view it optimistically, we have traded a cultural and visual diversity for a more varied personal life. Or a more varied and interesting intellectual and technical life.

At a time when it is hard to tell one computer book from another, Manning celebrates the inventiveness and initiative of the computer business with book covers based on the rich diversity of regional life of two centuries ago, brought back to life by Jefferys' pictures.

Part 1

Foundations

Even the most elaborate mansion must begin with a firm if humble foundation. We begin here by pouring a foundation of knowledge on which you'll be able to build a solid understanding about Clojure's less familiar ways. This foundation includes, among other things, the philosophy of programming underlying Clojure, sturdy walls of data and functions, and REPLs and nil puns.

Clojure philosophy

This chapter covers

- The Clojure way
- Why a(nother) Lisp?
- Functional programming
- Why Clojure isn't especially object-oriented

Learning a new language generally requires significant investment of thought and effort, and it's only fair that programmers expect each language they consider learning to justify that investment. Clojure was born out of creator Rich Hickey's desire to avoid many of the complications, both inherent and incidental, of managing state using traditional object-oriented techniques. Thanks to a thoughtful design based in rigorous programming language research, coupled with a fervent look toward practicality, Clojure has blossomed into a programming language playing an undeniably important role in the current state of the art in language design.

In the grand timeline of programming language history, Clojure is an infant, but its colloquialisms (loosely translated as "best practices" or idioms) are rooted in 50+ years of Lisp, as well as 15+ years of Java history.[1] Additionally, the enthusiastic

---

[1] Although it draws on the traditions of Lisps (in general) and Java, Clojure in many ways stands as a direct challenge to them for change.

community that has exploded since its introduction has cultivated its own set of unique idioms.

In this chapter, we'll discuss the weaknesses in existing languages that Clojure was designed to address, how it provides strength in those areas, and many of the design decisions Clojure embodies. We'll also look at some of the ways existing languages have influenced Clojure, and define many of the terms used throughout the book. We assume some familiarity with Clojure, although if you feel like you're getting lost, jumping to chapter 2 for a quick language tutorial will help. This chapter only scratches the surface of the topics that we'll cover in this book, but it serves as a nice basis for understanding not only the "how" of Clojure, but also the "why."

1.1   *The Clojure way*

We'll start slowly.

Clojure is an opinionated language—it doesn't try to cover all paradigms or provide every checklist bullet-point feature. Instead, it provides the features needed to solve all kinds of real-world problems the Clojure way. To reap the most benefit from Clojure, you'll want to write your code with the same vision as the language itself. As we walk through the language features in the rest of the book, we'll mention not just what a feature does, but also why it's there and how best to take advantage of it.

But before we get to that, we'll first take a high-level look at some of

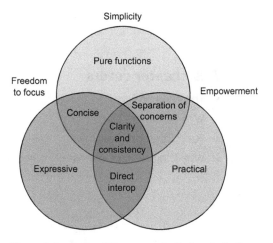

Figure 1.1   Some of the concepts that underlie the Clojure philosophy, and how they intersect

Clojure's most important philosophical underpinnings. Figure 1.1 lists some broad goals that Rich Hickey had in mind while designing Clojure and some of the more specific decisions that are built into the language to support these goals. As the figure illustrates, Clojure's broad goals are formed from a confluence of supporting goals and functionality, which we'll touch on in the following subsections.

1.1.1   *Simplicity*

It's hard to write simple solutions to complex problems. But every experienced programmer has also stumbled on areas where we've made things more complex than necessary—what you might call *incidental complexity* as opposed to complexity that's *essential* to the task at hand (Moseley 2006). Clojure strives to let you tackle complex problems involving a wide variety of data requirements, multiple concurrent threads, independently developed libraries, and so on without adding incidental complexity. It also provides tools to reduce what at first glance may seem like essential complexity.

Clojure is built on the premise of providing a key set of *simple* (consisting of few, orthogonal parts) abstractions and building blocks that you can use to form different and more powerful capabilities. The resulting set of features may not always seem easy (or familiar), but as you read this book, we think you'll come to see how much complexity Clojure helps strip away.

One example of incidental complexity is the tendency of modern object-oriented languages to require that every piece of runnable code be packaged in layers of class definitions, inheritance, and type declarations. Clojure cuts through all this by championing the *pure function*, which takes a few arguments and produces a return value based solely on those arguments. An enormous amount of Clojure is built from such functions, and most applications can be, too, which means there's less to think about when you're trying to solve the problem at hand.

1.1.2 Freedom to focus

Writing code is often a constant struggle against distraction, and every time a language requires you to think about syntax, operator precedence, or inheritance hierarchies, it exacerbates the problem. Clojure tries to stay out of your way by keeping things as simple as possible, not requiring you to go through a compile-and-run cycle to explore an idea, not requiring type declarations, and so on. It also gives you tools to mold the language itself so that the vocabulary and grammar available to you fit as well as possible to your problem domain. Clojure is *expressive*. It packs a punch, allowing you to perform highly complicated tasks succinctly without sacrificing comprehensibility.

One key to delivering this freedom is a commitment to dynamic systems. Almost everything defined in a Clojure program can be redefined, even while the program is running: functions, multimethods, types, type hierarchies, and even Java method implementations. Although redefining things on the fly might be scary on a production system, it opens a world of amazing possibilities in how you think about writing programs. It allows for more experimentation and exploration of unfamiliar APIs, and it adds an element of fun that can sometimes be impeded by more static languages and long compilation cycles.

But Clojure's not just about having fun. The fun is a byproduct of giving programmers the power to be more productive than they ever thought imaginable.

1.1.3 Empowerment

Some programming languages have been created primarily to demonstrate a particular nugget of academia or to explore certain theories of computation. Clojure is *not* one of these. Rich Hickey has said on numerous occasions that Clojure has value to the degree that it lets you build interesting and useful applications.

To serve this goal, Clojure strives to be practical—a tool for getting the job done. If a decision about some design point in Clojure had to weigh the trade-offs between the practical solution and a clever, fancy, or theoretically pure solution, usually the practical solution won out. Clojure could try to shield you from Java by inserting a comprehensive API between the programmer and the libraries, but this could make the use of third-party Java libraries clumsier. So Clojure went the other way: direct, wrapper-free, compiles-to-the-same-bytecode access to Java classes and methods. Clojure strings are Java strings, and ClojureScript strings are JavaScript strings; Clojure and ClojureScript function calls are native method calls—it's simple, direct, and practical.

The decisions to use the Java Virtual Machine (JVM) and target JavaScript are clear examples of this practicality. The JVM, for instance, is an amazingly practical platform—it's mature, fast, and widely deployed. It supports a variety of hardware and operating systems and has a staggering number of libraries and support tools available, all of which Clojure can take advantage of right out of the box. Likewise, in targeting JavaScript, ClojureScript can take advantage of its near-ubiquitous reach into the browser, server, and mobile devices, and even as a database processing script.

With direct method calls, proxy, gen-class, gen-interface (see chapter 10), reify, definterface, deftype, and defrecord (see section 9.3), Clojure works hard to provide a bevy of interoperability options, all in the name of helping you get your job done. Practicality is important to Clojure, but many other languages are practical as well. You'll start to see some ways that Clojure sets itself apart by looking at how it avoids muddles.

1.1.4   *Clarity*

> *When beetles battle beetles in a puddle paddle battle and the beetle battle puddle is a puddle in a bottle ... they call this a tweetle beetle bottle puddle paddle battle muddle.*
>
> —Dr. Seuss[2]

Consider what might be described as a simple snippet of code in a language like Python:

```
# This is Python code
x = [5]
process(x)
x[0] = x[0] + 1
```

After executing this code, what's the value of x? If you assume process doesn't change the contents of x at all, it should be [6], right? But how can you make that assumption? Without knowing exactly what process does, and what function it calls does, and so on, you can't be sure.

Even if you're sure process doesn't change the contents of x, add multithreading and now you have another set of concerns. What if some other thread changes x between the first and third lines? Worse yet, what if something is setting x at the moment the third line is doing its assignment—are you sure your platform guarantees an atomic write to that variable, or is it possible that the value will be a corrupted mix of multiple writes? We could continue this thought exercise in hopes of gaining some clarity, but the end result would be the same—what you have ends up not being clear, but the opposite: a muddle.

---

[2] *Fox in Socks* (Random House, 1965).

Clojure strives for code clarity by providing tools to ward off several different kinds of muddles. For the one just described, it provides immutable locals and persistent collections, which together eliminate most of the single- and multithreaded issues.

You can find yourself in several other kinds of muddles when the language you're using merges unrelated behavior into a single construct. Clojure fights this by being vigilant about separation of concerns. When things start off separated, it clarifies your thinking and allows you to recombine them only when and to the extent that doing so is useful for a particular problem. Table 1.1 contrasts common approaches that merge concepts in some other languages with separations of similar concepts in Clojure that will be explained in greater detail throughout this book.

Table 1.1 Separation of concerns in Clojure

Conflated	Separated	Where
Object with mutable fields	Values *from* identities	Chapter 4 and section 5.1
Class acts as a namespace for methods	Function namespaces *from* type namespaces	Sections 8.2 and 8.3
Inheritance hierarchy made of classes	Hierarchy of names *from* data and functions	Chapter 8
Data and methods bound together lexically	Data objects *from* functions	Sections 6.1 and 6.2 and chapter 8
Method implementations embedded throughout the class inheritance chain	Interface declarations *from* function implementations	Sections 8.2 and 8.3

It can be hard at times to tease apart these concepts in your mind, but accomplishing it can bring remarkable clarity and a sense of power and flexibility that's worth the effort. With all these different concepts at your disposal, it's important that the code and data you work with express this variety in a consistent way.

1.1.5 *Consistency*

Clojure works to provide consistency in two specific ways: consistency of syntax and of data structures. *Consistency of syntax* is about the similarity in form between related concepts. One simple but powerful example of this is the shared syntax of the `for` and `doseq` macros. They don't do the same thing—`for` returns a lazy seq, whereas `doseq` is for generating side effects—but both support the same mini-language of nested iteration, destructuring, and `:when` and `:while` guards.

The similarities stand out when comparing the following examples of Clojure code. Each example shows all possible pairs formed using one of the keywords a or b and a positive odd integer less than 5. The first example uses what's known as a for comprehension and returns a data structure of the pairs:

```
(for [x [:a :b], y (range 5) :when (odd? y)]
  [x y])

;;=> ([:a 1] [:a 3] [:b 1] [:b 3])
```

The second example uses a doseq to print the pairs:

```
(doseq [x [:a :b], y (range 5) :when (odd? y)]
  (prn x y))

; :a 1
; :a 3
; :b 1
; :b 3
;;=> nil
```

The value of this similarity is having to learn only one basic syntax for both situations, as well as the ease with which you can convert any particular usage of one form to the other if necessary.

Likewise, the *consistency of data structures* is the deliberate design of all of Clojure's persistent collection types to provide interfaces as similar to each other as possible, as well as to make them as broadly useful as possible. This is an extension of the classic Lisp "code is data" philosophy. Clojure data structures aren't used just for holding large amounts of application data, but also to hold the expression elements of the application itself. They're used to describe destructuring forms and to provide named options to various built-in functions. Where other object-oriented languages might encourage applications to define multiple incompatible classes to hold different kinds of application data, Clojure encourages the use of compatible map-like objects.

The benefit of this is that the same set of functions designed to work with Clojure data structures can be applied to all these contexts: large data stores, application code, and application data objects. You can use into to build any of these types, seq to get a lazy seq to walk through them, filter to select elements of any of them that satisfy a particular predicate, and so on. Once you've grown accustomed to having the richness of all these functions available everywhere, dealing with a Java or C++ application's Person or Address class will feel constraining.

Simplicity, freedom to focus, empowerment, consistency, and clarity—nearly every element of the Clojure programming language is designed to promote these goals. When writing Clojure code, if you keep in mind the desire to maximize simplicity, empowerment, and the freedom to focus on the real problem at hand, we think you'll find Clojure provides you the tools you need to succeed.

1.2   Why a(nother) Lisp?

> *By relieving the brain of all unnecessary work, a good notation sets it free to concentrate on more advanced problems.*
> —Alfred North Whitehead[3]

Go to any open source project hosting site, and perform a search for the term *Lisp interpreter.* You'll likely get a cyclopean mountain[4] of results from this seemingly innocuous term. The fact of the matter is that the history of computer science is littered

---

[3]   Quoted in Philip J. Davis and Reuben Hersh, *The Mathematical Experience* (Birkhäuser, 1981).

[4]   ... of madness.

(Fogus 2009) with the abandoned husks of Lisp implementations. Well-intentioned Lisps have come and gone and been ridiculed along the way, and yet tomorrow, search results for hobby and academic Lisps will have grown almost without bounds. Bearing in mind this legacy of brutality, why would anyone want to base their brand-new programming language on the Lisp model?

1.2.1 Beauty

Lisp has attracted some of the brightest minds in the history of computer science. But an argument from authority is insufficient, so you shouldn't judge Lisp on this alone. The real value in the Lisp family of languages can be directly observed through the activity of using it to write applications. The Lisp style is one of expressivity, empowerment, and, in many cases, outright beauty. Joy awaits the Lisp neophyte. The original Lisp language, as defined by John McCarthy in his earth-shattering essay "Recursive Functions of Symbolic Expressions and Their Computation by Machine, Part I" (McCarthy 1960), defined the entire language in terms of only seven functions and two special forms: atom, car, cdr, cond, cons, eq, quote, lambda, and label.

Through the composition of those nine forms, McCarthy was able to describe the whole of computation in a way that takes our breath away. Computer programmers are perpetually in search of beauty, and, more often than not, this beauty presents itself in the form of simplicity. Seven functions and two special forms—it doesn't get more beautiful than that.

1.2.2 But what's with all the parentheses?

Why has Lisp persevered for more than 50 years while countless other languages have come and gone? There are probably complex reasons, but chief among them is likely the fact that Lisp as a language genotype (Tarver 2008) fosters language flexibility in the extreme. Newcomers to Lisp are sometimes unnerved by its pervasive use of parentheses and prefix notation, which is different than non-Lisp programming languages. The regularity of this behavior not only reduces the number of syntax rules you have to remember, but also makes writing macros trivial. Macros let you introduce new syntax into Lisp to make it easy to handle specific tasks; in other words, you can easily create *domain-specific languages (DSLs)* to customize Lisp to your immediate needs. We'll look at macros in more detail in chapter 8; but to whet your appetite, we'll talk about how Clojure's seemingly odd syntax makes using them easy.

Clojure looks unlike almost every other popular language in use today. When you first encounter nearly every Lisp-based language, one thing stands out: the parentheses are in the wrong place! If you're familiar with a language like C, Java, JavaScript, or C#, then function and method calls look like the following:

```
myFunction(arg1, arg2);

myThing.myMethod(arg1, arg2);
```

Likewise, arithmetic operations tend to always look like the following:

```
// THIS IS NOT CLOJURE CODE
1 + 2 * 3;
//=> 7
```

But in Clojure, a function and a method call look like this:

```
(my-function arg1 arg2)

(.myMethod my-thing arg1 arg2)
```

Even more astonishing, mathematical operations look the same and likewise evaluate from the innermost nested parentheses to the outer:

```
(+ 1 (* 2 3))
;;=> 7
```

We come from a background in languages with C-like syntax, and the Lispy *prefix notation* took some getting used to. Clojure's extreme flexibility allows you to mold it in many ways to suit your personal style. For example, let's assume that you didn't want to deal with the Lispy prefix notation and instead wanted something more akin to APL (Iverson 1962), where every mathematical operation is strictly evaluated from right to left. A function that handles right-to-left evaluation of mathematical equations of up to four variables is shown next.

> **Listing 1.1   Function that solves math equations, evaluated right to left**

```
(defn r->lfix
  ([a op b]                (op a b))
  ([a op1 b op2 c]         (op1 a (op2 b c)))
  ([a op1 b op2 c op3 d]   (op1 a (op2 b (op3 c d)))))
```

Perhaps you see how this works; but just in case, figure 1.2 shows how the operators are shuffled.

   The operation of r->lfix is as follows:

```
(r->lfix 1 + 2)
;;=> 3
(r->lfix 1 + 2 + 3)
;;=> 6
```

As shown, the basic cases using only a single operator type work as expected. Likewise, mixing operator types seems to work fine:

```
(r->lfix 1 + 2 * 3)
;;=> 7
```

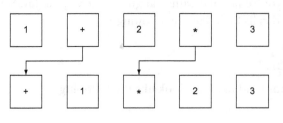

Figure 1.2   Right-to-left shuffle: the r->lfix function shuffles math operators, moving the rightmost infix operations to the innermost nested parentheses to ensure that they execute first.

But changing numbers and shifting operators around shows a potential problem:

```
(r->lfix 10 * 2 + 3)
;;=> 50
```

You might've hoped for 23 because you, like us, were taught that multiplication has a higher precedence than addition and should be performed first. Indeed, 23 is the answer in most C-like languages with infix math operators:

```
// THIS IS NOT CLOJURE CODE

10 * 2 + 3
//=> 23
```

That's OK, because we can change our function to instead use a more Smalltalk-like evaluation order, where mathematical operations are performed strictly from left to right.

Listing 1.2 Function that solves math equations, evaluated left to right

```
(defn 1->rfix
  ([a op b]              (op a b))
  ([a op1 b op2 c]       (op2 c (op1 a b)))
  ([a op1 b op2 c op3 d] (op3 d (op2 c (op1 a b)))))
```

A visualization of how this new operator-shuffling function works is shown in figure 1.3. The multiplication is nested so as to be the first evaluation.

To be doubly sure that everything seems correct, we can try the new function:

```
(1->rfix 10 * 2 + 3)
;;=> 23
```

Looks good. What about some of the other equations? Observe:

```
(1->rfix 1 + 2 + 3)
;;=> 6
```

By now you've probably realized that we're being silly. You could easily break our grade-school expectations with the following:

```
(1->rfix 1 + 2 * 3)
;;=> 9
```

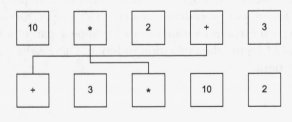

Figure 1.3 Left-to-right shuffle: the `1->rfix` function shuffles math operators, moving the leftmost infix operations to the inner-most nested parentheses to ensure that they execute first.

Just sticking to a strict right-to-left and left-to-right evaluation isn't going to allow us to observe proper operator precedence. Instead, we'd like to devise a way to describe the correct order of operations. For our purposes, a simple map will suffice:

```
(def order {+ 0   - 0
            * 1   / 1})
```

The `order` map describes what the teachers of our youth tried to explain—the multiplication and division operators are weighted more than addition and subtraction and therefore should be used first. To keep things simple, we'll write a new function, `infix3`, that observes the operator weights only for equations of three variables.

Listing 1.3 Function that changes evaluation order depending on operation weights

```
(defn infix3 [a op1 b op2 c]
  (if (< (get order op1) (get order op2))
    (r->lfix a op1 b op2 c)
    (l->rfix a op1 b op2 c)))
```

As you may notice, the operators are looked up in the `order` map and compared. If the leftmost operator is weighted less than the rightmost, we know that the evaluation order should go the other way (right to left). In general terms, the evaluation order should occur starting on the side with the operator with higher precedence.

Checking out the new function shows that everything seems in order:

```
(infix3 1 + 2 * 3)
;;=> 7

(infix3 10 * 2 + 3)
;;=> 23
```

The syntax of any Lisp, and Clojure in particular, seems so different from the norm that many people mistakenly assume the language requires a superhuman effort to learn. Certainly it's possible to expand the `infix3` function to handle any number of nested arithmetic operations,[5] and perhaps that would make such math easier to read, but there are good reasons why Clojure has the syntax it does.

No precedence rules

It seems obvious to us that multiplication has a higher precedence than addition, because that's what we've been taught from time out of mind. But what are the precedence rules for operators like less-than, equals, bitwise-or, and modulo? We personally find it difficult to remember the proper precedence of all the C-like operators and as a result can't immediately type the correct incantation of grouping parentheses to control the evaluation order. In Clojure, the evaluation ordering is always the same—from innermost to out, left to right:

```
(< (+ 1 (* 2 3))
   (* 2 (+ 1 3)))

;;=> true
```

---

[5] We created an example infix parser at www.github.com/joyofclojure/unfix that fits in about 20 lines of code.

We frankly don't buy the precedence argument for why Lisp syntax is great. Certainly it's nice to not worry about precedence rules, but we don't write a huge amount of code that requires us to memorize them. We're personally happy to crack open a Java book or perform a web search to refresh our memories when we forget. But this points to a larger issue. In Clojure, parentheses mean only one thing to the evaluation scheme: aggregating a bunch of things together into a list where the head is a function and the rest of the things are its arguments. In a language like C or Java, the parentheses serve any of the following purposes:

- Aggregating the method, constructor, or function arguments
- A syntax to group method, constructor, or function parameters
- A way to control the evaluation order of a mathematical expression
- The syntax elements of for and while loops
- A way to properly resolve reference casting
- An optional way to group expressions in a return
- A way to group expressions to serve as a method-call target
- General-purpose expression grouping
- Creating capture groups in regular expressions

If you come from a language where parentheses are so overloaded, it's understandable that you might be leery about a Lisp.

ADAPTABILITY IS KEY

As we've mentioned, calls to Clojure functions all look the same:

```
(a-function arg1 arg2)
```

The mathematical operators in Clojure are also functions. In a language like Java, mathematical operators are special and only exist as members of special math expressions. Because a Clojure mathematical operator is instead a function, it can do anything that functions can do, including take any number of arguments:

```
(+ 1 2 3 4 5 6 7 8 9 10)
;;=> 55
```

If all function calls look the same to Clojure, then it's easy to call functions with any number of arguments, because the call and its arguments are bound by the parentheses. The same expression in C or Java would look as follows:

```
// THIS IS NOT CLOJURE CODE

1 + 2 + 3 + 4 + 5 + 6 + 7 + 8 + 9 + 10;
//=> 55
```

Honestly, how often do you need to write something like this? Probably not often at all. But because C and Java operators can only take two arguments, a left side and a right side, performing math on an arbitrary number of numbers requires a completely separate looping construct:

```
int numbers[] = {1,2,3,4,5,6,7,8,9,10};
int sum = 0;

for (int n : numbers) {
    sum += n;
}
```

In Clojure, you can use the `apply` function to send a sequence of numbers to a function as if they were sent as arguments:

```
(def numbers [1 2 3 4 5 6 7 8 9 10])

(apply + numbers)
```

This is nice. Certainly you could create a specialized utility class to hold an array-summation function, but what if you needed a method to multiply a bunch of numbers in an array? You'd need to add it as well. Not a big deal, right? Maybe not, but the Lispy syntax that Clojure uses facilitates viewing functions as operating on collections of data by default. An interesting example is the less-than operator, used in many programming languages as follows:

```
// THIS IS NOT CLOJURE CODE

0 < 42;
//=> true
```

Clojure provides the same kind of behavior:

```
(< 0 42)
;;=> true
```

But the fact that Clojure's < function takes any number of arguments means you can directly express the idea of *monotonically increasing*, best defined with an example:

```
(< 0 1 3 9 36 42 108)
;;=> true
```

If any of the given numbers were not increasing, then the call would be `false`:

```
(< 0 1 3 9 36 -1000 42 108)
;;=> false
```

And this is a key point. The consistency of the function call form allows a great deal of flexibility in the way that functions receive arguments.

REPL PHASES

Clojure programs are composed of data structures. For example, Clojure can see the textual form (+ 1 2) one of two ways:

- The function call to + with the arguments 1 and 2
- The list of the symbol +, number 1, and number 2

What Clojure does with these two different things depends on context. If you open a Clojure REPL and type the following, then an evaluation occurs:

```
(+ 1 2)
;;=> 3
```

This is probably what you'd expect. But Clojure's evaluation model has multiple phases, only one of which is the evaluation phase. The word *REPL* refers to the *Read-Eval-Print Loop* phases shown in figure 1.4.

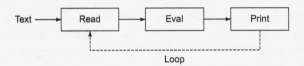

Figure 1.4 The word *REPL* hints at three repeated or looped phases: read, eval, and print.

Most Lisps have the same high-level *phase distinction* separating the text read, from the eval step, from the printing step. But a more realistic picture of Clojure's evaluation phases looks like figure 1.5.

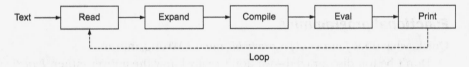

Figure 1.5 More REPL phases: Clojure also has macro-expansion and compilation phases.

The addition of the *expand* and *compile* phases hints at an interesting aspect of most Lisps—macros.

MACROS

We'll talk more about macros in chapter 8, but here we'll spend a page or two discussing the high-level idea behind Clojure macros. By splitting the evaluation into distinct phases, Clojure allows you to tap into some of these phases to manipulate the way that programs are evaluated. Recall from the previous section that to Clojure, (+ 1 2) can be either a list or a function call; the distinction is a matter of context. When you look at the characters on the screen or in this book, the text *(+ 1 2)* is just text. As shown in figure 1.6, after the read phase, Clojure doesn't deal with parentheses, which are just textual demarcations of lists. Instead, after the read phase, Clojure deals exclusively with data structures residing in memory.

But the textual characters work to easily demarcate lists to the reader.[6] Lisps (and Clojure is no exception) have chosen to mirror the list-like textual syntax with the list data structure.[7] By mirroring the syntax with the underlying data representation of code, there's little conceptual distance between the form of the code on the screen and the code that's fed

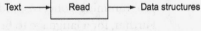

Figure 1.6 The reader takes a textual representation of a Clojure program and produces the corresponding data structures.

---

[6] And for that matter, an editor also, as users of Paredit can attest.

[7] And as you'll soon see, Clojure's textual representation is likewise conceptually tied to the corresponding data structure.

into the compiler. This short conceptual gap facilitates the manipulation of the data that represents a program using Clojure.

The notion of "code is data" is difficult to grasp at first. Implementing a programming language where code shares the same footing as the data structures it comprises presupposes a fundamental malleability of the language. When your language is represented as the inherent data structures, the language can manipulate its own structure and behavior (Graham 1995). Lisp can be likened to a self-licking lollipop—more formally defined as *homoiconicity*. Lisp's homoiconicity requires a great conceptual leap in order for you to fully grasp it, but we'll lead you toward that understanding throughout this book in hopes that you too will come to realize its inherent power.[8]

As we hope you understand, Lisp has its syntax for an excellent reason: to simplify the conceptual model needed for direct program manipulation by the programs themselves. There's a joy in learning Lisp for the first time, and if that's your experience coming into this book, we welcome you—and envy you.

1.3 Functional programming

Quick, what does *functional programming* mean? Wrong answer.

Don't be too discouraged—we don't really know the answer either. *Functional programming* is one of those computing terms[9] that has an amorphous definition. If you ask 100 programmers for their definition, you'll likely receive 100 different answers. Sure, some definitions will be similar, but like snowflakes, no two will be exactly the same. To further muddy the waters, the cognoscenti of computer science will often contradict one another in their own independent definitions. Likewise, the basic structure of any definition of functional programming will be different depending on whether your answer comes from someone who favors writing their programs in Haskell, ML, Factor, Unlambda, Ruby, Shen, or even Clojure. How can *any* person, book, or language claim authority for functional programming? As it turns out, just as the multitudes of unique snowflakes are all made mostly of water, the core of functional programming across all meanings has its core tenets.

1.3.1 A workable definition of functional programming

Whether your own definition of functional programming hinges on the lambda calculus, monadic I/O, delegates, or `java.lang.Runnable`, your basic unit of currency is likely some form of procedure, function, or method—herein lies the root. Functional programming concerns and facilitates the application and composition of functions. Further, for a language to be considered functional, its notion of function must be *first-class*. First-class functions can be stored, passed, and returned just like any other piece of data. Beyond this core concept, the definitions branch toward infinity; but, thankfully, it's enough to start. Of course, we'll also present a further definition of Clojure's

---

[8] Chapters 8 and 14 are especially key in understanding macros.

[9] Quick, what's the definition of *combinator*? How about *cloud computing*? *Enterprise*? *SOA*? *Web 2.0*? *Real-world*? *Hacker*? Often it seems that the only term with a definitive meaning is *yak shaving*.

style of functional programming that includes such topics as purity, immutability, recursion, laziness, and referential transparency, but that will come later, in chapter 7.

1.3.2 *The implications of functional programming*

Object-oriented programmers and functional programmers often see and solve a problem in different ways. Whereas an object-oriented mindset fosters the approach of defining an application domain as a set of nouns (classes), the functional mind sees the solution as the composition or verbs (functions). Although both programmers may generate equivalent results, the functional solution will be more succinct, understandable, and reusable. Grand claims, indeed! We hope that by the end of this book you'll agree that functional programming fosters elegance in programming. It takes a shift in mindset to go from thinking in nouns to thinking in verbs, but the journey will be worthwhile. In any case, we think there's much that you can take from Clojure to apply to your chosen language—if only you approach the subject with an open mind.

1.4 Why Clojure isn't especially object-oriented

Elegance and familiarity are orthogonal.

—Rich Hickey

Clojure was born out of frustration provoked in large part by the complexities of concurrent programming, complicated by the weaknesses of object-oriented programming in facilitating it. This section explores these weaknesses and lays the groundwork for why Clojure is functional and not object-oriented.

1.4.1 *Defining terms*

Before we begin, it's useful to define terms.[10]

The first important term to define is *time*. Simply put, time refers to the relative moments when events occur. Over time, the properties associated with an entity—both static and changing, singular or composite—will form a concrescence (Whitehead 1929), or, in other words, its *identity*. It follows that at any given time, a snapshot can be taken of an entity's properties, defining its *state*. This notion of state is an immutable one because it's not defined as a mutation in the entity itself, but only as a manifestation of its properties at a given moment in time. Imagine a child's flip book, as shown in figure 1.7, to understand the terms fully.

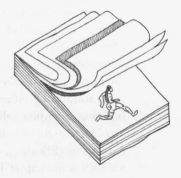

Figure 1.7 The Runner. A child's flip book serves to illustrate Clojure's notions of state, time, and identity. The book itself represents the identity. Whenever you wish to show a change in the illustration, you draw another picture and add it to the end of your flip book. The act of flipping the pages therefore represents the states over time of the image within. Stopping at any given page and observing the particular picture represents the state of the Runner at that moment in time.

---

[10] These terms are also defined and elaborated on in Rich Hickey's presentation "Are We There Yet?" (Hickey 2009).

It's important to note that in the canon of object-oriented programming (OOP), there's no clear distinction between state and identity. In other words, these two ideas are conflated into what's commonly referred to as *mutable state.* The classical object-oriented model allows unrestrained mutation of object properties without a willingness to preserve historical states. Clojure's implementation attempts to draw a clear separation between an object's state and identity as they relate to time. To state the difference from Clojure's model in terms of the aforementioned flip book, the mutable state model is different, as shown in figure 1.8.

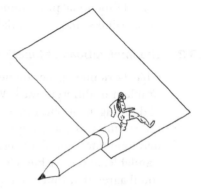

Figure 1.8 **The Mutable Runner.**
Modeling state change with mutation requires that you stock up on erasers. Your book becomes a single page: in order to model changes, you must physically erase and redraw the parts of the picture requiring change. Using this model, you should see that mutation destroys all notion of time, and state and identity become one.

Immutability lies at the cornerstone of Clojure, and much of the implementation ensures that immutability is supported efficiently. By focusing on immutability, Clojure eliminates the notion of mutable state (which is an oxymoron) and instead expounds that most of what's meant by *objects* are instead *values. Value* by definition refers to an object's constant representative amount,[11] magnitude, or epoch. You might ask yourself: what are the implications of the value-based programming semantics of Clojure?

Naturally, by adhering to a strict model of immutability, concurrency suddenly becomes a simpler (although not simple) problem, meaning if you have no fear that an object's state will change, then you can promiscuously share it without fear of concurrent modification. Clojure instead isolates value change to its reference types, as we'll show in chapter 11. Clojure's reference types provide a level of indirection to an identity that can be used to obtain consistent, if not always current, states.

1.4.2 *Imperative "baked in"*

Imperative programming is the dominant programming paradigm today. The most unadulterated definition of an imperative programming language is one where a sequence of statements mutates program state. During the writing of this book (and likely for some time beyond), the preferred flavor of imperative programming is the object-oriented style. This fact isn't inherently bad, because countless successful software projects have been built using object-oriented imperative programming techniques. But from the context of concurrent programming, the object-oriented imperative model is self-cannibalizing. By allowing (and even promoting) unrestrained mutation via *variables,* the imperative model doesn't directly support concurrency.

---

[11] Some entities have no representative value—pi is an example. But in the realm of computing, where we're ultimately referring to finite things, this is a moot point.

Instead, by allowing a maenadic[12] approach to mutation, there are no guarantees that any variable contains the expected value. Object-oriented programming takes this one step further by aggregating state in object internals. Although individual methods may be thread-safe through locking schemes, there's no way to ensure a consistent object state across multiple method calls without expanding the scope of potentially complex locking scheme(s). Clojure instead focuses on functional programming, immutability, and the distinction between state, time, and identity. But OOP isn't a lost cause. In fact, many aspects are conducive to powerful programming practice.

1.4.3 Most of what OOP gives you, Clojure provides

It should be made clear that we're not attempting to mark object-oriented programmers as pariahs. Instead, it's important that we identify the shortcomings of OOP if we're ever to improve our craft. In the next few subsections, we'll touch on the powerful aspects of OOP and how they're adopted and, in some cases, improved by Clojure. To start, we'll discuss Clojure's flavor of polymorphism, expressed via its protocol feature, an example of which is shown next.

> **Listing 1.4   Polymorphic `Concatenatable` protocol**

```
(defprotocol Concatenatable
  (cat [this other]))
```

Protocols are somewhat related to Java interfaces and a distillation of what are commonly known as *mix-ins*. The `Concatenatable` protocol defines a single function `cat` that takes two arguments, the target object and another object, to concatenate to it. But the `Concatenatable` protocol describes only a sketch of the functions that form a protocol for concatenation—there is as of yet no implementation of this protocol. In the next section, we'll discuss protocols in more detail, including their extension to new and existing types.

POLYMORPHISM AND THE EXPRESSION PROBLEM

Polymorphism is the ability of a function or method to perform different actions depending on the type of its arguments or a target object. Clojure provides polymorphism via *protocols*,[13] which let you attach a set of behaviors to any number of existing types and classes; they're similar to what are sometimes called *mix-ins, traits,* or *interfaces* in other languages and are more open and extensible than polymorphism in many languages.

To reiterate, what we've done in listing 1.4 is to define a *protocol* named `Concatenatable` that groups one or more functions (in this case only one, `cat`) defining the set of behaviors provided. That means the function `cat` will work for any object that fully satisfies the protocol `Concatenatable`. We can then *extend* this protocol to the

---

[12] Wild and unrestrained; from the Greek term for a follower of the god Dionysus, the god of wine and patron saint of party animals.

[13] Clojure also provides polymorphic multimethods, covered in depth in section 9.2.

String class and define the specific implementation—a function body that concatenates the argument other onto the string this:

```
(extend-type String
  Concatenatable
  (cat [this other]
    (.concat this other)))
;;=> nil

(cat "House" " of Leaves")

;;=> "House of Leaves"
```

We can also extend this protocol to the type java.util.List, so that the cat function can be called on either type:

```
(extend-type java.util.List
  Concatenatable
  (cat [this other]
    (concat this other)))

(cat [1 2 3] [4 5 6])

;;=> (1 2 3 4 5 6)
```

Now the protocol has been extended to two different types, String and java.util.List, and thus the cat function can be called with either type as its first argument—the appropriate implementation will be invoked.

Note that String was already defined (in this case by Java itself) before we defined the protocol, and yet we were able to successfully extend the new protocol to it. This isn't possible in many languages. For example, Java requires that you define all the method names and their groupings (known as *interfaces*) before you can define a class that implements them, a restriction that's known as the *expression problem.*

A Clojure protocol can be extended to any type where it makes sense, even those that were never anticipated by the original implementer of the type or the original designer of the protocol. We'll dive deeper into Clojure's flavor of polymorphism in chapter 9, but we hope now you have a basic idea of how it works.

The expression problem

The *expression problem* refers to the desire to implement an existing set of abstract methods for an existing concrete class without having to change the code that defines either. Object-oriented languages allow you to implement an existing abstract method in a concrete class you control (interface inheritance), but if the concrete class is outside your control, the options for making it implement new or existing abstract methods tend to be sparse. Many popular programming languages such as Ruby, Scala, C#, Groovy, and JavaScript provide partial solutions to this problem by allowing you to add methods to an existing concrete object, a feature sometimes known as *monkey-patching*; or you can interpose a different object between mismatched types via *implicit conversion*.

SUBTYPING AND INTERFACE-ORIENTED PROGRAMMING

Clojure provides a form of subtyping by allowing the creation of ad hoc hierarchies: inheritance relationships you can define among data types or even among symbols, which let you easily use the principles of polymorphism. We'll delve into using the ad hoc hierarchy facility later, in section 9.2. As shown before, Clojure provides a capability similar to Java's interfaces via its protocol mechanism. By defining a logically grouped set of functions, you can begin to define *protocols* to which data-type abstractions must adhere. This *abstraction-oriented programming* model is key in building large-scale applications, as you'll discover in section 9.3 and beyond.

ENCAPSULATION

If Clojure isn't oriented around classes, then how does it provide encapsulation? Imagine that you need a function that, given a representation of a chessboard and a coordinate, returns a basic representation of the piece at the given square. To keep the implementation as simple as possible, we'll use a vector containing a set of characters corresponding to the colored chess pieces, as shown in the following listing.

> **Listing 1.5 Simple chessboard representation in Clojure**

```
(ns joy.chess)

(defn initial-board []
  [\r \n \b \q \k \b \n \r
   \p \p \p \p \p \p \p \p          <─── Lowercase are black
   \- \- \- \- \- \- \- \-
   \- \- \- \- \- \- \- \-
   \- \- \- \- \- \- \- \-
   \- \- \- \- \- \- \- \-
   \P \P \P \P \P \P \P \P          <─── Uppercase are white
   \R \N \B \Q \K \B \N \R])
```

There's no need to complicate matters with the chessboard representation; chess is hard enough. This data structure in the code corresponds directly to an actual chessboard in the starting position, as shown in figure 1.9.

From the figure, you can gather that the black pieces are lowercase characters and white pieces are uppercase. You can name any square on the chessboard using a standard rank-and-file notation—using a letter for the column and a number for the row. For example, *a1* indicates the square at lower left, containing a white rook. This kind of structure likely isn't optimal for an enterprise-ready chess

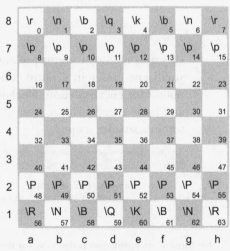

Figure 1.9 The corresponding chessboard layout

application, but it's a good start. You can ignore the actual implementation details for now and focus on the client interface to query the board for square occupations. This is a perfect opportunity to enforce encapsulation to avoid drowning the client in board-implementation details. Clojure has *closures*, and closures are an excellent way to group functions (Crockford 2008) with their supporting data.[14]

The code in the next listing provides a function named `lookup` that returns the contents of a square on the chessboard, given the name of the square in standard rank-and-file notation. It also defines a few supporting functions[15] that are used in the implementation of `lookup`; these are encapsulated at the level of the namespace `joy.chess` through the use of the `defn-` macro that creates namespace private functions.

Listing 1.6 Querying the squares of a chessboard

```
(def ^:dynamic *file-key* \a)
(def ^:dynamic *rank-key* \0)

(defn- file-component [file]
  (- (int file) (int *file-key*)))          Calculate the file
                                            (horizontal)
                                            projection

(defn- rank-component [rank]
  (->> (int *rank-key*)
       (- (int rank))                       Calculate the rank
       (- 8)                                (vertical) projection
       (* 8)))

(defn- index [file rank]
  (+ (file-component file) (rank-
     component rank)))                       Project the ID layout onto a
                                            logical 2D chessboard

(defn lookup [board pos]
  (let [[file rank] pos]
    (board (index file rank))))

(lookup (initial-board) "a1")
;;=> \R
```

Clojure's namespace encapsulation is the most prevalent form of encapsulation that you'll encounter in Clojure code. But the use of lexical closures provides another option for encapsulation: block-level encapsulation, as shown in the following listing, and local encapsulation, both of which effectively aggregate implementation details within a smaller scope.

Listing 1.7 Using block-level encapsulation

```
(letfn [(index [file rank]
          (let [f (- (int file) (int \a))
                r (* 8 (- 8 (- (int rank) (int \0))))]
```

---

[14] This form of encapsulation is described as the *module pattern*. But the module pattern as implemented with JavaScript provides some level of data hiding also, whereas in Clojure—not so much.

[15] And as a nice bonus, these functions can be generalized to project a 2D structure of any size to a 1D representation—which we leave to you as an exercise.

```
        (+ f r)))]
(defn lookup2 [board pos]
  (let [[file rank] pos]
    (board (index file rank))))))
```

```
(lookup2 (initial-board) "a1")
;;=> \R
```

When possible, it's a good idea to aggregate relevant data, functions, and macros at their most specific scope. You still call `lookup2` as before, but now the ancillary functions aren't readily visible to the larger enclosing scope—in this case, the namespace `joy.chess`. In the preceding code, we take the `file-component` and `rank-component` functions and the `*file-key*` and `*rank-key*` values out of the namespace proper and roll them into a block-level `index` function defined with the body of the `letfn` macro. Within this body, we then define the `lookup` function, thus limiting the client exposure to the chessboard API and hiding the implementation-specific functions and forms. But we can further limit the scope of the encapsulation, as shown in the next listing, by shrinking the scope even more to a truly function-local context.

> **Listing 1.8 Local encapsulation**

```
(defn lookup3 [board pos]
  (let [[file rank] (map int pos)
        [fc rc]     (map int [\a \0])
        f (- file fc)
        r (* 8 (- 8 (- rank rc)))
        index (+ f r)]
    (board index)))
```

```
(lookup3 (initial-board) "a1")
;;=> \R
```

Finally, we've pulled *all* the implementation-specific details into the body of the `lookup3` function. This localizes the scope of the `index` function and all auxiliary values to only the relevant party—`lookup3`. As a nice bonus, `lookup3` is simple and compact without sacrificing readability.

NOT EVERYTHING IS AN OBJECT

Another downside to OOP is the tight coupling between function and data. The Java programming language forces you to build programs entirely from class hierarchies, restricting all functionality to containing methods in a highly restrictive "Kingdom of Nouns" (Yegge 2006). This environment is so restrictive that programmers are often forced to turn a blind eye to awkward attachments of inappropriately grouped methods and classes.[16] It's because of the proliferation of this stringent object-centric viewpoint that Java code tends toward being verbose and complex (Budd 1995). Clojure functions are data, yet this in no way restricts the decoupling of data and the functions

---

[16] We like to call this condition *the fallacy of misplaced concretions*, taken from Whitehead—be careful using this term in mixed company.

that work on it.[17] Many of what programmers perceive to be classes are data tables that Clojure provides via maps[18] and records. The final strike against viewing everything as an object is that mathematicians view little (if anything) as objects (Abadi 1996). Instead, mathematics is built on the relationships between one set of elements and another through the application of functions.

1.5   Summary

We've covered a lot of conceptual ground in this chapter, but it was necessary to define the terms used throughout the remainder of the book. Likewise, it's important to understand Clojure's terminology (some familiar and some new) to frame our discussion. If you're still not sure what to make of Clojure, it's OK—we understand that it may be a lot to take in all at once. Understanding will come gradually as we piece together Clojure's story. If you're coming from a functional programming background, you'll likely have recognized much of the discussion in the previous sections, but perhaps with some surprising twists. Conversely, if your background is more rooted in OOP, you may get the feeling that Clojure is very different than you're accustomed to. Although in many ways this is true, in the coming chapters you'll see how Clojure elegantly solves many of the problems that you deal with on a daily basis. Clojure approaches solving software problems from a different angle than classical object-oriented techniques, but it does so having been motivated by their fundamental strengths and shortcomings.[19]

With this conceptual underpinning in place, it's time to make a brief run through Clojure's technical basics and syntax. We'll be moving fairly quickly, but no faster than necessary to get to the deeper topics in following chapters. So hang on to your REPL, here we go …

---

[17] Realize that at some point in your program you'll need to know the keys on a map or the position of an element in a vector; we don't mean to say that these precise details of structure are never important. Instead, Clojure lets you operate on data abstractions in the aggregate, allowing you to defer fine details until needed.

[18] See section 5.6 for more discussion on this idea.

[19] Although it's wonderful when programming languages can positively influence the creation of new languages, a negative influence has proven much more motivating.

Drinking from the
Clojure fire hose

2

This chapter covers

- Scalars: the base data types
- Putting things together: collections
- Making things happen: functions
- Vars are not variables
- Locals, loops, and blocks
- Preventing things from happening: quoting
- Using host libraries via interop
- Exceptional circumstances
- Modularizing code with namespaces

This chapter provides a quick tour of the bare necessities—the things you'll need to know to understand the rest of this book. It may seem odd to provide a tutorial-like chapter right away, but we felt that it was more important to introduce the ideas of the language first rather than the mechanics.[1] If you've been programming with Clojure for a while, this may be a review, but otherwise it should give you everything you need to start writing Clojure code. In most cases throughout this chapter, the examples provided will be perfunctory in order to highlight the immediate point. Later in the book, we'll build on these topics and many more, so don't worry if you don't grasp every feature now—you'll get there.

Interaction with Clojure is often performed at the *Read-Eval-Print Loop (REPL)*. When starting a new REPL session, you're presented with a simple prompt:

```
user>
```

The `user` prompt refers to the top-level namespace of the default REPL. It's at this point that Clojure waits for input expressions. Valid Clojure expressions consist of numbers, symbols, keywords, Booleans, characters, functions, function calls, macros, strings, literal maps, vectors, queues, records, and sets. Some expressions, such as numbers, strings, and keywords, are self evaluating—when entered, they evaluate to themselves. The Clojure REPL also accepts source comments, which are marked by the semicolon ; and continue to a newline:

```
user> 42     ; numbers evaluate to themselves
;=> 42
user> "The Misfits" ; strings do too
;=> "The Misfits"
user> :pyotr   ; as do keywords
;=> :pyotr
```

Now that you've seen several scalar data types, let's take a closer look at each of them.

2.1 Scalars: the base data types

The Clojure language has a rich set of data types. Like most programming languages, it provides scalar types such as integers, strings, and floating-point numbers, each representing a single unit of data. Clojure provides several different categories of scalar data types: integers, floats, rationals, symbols, keywords, strings, characters, Booleans, and regex patterns.[2] In this section, we'll address most of these categories in turn, providing examples of each.

2.1.1 Numbers

A number can consist of only the digits 0–9, a decimal point (.), a sign (+ or -), and an optional *e* for numbers written in exponential notation. In addition to these elements, numbers in Clojure can take either octal or hexadecimal form and also include an optional *M* or *N* flag that indicates arbitrary precision or arbitrarily sized integers, respectively. In many programming languages, the precision[3] of numbers is restricted

---

[1] Clojure is a language built on thoughtful design. In many ways, we see the ideas behind Clojure's design as more important than the language itself.

[2] We won't look at regular expression patterns here, but for details on everything regex-related you can flip forward to section 4.5.

[3] With caveats, as we'll describe in chapter 4.

by the host platform or, in the case of Java and C#, defined by the language specification. Although Clojure provides arbitrary-precision numbers, by default it uses the host language's (Java or JavaScript) primitive numbers. For the JVM, it then also throws exceptions when numbers would overflow, to provide generally desirable safety.

2.1.2 *Integers*

Integers comprise the entire number set, both positive and negative. Any number starting with an optional sign or digit followed exclusively by digits is considered and stored as some form of integer, although several different concrete types are used depending on the circumstance. Integers in Clojure can theoretically take an infinitely large value, but in practice the size is limited by the memory available. The following numbers are recognized by Clojure as integers:

```
42
+9
-107
9917786472619488492228198283114910358867343858270281187076768483007166514
```

All the numbers shown, except the last one, are read as primitive Java longs; the last is too big to fit in a long and thus is read as a BigInt (which is printed with a trailing *N*). The following illustrates the use of decimal, hexadecimal, octal, radix-32, and binary literals, respectively, all representing the same number:

```
[127 0x7F 0177 32r3V 2r01111111]
;=> [127 127 127 127 127]
```

The radix notation supports up to base 36, including both hexadecimal (16r7F) and octal (8r177). When using the higher bases (hexadecimal might spring to mind), you'll notice ASCII letters are needed to supplement the digits 0–9. The fact that there are only 26 usable ASCII characters limits the range of bases to a maximum of 36: 10 numbers between 0 and 9 plus 26 letters. Finally, adding signs to the front of each of the integer literals is also legal.

2.1.3 *Floating-point numbers*

Floating-point numbers are the decimal expansion of rational numbers. Like Clojure's implementation of integers, the floating-point values can be arbitrarily precise.[4] Floating-point numbers can take the traditional form of some number of digits and then a decimal point, followed by some number of digits. But floating-point numbers can also take an exponential form (scientific notation) where a significant part is followed by an exponent part separated by a lowercase or uppercase *E*. The following numbers are examples of valid floating-point numbers:

```
1.17
+1.22
-2.
```

---

[4] With some caveats, as we'll discuss in section 4.1.

```
366e7
32e-14
10.7e-3
```

Numbers are largely the same across most programming languages, so we'll move on to some scalar types that are more distinct to Lisp and Lisp-inspired languages.

2.1.4   *Rationals*

Clojure provides a rational type in addition to integer and floating-point numbers. Rational numbers offer a more compact and precise representation of a given value over floating-point. Rationals are represented classically by an integer numerator and denominator, and that's exactly how they're represented in Clojure. The following numbers are examples of valid rational numbers:

```
22/7
-7/22
1028798300029763676767687409028872/88829897008789478784
-103/4
```

Something to note about rational numbers in Clojure is that they'll be simplified if they can—the rational 100/4 will resolve to the integer 25.

2.1.5   *Symbols*

Symbols in Clojure are objects in their own right but are often used to represent another value:

```
(def yucky-pi 22/7)

yucky-pi
;;=> 22/7
```

When a number or a string is evaluated, you get back exactly the same object; but when a symbol is evaluated, you get back whatever value that symbol is referring to in the current context. In other words, symbols are typically used to refer to function parameters, local variables, globals, and Java classes.

2.1.6   *Keywords*

Keywords are similar to symbols, except that they always evaluate to themselves. You're likely to see the use of keywords far more in Clojure than symbols. The form of a keyword's literal syntax is as follows:

```
:chumby
:2
:?
:ThisIsTheNameOfaKeyword
```

Although keywords are prefixed by a colon :, it's only part of the literal syntax and not part of the name itself. We go into further detail about keywords in section 4.3.

2.1.7 Strings

Strings in Clojure are represented similarly to the way they're used in many programming languages. A string is any sequence of characters enclosed within a set of double quotes, including newlines, as shown:

```
"This is a string"
"This is also a
        String"
```

Both will be stored as written, but when printed at the REPL, multiline strings include escapes for the literal newline characters: for example, `"This is also a\n String"`.

2.1.8 Characters

Clojure characters are written with a literal syntax prefixed with a backslash and are stored as Java `Character` objects:

```
\a        ; The character lowercase a
\A        ; The character uppercase A
\u0042    ; The Unicode character uppercase B
\\        ; The back-slash character \
\u30DE    ; The Unicode katakana character ?
```

And that's it for Clojure's scalar data types. In the next section, we'll discuss Clojure's collection data types, which is where the real fun begins.

2.2 Putting things together: collections

We'll cover the collection types in greater detail in chapter 5. But because Clojure programs are made up of various kinds of literal collections, it's helpful to at least glance at the basics of lists, vectors, maps, and sets.

2.2.1 Lists

Lists are the classic collection type in Lisp (the name comes from *list processing*, after all) languages, and Clojure is no exception. Literal lists are written with parentheses:

```
(yankee hotel foxtrot)
```

When a list is evaluated, the first item of the list—yankee in this case—is resolved to a function, macro, or special operator. If yankee is a function, the remaining items in the list are evaluated in order, and the results are passed to yankee as its parameters.

> **NOTE** A *form* is any Clojure object meant to be evaluated, including but not limited to lists, vectors, maps, numbers, keywords, and symbols. A *special form* is a form with special syntax or special evaluation rules that typically aren't implemented using the base Clojure forms. An example of a special form is the . (dot) operator used for Java interoperability purposes.

If yankee is a macro or special operator, the remaining items in the list aren't necessarily evaluated, but are processed as defined by the macro or operator.

Lists can contain items of any type, including other collections. Here are some more examples:

```
(1 2 3 4)
()
(:fred ethel)
(1 2 (a b c) 4 5)
```

Note that unlike in some Lisps, the empty list in Clojure, written as (), isn't the same as nil.

2.2.2 Vectors

Like lists, vectors store a series of values. Several differences are described in section 5.4, but for now only two are important. First, vectors have a literal syntax using square brackets:

```
[1 2 :a :b :c]
```

The other important difference is that vectors evaluate each item in order. No function or macro call is performed on the vector itself, although if a list appears within the vector, that list is evaluated following the normal rules for a list. Like lists, vectors are type heterogeneous; and as you might guess, the empty vector [] isn't the same as nil.

2.2.3 Maps

Maps store unique keys and one value per key—similar to what some languages and libraries call *dictionaries* or *hashes*. Clojure has several types of maps with different properties, but don't worry about that for now. Maps can be written using a literal syntax with alternating keys and values inside curly braces. Commas are frequently used between pairs, but they're whitespace as they are everywhere else in Clojure:

```
{1 "one", 2 "two", 3 "three"}
```

As with vectors, every item in a map literal (each key and each value) is evaluated before the result is stored in the map. Unlike with vectors, the order in which they're evaluated isn't guaranteed. Maps can have items of any type for both keys and values, and the empty map {} isn't the same as nil.

2.2.4 Sets

Sets store zero or more unique items. They're written using curly braces with a leading hash:

```
#{1 2 "three" :four 0x5}
```

Again, the empty set #{} isn't the same as nil.

That's all for now regarding the basic collection types. Chapter 4 will cover the use of each type, including their relative strengths and weaknesses, in addition to covering queues.

2.3 *Making things happen: calling functions*

Functions in Clojure are a first-class type, meaning they can be used the same as any value. Functions can be stored in vars, held in lists and other collection types, and passed as arguments to and returned as the result of other functions.

Clojure borrows its function-calling syntax, known as *prefix notation*, from Lisp:

```
(vector 1 2 3)        <— Passing I, 2, and 3 to vector function

;;=> [1 2 3]          <— Returns a vector
```

The immediately obvious advantage of prefix notation over infix notation used by C-style languages[5] is that the former allows any number of operands per operator, whereas infix allows only two. Another, less obvious advantage to structuring code as prefix notation is that it eliminates the problem of operator precedence. Clojure makes no distinction between operator notation and regular function calls—all Clojure constructs, functions, macros, and operators are formed using prefix, or fully parenthesized, notation. This uniform structure forms the basis for the incredible flexibility that Lisp-like languages provide.

2.4 *Vars are not variables*

Programmers are typically accustomed to dealing with variables and mutation. Clojure's closest analogy to the variable is the *var*. A var is named by a symbol and holds a single value. Its value can be changed while the program is running, but this is best reserved for the programmer making manual changes. A var's value can also be *shadowed* (assigned a local value) by function parameters and locals, although shadowing doesn't change its original value.

Using def is the most common way to create vars in Clojure:

```
(def x 42)
```

Using def to associate the value 42 to the symbol x assigns the value to the var, creating what's known as a *root binding*.[6]

The trivial case is that the symbol x is bound to the value 42, but vars don't require a value:[7]

```
(def y)
y
;=> java.lang.IllegalStateException: Var user/y is unbound.
```

---

[5] Of course, Java uses infix notation in only a few instances. The remainder of the language forms tend toward C-style ad hoc debauchery.

[6] There's more to root bindings than acting as a default value. Instead, a root is the binding that's the same across all threads, unless otherwise re-bound relative to specific threads. By default, all threads start with the root binding, which is their associated value in the absence of a thread-bound value. We don't talk about threads and rebinding until chapter 11, so don't fret about root bindings for now.

[7] Instead you can declare them and defer the responsibility of binding their values to individual threads. We'll talk more about per-thread bindings in chapter 11.

Functions and vars theoretically provide all you need to implement any algorithm, and some languages leave you with exactly these "atomic" constructs. Speaking of which, we should probably transition into functions; their relationship to vars is important.

2.5   Functions

We've already shown how you can call a Clojure function using the (some-function arguments...) notation, but it's high time that we explain how to define your own. In this section, we'll discuss the most relevant points regarding function definition, starting with anonymous or in-place function definitions.

2.5.1   Anonymous functions

An anonymous (unnamed) Clojure function can be defined using a special form. A *special form* is a Clojure expression that's part of the core language but not created in terms of functions, types, or macros.

Here's an example of a function that takes two elements and returns a set of those elements:

```
(fn [x y]                          A vector of the
                                   function parameters
    (println "Making a set")     ←── Function body

    #{x y})                        The last expression
                                   gives the return value.
```

```
;;=> #<user$eval1027$fn__1028 user$eval1027$fn__1028@e324105>
```

Entering this function definition in a Clojure REPL gives a seemingly strange result. This is because the REPL is showing its internal name for the function object returned by the fn special form. This is far from satisfying, because now that the function has been defined, there's no apparent way to execute it. But recall from the previous chapter that the function call form is always (some-function arguments). You can define a function and call it in a single expression, as in this example:

```
((fn [x y]                            Define a function,
    (println "Making a set")          and call it right away.
   #{x y})

  1 2)                            ←── Pass 1 and 2 to the function.

;; Making a set                   ←── Prints and returns a set
 ;;=> #{1 2}
```

Although anonymous functions are useful and have their purpose, for the most part you'll probably want to give your functions names for easy reference. Clojure provides a couple of straightforward ways to define named functions, as we'll show next.

2.5.2 *Creating named functions with def and defn*

The def special form is a way to assign a symbolic name to a piece of Clojure data. Clojure functions are first class; they're equal citizens with data, allowing assignment to vars, storage in collections, and passing as arguments to (or returning from) other functions. This is different from programming languages where functions are functions and data is data, and a world of capability is available to the former that's incongruous to the latter.

Therefore, in order to associate a name with the previous function using def, you use

```
(def make-set
  (fn [x y]
    (println "Making a set")
    #{x y})))
```

And you can now call it in a more intuitive way:

```
(make-set 1 2)

;; Making a set
;;=> #{1 2}
```

Another way to define functions in Clojure is using the defn macro. Although def is one way to define functions by name, as shown it's cumbersome to use. The defn macro is a more convenient and concise way to create named functions. It provides a syntax similar to the original fn form and also allows an additional documentation string:

```
(defn make-set
  "Takes two values and makes a set from them."
  [x y]
  (println "Making a set")
  #{x y})
```

The function can be called the same as you saw before.

Clojure also provides a way to define functions that execute different bodies depending on the number of arguments sent to them. The argument count, known as *arity*, is described next.

2.5.3 *Functions with multiple arities*

The second form to define functions allows for arity overloading of the invocations of a function. *Arity* refers to the differences in the argument count that a function will accept. Changing the previous simple set-creating function to accept either one or two arguments is represented as

```
(defn make-set
  ([x]   #{x})
  ([x y] #{x y}))
```

The difference from the previous form is that you can now have any number of argument/body pairs as long as the arities of the arguments differ. Naturally, the execution of such a function for one argument is

```
(make-set 42)
;;=> #{42}
```

As you saw, arguments to functions are bound one for one to symbols during the function call, but there's a way for functions to accept a variable number of arguments:[8]

```
(make-set 1 2 3)
;; ArityException Wrong number of args passed...
```

As shown, calling the `make-set` function with three arguments won't work. But what if you want it to take any number of arguments? The way to denote variable arguments is to use the `&` symbol followed by symbols or *destructuring* forms (covered in the next chapter). Every symbol in the arguments list before the `&` is still bound one for one to the same number of arguments passed during the function call. But any additional arguments are aggregated in a sequence bound to the symbol following the `&` symbol:

```
(defn arity2+ [first second & more]         ◁─┐  Define function taking
  (vector first second more))                   │  2 or more args.

(arity2+ 1 2)                  ◁─── Extra args are nil.
 ;;=> [1 2 nil]

(arity2+ 1 2 3 4)             ◁─── Extra args are a list.
 ;;=> [1 2 (3 4)]

(arity2+ 1)                        ◁─── Too few args is an error.
 ;; ArityException Wrong number of args passed...
```

Of course, `arity2+` still requires at least two arguments, so to pass fewer is an error.

To round off our preliminary coverage of functions, we'll talk about the short way to create anonymous functions using the `#()` syntax.

2.5.4 In-place functions with #()

Clojure provides a shorthand notation for creating an anonymous function using the `#()` reader feature. In a nutshell, *reader features* are loosely analogous to C++ preprocessor directives in that they signify that some given form should be replaced with another at read time. In the case of the `#()` form, it's effectively replaced with the special form `fn`, described earlier in this section. Anywhere that it's appropriate to use `#()`, it's likewise appropriate for the `fn` special form.

The `#()` form can also accept arguments that are implicitly declared through the use of special symbols prefixed with `%`:

---

[8] The implementation details of Clojure prevent the creation of functions with an arity larger than 20, but in practice this should rarely, if ever, be an issue.

```
(def make-list0  #(list))                    <--- Takes no args

(make-list0)
;;=> ()

(def make-list2  #(list %1 %2))              <--- Takes exactly two args

(make-list2 1 2)
;;=> (1 2)

(def make-list2+ #(list %1 %2 %&))           <--- Takes two or more args

(make-list2+ 1 2 3 4 5)
;;=> (1 2 (3 4 5))
```

A couple of notes about these examples are worth mentioning. First, a function taking one argument can be written using either the explicit #(list %1) or the implicit #(list %). The % symbol means the same as %1, but we prefer the numbered version. Also note that the %& symbol in make-a-list2+ is used to refer to the variable arguments passed as arguments.

2.6 Locals, loops, and blocks

Clojure's function and value-binding capabilities provide a basis for much of what you need in order to start writing operational code, but a large part of the story is missing. Clojure also provides capabilities for creating local value bindings, building looping constructs, and aggregating blocks of functionality.

2.6.1 Blocks

Use the do form when you have a series or block of expressions that need to be treated as one. All the expressions are evaluated, but only the last one is returned:

```
(do
  (def x 5)
  (def y 4)
  (+ x y)
  [x y])

;;=> [5 4]
```

The expressions (def x 5), (def y 4), and (+ x y) are executed one by one in the body of the do block. Even the addition (+ x y) is executed, but the value is thrown away—only the final expression [x y] is returned. The middle bits of the do block are typically where the side effects occur, as shown with the use of def. Whenever you see a Clojure form with a name starting with do, you can assume that its purpose is related to side-effectful activities like defining a var, printing, and so on.

2.6.2 Locals

Clojure doesn't have local variables, but it does have locals; they just can't vary. Locals are created and their scope is defined using a let form, which starts with a vector that defines the bindings, followed by any number of expressions that make up the body. The vector begins with a binding form (usually a symbol), which is the name of a new local. This is followed by an expression whose value is bound to this new local for the remainder of the let form. You can continue pairing binding names and expressions to create as many locals as you need. All of them are available in the body of the let:

```
(let [r          5
      pi         3.1415
      r-squared (* r r)]
  (println "radius is" r)
  (* pi r-squared))

;; radius is 5
;;=> 78.53750000000001
```

The body is sometimes described as an *implicit do* because it follows the same rules: you may include any number of expressions, and all are evaluated, but only the value of the last one is returned.

All the binding forms in the previous example are simple symbols: r, pi, and r-squared. More complex binding expressions can be used to pull apart expressions that return collections. This feature is called *destructuring*: see section 3.3 for details.

Because they're immutable, locals can't be used to accumulate results. Instead, you use a high-level function or loop/recur form.

2.6.3   Loops

The classic way to build a loop in a Lisp is a recursive call, and this is true in Clojure as well. Using recursion sometimes requires thinking about your problem in a different way than imperative languages encourage; but recursion from a tail position is in many ways like a structured goto and has more in common with an imperative loop than it does with other kinds of recursion.

RECUR

Clojure has a special form called recur that's specifically for tail recursion. The following function prints the integers from x to 1, counting backward:

```
(defn print-down-from [x]
  (when (pos? x)              ◁— Perform while still positive.
    (println x)                       ◁— Print the current x.
    (recur (dec x))))                  ◁— Recurse with x minus 1.
```

This is nearly identical to how you'd structure a while loop in an imperative language. One significant difference is that the value of x isn't decremented somewhere in the body of the loop. Instead, a new value is calculated as a parameter to recur, which immediately does two things: rebinds x to the new value and returns control to the top of print-down-from.

If the function has multiple arguments, the recur call must as well, just as if you were calling the function by name instead of using the recur special form. And just as with a function call, the expressions in the `recur` are evaluated in order first and only then bound to the function arguments simultaneously.

The previous example doesn't concern itself with return values; it's just about the `println` side effects. Here's a similar loop that builds up an accumulator named `sum`, which adds the numbers between 1 and x, inclusive, and returns the sum:

```
(defn sum-down-from [sum x]     ◁━❶ Take counter
  (if (pos? x)                              ◁━❷ If positive ...
    (recur (+ sum x) (dec x))      ◁━❸ ... then recurse
    sum))                                    ◁━❹ ... else return sum
```

First, `sum-down-from` accepts a partial sum and an upper limit for the remaining sum as arguments ❶. Although recursive, `sum-down-from` will recur only if x is greater than 0 ❷. When it does recur, it adds x to the `sum`, decrements x, and passes these values to the recursive call ❸. Otherwise, if x is 0, `sum-down-from` returns the `sum`, thus terminating the recursion ❹. The only ways out of the function are `recur`, which isn't really a way out, and `sum`. So when x is no longer positive, the function returns the value of `sum`:

```
(sum-down-from 0 10)
;=> 55
```

Graphically, `sum-down-from` can be represented as in figure 2.1.

Note that the return value of the recursive call becomes the value of the `if` when that branch is taken, and that, in turn, becomes the return value of the function. The value of `sum` when x is 0 therefore ultimately becomes the return value of the original invocation of `sum-down-from`.

You may have noticed that the two preceding functions use different blocks: the first `when` and the second `if`. You'll often see one or the other used as a conditional,

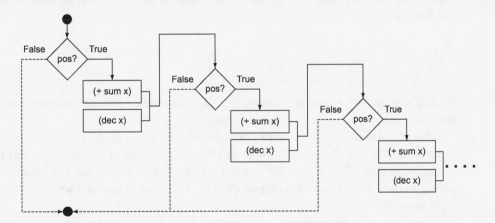

Figure 2.1   A graphical representation of the `sum-down-from` function

but it's not always immediately apparent why. In general, you should use when in these cases:

- No else part is associated with the result of a conditional.
- You require an implicit do in order to perform side effects.

If neither of these is true, you should use if.

LOOP

Sometimes you want to loop back not to the top of the function, but to somewhere inside it. For example, in sum-down-from, you might prefer that callers not have to provide an initial value for sum. To help, there's a loop form that acts exactly like let but provides a target for recur to jump to. It's used like this:

```
(defn sum-down-from [initial-x]
  (loop [sum 0, x initial-x]          <—— Set up recursion target
    (if (pos? x)
      (recur (+ sum x) (dec x))       <—— Jump to recursion target
      sum)))
```

Upon entering the loop form, the locals sum and x are initialized, just as they would be for a let.

A recur always loops back to the closest enclosing loop or fn, so in this case it goes to loop. The loop locals are re-bound to the values given in recur. The looping and rebinding continue until finally x is no longer positive. The return value of the entire loop expression is sum, just as it was for the earlier function.

TAIL POSITION

Now that we've looked at a couple of examples of how to use recur, we must discuss an important restriction. The recur form can only appear in the tail position of a function or loop. What's a tail position? Succinctly, a form is in a *tail position* of an expression when its value may be the return value of the entire expression. Consider this function:

```
(defn absolute-value [x]
  (if (pos? x)
    x              ; "then" clause
    (- x)))        ; "else" clause
```

It takes a single parameter and names it x. If x is already a positive number, then x is returned; otherwise the opposite of x is returned.

The if form is in a tail position because whatever it returns, the entire function will return. The x in the then clause is also in a tail position of the function. But the x in the else clause is *not* in a tail position of the function because the value of x is passed to the - function, not returned directly. The else clause as a whole (- x) is in a tail position.

If you try to use the recur form somewhere other than a tail position, Clojure will remind you at compile time:

```
(fn [x] (recur x) (println x))
; java.lang.UnsupportedOperationException:
;     Can only recur from tail position
```

You've seen how Clojure provides core functionality available to most popular programming languages, albeit from a different bent. But in the next section, we'll cover the notion of quoting forms, which are in many ways unique to the Lisp family of languages and may seem alien to programmers coming from classically imperative and/or object-oriented languages.

2.7 Preventing things from happening: quoting

Clojure has two quoting forms: quote and syntax-quote. Both are simple bits of syntax you can put in front of a form in your program. They're the primary ways to include literal scalars and composites in your Clojure program *without* evaluating them as code. But before quoting forms can make sense, you need a solid understanding of how expressions are evaluated.

2.7.1 Evaluation

When a collection is evaluated, each of its contained items is evaluated first:[9]

```
(cons 1 [2 3])
```

If you enter this at the REPL, the form as a whole is evaluated, giving (1 2 3). In this specific example, the function cons "constructs" a new sequence with its first argument in the front of the sequence provided as its second. Because the form is a list, each of the items is evaluated first. A symbol, when evaluated, is resolved to a local, a var, or a Java class name. If a local or a var, its value is returned:

```
cons
;=> #<core$cons__3806 clojure.core$cons__3806@24442c76>
```

Literal scalar values evaluate to themselves—evaluating one just returns the same thing:

```
1
;=> 1
```

The evaluation of another kind of collection, a vector, starts again by evaluating the items it contains. Because they're literal scalars, nothing much happens. Once that's done, evaluation of the vector can proceed. Vectors, like scalars and maps, evaluate to themselves:

```
[2 3]
;=> [2 3]
```

Now that all the items of the original list have been evaluated (to a function, the number 1, and the vector [2 3]), evaluation of the entire list can proceed. Lists are

---

[9] ... unless it's a list that starts with the name of a macro or special operator. We'll get to that later.

evaluated differently from vectors and maps; they call functions, or trigger special operations, as shown:

```
(cons 1 [2 3])
;=> (1 2 3)
```

Whatever function was at the head of the list, cons in this case, is called with the remaining items of the list as arguments.

2.7.2 Quoting

Using a special operator looks like calling a function—a symbol as the first item of a list:

```
(quote age)
```

Each special operator has its own evaluation rules. The quote special operator prevents its argument from being evaluated at all. Although the symbol age by itself might evaluate to the value of a var, when it's inside a quote form, it isn't:

```
(def age 9)
(quote age)
;=> age
```

Instead, the entire form evaluates to just the symbol. This works for arbitrarily complex arguments to quote: nested vectors, maps, and even lists that would otherwise be function calls, macro calls, or other special forms. The whole thing is returned:

```
(quote (cons 1 [2 3]))
;=> (cons 1 [2 3])
```

There are a few reasons why you might use the quote form, but by far the most common is so that you can use a literal list as a data collection without having Clojure try to call a function. We've been careful to use vectors in the examples so far in this section because vectors are never function calls. But if you wanted to use a list instead, a naive attempt would fail:

```
(cons 1 (2 3))
; java.lang.ClassCastException:
;    java.lang.Integer cannot be cast to clojure.lang.IFn
```

That's Clojure telling you that an integer (the number 2 here) can't be used as a function. You have to prevent the form (2 3) from being treated like a function call—which is exactly what quote is for:

```
(cons 1 (quote (2 3)))
;=> (1 2 3)
```

In other Lisps, this need is so common that they provide a shortcut: a single quote. Although this is used less in Clojure, it's still provided. The previous example can also be written as follows:

```
(cons 1 '(2 3))
;=> (1 2 3)
```

And look at that: one less pair of parentheses—always welcome in a Lisp. Remember, though, that quote affects all of its argument, not just the top level. Even though it worked in the preceding examples to replace [] with '(), this may not always give the results you want:

```
[1 (+ 2 3)]        ;=> [1 5]
'(1 (+ 2 3))       ;=> (1 (+ 2 3))
```

Finally, note that the empty list () already evaluates to itself; it doesn't need to be quoted. Quoting the empty list isn't required in Clojure.

SYNTAX-QUOTE

Like quote, the syntax-quote prevents its argument and subforms from being evaluated. Unlike quote, it has a few extra features that make it ideal for constructing collections to be used as code.

Syntax-quote is written as a single back-quote (`):

```
`(1 2 3)
;=> (1 2 3)
```

It doesn't expand to a simple form like quote, but to whatever set of expressions is required to support the following features.

SYMBOL AUTO-QUALIFICATION

A symbol can begin with a namespace and a slash (/). These can be called *qualified symbols*:

```
clojure.core/map
clojure.set/union
i.just.made.this.up/quux
```

Syntax-quote automatically qualifies all unqualified symbols in its argument:

```
`map
;=> clojure.core/map
`Integer
;=> java.lang.Integer
`(map even? [1 2 3])
;=> (clojure.core/map clojure.core/even? [1 2 3])
```

If the symbol doesn't name a var or class that exists yet, syntax-quote uses the current namespace:

```
`is-always-right
;=> user/is-always-right
```

This behavior will come in handy in chapter 8, when we discuss macros.

2.7.3   *Unquote*

As you discovered, the quote special operator prevents its argument, and all of its subforms, from being evaluated. But there will come a time when you'll want *some* of its constituent forms to be evaluated. The way to accomplish this feat is to use what's known as an *unquote*. An unquote is used to demarcate specific forms as requiring evaluation by prefixing them with the symbol ~ within the body of a syntax-quote:

```
`(+ 10 (* 3 2))
;=> (clojure.core/+ 10 (clojure.core/* 3 2))

`(+ 10 ~(* 3 2))
;=> (clojure.core/+ 10 6)
```

What just happened? The final form uses an unquote to evaluate the subform (* 3 2), performing a multiplication of 3 and 2, thus inserting the result into the outermost syntax-quoted form. The unquote is used to denote any Clojure expression as requiring evaluation:

```
(let [x 2]
`(1 ~x 3))
;=> (1 2 3)

`(1 ~(2 3))
;; ClassCastException java.lang.Long
;;   cannot be cast to clojure.lang.IFn
```

Whoops! Using the unquote told Clojure that the marked form should be evaluated. But the marked form here is (2 3); and remember what happens when Clojure encounters an expression like this? It attempts to evaluate it as a function! Therefore, you should take care with unquote to ensure that the form requiring evaluation is the form you expect. The more appropriate way to perform the previous task would be

```
(let [x '(2 3)] `(1 ~x))
;=> (1 (2 3))
```

This provides a level of indirection such that the expression being evaluated is no longer (2 3) but x. But this new way breaks the pattern of the previous examples that returned a list of (1 2 3).

2.7.4   *Unquote-splicing*

Clojure provides a handy feature to solve exactly the problem posed earlier. A variant of unquote called *unquote-splicing* works similarly to unquote, but a little differently:

```
(let [x '(2 3)] `(1 ~@x))
;=> (1 2 3)
```

Note the @ in ~@, which tells Clojure to unpack the sequence x, splicing it into the resulting list rather than inserting it as a nested list.

2.7.5   *Auto-gensym*

Sometimes you need a unique symbol, such as for a parameter or let local name. The easiest way to do this inside a syntax-quote is to append a # to the symbol name. This causes Clojure to create a new, unqualified, automatically generated symbol:

```
`potion#
;=> potion__211__auto__
```

Sometimes even this isn't enough, either because you need to refer to the same symbol in multiple syntax-quotes or because you want to capture a particular unqualified symbol. We'll talk more about this circumstance in section 8.5.1.

Until this point, we've covered many of the basic features that make Clojure a unique flavor of Lisp. Something that Clojure and ClojureScript excel at is interoperability with their host language and runtime: Java, the Java Virtual Machine (JVM), or a JavaScript runtime.

2.8   *Using host libraries via interop*

Clojure is symbiotic with its host,[10] providing its rich and powerful features, whereas Java provides an object model, libraries, and runtime support. In this section, we'll take a brief look at how Clojure allows you to access Java classes and class members, and how you can create instances and access their members. This interaction with Java classes via Clojure is known as interoperability, or *interop* for short.

2.8.1   *Accessing static class members (Clojure only)*

Clojure provides powerful mechanisms for accessing, creating, and mutating Java classes and instances. The trivial case is accessing static class properties:

```
java.util.Locale/JAPAN
;=> #<Locale ja_JP>
```

Clojure programmers usually prefer to access static class members using a syntax that's like accessing a namespace-qualified var:

```
(Math/sqrt 9)
;=> 3.0
```

The preceding call is to the `java.lang.Math#sqrt` static method. By default, all classes in the root `java.lang` package are available for immediate use. ClojureScript doesn't provide access to static members because JavaScript has no such feature.

2.8.2   *Creating instances*

Creating instances is likewise a trivial matter with Clojure. The new special operator closely mirrors the Java and JavaScript models:

```
(new java.awt.Point 0 1)

;=> #<Point java.awt.Point[x=0,y=1]>
```

This example creates an instance of `java.awt.Point` with the numbers 0 and 1 passed in as constructor arguments. An interesting aspect of Clojure is that its core collection types can be used as arguments to Java constructors for the purpose of initialization. Observe how you can use a Clojure map to initialize a Java map:

---

[10] We'll focus on the JVM and JavaScript throughout this book, but Clojure has also been hosted on the .NET Common Language Runtime (CLR), Scheme, Lua, Python, and ClojureScript (http://clojurescript.net).

```
(new java.util.HashMap {"foo" 42 "bar" 9 "baz" "quux"})
;=> {"baz" "quux", "foo" 42, "bar" 9}
```

The second, more succinct, Clojure form to create instances is the preferred form:

```
(java.util.HashMap. {"foo" 42 "bar" 9 "baz" "quux"})
;=> {"baz" "quux", "foo" 42, "bar" 9}
```

As you can see, the class name is followed by a dot in order to signify a constructor call. The same capability exists in ClojureScript, except that when referencing core or globally accessible JavaScript types, you need to prefix the type with the js namespace symbol:

```
(js/Date.)
;=> #inst "2013-02-01T15:10:44.727-00:00"
```

There are subtle differences like this (although relatively few) between Clojure and ClojureScript, and as needed we'll highlight and explain them.

2.8.3 Accessing instance members with the . operator

To access public instance variables, precede the field name with a dot and a hyphen:

```
(.-x (java.awt.Point. 10 20))
;=> 10
```

This returns the value of the field x from the Point instance given.

To access instance methods, the dot form allows an additional argument to be passed to the method:

```
(.divide (java.math.BigDecimal. "42") 2M)
;=> 21M
```

This example calls the #divide method on the class BigDecimal. Notice that the instance you're accessing is explicitly given as the first argument to the .divide call. This inverts the way that Java instance calls happen, where the instance is the implicit method target. Note that the example also uses the 2M literal to denote that you want to use an arbitrarily precise numeric value.

2.8.4 Setting instance fields

Instance fields can be set via the set! function:

```
(let [origin (java.awt.Point. 0 0)]
  (set! (.-x origin) 15)
  (str origin))
;=> "java.awt.Point[x=15,y=0]"
```

The first argument to set! is the instance member access form.

2.8.5 The .. macro

When working with Java, it's common practice to chain together a sequence of method calls on the return type of the previous method call:

```
new java.util.Date().toString().endsWith("2014") /* Java code */
```

Using Clojure's dot special operator, the following code is equivalent:[11]

```
(.endsWith (.toString (java.util.Date.)) "2014") ; Clojure code
;=> true
```

Although correct, the preceding code is difficult to read and will only become more so when you lengthen the chain of method calls. To combat this, Clojure provides the .. macro, which can simplify the call chain as follows:

```
(.. (java.util.Date.) toString (endsWith "2014"))
;=> true
```

This .. call closely follows the equivalent Java code and is much easier to read. Bear in mind, you may not see .. used often in Clojure code found in the wild, outside the context of macro definitions. Instead, Clojure provides the -> and ->> macros, which can be used similarly to the .. macro but are also useful in non-interop situations; this makes them the preferred method-call facilities in most cases. The -> and ->> macros are covered in more depth in the introduction to chapter 8.

2.8.6 *The doto macro*

When working with Java, it's also common to initialize a fresh instance by calling a set of mutators:

```
// This is Java, not Clojure
java.util.HashMap props = new java.util.HashMap();
props.put("HOME", "/home/me");          /* More java code. Sorry. */
props.put("SRC",  "src");
props.put("BIN",  "classes");
```

But using this method is overly verbose and can be streamlined using the doto macro, which takes the form

```
(doto (java.util.HashMap.)
  (.put "HOME" "/home/me")
  (.put "SRC"  "src")
  (.put "BIN"  "classes"))

;=> {"HOME" "/home/me", "BIN" "classes", "SRC" "src"}
```

These kinds of Java and Clojure comparisons are useful for understanding Clojure's interoperability offerings.

2.8.7 *Defining classes*

Clojure provides the reify and deftype macros as possible ways to create realizations of Java interfaces, but we'll defer covering them until chapter 9. Additionally, Clojure provides a macro named proxy that can be used to implement interfaces and extend

---

[11] Depending on when you run this code, you may get false as the answer. To fix that, change the string "2013" to whatever year it happens to be (for example, "2112").

base classes on the fly. Similarly, using the gen-class macro, you can generate statically named classes. More details about proxy and gen-class are available in chapter 12.

2.9   *Exceptional circumstances*

We'll now talk briefly about Clojure's facilities for handling exceptions. Like Java, Clojure provides a couple of forms for throwing and catching runtime exceptions: throw and catch, respectively. Although throw and catch map almost directly down to Java and JavaScript, they're considered the standard way of dealing with error handling. In other words, even in the absence of interoperability, most Clojure code uses throw and catch to perform error handling.

2.9.1   *Throwing and catching*

The mechanism to throw an exception is fairly straightforward:

```
(throw (Exception. "I done throwed"))
;=> java.lang.Exception: I done throwed ...
```

The syntax for catching exceptions in Clojure is similar to that of Java:

```
(defn throw-catch [f]
  [(try
    (f)
    (catch ArithmeticException e "No dividing by zero!")
    (catch Exception e (str "You are so bad " (.getMessage e)))
    (finally (println "returning... ")))])

(throw-catch #(/ 10 5))
; returning...
;=> [2]

(throw-catch #(/ 10 0))
; returning...
;=> ["No dividing by zero!"]

(throw-catch #(throw (Exception. "Crybaby")))
; returning...
;=> ["You are so bad Crybaby"]
```

The major difference between how Java and Clojure handle exceptions is that Clojure doesn't adhere to checked-exception requirements. The ClojureScript catch form looks similar except for the need to use js to catch core error types, as shown next:

```
(try
  (throw (Error. "I done throwed in CLJS"))
  (catch js/Error err "I done catched in CLJS"))
;=> "I done catched in CLJS"
```

In the next and final section of this introduction to Clojure, we'll present namespaces, which may look vaguely familiar if you're familiar with Java or Common Lisp.

2.10 *Modularizing code with namespaces*

Clojure's namespaces provide a way to bundle related functions, macros, and values. In this section, we'll briefly talk about how to create namespaces and how to reference and use things from other namespaces. This section will focus on the Clojure (Java targeted) namespacing functionality. For a discussion with a ClojureScript-specific focus on namespaces, see chapter 13.

2.10.1 *Creating namespaces using ns*

To create a new namespace, you can use the ns macro:

```
(ns joy.ch2)
```

Your REPL prompt now displays

```
joy.ch2=>
```

This prompt shows that you're working in the context of the joy.ch2 namespace. Clojure also provides a var *ns* that refers to the current namespace. Any var created is a member of the current namespace:

```
joy.ch2=> (defn hello []
  (println "Hello Cleveland!"))

joy.ch2=> (defn report-ns []
  (str "The current namespace is " *ns*))

joy.ch2=> (report-ns)
;=> "The current namespace is joy.ch2"
```

Entering a symbol in a namespace causes Clojure to attempt to look up its value in the current namespace:

```
joy.ch2=> hello
;=> #<ch2$hello joy.ch2$hello@2af8f5>
```

You can create new namespaces at any time:

```
(ns joy.another)
```

```
joy.another=>
```

Again, notice that the prompt has changed, indicating that the new context is joy.another. By using the ns form, you tell Clojure to create another namespace and switch over to it. Because the joy.another namespace is new and not nested inside of nor in any way part of the previously created joy.ch2 namespace, attempting to run report-ns will no longer work:

```
joy.another=> (report-ns)
; java.lang.Exception:
;   Unable to resolve symbol: report-ns in this context
```

This is because report-ns exists in the joy.ch2 namespace and is only accessible via its fully qualified name, joy.ch2/report-ns. Any namespaces referenced must already be loaded implicitly by being previously defined or by being one of Clojure's core namespaces, or explicitly loaded through the use of :require, which we'll discuss next.

2.10.2   Loading other namespaces with :require

Creating a namespace at the REPL is straightforward. But just because you've created one and populated it with useful functions doesn't mean its awesomeness is available for use by any other namespace you create. Instead, in order to use functions from any given namespace, you need to load it from disk. But how do you load namespaces? Clojure provides the convenience directive :require to take care of this task. Here's an example:

```
(ns joy.req
  (:require clojure.set))

(clojure.set/intersection #{1 2 3} #{3 4 5})

;;=> #{3}
```

Call a function in the clojure.set namespace.

Using :require indicates that you want the clojure.set namespace loaded. You can also use the :as directive to create an additional alias to clojure.set:

```
(ns joy.req-alias
  (:require [clojure.set :as s]))

(s/intersection #{1 2 3} #{3 4 5})
;=> #{3}
```

The qualified namespace form looks the same as a call to a static class method. The difference is that a namespace symbol can only be used as a qualifier, whereas a class symbol can also be referenced independently:

```
clojure.set                              ⟵— Namespace symbol
  ; java.lang.ClassNotFoundException: clojure.set

java.lang.Object            ⟵— Class symbol
  ;=> java.lang.Object
```

The vagaries of namespace mappings from symbols to vars, both qualified and unqualified, can cause confusion between class names and static methods in the beginning, but the differences will begin to feel natural as you progress. In addition, Clojure code in the wild tends to use my.Class and my.ns for naming classes and namespaces, respectively, to help eliminate potential confusion.

2.10.3   Loading and creating mappings with :refer

Sometimes you'll want to create mappings from vars in another namespace to names in your own, in order to avoid calling each function or macro with the qualifying namespace symbol. To create these unqualified mappings, Clojure provides the :refer option of the :require directive:

```
(ns joy.use-ex
  (:require [clojure.string :refer (capitalize)]))
(map capitalize ["kilgore" "trout"])
;=> ("Kilgore" "Trout")
```

The :refer option indicates that only the function capitalize should be mapped in the namespace joy.use-ex. Although you can bring in all public vars from the specified namespace by using :refer :all (or the older :use directive), we don't generally recommend these. Explicitly specifying the vars you'd like to refer is good practice in Clojure, because it avoids creating unnecessary names in a namespace. Unnecessary names increase the odds of name clashes and make it more difficult for people reading your code to discover the definitions of the vars you use.

2.10.4 Creating mappings with :refer

Clojure also provides a :refer directive that works almost exactly like the option of the same name in the :require directive, except that it only creates mappings for libraries that have already been loaded:

```
(ns joy.yet-another
  (:refer joy.ch2))

(report-ns)
;=> "The current namespace is joy.yet-another"
```

Using :refer this way creates a mapping from the name report-ns to the actual function located in the namespace joy.ch2 so that the function can be called normally. You can also set an alias for the same function using the :rename keyword taking a map, as shown here:

```
(ns joy.yet-another
  (:refer clojure.set :rename {union onion}))

(onion #{1 2} #{4 5})
;=> #{1 2 4 5}
```

Note that :rename also works with the :require directive.

2.10.5 Loading Java classes with :import

To use unqualified Java classes in any given namespace, you should import them via the :import directive:

```
(ns joy.java
  (:import [java.util HashMap]
           [java.util.concurrent.atomic AtomicLong]))

(HashMap. {"happy?" true})
;=> {"happy?" true}

(AtomicLong. 42)
;=> 42
```

But fully qualified Java class names are always available without any import. Finally, any classes in the Java `java.lang` package are automatically imported when namespaces are created. We'll discuss namespaces in more detail in sections 9.1 and 10.1.

2.11 Summary

We named this chapter "Drinking from the Clojure fire hose"—and you've made it through! How does it feel? We've only provided an overview of the topics needed to move on to the following chapters, instead of a full-featured language tutorial. Don't worry if you don't fully grasp the entirety of the Clojure programming language; understanding will come as you work your way through the book.

In the next chapter, we'll take a step back and delve into some topics that can't be easily categorized but that deserve attention because of their ubiquity. It'll be short and sweet and give you a chance to take a breath before moving into the deeper discussions on Clojure later in the book.

*Dipping your toes
in the pool*

3

Deeper and broader topics will be covered in later chapters, but now's a good time to pick through an eclectic selection of smaller topics. The topics covered in this chapter stand alone but are important. Covering them now will be a fun way to start digging into practical matters of how to use Clojure.

We covered a lot of conceptual ground in the previous chapter and built your Clojure lexicon. In this chapter, we'll take a detour into some fundamental underpinnings relevant to every Clojure project. First we'll explore Clojure's straightforward notions of *truthiness*,[1] or the distinctions between values considered logical

---

[1] As a deviation from the definition coined by Stephen Colbert in his television show *The Colbert Report*. Ours isn't about matters of gut feeling but rather about matters of Clojure's logical truth ideal.

true and those considered logical false. We'll discuss Clojure's extremely simple rules followed by the notion of *nil punning*, or treating an empty sequence as nil. Those of you coming from a background in Lisp may recognize the term, but Clojure handles nil punning differently. We'll discuss the idioms related to nil punning in Clojure and their rationale. We'll then cover destructuring—a powerful mechanism for pulling apart collection types and binding their constituent parts as individual values. Using destructuring in your own code can often lead to extremely concise and elegant solutions, and we'll provide some examples to illustrate this. Finally, we'll sit down and pair-program together to help you gain an appreciation for the power of Clojure's Read-Eval-Print Loop (REPL).

3.1   Truthiness

Truthfulness may be an important virtue, but it doesn't come up much in programming. On the other hand, *truthiness*, or the matter of logical truth values in Clojure, is critical.

Clojure has one Boolean context: the test expression of the if form. Other forms that expect Booleans—and, or, when, and so forth—are macros built on top of if. It's here that truthiness matters.

3.1.1   What's truth?

Every value looks like true to if, except for false and nil. That means values some languages treat as false—zero-length strings, empty lists, the number zero, and so on—are all treated as true in Clojure:

```
(if true :truthy :falsey)  ;=> :truthy
(if [] :truthy :falsey)    ;=> :truthy
(if nil :truthy :falsey)   ;=> :falsey
(if false :truthy :falsey) ;=> :falsey
```

This may feel uncomfortable to you, depending on your background. But because branches in a program's logic are already one of the most likely places for complexity and bugs, Clojure has opted for a simple rule. There's no need to check a class's definition to see if it acts like "false" when you think it should (as is sometimes required in Python, for example). Every object is "true" all the time, unless it's nil or false.

3.1.2   Don't create Boolean objects

It's possible to create an object that looks a lot like, but isn't actually, false. Java has left a land mine for you here, so take a moment to look at it so that you can step past it gingerly and get on with your life:

```
(def evil-false (Boolean. "false")) ; NEVER do this
```

This creates a new instance of Boolean—and that's already wrong! Because there are only two possible values of Boolean, an instance of each has already been made for us—they're named true and false.[2] But here we've gone and done it anyway, created a new instance of Boolean and stored it in a var named evil-false. It looks like false:

```
evil-false
;=> false
```

Sometimes it even acts like false:

```
(= false evil-false)
;=> true
```

But once it gains your trust, it'll show you just how wicked it is by acting like true:

```
(if evil-false :truthy :falsey)
;=> :truthy
```

Java's own documentation warns against the creation of this evil thing, and now you've been warned again. If you want to parse a string, use the Boolean class's static valueOf method instead of its constructor. This is the right way:

```
(if (Boolean/valueOf "false") :truthy :falsey)
;=> :falsey
```

3.1.3 *nil vs. false*

Rarely do you need to differentiate between the two non-truthy values, but if you do, you can use nil? and false?:

```
(when (nil? nil) "Actually nil, not false")
;=> "Actually nil, not false"
```

Keeping in mind the basic rule that everything in Clojure is truthy unless it's false or nil is an astonishingly powerful concept, allowing for elegant solutions. Often programming languages have complicated semantics for truthiness, but Clojure manages to avoid those matters nicely.

Building on that theme, we'll now discuss the matter of *nil punning*, which may or may not surprise you, depending on your background.

3.2 *Nil pun with care*

Because empty collections act like true in Boolean contexts, you need an idiom for testing whether there's anything in a collection to process. Thankfully, Clojure provides such a technique:

```
(seq [1 2 3])
;=> (1 2 3)

(seq [])
;=> nil
```

---

[2] Clojure's true and false instances are the same as Java's Boolean/TRUE and Boolean/FALSE, respectively.

The seq function returns a sequence view of a collection, or nil if the collection is empty. In a language like Common Lisp, an empty list acts as a false value and can be used as a *pun* (a term with the same behavior) for such in determining a looping termination. As you saw in section 3.1, Clojure's empty sequences are instead truthy, and therefore to use one as a pun for falsity will lead to heartache and despair. One solution that might come to mind is to use empty? in the test, leading to the awkward phrase (when-not (empty? s) ...). A better solution is to use seq as a termination condition, as in the following function print-seq:

```
(defn print-seq [s]
   (when (seq s)                    ⬩—❶ Check for empty
     (prn (first s))
     (recur (rest s))))))           ⬩—❷ Recurse
```

There are a number of points to take away from this example. First, the use of seq as a terminating condition is the preferred way to test whether a sequence is empty ❶. If you tested just s instead of (seq s), then the terminating condition wouldn't occur even for empty collections, leading to an infinite loop. Thankfully, the use of seq allows you to properly check for an empty collection:

```
(print-seq [])
;=> nil
```

Second, rest is used instead of next to consume the sequence on the recursive call. Although they're nearly identical in behavior, rest can return a sequence that's either empty or not empty (has elements) ❷, but it never returns nil. On the other hand, next returns a seq of the rest, or (seq (rest s)), and thus never returns an empty sequence, returning nil in its place. It's appropriate to use rest here because you're using seq explicitly in each subsequent iteration. Observe:

```
(print-seq [1 2])
; 1
; 2
;=> nil
```

As shown, the print-seq function uses seq and recursion (via recur) to "consume" a collection, printing its elements along the way using prn. In fact, print-seq is a template for most functions in Clojure: it shows that you generally shouldn't assume seq has been called on your collection arguments, but instead call seq in the function itself and process based on its result. Using this approach fosters a more generic handling of collections, a topic that we explore in great detail in chapter 5. In the meantime, it's important to keep in mind the difference between empty collections and false values; otherwise your attempts at nil punning may cause groans all around.

> **NOTE** An important point to mention is that it would be best to use doseq to iterate over the collection rather than an explicit recursion (see section 1.1.5), but that wouldn't allow us to illustrate the point at hand: the Clojure forms named with do at the start (doseq, dotimes, do, and so on) are intended for side effects in their bodies and generally return nil as their results.

To top off our trifecta of core Clojure concepts, we next explore the most powerful of the three: destructuring. You'll see how powerful this mini-language in Clojure can be toward developing elegant and often beautiful solutions.

3.3 *Destructuring*

In the previous section, we briefly described Clojure's destructuring facility as a mini-language embedded in Clojure. *Destructuring* allows you to positionally bind locals based on an expected form for a composite data structure. In this section, we'll explore how destructuring can be used to pull apart composite structures into bindings through the lens of a simple rolodex example project.

> **NOTE** Destructuring is loosely related to pattern matching found in Haskell, KRC, or Scala, but it only provides place binding and not conditional binding. For full-featured pattern matching in Clojure, consider using http://github.com/clojure/core.match, which might become a core feature one day.

3.3.1 *Your assignment, should you choose to accept it*

You've heard that the rolodex project has been overdue, but now every developer assigned to it is out sick. The QA team is ready to go, but one function is still missing, and it's a show-stopper. You're told to drop everything and write the function ASAP.

The design? Take a vector of length 3 that represents a person's first, middle, and last names, and return a string that will sort in the normal way, like "Steele, Guy Lewis". What are you waiting for? Why aren't you done yet?!?!

```
(def guys-whole-name ["Guy" "Lewis" "Steele"])

(str (nth guys-whole-name 2) ", "
     (nth guys-whole-name 0) " "
     (nth guys-whole-name 1))
;=> "Steele, Guy Lewis"
```

Alas, by the time you've finished typing guys-whole-name for the fourth time, it's too late. The customers have cancelled their orders, and the whole department has been downsized.

If only you'd known about destructuring.

OK, so you're not likely to lose your job because your function is twice as many lines as it needs to be, but still, that's a lot of code repeated in a pretty small function. And using index numbers instead of named locals makes the purpose of the function more obscure than necessary.

Destructuring solves both these problems by allowing you to place a collection of names in a binding form where normally you'd put a single name. One kind of binding form is the list of parameters given in a function definition.

3.3.2   *Destructuring with a vector*

Let's try that again but use destructuring with `let` to create more convenient locals for the parts of Guy's name:

```
(let [[f-name m-name l-name] guys-whole-name]
  (str l-name ", " f-name " " m-name))
```

> **Positional destructuring**
>
> This positional destructuring doesn't work on maps and sets because they're not logically[3] aligned sequentially. Interestingly, positional destructuring works with Java's `java.util.regex.Matcher`:
>
> ```
> (def date-regex #"(\d{1,2})\/(\d{1,2})\/(\d{4})")
>
> (let [rem (re-matcher date-regex "12/02/1975")]
>   (when (.find rem)
>     (let [[_ m d] rem]
>       {:month m :day d})))
>
> ;;=> {:month "12", :day "02"}
> ```
>
> Although it's possible to destructure a `Matcher` object, a better solution would be to destructure the result of `(re-find rem)` instead. Finally, positional destructuring also works for anything implementing the `CharSequence` and `java.util.Random-Access` interfaces.

This is the simplest form of destructuring, where you want to pick apart a sequential thing (a vector of strings in this case, although a list or other sequential collection would work as well), giving each item a name.

You don't need it here, but you can also use an ampersand in a destructuring vector to indicate that any remaining values of the input should be collected into a (possibly lazy) seq:

```
(let [[a b c & more] (range 10)]
  (println "a b c are:" a b c)
  (println "more is:" more))
; a b c are: 0 1 2
; more is: (3 4 5 6 7 8 9)
;=> nil
```

Here the locals a, b, and c are created and bound to the first three values of the range. Because the next symbol is an ampersand, the remaining values are made available as a seq bound to more.

The final feature of vector destructuring is `:as`, which can be used to bind a local to the entire collection. It must be placed after the `&` local, if there is one, at the end of the destructuring vector:

---

[3] Technically, positional destructuring might make sense with sorted sets and maps, but alas it doesn't operate as such because Clojure doesn't consider them to be sequential collections. See section 5.2.

```
(let [range-vec (vec (range 10))
      [a b c & more :as all] range-vec]
  (println "a b c are:" a b c)
  (println "more is:" more)
  (println "all is:" all))
; a b c are: 0 1 2
; more is: (3 4 5 6 7 8 9)
; all is: [0 1 2 3 4 5 6 7 8 9]
;=> nil
```

range-vec is a vector in this example, and the directive :as binds the input collection as is, entirely unmolested, so that the vector stays a vector. This is in contrast to &, which binds more to a seq, not a vector.

3.3.3 *Destructuring with a map*

Perhaps passing a name as a three-part vector wasn't a good idea in the first place. It might be better stored in a map:

```
(def guys-name-map
  {:f-name "Guy" :m-name "Lewis" :l-name "Steele"})
```

But now you can't use a vector to pick it apart. Instead, you use a map:

```
(let [{f-name :f-name, m-name :m-name, l-name :l-name} guys-name-map]
  (str l-name ", " f-name " " m-name))

;=> "Steele, Guy Lewis"
```

A couple things about this example may jump out at you. One might be that it still seems repetitive—we'll get to that in a moment.

Another might be that the way the keywords are organized looks unusual. The example has its keywords like :f-name on the right side of each pair, even though the input map had keywords on the left. There are a couple reasons for that. The first is to help keep the pattern of the name on the left getting the value specified by the thing on the right. So the new local f-name gets the value looked up in the map by the key :f-name, just as the whole map gets its value from guys-name-map in the earlier def form.

The second reason is because it allows you to conjure up other destructuring features by using forms that would otherwise make no sense. Because the item on the left of each pair will be a new local name, it must be a symbol or possibly a nested destructuring form. But one thing it can't be is a keyword, unless the keyword is a specially supported feature such as :keys, :strs, :syms, :as, and :or.

We'll discuss the :keys feature first because it nicely handles the repetitiveness we mentioned earlier. It allows you to rewrite your solution like this:

```
(let [{:keys [f-name m-name l-name]} guys-name-map]
  (str l-name ", " f-name " " m-name))

;=> "Steele, Guy Lewis"
```

So by using :keys instead of a binding form, you're telling Clojure that the next form will be a vector of names that it should convert to keywords such as :f-name in order to look up their values in the input map. Similarly, if you'd used :strs, Clojure would be looking for items in the map with string keys such as "f-name", and :syms would indicate symbol keys.

The directives :keys, :strs, :syms, and regular named bindings can appear in any combination and in any order. But sometimes you'll want to get at the original map—in other words, the keys you didn't name individually by any of the methods just described. For that, you want :as, which works just like it does with vector destructuring:

```
(let [{f-name :f-name, :as whole-name} guys-name-map]
  (println "First name is" f-name)
  (println "Whole name is below:")
  whole-name)
;; First name is Guy
;; Whole name is below:
;;=> {:f-name "Guy", :m-name "Lewis", :l-name "Steele"}
```

If the destructuring map looks up a key that's not in the source map, it's normally bound to nil, but you can provide different defaults with :or:

```
(let [{:keys [title f-name m-name l-name],
       :or {title "Mr."}} guys-name-map]
  (println title f-name m-name l-name))

; Mr. Guy Lewis Steele
;=> nil
```

All of these map destructuring features also work on lists, a feature that's primarily used by functions so as to accept keyword arguments:

```
(defn whole-name [& args]
  (let [{:keys [f-name m-name l-name]} args]
    (str l-name ", " f-name " " m-name)))

(whole-name :f-name "Guy" :m-name "Lewis" :l-name "Steele")
;=> "Steele, Guy Lewis"
```

Note that when defined this way, whole-name isn't called with a map parameter, but rather with arguments that alternate between keys and values. Using a map to destructure this list of arguments causes the list to first be poured into a map collection before then being destructured as usual.

ASSOCIATIVE DESTRUCTURING

One final technique worth mentioning is associative destructuring. Using a map to define a number of destructure bindings isn't limited to maps. You can also destructure a vector by providing a map declaring the local name as indices into them, as shown:

```
(let [{first-thing 0, last-thing 3} [1 2 3 4]]
  [first-thing last-thing])
;=> [1 4]
```

You've seen the shapes that destructuring takes in the let form, but you're not limited to that exclusively, as we'll explore next.

3.3.4 Destructuring in function parameters

All the preceding examples use let to do their destructuring, but exactly the same features are available in function parameters. Each function parameter can destructure a map or sequence:

```
(defn print-last-name [{:keys [l-name]}]
  (println l-name))

(print-last-name guys-name-map)
; Steele
```

Note that function arguments can include an ampersand as well, but this isn't the same as destructuring. Instead, that's part of their general support for multiple function bodies, each with its own number of parameters.

3.3.5 Destructuring vs. accessor methods

In many object-oriented languages, you might create new classes to manage your application data objects, each with its own set of getter and setter methods. Clojure instead is built to facilitate the use of maps and vectors to create abstractions. This makes destructuring natural and straightforward. Any time you find that you're calling nth on the same collection a few times, or looking up constants in a map, or using first or next, consider using destructuring instead.

Now that we've made it through the cursory introduction to Clojure, let's take some time to pair-program (Williams 2002). In the next section, we'll take many of the bare necessities that you've just learned and walk through the creation of a couple interesting functions for drawing pretty pictures in Clojure's REPL.

3.4 Using the REPL to experiment

Most software development projects include a stage where you're not sure what needs to happen next. Perhaps you need to use a library or part of a library you've never touched before. Or perhaps you know what your input to a particular function will be, and what the output should be, but you aren't sure how to get from one to the other. In some programming languages, this can be time-consuming and frustrating; but by using the power of the Clojure REPL, the interactive command prompt, it can be fun.

3.4.1 Experimenting with seqs

Say someone suggests to you that coloring every pixel of a canvas with the xor of its x and y coordinates might produce an interesting image. It shouldn't be too hard, so you can jump right in. You'll need to perform an operation on every x and y in a pair of ranges. Do you know how `range` works?

```
(range 5)
;=> (0 1 2 3 4)
```

That should do nicely for one coordinate. To nest seqs, `for` often does the trick. But again, rather than writing code and waiting until you have enough to warrant compiling and testing, you can try it:

```
(for [x (range 2) y (range 2)] [x y])
;=> ([0 0] [0 1] [1 0] [1 1])
```

There are the coordinates that will form your input. Now you need to xor them:

```
(xor 1 2)
;=> java.lang.Exception: Unable to resolve symbol: xor in this context
```

Bother—no function named xor. Fortunately, Clojure provides `find-doc`, which searches not just function names but also their doc strings for the given term:[4]

```
(find-doc "xor")
; -------------------------
; clojure.core/bit-xor
; ([x y]) ([x y & more])
;   Bitwise exclusive or
;=> nil
```

So the function you need is called `bit-xor`:

```
(bit-xor 1 2)
;=> 3
```

Perfect! Next you want to adjust the earlier `for` form to return `bit-xor` along with x and y. The easiest way to do this depends on what tool is hosting your REPL. In many, you can press the up-arrow key on your keyboard a couple of times to bring back the earlier `for` form. You won't want to retype things to make minor adjustments, so take a moment right now to figure out a method you like that will let you make a tweak like this by inserting the `bit-xor` call:

```
(for [x (range 2) y (range 2)]
    [x y (bit-xor x y)])

;=> ([0 0 0] [0 1 1] [1 0 1] [1 1 0])
```

That looks about right. We're about to shift gears to pursue the graphics side of this problem, so tuck away that bit of code in a function so it'll be easy to use later:

```
(defn xors [max-x max-y]
    (for [x (range max-x) y (range max-y)]
        [x y (bit-xor x y)]))
```

---

[4] Two community-run sources of Clojure information worth bookmarking are http://clojuredocs.org, a site providing API documentation and examples, and http://clojure-doc.org, a site providing tutorials, guides, and cookbooks.

```
(xors 2 2)
;=> ([0 0 0] [0 1 1] [1 0 1] [1 1 0])
```

You might even save that into a .clj file, if you haven't already. It's worth mentioning that saving files with the .clj extension is standard for Clojure source code, whereas .cljs is standard for ClojureScript files.

3.4.2 Experimenting with graphics

Clojure's REPL isn't just for playing around; it's also great for experimenting with Java libraries. We believe there's no better environment for exploring a Java API than Clojure's REPL. To illustrate, poke around with java.awt, starting with a Frame:

```
(def frame (java.awt.Frame.))
;=> #'user/frame
```

That should have created a Frame, but no window appeared. Did it work at all?

```
frame
;=> #<Frame java.awt.Frame[frame0,0,22,0x0,invalid,hidden,...]>
```

Well, you have a Frame object, but perhaps the reason you can't see it is hinted at by the word *hidden* in the #<Frame...> printout. Perhaps the Frame has a method you need to call to make it visible. One way to find out would be to check the Javadoc of the object, but because you're at the REPL already, let's try something else. You've already seen how the for macro works, so maybe you can check a class for which methods it has to see whether one you can use is available:

```
(for [meth (.getMethods java.awt.Frame)        ⟵─❶ Iterate over class methods
      :let [name (.getName meth)]               ⟵─❷ Bind a variable name
      :when (re-find #"Vis" name)]              ⟵─❸ Build a seq of matched names
  name)

;=> ("setVisible" "isVisible")
```

The for macro provides a way to iterate over a collection, performing some action on each item and collecting the results into a sequence. The preceding example iterates over a sequence of the methods available on the java.awt.Frame class ❶. Whenever Clojure encounters a symbol that looks like a Java class name, it attempts to resolve it as a class. This behavior allows you to then call the getMethods method directly on the class. Next, a :let flag and bindings vector is used ❷, working similarly to the let special form that you use to bind the local method-name to the result of calling the method .getName on each method in turn. The :when is used to limit the elements used in its body to only those that return a truthy value in the expression after the directive ❸. Using these directives lets you iterate through the methods and build a seq of those whose names match a regular expression #"Vis". We'll cover Clojure's regular-expression syntax in section 3.5.

Your query returns two potential methods, so try each of them:

```
(.isVisible frame)
;=> false
```

That's false, as you might have suspected. Will setting it to true make any difference?

```
(.setVisible frame true)
;=> nil
```

It did, but it's so tiny! Not to worry, because a Frame class also has a .setSize method you can use:

```
(.setSize frame (java.awt.Dimension. 200 200))
;=> nil
```

And up pops a blank window for you to draw on. At this point, we'll guide you through the rest of this section; but keep in mind that Java's official API might be of interest, should you choose to extend the example program.

> **NOTE**   The Clojure clojure.java.javadoc namespace has a javadoc function to query and view official API documentation: (javadoc frame). This should return a string corresponding to a URL and open a browser window for the right page of documentation. Prior to Clojure 1.2, this function was in clojure.contrib.repl-utils.

What you need to draw into your Frame is its graphics context, which can be fetched as shown:

```
(def gfx (.getGraphics frame))
;=> #'user/gfx
```

Then, to draw, you can try out the fillRect method of that graphics context. If you're trying this yourself, make sure the blank window is positioned so that it's unobscured while you're typing into your REPL:

```
(.fillRect gfx 100 100 50 75)
```

And just like that, you're drawing on the screen interactively. You should see a single black rectangle in the formerly empty window. Exciting, isn't it? You could be a kid playing with turtle graphics for the first time, it's so much fun. But what it needs is a dash of color:

```
(.setColor gfx (java.awt.Color. 255 128 0))
(.fillRect gfx 100 150 75 50)
```

Now there should be an orange rectangle as well. Perhaps the coloring would make Martha Stewart cry, but you've tried all the basic building blocks you'll need to complete the original task: you have a function that returns a seq of coordinates and their xor values, you have a window you can draw into, and you know how to draw rectangles of different colors. Bear in mind that if you move the frame with the mouse, your beautiful graphics may disappear (depending on your OS and window manager). This is an artifact of this limited experiment and can be avoided using the full Java Swing capabilities.[5]

3.4.3 Putting it all together

What's left to do? Use the graphics functions you just saw to draw the xor values:

```
(doseq [[x y xor] (xors 200 200)]
  (.setColor gfx (java.awt.Color. xor xor xor))
  (.fillRect gfx x y 1 1))
```

The xors function you created earlier generates a seq of vectors, if you remember, where each vector has three elements: the x and y for your coordinates and the xor value that goes with them. The first line here uses destructuring to assign each of those three values to new locals x, y, and xor, respectively.

The second line sets the "pen" color to a gray level based on the xor value, and the final line draws a single-pixel rectangle at the current coordinates. The resulting graphic is shown in figure 3.1.

Figure 3.1 Visualization of xor. This is the graphic drawn by the 10 or so lines of code we've looked at so far—a visual representation of Clojure's `bit-xor` function.

But just because you've succeeded doesn't mean you have to quit. You've built up some knowledge and a bit of a toolbox, so why not play with it a little?

3.4.4 When things go wrong

For example, the pattern appears to cut off in the middle—perhaps you'd like to see more. Re-enter that last expression, but this time try larger limits:

```
(doseq [[x y xor] (xors 500 500)]
  (.setColor gfx (java.awt.Color. xor xor xor))
  (.fillRect gfx x y 1 1))
; java.lang.IllegalArgumentException:
;    Color parameter outside of expected range: Red Green Blue
```

Whoops. Something went wrong, but what exactly? This gives you a perfect opportunity to try one final REPL tool. When an exception is thrown from something you try at the REPL, the result is stored in a var named *e. This allows you to get more detail about the expression, such as the stack trace:

```
(.printStackTrace *e)
; java.lang.IllegalArgumentException: Color parameter outside of
;         expected range: Red Green Blue
; at clojure.lang.Compiler.eval(Compiler.java:4639)
; at clojure.core$eval__5182.invoke(core.clj:1966)
; at clojure.main$repl__7283$read_eval_print__7295.invoke(main.clj:180)
; ...skipping a bit here...
; Caused by: java.lang.IllegalArgumentException: Color parameter
```

---

[5] A nice open source Swing library for Clojure is Seesaw, available at http://github.com/daveray/seesaw.

```
;          outside of expected range: Red Green Blue
; at java.awt.Color.testColorValueRange(Color.java:298)
; at java.awt.Color.<init>(Color.java:382)
; ...skipping a bit more...
; ... 11 more
;=> nil
```

That's a lot of text, but don't panic. Learning to read Java stack traces is useful, so let's pick it apart.

The first thing to understand is the overall structure of the trace—there are two "causes." The original or root cause of the exception is listed last—this is the best place to look first.[6] The name and text of the exception there are the same as the REPL printed for you in the first place, although they won't always be. So let's look at that next line:

```
at java.awt.Color.testColorValueRange(Color.java:298)
```

Like most lines in the stack trace, this has four parts—the name of the class, the name of the method, the filename, and finally the line number:

```
at <class>.<method or constructor>(<filename>:<line>)
```

In this case, the function name is testColorValueRange, which is defined in Java's own Color.java file. Unless this means more to you than it does to us, let's move on to the next line:

```
at java.awt.Color.<init>(Color.java:382)
```

It appears that it was the Color's constructor (called <init> in stack traces) that called the test function you saw earlier. So now the picture is pretty clear—when you constructed a Color instance, it checked the values you passed in, decided they were invalid, and threw an appropriate exception.

If this isn't enough, you can continue walking down the stack trace until the line

```
... 11 more
```

This is your cue to jump up to the cause listed before this one to find out what the next 11 stack frames were.

To fix your invalid Color argument, you can adjust the xors function to return only legal values using the rem function, which returns the remainder so you can keep the results under 256:

```
(defn xors [xs ys]
  (for [x (range xs) y (range ys)]
    [x y (rem (bit-xor x y) 256)]))
```

---

[6] This is a runtime exception, the most common kind. If you misuse a macro or find a bug in one, you may see compile-time exceptions. The trace will look similar but will have many more references to Compiler.java. For these traces, the most recent exception (listed first) may be the only one that identifies the filename and line number in your code that's at fault.

Note that you're redefining an existing function here. This is perfectly acceptable and well-supported behavior. Before moving on, create a function that takes a graphics object and clears it:

```
(defn clear [g] (.clearRect g 0 0 200 200))
```

Calling (clear gfx) clears the frame, allowing the doseq form you tried before to work perfectly.

3.4.5 *Just for fun*

The bit-xor function does produce an interesting image, but it would be fun to explore what different functions look like. Try adding another parameter to xors so that you can pass in whatever function you'd like to look at. Because it's not just bit-xor anymore, change the name while you're at it:

```
(defn f-values [f xs ys]
  (for [x (range xs) y (range ys)]
    [x y (rem (f x y) 256)]))
```

You might as well wrap your call to setSize, clear, and the doseq form in a function as well:

```
(defn draw-values [f xs ys]
  (clear gfx)
  (.setSize frame (java.awt.Dimension. xs ys))
  (doseq [[x y v] (f-values f xs ys)]
    (.setColor gfx (java.awt.Color. v v v))
    (.fillRect gfx x y 1 1)))
```

This allows you to try different functions and ranges easily. More nice examples are shown in figure 3.2, resulting from the following:

```
(draw-values bit-and 256 256)
(draw-values + 256 256)
(draw-values * 256 256)
```

If this were the beginning or some awkward middle stage of a large project, you'd have succeeded in pushing past this troubling point and could now take the functions you've built and drop them into the larger project.

By trying everything out at the REPL, you're encouraged to try smaller pieces rather than larger ones. The smaller the piece, the shorter the distance down an incorrect path you're likely to go. Not only does this reduce the overall development time, but it provides developers more frequent successes that can help keep morale and motivation high through even tough stages of a project. But trial-and-error exploration isn't enough. An intuitive basis in Clojure is also needed to become highly

Figure 3.2 The draw-values function you've written can be used to create a variety of graphics. Here are examples, from left to right, of bit-and, +, and *.

effective. Throughout this book, we'll help you to build your intuition in Clojure through discussions of its idioms and its motivating factors and rationale.

3.5   *Summary*

We started slowly in this chapter in order to take a breather from the sprint that was chapter 2. Truthiness in Clojure observes a simple rule: every object is `true` all the time, unless it's `nil` or `false`. Second, in many Lisp-like languages, the empty list `()` and the truth value `nil` are analogous—this is known as *nil punning*—but in Clojure this isn't the case. Instead, Clojure employs the `(seq (rest _))` idiom in the form of the `next` function to provide a mechanism fostering "form follows function" and also to eliminate errors associated with falsity/empty-seq disparity. Finally, destructuring provides a powerful mechanism, a mini-language for binding if you will, for partially or entirely pulling apart the constituent components of composite types. Our trek through the REPL illustrated the power in having the whole language (Graham 2001) at your disposal. As a Clojure programmer, you'll spend a lot of time in the REPL, and pretty soon you won't know how you lived without it.

In the next chapter, we'll touch on matters concerning Clojure's seemingly innocent scalar data types. Although in most cases these scalars will expose powerful programming techniques, be forewarned: as you'll see, the picture isn't always rosy.

Part 2

Data types

Clojure has squirreled away interesting tidbits even among its data types. The scalar types include some less common items such as keywords and rational numbers, and the composite types are all immutable. In this part of the book, we'll explore all of them in detail.

On scalars

*It requires a very unusual mind
to undertake the analysis of the obvious.*
—Alfred North Whitehead[1]

> **This chapter covers**
> - Understanding precision
> - Trying to be rational
> - When to use keywords
> - Symbolic resolution
> - Regular expressions—the second problem

So far, we've covered a somewhat eclectic mix of fun and practical concerns. This brings us to a point where we can dive deeper into a fundamental topic: how Clojure deals with scalar values, including numeric, symbolic, and regular expression values, and how they behave as data and sometimes as code.

A scalar data type represents a singular value of one of the following types: number, symbol, keyword, string, or character. Most of the use cases for Clojure's scalar data types will be familiar to you, but there are nuances that should be observed. Clojure's scalar data types exist in an interesting conceptual space. Because of Clojure's symbiotic relationship with the host language it's embedded in, some of the

---

[1] *Science and the Modern World* (Macmillan, 1925).

scalar type behaviors walk a conceptual line between pure Clojure semantics and host semantics. This chapter provides a rundown of some of the common uses of Clojure's scalar data types as well as some pitfalls you might encounter. In most cases, Clojure will shield you from the quirks of its host, but there are times when they'll demand attention. We'll talk about their limitations and possible mitigation techniques. Additionally, we'll address the age-old topic of Lisp-1 versus Lisp-2 implementations and how Clojure approaches the matter. Finally, we'll talk briefly about Clojure's regular expression literals and how they're typically used.

We'll first cover matters of numerical precision and how the Java Virtual Machine works to thwart your attempts at mathematical nirvana.

4.1 *Understanding precision*

Numbers in Clojure are by default as precise as they need to be. Given enough memory, you could store the value of pi accurately up to a billion places and beyond; in practice, values that large are rarely needed. But it's sometimes important to provide perfect accuracy at less-precise values. When dealing with raw Clojure functions and forms, it's a trivial matter to ensure such accuracy; it's handled automatically. Because Clojure encourages interoperability with its host platform, the matter of accuracy becomes less than certain. This section will talk about real matters of precision related to Clojure's support for the Java Virtual Machine. As it pertains to programming languages, numerical precision[2] is proportional to the mechanisms used for storing numerical representations. The Java language specification describes the internal representation of its primitive types, thus limiting their precision. Depending on the class of application specialization, a programmer could go an entire career and never be affected by Java's precision limitations. But many industries require perfect accuracy of arbitrarily precise computations, and here Clojure can provide a great boon; but with this power come some pointy edges, as we'll discuss shortly.

4.1.1 *Truncation*

Truncation refers to limiting accuracy for a floating-point number based on a deficiency in the corresponding representation. When a number is truncated, its precision is limited such that the maximum number of digits of accuracy is bound by the number of bits that can "fit" into the storage space allowed by its representation. For floating-point values, Clojure truncates by default. Therefore, if high precision is required for your floating-point operations, then explicit typing is required, as seen with the use of the M literal in the following:

```
(let [imadeuapi 3.14159265358979323846264338327950288419716939937M]
  (println (class imadeuapi))
  imadeuapi)
; java.math.BigDecimal
;=> 3.14159265358979323846264338327950288419716939937M
```

---

[2] As opposed to arithmetic precision.

```
(let [butieatedit 3.1415926535897932384626433832795028841971693993
  (println (class butieatedit))
  butieatedit)
; java.lang.Double
;=> 3.141592653589793
```

As we show, the local `butieatedit` is truncated because the default Java double type is insufficient. On the other hand, `imadeuapi` uses Clojure's literal notation, a suffix character `M`, to declare a value as requiring arbitrary decimal representation. This is one possible way to mitigate truncation for an immensely large range of values, but as we'll explore in section 4.2, it's not a guarantee of perfect precision.

4.1.2 Promotion

Clojure is able to detect when overflow occurs, and it promotes the value to a numerical representation that can accommodate larger values. In many cases, promotion results in the usage of a pair of classes used to hold exceptionally large values. This promotion in Clojure is automatic, because the primary focus is first correctness of numerical values, then raw speed. It's important to remember that this promotion *will* occur, as shown in the following snippet, and your code should accommodate this certainty:[3]

```
(def clueless 9)

(class clueless)
;=> java.lang.Long              <── Long by default

(class (+ clueless 9000000000000000))
;=> java.lang.Long              Long can hold
                                 large values

(class (+ clueless 90000000000000000000))
;=> clojure.lang.BigInt         But when too large, the
                                 type promotes to BigInt

(class (+ clueless 9.0))        Floating-point doubles
;=> java.lang.Double            are contagious
```

Java has a bevy of contexts under which automatic type conversion occurs, so we advise you to familiarize yourself with them (Lindholm 1999) when dealing with Java native libraries.

4.1.3 Overflow

Integer and long values in Java are subject to overflow errors. When a numeric calculation results in a value that's larger than 32 bits of representation will allow, the bits of storage wrap around. When you're operating in Clojure, overflow isn't an issue for most cases, thanks to promotion. But when you're dealing with numeric operations on primitive types, overflow can occur. Fortunately, in these instances an exception will occur rather than propagating inaccuracies:

---

[3] In the example, it's important to realize that the actual class of the value is changing, so any functions or methods reliant on specific types might not work as expected.

```
(+ Long/MAX_VALUE Long/MAX_VALUE)
;=> java.lang.ArithmeticException: integer overflow
```

Clojure provides a class of unchecked integer and long mathematical operations that assume their arguments are primitive types. These unchecked operations *will* overflow if given excessively large values:

```
(unchecked-add (Long/MAX_VALUE) (Long/MAX_VALUE))
;=> -2
```

You should take care with unchecked operations, because there's no way to detect overflowing values and no reliable way to return from them. Use the unchecked functions only when overflow is desired.

4.1.4   Underflow

Underflow is the inverse of overflow, where a number is so small that its value collapses into zero. Here are simple examples of underflow for floats and doubles:

```
(float 0.0000000000000000000000000000000000000000000001)
;=> 0.0

1.0E-430
;=> 0.0
```

Underflow presents a danger similar to overflow, except that it occurs only with floating-point numbers.

4.1.5   Rounding errors

When the representation of a floating-point value isn't sufficient for storing its actual value, then rounding errors will occur (Goldberg 1991). Rounding errors are an especially insidious numerical inaccuracy, because they have a habit of propagating throughout a computation and/or build over time, leading to difficulties in debugging. There's a famous case involving the failure of a Patriot missile caused by a rounding error, resulting in the death of 28 U.S. soldiers in the first Gulf War (Skeel 1992). This occurred due to a rounding error in the representation of a count register's update interval. The timer register was meant to update once every 0.1 seconds, but because the hardware couldn't represent 0.1 directly, an approximation was used instead. Tragically, the approximation used was subject to rounding error. Therefore, over the course of 100 hours, the rounding accumulated into a timing error of approximately 0.34 seconds:

```
(let [approx-interval  (/ 209715 2097152)      <— Patriot's approx 0.1
      actual-interval (/ 1 10)                  <—┐
      hours            (* 3600 100 10)            │ Clojure can
      actual-total    (double (* hours actual-interval))   │ accurately
      approx-total    (double (* hours approx-interval))]  ┘ represent 0.1
  (- actual-total approx-total))

;=> 0.34332275390625
```

In the case of the Patriot missile, the deviation of 0.34 seconds was enough to cause a catastrophic software error, resulting in the missile's ineffectiveness. When human lives are at stake, the inaccuracies wrought from rounding errors are unacceptable. For the most part, Clojure can maintain arithmetic accuracies in a certain range, but you shouldn't take for granted that such will be the case when interacting with Java libraries.

One way to contribute to rounding errors is to introduce doubles and floats into an operation. In Clojure, any computation involving even a single double results in a value that's a double:

```
(+ 0.1M 0.1M 0.1M 0.1 0.1M 0.1M 0.1M 0.1M 0.1M 0.1M)
;=> 0.9999999999999999
```

Can you spot the double?

This discussion was Java-centric, but Clojure's ultimate goal is to be platform agnostic, and the problem of numerical consistency across platforms is a nontrivial matter. It's still unknown whether the preceding points will be universal across host platforms, so bear in mind that they should be reexamined when using Clojure outside the context of the JVM. Now that we've identified the root issues when dealing with numbers in Clojure, we'll dive into a successful mitigation technique for dealing with them: rationals.

4.2 Trying to be rational

Clojure provides a data type representing a rational number, and all of its core mathematical functions operate with rational numbers. A *rational number* is a fraction consisting of an arbitrary-precision integer numerator and denominator of the form 22/7. Clojure's rational type allows for arbitrarily large numerators and denominators. We won't go into depth about the limitations of floating-point operations, but the problem can be summarized simply. Given a finite representation of an infinitely large set, a determination must be made which finite subset *is* represented. In the case of standard floating-point numbers as representations of real numbers, the distribution of represented numbers is logarithmic (Kuki 1973) and not one for one. What does this mean in practice? That requiring more accuracy in your floating-point operations increases the probability that the corresponding representation won't be available. In these circumstances, you have to settle for approximations. But Clojure's rational number type provides a way to retain perfect accuracy when needed.

4.2.1 Why be rational?

Of course, Clojure provides a decimal type that's boundless relative to your computer memory, so why wouldn't you use that? In short, you can, but decimal operations can be easily corrupted—especially when you're working with existing Java libraries (Kahan 1998), taking and returning primitive types. Additionally, in the case of Java, its underlying `BigDecimal` class is finite in that it uses a 32-bit integer to represent the number of digits to the right of the decimal place. This can represent an extremely large range of values perfectly, but it's still subject to error:

```
1.0E-430000000M
;=> 1.0E-430000000M

1.0E-4300000000M
;=> java.lang.RuntimeException: java.lang.NumberFormatException
```

Even if you manage to ensure that your `BigDecimal` values are free from floating-point corruption, you can never protect them from themselves. At some point, a floating-point calculation will encounter a number such as 2/3 that *always* requires rounding, leading to subtle yet propagating errors. Finally, floating-point arithmetic is neither associative nor distributive, which may lead to the shocking result that many floating-point calculations are dependent on the order in which they're carried out:

```
(def a  1.0e50)
(def b -1.0e50)
(def c 17.0e00)

(+ (+ a b) c)               Associativity should
;;=> 17.0                   guarantee 17.0 for both

(+ a (+ b c))
;;=> 0.0
```

As shown, by selectively wrapping parentheses, we've changed the order of operations and, amazingly, changed the answer! Therefore, for absolutely precise calculations, rationals are the best choice.[4]

4.2.2   *How to be rational*

Aside from the rational data type, Clojure provides functions that can help maintain your sanity: `ratio?`, `rational?`, and `rationalize`. Taking apart rationals is also a trivial matter.

The best way to ensure that your calculations remain as accurate as possible is to do them all using rational numbers. As shown next, the shocking results from using floating-point numbers have been eliminated:

```
(def a (rationalize 1.0e50))
(def b (rationalize -1.0e50))
(def c (rationalize 17.0e00))

(+ (+ a b) c)
;;=> 17N                    <— Associativity preserved

(+ a (+ b c))
;;=> 17N
```

---

[4] In the case of irrational numbers like pi, all bets are off.

You can use `rational?` to check whether a given number is a rational and then use `rationalize` to convert it to one. There are a few rules of thumb to remember if you want to maintain perfect accuracy in your computations:

- Never use Java math libraries unless they return results of `BigDecimal`, and even then be suspicious.
- Don't `rationalize` values that are Java float or double primitives.
- If you must write your own high-precision calculations, do so with rationals.
- Only convert to a floating-point representation as a last resort.

Finally, you can extract the constituent parts of a rational using the `numerator` and `denominator` functions:

```
(numerator (/ 123 10))
;=> 123
(denominator (/ 123 10))
;=> 10
```

You might never need perfect accuracy in your calculations. When you do, Clojure provides tools for maintaining sanity, but the responsibility to maintain rigor lies with you.

4.2.3 *Caveats of rationality*

Like any programming language feature, Clojure's rational type has its share of trade-offs. The calculation of rational math, although accurate, isn't nearly as fast as with floats or doubles. Each operation in rational math has an overhead cost (such as finding the least common denominator) that should be accounted for. It does you no good to use rational operations if speed is a greater concern than accuracy.

That covers the numerical scalars, so we'll move on to two data types that you may not be familiar with unless you come from a background in the Lisp family of languages: keywords and symbols.

4.3 *When to use keywords*

If you'll recall from section 2.1.6, *keywords* are self-evaluating types that are prefixed by one or more colons, as shown next:

```
:a-keyword
;;=> :a-keyword
::also-a-keyword
;;=> :user/also-a-keyword
```

Knowing how to type a keyword is important,[5] but the purpose of Clojure keywords can sometimes lead to confusion for first-time Clojure programmers, because their

---

[5] You'll notice that the third keyword has two colons in the front. This is a *qualified keyword* and is discussed in section 4.3.2.

analogue isn't often found[6] in other languages. This section attempts to alleviate the confusion and provides some tips for how keywords are typically used.

4.3.1 Applications of keywords

Keywords *always* refer to themselves, whereas symbols don't. What this means is that the keyword :magma always has the value :magma, whereas the symbol ruins may refer to any legal Clojure value or reference.

AS KEYS

In Clojure code in the wild, keywords are almost always used as map keys:

```
(def population {:zombies 2700, :humans 9})

(get population :zombies)
;=> 2700

(println (/ (get population :zombies)
            (get population :humans))
         "zombies per capita")
; 300 zombies per capita
```

The use of the get function does what you might expect. That is, get takes a collection and attempts to look up its keyed value. But there's a special property of keywords that makes this lookup more concise.

AS FUNCTIONS

So far, we've somewhat oversimplified the capabilities of keywords. Although they're self-evaluating, they're also sometimes evaluated as functions. When a keyword appears in the function position, it's treated as a function. Therefore, another important reason to use keywords as map keys is that they're also functions that take a map as an argument to perform lookups of themselves:

```
(:zombies population)
;=> 2700

(println (/ (:zombies population)
            (:humans population))
         "zombies per capita")
; 300 zombies per capita
```

Using keywords as map-lookup functions leads to much more concise code.

AS ENUMERATIONS

Often, Clojure code uses keywords as enumeration values, such as :small, :medium, and :large. This provides a nice visual delineation in the source code.

AS MULTIMETHOD DISPATCH VALUES

Because keywords are used often as enumerations, they're ideal candidates for dispatch values for multimethods, which we'll explore in more detail in section 9.2.

---

[6] Ruby has a symbol type that acts, looks, and is used similarly to Clojure keywords.

AS DIRECTIVES

Another common use for keywords is to provide a directive to a function, multi-method, or macro. A simple way to illustrate this is to imagine a simple function pour, shown in listing 4.1, which takes two numbers and returns a lazy sequence of the range of those numbers. But there's also a mode for this function that takes a keyword :toujours, which instead returns an infinite lazy range starting with the first number and continuing "forever."

Listing 4.1   Using a keyword as a function directive

```
(defn pour [lb ub]
  (cond
    (= ub :toujours) (iterate inc lb)
    :else (range lb ub)))
```
Called with lower and upper bounds, returns a range
```
(pour 1 10)
;=> (1 2 3 4 5 6 7 8 9)

(pour 1 :toujours)
; ... runs forever
```
Called with a keyword argument, iterates forever

An illustrative bonus with pour is that the macro cond uses a directive :else to mark the default conditional case. In this case, cond uses the fact that the keyword :else is truthy; any keyword (or truthy value) would work just as well.

4.3.2   Qualifying your keywords

Keywords don't belong to any specific namespace, although they may appear to if you start them with two colons rather than only one:

```
::not-in-ns
;=> :user/not-in-ns
```

When Clojure sees a double colon, it assumes that the programmer wants a qualified, or prefixed keyword. Because this example doesn't specify an exact prefix, Clojure uses the current namespace name—in this case, user—to automatically qualify the keyword. But the prefix portion of the keyword marked as :user/ only looks like it's denoting a namespace, when in fact it's a prefix gathered from the current namespace by the Clojure reader. This may seem like a distinction without a difference—we'll show how the prefix is arbitrary in relation to existing namespaces. First, you create a new namespace and manually create a prefixed keyword:

```
(ns another)

another=> :user/in-another

;=> :user/in-another
```

This example creates a namespace another and a keyword :user/in-another that appears to belong to the preexisting user namespace but in fact is only prefixed to look that way. The prefix on a keyword is arbitrary and in no way associates it with a given namespace as far as Clojure is concerned. You can even create a keyword with a prefix that's not named the same as any existing namespace:

```
:haunted/name
;=> :haunted/name
```

You create a keyword :haunted/name, showing that the prefix doesn't have to be an existing namespace name. But the fact that keywords aren't members of any given namespace doesn't mean namespace-qualifying them is pointless. Instead, it's often clearer to do so, especially when a namespace aggregates a specific functionality and its keywords are meaningful in that context.

Separating the plumbing from the domain

Even though qualified keywords can have any arbitrary prefix, sometimes it's useful to use namespaces to provide special information for keywords. In a namespace named crypto, the keywords ::rsa and ::blowfish make sense as being namespace qualified. Similarly, if you create a namespace aquarium, then using ::blowfish in it is contextually meaningful. Likewise, when adding metadata to structures, you should consider using qualified keywords as keys and directives if their intention is domain oriented. Consider the following code:

```
(defn do-blowfish [directive]
  (case directive
    :aquarium/blowfish (println "feed the fish")
    :crypto/blowfish   (println "encode the message")
    :blowfish          (println "not sure what to do")))
(ns crypto)
(user/do-blowfish :blowfish)
; not sure what to do

(user/do-blowfish ::blowfish)
; encode the message
(ns aquarium)
(user/do-blowfish :blowfish)
; not sure what to do
(user/do-blowfish ::blowfish)
; feed the fish
```

When switching to different namespaces using ns, you can use the namespace-qualified keyword syntax to ensure that the correct domain-specific code path is executed.

Namespace qualification is especially important when you're creating ad hoc hierarchies and defining multimethods, both discussed in section XREF ch09lev1sec2.

4.4   *Symbolic resolution*

In the previous section, we covered the differences between symbols and keywords. Whereas keywords are fairly straightforward, symbols abide by a slightly more complicated system for lookup resolution.

Symbols in Clojure are roughly analogous to identifiers in many other languages—words that refer to other things. In a nutshell, symbols are primarily used to provide a name for a given value. But in Clojure, symbols can also be referred to directly, by using the symbol or quote function or the ' special operator. Symbols tend to be discrete entities from one lexical contour (or scope) to another, and often even in a single contour. Unlike keywords, symbols aren't unique based solely on name alone, as you can see in the following:

```
(identical? 'goat 'goat)
;=> false
```

identical? returns false in this example because each goat symbol is a discrete object that only happens to share a name and therefore a symbolic representation. But that name is the basis for symbol equality:

```
(= 'goat 'goat)
;=> true

(name 'goat)
"goat"
```

The identical? function in Clojure only ever returns true when the symbols are the same object:

```
(let [x 'goat, y x]
  (identical? x y))

;=> true
```

In the preceding example, x is also a symbol; but when evaluated in the (identical? x y) form, it returns the symbol goat, which is being stored on the runtime call stack. The question arises: why not make two identically named symbols the same object? The answer lies in metadata, which we discuss next.

4.4.1 Metadata

Clojure lets you attach metadata to various objects, but for now we'll focus on attaching metadata to symbols. The with-meta function takes an object and a map and returns another object of the same type with the metadata attached. Equally named symbols often aren't the same instance because each can have its own unique metadata:

```
(let [x (with-meta 'goat {:ornery true})
      y (with-meta 'goat {:ornery false})]
  [(= x y)
   (identical? x y)
   (meta x)
   (meta y)])

;=> [true false {:ornery true} {:ornery false}]
```

The two locals x and y both hold an equal symbol 'goat, but they're different instances, each containing separate metadata maps obtained with the meta function.

So you see, symbol equality depends on neither metadata nor identity. This equality semantic isn't limited to symbols but is pervasive in Clojure, as we'll demonstrate throughout this book. You'll find that keywords can't hold metadata[7] because any equally named keyword is the same object.

4.4.2   *Symbols and namespaces*

Like keywords, symbols don't belong to any specific namespace. Take, for example, the following code:

```
(ns where-is)
(def a-symbol 'where-am-i)

a-symbol
;=> where-am-i

(resolve 'a-symbol)
;=> #'where-is/a-symbol

`a-symbol
;=> where-is/a-symbol
```

The initial evaluation of a-symbol shows the expected value where-am-i. But attempting to resolve the symbol using resolve and using syntax-quote returns what looks like (as printed at the REPL) a namespace-qualified symbol. This is because a symbol's qualification is a characteristic of evaluation and not necessarily inherent in the symbol. This also applies to symbols qualified with class names. This evaluation behavior will prove beneficial when we discuss macros in chapter 8, but for now we can summarize the overarching idea known as Lisp-1 (Gabriel 2001).

4.4.3   *Lisp-1*

Clojure is what's known as a Lisp-1,[8] which in simple terms means it uses the same name resolution for function and value bindings. In a Lisp-2 programming language like Common Lisp, these name resolutions are performed differently depending on the context of the symbol, be it in a function-call position or a function-argument position. There are many arguments for and against both Lisp-1 and Lisp-2, but one downside of Lisp-1 bears consideration. Because the same name-resolution scheme is used for functions and their arguments, there's a real possibility of shadowing existing functions with other locals or vars. Name shadowing isn't necessarily bad if done thoughtfully, but if done accidentally it can lead to unexpected and obscure errors. You should take care when naming locals and defining new functions so that name-shadowing complications can be avoided.

Because name-shadowing errors tend to be rare, the benefits of a simplified mechanism for calling and passing first-class functions far outweigh the detriments. Clojure's

---

[7]   Java class instances, including strings, can't hold metadata either.

[8]   It's more like a Lisp-1.5, because like keywords, symbols can be used as functions when placed in the function-call position. This doesn't have anything to do with name resolution, however, so it's a minor point.

adoption of a Lisp-1 resolution scheme makes for cleaner implementations and therefore highlights the solution rather than muddying the waters with the nuances of symbolic lookup. For example, the best function highlights this perfectly in the way that it takes the greater-than function > and calls it in its body as f:

```
(defn best [f xs]
  (reduce #(if (f % %2) % %2) xs))

(best > [1 3 4 2 7 5 3])
;=> 7
```

A similar function body using a Lisp-2 language requires the intervention of another function (in this case, funcall) responsible for invoking the function explicitly. Likewise, passing any function requires the use of a qualifying tag marking it as a function object, as shown here:

```
;; This is Common Lisp and NOT Clojure code
(defun best (f xs)
  (reduce #'(lambda (l r)
              (if (funcall f l r) l r))
          xs))

(best #'> '(1 3 4 2 7 5 3))
;=> 7
```

This section isn't intended to champion the cause of Lisp-1 over Lisp-2, but rather to highlight the differences between the two. Many of the design decisions in Clojure provide succinctness in implementation, and Lisp-1 is no exception. The preference for Lisp-1 versus Lisp-2 typically boils down to matters of style and taste; by all practical measures, they're equivalent.

Having covered the two symbolic scalar types, we now move into a type that you're (for better or worse) likely familiar with: the regular expression.

4.5   Regular expressions—the second problem

> *Some people, when confronted with a problem, think "I know, I'll use regular expressions." Now they have two problems.*
>
> —Jamie Zawinski[9]

Regular expressions are a powerful and compact way to find specific patterns in text strings. Although we sympathize with Zawinski's attitude and appreciate his wit, sometimes regular expressions are a useful tool to have on hand. The full capabilities of regular expressions (or regexes) are well beyond the scope of this section (Friedl 1997), but we'll look at some of the ways Clojure uses Java's regex capabilities.

Java's regular-expression engine is reasonably powerful, supporting Unicode and features such as reluctant quantifiers and look-around clauses. Clojure doesn't try to reinvent the wheel and instead provides special syntax for literal Java regex patterns plus a few functions to help Java's regex capabilities fit better with the rest of Clojure.

---

[9] Usenet post, 12 August 1997, alt.religion.emacs.

4.5.1 *Syntax*

A literal regular expression in Clojure[10] looks like this:

```
#"an example pattern"
```

This produces[11] a compiled regex object that can be used either directly with Java interop method calls or with any of the Clojure regex functions described later:

```
(class #"example")
;=> java.util.regex.Pattern
```

Although the pattern is surrounded with double quotes like string literals, the way things are escaped within the quotes isn't the same. If you've written regexes in Java, you know that any backslashes intended for consumption by the regex compiler must be doubled, as shown in the following `compile` call. This isn't necessary in Clojure regex literals, as shown by the undoubled return value:

```
(java.util.regex.Pattern/compile "\\d")
;=> #"\d"
```

In short, the only rules you need to know for embedding unusual literal characters or predefined character classes are listed in the Javadoc for `Pattern`.[12]

Regular expressions accept option flags, shown in table 4.1, that can make a pattern case-insensitive or enable multiline mode. Clojure's regex literals starting with `(?<flag>)` set the mode for the rest of the pattern. For example, the pattern `#"(?i)yo"` matches the strings "yo", "yO", "Yo", and "YO".

Table 4.1 Flags that can be used in Clojure regular-expression patterns, along with their long name and a description of what they do. See Java's documentation for the `java.util.regex.Pattern` class for more details.

Flag	Flag name	Description
d	UNIX_LINES	`.`, `^`, and `$` match only the Unix line terminator `'\n'`.
i	CASE_INSENSITIVE	ASCII characters are matched without regard to uppercase or lowercase.
x	COMMENTS	Whitespace and comments in the pattern are ignored.
m	MULTILINE	`^` and `$` match near line terminators instead of only at the beginning or end of the entire input string.
s	DOTALL	`.` matches any character including the line terminator.
u	UNICODE_CASE	Causes the i flag to use Unicode case insensitivity instead of ASCII.

---

[10] This section is Clojure-specific. ClojureScript's regular expressions are notably different, and we'll defer discussing them until chapter 13.

[11] Literal regex patterns are compiled to `java.util.regex.Pattern` instances at read-time. This means, for example, if you use a literal regex in a loop, it's *not* recompiled each time through the loop, but just once when the surrounding code is compiled.

[12] See the online `Pattern` reference at http://mng.bz/qp77.

4.5.2 *Regular-expression functions*

The re-seq function is Clojure's regex workhorse. It returns a lazy seq of all matches in a string, which means it can be used to efficiently test whether a string matches or to find all matches in a string or a mapped file:

```
(re-seq #"\w+" "one-two/three")
;=> ("one" "two" "three")
```

The preceding regular expression has no capturing groups, so each match in the returned seq is a string. A *capturing group* (subsegments that are accessible via the returned match object) in the regex causes each returned item to be a vector:

```
(re-seq #"\w*(\w)" "one-two/three")
;=> (["one" "e"] ["two" "o"] ["three" "e"])
```

Now that we've looked at some nice functions you can use, we'll talk about one object you shouldn't.

4.5.3 *Beware of mutable matchers*

Java's regular-expression engine includes a Matcher object that mutates in a non-thread-safe way as it walks through a string finding matches. This object is exposed by Clojure via the re-matcher function and can be used as an argument to re-groups and the single-parameter form of re-find. We highly recommend avoiding all of these unless you're certain you know what you're doing. These dangerous functions are used internally by the implementations of some of the recommended functions described earlier, but in each case they're careful to disallow access to the Matcher object they use. Use matchers at your own risk, or better yet don't use them directly at all.[13]

4.6 *Summary*

Clojure's scalar types generally work as expected, but its numerical types have the potential to cause frustration in certain situations. Although you may rarely encounter issues with numerical precision, keeping in mind the circumstances under which they occur may prove useful in the future. Given its inherent arbitrary-precision big decimal and rational numerics, Clojure provides the tools for perfectly accurate calculations. Keywords serve many purposes and are ubiquitous in Clojure code. When dealing directly with symbols, Clojure's nature as a Lisp-1 defines the nature of how symbolic resolution occurs. Finally, Clojure provides regular expressions as first-class data types, and their usage is encouraged where appropriate.

As you might have speculated, this chapter was nice and short due to the relative simplicity of scalar types. In the following chapter, we'll step it up a notch or 10 when covering Clojure's composite data types. Although scalars are interesting and deeper than expected, the next chapter will start you on your way to understanding Clojure's true goal: providing a sane approach to application state.

---

[13] The clojure.string namespace has a bevy of functions that are handy for using regular expressions.

Collection types

It's better to have 100 functions operate on one data structure than 10 functions on 10 data structures.

—Alan Perlis[1]

This chapter covers

- Persistence, sequences, and complexity
- Vectors: creating and using them in all their varieties
- Lists: Clojure's code form data structure
- How to use persistent queues
- Persistent sets
- Thinking in maps
- Finding the position of items in a sequence

Clojure provides a rich set of composite data types, or collection types, and we'll cover them all: vectors, lists, queues, sets, and maps. In this chapter, we'll dig into the strengths and weaknesses of each. We'll spend more time on vectors and maps than on the other types, because those two are used in a wider variety of circumstances and warrant the extra discussion. Finally, we'll discuss the design of a simple

---

[1] "Epigrams on Programming," *ACM SIGPLAN* 17, no. 9 (September 1982).

function to use many of the lessons learned in this chapter, and you'll gain specific insight into the preceding quote.

Before we look at the primary collection types individually, we'll discuss the things they have in common. For example, you may have heard of Clojure's *sequence abstraction*—all the persistent collections use it, so we'll examine that as well as some algorithmic complexity concepts we'll refer to throughout the chapter.

5.1 *Persistence, sequences, and complexity*

Clojure's collection data types have some unique properties compared to collections in many mainstream languages. Terms such as *persistent* and *sequence* come up, and not always in a way that makes their meaning clear. In this section, we'll define their meanings carefully. We'll also briefly examine the topic of algorithmic complexity and Big-O notation as they apply to Clojure collections.

The term *persistent* is particularly problematic because it means something different in other contexts. In the case of Clojure, we believe that a phrase immortalized by Inigo Montoya from the novel and subsequent film *The Princess Bride* summarizes your likely initial reaction …

5.1.1 *"You keep using that word. I do not think it means what you think it means."*

Although storage to disk may be the more common meaning of *persistent* today, Clojure uses an older meaning of the word having to do with immutable in-memory collections with specific properties. In particular, a persistent collection in Clojure allows you to preserve historical versions (Okasaki 1999) of its state and promises that all versions will have the same update and lookup complexity guarantees. The specific guarantees depend on the collection type, and we'll cover those details along with each kind of collection.

Here you can see the difference between a persistent data structure and one that's not by using a Java array:

```
(def ds (into-array [:willie :barnabas :adam]))    ⟵── into-array can make a
(seq ds)                                                Java/JavaScript array
;=> (:willie :barnabas :adam)                           out of a vector
```

This example creates a three-element array of keywords and uses seq to produce an object that displays nicely in the REPL. Any change to the array ds happens in place, thus obliterating any historical version:

```
(aset ds 1 :quentin)    ⟵── aset sets the value
;=> :quentin                in an array slot

(seq ds)
;=> (:willie :quentin :adam)
```

But using one of Clojure's persistent data structures paints a different picture:

```
(def ds [:willie :barnabas :adam])
ds
;=> [:willie :barnabas :adam]

(def ds1 (replace {:barnabas :quentin} ds))
ds
;=> [:willie :barnabas :adam]

ds1
;=> [:willie :quentin :adam]
```

> This time create a vector instead of an array

> ds is unchanged

> ds1 is a modified version of the original vector

The original vector ds did *not* change on the replacement of the keyword :barnabas but instead created another vector with the changed value. A natural concern when confronted with this picture of persistence is that a naive implementation would copy the entire collection on each change, leading to slow operations and poor use of memory. Clojure's implementations (Bagwell 2001) are instead efficient by sharing structural elements from one version of a persistent structure to another. This may seem magical, but we'll demystify it in the next chapter. For now it's sufficient to understand that each instance of a collection is immutable and efficient. This fact opens numerous possibilities that wouldn't work for standard mutable collections. One of these is the sequence abstraction.

5.1.2   *Sequence terms and what they mean*

The words *sequential, sequence,* and *seq* don't sound very different from each other, but they mean specific things in Clojure. We'll start with specific definitions of each term to help you tell them apart, and then go into a bit of detail about how they relate to equality partitions and the sequence abstraction.

SEQS, SEQUENTIALS, AND SEQUENCES ... OH MY

A *sequential* collection is one that holds a series of values without reordering them. As such, it's one of three broad categories of collection types along with sets and maps.

A *sequence* is a sequential collection that represents a series of values that may or may not exist yet. They may be values from a concrete collection or values that are computed as necessary. A sequence may also be empty.

Clojure has a simple API called *seq* for navigating collections. It consist of two functions: first and rest. If the collection has anything in it, (first coll) returns the first element; otherwise it returns nil. (rest coll) returns a sequence of the items other than the first. If there are no other items, rest returns an empty sequence and never nil. As you may recall from sections 3.1 and 3.2, the way that Clojure treats nil versus empty collections motivates the iteration patterns used in the language. Clojure functions that promise to return sequences, such as map and filter, work the same way as rest. A *seq* is any object that implements the seq API, thereby supporting the functions first and rest. You might consider it an immutable variant of an enumerator or iterator where the lack of internal state allows near limitless concurrent and parallel iteration over the same seq.

Throughout this book, we'll use very precise terms for certain aspects and features of Clojure. Table 5.1 provides a summary of some of the collection-specific terms.

Table 5.1　Sequence terms in brief

Term	Brief description	Example(s)
Collection	A composite data type	`[1 2]`, `{:a 1}`, `#{1 2}`, and lists and arrays
Sequential	Ordered series of values	`[1 2 3 4]`, `(1 2 3 4)`
Sequence	A sequential collection that may or may not exist yet	The result of `(map a-fun a-collection)`
Seq	Simple API for navigating collections	`first`, `rest`, `nil`, and `()`
`clojure.core/seq`	A function that returns an object implementing the seq API	`(seq [])  ;;=> nil` and `(seq [1 2])  ;;=> (1 2)`

There's also a function called `seq` that accepts a wide variety of collection-like objects. Some collections, such as lists, implement the seq API directly, so calling `seq` on them returns the collection itself. More often, calling `seq` on a collection returns a new seq object for navigating that collection. In either case, if the collection is empty, `seq` returns `nil` and never an empty sequence. Functions that promise to return seqs (not sequences), such as `next`, work the same way.

Clojure's sequence library manipulates collections, strings, arrays, and so on as if they were sequences, using the `seq` function and seq API.

Beware type-based predicates

Clojure includes a few predicates with names like the words just defined. Although they're not frequently used, it seems worth mentioning that they may not mean exactly what the definitions here might suggest. For example, every object for which `sequential?` returns `true` is a sequential collection, but it returns `false` for some that are also sequential. This is because of implementation details that may be improved in a future version of Clojure.

EQUALITY PARTITIONS

As we mentioned previously, Clojure classifies each collection data type into one of three logical categories or partitions: sequentials, maps, and sets. These divisions draw clear distinctions between the types and help define equality semantics. Specifically, two objects will never be equal if they belong to different partitions. Few collection types are actually *sequences*, although several such as vectors are *sequential.*

If two sequentials have the same values in the same order, = returns true for them, even if their concrete types are different, as shown:

```
(= [1 2 3] '(1 2 3))
;=> true
```

Conversely, even if two collections have the same exact values, if one is a sequential collection and the other isn't, = returns false:

```
(= [1 2 3] #{1 2 3})
;=> false
```

Examples of things that are sequential include Clojure lists and vectors, and Java lists such as java.util.ArrayList. In fact, everything that implements java.util.List is included in the sequential partition.

Generally, things that fall into the other partitions include *set* or *map* in their name and so are easy to identify.

THE SEQUENCE ABSTRACTION

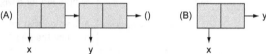

Many Lisps build their data types (McCarthy 1962) on the *cons-cell abstraction*, an elegant two-element structure illustrated in figure 5.1. The cons-cell is used to build a linked list structure akin to the java.util.LinkedList type in the Java core library. In fact, although the cons-cell is the base structure

Figure 5.1 Each cons-cell is a simple pair, a car and a cdr. (A) A list with two cells, each of which has a value— x and y, respectively—as the head (the car in Lisp terminology) and a list as the tail (the cdr). This is very similar to first and rest in Clojure sequences. (B) A cons-cell with a simple value for both the head and tail. This is called a *dotted pair* but is not supported by any of Clojure's built-in types.

on which traditional Lisps are built, the name Lisp comes from its focus on *list processing*.

Clojure also has a couple of cons-cell-like structures that are covered in section 5.4, but they're not central to Clojure's design. Instead, the conceptual interface fulfilled by the cons-cell has been lifted off the concrete structure illustrated previously and been named *sequence*. All an object needs to do to be a sequence is to support the two core functions: first and rest. This isn't much, but it's all that's required for the bulk of Clojure's powerful library of sequence functions and macros to be able to operate on the collection: filter, map, for, doseq, take, partition … the list goes on.

At the same time, a wide variety of objects satisfy this interface. Every Clojure collection provides at least one kind of seq object for walking through its contents, exposed via the seq function. Some collections provide more than one; for example, vectors support rseq, and maps support the functions keys and vals. All of these functions return a seq or, if the collection is empty, nil.

You can see examples of this by looking at the types of objects returned by various expressions. Here's the map class:

```
(class (hash-map :a 1))
;=> clojure.lang.PersistentHashMap
```

Unsurprisingly, the `hash-map` function returns an object of type `PersistentHashMap`. Passing that map object to `seq` returns an entirely new kind of object:

```
(seq (hash-map :a 1))
;=> ([:a 1])

(class (seq (hash-map :a 1)))
;=> clojure.lang.PersistentHashMap$NodeSeq
```

This class name suggests it's a seq of nodes on a hash map. Similarly, you can get a seq of keys on the same map:

```
(seq (keys (hash-map :a 1)))
;=> (:a)

(class (keys (hash-map :a 1)))
;=> clojure.lang.APersistentMap$KeySeq
```

Note that these specific class names are an implementation detail that may change in the future, but the concepts they embody are central to Clojure and unlikely to change.

Having laid the foundation for a deeper dive into the sequence abstraction, we now must quickly diverge into a simplified discussion of asymptotic complexity of algorithms and Big-O notation. If you're already comfortable with these topics, by all means skip to section 5.2. If you need a refresher or an overview, then the next section is a minimalist introduction (Cormen 2009) to the topic.

5.1.3 *Big-O*

This book isn't heavily focused on asymptotic complexity, but we do mention it a handful of times throughout, so here we'll cover the minimum required for understanding these few mentions. You may have gone your entire career without having to understand Big-O notation, and you may go the remainder similarly. But that's no reason not to learn more; and a bit of understanding about Big-O and its implications will go a long way toward helping you choose between Clojure collections, as well as design and analyze algorithms in general.

Algorithmic complexity is a system for describing the *relative* space and time costs for algorithms. Typically the complexity of an algorithm is described using what's known as *Big-O notation*. For example, you may have heard that finding an element in a linked list is $O(n)$, which is read as *order n*. This means if you have a list `(:a :b :c)` of length 3, then verifying that the keyword `:c` is in that list requires three comparisons. This highlights the *worst case* of list access because `:c` is at the end of the list, but you don't need to worry too much about the worst-case scenario unless that's the only difference between two algorithms. On the other hand, to verify that `:a` is in the same list is $O(1)$, which is read as *constant time*. Finding `:a` represents the *best case* for list access because it's at the front of the list. But you shouldn't build your hopes that elements will always be at the front—in analyzing algorithms, the best-case scenario is too rare to matter much. What you care about when analyzing algorithms is the *expected case*, or what you're likely to see in practice. When looking at a few million runs of verifying that some value is contained in a million different lists, you inevitably see that the average number of comparisons required approaches the length of the list, divided by two. But because doubling the length of the list would also double the number of comparisons done in both the expected and worst cases, they're grouped into the same Big-O category: O(n), also known as *linear time.*

Thus two algorithms that are in the same Big-O category may perform very differently, especially on small workloads. This makes the most difference when there's a large *constant term*: work that the algorithm has to do up front regardless of the size of the workload.

When the workload is small, an O(1) algorithm with a large constant factor may be more costly than an O(n) algorithm that's without extra costs. But as the workload increases, an O(1) algorithm *always* overtakes the O(n) algorithm, as shown in figure 5.2. Big-O doesn't concern itself with these constant factors or small workloads.

When learning about Clojure's persistent data structures, you're likely to hear the term $O(\log_{32} n)$ for those based on the persistent hash trie and $O(\log_2 n)$ for the sorted structures. Accessing an element in a Clojure persistent structure by index is O(log n), or logarithmic. Logarithmic complexity describes a class of algorithms that are effectively immune to large changes in the size of their data. In the case of Clojure's persistent structures, this means there's little difference in "hops" (such as comparisons) between locating an element in a structure containing 100 elements and one containing 1 million elements. In practice you may notice some difference, because for a billion objects $O(\log_2 n)$ would require approximately 30 comparisons for a lookup, whereas $O(\log_{32} n)$ would require only about 6. Given the smaller number of operations required for the $O(\log_{32} n)$ data structures, they can be viewed as providing a nearly O(1) lookup and update.[2]

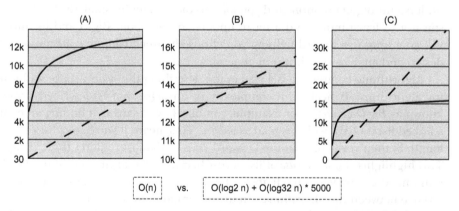

Figure 5.2   In Big-O, regardless of the other ancillary costs, the higher order of magnitude always overtakes the lower eventually.

---

[2]   Logarithms in Big-O notation are specified without a base because they differ from one another only by a constant factor. Both $\log_{32} n$ and $\log_2 n$ scale *exactly the same way*; they're just multiplied by a smaller constant. In no way is $O(\log_{32} n)$ more like O(1) then $O(l_n n)$—in formal Big-O notation, they're exactly the same.

We've covered the basic ideas behind persistence and the sequence abstraction and even touched on the basics of Big-O notation. Now we'll discuss Clojure's primary collection types and how these concepts apply to each, starting with vectors.

5.2 Vectors: creating and using them in all their varieties

Vectors store zero or more values sequentially, indexed by number; they're a bit like arrays but are immutable and persistent. They're versatile and make efficient use of memory and processor resources at both small and large sizes.

Vectors are probably the most frequently used collection type in Clojure code. They're used as literals for argument lists and `let` bindings, for holding large amounts of application data, as stacks, and as map entries. We'll also address efficiency considerations, including growing on the right end, subvectors, and reversals, and finally we'll discuss cases in which vectors aren't an optimal solution.

5.2.1 Building vectors

The vector's literal square-bracket syntax is one reason you may choose to use a vector over a list. For example, the `let` form would work perfectly well, and with a nearly identical implementation, if it took a literal *list* of bindings instead of a literal *vector*. But the square brackets are visually different from the round parentheses surrounding the `let` form itself as well as the likely function calls in the body of the `let` form, and this is useful for humans (so we hear). Using vectors to indicate bindings for `let`, `with-open`, `fn`, and such is idiomatic Clojure practice and is a pattern you're encouraged to follow in any similar macros you write.

The most common way to create a vector is with the literal syntax like [1 2 3]. But in many cases, you'll want to create a vector out of the contents of some other kind of collection. For this, there's the function vec:

```
(vec (range 10))
;=> [0 1 2 3 4 5 6 7 8 9]
```

If you already have a vector but want to pour several values into it, then `into` is your friend:

```
(let [my-vector [:a :b :c]]
  (into my-vector (range 10)))
;=> [:a :b :c 0 1 2 3 4 5 6 7 8 9]
```

If you want it to return a vector, the first argument to `into` *must* be a vector. The second arg can be any sequence, such as what `range` returns, or anything else that works with the `seq` function. You can view the operation of `into` as similar to an $O(n)$ concatenation based on the size of the second argument.[3] Clojure also provides a `vector` function to build a vector from its arguments, which is handy for constructs like (map vector a b).

---

[3] Vectors can't be concatenated any more efficiently than $O(n)$.

Clojure can store primitive types inside of vectors using the `vector-of` function, which takes any of `:int`, `:long`, `:float`, `:double`, `:byte`, `:short`, `:boolean`, or `:char` as its argument and returns an empty vector. This returned vector acts like any other vector, except that it stores its contents as primitives internally. All the normal vector operations still apply, and the new vector attempts to coerce any additions into its internal type when being added:

```
(into (vector-of :int) [Math/PI 2 1.3])
;=> [3 2 1]
(into (vector-of :char) [100 101 102])
;=> [\d \e \f]
(into (vector-of :int) [1 2 623876371267813267326786327863])
;  java.lang.IllegalArgumentException: Value out of range for int:
     -8359803716404783817
```

In addition, all caveats mentioned in section 4.1 regarding overflow, underflow, and so forth also apply to vectors of primitives.

Using `vec` and `into`, it's easy to build vectors much larger than can be conveniently built using vector literals. But once you have a large vector like that, what are you going to do with it?

5.2.2   *Large vectors*

When collections are small, the performance differences between vectors and lists hardly matter. But as both get larger, each becomes dramatically slower at operations the other can still perform efficiently. Vectors are particularly efficient at three things relative to lists: adding or removing things from the right end of the collection, accessing or changing items in the interior of the collection by numeric index, and walking in reverse order. Adding and removing from the end is done by treating the vector as a stack—we'll cover that in section 5.2.3.

Any item in a vector can be accessed by its index number from 0 up to but not including (`count my-vector`) in essentially constant time.[4] You can do this using the function `nth`; using the function `get`, essentially treating the vector like a map; or by invoking the vector as a function. Look at each of these as applied to this example vector:

```
(def a-to-j (vec (map char (range 65 75))))     ◁─┐ Characters can be built
                                                  │ from the ASCII code
a-to-j
;;=> [\A \B \C \D \E \F \G \H \I \J]
```

All three of these do the same work, and each returns `\E`:

```
(nth a-to-j 4)
;;=> \E

(get a-to-j 4)
;;=> \E

(a-to-j 4)
;;=> \E
```

---

[4] Several operations on Clojure's persistent data structures are described in this book as "essentially constant time." In all cases, these are $O(\log_{32} n)$.

Which to use is a judgment call, but table 5.2 highlights some points you might consider when choosing.

Table 5.2 Vector lookup options: the three ways to look up an item in a vector, and how each responds to different exceptional circumstances

	nth	get	Vector as a function
If the vector is `nil`	Returns `nil`	Returns `nil`	Throws an exception
If the index is out of range	Throws exception by default or returns a "not found" if supplied	Returns `nil`	Throws an exception
Supports a "not found" arg	Yes `(nth [] 9 :whoops)`	Yes `(get [] 9 :whoops)`	No

Because vectors are indexed, they can be efficiently walked in either direction, left to right or right to left. The `seq` and `rseq` functions return sequences that do exactly that:

```
(seq a-to-j)
;=> (\A \B \C \D \E \F \G \H \I \J)

(rseq a-to-j)
;=> (\J \I \H \G \F \E \D \C \B \A)
```

Any item in a vector can be changed using the `assoc` function. Clojure does this in essentially constant time using structural sharing between the old and new vectors as described at the beginning of this chapter:

```
(assoc a-to-j 4 "no longer E")
;=> [\A \B \C \D "no longer E" \F \G \H \I \J]
```

The `assoc` function for vectors only works on indices that already exist in the vector or, as a special case, exactly one step past the end. In this case, the returned vector is one item larger than the input vector. More frequently, vectors are grown using the `conj` function, as you'll see in the next section.

A few higher-powered functions are provided that use `assoc` internally. For example, the `replace` function works on both seqs and vectors, but when given a vector, it uses `assoc` to fix up and return a new vector:

```
(replace {2 :a, 4 :b} [1 2 3 2 3 4])
;=> [1 :a 3 :a 3 :b]
```

The functions `assoc-in` and `update-in` are for working with nested structures of vectors and/or maps, like this one:[5]

```
(def matrix
    [[1 2 3]
```

---

[5] Nested vectors are far from the most efficient way to store or process matrices, but they're convenient to manipulate in Clojure and so make a good example here. More efficient options include a single vector, arrays, or a library for matrix processing such as Colt or Incanter (http://incanter.org).

```
    [4 5 6]
    [7 8 9]])
```

assoc-in, get-in, and update-in take a series of indices to pick items from each more deeply nested level. For a vector arranged like the earlier matrix example, this amounts to row and column coordinates:

```
(get-in matrix [1 2])
;=> 6

(assoc-in matrix [1 2] 'x)
;=> [[1 2 3] [4 5 x] [7 8 9]]
```

The update-in function works the same way, but instead of taking a value to *overwrite* an existing value, it takes a function to *apply* to an existing value. It replaces the value at the given coordinates with the return value of the function given:

```
(update-in matrix [1 2] * 100)
;=> [[1 2 3] [4 5 600] [7 8 9]]
```

The coordinates refer to the value 6, and the function given here is * taking an argument 100, so the slot becomes the return value of (* 6 100). There's also a function get-in for retrieving a value in a nested vector. Before exploring its operation, let's create a function neighbors in the following listing that, given a y-x location in an square 2D matrix, returns a sequence of the locations surrounding it.

Listing 5.1   Function for finding the neighbors of a spot on a 2D matrix

```
(defn neighbors
  ([size yx] (neighbors [[-1 0] [1 0] [0 -1] [0 1]]     ◁─┐  Define neighbors to be
                        size                                │  one spot away, crosswise
                        yx))
  ([deltas size yx]
     (filter (fn [new-yx]                               ◁──  Remove illegal coordinates
               (every? #(< -1 % size) new-yx))
             (map #(vec (map + yx %))                      │  Blindly calculate possible
                  deltas))))                            ◁─┘  coordinates
```

The operation of neighbors is fairly straightforward, but let's walk through it a little. The deltas local describes that a neighbor can be one spot away, but only along the x or y axis (not diagonally). The function first walks through deltas and builds a vector of each added to the yx point provided. This operation of course generates illegal point coordinates, so those are removed using filter, which checks to ensure that the indices lie between -1 and the provided size.

To show this in action, you can call neighbors, indicating a 3 x 3 matrix and asking for the neighbors of the top-left cell:

```
(neighbors 3 [0 0])

;;=> ((1 0) (0 1))
```

The result indicates that the crosswise neighbors of cell y=0|x=0 are the cells y=1|x=0 and y=0|x=1. You can see how this result is correct graphically in figure 5.3.

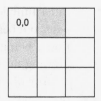

You can also call `neighbors` with the same-sized matrix but asking for the neighbors of the center cell:

```
(neighbors 3 [1 1])

;;=> ((0 1) (2 1) (1 0) (1 2))
```

Figure 5.3 The crosswise neighbors of cell 0,0

The result indicates that the crosswise neighbors of the center cell at y=1|x=1 are the cells forming a plus, as shown in figure 5.4.

You can test the result of `neighbors` on cell 0,0 using `get-in` as follows:

```
(map #(get-in matrix %) (neighbors 3 [0 0]))
;=> (4 2)
```

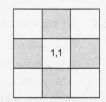

For each neighbor coordinate returned from `neighbors`, you use `get-in` to retrieve the value at that point. The position

Figure 5.4 The crosswise neighbors of cell 1,1

[0 0] corresponding to the value 1 has the neighboring values 4 and 2. You'll use `neighbors` again in section 7.4; but next we'll look at growing and shrinking vectors—treating them like stacks.

5.2.3 Vectors as stacks

Classic stacks have at least two operations, *push* and *pop*. With respect to Clojure vectors, these operations are called `conj` and `pop`, respectively. The `conj` function adds elements to, and `pop` removes elements from, the right side of the stack. Because vectors are immutable, `pop` returns a new vector with the rightmost item dropped—this is different from many mutable stack APIs, which generally return the dropped item. Consequently, `peek` becomes more important as the primary way to get an item from the top of the stack:

```
(def my-stack [1 2 3])

(peek my-stack)
;=> 3

(pop my-stack)
;=> [1 2]

(conj my-stack 4)
;=> [1 2 3 4]

(+ (peek my-stack) (peek (pop my-stack)))
;=> 5
```

Each of these operations completes in essentially constant time. Most of the time, a vector that's used as a stack is used that way throughout its life. It's helpful to future readers of your code to keep this is mind and use the stack operations consistently, even when other functions might work. For example, `last` on a vector returns the same thing as `peek`; but besides being slower,[6] it leads to unnecessary confusion about how the collection is being used. If the algorithm involved calls for a stack, use `conj`, not `assoc`, for growing the vector; `peek`, not `last`; and `pop`, not `dissoc`, for shrinking it.

Any object that implements `clojure.lang.IPersistentStack`[7] can use the functions `conj`, `pop`, and `peek`. In addition to vectors, Clojure lists also implement this interface, but the functions operate on the left side of lists instead of the right side as with vectors. When operating on either via the stack discipline, it's best to ignore the ordering, because it tends to add confusion.

5.2.4   *Using vectors instead of reverse*

The ability of vectors to grow efficiently on the right side and then be walked right to left produces a noteworthy emergent behavior: you rarely need the `reverse` function. This is different from most Lisps and schemes. When processing a list, it's pretty common to want to produce a new list in the same order. But if all you have are classic Lisp lists, often the most natural algorithm[8] leaves you with a backward list that needs to be reversed. Here's an example of a function similar to Clojure's `map`:

```
(defn strict-map1 [f coll]                    Accumulator
  (loop [coll coll, acc nil]                  starts as nil
    (if (empty? coll)
        (reverse acc)                   Final result is reversed
        (recur (next coll)
               (cons (f (first coll)) acc)))))    Put the element onto the
(strict-map1 - (range 5))                          front of the accumulator
;;=> (0 -1 -2 -3 -4)
```

This is adequate code, except for that glaring `reverse` of the final return value. After the entire list has been walked once to produce the desired values, `reverse` walks it again to get the values in the right order. This is both inefficient and unnecessary. One way to get rid of the `reverse` is to use a vector instead of a list as the accumulator:

```
(defn strict-map2 [f coll]                    Accumulator now
  (loop [coll coll, acc []]                   starts as a vector
    (if (empty? coll)
        acc                             Final result is unchanged
        (recur (next coll)
               (conj acc (f (first coll)))))))    Put the element onto the rear
(strict-map2 - (range 5))                          of the vector accumulator
;=> [0 -1 -2 -3 -4]
```

---

[6] `last` is slower than `peek` for a vector because `last` always walks to the end of the collection given to it, whereas `peek` is defined in terms of the most efficient operation for the collection type.

[7] The `conj` function also works with all Clojure's other persistent collection types, even if they don't implement `clojure.lang.IPersistentStack`.

[8] ... the most natural *tail-recursive* algorithm, anyway.

A small change, but the code is now a touch cleaner and faster. It does return a vector instead of a list, but this is rarely a problem, because any client code that wants to treat this as a seq can usually do so automatically.[9]

The examples we've shown so far have all been plain vectors, but we'll turn now to the special features of some other vector types, starting with subvectors.

5.2.5 *Subvectors*

Although items can't be removed efficiently from a vector (except the rightmost item), Clojure provide a fast way to take a slice of an existing vector such as `a-to-j` (previously defined as `[\A \B \C \D \E \F \G \H \I \J]`) based on start and end indices with the `subvec` function:

```
(subvec a-to-j 3 6)
;=> [\D \E \F]
```

The first index given to `subvec` is inclusive (starts *at* index 3), but the second is exclusive (ends *before* index 6). The new subvector internally hangs on to the entire original `a-to-j` vector, making each lookup performed on the new vector cause the subvector to do a little offset math and then look it up in the original. This makes creating a subvector fast. You can use `subvec` on any kind of vector, and it'll work fine. But there's special logic for taking a subvec of a subvec, in which case the newest subvector keeps a reference to the *original* vector, not the intermediate subvector. This prevents subvectors of subvectors from stacking up needlessly, and it keeps both the creation and use of the sub-subvecs fast and efficient.

5.2.6 *Vectors as map entries*

Clojure's hash map, just like hash tables or dictionaries in many other languages, has a mechanism to iterate through the entire collection. Clojure's solution for this iterator is, unsurprisingly, a seq. Each item of this seq needs to include both the key and the value, so they're wrapped in a map entry. When printed, each entry looks like a vector:[10]

```
(first {:width 10, :height 20, :depth 15})
;=> [:depth 15]
```

But not only does a map entry *look* like a vector, it really *is* one:

```
(vector? (first {:width 10, :height 20, :depth 15}))
;=> true
```

This means you can use all the regular vector functions on it: `conj`, `get`, and so on. It even supports destructuring, which can be handy. For example, the following locals `dimension` and `amount` take on the value of each key/value pair in turn:

---

[9] Another way to get rid of a `reverse` is to build a lazy sequence instead of accumulating a strict collection. This is how Clojure's own `map` function is implemented; type `(source map)` in your REPL to see it.

[10] In the version of Clojure used while writing the book, we got `[:depth 15]` as our answer. But because map entry order isn't guaranteed, you may see something different with a different version of Clojure.

```
(doseq [[dimension amount] {:width 10, :height 20, :depth 15}]
  (println (str (name dimension) ":") amount "inches"))
; width: 10 inches
; height: 20 inches
; depth: 15 inches
;=> nil
```

A `MapEntry` is its own type and has two functions for retrieving its contents: `key` and `val`, which do exactly the same thing as `(nth my-map 0)` and `(nth my-map 1)`, respectively. These are sometimes useful for the clarity they can bring to your code, but frequently destructuring is used instead, because it's so darned handy.

Now you know what vectors are, what specific kinds of vectors are included in Clojure, and some of the things they're good at doing. To round out your understanding of vectors, we'll conclude with a brief look at things that vectors are *bad* at doing.

5.2.7 *What vectors aren't*

Vectors are versatile, but there are some commonly desired patterns for which they might *seem* like a good solution but in fact aren't. Although we prefer to focus on the positive, we hope a few negative examples will help you avoid using the wrong tool for the job.

VECTORS AREN'T SPARSE

If you have a vector of length *n*, the only position where you can insert a value is at index *n*—appending to the far-right end. You can't skip some indices and insert at a higher index number. If you want a collection indexed by nonsequential numbers, consider a hash map or sorted map. Although you can replace values in a vector, you can't insert or delete items such that indices for the subsequent items would have to be adjusted. Clojure doesn't currently have a native persistent collection that supports this kind of operation, but a Clojure contrib library aptly named `data.finger-tree`[11] supporting a structure called *finger trees* may help for these use cases.

VECTORS AREN'T QUEUES

Some people have tried to use vectors as queues. One approach would be to push items onto the right end of the vector using `conj` and then to pop items off the left using `rest` or `next`. The problem with this is that `rest` and `next` return seqs, not vectors, so subsequent `conj` operations wouldn't behave as desired. Using `into` to convert the seq back into a vector is O(n), which is less than ideal for every `pop`.

Another approach is to use `subvec` as a "pop," leaving off the leftmost item. Because `subvec` does return a vector, subsequent `conj` operations will push onto the right end as desired. But as explained earlier, `subvec` maintains a reference to the entire underlying vector, so none of the items being popped this way will ever be garbage collected. Also less than ideal.

So what *would* be the ideal way to do queue operations on a persistent collection? Why, use a `PersistentQueue`, of course. See section 5.5 for details.

---

[11] The `data.finger-tree` library is located at https://github.com/clojure/data.finger-tree.

VECTORS AREN'T SETS

If you want to find out whether a vector contains a particular value, you might be tempted to use the contains? function, but you'd be disappointed by the results. Clojure's contains? is for asking whether a particular *key*, not *value*, is in a collection. So for a vector, the "keys" are the indices of its elements (the first element is at index 0, and so on). Although it's sometimes useful to check whether an index is contained in a vector using contains?, more often than not you want to find a value.

In this section, we showed how to create vectors using literal syntax or by building them up programmatically. We looked at how to push them, pop them, and slice them. We also looked at some of the things vectors can't do well. One of these is adding and removing items from the left side; although vectors can't do this, lists can, as we'll discuss next.

5.3 Lists: Clojure's code-form data structure

Clojure's PersistentLists are by far the simplest of Clojure's persistent collection types. A PersistentList is a singly linked list where each node knows its distance from the end. List elements can only be found by starting with the first element and walking each prior node in order, and can only be added or removed from the left end.

Lists are almost exclusively used to represent code forms. They're used literally in code to call functions, macros, and so forth, as we'll discuss shortly. Code forms are also built programmatically to then be evaled or used as the return value for a macro. If the final usage of a collection isn't as Clojure code, lists rarely offer any value over vectors and are thus rarely used. But lists have a rich heritage in Lisps, so we'll discuss when they should be used in Clojure, and also when they shouldn't—situations in which there are now better options.

5.3.1 Lists like Lisps like

All flavors of Lisp have lists that they like to use, and Clojure lists, already introduced in chapter 2, are similar enough to be familiar. The functions have different names, but what other Lisps call car is the same as first on a Clojure list. Similarly, cdr is the same as next. But there are substantial differences as well. Perhaps the most surprising is the behavior of cons. Both cons and conj add something to the front of a list, but the order of their arguments is different:

```
(cons 1 '(2 3))
;=> (1 2 3)

(conj '(2 3) 1)
;=> (1 2 3)
```

In a departure from classic Lisps, the "right" way to add to the front of a list is with conj. For each concrete type, conj adds elements in the most efficient way, and for lists this means at the left side. Additionally, a list built using conj is homogeneous— all the objects on its next chain are guaranteed to be lists, whereas sequences built with cons only promise that the result will be some kind of seq. So you can use cons to add to the front of a lazy seq, a range, or any other type of seq, but the only way to get a bigger list is to use conj.[12] Either way, the next part has to be some kind of sequence, which points out another difference from other Lisps: Clojure has no *dotted pair*, a cons-cell whose cdr is a value, not another cons, as we showed earlier in figure 5.1. All you need to know is that if you want a simple pair in a Clojure program, you should use a vector of two items.

All seqs print with rounded parentheses, but this does *not* mean they're the same type or will behave the same way. For example, many of these seq types don't know their own size the way lists do, so calling count on them may be O(n) instead of O(1).[13] An unsurprising difference between lists in Clojure and other Lisps is that they're immutable. At least that had better not be surprising anymore. Changing values in a list is generally discouraged in other Lisps anyway, but in Clojure it's impossible.

5.3.2   *Lists as stacks*

Lists in all Lisps can be used as stacks, but Clojure goes further by supporting the IPersistentStack interface. This means you can use the functions peek and pop to do roughly the same thing as first and next. Two details are worth noting. One is that next and rest are legal on an empty list, but pop throws an exception. The other is that next on a one-item list returns nil, whereas rest and pop both return an empty list.

When you want a stack, the choice between using a list and a vector is a somewhat subtle decision. Their memory organization is different, so it may be worth testing your usage to see which performs better. Also, the order of values returned by seq on a list is backward compared to seq on a vector, and in rare cases this can point to one or the other as the best solution. In the end, it may come down primarily to personal taste.

5.3.3   *What lists aren't*

Probably the most common misuse of lists is to hold items that will be looked up by index. Although you can use nth to get the 42nd (or any other) item from a list, Clojure has to walk the list from the beginning to find it. Don't do that. In fact, this is a practical reason why lists can't be used as functions, as in ((list :a) 0). Vectors are good at looking things up by index, so use one of those instead.

Lists are also not sets. All the reasons we gave in the previous section for why it's a bad idea to frequently search a vector looking for a particular value apply to lists as well. Even more so because contains? *always* returns false for a list. See section 5.5.

Finally, lists aren't queues. You can add items to one end of a list, but you can't remove things from the other end. So what should you use when you need a queue? Funny you should ask …

---

[12] Or to conj or cons onto nil. This is a special case, because nil isn't the same as an empty collection of any specific type. Clojure *could* have left this unsupported, perhaps throwing an exception if you did (cons 1 nil), but instead it provides a reasonable default behavior: building a list one item long.

[13] You can test for this property of being countable in constant time using the counted? function. For example, (counted? (range 10)) returns true in Clojure 1.0 but false in 1.1, because the implementation of range changed between those versions and no longer provides O(1) counting.

5.4　*How to use persistent queues*

We mentioned in section 5.2 that new Clojure developers often attempt to implement simple queues using vectors. Although this is possible, such an implementation leaves much to be desired. Instead, Clojure provides a persistent immutable queue that will serve all your queueing needs. In this section, we'll touch on the usage of the PersistentQueue class, where its first-in-first-out (FIFO) queueing discipline (Knuth 1997) is described by conj adding to the rear, pop removing from the front, and peek returning the front element without removal.

Before going further, it's important to point out that Clojure's PersistentQueue is a collection, not a workflow mechanism. Java has classes deriving from the java.util.concurrent.BlockingQueue interface for workflow, which often are useful in Clojure programs, and those aren't these. If you find yourself wanting to repeatedly check a work queue to see if there's an item of work to be popped off, or if you want to use a queue to send a task to another thread, you do *not* want the Persistent-Queue, because it's an immutable structure; thus there's no way to inherently communicate changes from one worker to another.

5.4.1　*A queue about nothing*

Search all you like, but the current implementation of Clojure doesn't provide special syntax like the vector, set, and map literals for creating persistent queues.[14] That being the case, how would you go about creating a queue? The answer is that there's a readily available empty queue instance to use, clojure.lang.PersistentQueue/EMPTY. The printed representation for Clojure's queues isn't incredibly informative, but you can change that by providing a method on the print-method multimethod:

```
(defmethod print-method clojure.lang.PersistentQueue      Overload the printer
  [q, w]                                                   for queues so they
                                                           look like fish

  (print-method '<- w)
  (print-method (seq q) w)       Delegate to other methods
  (print-method '-< w))          to print the queue's parts

clojure.lang.PersistentQueue/EMPTY
;=> <-nil-<
```

Defining print-method implementations is a convenient mechanism for printing types in logical ways. This fun format, that we call the *queue fish*, indicates a direction of flow for conj and pop.

You might think that popping an empty queue would raise an exception, but the fact is that this action results in another empty queue. Likewise, peeking an empty queue returns nil. Not breathtaking, for sure, but this behavior helps to ensure that queues work in place of other sequences. The functions first, rest, and next also

---

[14] The Clojure core language grows carefully, tending to incorporate only features that have proven useful. Queues currently stand at the edge of this growth, meaning there might be more (or less) support for them in the future.

work on queues and give the results you might expect, although `rest` and `next` return seqs, not queues. Therefore, if you're using a queue as a queue, it's best to use the functions designed for this purpose: `peek`, `pop`, and `conj`.

5.4.2 *Putting things on*

The mechanism for adding elements to a queue is `conj`:

```
(def schedule
  (conj clojure.lang.PersistentQueue/EMPTY
        :wake-up :shower :brush-teeth))

schedule
;=> <-(:wake-up :shower :brush-teeth)-<
```

Clojure's persistent queue is implemented internally using two separate collections, the front being a seq and the rear being a vector, as shown in figure 5.5. All insertions occur in the rear vector, and all removals occur in the front seq, taking advantage of each collection's strength. When all the items from the front list have been popped, the back vector is wrapped in a seq to become the new front, and an empty vector is used as the new back.

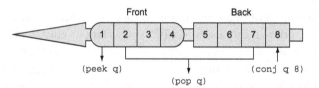

Figure 5.5 **The two collections used internally in a single queue. peek returns the front item of the seq, pop returns a new queue with the front of the seq left off, and conj adds a new item to the back of the vector.**

Typically, an immutable queue such as this is implemented with the rear as a list in reverse order, because insertion to the front of a list is an efficient operation. But using a Clojure vector eliminates the need for a reversed list.

5.4.3 *Getting things*

Clojure provides the `peek` function to get the front element in a queue:

```
(peek schedule)
;=> :wake-up
```

The fact that performing `peek` doesn't modify the contents of a persistent queue should be no surprise by now.

5.4.4 *Taking things off*

To remove elements from the front of a queue, use the `pop` function and not `rest`:

```
(pop schedule)
;=> <-(:shower :brush-teeth)-<

(rest schedule)
;=> (:shower :brush-teeth)
```

Although rest returns something with the same values and even prints the same thing pop returns, the former is a seq, not a queue. This is potentially the source of subtle bugs, because subsequent attempts to use conj on the returned seq won't preserve the speed guarantees of the queue type, and the queue functions pop, peek, and conj won't behave as expected.

We've talked numerous times in this chapter about the sequence abstraction, and although it's an important consideration, it shouldn't *always* be used. Instead, it's important to know your data structures, their sweet spots, and their operations. By doing so, you can write code that's specialized in ways that use the performance characteristics you need for a given problem space. Clojure's persistent queues illustrate this fact perfectly. To further highlight this point, we'll now explore Clojure's set type.

5.5 Persistent sets

Clojure sets work the same as mathematical sets, in that they're collections of unsorted unique elements. In this section, we'll cover sets by explaining their strong points, weaknesses, and idioms. We'll also cover some of the functions from the clojure.set namespace.

5.5.1 Basic properties of Clojure sets

Sets are functions of their elements that return the matched element or nil:

```
(#{:a :b :c :d} :c)
;=> :c

(#{:a :b :c :d} :e)
;=> nil
```

Set elements can be accessed via the get function, which returns the queried value if it exists in the given set:

```
(get #{:a 1 :b 2} :b)
;=> :b

(get #{:a 1 :b 2} :z :nothing-doing)
;=> :nothing-doing
```

An added advantage of using get is shown here in the second call: get allows a third argument that is used as the "not found" value, should a key lookup fail. As a final point, sets, like all Clojure's collections, support heterogeneous values.

How Clojure populates sets

The key to understanding how Clojure sets determine which elements are discrete lies in one simple statement. Given two elements evaluating as equal, a set will contain only one, independent of concrete types:

```
(into #{[]} [()])
;;=> #{[]}

(into #{[1 2]} '[(1 2)])
;;=> #{[1 2]}
```

```
(into #{[] #{} {}} [()])
;;=> #{#{} {} []}
```

From the first two examples, even though `[]` and `()` are of differing types, they're considered equal because their elements are equal or (in this case) empty. But the last example illustrates nicely that collections in an equality partition (as described in section 5.1.2) will always be equal if their elements are equal, but will never be considered equal if the collections are of types in different equality partitions.

> ## Finding items in a sequence using a set and the some function
>
> As we'll explain in section 5.5.3, trying to find a value in a vector using the `contains?` function doesn't work the way we'd hope. Instead, the `some` function takes a predicate and a sequence. It applies the predicate to each element in turn, returning the first truthy value returned by the predicate or else `nil`:
>
> ```
> (some #{:b} [:a 1 :b 2])
> ;=> :b
> ```
>
> ```
> (some #{1 :b} [:a 1 :b 2])
> ;=> 1
> ```
>
> Using a set as the predicate supplied to `some` allows you to check whether *any of the* truthy values in the set are contained within the given sequence. *This is a frequently used Clojure idiom for searching for containment within a sequence.*

5.5.2 *Keeping your sets in order with sorted-set*

There's not much to say about creating sorted sets with the `sorted-set` function. But there's a simple rule you should bear in mind:

```
(sorted-set :b :c :a)
;=> #{:a :b :c}

(sorted-set [3 4] [1 2])
;=> #{[1 2] [3 4]}

(sorted-set :b 2 :c :a 3 1)
; java.lang.ClassCastException: clojure.lang.Keyword cannot be cast to
      java.lang.Number
```

As long as the arguments to the `sorted-set` function are mutually comparable, you'll receive a sorted set; otherwise an exception is thrown. This can manifest itself when you're dealing with sorted sets downstream from their point of creation, leading to potential confusion:

```
(def my-set (sorted-set :a :b))

;; ... some time later
(conj my-set "a")
;=> java.lang.ClassCastException: clojure.lang.Keyword cannot be cast to
      java.lang.String
```

The difficulty in finding the reason for this exception will increase as the distance between the creation of my-set and the call to conj increases. You can adjust this rule a bit by using sorted-set-by instead and providing your own comparator. This works exactly like the comparator for sorted-map-by, which we'll cover in section 5.6.2. Sorted maps and sorted sets are also similar in their support of subseq, to allow efficiently jumping to a particular key in the collection and walking through it from there. This is covered in section 5.6.

5.5.3 *The contains? function*

As we touched on in section 5.2, there's sometimes confusion regarding the usage of Clojure's contains? function. Many newcomers to Clojure expect this function to work the same as Java's java.util.Collection#contains method; this assumption is false, as shown:

```
(contains? #{1 2 4 3} 4)
;=> true

(contains? [1 2 4 3] 4)
;=> false
```

If you were to draw a false analogy between Java's .contains methods and contains?, then both of the function calls noted here should return true. The official documentation for contains? describes it as a function that returns true if a given *key* exists in a collection. When reading the word *key*, the notion of a map springs to mind, but the fact that this function also works on sets hints at their implementation details. Sets are implemented as maps with the same element as the key *and* value,[15] but there's an additional check for containment before insertion.

5.5.4 *The clojure.set namespace*

Mathematical sets form the basis of much of modern mathematical thought, and Clojure's basic set functions in the clojure.set namespace are a clear reflection of the classical set operations. In this subsection, we'll briefly cover each function and talk about how, when applicable, they differ from the mathematical model. To start using the functions in the clojure.set namespace, enter the following into your REPL:

```
(require 'clojure.set)
```

Or, if you wish to use these functions in your namespace, use the following inclusion:

```
(ns my.cool.lib
  (:require clojure.set))
```

To describe some of the functions in the clojure.set namespace, let's start with a simple picture. Figure 5.6 describes the nature of Clojure's set functions, each of which will be shown presently. Note that Clojure's set functions take an arbitrary number of sets and apply the operation incrementally.

---

[15] All implementation caveats apply.

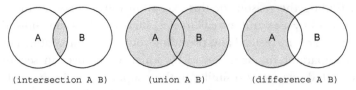

Figure 5.6 The three Venn diagrams show a graphical representation of Clojure's set functions: `intersection`, `union`, and `difference`.

(intersection A B)   (union A B)   (difference A B)

THE INTERSECTION FUNCTION

Clojure's `clojure.set/intersection` function works as you might expect. Given two sets, `intersection` returns a set of the common elements. Given n sets, it incrementally returns the intersection of resulting sets and the next set, as shown in the following code:

```
(clojure.set/intersection #{:humans :fruit-bats :zombies}
                          #{:chupacabra :zombies :humans})
;=> #{:zombies :humans}

(clojure.set/intersection #{:pez :gum :dots :skor}
                          #{:pez :skor :pocky}
                          #{:pocky :gum :skor})
;=> #{:skor}
```

In the first example, the resulting set is the common elements between the given sets. The second example is the result of the intersection of the first two sets then intersected with the final set.

THE UNION FUNCTION

There's also likely no surprise when using the `clojure.set/union` function:

```
(clojure.set/union #{:humans :fruit-bats :zombies}
                   #{:chupacabra :zombies :humans})
;=> #{:chupacabra :fruit-bats :zombies :humans}

(clojure.set/union #{:pez :gum :dots :skor}
                   #{:pez :skor :pocky}
                   #{:pocky :gum :skor})
;=> #{:pez :pocky :gum :skor :dots}
```

Given two sets, the resulting set contains all the distinct elements from both. In the first example, this means `:zombies` and `:humans` show up only once each in the return value. Note in the second example that more than two sets may be given to `union`, but as expected each value given in any of the input sets is included exactly once in the output set.

THE DIFFERENCE FUNCTION

The only set function that could potentially cause confusion on first glance is `clojure.set/difference`, which by name implies some sort of opposition to a union operation. Working under this false assumption, you might assume that `difference` would operate thusly:

```
;; This is not what really happens

(clojure.set/difference #{1 2 3 4} #{3 4 5 6})
;=> #{1 2 5 6}
```

But if you were to evaluate this expression in your REPL, you'd receive a very different result:

```
(clojure.set/difference #{1 2 3 4} #{3 4 5 6})
;=> #{1 2}
```

The reason for this result is that Clojure's difference function calculates what's known as a *relative complement* (Stewart 1995) between two sets. In other words, difference can be viewed as a set-subtraction function, "removing" all elements in a set A that are also in another set B.

5.6 *Thinking in maps*

It's difficult to write a program of any significant size without the need for a map of some sort. The use of maps is ubiquitous in writing software because, frankly, it's hard to imagine a more robust data structure. But we as programmers tend to view maps as a special case structure outside the normal realm of data objects and classes. The object-oriented school of thought has relegated the map to being a supporting player in favor of the class. We're not going to talk about the merits (or lack thereof) for this relegation here, but in upcoming sections we'll discuss moving away from thinking in classes and instead thinking in the sequence abstraction, maps, protocols, and types. Having said all that, it need hardly be mentioned that maps should be used to store named values. In this section, we'll talk about the different types of maps and the trade-offs surrounding each.

5.6.1 *Hash maps*

Arguably, the most ubiquitous[16] form of map found in Clojure programs is the hash map, which provides an unsorted key/value associative structure. In addition to the literal syntax touched on in chapter 2, hash maps can be created using the hash-map function, which likewise takes alternating key/value pairs, with or without commas:

```
(hash-map :a 1, :b 2, :c 3, :d 4, :e 5)
;=> {:a 1, :c 3, :b 2, :d 4, :e 5}
```

Clojure hash maps support heterogeneous keys, meaning they can be of any type and each key can be of a differing type, as this code shows:

```
(let [m {:a 1, 1 :b, [1 2 3] "4 5 6"}]
  [(get m :a) (get m [1 2 3])])
;=> [1 "4 5 6"]
```

As we mentioned at the beginning of this chapter, many of Clojure's collection types can be used as functions, and in the case of maps they're functions of their keys. Using maps this way acts the same as the use of the get function in the previous code example, as shown when building a vector of two elements:

---

[16] Although with the pervasiveness of the map literal, the ubiquity may instead fall to the array map.

```
(let [m {:a 1, 1 :b, [1 2 3] "4 5 6"}]
  [(m :a) (m [1 2 3])])
;=> [1 "4 5 6"]
```

Providing a map to the seq function returns a sequence of map entries:

```
(seq {:a 1, :b 2})
;=> ([:a 1] [:b 2])
```

This sequence appears to be composed of the sets of key/value pairs contained in vectors, and for all practical purposes it should be treated as such. In fact, you can create a new hash map using this precise structure:

```
(into {} [[:a 1] [:b 2]])
;=> {:a 1, :b 2}
```

Even if your embedded pairs aren't vectors, they can be made to be for building a new map:

```
(into {} (map vec '[(:a 1) (:b 2)]))
;=> {:a 1, :b 2}
```

Your pairs don't have to be explicitly grouped, because you can use apply to create a hash map given that the key/value pairs are laid out in a sequence consecutively:

```
(apply hash-map [:a 1 :b 2])
;=> {:a 1, :b 2}
```

You can also use apply this way with sorted-map and array-map. Another fun way to build a map is to use zipmap to "zip" together two sequences, the first of which contains the desired keys and the second their corresponding values:

```
(zipmap [:a :b] [1 2])
;=> {:b 2, :a 1}
```

The use of zipmap illustrates nicely the final property of map collections. Hash maps in Clojure have no order guarantees. If you do require ordering, then you should use sorted maps, discussed next.

5.6.2   *Keeping your keys in order with sorted maps*

It's impossible to rely on a specific ordering of the key/value pairs for a standard Clojure map, because there are no order guarantees. Using the sorted-map and sorted-map-by functions, you can construct maps with order assurances. By default, the function sorted-map builds a map sorted by the comparison of its keys:

```
(sorted-map :thx 1138 :r2d 2)
;=> {:r2d 2, :thx 1138}
```

You may require an alternative key ordering, or perhaps an ordering for keys that aren't easily comparable. In these cases, you must use sorted-map-by, which takes an additional comparison function:[17]

---

[17] Note that simple Boolean functions like > can be used as comparison functions.

```
(sorted-map "bac" 2 "abc" 9)
;=> {"abc" 9, "bac" 2}

(sorted-map-by #(compare (subs %1 1) (subs %2 1)) "bac" 2 "abc" 9)
;=> {"bac" 2, "abc" 9}
```

This means sorted maps don't generally support heterogeneous keys the same as hash maps, although it depends on the comparison function provided. For example, the preceding examples assume all keys are strings. The default sorted-map comparison function compare supports maps whose keys are all mutually comparable with each other. Attempts to use keys that aren't supported by whichever comparison function you're using will generally result in a cast exception:

```
(sorted-map :a 1, "b" 2)
;=> java.lang.ClassCastException: clojure.lang.Keyword cannot be cast to
         java.lang.String
```

One remarkable feature supported by sorted maps (and also sorted sets) is the ability to jump efficiently to a particular key and walk forward or backward from there through the collection. This is done with the subseq and rsubseq functions for forward and backward, respectively. Even if you don't know the exact key you want, these functions can be used to "round up" the next closest key that exists.

Another way that sorted maps and hash maps differ is in their handling of numeric keys. A number of a given magnitude can be represented by many different types; for example, 42 can be a long, an int, a float, and so on. Hash maps treat each of these different objects as *different*, whereas a sorted map treats them as the same. You can see the contrast in this example, where the hash map keeps both keys but the sorted map keeps just one:

```
(assoc {1 :int} 1.0 :float)
;=> {1.0 :float, 1 :int}

(assoc (sorted-map 1 :int) 1.0 :float)
;=> {1 :float}
```

This is because the comparison function used by the sorted map determines order by equality, and if two keys compare as equal, only one is kept. This applies to comparison functions provided to sorted-map-by as well as the default comparator shown previously.

Sorted maps otherwise work just like hash maps and can be used interchangeably. You should use sorted maps if you need to specify or guarantee a specific key ordering. On the other hand, if you need to maintain insertion ordering, then the use of array maps is required, as you'll see.

5.6.3 *Keeping your insertions in order with array maps*

If you hope to perform an action under the assumption that a given map is insertion ordered, then you're setting yourself up for disappointment. But you might already know that Clojure provides a special map, called an *array map*, that ensures insertion ordering:

```
(seq (hash-map :a 1, :b 2, :c 3))
;=> ([:a 1] [:c 3] [:b 2])

(seq (array-map :a 1, :b 2, :c 3))
;=> ([:a 1] [:b 2] [:c 3])
```

When insertion order is important, you should explicitly use an array map. Array maps can be populated quickly by ignoring the form of the key/value pairs and blindly copying them into place. For structures sized below a certain count, the cost associated with map lookup bridges the gap between a linear search through an equally sized array or list. That's not to say that the map will be slower; instead, it allows the map and linear implementations to be comparable. Sometimes your best choice for a map is not a map at all, and like most things in life, there are trade-offs. Fortunately, Clojure takes care of these considerations for you by adjusting the concrete implementations behind the scenes as the size of the map increases. The precise types in play aren't important, because Clojure is careful to document its promises and to leave undefined aspects subject to change and/or improvement. It's usually a bad idea to build your programs around concrete types, and it's always bad to build around undocumented behaviors. *Clojure handles the underlying efficiency considerations so you don't have to.* But be aware that if ordering is important, you should avoid operations that inadvertently change the underlying map implementation from an array map.

We've covered the basics of Clojure maps in this section, including common usage and construction techniques. Clojure maps, minus some implementation details, shouldn't be surprising to anyone. It'll take a while to grow accustomed to dealing with immutable maps, but in time even this nuance will become second nature.

Now that we've looked at Clojure's primary collection types and their differences in detail, we'll take some time to work through a simple case study. This case study, creating a function named pos, will illustrate the thought processes you may consider on your way toward designing an API built on the principles of the sequence abstraction.

5.7   *Putting it all together: finding the position of items in a sequence*

> *We sometimes underestimate the influence of little things.*
>
> —Charles W. Chesnutt[18]

The case study for this chapter is to design and implement a simple function to locate the positional index of an element in a sequence.[19] We're going to pool together much of the knowledge gained in this chapter in order to illustrate the steps you

---

[18] "Obliterating the Color Line," *Cleveland World*, October 23, 1901.

[19] Stuart Halloway and Aaron Bedra describe a similar function, index-of-any, in their book *Programming Clojure* (Pragmatic Bookshelf, 2012) that views the problem largely through the lens of reduced complexity. We like their example and the example in this section because they're simple yet powerful and nicely illustrative of the way that Clojure functions should be written.

might take in designing, writing, and ultimately optimizing a Clojure collection function. Of course, we'll work against the sequence abstraction and therefore design the solution accordingly.

The function, named pos, *must*

- Work on any collection type, returning indices corresponding to some value
- Return a numerical index for sequential collections or associated key for maps and sets
- Otherwise return nil

Now that we've outlined the basic requirements of pos, we'll run through a few implementations, discussing each along the way toward a Clojure-optimal version.

5.7.1 Implementation

If we were to address each of the requirements for pos literally and directly, we might come up with a function that looks like the following listing.

Listing 5.2 First cut of the position function

```
(defn pos [e coll]
  (let [cmp (if (map? coll)
              #(= (second %1) %2)        <— Map compare
              #(= %1 %2))]               <— Default compare
    (loop [s coll idx 0]         <— Start at the beginning
      (when (seq s)
        (if (cmp (first s) e)          <— Compare
          (if (map? coll)
            (first (first s))          <— Map returns key
            idx)                       <— ... Else index
          (recur (next s) (inc idx)))))))
```

Pretty hideous, right? We think so too, but let's at least check whether it works as desired:

```
(pos 3 [:a 1 :b 2 :c 3 :d 4])
;;=> 5

(pos :foo [:a 1 :b 2 :c 3 :d 4])
;;=> nil

(pos 3 {:a 1 :b 2 :c 3 :d 4})
;;=> :c

(pos \3 ":a 1 :b 2 :c 3 :d 4")
;;=> 13
```

Apart from being overly complicated, it'd likely be more useful if it instead returned a sequence of *all* the indices matching the item, so let's add that to the requirements. But we've built a heavy load with the first cut at pos and should probably step back a moment to reflect. First, it's probably the wrong approach to handle map types and other sequence types differently. The use of the predicate `map?` to detect the type of the passed collection is incredibly constraining, in that it forces different collections to be processed differently, and sets are not handled correctly at all. That's not to say the use of type-based predicates is strictly prohibited, only that you should try to favor more generic algorithms or at least minimize their usage.

As chance has it, the exact nature of the problem demands that we view collections as a set of values paired with a given index, be it explicit in the case of maps or implicit in the case of other sequences' positional information. Therefore, imagine how easy this problem would be if all collections were laid out as sequences of pairs (`[index1 value1]` `[index2 value2]` ... `[indexn valuen]`). Well, there's no reason why they can't be, as shown next:

```
(defn index [coll]
  (cond
    (map? coll) (seq coll)
    (set? coll) (map vector coll coll)
    :else (map vector (iterate inc 0) coll)))
```

This simple function[20] can generate a uniform representation for indexed collections:

```
(index [:a 1 :b 2 :c 3 :d 4])
;=> ([0 :a] [1 1] [2 :b] [3 2] [4 :c] [5 3] [6 :d] [7 4])

(index {:a 1 :b 2 :c 3 :d 4})
;=> ([:a 1] [:b 2] [:c 3] [:d 4])

(index #{:a 1 :b 2 :c 3 :d 4})
;=> ([1 1] [2 2] [3 3] [4 4] [:a :a] [:c :c] [:b :b] [:d :d])
```

As shown, we're still using type-based predicates, but we've raised the level of abstraction to the equality partitions in order to build contextually relevant indices. Now, the function for finding the positional indices for the desired value is trivial:

```
(defn pos [e coll]
  (for [[i v] (index coll) :when (= e v)] i))

(pos 3 [:a 1 :b 2 :c 3 :d 4])
;=> (5)
(pos 3 {:a 1, :b 2, :c 3, :d 4})
;=> (:c)
(pos 3 [:a 3 :b 3 :c 3 :d 4])
;=> (1 3 5)
(pos 3 {:a 3, :b 3, :c 3, :d 4})
;=> (:a :c :b)
```

Much better! But there's one more deficiency with the `pos` function from a Clojure perspective. Typically in Clojure it's more useful to pass a predicate function in cases such as these, so that instead of `pos` determining raw equality, it can build its result along any dimension:

---

[20] Clojure has a core function, `keep-indexed`, that works similarly but doesn't implicitly build indices along equality partitions. For a vector, you could build the index as (`keep-indexed #(-> [% %2])` `[:a :b :c :d]`).

```
(pos #{3 4} {:a 1 :b 2 :c 3 :d 4})
;=> (:c :d)

(pos even? [2 3 6 7])
;=> (0 2)
```

We can modify pos only slightly to achieve the ideal level of flexibility.

> **Listing 5.3 Final version of pos**

```
(defn pos [pred coll]
  (for [[i v] (index coll) :when (pred v)] i))
```

We've vastly simplified the original solution and generated two potentially useful functions (Martin 2002) in the process. By following some simple Clojure principles, we solved the original problem statement in a concise and elegant manner.

5.8   Summary

Clojure favors simplicity in the face of growing software complexity. If problems are easily solved by collection abstractions, then those abstractions should be used. Most problems can be modeled on such simple types, yet we continue to build monolithic class hierarchies in a fruitless race toward mirroring the "real world"—whatever that means. Perhaps it's time to realize that we no longer need to layer self-imposed complexities on top of software solutions that are already inherently complex. Not only does Clojure provide the sequential, set, and map types useful for pulling ourselves from the doldrums of software complexity, but it's also optimized for dealing with them.

Now that we've discussed each of these types in detail, let's take a step back and talk about three important properties of Clojure's collection types that until now we've only touched on lightly: immutability, persistence, and laziness.

Part 3

Functional programming techniques

In this part of the book, we'll expose some of the underpinnings of Clojure's approach to functional programming, as well as some practical uses of it. Clojure provides mechanisms for immutability, deferred execution, closures, and recursion. We'll show examples of how these can work together to let you create data structures of your own, and find routes through a weighted graph.

Part 3

Functional
programming techniques

6
Being lazy and
set in your ways

This chapter covers

- Immutability
- Designing a persistent toy
- Laziness
- A lazy quicksort

We mentioned in section 1.3 that the definitions of functional programming are widely disparate, and unfortunately this book won't work to unify them. Instead, we'll start in this chapter to build a basis for Clojure's style of functional programming by digging into its core supporting maxims: immutable data and laziness. In addition, this chapter covers in greater depth the parts of Clojure's composite types that we've only touched on. It will conclude with a sorting function that uses both maxims in a way we find to be mentally invigorating.

6.1 On immutability: being set in your ways

We've touched on immutability throughout this book, but we've avoided discussing why Clojure has chosen it as a cornerstone principle. Although it's no panacea, fostering immutability at the language level solves many difficult problems right out of the box while simplifying many others. If you're coming from a language background where mutability interwoven with imperative programming methods reign, it often requires a significant conceptual leap to twist your mind to accept and utilize immutability and functional programming. In this section, we'll build a conceptual basis for immutability as it relates to Clojure's underlying philosophy, as well as why you should work to foster immutability even when outside the warming confines of Clojure proper.

6.1.1   *What is immutability?*

In many cases, when talking specifically about Clojure's immutable data structures, we could be talking about the broader category of immutable objects without loss of meaning. But we should probably set down some conditions defining what's meant by immutability.

EVERY DAY IS LIKE SUNDAY

An entire branch of philosophy named *predestination* is devoted to exploring the notion that there's no such thing as free will, but that instead, everything that we are or ever will be is determined beforehand. Although this possibility for our own lives may seem bleak, the notion does nicely encapsulate the first principle of immutability: all the possible properties of immutable objects are defined at the time of their construction and can't be changed thereafter.

IMMUTABILITY THROUGH CONVENTION

Computer systems are in many ways open systems, providing the keys to the vault if you're so inclined to grab them. But in order to foster an air of immutability in your own systems, it's important to create a facade of immutability. Creating immutable classes in Java requires a few steps (Goetz 2006). First, a class itself and all of its fields should be labeled as `final`. Next, in no way should an object's `this` reference escape during construction. And finally, any internal mutable objects should originate, either whole-cloth or through a copy, in the class itself and never escape. Obviously we're simplifying, because there are finer details to this recipe for Java immutability. Our point is that by observing convention, even an inherently mutable language such as Java can be made immutable. Clojure directly supports immutability as a language feature[1] with its core data structures. By providing immutable data structures as a primary language feature, Clojure separates (Braithwaite 2007) the complexity of working with immutable structures from the complexities of their implementation. By providing immutability, either as a core language feature or through convention, you can reap enormous benefits.

---

[1] We're intentionally glossing over Clojure's features that support mutability, such as reference types and transients, in order to keep this section focused. Read chapters 10 and 11 for more details on such matters.

6.1.2　*What is immutability for?*

Clojure's immutable data structures aren't bolted onto the language as an after-thought. Instead, their inclusion in the language runs deep to its philosophical core.

INVARIANTS

Invariant-based programming involves the definition of constraints on classes and functions in order to provide assurances that if instances enter into certain states, assertion errors will arise. Providing invariants in a mutable system requires a fair amount of assertion weaving in the methods of any given class. But by observing a practice of immutability, invariants are defined solely within the construction mechanism and can never be violated thereafter.

REASONING

Because the life of an immutable object is one of predestiny, the matter of reasoning about its possible states is simplified. It follows that the act of testing such a system is simplified, in that the set of possible states and transitions is constrained.

EQUALITY HAS MEANING

Equality in the presence of mutability has no meaning. Equality in the face of mutability and concurrency is utter lunacy. If any two objects resolve as being equal now, then there's no guarantee that they will a moment from now. And if two objects aren't equal forever, then they're technically never equal (Baker 1993). Providing immutable objects once again assigns meaning to equality, in that if two objects are equal now, they'll always be so.

SHARING IS CHEAP

If you're certain that an object will never change, then sharing said object becomes a simple matter of providing a reference to it. In Java, to do so often requires a lot of defensive copying. Along this vein, because you can freely share references for immutable objects, you can likewise intern them for free.

FLATTENING THE LEVELS OF INDIRECTION

There's a marked difference between a mutable object and a mutable reference. The default in Java is that there are references that might point to mutable data. But in Clojure, there are only mutable references. This may seem like a minor detail, but it certainly works to reduce unnecessary complexities.

IMMUTABILITY FOSTERS CONCURRENT PROGRAMMING

> *Immutable objects are always thread safe.*
> —Brian Goetz[2]

If an object can't change, it can be shared freely between different threads of execution without fear of concurrent modification errors. There can be little debate about this particular point, but that fact doesn't answer the question of how mutation occurs. Without delving into the specifics, you likely already know that Clojure

---

[2] *Java Concurrency in Practice* (Addison-Wesley Professional, 2006).

isolates mutation to its reference types while the data wrapped with them is left unchanged. We'll leave this alone for now, because we'll devote chapter 10 to this and related topics.

6.2   *Structural sharing: a persistent toy*

We won't go into terrible detail about the internals of Clojure's persistent data structures—we'll leave that to others (Krukow 2009). But we do want to explore the notion of structural sharing. Our example will be highly simplified compared to Clojure's implementations, but it should help clarify some of the techniques used.

The simplest shared-structure type is the list. Two different items can be added to the front of the same list, producing two new lists that share their next parts. Let's try this by creating a base list and then two new lists from that same base:

```
(def baselist (list :barnabas :adam))
(def lst1 (cons :willie baselist))
(def lst2 (cons :phoenix baselist))

lst1
;=> (:willie :barnabas :adam)

lst2
;=> (:phoenix :barnabas :adam)
```

You can think of `baselist` as a historical version of both `lst1` and `lst2`. But it's also the shared part of both lists. More than being equal, the `next` parts of both lists are *identical*—the same instance:

```
(= (next lst1) (next lst2))

;=> true
```
◁ **Not only are the nexts equal ...**

```
(identical? (next lst1) (next lst2))

;=> true
```
◁ **... but they're the same exact objects**

That's not too complicated, right? But the features supported by lists are also limited. Clojure's vectors and maps also provide structural sharing, while allowing you to change values anywhere in the collection, not just on one end. The key is the structure each of these datatypes uses internally. You'll now build a simple tree to help demonstrate how a tree can allow interior changes and maintain shared structure at the same time.

Each node of your tree will have three fields: a value, a left branch, and a right branch. You'll put them in a map, like this:

```
{:val 5, :L nil, :R nil}
```

That's the simplest possible tree—a single node holding the value 5, with empty left and right branches. This is exactly the kind of tree you want to return when a single item is added to an empty tree. To represent an empty tree, you'll use `nil`. With the structure decision made, you can write your own `conj` function, `xconj`, to build up your tree, starting with the code for this initial case:

```
(defn xconj [t v]
  (cond
    (nil? t) {:val v, :L nil, :R nil}))
```

⌐ **Start with a tree t
and a value to add v**

```
(xconj nil 5)
;=> {:val 5, :L nil, :R nil}
```

Hey, it works! Not too impressive yet, though, so you need to handle the case where an item is being added to a nonempty tree. Keep the tree in order by putting values less than a node's :val in the left branch, and other values in the right branch. That means you need a test like this:

```
(< v (:val t))
```

When that's true, you need the new value v to go into the left branch, (:L t). If this were a mutable tree, you'd *change* the value of :L to be the new node. Instead, you should build a *new* node, copying in the parts of the old node that don't need to change. Something like this:

```
{:val (:val t),
 :L (insert-new-val-here),
 :R (:R t)}
```

Keywords as functions for true-power elegance

A point of deep significance in understanding the fragment using :val and :R in the function position is how Clojure uses keywords as functions. In section 4.3.1, we said that keywords, when placed in a function call position, work as functions taking a map that then look up themselves (as keywords) in said map. Therefore, the snippet (:val t) states that the keyword :val takes the map t and looks itself up in the map. This is functionally equivalent to (get t :val). Although we prefer the keyword-as-function approach used in xconj, you'll sometimes be faced with a decision and may instead choose to use get. Either choice is fine, and your decision is stylistic. A nice rule of thumb to follow is that if a keyword is stored in a local or var, using get is often clearer in its "lookup" intent:

```
(let [some-local :a-key]
  (get {:a-key 42} :a-key))

;;=> 42
```

That is, the preceding is more clear than (some-local a-map).

This map will be the new root node. Now you need to figure out what to put for insert-new-val-here. If the old value of :L is nil, you need a new single-node tree—you even have code for that already, so you could use (xconj nil v). But what if :L isn't nil? In that case, you want to insert v in its proper place in whatever tree :L is pointing to—so (:L t) instead of nil:

```
(defn xconj [t v]
  (cond
    (nil? t)        {:val v, :L nil, :R nil}
```

```
            (< v (:val t)) {:val (:val t),
                            :L (xconj (:L t) v),
                            :R (:R t)}}))
(def tree1 (xconj nil 5))
tree1
;=> {:val 5, :L nil, :R nil}

(def tree1 (xconj tree1 3))
tree1
;=> {:val 5, :L {:val 3, :L nil, :R nil}, :R nil}

(def tree1 (xconj tree1 2))
tree1
;=> {:val 5, :L {:val 3, :L {:val 2, :L nil, :R nil}, :R nil}, :R nil}
```

There, it's working. At least it seems to be—there's a lot of noise in that output, making it difficult to read. Here's a function to traverse the tree in sorted order, converting it to a seq that will print more succinctly:

```
(defn xseq [t]
  (when t
    (concat (xseq (:L t)) [(:val t)] (xseq (:R t)))))

(xseq tree1)
;=> (2 3 5)
```

Now you need a final condition for handling the insertion of values that are *not* less than the node value:

```
(defn xconj [t v]
  (cond
    (nil? t)        {:val v, :L nil, :R nil}        ←—  Nil nodes start with v
    (< v (:val t))  {:val (:val t),                 ←┐
                     :L (xconj (:L t) v),            │ When v is less than the value at the
                     :R (:R t)}                      │ current node, it's pushed left
    :else           {:val (:val t),                 ←┐
                     :L (:L t),                       │ Otherwise it's
                     :R (xconj (:R t) v)}}))          │ pushed right
```

Now that you have the thing built, we hope you understand well enough how it's put together that this demonstration of the shared structure is unsurprising:

```
(def tree2 (xconj tree1 7))
(xseq tree2)
;=> (2 3 5 7)

(identical? (:L tree1) (:L tree2))
;=> true
```

Both tree1 and tree2 share a common structure, which is more easily visualized in figure 6.1.

This example demonstrates several features that it has in common with all of Clojure's persistent collections:

- Every "change" creates at least a new root node, plus new nodes as needed in the path through the tree to where the new value is being inserted.

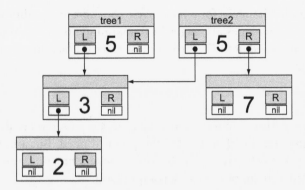

Figure 6.1 Shared structure tree: no matter how big the left side of a tree's root node is, something can be inserted on the right side without copying, changing, or even examining the left side. All those values will be included in the new tree, along with the inserted value.

- Values and unchanged branches are never copied, but references to them are copied from nodes in the old tree to nodes in the new one.
- This implementation is completely thread-safe in a way that's easy to check—no object that existed before a call to xconj is changed in any way, and newly created nodes are in their final state before being returned. There's no way for any other thread, or even any other functions in the same thread, to see anything in an inconsistent state.

The example fails, though, when compared to Clojure's production-quality code:

- It's a binary tree.[3]
- It can only store numbers.
- It'll overflow the stack if the tree gets too deep.
- It produces (via xseq) a non-lazy seq that will contain an entire copy of the tree.
- It can create unbalanced trees that have worst-case algorithmic complexity.[4]

Although structural sharing as described using xconj as a basis example can reduce the memory footprint of persistent data structures, it alone is insufficient. Instead, Clojure leans heavily on the notion of lazy sequences to further reduce its memory footprint, as we'll explore further in the next section.

6.3 Laziness

Through all the windows I only see infinity.

—Mark Z. Danielewski[5]

Clojure is partially a lazy language. This isn't to say that Clojure vectors lie around the house every day after school playing video games and refusing to get a job. Instead, Clojure is lazy in the way it handles its sequence types—but what does that mean?

---

[3] Clojure's sorted collections are binary trees, but its hash maps, hash sets, and vectors all have up to 32 branches per node. This results in dramatically shallower trees and, therefore, faster lookups and updates.

[4] Clojure's sorted map and sorted set do use a binary tree internally, but they implement red-black trees to keep the left and right sides nicely balanced.

[5] *House of Leaves* (Pantheon, 2000).

First, we'll start by defining what it means for a language to be *eager*, or, in other words, not lazy. Many programming languages are eager in that arguments to functions are immediately evaluated when passed, and Clojure in most cases follows this pattern as well. Observe the following:

```
(- 13 (+ 2 2))
;=> 9
```

The expression (+ 2 2) is eagerly evaluated, in that its result 4 is passed on to the subtraction function during the actual call and *not* at the point of need. But a lazy programming language such as Haskell (Hudak 2000) will evaluate a function argument only if that argument is needed in an overarching computation.

In this section, we'll discuss how you can use laziness to avoid nontermination, unnecessary calculations, and even combinatorially exploding computations. We'll also discuss the matter of utilizing infinite sequences, a surprisingly powerful technique. Finally, you'll use Clojure's delay and force to build a simple lazy structure. First, we'll start with a simple example of laziness that you may be familiar with from Java.

6.3.1   *Familiar laziness with logical-and*

Laziness isn't limited to the case of the evaluation of function arguments; a common example can be found even in eager programming languages. Take the case of Java's logical-and operator &&. Java implementations, by dictate of the specification, optimize this particular operator to avoid performing unnecessary operations should an early subexpression evaluate to false. This lazy evaluation in Java allows the following idiom:

```
if (obj != null && obj.isWhatiz()) {
   ...
}
```

For those of you unfamiliar with Java, the preceding code says, "If the object obj isn't null, then call the method isWhatiz." Without a short-circuiting (or lazy, if you will) && operator, the preceding operation would always throw a java.lang.NullPointer-Exception whenever obj was set to null. Although this simple example doesn't qualify Java as a lazy language, it does illustrate the first advantage of lazy evaluation: *laziness allows the avoidance of errors in the evaluation of compound structures.*

Clojure's and operator also works this way, as do a number of other operators, but we won't discuss this type of short-circuiting laziness too deeply. The following listing illustrates what we mean, using the case of a series of nested if expressions.

> **Listing 6.1   Short-circuiting `if` expression**

```
(defn if-chain [x y z]
  (if x
    (if y
      (if z
```

```
        (do
          (println "Made it!")
          :all-truthy)))))
(if-chain () 42 true)
; Made it!
;=> :all-truthy

(if-chain true true  false)
;=> nil
```

The call to `println` is evaluated only in the case of three truthy arguments. But you can perform the equivalent action given only the and macro:

```
(defn and-chain [x y z]
  (and x y z (do (println "Made it!") :all-truthy)))

(and-chain () 42 true)
; Made it!
;=> :all-truthy

(and-chain true false true)
;=> false
```

You may see tricks like this from time to time, but they're not often found in Clojure code. Regardless, we've presented them as a launching point for the rest of the discussion in the section. We'll now proceed to discuss how your own Clojure programs can be made more generally lazy by following an important recipe.

6.3.2 *Understanding the lazy-seq recipe*

Here's a seemingly simple function, `steps`, that takes a sequence and makes a deeply nested structure from it:

```
(steps [1 2 3 4])
;=> [1 [2 [3 [4 []]]]]
```

Seems simple enough, no? Your first instinct might be to tackle this problem recursively, as suggested by the form of the desired result:

```
(defn rec-step [[x & xs]]
  (if x
    [x (rec-step xs)]
    []))
(rec-step [1 2 3 4])
;=> [1 [2 [3 [4 []]]]]
```

Things look beautiful at this point; you've created a simple solution to a simple problem. But therein bugbears lurk. What would happen if you ran this same function on a large set?

```
(rec-step (range 200000))
;=> java.lang.StackOverflowError
```

Observing the example, running the same function over a sequence of 200,000 elements[6] causes a stack overflow. How can you fix this problem? Perhaps it's fine to say that you'll never encounter such a large input set in your own programs; such trade-offs are made all the time. But Clojure provides lazy sequences to help tackle such problems without significantly complicating your source code. Additionally, your code should strive to deal with, and produce, lazy sequences.

Stepping back a bit, let's examine the `lazy-seq` recipe for applying laziness to your own functions:

1 Use the `lazy-seq` macro at the outermost level of your lazy sequence–producing expression(s).
2 If you happen to be consuming another sequence during your operations, then use `rest` instead of `next`.
3 Prefer higher-order functions when processing sequences.
4 Don't hold on to your head.

These rules of thumb are simple, but they take some practice to utilize to their fullest. For example, #4 is especially subtle in that the trivial case is easy to conceptualize, but it's more complex to implement in large cases. For now we'll gloss over #3, because we'll talk about that approach separately in section 7.1.

So how can you use these rules of thumb to ensure laziness?

rest vs. next

What happens when you create a potentially infinite sequence of integers using `iterate`, printing a dot each time you generate a new value, and then use either `rest` or `next` to return the first three values of the sequence? The difference between `rest` and `next` can be seen in the following example:

```
(def very-lazy (-> (iterate #(do (print \.) (inc %)) 1)
                   rest rest rest))
;=> ..#'user/very-lazy

(def less-lazy (-> (iterate #(do (print \.) (inc %)) 1)
                   next next next))
;=> ...#'user/less-lazy
```

As shown, the `next` version printed three dots, whereas the `rest` version printed only two. When building a lazy seq from another, `rest` doesn't cause the calculation of (or *realize*) any more elements than it needs to; `next` does. In order to determine whether a seq is empty, `next` needs to check whether there's at least one thing in it, thus potentially causing one extra realization. Here's an example:

```
(println (first very-lazy)) ; .4

(println (first less-lazy)) ; 4
```

---

[6] On our machines, 200,000 elements are enough to cause a stack overflow, but your machine may require more or fewer depending on your JVM configuration.

Grabbing the first element in a lazy seq built with `rest` causes a realization as expected. But the same doesn't happen for a seq built with `next` because it's already been previously realized. Using `next` causes a lazy seq to be one element less lazy, which might not be desired if the cost of realization is expensive. In general, we recommend that you use `next` unless you're specifically trying to write code to be as lazy as possible.

USING LAZY-SEQ AND REST

In order to be a proper lazy citizen, you should produce lazy sequences using the `lazy-seq` macro. Here's a lazy version of `rec-step` that addresses the problems with the previous implementation.

> **Listing 6.2 Using `lazy-seq` to avoid stack overflows**

```
(defn lz-rec-step [s]
  (lazy-seq
    (if (seq s)
      [(first s) (lz-rec-step (rest s))]
      [])))

(lz-rec-step [1 2 3 4])
;=> (1 (2 (3 (4 ()))))

(class (lz-rec-step [1 2 3 4]))
;=> clojure.lang.LazySeq

(dorun (lz-rec-step (range 200000)))          No longer produces a
                                              stack overflow
;=> nil
```

There are a few points of note for this new implementation. As we mentioned in our rules of thumb, when consuming a sequence in the body of a `lazy-seq`, you want to use rest, as in `lz-rec-step`. Second, you're no longer producing nested vectors as the output of the function, but instead a lazy sequence `LazySeq`, which is the byproduct of the `lazy-seq` macro.

With only minor adjustments, you've created a lazy version of the step function while also maintaining simplicity. The first two rules of the lazy-sequence recipe can be used in all cases when producing lazy sequences. Note them in the previous example—the use of `lazy-seq` as the outermost form in the function and the use of rest. You'll see this pattern over and over in Clojure code found in the wild.

If what's going on here still doesn't quite make sense to you, consider this even simpler example:

```
(defn simple-range [i limit]
  (lazy-seq
    (when (< i limit)
      (cons i (simple-range (inc i) limit)))))
```

This behaves similarly to Clojure's built-in function `range`, but it's simpler in that it doesn't accept a `step` argument and has no support for producing chunked seqs:[7]

```
(simple-range 0 9)
;=> (0 1 2 3 4 5 6 7 8)
```

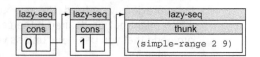

Note that it follows all the lazy-seq recipe rules you've seen so far. Figure 6.2 is a representation of what's in memory when the REPL has printed the first two items in a `simple-range` seq but hasn't yet printed any more than that.

Complications may arise if you accidentally hold on to the head of a lazy sequence. This is addressed by the fourth rule of lazy sequences.

Figure 6.2 Each step of a lazy seq may be in one of two states. If the step is unrealized, it contains a function or closure of no arguments that can be called later to realize the step. When this happens, the thunk's return value is cached instead, and the thunk itself is released as pictured in the first two lazy seq boxes, transitioning the step to the realized state. Note that although not shown here, a realized lazy seq may contain nothing at all, called `nil`, indicating the end of the seq.

6.3.3 *Losing your head*

The primary advantage of laziness in Clojure is that it prevents the full realization of interim results during a calculation. If you manage to hold on to the head of a sequence somewhere within a function, then that sequence will be prevented from being garbage collected. The simplest way to retain the head of a sequence is to bind it to a local. This condition can occur with any type of value bind, be it to a reference type or through the usage of `let` or `binding`:[8]

```
(let [r (range 1e9)]
  (first r)
  (last r))
;=> 999999999

(let [r (range 1e9)]
  (last r)
  (first r))
; java.lang.OutOfMemoryError: GC overhead limit exceeded
```

Clojure's compiler can deduce that in the first example, the retention of `r` is no longer needed when the computation of `(last r)` occurs, and therefore Clojure aggressively clears it. But in the second example, the head is needed later in the overall computation and can no longer be safely cleared. Of course, the compiler could perform some rearranging with the order of operations for this case, but it doesn't because in order to do so safely it would have to guarantee that all the composite functions were pure. It's OK if you're not clear on what a pure function is right now—we'll cover it in section 7.1. In a nutshell, take to heart that Clojure can't rearrange operations, because there's no way to guarantee that order is unimportant. This is one area

---

[7] Chunked seqs are a technique for improving performance that we cover in chapter 15.

[8] When running this code, our laptop got very hot. Be warned that your lap may get toasty—please don't sue us.

where a purely functional lazy language such as Haskell (Thompson 1999) shines by comparison.

6.3.4 *Employing infinite sequences*

Because Clojure's sequences are lazy, they have the potential to be infinitely long. Clojure provides a number of functions for generating and working with infinite sequences:

```
; Run at your own risk
(iterate (fn [n] (/ n 2)) 1)
;=> (1 1/2 1/4 1/8 ...)
```

It sure is a nice trick (although you might not think so had you chosen to ignore our warning), but what could you possibly use infinite sequences for? Working with infinite sequences often fosters more declarative solutions. Take a simple example as a start. Imagine that you have a function that calculates a triangle number[9] for a given integer:

```
(defn triangle [n]
(/ (* n (+ n 1)) 2))

(triangle 10)
;=> 55
```

The function `triangle` can then be used to build a sequence of the first 10 triangle numbers:

```
(map triangle (range 1 11))
;=> (1 3 6 10 15 21 28 36 45 55)
```

There's nothing wrong with the preceding solution, but it suffers from a lack of flexibility in that it does what it does and that's all. By defining a sequence of *all* the triangle numbers, as in the following listing, you can perform more interesting "queries" in order to retrieve the desired elements.

Listing 6.3 Infinite sequences fostering declarative solutions

```
(def tri-nums (map triangle (iterate inc 1)))

(take 10 tri-nums)                               ← Get the first 10
;=> (1 3 6 10 15 21 28 36 45 55)

(take 10 (filter even? tri-nums))                ← Get the first 10 even
;=> (6 10 28 36 66 78 120 136 190 210)

(nth tri-nums 99)                                ← What Gauss found
;=> 5050

(double (reduce + (take 1000 (map / tri-nums)))) ← Converge on 2
;=> 1.998001998001998
```

---

[9] If you've ever gone bowling, you may know what a triangle number is without realizing it. The game has 10 pins arranged in a triangular formation, where the first row has one pin and the last row has four. Therefore, the triangle number of four is 10 $(1 + 2 + 3 + 4 = 10)$.

```
(take 2 (drop-while #(< % 10000) tri-nums))     ◁— First 2 greater than 10,000
;=> (10011 10153)
```

The queries use three ubiquitous Clojure functions: map, reduce, and filter. The map function applies a function to each element in a sequence and returns the resulting sequence. The reduce function applies a function to each value in the sequence *and* the running result to accumulate a final value. Finally, the filter function applies a function to each element in a sequence and returns a new sequence of those elements where said function returned a truthy value. All three of these functions retain the laziness of a given sequence.

Defining the infinite sequence of triangle numbers allows you to take elements from it as needed, only calculating those particular items.

6.3.5   *The delay and force macros*

Although Clojure sequences are largely lazy, Clojure itself isn't. In most cases, expressions in Clojure are evaluated once prior to their being passed into a function rather than at the time of need. But Clojure does provide mechanisms for implementing what are known as *call-by-need semantics*. The most obvious of these mechanisms is its macro facilities, but we'll defer that discussion until chapter 8. The other mechanism for providing what we'll call *explicit laziness* uses Clojure's delay and force. In short, the delay macro is used to defer the evaluation of an expression until explicitly forced using the force function. Using these laziness primitives, you can wrap an expression in a call to delay and use it only if necessary on the callee's side:[10]

```
(defn defer-expensive [cheap expensive]
  (if-let [good-enough (force cheap)]        ◁—┐ Perform the "then" part only if
    good-enough                                 │ a truthy value is returned
    (force expensive)))

(defer-expensive (delay :cheap)
                 (delay (do (Thread/sleep 5000) :expensive)))
;=> :cheap

(defer-expensive (delay false)
                 (delay (do (Thread/sleep 5000) :expensive)))
;=> :expensive
```

You can simulate this behavior with the use of anonymous functions, where delay is replaced by (fn [] expr) and force by (delayed-fn), but using delay/force lets you explicitly check for delayed computations using delay?. Additionally, delay caches its calculation, therefore allowing its wrapped expression to be calculated only once. Of course, you could simulate the same behavior using memoization,[11] but why would you in this case when delay and force solve the problem more succinctly?

---

[10] See the sidebar at the top of the next page for a description of if-let.
[11] We'll cover memoization in chapter 14.

if-let and when-let

The `if-let` and `when-let` macros are useful when you'd like to bind the results of an expression based on whether it returns a truthy value. This helps to avoid the need to nest `if`/`when` and `let` as shown:

```
(if :truthy-thing
  (let [res :truthy-thing] (println res)))
; :truthy-thing

(if-let [res :truthy-thing] (println res))
; :truthy-thing
```

The latter is much more succinct.

There are more complicated usage patterns for `delay` and `force` besides the simple scheme outlined previously. For example, you can implement a version of the lazy sequence of triangular numbers from a few sections prior using `delay` and `force`:

```
(defn inf-triangles [n]
  {:head (triangle n)
   :tail (delay (inf-triangles (inc n)))})

(defn head [l]    (:head l))
(defn tail [l]    (force (:tail l)))
```

The function `inf-triangles` creates a lazy linked list of nodes. Each node is a map containing a value mapped to `:head` and a link to the remainder of the list keyed as `:tail`. The head of the list is the result of applying the function `triangle` to the incrementing counter passed recursively within the body of `delay`. As you can imagine, the head of a node is always calculated as you walk down the linked list, even if it's never accessed. This type of lazy structure is known as *head strict* but differs from Clojure's `lazy-seq`, which delays both the head and tail and then realizes them at the same time.

You can now create a structure similar to the original `tri-nums` and start getting at its contained elements:

```
(def tri-nums (inf-triangles 1))

(head tri-nums)
;=> 1
(head (tail tri-nums))
;=> 3
(head (tail (tail tri-nums)))
;=> 6
```

One thing to note about the preceding code is that accessing the values 3 and 6 involves deferred calculations that occur only on demand. The structure of the example is shown in figure 6.3.

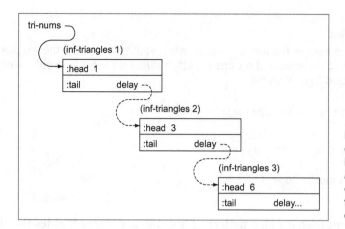

Figure 6.3   Lazy linked-list example. Each node of this linked list contains a value (the *head*) and a delay (the *tail*). The creation of the next part is forced by a call to `tail`—it doesn't exist until then.

Although you can navigate the entire chain of triangular numbers using only `head` and `tail`, it's probably a better idea[12] to use them as primitives for more complicated functions:

```
(defn taker [n l]
  (loop [t n, src l, ret []]
    (if (zero? t)
      ret
      (recur (dec t) (tail src) (conj ret (head src))))))
(defn nthr [l n]
  (if (zero? n)
    (head l)
    (recur (tail l) (dec n))))
(taker 10 tri-nums)
;=> [1 3 6 10 15 21 28 36 45 55]

(nthr tri-nums 99)
;=> 5050
```

Of course, writing programs using `delay` and `force` is an onerous way to go about the problem of laziness, and you'd be better served by using Clojure's lazy sequences to full effect rather than building your own from these basic blocks. But the preceding code, in addition to being simple to understand, harkens back to chapter 5 and the entire sequence "protocol" being built entirely on the functions `first` and `rest`. Pretty cool, right?

6.4   *Putting it all together: a lazy quicksort*

In a time when the landscape is rife with new programming languages and pregnant with more, it seems inconceivable that the world would need another quicksort implementation. Inconceivable or not, we won't be deterred from adding yet another to the rich ecosystem of pet problems. This implementation of quicksort differs from many in

---

[12] And as we'll cover in section 9.3, participating in the ISeq protocol is even better.

a few key ways. First, you'll implement a lazy, tail-recursive version. Second, you'll split the problem such that it can be executed incrementally. Only the calculations required to obtain the part of a sequence desired will be calculated. This will illustrate the fundamental reason for laziness in Clojure: *the avoidance of full realization of interim results.*

6.4.1 The implementation

Without further ado, we present our quicksort implementation, starting with a simple function named rand-ints that generates a seq of pseudo-random integers sized according to its given argument n with numbers ranging from zero to n, inclusive:

```
(ns joy.q)
```

```
(defn rand-ints [n]
  (take n (repeatedly #(rand-int n))))
```

The rand-ints function works as you might expect:

```
(rand-ints 10)
```

```
;;=> (0 1 5 7 3 5 6 4 9 0)
```

The bulk of this lazy quicksort implementation[13] is as shown in the following listing.

Listing 6.4 Lazy, tail-recursive, incremental quicksort

```
(defn sort-parts [work]
  (lazy-seq
    (loop [[part & parts] work]          <— Pull apart work
      (if-let [[pivot & xs] (seq part)]
        (let [smaller? #(< % pivot)]      <— Define pivot comparison fn
          (recur (list*
                   (filter smaller? xs)   <— Work all < pivot
                   pivot                  <— Work the pivot itself
                   (remove smaller? xs)   <— Work all > pivot
                   parts)))               <— Concat parts
        (when-let [[x & parts] parts]
          (cons x (sort-parts parts)))))))  <— Sort the rest if more parts
```

The key detail in the preceding code is that sort-parts works not on a plain sequence of elements but on a carefully constructed list that alternates between lazy seqs and pivots. Every element before each pivot is guaranteed to be less than the pivot, and everything after will be greater, but the sequences between the pivots are as yet unsorted. When qsort is given an input sequence of numbers to sort, it creates a new work list consisting of just that input sequence and passes this work to sort-parts. The loop inside sort-parts pulls apart the work, always assuming that the first

---

[13] This listing uses the list* function, which for some reason is rarely seen. In cases like this, though, it's exactly what you need. list* is like list except it expects its last argument to be a list on which to prepend its other arguments. You'll use it again in chapter 8.

item, which it binds to part, is an unsorted sequence. It also assumes that if there is a second item, which will be at the head of parts, then that item is a pivot. It recurs on the sequence at the head of work, splitting out pivots and lazy seqs until the sequence of items less than the most recent pivot is empty, in which case the if-let test is false, and that most recent pivot is returned as the first item in the sorted seq. The rest of the built-up list of work is held by the returned lazy sequence to be passed into sort-parts again when subsequent sorted items are needed.

You can see a snapshot of the work list for the function call (qsort [2 1 4 3]) in figure 6.4, at an intermediate point in its process.

The figure includes the characteristics of a standard quicksort implementation, which you can finalize with another function that starts sort-parts running properly:

Figure 6.4 The qsort function shown earlier uses a structure like this for its work list when sorting the vector [2 1 4 3]. Note that all the parts described by a standard quicksort implementation are represented here.

```
(defn qsort [xs]
  (sort-parts (list xs)))
```

You can run qsort as follows to sort a given sequence:

```
(qsort [2 1 4 3])
;=> (1 2 3 4)

(qsort (rand-ints 20))
;=> (0 2 3 5 6 7 7 8 9 10 11 11 11 12 12 13 14 16 17 19)
```

The implementation of the sort-parts function works to provide an incremental solution for a lazy quicksort. This incremental approach stands in opposition to a monolithic approach (Okasaki 1996) defined by its performance of the entire calculation when any segment of the sequence is accessed. For example, grabbing the first element in a lazy sequence returned from qsort performs *only* the necessary calculations required to get that first item:

```
(first (qsort (rand-ints 100)))
;=> 1
```

Of course, the number returned here will likely be different in your REPL, but the underlying structure of the lazy sequence used internally by sort-parts will be similar to that shown in figure 6.5.

The lazy qsort can gather the first element because it takes only some small subset of comparisons to gather the numbers into left-side smaller and right-side larger partitions and sort those smaller pieces only. The characteristic of the quicksort algorithm is especially conducive to laziness, because it's fairly cheap to make and shuffle partitions where those with a smaller magnitude can be shuffled first. What then are the benefits of a lazy, tail-recursive, incremental quicksort? The answer is that you can take

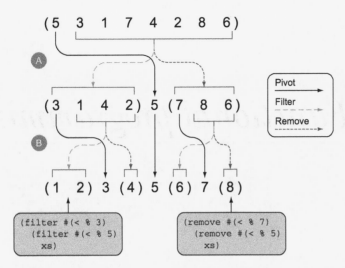

Figure 6.5 Internal structure of `qsort`. Each `filter` and `remove` lazily returns items from its parent sequence only as required. So, to return the first two items of the seq returned by `qsort`, no `remove` steps are required from either level A or level B. To generate the sequence `(4)`, a single `remove` step at level B is needed to eliminate everything less than 3. As more items are forced from the seq returned by `qsort`, more of the internal `filter` and `remove` steps are run.

sorted portions of a large sequence without having to pay the cost of sorting its entirety, as the following command hints:

```
(take 10 (qsort (rand-ints 10000)))
;=> (0 0 0 4 4 7 7 8 9 9)
```

On our machines, this command required roughly 11,000 comparisons, which for all intents and purposes is an O(n) operation—an order of magnitude less than the quicksorts's best case. Bear in mind that as the `take` value gets closer to the actual number of elements, this difference in asymptotic complexity will shrink. But it's a reasonably efficient way to determine the smallest *n* values in a large unsorted (Knuth 1997) sequence, especially given that it doesn't sort its elements in place.

6.5 Summary

We've covered the topics of immutability, persistence, and laziness in this chapter. Clojure's core composite data types are all immutable and persistent by default, and although this fact might presuppose fundamental inefficiencies, we've shown how Clojure addresses them. The implementation of a persistent sorted binary tree demonstrated how structural sharing eliminated the need for full copy on write. But structural sharing isn't enough to guarantee memory efficiency, and that's where the benefits of laziness come into the fold. The implementation of a lazy, tail-recursive quicksort demonstrates that laziness guarantees that sequences aren't fully realized in memory at any given step.

In the next chapter, we'll dive into Clojure's notion of functional programming. Along the way, you'll notice that much of the shape of functional implementations in Clojure is influenced by the topics discussed in this chapter.

Functional programming

This chapter covers
- Functions in all their forms
- Closures
- Thinking recursively
- A* pathfinding

At the core of functional programming is a formal system of computation known as the *lambda calculus* (Pierce 2002). Clojure functions, in adherence with the lambda calculus, are first class—they can be both passed as arguments and returned as results from other functions. This book isn't about the lambda calculus. Instead, we'll explore Clojure's particular flavor of functional programming. We'll cover a vast array of useful topics, including function composition, partial evaluation, recursion, lexical closures, pure functions, function constraints, higher-order functions, and first-class functions. We'll use that last item as our starting point.

7.1 Functions in all their forms

In chapter 5, we mentioned that most of Clojure's composite types can be used as functions of their elements. As a refresher, recall that vectors are functions of their indices, so executing (`[:a :b] 0`) returns `:a`. But this can be used to greater effect by passing the vector as a function argument:

```
(map [:chthon :phthor :beowulf :grendel] #{0 3})

;;=> (:chthon :grendel)    <— Collect the results in a seq
```

<— Call the vector as a function, passing numbers as args

The example uses the vector as the function to map over a set of indices, indicating its first and fourth elements by index. Clojure collections offer an interesting juxtaposition, in that not only can Clojure collections act as functions, but Clojure functions can also act as data—an idea known as *first-class functions*.

7.1.1 *First-class functions*

In a programming language such as Java, there's no notion of a standalone function.[1] Instead, every problem solvable by Java must be performed with the fundamental philosophy that everything is an object. This view on writing programs is therefore rooted in the idea that behaviors in a program must be either modeled as class instances or attached to them—wise or not. Clojure, on the other hand, is a functional programming language and views the problem of software development as the application of functions to data. Likewise, functions in Clojure enjoy equal standing with data—functions are first-class citizens. Before we start, we should define what makes something first class:

- It can be created on demand.
- It can be stored in a data structure.
- It can be passed as an argument to a function.
- It can be returned as the value of a function.

Those of you coming from a background in Java might find the idea of creating functions on demand analogous to the practice of creating anonymous inner classes to handle Swing events (to name only one use case). Although similar enough to start on the way toward understanding functional programming, it's not a concept likely to bear fruit, so don't draw conclusions from this analogy.

CREATING FUNCTIONS ON DEMAND USING COMPOSITION

Even a cursory glance at Clojure is enough to confirm that its primary unit of computation is the function, be it created or composed of other functions:

```
(def fifth (comp first rest rest rest rest))
(fifth [1 2 3 4 5])
;=> 5
```

The function `fifth` isn't defined with `fn` or `defn` forms shown before, but instead built from existing parts using the `comp` (compose) function. But it may be more

---

[1] Although the likely inclusion of closures in some future version of Java should go a long way toward invalidating this. Additionally, for those of you coming from a language such as Python, Scala, or another Lisp, the notion of a first-class function is likely not as foreign as we make it out to be.

interesting to take the idea one step further by instead proving a way to build arbitrary *nth* functions[2] as shown here:

```
(defn fnth [n]
  (apply comp
         (cons first
               (take (dec n) (repeat rest)))))
((fnth 5) '[a b c d e])
;=> e
```

The function fnth builds a list of the function rest of the appropriate length with a final first consed onto the front. This list is then fed into the comp function via apply, which takes a function and a sequence of things and effectively calls the function with the list elements as its arguments. At this point, there's no longer any doubt that the function fnth builds new functions on the fly based on its arguments. Creating new functions this way is a powerful technique, but it takes some practice to think in a compositional way. It's relatively rare to see more than one open parenthesis in a row like this in Clojure, but when you see it, it's almost always because a function (such as fnth) is creating and returning a function that's called immediately. A general rule of thumb is that if you need a function that applies a number of functions serially to the return of the former, then composition is a good fit:

```
(map (comp              <—— Compose fn
      keyword           <—— ... make a keyword
      #(.toLowerCase %) <—— ... from a lowercase
      name)             <—— ... string name
     '(a B C))          <—— Mapped over a list of symbols

;;=> (:a :b :c)
```

Splitting functions into smaller, well-defined pieces fosters composability and, as a result, reuse.

CREATING FUNCTIONS ON DEMAND USING PARTIAL FUNCTIONS

There may be times when instead of building a new function from chains of other functions as comp allows, you need to build a function from the partial application of another:

```
((partial + 5) 100 200)
;=> 305
```

The function partial builds (Tarver 2008) a new function that partially applies the single argument 5 to the addition function. When the returned partial function is passed the arguments 100 and 200, the result is their summation plus that of the value 5 *captured* by partial.

---

[2] We know that Clojure provides an nth function that works slightly differently, but in this case please indulge our obtuseness.

NOTE The use of `partial` differs from the notion of *currying* in a fundamental way. A function built with `partial` attempts to evaluate whenever it's given another argument. A curried function returns another curried function until it receives a predetermined number of arguments—only then does it evaluate. Because Clojure allows functions with a variable number of arguments, currying makes little sense.

We'll discuss more about using `partial` later in this section, but as a final point observe that ((partial + 5) 100 200) is equivalent to (#(apply + 5 %&) 100 200).

REVERSING TRUTH WITH COMPLEMENT

One final function builder is the `complement` function. This function takes a function that returns a truthy value and returns the opposite truthy value:

```
(let [truthiness (fn [v] v)]
  [((complement truthiness) true)
   ((complement truthiness) 42)
   ((complement truthiness) false)
   ((complement truthiness) nil)])

;=> [false false true true]

((complement even?) 2)
;=> false
```

Note that (complement even?) is equivalent to (comp not even?) or #(not (even? %)).

USING FUNCTIONS AS DATA

First-class functions can not only be treated as data; they *are* data. Because a function is first class, it can be stored in a container expecting a piece of data, be it a local, a reference, collections, or anything able to store a `java.lang.Object`. This is a significant departure from Java, where methods are part of a class but don't stand alone at runtime (Forman 2004). One particularly useful method for treating functions as data is the way that Clojure's testing framework `clojure.test` stores and validates unit tests in the metadata (as discussed in section 14.2) of a var holding a function. These unit tests are keyed with the `:test` keyword, laid out as follows:

```
(defn join
  {:test (fn []
           (assert
             (= (join "," [1 2 3]) "1,3,3")))}
  [sep s]
  (apply str (interpose sep s)))
```

The faces of defn metadata

As shown in the definition of the `join` function with built-in tests, placing a map before a function's parameters is one way of assigning metadata to a function using the `defn` macro. Another way is to use the shorthand notation before the function name, like so:

> *(continued)*
>
> ```
> (defn ^:private ^:dynamic sum [nums]
>   (map + nums))
> ```
>
> The use of the shorthand ^:private and ^:dynamic is the same as saying
>
> ```
> (defn ^{:private true, :dynamic true} sum [nums]
>   (map + nums))
> ```
>
> which is the same as saying
>
> ```
> (defn sum {:private true, :dynamic true} [nums]
>   (map + nums))
> ```
>
> which is also the same as saying
>
> ```
> (defn sum
>   ([nums]
>      (map + nums))
>   {:private true, :dynamic true})
> ```
>
> The differing choices come in handy usually in different macro metaprogramming sce-
> narios. For most human-typed functions, the shorthand form works fine.

You've modified join by attaching some metadata containing a *faulty* unit test. Of
course, by that we mean the attached unit test is meant to fail in this case. The
clojure.test/run-tests function is useful for running attached unit tests in the current namespace:

```
(use '[clojure.test :as t])
(t/run-tests)
; Testing user
;
; ERROR in (join) (test.clj:646)
; ...
; actual: java.lang.AssertionError:
;  Assert failed: (= (join "," [1 2 3]) "1,3,3")
; ...
```

As expected, the faulty unit test for join fails. Unit tests in Clojure only scratch the
surface of the boundless spectrum of examples using functions as data, but for now
they'll do, as we move on to the notion of higher-order functions.

7.1.2 *Higher-order functions*

A *higher-order function* is a function that does at least one of the following:

- Takes one or more functions as arguments
- Returns a function as a result

A Java programmer may be familiar with the practices of subscriber patterns or
schemes using more general-purpose callback objects. There are scenarios such as
these where Java treats objects like functions, but as with anything in Java, you're really
dealing with objects containing privileged methods.

FUNCTIONS AS ARGUMENTS

In this book, we use and advocate the use of the sequence functions map, reduce, and filter—all of which expect a function argument that's applied to the elements of the sequence arguments. The use of functions in this way is ubiquitous in Clojure and can make for truly elegant solutions. Another interesting example of a function that takes a function as an argument is the sort-by function. Before we dig into that, allow us to explain the motivation behind it. Specifically, Clojure provides a function named sort that works exactly as you might expect:

```
(sort [1 5 7 0 -42 13])
;;=> (-42 0 1 5 7 13)
```

The sort function works on many different types of elements:[3]

```
(sort ["z" "x" "a" "aa"])
;;=> ("a" "aa" "x" "z")

(sort [(java.util.Date.) (java.util.Date. 100)])
;;=> (#inst "1970-01-01T00:00:00.100-00:00"
;;    #inst "2013-06-18T02:49:53.544-00:00")

(sort [[1 2 3], [-1, 0, 1], [3 2 1]])
;;=> ([-1 0 1] [1 2 3] [3 2 1])
```

But if you want to sort by different criteria, such as from greatest to least, then you can pass a function in to sort for use as the sorting criteria:

```
(sort > [7 1 4])
;;=> (7 4 1)
```

But sort fails if given seqs containing elements that aren't mutually comparable:

```
(sort ["z" "x" "a" "aa" 1 5 8])
;; ClassCastException java.lang.Long cannot be cast to java.lang.String

(sort [{:age 99}, {:age 13}, {:age 7}])
;; ClassCastException clojure.lang.PersistentArrayMap cannot be ...
```

Likewise, it gives unwanted results if you try to compare sub-elements of a type that it sorts as an aggregate rather than by specific parts:

```
(sort [[:a 7], [:c 13], [:b 21]])
;;=> ([:a 7] [:b 21] [:c 13])
```

That is, in this example you want to sort by the *second* element in the vectors, but passing the second function into sort is not the solution:

```
(sort second [[:a 7], [:c 13], [:b 21]])
;; ArityException Wrong number of args (2) passed to: core$second
```

---

[3] The odd-looking printout of the Date instances are what are known as *tagged literals*, which we'll talk about in chapter 14.

Instead, Clojure provides the `sort-by` function, which takes a function as an argument that is used to preprocess each sortable element into something that is mutually comparable to the others:

```
(sort-by second [[:a 7], [:c 13], [:b 21]])
;;=> ([:a 7] [:c 13] [:b 21])
```

That looks better. And likewise for the other failed examples shown earlier, `sort-by` is key:

```
(sort-by str ["z" "x" "a" "aa" 1 5 8])
;;=> (1 5 8 "a" "aa" "x" "z")

(sort-by :age [{:age 99}, {:age 13}, {:age 7}])
;;=> ({:age 7} {:age 13} {:age 99})
```

The fact that `sort-by` takes an arbitrary function (and function-like thing, as shown when you used the keyword earlier) to preprocess elements allows for powerful sorting techniques. For example, let's look at an example of a function that takes a sequence of maps and a function working on each, and returns a sequence sorted by the results of the function. The implementation in Clojure is straightforward and clean:

```
(def plays [{:band "Burial",     :plays 979,  :loved 9}
            {:band "Eno",        :plays 2333, :loved 15}
            {:band "Bill Evans", :plays 979,  :loved 9}
            {:band "Magma",      :plays 2665, :loved 31}])

(def sort-by-loved-ratio (partial sort-by #(/ (:plays %) (:loved %))))
```

The function with the overly descriptive name `sort-by-loved-ratio` is built from the partial application of the function `sort-by` and an anonymous function dividing the `:plays` field by the `:loved` field. This is a simple solution to the problem presented, and its usage is equally so:

```
(sort-by-loved-ratio plays)
;=> ({:band "Magma",     :plays 2665, :loved 31}
     {:band "Burial",    :plays 979,  :loved 9}
     {:band "Bill Evans",:plays 979,  :loved 9}
     {:band "Eno",       :plays 2333, :loved 15})
```

This example intentionally uses the additional higher-order function `sort-by` to avoid reimplementing core functions and instead *build the program from existing parts.* You should strive to do this whenever possible.

FUNCTIONS AS RETURN VALUES

You've already used functions returning functions in this chapter with `comp`, `partial`, and `complement`, but you can build functions that do the same. Let's extend the earlier example to provide a function that sorts rows based on some number of column values. This is similar to the way spreadsheets operate, in that you can sort on a primary column while falling back on a secondary column to provide the sort order on matching results in the primary. This behavior is typically performed along any number of columns, cascading down from the primary column to the last; each subgroup is sorted appropriately, as the expected result illustrates:

```
(sort-by (columns [:plays :loved :band]) plays)
;=> ({:band "Bill Evans", :plays 979,  :loved 9}
      {:band "Burial",     :plays 979,  :loved 9}
      {:band "Eno",        :plays 2333, :loved 15}
      {:band "Magma",      :plays 2665, :loved 31})
```

This kind of behavior sounds complex on the surface but is shockingly simple[4] in its Clojure implementation:

```
(defn columns [column-names]
  (fn [row]
    (vec (map row column-names))))
```

A quick example of what columns provides will help to clarify its intent:

```
(columns [:plays :loved :band])
;;=> #<user$columns$fn__1076 user$columns$fn__1076@689ba632>

((columns [:plays :loved :band])
  {:band "Burial", :plays 979, :loved 9})

;;=> [979 9 "Burial"]
```

Running the preceding expression shows that the row for Burial has a tertiary column sorting, represented as a vector of three elements that correspond to the listed column names. Specifically, the function columns returns another function expecting a map. This return function is then supplied to sort-by to provide the value on which the plays vector would be sorted. Perhaps you see a familiar pattern: you apply the column-names vector as a function across a set of indices, building a sequence of its elements *at* those indices. This action returns a sequence of the values of that row for the supplied column names, which is then turned into a vector so that it can be used as the sorting function,[5] as structured here:

```
(vec (map (plays 0) [:plays :loved :band]))
;=> [979 9 "Burial"]
```

This resulting vector is then used by sort-by to provide the final ordering.

Building your programs using first-class functions in concert with higher-order functions reduces complexities and makes your code base more robust and extensible. In the next subsection, we'll explore pure functions, which all prior functions in this section have been, and explain why your applications should strive toward purity.

---

[4] Strictly speaking, the implementation of columns should use #(% row) instead of just row, because you can't always assume that the row is implemented as a map (a record might be used instead) and therefore directly usable as a function. Records are discussed further in chapter 9.

[5] Because sort-by is higher order, it naturally expects a function argument. As mentioned, vectors can also be used as functions. But as we'll discuss in detail in section 12.4, all closure functions implement the java.util.Comparator interface, which in this case is the driving force behind the sorting logic of sort-by!

Prefer higher-order functions when processing sequences

We mentioned in section 6.3 that one way to ensure that lazy sequences are never fully realized in memory is to prefer (Hutton 1999) higher-order functions for processing. Most collection processing can be performed with some combination of the following functions: `map`, `reduce`, `filter`, `for`, `some`, `repeatedly`, `sort-by`, `keep`, `take-while`, and `drop-while`.

But higher-order functions aren't a panacea for every solution. Therefore, we'll cover the topic of recursive solutions in greater depth in section 7.3 for those cases when higher-order functions fail or are less than clear.

7.1.3 Pure functions

Pure functions are regular functions that, through convention, conform to the following simple guidelines:

- The function *always* returns the same result, given the *same* arguments.
- The function doesn't cause any *observable* side effects.

Although Clojure is designed to minimize and isolate side effects, it's by no means a purely functional language. But there are a number of reasons why you'd want to build as much of your system as possible from pure functions, and we'll enumerate a few presently.

REFERENTIAL TRANSPARENCY

If a function of some arguments always results in the same value and changes no other values in the greater system, then it's essentially a constant, or referentially transparent (the reference to the function is transparent to time). Take a look at pure function `keys-apply`:

```
(defn keys-apply [f ks m]                    Get exact entries
  (let [only (select-keys m ks)]
    (zipmap (keys only)                      Zip the keys and processed
            (map f (vals only)))))           values back into a map
```

The action of `keys-apply` is as follows (recall that `plays` is a sequence of maps, defined in the previous section):

```
(keys-apply #(.toUpperCase %) #{:band} (plays 0))
;;=> {:band "BURIAL"}
```

Using another pure function `manip-map`, you can then manipulate a set of keys based on a given function:

```
(defn manip-map [f ks m]                    Manipulate only the given keys, and then
  (merge m (keys-apply f ks m)))            merge the changes into the original
```

And the use of `manip-map` to halve the values keyed at `:plays` and `:loved` is as follows:

```
(manip-map #(int (/ % 2)) #{:plays :loved} (plays 0))

;;=> {:band "Burial", :plays 489, :loved 4}
```

keys-apply and manip-map are both pure functions,[6] illustrated by the fact that you can replace them in the context of a larger program with their expected return values and not change the outcome. Pure functions exist outside the bounds of time. But if you make either keys-apply or manip-map reliant on anything but its arguments or generate a side effect within, then referential transparency dissolves. Let's add one more function to illustrate this:

```
(defn mega-love! [ks]
  (map (partial manip-map #(int (* % 1000)) ks) plays))

(mega-love! [:loved])
;;=> ({:band "Burial",     :plays 979,  :loved 9000}
      {:band "Eno",        :plays 2333, :loved 15000}
      {:band "Bill Evans", :plays 979,  :loved 9000}
      {:band "Magma",      :plays 2665, :loved 31000})
```

The function mega-love! works against the global var plays and is no longer limited to generating results solely from its arguments. Because plays could change at any moment, there's no guarantee that mega-love! would return the same value given any particular argument.

OPTIMIZATION

If a function is referentially transparent, then it can more easily be optimized using techniques such as memoization (discussed in chapter 14) and algebraic manipulations (Wadler 1989).

TESTABILITY

If a function is referentially transparent, then it's easier to reason about and therefore more straightforward to test. Building mega-love! as an impure function forces the need to test against the possibility that plays could change at any time, complicating matters substantially. Imagine the confusion should you add further impure functions based on further external transient values.

7.1.4 Named arguments

Some programming languages allow functions to take named arguments. Python is one such language, as shown here:

```
def slope(p1=(0,0), p2=(1,1)):
    return (float(p2[1] - p1[1])) / (p2[0] - p1[0])

slope((4,15), (3,21))
#=> -6.0

slope(p2=(2,1))
#=> 0.5
```

---

[6] These functions are based on a similar implementation created by Steven Gilardi.

```
slope()
#=> 1.0
```

The Python function `slope` calculates the slope of a line given two tuples defining points on a line. The tuples `p1` and `p2` are defined as named parameters, allowing either or both to be omitted in favor of default values or passed in any order as named parameters. Clojure provides a similar feature, using its destructuring mechanism coupled with the optional arguments flag `&`. The same function can be written using Clojure's named arguments as follows:

```
(defn slope
  [& {:keys [p1 p2] :or {p1 [0 0] p2 [1 1]}}]
  (float (/ (- (p2 1) (p1 1))
            (- (p2 0) (p1 0)))))

(slope :p1 [4 15] :p2 [3 21])
;=> -6.0

(slope :p2 [2 1])
;=> 0.5

(slope)
;=> 1.0
```

Clojure's named arguments are built on the destructuring mechanism outlined in section 3.3, allowing much richer ways to declare them.

7.1.5   *Constraining functions with pre- and postconditions*

Every function in Clojure can potentially be constrained on its inputs, its output, and some arbitrary relationship between them. These constraints take the form of pre- and postcondition vectors contained in a map defined in the function body. Let's simplify the `slope` function to the base case to more clearly illustrate the matter of constraints:

```
(defn slope [p1 p2]
  {:pre [(not= p1 p2) (vector? p1) (vector? p2)]
   :post [(float? %)]}
  (/ (- (p2 1) (p1 1))
     (- (p2 0) (p1 0))))
```

The constraint map defines two entries: `:pre` constraining the input parameters and `:post` constraining the return value. The function calls in the constraint vectors are all expected to return `true` for the constraints to pass (via logical and). In the case of the revised `slope` function, the input constraints are that the points must not be equal and they must both be vectors. In the postcondition, the constraint is that the return result must be a floating-point value. The following example runs through a few scenarios to show how the new implementation works:

```
(slope [10 10] [10 10])                          ⟵— Same points
; java.lang.AssertionError: Assert failed: (not= p1 p2)

(slope [10 1] '(1 20))                            ⟵— p2 is a List
; java.lang.AssertionError: Assert failed: (vector? p2)
```

```
(slope [10 1] [1 20])                        ⟵ Float isn't returned
; java.lang.AssertionError: Assert failed: (float? %)

(slope [10.0 1] [1 20])                      ⟵ Any/all as a floating point
 ;=> -2.111111111111111
```

Clojure also provides a simple assertion macro that can be used to emulate some pre-
and postconditions. Using assert instead of :pre is typically fairly straightforward.
But using assert instead of :post is cumbersome and awkward. On the contrary,
restricting yourself to constraint maps will cover most of the expected cases covered by
assert, which can be used to fill in the remaining holes (such as loop invariants). In
any case, constraint maps provide standard hooks into the assertion machinery of Clojure, whereas using assert is by its nature ad hoc. Yet another advantage of :pre and
:post is that they allow the assertions to come from a different source than the body
of the function, which we'll address next.

> **TIP** To turn off :pre and :post checks for a specific file, add the line (set!
> *assert* false) to a source file somewhere near the top, but after the
> namespace declaration.

DECOUPLING ASSERTIONS FROM FUNCTIONS

The implementation of slope corresponds to a well-established mathematical property. As a result, it makes perfect sense to tightly couple the constraints and the work
to be done to perform the calculation. But not all functions are as well defined as
slope, and therefore they could benefit from some flexibility in their constraints.
Imagine a function that takes a map, puts some keys into it, and returns the new map,
defined as follows:

```
(defn put-things [m]
  (into m {:meat "beef" :veggie "broccoli"}))

(put-things {})
;=> {:meat "beef", :veggie "broccoli"}
```

How would you add constraints to put-things? You could add them directly to the
function definition, but the consumers of the map might have differing requirements
for the entries added. Instead, here's how you can abstract the constraints into
another function:

```
(defn vegan-constraints [f m]
  {:pre [(:veggie m)]
   :post [(:veggie %) (nil? (:meat %))]}
  (f m))

(vegan-constraints put-things {:veggie "carrot"})
; java.lang.AssertionError: Assert failed: (nil? (:meat %))
```

The vegan-constraints function applies specific constraints to an incoming function,
stating that the map coming in and going out should have some kind of veggie and
should never have meat in the result. The beauty of this scheme is that you can create
contextual constraints based on the appropriate expected results, as shown next:

```
(defn balanced-diet [f m]
  {:post [(:meat %) (:veggie %)]}
  (f m))
```
◁─┐ **Make sure there is a**
  │ **meat and a veggie**
```
(balanced-diet put-things {})
;=> {:veggie "broccoli", :meat "beef"}

(defn finicky [f m]
  {:post [(= (:meat %) (:meat m))]}
  (f m))
```
◁── **Never change the meat**
```
(finicky put-things {:meat "chicken"})
; java.lang.AssertionError: Assert failed: (= (:meat %) (:meat m))
```

Recall that the put-things function returns a new map augmented with certain food-stuffs. Therefore, the assertion failure in the last example happens because the new map is compared with the original map passed to finicky as an argument. By pulling out the assertions into a wrapper function, you detach some domain-specific requirements from a potentially globally useful function and isolate them in *aspects* (Laddad 2003). By detaching pre- and postconditions from the functions themselves, you can mix in any implementation you please, knowing that as long as it fulfills the contract (Meyer 1991), its interposition is transparent. This is only the beginning of the power of Clojure's pre- and postconditions, and we'll come back to it a few times more to see how it can be extended and utilized.

Now that we've covered some of the powerful features available via Clojure's functions, we'll take a step further by exploring lexical closures.

7.2   On closures

> On his next walk with Qc Na, Anton attempted to impress his master by saying "Master, I have diligently studied the matter, and now understand that objects are truly a poor man's closures." Qc Na responded by hitting Anton with his stick, saying "When will you learn? Closures are a poor man's object." At that moment, Anton became enlightened.
>
> —Anton van Straaten[7]

It took only 30 years, but closures (Sussman 1975) are now a key feature of mainstream programming languages—Perl and Ruby support them, and JavaScript derives much of what power it has from closures. So what's a closure? In a sentence, a *closure* is a function that has access to locals from the context where it was created:

```
(def times-two
  (let [x 2]
    (fn [y] (* y x))))
```

The fn form defines a function and uses def to store it in a var named times-two. The let forms a lexical scope in which the function was defined, so the function gains access to all the locals in that lexical context. That's what makes this function a closure: it uses the local x that was defined *outside* the body of the function, and so the

---

[7] Email message to Guy Steele, June 4, 2003, http://mng.bz/7xFk.

local and its value become a property of the function itself. The function is said to *close over* the local x, as in the following example:[8]

```
(times-two 5)
;=> 10
```

This isn't terribly interesting, but one way to make a more exciting closure is to have it close over something mutable:

```
(def add-and-get
  (let [ai (java.util.concurrent.atomic.AtomicInteger.)]
    (fn [y] (.addAndGet ai y))))

(add-and-get 2)
;=> 2
(add-and-get 2)
;=> 4
(add-and-get 7)
;=> 11
```

The `java.util.concurrent.atomic.AtomicInteger` class holds an integer value, and its `.addAndGet` method adds to its value, stores the result, and also returns the result. The function `add-and-get` is holding on to the same instance of `Atomic-Integer`, and each time it's called, the value of that instance is modified. Unlike the earlier `times-two` function, this one can't be rewritten with the local `ai` defined in the function. If you tried, then each time the function was called, it would create a new instance with a default value of 0 to be created and stored in `ai`—clearly not what should happen. A point of note about this technique is that when closing over something mutable, you run the risk of making your functions impure and thus more difficult to test and reason about, especially if the mutable local is shared.

7.2.1 *Functions returning closures*

Each of the previous examples creates a single closure, but by wrapping similar code in another function definition, you can create more closures on demand. For example, you can take the earlier `times-two` example and generalize it to take an argument instead of using 2 directly:

```
(defn times-n [n]
  (let [x n]
    (fn [y] (* y x))))
```

We've covered functions returning functions before, but if you're not already familiar with closures, this may be a stretch. You now have an outer function stored in a var named `times-n`—note that you use `defn` instead of `def`. When `times-n` is called with an argument, it returns a new closure created by the `fn` form and closing over the local x. The value of x for this closure is whatever is passed in to `times-n`:

---

[8] Locals like x in this example are sometimes called *free variables*. We don't use the term because Clojure locals are immutable.

```
(times-n 4)
;=> #<user$times_n$fn__39 user$times_n$fn__39@427be8c2>
```

Viewing the function form for this closure isn't too useful, so instead you can store it in a var, allowing you to call it by a friendlier name such as `times-four`:

```
(def times-four (times-n 4))
```

Here you're using `def` again to store what `times-n` returns—a closure over the number 4. Thus when you call this closure with an argument of its own, it returns the value of y times x, as shown:

```
(times-four 10)
;=> 40
```

Note that when you call the closure stored in `times-four`, it uses the local it closed over as well as the argument in the call.

7.2.2 Closing over parameters

The definition of `times-n` creates a local x using `let` and closes over that instead of closing over the argument n directly. But this was only to help focus the discussion on other parts of the function. In fact, closures close over parameters of outer functions the same way they do over `let` locals. Thus `times-n` can be defined without any `let` at all:

```
(defn times-n [n]
  (fn [y] (* y n)))
```

All the preceding examples would work exactly the same. Here's another function that creates and returns a closure in a similar way. Note again that the inner function maintains access to the outer parameter even after the outer function has returned:

```
(defn divisible [denom]
  (fn [num]
    (zero? (rem num denom))))
```

You don't have to store a closure in a var; you can instead create one and call it immediately:

```
((divisible 3) 6)
;=> true
```

```
((divisible 3) 7)
;=> false
```

Instead of storing or calling a closure, a particular need is best served by passing a closure along to another function that will use it.

7.2.3 Passing closures as functions

We've shown many examples in previous chapters of higher-order functions built in to Clojure's core libraries. What we've glossed over so far is that anywhere a function is expected, a closure can be used instead. This has dramatic consequences for how powerful these functions can be.

For example, `filter` takes a function (called a *predicate* in this case) and a sequence, applies the predicate to each value of the sequence,[9] and returns a sequence of just the values for which the predicate returned something truthy. A simple example of its use returns only the even numbers from a sequence of numbers:

```
(filter even? (range 10))
;=> (0 2 4 6 8)
```

Note that `filter` only ever passes a single argument to the predicate given it. Without closures, this might be restrictive, but with them you can close over the values needed:

```
(filter (divisible 4) (range 10))
;=> (0 4 8)
```

It's common to define a closure right on the spot where it's used, closing over whatever local context is needed:

```
(defn filter-divisible [denom s]
  (filter (fn [num] (zero? (rem num denom))) s))

(filter-divisible 4 (range 10))
;=> (0 4 8)
```

This kind of on-the-spot anonymous function definition is desired frequently enough that Clojure spends a little of its small syntax budget on the reader feature to make such cases more succinct. This `#()` form was first introduced in chapter 2 and in this case can be used to write the definition of `filter-divisible` as follows:

```
(defn filter-divisible [denom s]
  (filter #(zero? (rem % denom)) s))

(filter-divisible 5 (range 20))
;=> (0 5 10 15)
```

Although certainly more succinct than the extended anonymous function form and the earlier example using a separate `divisible` function with `filter`, there's a fine line to balance between reuse and clarity.[10] Thankfully, in any case the performance differences among the three choices are nominal.

7.2.4 Sharing closure context

So far, the closures we've shown have stood alone, but it's sometimes useful to have multiple closures closing over the same values. This may take the form of an ad hoc set of closures in a complex lexical environment, such as event callbacks or timer handlers

---

[9] Please don't construe from this wording that `filter` always iterates through the entire input sequence. Like most of the seq library, it's lazy and only consumes as much of the input sequence as needed to produce the values demanded of it.

[10] Hiding `divisible` as an anonymous function inside `filter-divisible` reduces the reusability of the code with no real benefit. Anonymous functions are best reserved for when the lexical context being closed over is more complex or the body of the function is too narrow in use to warrant being its own named function.

in a nested GUI builder. Or it may be a tidy, specifically designed bundle of values and related functions—something that can be thought of as an object.

To demonstrate this, let's build a robot object that has functions for moving it around a grid based on its current position and bearing. For this you need a list of coordinate deltas for compass bearings, starting with north and going clockwise:

```
(def bearings [{:x  0, :y  1}    ; north
               {:x  1, :y  0}    ; east
               {:x  0, :y -1}    ; south
               {:x -1, :y  0}])  ; west
```

Note that this is on a grid where y increases as you go north and x increases as you go east—mathematical coordinate style rather than spreadsheet cells.

With this in place, it's easy to write a function `forward` that takes a coordinate and a bearing and returns a new coordinate, having moved forward one step in the direction of the bearing:

```
(defn forward [x y bearing-num]
  [(+ x (:x (bearings bearing-num)))
   (+ y (:y (bearings bearing-num)))])
```

Starting with a bearing of 0 (north) at 5,5 and going one step brings the bot to 5,6:

```
(forward 5 5 0)
;=> [5 6]
```

You can also try starting at 5,5 and with bearing 1 (east) or bearing 2 (south) and see the desired results:

```
(forward 5 5 1)
;=> [6 5]

(forward 5 5 2)
;=> [5 4]
```

But you have no closures yet, so you'll build a bot object that keeps not just its coordinates, but also its bearing. In the process, you'll move this standalone `forward` function into the bot object. By making this a closure, you'll also open up possibilities for polymorphism later. So here's a bot that knows how to move itself forward:

```
(defn bot [x y bearing-num]
  {:coords  [x y]
   :bearing ([:north :east :south :west] bearing-num)
   :forward (fn [] (bot (+ x (:x (bearings bearing-num)))
                        (+ y (:y  (bearings bearing-num)))
                        bearing-num))})
```

You can create an instance of this bot and query it for its coordinates or its bearing:

```
(:coords (bot 5 5 0))
;=> [5 5]

(:bearing (bot 5 5 0))
;=> :north
```

But now that you've moved the forward function inside, you no longer pass in parameters, because it gets everything it needs to know from the state of the bot that it closes over. Instead, you use :forward to fetch the closure from inside the bot object and then use an extra set of parentheses to invoke it with no arguments:

```
(:coords ((:forward (bot 5 5 0))))
;=> [5 6]
```

Now you have a somewhat complicated beastie, but there's still only a single closure in the mix. Note that the inner set of parentheses is for the call of :forward, which returns the anonymous function; the outer set then calls that function. To make things more interesting, let's add turn-left and turn-right[11] functions and store them right there in the object with :forward:

```
(defn bot [x y bearing-num]
  {:coords    [x y]
   :bearing   ([:north :east :south :west] bearing-num)
   :forward   (fn [] (bot (+ x (:x (bearings bearing-num)))
                          (+ y (:y (bearings bearing-num)))
                          bearing-num))
   :turn-right (fn [] (bot x y (mod (+ 1 bearing-num) 4)))
   :turn-left  (fn [] (bot x y (mod (- 1 bearing-num) 4)))})

(:bearing ((:forward ((:forward ((:turn-right (bot 5 5 0)))))))))
;=> :east

(:coords ((:forward ((:forward ((:turn-right (bot 5 5 0)))))))))
;=> [7 5]
```

We won't talk about the verbosity of using the bot object yet; instead we'll focus on the features used in the definition of bot. You're freely mixing values computed when a bot is created (such as the :bearing) and functions that create values when called later. The functions are closures, and each has full access to the lexical environment. The fact that there are multiple closures sharing the same environment isn't awkward or unnatural and flows easily from the properties of closures already shown.

We'd like to demonstrate one final feature of this pattern for building objects: polymorphism. For example, here's the definition of a bot that supports all the same usage as earlier, but this one has its wires crossed or perhaps is designed to work sensibly in Alice's Wonderland. Specifically, like the bots defined previously, the mirror-bot in the following code has all the same names for its fields—a form of *duck typing*. When told to go forward, mirror-bot instead reverses, and it turns left instead of right and vice versa:

```
(defn mirror-bot [x y bearing-num]
  {:coords    [x y]
   :bearing   ([:north :east :south :west] bearing-num)
   :forward   (fn [] (mirror-bot (- x (:x (bearings bearing-num)))
```

---

[11] The :turn-right function uses (+ 1 foo), even though in general (inc foo) would be idiomatic. Here it helps highlight the symmetry between turn-right and turn-left, for anyone reading the code. In this case, using + is more readable than using inc and so is preferred.

```
                              (- y (:y (bearings bearing-num)))
                            bearing-num))
    :turn-right (fn [] (mirror-bot x y (mod (- 1 bearing-num) 4)))
    :turn-left  (fn [] (mirror-bot x y (mod (+ 1 bearing-num) 4)))})
```

By bundling the functions that operate on data inside the same structure as the data itself, simple polymorphism is possible. Because each function is a closure, no object state needs to be explicitly passed; instead, each function uses any locals required to do its job.

You probably cringed at the number of parentheses required to call these particular object closures, and rightfully so. We encourage you to extrapolate from the closure examples when dealing with your own applications and see how they can solve a variety of tricky and unusual problems. Although this kind of structure is simple and powerful[12] and may be warranted in some situations, Clojure provides other ways of associating functions with data objects that are more flexible. In fact, the desire to avoid a widespread need for this type of ad hoc implementation inspired the creation of Clojure's reify macro, which we'll cover in section 9.3.2.

COMPILE-TIME VS. RUNTIME

When you look at code that includes a closure, it's not immediately obvious how the work is distributed between compile-time and runtime. In particular, when you see a lot of code or processor-intensive work being done in a closure, you may wonder about the cost of calling the function that creates the closure:

```
(defn do-thing-builder [x y z]
  (fn do-thing [a b]
    . . .
    (massive-calculation x y z)
    ...))
```

But you don't need to worry. When this entire expression is compiled, bytecode for the bodies of do-thing and do-thing-builder is generated and stored in memory.[13] In current versions of Clojure, each function definition gets its own class. But when do-thing-builder is called, it doesn't matter how large or slow the body of do-thing is—all that's done at runtime is the creation of an *instance* of do-thing's class. This is lightweight and fast. Not until the closure *returned* by do-thing-builder is called does the complexity or speed of the body of that inner function matter at all.

In this section, you learned that closures are functions that close over lexical locals, how to create them from inside other functions, how to pass them around and call them, and even how to build lightweight objects using them. Next, we'll look at how functions and closures behave when they call themselves, a pattern lovingly known as *recursion*.

---

[12] ... a fact any sufficiently experienced JavaScript programmer would be able to confirm.

[13] If the code is being compiled ahead of time by the compile function, the generated bytecode is also written to disk in .class files.

7.3 *Thinking recursively*

You're likely already familiar with the basics of recursion, and as a result you can take heart that we won't force you to read a beginner's tutorial again. But because recursive solutions are prevalent in Clojure code, it's important for us to cover it well enough that you can fully understand Clojure's recursive offerings.

Recursion is often viewed as a low-level operation reserved for times when solutions involving higher-order functions either fail or lead to obfuscation. Granted, it's fun to solve problems recursively because even for those of us who've attained some level of acumen with functional programming, finding a recursive solution still injects a bit of magic into our day. Recursion is a perfect building block for creating higher-level looping constructs and functions, as we'll show in this section.

7.3.1 *Mundane recursion*

A classically recursive algorithm is that of calculating some base number raised to an exponent, or the pow function. A straightforward[14] way to solve this problem recursively is to multiply the base by each successively smaller value of the exponent, as implemented here:

```
(defn pow [base exp]
  (if (zero? exp)
    1
    (* base (pow base (dec exp))))))

(pow 2 10)
;=> 1024
(pow 1.01 925)
;=> 9937.353723241924
```

We say that the recursive call is *mundane*[15] because it's named explicitly rather than through mutual recursion or implicitly with the recur special form. Why is this a problem? The answer lies in what happens when you try to call pow with a large value:

```
(pow 2 10000)
; java.lang.StackOverflowError
```

The implementation of pow is doomed to throw java.lang.StackOverflowError because the recursive call is trapped by the multiplication operation. The ideal solution is a tail-recursive version that uses the explicit recur form, thus avoiding stack consumption and the resulting exception. One way to remove the mundane recursive call is to perform the multiplication at a different point, thus freeing the recursive call to occur in the tail position, as shown next:

```
(defn pow [base exp]
  (letfn [(kapow [base exp acc]
            (if (zero? exp)
```

---

[14] Yes, we're aware of Math/pow.

[15] Typically, mundane recursion is referred to as *linear*, or the case where the space requirement needed to perform the recursion is proportional to the magnitude of the input.

```
                acc
               (recur base (dec exp) (* base acc)))))]
      (kapow base exp 1)))
```

```
(pow 2N 10000)
;=> ... A very big number
```

This new version of pow uses two common techniques for converting mundane recursion to tail recursion. First, it uses a helper function kapow that does the majority of the work. Second, kapow uses an accumulator acc that holds the result of the multiplication. The exponent exp is no longer used as a multiplicative value but instead functions as a decrementing counter, eliminating a stack explosion.

REGULAR RECURSION IS FUN AGAIN WITH LAZY-SEQ

As mentioned in section 6.3, the lazy-seq recipe rule of thumb #1 states that you should wrap outer-layer function bodies with the lazy-seq macro when generating lazy seqs. The implementation of lz-rec-step used mundane recursion but managed to avoid stack-overflow exceptions thanks to the use of lazy-seq. For functions generating sequences, the use of lazy-seq might be a better choice than tail recursion, because often the regular (mundane) recursive definition is the most natural and understandable.

A RECURSIVE UNITS CALCULATOR

Some problems scream out for a recursive solution; take for example the problem of unit conversions. A kilometer consists of 1,000 meters, each made of 100 centimeters, each of which is 10 millimeters, each of which is 1/1,000 of a meter. These types of conversions are often needed in far-ranging applications.

If you wanted to describe this relationship in terms of a data structure, then you might land on something like the map that follows:

```
(ns joy.units)

(def simple-metric {:meter 1,
                     :km 1000,
                     :cm 1/100,
                     :mm [1/10 :cm]})
```

The map simple-metric uses the :meter value as the base unit, or the unit used as the reference point for every other unit. To calculate the answer to "How many meters are in 3 kilometers, 10 meters, 80 centimeters, 10 millimeters?" you could use the map as follows:

```
(->    (* 3  (:km simple-metric))
    (+ (* 10 (:meter simple-metric)))
    (+ (* 80 (:cm simple-metric)))
    (+ (* (:cm simple-metric)
          (* 10 (first (:mm simple-metric)))))
    float)
;;=> 3010.81
```

Although the map is certainly usable this way, the user experience of traversing simple-metric directly is less than stellar. Instead, it would be nicer to define a function named convert, shown in the following listing, that essentially performs these mathematical operations.

Listing 7.1 Function to recursively convert units of measure

```
(defn convert [context descriptor]
   (reduce (fn [result [mag unit]]      <──❶ Destructure aggregates
              (+ result
                 (let [val (get context unit)]    <──❷ Look up the relative value
                   (if (vector? val)
                       (* mag (convert context val))    <──❸ Process the aggregate
                       (* mag val)))))              <┐
             0                                       │  Perform the final
             (partition 2 descriptor)))             ❹  calculation
```

The action of the convert function programmatically mirrors the manual use of simple-metric shown earlier. The form of the descriptor coming into the function and mirrored in the destructuring form ❶ is the opposite of the key/value mapping in the context map. This is because it allows the descriptor to take a more linguistically natural form where the magnitude precedes the unit name (such as 1 :meter).

After binding the magnitude mag and the unit name, the value associated with the unit is retrieved ❷. In the case where a straight lookup results in a number, the :default case takes over and results in a magnitude multiplication. This straightforward multiplication is the recursion's terminating condition. In the case where a lookup results in a vector, the recursion continues with the vector itself for the purpose of traversing the recursive unit definitions ❸. Eventually, the function should bottom out on a nonvector, thus allowing the final magnitude multiplication ❹. Because of the recursion, the multiplication rolls up through all the intermediate relative unit values.

You can see convert in action next:

```
(convert simple-metric [1 :meter])
;;=> 1

(convert simple-metric [50 :cm])
;;=> 1/2

(convert simple-metric [100 :mm])
;;=> 1/10
```

And of course, convert should handle compounds:

```
(float (convert simple-metric [3 :km 10 :meter 80 :cm 10 :mm]))
;;=> 3010.81
```

The beauty of convert is that it's not bound to units of length. Through a synergy between recursive data and recursive function, you've defined a generic unit-conversion specification, allowing other unit types:

```
(convert {:bit 1, :byte 8, :nibble [1/2 :byte]} [32 :nibble])
;;=> 128N
```

You'll see convert again in chapter 14, but for now we'll move on to matters of finding and using a function's tail.

7.3.2 *Tail calls and recur*

In a language such as Clojure, where function locals are immutable, the benefit of tail recursion is especially important for implementing algorithms that require the consumption of a value or the accumulation of a result. Before we get deeper into implementing tail recursion, we'll take a moment to appreciate the historical underpinnings of tail-call recursion and expound on its further role in Clojure.

GENERALIZED TAIL-CALL OPTIMIZATION (TCO)

In their "Lambda Papers" (MIT AI Lab, AI Lab Memos, 1975–1980), Guy L. Steele and Gerald Sussman describe their experiences with the research and implementation of the early versions of the Scheme programming language. The first versions of the interpreter served as a model for Carl Hewitt's Actor model (Hewitt 1973) of concurrent computation, implementing both actors and functions. As a quick summary, you can think of the Actor model as one where each actor is a process with local state and an event loop processing messages from other actors to read, write, and compute on that state. In any case, one day, while eating Ho-Hos,[16] Steele and Sussman noticed that the implementation of control flow in Scheme, implemented using actors, always ended with one actor calling another in its tail position, with the return to the callee being deferred. Armed with their intimate knowledge of the Scheme compiler, Steele and Sussman were able to infer that because the underlying architecture dealing with actors and functions was the same, retaining both was redundant. Therefore, actors were removed from the language and functions remained as the more general construct. Thus, generalized tail-call optimization was thrust (Steele 1977) into the world of computer science.

Generalized tail-call optimization as found in Scheme (Abelson 1996) can be viewed as analogous to object delegation. Hewitt's original Actor model was rooted heavily in message delegation of arbitrary depth, with data manipulation occurring at any and all levels along the chain. This is similar to an adapter, except that there's an implicit resource-management element involved. In Scheme, any tail call from a function A to a function B results in the deallocation of all of A local resources and the full delegation of execution to B.[17] As a result of this generalized tail-call optimization, the return to the original caller of A is directly from B instead of back down the call chain through A again, as shown in figure 7.1.

---

[16] This isn't true, but wouldn't it be great if it were?

[17] Bear in mind that in this scenario, A and B can be different functions or the same function.

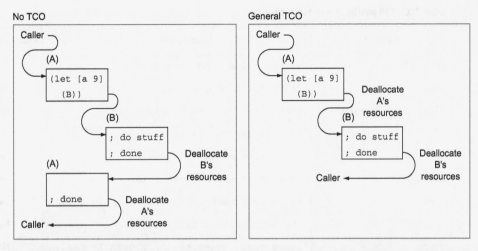

Figure 7.1 Generalized tail-call optimization: if you know that A calls B in the tail position, then you also know that A's resources are no longer needed, allowing Scheme to deallocate them and defer to B for the return call instead.

Unfortunately for Clojure, neither the Java Virtual Machine nor its bytecode provide generalized tail-call optimization facilities. Clojure does provide a tail call special form recur, but it only optimizes the case of a tail-recursive self call and not the generalized tail call. In the general case, there's currently no way to reliably optimize (Clinger 1998) tail calls.

TAIL RECURSION

The following function calculates the greatest common denominator of two numbers:

```
(defn gcd [x y]
  (cond
    (> x y) (gcd (- x y) y)
    (< x y) (gcd x (- y x))
    :else x))
```

The implementation of gcd is straightforward, but notice that it uses mundane recursion instead of tail recursion via recur. In a language such as Scheme, containing generalized tail-call optimization, the recursive calls are optimized automatically. On the other hand, because of the JVM's lack of tail-call optimization, the recur is needed in order to avoid stack-overflow errors.

Using the information in table 7.1, you can replace the mundane recursive calls with the recur form, causing gcd to be optimized by Clojure's compiler.[18]

---

[18] Possibly the first instance of a compiler that converted tail recursion into an iterative loop was the LISP 1.5 compiler written by Tim Hart and Mike Levin around the summer of 1961. Buried in the compiler's implementation was a function named PROGITER that was responsible for searching through an expression for a given name (the recursive call name, that is) and, when found, replacing its call with the proper incantation of PROG, GO, SETQ, and RETURN to create a looping program (Levin 1963).

Table 7.1 Tail positions and recur targets

Form(s)	Tail position	Recur target?
fn, defn	(fn [args] expressions tail)	Yes
loop	(loop [bindings] expressions tail)	Yes
let, letfn, binding	(let [bindings] expressions tail)	No
do	(do expressions tail)	No
if, if-not	(if test then-tailelse-tail)	No
when, when-not	(when test expressions tail)	No
cond	(cond test test tail ...:else else tail)	No
or, and	(or test test... tail)	No
case	(case const const tail ... default tail)	No

WHY RECUR?

If you think you understand why Clojure provides an explicit tail-call optimization form rather than an implicit one, then go ahead and skip to the next section.

There's no technical reason why Clojure couldn't automatically detect and optimize recursive tail calls—Scala does this—but there are valid reasons why Clojure doesn't. First, because there's no generalized TCO in the JVM, Clojure can only provide a subset of tail-call optimizations: the recursive case and the mutually recursive case (see the next section). By making recur an explicit optimization, Clojure doesn't give the pretense of providing full TCO.

Second, having recur as an explicit form allows the Clojure compiler to detect errors caused by an expected tail call being pushed out of the tail position. If you change gcd to always return an integer, then an exception is thrown because the recur call is pushed out of the tail position:

```
(defn gcd [x y]
  (int
    (cond
      (> x y) (recur (- x y) y)
      (< x y) (recur x (- y x))
      :else x)))
```

```
; java.lang.UnsupportedOperationException: Can only recur from tail...
```

With automatic recursive tail-call optimization, the addition of an outer int call wouldn't necessarily trigger[19] an error condition (Wampler 2009). But Clojure enforces that a call to recur be in the tail position. This benefit will likely cause recur to live on, even should the JVM acquire TCO.

---

[19] The Scala 2.8 compiler recognizes a @tailrec annotation and triggers an error whenever a marked function or method can't be optimized.

The final benefit of recur is that it allows the forms fn and loop to act as anonymous recursion points. Why recur, indeed.

7.3.3 *Don't forget your trampoline*

We touched briefly on the fact that Clojure can also optimize a mutually recursive function relationship, but like the tail-recursive case, it's done explicitly. Mutually recursive functions are nice for implementing finite state machines (FSAs), and in this section we'll show an example of a simple state machine modeling the operation of an elevator (Mozgovoy 2009) for a two-story building. The elevator FSA allows only four states: on the first floor with the doors open or closed, and on the second floor with the doors open or closed. The elevator can also take four distinct commands: open doors, close doors, go up, and go down. Each command is valid only in a certain context: for example, the close command is valid only when the elevator door is open. Likewise, the elevator can only go up when on the first floor and can only go down when on the second floor, and the door must be shut in both instances.

You can directly translate these states and transitions into a set of mutually recursive functions by associating the states as a set of functions ff-open, ff-closed, sf-closed, and sf-open, and the transitions :open, :close, :up, and :down, as conditions for calling the next function. Let's create a function elevator that starts in the ff-open state, takes a sequence of commands, and returns true or false if the commands correspond to a legal schedule according to the FSA. For example, the sequence [:close :open :done] would be legal, if pointless, whereas [:open :open :done] wouldn't be legal, because an open door can't be reopened. The function elevator can be implemented as shown next.

Listing 7.2 Using mutually recursive functions to implement a finite state machine

```
(defn elevator [commands]
  (letfn                                      <— Local functions
    [(ff-open [[_ & r]]                        <— lst floor open
       "When the elevator is open on the 1st floor
        it can either close or be done."
       #(case _
          :close (ff-closed r)
          :done  true
          false))
     (ff-closed [[_ & r]                       <— lst floor closed
       "When the elevator is closed on the 1st floor
        it can either open or go up."
       #(case _
          :open (ff-open r)
          :up   (sf-closed r)
          false))
     (sf-closed [[_ & r]]                       <— 2nd floor closed
       "When the elevator is closed on the 2nd floor
        it can either go down or open."
       #(case _
          :down (ff-closed r)
```

```
        :open (sf-open r)
        false))
    (sf-open [[_ & r]]                               ⟵── 2nd floor open
      "When the elevator is open on the 2nd floor
       it can either close or be done"
      #(case _
         :close (sf-closed r)
         :done  true
         false))]
    (trampoline ff-open commands)))                  ⟵── Trampoline call
```

Using letfn this way allows you to create local functions that reference each other, whereas (let [ff-open #(...)] ...) wouldn't, because it executes its bindings serially.[20] Each state function contains a case macro that dispatches to the next state based on a contextually valid command. For example, the sf-open state transitions to the sf-closed state given a :close command, returns true on a :done command (corresponding to a legal schedule), or otherwise returns false. Each state is similar in that the default case command is to return false, indicating an illegal schedule. One other point of note is that each state function returns a function returning a value, rather than directly returning the value. This is done so that the trampoline function can manage the stack on the mutually recursive calls, thus avoiding cases where a long schedule would blow the stack. The trampoline manages the process of the self calls through the placement of the functions in a list, where each function is bounced back and forth explicitly, as shown in figure 7.2.

Here's the operation of elevator given a few example schedules:

```
(elevator [:close :open :close :up :open :open :done])
;=> false

(elevator [:close :up :open :close :down :open :done])
;=> true

;; run at your own risk!
(elevator (cycle [:close :open]))
; ... runs forever
```

Like the recur special form, the trampoline for mutual recursion has a definitive syntactic and semantic cost on the structure of your code. But whereas the call to recur

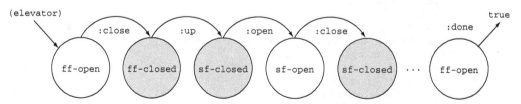

Figure 7.2   Elevator trampoline: the trampoline function explicitly bounces between mutually recursive calls.

---

[20] In other words, a function defined in a let can't refer to a function defined later in the bindings vector because let doesn't set up forward declarations, whereas letfn does.

can be replaced by mundane recursion without too much effect, except at the edges, the rules for mutual recursion aren't general. Having said that, the actual rules are simple:

1 Make all functions participating in the mutual recursion return a function instead of their normal result. Normally this is as simple as tacking a # onto the front of the outer level of the function body.

2 Invoke the first function in the mutual chain via the `trampoline` function.

The final example doesn't cause a stack overflow because the `trampoline` function handles the calls explicitly. The typical use case for mutually recursive functions is a state machine, of which the `elevator` FSA is only a simple case.

7.3.4 *Continuation-passing style*

Before wrapping up this chapter, we'll take time to talk about a style of programming not necessarily prevalent in Clojure, but more so in the functional tradition: *continuation-passing style*. Continuation-passing style (CPS) is a hybrid between recursion and mutual recursion, but with its own set of idioms. We won't give you a deep survey of CPS, but this subsection should provide a reasonable overview for deeper exploration if you're inclined.

The nutshell version of CPS is that it's a way of generalizing a computation (Friedman 2001) by viewing it in terms of up to three functions:

- *Accept*—Decides when a computation should terminate
- *Return*—Wraps the return values
- *Continuation*—Provides the next step in the computation

There's a reason many sources on CPS use the factorial function as a base example: because it's exceptionally illustrative. Here's an example:

```
(defn fac-cps [n k]
  (letfn [(cont [v] (k (* v n)))]        <--- Next
    (if (zero? n)                         <--- Accept
      (k 1)                               <--- Return
      (recur (dec n) cont))))

(defn fac [n]
  (fac-cps n identity))

(fac 10)
;=> 3628800
```

Although this approach is definitely different than the normal functional structure, it's not exactly interesting in and of itself. The power of CPS is that you can extract more generic function builders using CPS. One such builder, shown next, can be used to make a range of functions that happen to fall into the same mold of a mathematical folding function.

```
(defn mk-cps [accept? kend kont]
  (fn [n]
```

```
((fn [n k]
  (let [cont (fn [v]                       ←— Next
              (k ((partial kont v) n)))]
    (if (accept? n)                        ←— Accept
      (k 1)                                ←— Return
      (recur (dec n) cont))))
  n kend)))
```

If you look at the mk-cps function a little closer, you'll notice that it builds the same structured code as fac-cps. The difference is that whereas fac-cps has its continuation calls hard-coded into the source, mk-cps takes its continuations as arguments and returns a closure that calls out to them later. Here's an example of the use of mk-cps:

```
(def fac                       ←— Factorial
  (mk-cps zero?                   ←— … ends when 0
          identity                ←— … returns 1 when done
          #(* %1 %2)))            ←— … multiplies up the stack


(fac 10)
;;=> 3628800
(def tri                       ←— Triangles
  (mk-cps #(== 1 %)               ←— … ends when 1
          identity                ←— … returns 0 when done
          #(+ %1 %2)))            ←— … sums up the stack


(tri 10)
;;=> 55
```

Although this is potentially a powerful technique, there are a number of reasons preventing its widespread adoption in Clojure:

- Without generalized tail-call optimization, the number of continuation calls is bounded by the size of the stack. If your applications can guarantee a bounded execution path for the CPS calls, then this may not be a problem in practice.
- In the case of exception handling, CPS can cause the point of failure to bubble out, especially on deferred computations such as in using delay, future, or promise.[21] In the abstract this may not seem to be a problem; but if your continuation function is supposed to throw the error, but an outer layer function is doing so instead, then bugs may be difficult to track down.
- In a language such as Haskell that has ubiquitous lazy evaluation and pure functions, it's often not necessary to impose a strict order of execution. One way to impose a strict order of execution is to design your programs along the continuation-passing style. Although Clojure isn't entirely lazy, the matter of out-of-order execution isn't a factor against CPS. But CPS isn't conducive to parallelization, which is antithetical to Clojure's nature.

---

[21] Clojure's future and promise will be discussed in detail in chapter 11.

7.4 Putting it all together: A* pathfinding

A* is a best-first pathfinding algorithm that maintains a set of candidate paths through a "world" with the purpose of finding the least-difficult (Bratko 2000) path to some goal. The difficulty (or cost) of a path is garnered by the A* algorithm through the use of a function, which in this example is called total-cost, that builds an estimate of the total cost from a start point to the goal. The application of this cost-estimate function total-cost is used to sort the candidate paths (Hart 1968) in the order most likely to prove least costly.

7.4.1 The world

To represent the world, you'll again use a simple 2D matrix representation:

```
(def world [[  1   1   1   1    1]
            [999 999 999 999    1]
            [  1   1   1   1    1]
            [  1 999 999 999  999]
            [  1   1   1   1    1]])
```

The world structure is made from the values 1 and 999 respectively, corresponding to flat ground and cyclopean mountains. What would you assume is the optimal path from the upper-left corner [0 0] to the lower-right [4 4]? Clearly the optimal (and only) option is the Z-shaped path around the walls. Implementing an A* algorithm should fit the bill, but first, we'll talk a bit about how to do so.

7.4.2 Neighbors

For any given spot in the world, you need a way to calculate possible next steps. You can do this using brute force for small worlds, but a more general function is preferable. It turns out that if you restrict the possible moves to north, south, east, and west, then any given move is +/-1 along the x or y axis. Taking advantage of this fact, you can use the neighbors function from listing 5.1 as shown here:

```
(neighbors 5 [0 0])
;=> ([1 0] [0 1])
```

From the upper-left point, the only next steps are y=0, x=1 or y=1, x=0. Now that you have that, think about how you might estimate the path cost from any given point. A simple cost estimate turns out to be described as, "From the current point, calculate the expected cost by assuming you can travel to the right edge and then down to the lower-right." An implementation of a function named estimate-cost[22] that estimates the remaining path cost is shown next.

Listing 7.3 Function to estimate the straight-line remaining path cost

```
(defn estimate-cost [step-cost-est size y x]
  (* step-cost-est
```

---

[22] In the literature on the A* algorithm, this function is typically called h.

```
        (- (+ size size) y x 2)))
(estimate-cost 900 5 0 0)
;=> 7200

(estimate-cost 900 5 4 4)
;=> 0
```

From the y-x point [0 0], the cost of traveling 5 right and 5 down given an estimated single-step cost step-cost-est is 7200. This is a pretty straightforward estimate based on a straight-line path. Likewise, starting at the goal state [4 4] would cost nothing. Still needed is a function to calculate the cost of the path so far, named path-cost, which is provided in the following listing.[23]

Listing 7.4 Function to calculate the cost of the path traversed so far

```
(defn path-cost [node-cost cheapest-nbr]
  (+ node-cost
      (or (:cost cheapest-nbr) 0)))      ◁────┐ Add cheapest neighbor
(path-cost 900 {:cost 1})                     │ cost, else 0
;=> 901
```

Now that you've created an estimated-cost function and a current-cost function, you can implement a simple total-cost function.[24]

Listing 7.5 Function to calculate the estimated total cost of the path

```
(defn total-cost [newcost step-cost-est size y x]
  (+ newcost
      (estimate-cost step-cost-est size y x)))

(total-cost 0 900 5 0 0)
;=> 7200

(total-cost 1000 900 5 3 4)
;=> 1900

(total-cost (path-cost 900 {:cost 1}) 900 5 3 4)
;=> 1801
```

The second example shows that if you're one step away with a current cost of 1000, the total estimated cost is 1900, which is expected. The third example uses the result of path-cost to derive a total step cost, which is emblematic of how the two functions relate in the final A* implementation.

Now you have all the heuristic pieces in place. You may think we've simplified the heuristic needs of A*, but in fact this is all that there is to it. The actual implementation is complex, and you'll it tackle next.

---

[23] In the literature on the A* algorithm, this function is typically called g.
[24] In the literature on the A* algorithm, this function is typically called f and is implemented as (+ (g ...) (h ...)).

7.4.3 The A* implementation

Before we show the implementation of A*, you need one more auxiliary function, min-by, which retrieves from a collection the minimum value dictated by some function. The implementation of min-by is naturally a straightforward higher-order function, as shown next.

Listing 7.6 Function to retrieve the minimum value based on a criteria function

```
(defn min-by [f coll]
  (when (seq coll)
    (reduce (fn [min other]          ←— Process each elem
              (if (> (f min) (f other))  ←—┐
                other                       │ Successively bubble the minimal
                min))                       │ value out to the return
            coll)))

(min-by :cost [{:cost 100} {:cost 36} {:cost 9}])

;;=> {:cost 9}
```

This function will come in handy when you want to grab the cheapest path determined by the cost heuristic.

  We've delayed enough! Let's finally implement the A* algorithm so that you navigate around the world. The following listing shows a tail-recursive solution.

Listing 7.7 Main A* algorithm

```
(defn astar [start-yx step-est cell-costs]
  (let [size (count cell-costs)]
    (loop [steps 0
           routes (vec (replicate size (vec (replicate size nil))))
           work-todo (sorted-set [0 start-yx])]
      (if (empty? work-todo)                    ←— Check done
```

Grab the first route → `        [(peek (peek routes)) :steps steps]`

```
        (let [[_ yx :as work-item] (first work-todo)   ←— Get the next work
              rest-work-todo (disj work-todo work-item)  ←— Clear from todo
              nbr-yxs (neighbors size yx)                ←—┐ Get
```
Calculate the least cost → `              cheapest-nbr (min-by :cost`   `│ neighbors`
```
                             (keep #(get-in routes %)
                                   nbr-yxs))
              newcost (path-cost (get-in cell-costs yx)   ←—┐ Calculate the
                                 cheapest-nbr)               │ path so far
              oldcost (:cost (get-in routes yx))]
```
Check if new is worse → `          (if (and oldcost (>= newcost oldcost))`
```
            (recur (inc steps) routes rest-work-todo)
            (recur (inc steps)                           ←—┐ Place a new path
                   (assoc-in routes yx                     │ in the routes
```

```
                     {:cost newcost
                      :yxs (conj (:yxs cheapest-nbr [])
                                 yx)})
        (into rest-work-todo          ◄──┐  Add the estimated path
           (map                          │  to the todo, and recur
            (fn [w]
              (let [[y x] w]
                [(total-cost newcost step-est size y x) w]))
             nbr-yxs)))))))))
```

The main thrust of the astar function occurs when you check that (>= newcost oldcost). Once you've calculated newcost (the cost so far for the cheapest neighbor) and the cost-so-far oldcost, you perform one of two actions. The first action occurs when newcost is greater than or equal to oldcost: you throw away this new path, because it's clearly a worse alternative. The other action is the core functionality corresponding to the constant sorting of work-todo, based on the cost of the path as determined by the heuristic function total-cost. The soul of A* is based on the fact that the potential paths stored in work-todo are always sorted and distinct (through the use of a sorted set) based on the estimated path cost function. Each recursive loop through the astar function maintains the sorted routes based on the current-cost knowledge of the path added to the estimated total cost.

The results given by the astar function for the Z-shaped world are shown in the next listing.

Listing 7.8   Running the A* algorithm on Z World

```
(astar [0 0]
       900
       world)

;=> [{:cost 17,
      :yxs [[0 0] [0 1] [0 2] [0 3] [0 4] [1 4] [2 4]
            [2 3] [2 2] [2 1] [2 0] [3 0] [4 0] [4 1]
            [4 2] [4 3] [4 4]]}
     :steps 94]
```

By following the y-x indices, you'll notice that the astar function traverses Z World along the path where cost is 1, as shown in figure 7.3.

You can also build another world called Shrubbery World, shown next, that contains a single weakling shrubbery at position [0 3] (represented by the number 2), and see how astar navigates it.

Figure 7.3   A graphical representation of Z World clearly shows the optimal/only path.

Listing 7.9   Shrubbery World

```
(astar [0 0]
       900
       [[  1   1   1   2   1]              <— Shrubbery is 2
        [  1   1   1 999   1]
        [  1   1   1 999   1]
        [  1   1   1 999   1]
        [  1   1   1   1   1]])            <— Clear path

;=> [{:cost 9,
      :yxs [[0 0] [0 1] [0 2]
            [1 2]
            [2 2]                          <— Sequence of squares to walk the path
            [3 2]
            [4 2] [4 3] [4 4]]}
      :steps 134]
```

When tracing the best path, you see that the astar function prefers the non-shrubbery path. But what would happen if you placed a man-eating bunny along the previously safe path, represented by an ominously large number?

Listing 7.10   Bunny World

```
(astar [0 0]
       900
       [[  1   1   1   2   1]              <— Shrubbery looks inviting
        [  1   1   1 999   1]
        [  1   1   1 999   1]
        [  1   1   1 999   1]
        [  1   1   1 666   1]])            <— Bunny lies in wait

;=> [{:cost 10,
      :yxs [[0 0] [0 1] [0 2] [0 3] [0 4]
            [1 4]
            [2 4]                          <— Bunny-less path
            [3 4]
            [4 4]]}
      :steps 132]
```

As expected, the astar function picks the shrubbery path (2) instead of the evil-bunny path to reach the final destination.

7.4.4   *Notes about the A* implementation*

Each of the data structures, from the sorted set, to the tail-recursive astar function, to the higher-order function min-by, is functional in nature and therefore extensible as a result. We encourage you to explore the vast array of possible worlds traversable by the A* implementation and see what happens should you change the heuristic (Dijkstra 1959) functions along the way. Clojure encourages experimentation, and by partitioning the solution this way, we've enabled you to explore different heuristics.

7.5   *Summary*

We've covered a lot about Clojure's flavor of functional programming in this chapter, and you may have noticed that it looks like many others. Clojure favors an approach where immutable data is transformed through the application of functions. Additionally, Clojure prefers that functions be free of side effects and referentially transparent (pure) in order to reduce the complexities inherent in widespread data mutation. Lexical closures provide a simple yet powerful mechanism for defining functions that carry around with them the value context in which they were created. This allows certain information to exist beyond their lexical context, much like a poor-man's object. Finally, Clojure is built with this in mind, in that its primary form of iteration is through tail recursion as a natural result of its focus on immutability.

In the next chapter, we'll explore the feature most identified with Lisp: macros.

Part 4

Large-scale design

Clojure is a practical language, not an academic one; and in the real world, programs grow large, change over time, and are confronted with shifting requirements. In this part, we'll show how Clojure's Lisp heritage of "code is data" can help address these problems. We'll demonstrate the use of macros, how to create a fluent builder, and how Clojure addresses the mutability of the real world.

Macros 8

*If you give someone Fortran, he has
Fortran. If you give someone Lisp,
he has any language he pleases.*

—Guy Steele[1]

This chapter covers

- Data is code is data
- Defining control structures
- Macros combining forms
- Using macros to control symbolic resolution time
- Using macros to manage resources
- Macros returning functions

Macros are where the rubber of "code is data" meets the road of making programs simpler and cleaner. To fully understand macros, you need to understand the different *times* of Clojure: read time, macro-expansion time, compile time, and runtime. Macros perform the bulk of their work at compile time. We'll start by looking

---

[1] Afterword in *The Seasoned Schemer* by Daniel P. Friedman and Matthias Felleisen (MIT Press, 1995).

at what it means for code to be data and data to be used as code. This is the background you'll need to understand that control structures in Clojure are built out of macros, and how you can build your own. The mechanics of macros are relatively simple, and before you're halfway through this chapter you'll have learned all you technically need to write your own. Where macros get complicated is when you try to bring theoretical knowledge of them into the real world, so to help you combat that we'll lead you on a tour of practical applications of macros.

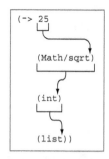

Figure 8.1 Arrow macro: each expression is inserted into the following one at compile time, allowing you to write the whole expression inside-out when that feels more natural.

What kinds of problems do macros solve? One extremely important role that macros perform is to let you transform an expression into something else, before runtime. Consider Clojure's `->` macro, which returns the result of evaluating a succession of functions on an initial value. To understand the arrow macro, we find it useful to think of it as an arrow indicating the flow of data from one function to another—the form `(-> 25 Math/sqrt int list)` can be read as follows:

1 Take the value 25.
2 Feed it into the method `Math/sqrt`.
3 Feed that result into the function `int`.
4 Feed that result into the function `list`. Graphically, this can be viewed as shown in figure 8.1.

It expands into the following expression:

```
(list (int (Math/sqrt 25)))
```

When viewed this way, the `->` macro can be said to *weave* a sequence of forms into each in turn. This weaving can be done in any form and is *always* stitched in as the first argument to the outermost expression.[2] Observe how the placement of snowmen provides visual markers for the weave point:

```
(-> (/ 144 12) (/ ☃ 2 3) str keyword list)
;=> (:2)

(-> (/ 144 12) (* ☃ 4 (/ 2 3)) str keyword (list ☃ :33))
;=> (:32 :33)
```

As shown via snowman, each expression is inserted into the following one at compile time, allowing you to write the whole expression inside-out. Using one of the arrow macros is useful when many sequential operations need to be applied to a single object. So this is a potential use case for macros: taking one form of an expression and

---

2 On the other hand, the `->>` macro threads the form as the last argument.

transforming it into another form. In this chapter, we'll also look at using macros to combine forms, change forms, control evaluation and resolution of arguments, manage resources, and build functions. But first, what does it mean that Clojure code is data, and why should you care?

8.1 Data is code is data

You're already familiar with textual representations of data in your programs, at least with strings, lists, vectors, maps, and so on. Clojure, like other Lisps, takes this one step further by having programs be made *entirely* out of data. Function definitions in Clojure programs are also represented using an aggregation of the various data structures mentioned in the previous chapters. Likewise, the expressions representing the execution of functions and the use of control structures are also data structures! These data representations of functions and their executions represent a concept different from the way other programming languages operate. Typically, there's a sharp distinction between data structures and functions of the language. In fact, most programming languages don't even remotely describe the form of functions in their textual representations. With Clojure, there's no distinction between the textual form and the actual form of a program. When a program is the data that composes the program, then you can write programs to write programs. This may seem like nonsense now, but as you'll see throughout this chapter, it's powerful.

To start with, look at the built-in Clojure function eval, whose purpose is to take a data structure representing a Clojure expression, evaluate it, and return the result. This behavior can be seen in the following examples:

```
(eval 42)
;=> 42

(eval '(list 1 2))
;=> (1 2)

(eval (list 1 2))
; java.lang.ClassCastException:
;   java.lang.Integer cannot be cast to clojure.lang.IFn
```

Why did we get an exception for the last example? The answer lies in the previous example. The quote in '(list 1 2) causes eval to view it as (list 1 2), which is the function call to create the resulting list. Likewise, for the final example eval received a list of (1 2) and attempted to use 1 as a function, thus failing. Not very exciting, is it? The excitement inherent in eval stems from something that we mentioned earlier[3]—if you provide eval a list in the form expected of a function call, then *something else* should happen. This *something else* is the evaluation of a function call and not of the data structure itself. Look at what happens if you try evaluating something more complicated:

```
(eval (list (symbol "+") 1 2))
;=> 3
```

---

[3] All the way back in section 2.5.

In words, the steps involved are as follows:

1 The function `symbol` receives a string + and returns a symbol data type of +.

2 The function `list` receives three arguments—a symbol +, the integer 1, and the integer 2—and returns a list of these elements.

3 The `eval` function receives a list data type of `(+ 1 2)`, recognizes it as the function call form, and executes the + function with the arguments 1 and 2, returning the integer 3.

8.1.1   *Syntax-quote, unquote, and splicing*

You'll often hear the phrase "eval is evil," but many of the problems that arise from the use of `eval` occur because the bindings it uses for evaluation are global. If we could instead restrict the use of specific bindings to `eval`, then perhaps we could convince it to be less evil. A function in the following snippet uses three features first shown in section 2.7—Clojure's syntax-quote (written as a single back-quote), unquote (written as ~), and unquote-splice (written as ~@) operations—to build a `let` structure around the form to evaluate:

```
(defn contextual-eval [ctx expr]
  (eval
    `(let [~@(mapcat (fn [[k v]] [k `'~v]) ctx)]     ⟵ Build let bindings
       ~expr)))                                          at compile time
```

The bindings created use the interesting `` `'~v `` pattern to garner the value of the built bindings at runtime. Observe how `contextual-eval` works:

```
(contextual-eval '{a 1, b 2} '(+ a b))
;;=> 3

(contextual-eval '{a 1, b 2} '(let [b 1000] (+ a b)))
;;=> 1001
```

> ### Handling nested syntax-quotes
>
> Dealing with nested syntax-quotes can at times be complicated. But you can visualize the way in which unquoting affects the nested structures as a result of repeated evaluations (Steele 1990) relative to its nesting level:
>
> ```
> (let [x 9, y '(- x)]
>   (println `y)
>   (println ``y)
>   (println ``~y)
>   (println ``~~y)
>   (contextual-eval {'x 36} ``~~y))
> ; user/y
> ; (quote user/y)
> ; user/y
> ; (- x)
> ;=> -36
> ```

The nesting of the syntax-quotes in the first two `println` calls takes the value of `y` further up the abstraction ladder. But by including a single unquote in the third `println`, we again bring it back down. Finally, by unquoting a second time, we've created a structure that can then be evaluated—and doing so yields the result `-36`. We had to use `contextual-eval` in the tail because core `eval` doesn't have access to local bindings—only var bindings. One final note is that had we attempted to unquote one extra time, we'd have seen the exception `java.lang.IllegalState-Exception: Var clojure.core/unquote is unbound`. The reason for this error is that unquote is the way to "jump" out of a syntax-quote, and to do so more than nesting allows will cause an error. You won't use this technique in this chapter, and in most cases you won't need to utilize it unless you're planning to create macro-defining macros—something you won't do until section 14.4.3.

In section 2.7, we mentioned quoting and its effects on evaluation, and in this chapter we'll expand on that theme fully as it relates to Clojure's macro facility. But the functionality of the quoting forms is orthogonal to macros, and they can be used independently. As we showed in the previous example,[4] using quoting and unquoting in a function allows you to create an evaluation function, `contextual-eval`, that takes an explicit context map. Rarely will you see the use of syntax-quote outside the body of a macro, but nothing prevents it from being used this way—and doing so is powerful. But the maximum power of quoting forms is fully realized when used with macros.

Working from a model where code is data, Clojure is able to manipulate structures into different executable forms at both runtime and compile time. We've already shown how you can do this at runtime using `eval` and `contextual-eval`, but this doesn't serve the purpose of compile-time manipulation. It probably doesn't need saying, but because this is a book about Clojure, we will: macros are the way to achieve this effect.

8.1.2 Macro rules of thumb

Before we begin, we should list a few rules of thumb to observe when writing macros:

- Don't write a macro if a function will do. Reserve macros to provide syntactic abstractions or create binding forms.
- Write an example usage.
- Expand your example usage by hand.
- Use `macroexpand`, `macroexpand-1`, and `clojure.walk/macroexpand-all`[5] liberally to understand how your implementation works.
- Experiment at the REPL.
- Break complicated macros into smaller functions whenever possible.

---

[4] Thanks to George Jahad for the implementation on which `contextual-eval` is based.

[5] The `macroexpand-all` function is a useful debugging aid, as we'll demonstrate in this chapter. But it's worth knowing that unlike the other `macroexpand` functions, it doesn't use exactly the same logic as the Clojure compiler and thus may in some unusual circumstances produce misleading results.

Throughout this chapter, you'll see all these rules to varying degrees. Obviously, we're trying to balance best practices, teaching, and page counts, so we may not always adhere entirely. Even so, we'll try to highlight those times when we do break from the recommended heuristics. Having said that, we'll talk first about the most ubiquitous use of macros: creating custom control structures.

8.2   *Defining control structures*

Most control structures in Clojure are implemented via macros, so they provide a nice starting point for learning how macros can be useful. Macros can be built with or without using syntax-quote, so we'll show examples of each.

In languages lacking macros, such as Haskell[6] for example, the definition of control structures relies on the use of higher-order functions such as we showed in section 7.1.2. Although this fact in no way limits the ability to create control structures in Haskell, the approach that Lisps take to the problem is different. The most obvious advantage of macros over higher-order functions is that the former manipulate compile-time forms, transforming them into runtime forms. This allows your programs to be written in ways natural to your problem domain, while still maintaining runtime efficiency. Clojure already provides a rich set of control structures, including but not limited to doseq, while, if, if-let, and do, but in this section you'll write a few others.

8.2.1   *Defining control structures without syntax-quote*

Because the arguments to defmacro aren't evaluated before being passed to the macro, they can be viewed as pure data structures and manipulated and analyzed as such. Because of this, amazing things can be done on the raw forms supplied to macros even in the absence of unquoting.

Imagine a macro named do-until that executes all of its clauses evaluating as true *until* it gets one that is falsey:

```
(do-until
  (even? 2) (println "Even")
  (odd?  3) (println "Odd")
  (zero? 1) (println "You never see me")
  :lollipop (println "Truthy thing"))
; Even
; Odd
;=> nil
```

A good example of this type of macro is Clojure's core macro cond, which with some minor modifications can be made to behave differently:

```
(defmacro do-until [& clauses]
  (when clauses
    (list 'clojure.core/when (first clauses)
          (if (next clauses)
```

When there
are clauses

... build a list of
each paired clause

---

[6]   Although there's a GHC extension named Template Haskell that provides a macro-like capability, this isn't the norm.

```
        (second clauses)
        (throw (IllegalArgumentException.
                 "do-until requires an even number of forms")))
    (cons 'do-until (nnext clauses)))))            <— ... recursively
```

The first expansion of do-until illustrates how this macro operates:

```
(macroexpand-1 '(do-until true (prn 1) false (prn 2)))
;=> (clojure.core/when true
  (prn 1) (do-until false (prn 2)))
```

do-until recursively expands into a series of when calls, which themselves expand into a series of if expressions (because when is a macro defined in terms of the built-in if):

```
(require '[clojure.walk :as walk])
(walk/macroexpand-all '(do-until true (prn 1) false (prn 2)))
;=> (if true (do (prn 1) (if false (do (prn 2) nil))))

(do-until true (prn 1) false (prn 2))
; 1
;=> nil
```

You could write out the nested if structure manually and achieve the same result, but the beauty of macros lies in the fact that they can do so on your behalf while presenting a lightweight and intuitive form. In cases where do-until can be used, it removes the need to write and maintain superfluous boilerplate code. This idea can be extended to macros in general and their propensity to reduce unneeded boilerplate for a large category of circumstances, as you desire. One thing to note about do-until is that it's meant to be used only for side effects, because it's designed to always return nil. Macros starting with do tend to act the same way.

8.2.2 *Defining control structures using syntax-quote and unquoting*

Not all control structures are as simple as do-until. Sometimes you'll want to selectively evaluate macro arguments, structures, or substructures. In this section, we'll explore one such macro named unless, implemented using unquote and unquote-splice.

Ruby provides a control structure named unless that reverses the sense (Olsen 2007) of a when statement, executing the body of a block when a given condition evaluates to false:

```
(unless (even? 3) "Now we see it...")
;=> "Now we see it..."

(unless (even? 2) "Now we don't.")
;=> nil
```

The maverick implementation[7] of unless as demonstrated previously and as shown next is straightforward:

---

[7] The proper way to define unless is either (defmacro unless [& args] `(when-not ~@args)) or (clojure.contrib.def/defalias unless when-not)—or just use when-not from the start.

```
(defmacro unless [condition & body]
  `(if (not ~condition)              <--- Unquote condition
     (do ~@body)))                   <--- Splice body
```

The body of the unless implementation uses syntax-quote, unquote, and unquote-splice. Syntax-quote allows the if form to act as a template for the expression that any use of the macro becomes when expanded. The unquote and splicing-unquote provide the "blanks" where the values for the parameters condition and body will be inserted. You can see unless in action next:

```
(unless true (println "nope"))
;;=> nil

(unless false (println "yep!"))
;; yep!
;;=> nil
```

Because unless relies on the result of a condition for its operation, it's imperative that it evaluate the condition part using unquote. If we didn't use unquote in our example, then instead of evaluating a function (even? 3), it would attempt to resolve a namespace var named condition that may not exist—and if it did exist, it might be arbitrarily truthy at the time of the macro call. Some of the unintended consequences of this mistake are shown here:

```
(macroexpand `(if (not condition) "got it"))       <--- Missing ~
;=> (if (clojure.core/not user/condition) "got it")    <--- Resolved to var

(eval `(if (not condition) "got it"))
; java.lang.Exception: No such var: user/condition    <--- Unbound var

(def condition false)                               <--- Bound the var
(eval `(if (not condition) "got it"))                <--- Resolved to var
;=> "got it"
```

Clearly this isn't the desired behavior. Instead, by unquoting the condition local, you ensure that the function call is used instead. It's easy to forget to add an unquote to the body of a macro, and depending on the condition of your runtime environment, the problem may not be immediately obvious.

8.3   *Macros combining forms*

Macros are often used for combining a number of forms and actions into one consistent view. You saw this behavior in the previous section with the do-until macro, but it's more general. In this section, we'll show how you can use macros to combine a number of tasks in order to simplify an API. Clojure's defn macro is an instance of this type of macro because it aggregates the processes of creating a function, including the following:

- Creating the corresponding function object using fn
- Checking for and attaching a documentation string
- Building the :arglists metadata

- Binding the function name to a var
- Attaching the collected metadata

You could perform all these steps over and over again every time you wanted to create a new function, but thanks to macros you can instead use the more convenient `defn` form. Regardless of your application domain and its implementation, programming language boilerplate code inevitably occurs and is a fertile place to hide subtle errors. But identifying these repetitive tasks and writing macros to simplify and reduce or eliminate the tedious copy-paste-tweak cycle can work to reduce the incidental complexities inherent in a project. Where macros differ from techniques familiar to proponents of Java's object-oriented style—including hierarchies, frameworks, inversion of control, and the like—is that they're treated no differently by the language itself. Clojure macros work to mold the language into the problem space rather than force you to mold the problem space into the constructs of the language. There's a specific term for this, *domain-specific language*, but in Lisp the distinction between DSL and API is thin to the point of transparency.

Envision a scenario where you want to be able to define vars that call a function whenever their root bindings change. You could do this using the `add-watch` function, which lets you attach a *watcher* to a reference type that's called whenever a change occurs within. The `add-watch` function takes three arguments: a reference, a watch function key, and a watch function called whenever a change occurs. You could enforce that every time someone wanted to define a new var, they would have to follow these steps:

1 Define the var.
2 Define a function (maybe inline to save a step) that will be the watcher.
3 Call `add-watch` with the proper values.

A meager three steps isn't too cumbersome a task to remember in a handful of uses, but over the course of a large project it's easy to forget and/or morph one of these steps when the need to perform them many times occurs. Therefore, perhaps a better approach is to define a macro to perform all these steps for you, as the following definition does:

```
(defmacro def-watched [name & value]
  `(do
     (def ~name ~@value)
     (add-watch (var ~name)
                :re-bind
                (fn [~'key ~'r old# new#]
                  (println old# " -> " new#)))))
```

Ignoring symbol resolution and auto-gensym, which we'll cover in upcoming sections, the macro called as `(def-watched x 2)` expands into roughly the following:

```
(do (def x 2)
    (add-watch (var x)
               :re-bind
```

```
       (fn [key r old new]
         (println old " -> " new))))
```

The results of `def-watched` are thus

```
(def-watched x (* 12 12))
x
;=> 144

(def x 0)
; 144 -> 0
```

Lisp programs in general (and Clojure programs specifically) use macros of this sort to vastly reduce the boilerplate needed to perform common tasks. Throughout this chapter, you'll see macros that combine forms, so there's no need to dwell on the matter here. Instead, we'll move on to a macro `domain` that does just that, with the added bonus of performing some interesting transformations in the process.

8.4   *Using macros to change forms*

One way to design macros is to start by writing out example code that you wish worked—code that has the minimal distance between what you must specify and the specific application domain in which you're working. Then, with the goal of making this code work, you begin writing macros and functions to fill in the missing pieces.

For example, when designing software systems, it's often useful to identify the "things" that make up your given application domain, including their logical groupings. The level of abstraction at this point in the design is best kept high (Rosenberg 2005) and shouldn't include details about implementation. Imagine that you want to describe a simple domain of the ongoing struggle between humans and monsters:

- Man versus monster
  - ◇ People
    - Men (humans)
      - Name
      - Have beards?
  - ◇ Monsters
    - Chupacabra
      - Eats goats?

Although this is a simple format, it needs work to be programmatically useful. Therefore, the goal of this section is to write macros that perform the steps to get from this simple representation to the one more conducive to processing. The outline form can be rendered in a Clojure form, assuming the existence of some macros and functions you've yet to define, like this:

```
(domain man-vs-monster
  (grouping people
    (Human "A stock human")

    (Man (isa Human)
```

```
     "A man, baby"
     [name]
     [has-beard?]]))
 (grouping monsters
  (Chupacabra
    "A fierce, yet elusive creature"
    [eats-goats?]])))
```

One possible structure underlying this sample format is a tree composed of individual generic nodes, each taking a form similar to the following:

```
{:tag <node form>,          ◄── Domain, grouping, and so on
 :attrs {},                 ◄── For example, :name people
 :content [<nodes>]}        ◄── For example, properties
```

You'd never say this is a beautiful format, but it does present practical advantages over the original format—it's a tree, it's composed of simple types, it's regular, and it's recognizable to some existing libraries.

CLOJURE APHORISM Clojure is a design language where the conceptual model is also Clojure.

Start with the outer-level element, domain:

```
(defmacro domain [name & body]
  `{:tag :domain,
    :attrs {:name (str '~name)},
    :content [~@body]})
```

The body of domain is fairly straightforward in that it sets the domain-level tree node and splices the body of the macro into the :content slot. After domain expands, you'd expect its body to be composed of a number of grouping forms, which are then handled by an aptly named macro:

```
(declare handle-things)

(defmacro grouping [name & body]
  `{:tag :grouping,
    :attrs {:name (str '~name)},
    :content [~@(handle-things body)]})
```

Similar to domain, grouping expands into a node with its body spliced into the :content slot. In its body, the grouping macro uses a form named handle-things that hasn't been written yet, so you have to use declare to avoid a compilation error. But grouping differs from domain in that it splices in the result of the call to a function, handle-things:

```
(declare grok-attrs grok-props)

(defn handle-things [things]
  (for [t things]
    {:tag :thing,
     :attrs (grok-attrs (take-while (comp not vector?) t))
     :content (if-let [c (grok-props (drop-while (comp not vector?) t))]
```

```
    [c]
    []})))
```

Because the body of a thing is fairly simple and regular, you can simplify the implementation of handle-things by again splitting it into two functions. The first function, grok-attrs, handles everything in the body of a thing that's not a vector, and
grok-props handles properties that are. In both cases, these leaf-level functions
return specifically formed maps:

```
(defn grok-attrs [attrs]
  (into {:name (str (first attrs))}
        (for [a (rest attrs)]
          (cond
            (list? a) [:isa (str (second a))]
            (string? a) [:comment a]))))
```

The implementation of grok-attrs may seem overly complex, especially given that
the sample domain model DSL only allows for a comment attribute and an optional isa
specification (as shown in the sample layout in the beginning of this section). But by
laying it out this way, you can easily expand the function to handle a richer set of attributes later. Likewise with grok-props, this more complicated function pulls apart the
vector representing a property so it's more conducive to expansion:

```
(defn grok-props [props]
  (when props
    {:tag :properties, :attrs nil,
     :content (apply vector (for [p props]
                {:tag :property,
                 :attrs {:name (str (first p))},
                 :content nil}))}))
```

Now that you've created the pieces, take a look at the new DSL in action:

```
(def d
  (domain man-vs-monster
    (grouping people                ⟵ Group of people
      (Human "A stock human")       ⟵ One kind of person

      (Man (isa Human)              ⟵ Another kind of person
        "A man, baby"
        [name]
        [has-beard?]))
    (grouping monsters              ⟵ Group of monsters
      (Chupacabra                   ⟵ One kind of monster
        "A fierce, yet elusive creature"
        [eats-goats?]))))
```

You can navigate this structure as follows:

```
(:tag d)
;=> :domain

(:tag (first (:content d)))
;=> :grouping
```

Maybe that's enough to prove to you that you've constructed the promised tree, but probably not. Therefore, you can pass a tree into a function that expects one of that form[8] and see what comes out on the other end:

```
(use '[clojure.xml :as xml])
(xml/emit d)
```

Performing this function call prints out the corresponding XML representation, minus the pretty printing:

```
<?xml version='1.0' encoding='UTF-8'?>                      | (domain ...)
<domain name='man-vs-monster'>                            ◄─┘
  <grouping name='people'>                        ◄─ (grouping ...)
    <thing name='Human' comment='A stock human'>          ◄─┐
      <properties></properties>                            | (Human ...)
    </thing>
    <thing name='Man' isa='Human' comment='A man, baby'>   ◄─ (Man ...)
      <properties>
        <property name='name'/>
        <property name='has-beard?'/>
      </properties>
    </thing>
  </grouping>                                              | (grouping ...)
  <grouping name='monsters'>                             ◄─┘
    <thing name='Chupacabra' comment='A fierce, yet elusive creature'>
      <properties>
        <property name='eats-goats?'/>
      </properties>
    </thing>
  </grouping>
</domain>
```

Our approach was to define a single macro entry point `domain`, intended to build the top-level layers of the output data structure and instead pass the remainder on to auxiliary functions for further processing. In this way, the body of the macro expands into a series of function calls, each taking some subset of the remaining structure and returning some result that's spliced into the final result. This functional composition approach is fairly common when defining macros. The entirety of the domain description could have been written in one monolithic macro, but by splitting the responsibilities, you can more easily extend the representations for the constituent parts.

Macros take data and return data, always. It so happens that in Clojure, code is data and data is code.

---

[8] The namespace `clojure.contrib.json` in the Clojure contrib library also contains some functions that can handle the domain DSL structure seamlessly. Additionally, Enlive (http://mng.bz/8Hh6) should also recognize the resultant structure.

8.5   *Using macros to control symbolic resolution time*

Whereas functions accept and return values that are meaningful to an application at runtime, macros accept and return code forms that are meaningful at compile time. Any symbol has subtleties depending on whether it's fully qualified, its resolution time, and its lexical context. These factors can be controlled in any particular case by the appropriate use of quoting and unquoting, which we explore in this section.

The term *name capture* refers to a potential problem in macro systems where a name generated at compile time clashes with a name that exists at runtime. Clojure macros are mostly safe from name capture, because the use of syntax-quote attempts to resolve symbols at macro-expansion time. This strategy reduces complexity by ensuring that symbols refer to those available at macro-expansion time, rather than to those unknown in the execution context.

For example, consider one of the simplest possible macros:

```
(defmacro resolution [] `x)
```

Viewing the expansion of this macro is illuminating in understanding how Clojure macros resolve symbols:

```
(macroexpand '(resolution))
;=> user/x
```

The expansion of the macro resolves the namespace of the syntax-quoted symbol x. This behavior is useful in Clojure because it helps to avoid problems with free name capturing that are possible in a macro system such as that found in Common Lisp.[9] Here's an example that would trip up a lesser implementation of syntax-quote, but which does just what you want in Clojure:

```
(def x 9)
(let [x 109] (resolution))
;=> 9
```

The x defined in the let isn't the same as the namespace-qualified user/x referred to by the macro resolution. As you might expect, the macro would throw an unbound var exception if you didn't first execute the call to def. If it didn't error out this way, the local version of x would be used instead, which might not be what you intend.

Clojure does provide a way to defer symbolic resolution for those instances where it may be useful to resolve it in the execution context, which we'll show now.

8.5.1   *Anaphora*

Anaphora[10] in spoken language is a term used in a sentence that refers back to a previously identified subject or object. It helps to reduce repetition in a phrase by replacing "Jim bought 6,000 Christmas lights and hung all the Christmas lights," with "Jim

---

[9]   One of the ways Common Lisp works to alleviate this kind of problem is the use of gensym. The key difference is that in Common Lisp, you have to be careful to avoid name capturing, whereas Clojure avoids it by default.

[10] Anaphora is pronounced *un-NAF-er-uh.*

bought 6,000 Christmas lights and hung *them* all." In this case, the word *them* is the anaphora. Some programming languages use anaphora, or allow for their simple definition. Scala has a rich set of anaphoric (Odersky 2008) patterns primarily focused around its _ operator:

```
// NOTE: This is Scala, not Clojure

Array(1, 2, 3, 4, 5).map(2 * _)
//=> res0: Array[Int] = Array(2, 4, 6, 8, 10)
```

In this Scala example, the underscore serves to refer back to an implicitly passed argument to the map function, which in this case would be each element of the array in succession. The same expression could be written with `(x) => 2 * x`—the syntax for an anonymous function—in the body of the map call, but that would be unnecessarily verbose.

Anaphora don't nest and as a result generally aren't employed in Clojure. Within a nested structure of anaphoric macros, you can only refer to the most immediate anaphoric binding, and never those from outer lexical contours, as demonstrated in the next example. For example, the Arc programming language (Graham Arc) contains a macro named awhen that is similar to Clojure's when, except that it implicitly defines a local named it used in its body to refer to the value of the checked expression. You can implement the same macro, called awhen in Clojure, as shown here:

```
(defmacro awhen [expr & body]
   `(let [~'it ~expr]                      <── Define anaphora
      (if ~'it
          (do ~@body))))                   <── Inline the body

(awhen [1 2 3] (it 2))                     <── Use "it" in the body
;=> 3

(awhen nil (println "Will never get here"))
;=> nil

(awhen 1 (awhen 2 [it]))                   <── Fail to nest
;=> [2]
```

Check its
truth

Clojure provides similar macros that do nest and replace the need for anaphora: if-let and when-let. When designing your own macros, it's preferable to build them along these lines so that the macro itself takes the name to be bound. But just because typical anaphorics are limited, that's not to say they're entirely useless. Instead, for your own libraries you may find that their usage is intuitive. You'll see the pattern ~'symbol at times in Clojure macros for selectively capturing a symbolic name in the body of a macro. The reason for this bit of awkwardness[11] is that Clojure's syntax-quote attempts to resolve symbols in the current context, resulting in fully qualified symbols. Therefore, ~' avoids that resolution by unquoting a quote.

---

[11] According to Christophe Grand (in a personal communication), "Awkwardness is good since it's a strong signal to make the user aware he is drifting away from the true path to Clojure enlightenment."

8.5.2   *(Arguably) useful selective name capturing*

We contend that there's only one case to be made for selective name capturing in Clojure macros: the case when you're forced to embed third-party macros and functions in your macros that rely on the existence of anaphora. One such macro is the `proxy` macro in Clojure's core libraries, which provides an anaphoric symbol named `this` in its body for use therein. We'll cover the `proxy` macro in depth in section 12.1, so there's no need to discuss it here. But bear in mind that should this macro ever be embedded in your own macros, you may be forced to use the `~'this` pattern.

> **Hygiene**
>
> A *hygienic* macro is one that doesn't cause name capturing at macro-expansion time. Clojure macros help to ensure hygiene by namespace-resolving symbols in the body of syntax-quote at macro-definition time. As you saw, symbols are expanded into the form `user/a-symbol` in the body of syntax-quote. To close this hygienic loop, Clojure also disallows the definition of qualified locals in the body of a macro. In order to selectively capture names in Clojure macros, you *must* explicitly do so via the `~'a-symbol` pattern.

Clojure prefers that symbols be either declared or bound at macro-definition time. But using the resolution-deferment strategy outlined earlier, you can relax this requirement for those instances where doing so would be useful.

8.6   *Using macros to manage resources*

Managing scarce resources or those with a finite lifetime is often viewed as a sweet spot for macro usage. In Java, such activities are almost always performed using the `try/catch/finally` idiom (Bloch 2008), as shown:[12]

```
// NOTE: This is Java, not Clojure

try {
    // open the resource
}
catch (Exception e) {
    // handle any errors
}
finally {
// in any case, release the resource
}
```

We showed in section 2.9 that Clojure also has a `try/catch/finally` form that can be used the same way, but as with the Java idiom, you must remember to explicitly close the resource in the `finally` block. Clojure provides a generic `with-open` macro,

---

[12] Java 7 introduces an `AutoCloseable` interface coupled with a `try-with-resources` statement that operates almost exactly like the `with-resource` macro. See "The try-with-resources Statement," The Java Tutorials, http://mng.bz/389y.

shown next, that when given a closeable object bound to a name, automatically calls its .close method (assuming that one exists) in a finally block:

```
(import [java.io BufferedReader InputStreamReader]
        [java.net URL])

(defn joc-www []
  (-> "http://joyofclojure.com/hello" URL.
      .openStream
      InputStreamReader.
      BufferedReader.))
```

```
(let [stream (joc-www)]
  (with-open [page stream]                         ⟵ Begin IO block
    (println (.readLine page))
    (print "The stream will now close... "))       ⟵ Close implicitly
  (println "but let's read from it anyway.")
  (.readLine stream))                              ⟵ Use illegally after close
```

```
; Hello Cleveland
; The stream will now close... but let's read from it anyway.
; java.io.IOException: Stream closed
```

Not all instances of resources in your own programs will be closeable. In these instances, we present a generic template for resource-allocating macros that can be used for many cases:

```
(defmacro with-resource [binding close-fn & body]
  `(let ~binding
     (try
       (do ~@body)
       (finally
         (~close-fn ~(binding 0))))))

(let [stream (joc-www)]
  (with-resource [page stream]
    #(.close %)
    (.readLine page)))
```

The macro with-resource is generic enough and so generally ubiquitous across differing flavors (Symbolics Inc.)[13] to almost be considered a Lisp design pattern. The macro with-resource differs from with-open in that it doesn't assume that its resource is closeable but instead delegates the task of closing the resource to a close-fn function taken as an argument. One final point is that with-resource avoids the nesting problem of anaphoric macros because it requires that the resource be named explicitly à la [stream (joc-www)]. This approach allows for the proper nesting of with-resource macros; and, in fact, the use of named bindings marked by vectors is ubiquitous in Clojure and has been adopted by most codebases in the wild.

---

[13] The spirit of this section was inspired by a similar discussion of "Writing Macros to Surround Code" ("Reference Guide to Symbolics Common Lisp: Language Concepts," Symbolics Release 7 Document Set, 1986). If you can get your hands on the original Symbolics manuals, do so—they contain a wealth of information.

8.7   *Putting it all together: macros returning functions*

In section 7.1, we introduced Clojure's constraint facility that uses pre- and postcondition checks on function arguments and return values, respectively, to ensure some assertions about said function. In that section, we talked briefly about how separating the constraints from the functions they're constraining allows you to more flexibly apply different assertion templates based on need and context.

> **CLOJURE APHORISM**   Clojure programmers don't write their apps in Clojure. They write the language that they use to write their apps in Clojure.

In this section, we'll take this idea one step further by introducing a macro named `contract` that implements a simple DSL to describe function constraints. For example, a proposed DSL should be nameable and describe its pre- and postconditions in an intuitive way, building a higher-order function that will be used to apply its constraints later. The following sketches a contract specifying that a function should take only a positive number and return its value multiplied by 2:

```
(contract doubler
  [x]
  (:require
    (pos? x))
  (:ensure
    (= (* 2 x) %)))
```

The contract's `:require` list (Meyer 2000) refers to the preconditions, and the `:ensure` list refers to the postconditions. Given this description, how would you start to implement a macro to realize this sketch? If you haven't already gathered from the section title and the initial problem statement, the macro must return a function, so let's start there.

Listing 8.1   Contract top-level macro

```
(declare collect-bodies)

(defmacro contract [name & forms]
  (list* `fn name (collect-bodies forms)))
```

Hold fast, because you're going to implement that necessary function soon. But first, imagine what the form of the returned function will be when it finally comes out of `contract`:

```
(fn doubler
  ([f x]
     {:post [(= (* 2 x) %)],
      :pre [(pos? x)]}
     (f x)))
```

You also want to allow for the multi-arity function definition form so that the `contract` can take more than one specification per arity function, each separated by a vector of symbols. The first step down that path starts with an implementation of collect-bodies:

```
(declare build-contract)

(defn collect-bodies [forms]
  (for [form (partition 3 forms)]
    (build-contract form)))
```

The primary task of collect-bodies is to build a list of the body portion of the contract, each partitioned into three segments. These partitions represent the arglist, requires, and ensures of the contract, which you'll then pass along to another function named build-contract, which will build the arity bodies and corresponding constraint maps. This is shown next.

Listing 8.2   Contract auxiliary function `build-contract`

```
(defn build-contract [c]
  (let [args (first c)]              <-- Grab args
    (list                            <-- Build a list
      (into '[f] args)               <-- Include fn and args
      (apply merge
             (for [con (rest c)]
               (cond (= (first con) 'require)
                   (assoc {} :pre (vec (rest con)))       <-- Process require
                   (= (first con) 'ensure)
                   (assoc {} :post (vec (rest con)))      <-- Process ensure
                   :else (throw (Exception.
                                  (str "Unknown tag "
                                       (first con)))))))
      (list* 'f args))))             <-- Build the call site
```

The function build-contract is where the heart of contract construction lies, building the arity bodies that contain constraint maps. The difference is that each body is a higher-order function that takes an additional function as an argument, to which the arguments are then delegated. This allows you to compose the contract function with a constrained function, as shown in the next listing.

Listing 8.3   Composition of the contract function and constrained function

```
(def doubler-contract                          <-- Define a contract
  (contract doubler
    [x]
    (require
      (pos? x))
    (ensure
      (= (* 2 x) %))))

(def times2 (partial doubler-contract #(* 2 %)))       <-- Test correct use

(times2 9)
;=> 18
```

```
(def times3 (partial doubler-contract #(* 3 %)))          ⟵ Test incorrect use
(times3 9)
; java.lang.AssertionError: Assert failed: (= (* 2 x) %)
```

As you might expect, times2 fulfills the contract, whereas times3 doesn't. You could extend doubler-contract to handle extended arities, as shown here.

Listing 8.4 Contract for multiple-arity functions

```
(def doubler-contract
  (contract doubler
    [x]                           ⟵ Define one-arg contract
    (require
      (pos? x))
    (ensure
      (= (* 2 x) %))
    [x y]                         ⟵ Define two-arg contract
      (require
        (pos? x)
        (pos? y))
      (ensure
        (= (* 2 (+ x y)) %)))))
((partial doubler-
      contract #(* 2 (+ %1 %2))) 2 3)          ⟵ Test a correct fn
;=> 10

((partial doubler-contract #(+ %1 %1 %2 %2)) 2 3)     ⟵ Test another correct fn
;=> 10

((partial doubler-contract #(* 3 (+ %1 %2))) 2 3)       ⟵ Test an incorrect fn
; java.lang.AssertionError: Assert failed: (= (* 2 (+ x y)) %)
```

You could extend the contract to cover any number of expected function arities using contract, independent of the functions themselves. This provides a nice separation of the work to be done from the expected work to be done. By using the contract macro, you provide a way to describe the expectations of a function, including but not limited to

- The possible types of its inputs and output
- The relationship of the function output to its inputs
- The expected function arities
- The "shape" of the inputs and output

The contract macro can be extended in many complementary ways. For example, Clojure's function constraints are verified using logical and—the implications being that any additional pre- or postcondition works to tighten the requirements. But there may be times when loosening the constraints on the inputs and tightening them on the output makes more sense. In any case, this section isn't about the nuances of contracts programming, and to dig deeper would elude the point that using macros to return functions is an extremely powerful way to extend the capabilities of Clojure itself.

8.8 *Summary*

We've explored various use cases for macros and given examples of each. We also tried to show how you can use macros to mold Clojure into the language that shortens the gap between your problem space and solution space. In your own unique programs, you should try to do the same. But the most important skill that you can learn on your path toward macro mastery is the ability to recognize when to avoid using them. The general answer, of course, is whenever and as often as you can.

In the next chapter, we'll cover various powerful ways to organize and categorize data types and functions using Clojure's namespaces, multimethods, types, and protocols.

Combining data and code

9

This chapter covers

- Namespaces
- Exploring Clojure multimethods with the Universal Design Pattern
- Types, protocols, and records
- A fluent builder for chess moves

Clojure provides powerful features for grouping and partitioning logical units of code and data. Most logical groupings occur in namespaces, Clojure's analogue to Java packages. We explore how to build, manipulate, and reason about them. Also, in this chapter we'll play with Clojure's powerful multimethods that provide polymorphism based on arbitrary dispatch functions. We'll then uncover recent additions to Clojure supporting *abstraction-oriented programming*—types, protocols, and records. Finally, the chapter concludes with the creation of a fluent chess-move facility, comparing a Java approach to solving the problem with a Clojure approach.

9.1 Namespaces

Newcomers to Clojure have a propensity to hack away at namespace declarations until they appear to work. This may work sometimes, but it delays the process of learning how to use namespaces more effectively.

From a high-level perspective, namespaces can be likened to a two-level mapping, where the first level is a symbol to a namespace containing mappings of symbols to vars, as shown in figure 9.1. This conceptual model[1] is slightly complicated by the fact that namespaces can be aliased, but even in these circumstances the model holds true.

In the simplest possible terms, qualified symbols of the form `joy.ns/authors` cause a two-level lookup—a symbol `joy.ns` used to look up a namespace map and a symbol `authors` used to retrieve a var, as shown here:

```
(in-ns 'joy.ns)                         ◄─┐ Create and switch
                                          │ to a namespace
(def authors ["Chouser"])

(in-ns 'your.ns)                        ◄── Create another

(clojure.core/refer 'joy.ns)            ◄── Pull in all the definitions
joy.ns/authors
;=> ["Chouser"]

(in-ns 'joy.ns)                         ◄── Switch namespaces
(def authors ["Chouser" "Fogus"])

(in-ns 'your.ns)                        ◄─┐ Switch back, and check the
joy.ns/authors                            │ value in the other namespace
;=> ["Chouser" "Fogus"]
```

Because a symbolic name refers to a var in the current namespace or another, it follows that any referred var always evaluates to the current value and not the value present at referral time.

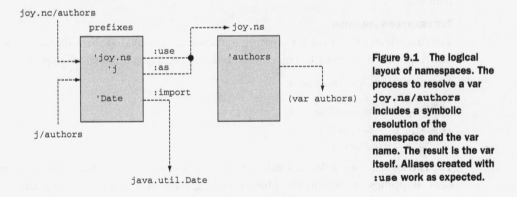

Figure 9.1 The logical layout of namespaces. The process to resolve a var `joy.ns/authors` includes a symbolic resolution of the namespace and the var name. The result is the var itself. Aliases created with `:use` work as expected.

---

[1] As always, we're trying to keep the level of discussion limited to abstractions rather than implementation details.

9.1.1 Creating namespaces

There are a number of ways to create a new namespace; each has its advantages and use cases. The choice of one namespace-creation mechanism over another amounts to choosing a level of control over the default symbolic mappings.

THE NS MACRO

Using the ns macro automatically conveys two sets of symbolic mappings—all classes in the java.lang package and all the functions, macros, and special forms in the clojure.core namespace:

```
(ns chimp)
(reduce + [1 2 (Integer. 3)])
;=> 6
```

Using the ns macro creates a namespace if it doesn't already exist, and switches to that namespace. The ns macro is intended for use in source code files and not in the REPL, although nothing prevents you from doing so.

THE IN-NS FUNCTION

Using the in-ns function imports the java.lang package like ns, but it doesn't create any mappings for functions or macros in clojure.core. The in-ns function also takes an explicit symbol used as the namespace qualifier, as shown here:

```
(in-ns 'gibbon)

(reduce + [1 2 (Integer. 3)])
; java.lang.Exception: Unable to resolve symbol: reduce in this context

(clojure.core/refer 'clojure.core)
(reduce + [1 2 (Integer. 3)])
;=> 6
```

in-ns is more amenable to REPL experimentation when dealing with namespaces than ns.

THE CREATE-NS FUNCTION

The finest level of control for creating namespaces is provided through the create-ns function, which when called takes a symbol and returns a namespace object:

```
(def b (create-ns 'bonobo))
b
;=> #<Namespace bonobo>

((ns-map b) 'String)
;=> java.lang.String
```

The call to create-ns doesn't switch to the named namespace, but it does create Java class mappings automatically. The preceding code shows this by using the ns-map function to get a map of the bindings in the bonobo namespace and checking that the symbol String is bound to the class java.lang.String. When given a namespace object (also retrieved using the find-ns function), you can manipulate its bindings programmatically using the functions intern and ns-unmap:

```
(intern b 'x 9)
;=> #'bonobo/x
bonobo/x
;=> 9
```

The preceding code binds the symbol x to the value 9 in the namespace bonobo and then references it directly using its qualified name bonobo/x. You can do the same thing for any type of var binding:

```
(intern b 'reduce clojure.core/reduce)
;=> #'bonobo/reduce

(intern b '+ clojure.core/+)
;=> #'bonobo/+

(in-ns 'bonobo)
(reduce + [1 2 3 4 5])
;=> 15
```

Because only Java class mappings are created by create-ns, you have to intern any Clojure core functions, as with + and reduce. You can even inspect the mappings in a namespace programmatically and likewise remove specific mappings:

```
(in-ns 'user)
(get (ns-map 'bonobo) 'reduce)
;=> #'bonobo/reduce

(ns-unmap 'bonobo 'reduce)   ;=> nil

(get (ns-map 'bonobo) 'reduce)
;=> nil
```

Finally, you can wipe a namespace using remove-ns:

```
(remove-ns 'bonobo)
;=> #<Namespace bonobo>

(all-ns)
;=> (#<Namespace clojure.set> #<Namespace clojure.main>
     #<Namespace clojure.core> #<Namespace clojure.zip>
     #<Namespace chimp> #<Namespace gibbon>
     #<Namespace clojure.xml>)
```

Be careful when populating namespaces using create-ns and intern, because these functions can cause potentially confusing side effects to occur. Their use is intended only for advanced techniques, and even then they should be used cautiously.

9.1.2 *Expose only what's needed*

Knowing that namespaces operate as two-level mappings will only get you so far in creating and using them effectively. You must understand other practical matters to use namespaces to their fullest. For example, for a given namespace joy.contracts, the directory structure could look like that in figure 9.2.

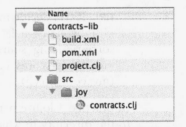

Figure 9.2 The directories layout for an illustrative joy.contracts namespace

This directory structure is fairly straight-forward, but there are a couple items to note. First, although the namespace is named joy.contracts, the corresponding Clojure source file is located in the contracts-lib/src/joy directory. This is a common technique in organizing Java and Clojure projects, where the actual source directories and files are located in a common src subdirectory in the main project directory. The addi-

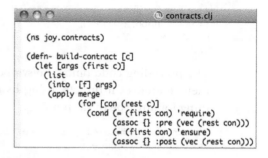

```
(ns joy.contracts)

(defn- build-contract [c]
  (let [args (first c)]
    (list
      (into '[f] args)
      (apply merge
        (for [con (rest c)]
          (cond (= (first con) 'require)
                (assoc {} :pre (vec (rest con)))
                (= (first con) 'ensure)
                (assoc {} :post (vec (rest con)))))))
```

Figure 9.3   The top of the source file for the joy.contracts namespace

tional files build.xml, pom.xml, and project.clj correspond to the build scripts for Apache Ant, Maven, and Leiningen, respectively. These build scripts will know, through either configuration or convention, that the src directory contains the directories and source files for Clojure namespaces and *not* part of the namespace logical layout. If you were to open the contracts.clj file located in contracts-lib/src/joy in your favorite editor, you might see something like figure 9.3.

The file contracts.clj defines the namespace joy.contracts and defines the function build-contract using the defn- macro. The use of defn- in this way indicates to Clojure that the build-contract function is private to the joy.contracts namespace. The defn- macro is provided for convenience and attaches privileged metadata to the var containing the function. You can attach the same namespace privacy metadata yourself, as shown:

```
(ns hider.ns)

(defn ^{:private true} answer [] 42)

(ns seeker.ns
  (:refer hider.ns))

(answer)
; java.lang.Exception: Unable to resolve symbol: answer in this context
```

Using ^{:private true} this way also works in a def and a defmacro, and for these cases it's required, because there are no corresponding def- and defmacro- in Clojure's core.

> **TIP** If you decide to name your namespaces with hyphens, à la my-cool-lib, then the corresponding source file *must* be named with underscores in place of the hyphens (my_cool_lib.clj).

In practice, Clojure namespace names are often tied to the directory in which they reside. Following this trend, you can create a certain directory structure conducive to hiding implementation details, as shown in figure 9.4.

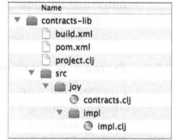

Figure 9.4   Private API directories: using the folder layout to hide namespace implementation details

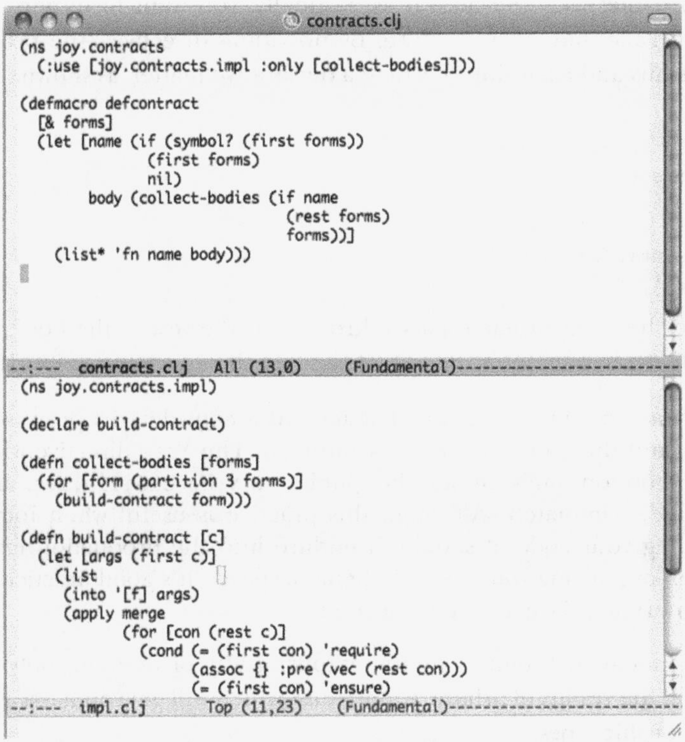

```
(ns joy.contracts
  (:use [joy.contracts.impl :only [collect-bodies]]))

(defmacro defcontract
  [& forms]
  (let [name (if (symbol? (first forms))
               (first forms)
               nil)
        body (collect-bodies (if name
                               (rest forms)
                               forms))]
    (list* 'fn name body)))
```

`--:--- contracts.clj   All (13,0)      (Fundamental)------------------`

```
(ns joy.contracts.impl)

(declare build-contract)

(defn collect-bodies [forms]
  (for [form (partition 3 forms)]
    (build-contract form)))

(defn build-contract [c]
  (let [args (first c)]
    (list
      (into '[f] args)
      (apply merge
        (for [con (rest c)]
          (cond (= (first con) 'require)
                  (assoc {} :pre (vec (rest con)))
                (= (first con) 'ensure)
```

`--:--- impl.clj      Top (11,23)      (Fundamental)------------------`

Figure 9.5 Private API source: the client-facing API is located in contracts.clj, and the private API in impl.clj.

By creating another subdirectory to contracts-lib/src/joy named impl, you can effectively hide implementation details for your code. The public-facing API would be located in contracts.clj, and the "hidden" implementation details in impl.clj. Your clients would be expected to refer only to the elements in contracts.clj, whereas your library could refer to elements in impl.clj, as shown in figure 9.5.

Of course, nothing's stopping code in other namespaces from also referencing the joy.contracts.impl namespace, but you do so at your own peril. There are never any guarantees that implementation details will remain the same from one release to the next.

9.1.3 *Declarative inclusions and exclusions*

When you're defining namespaces, it's important to include only the references that are likely to be used. Clojure prefers a fine-grained var mapping via a set of directives on the ns macro: :exclude, :only, :as, :refer-clojure, :import, :use, :load, and :require.

We'll describe a namespace named joy.ns-ex first in prose and then using ns and its directives. In this namespace, you want to exclude the defstruct macro from clojure.core. Next, you want to use everything in clojure.set and clojure.xml without namespace qualification. Likewise, you wish to use only the functions are and is from the clojure.test namespace without qualification. You then want to load the `clojure.zip` namespace and alias it as `z`. Finally, you want to import the Java classes `java.util.Date` and `java.io.File`. By providing directives, the problem of namespace inclusions and exclusions become a declarative matter, as shown:

```
(ns joy.ns-ex
  (:refer-clojure :exclude [defstruct])
  (:use (clojure set xml))
  (:use [clojure.test :only (are is)])
  (:require (clojure [zip :as z]))
  (:import (java.util Date)
           (java.io File)))
```

We'll touch on further uses of namespaces throughout the rest of the book, with an extensive example explaining their use as JVM class specifications in section 10.3.

> **NOTE**   The `(:use (clojure set xml))` statement is considered a promiscuous operation, and therefore its use is discouraged. The `:use` directive without the `:only` option pulls in all the public vars in `clojure.set` and `clojure.xml` indiscriminately. Although this practice is useful when incrementally building your code, it shouldn't endure into the production environment. When organizing your code along namespaces, it's good practice to export and import *only* those elements needed.

We now turn our focus to Clojure's multimethods, a way of defining polymorphic functions based on the results of arbitrary functions, which will get you halfway toward a system of polymorphic types.

9.2   *Exploring Clojure multimethods with the Universal Design Pattern*

> *The most specific event can serve as a general example of a class of events.*
>
> —Douglas R. Hofstadter

In Douglas Hofstadter's Pulitzer prize–winning work *Gödel, Escher, Bach: An Eternal Golden Braid*, he describes a notion of the *Prototype Principle*—the tendency of the human mind to use specific events as models for similar but different events or things. He presents the idea "that there is generality in the specific" (Hofstadter 1979). Building on this idea, programmer Steve Yegge coined the term *The Universal Design Pattern (UDP)*, extrapolating on Hofstadter's idea (Yegge 2008) and presenting it in terms of prototypal inheritance (Ungar 1987). The UDP is a reusable blueprint for designing software to fit any situation by building on a simple data (maps) and lookup model.

The UDP is built on the notion of a map or map-like object. Although not groundbreaking, the flexibility in the UDP derives from the fact that each map contains a reference to a *prototype* map used as a parent link to inherited fields. You might wonder how anyone could model a software problem in this way, but we assure you that countless programmers do so every day when they choose JavaScript (Flanagan 2006). In this section, we'll implement a subset of Yegge's UDP and discuss how it might be used as the basis for abstraction-oriented programming and polymorphism using Clojure's multimethods and ad hoc hierarchies.

9.2.1 *The parts*

In addition to the aforementioned prototype reference, the UDP requires a set of supporting functions to operate: `beget`, `get`, `put`, `has?`, and `forget`. The entire UDP is built on these five functions, but you'll need the first three for this section. To start, let's define the namespace in a somewhat interesting way:

```
(ns joy.udp                              Exclude clojure.core/get
  (:refer-clojure :exclude [get]))       from referral
```

Because you plan to define a function `get` in this UDP namespace, you want to explicitly exclude it from being automatically referred from Clojure's core library. This action is tantamount to overriding the core definition in your new namespace.

THE BEGET FUNCTION

The `beget` function performs a simple task. It takes a map and associates its prototype reference to another map, returning a new map:

```
(defn beget [this proto]              Takes a map and associates its prototype
  (assoc this ::prototype proto))     at the :joy.udp/prototype key
```

To participate in the UDP, maps must have a `:joy.udp/prototype` entry. Using `beget` ensures that the prototype object is attached using the correct key and layout, as shown next:

```
(beget {:sub 0} {:super 1})

;=> {:joy.udp/prototype {:super 1}, :sub 0}
```

Now that prototype map is in place, you can implement a function `get` to perform the (potentially) nested lookup.

THE GET FUNCTION

Because of the presence of the prototype link, `get` requires more than a simple one-level lookup. Instead, whenever a value isn't found in a given map, the prototype chain is followed until the end:

```
(defn get [m k]
  (when m
    (if-let [[_ v] (find m k)]
      v
      (recur (::prototype m) k))))

(get (beget {:sub 0} {:super 1})
     :super)
;=> 1
```

You don't explicitly handle the case of "removed" properties but instead treat them like any other associated value. This is fine because the "not found" value of nil is falsey. Most of the time, it's sufficient to rely on the fact that looking up a nonexistent key returns nil. But in cases where you want to allow users of your functions to store any value, including `nil`, you have to be careful to distinguish `nil` from "not found," and the `find` function is the best way to do this.

THE PUT FUNCTION

The function `put` takes a key and an associated value and puts them into the supplied map, overwriting any existing key of the same name:

```
(def put assoc)
```

The `put` function is asymmetric to the functionality of `get`. That is, `get` retrieves values anywhere along the prototype chain, whereas `put` only ever inserts at the level of the supplied map—which is why using `assoc` directly will work for you.

9.2.2   *Basic use of the Universal Design Pattern*

Using only `beget`, `put`, and `get`, you can use the UDP in some simple yet powerful ways. Assume that at birth, cats like dogs and only learn to despise them when goaded. Morris the cat has spent most of his life liking 9-Lives cat food and dogs, until the day comes when a surly Shih Tzu leaves him battered and bruised. We can model this unfortunate story as shown:

```
(def cat {:likes-dogs true, :ocd-bathing true})
(def morris (beget {:likes-9lives true} cat))
(def post-traumatic-morris (beget {:likes-dogs nil} morris))

(get cat :likes-dogs)
;=> true

(get morris :likes-dogs)
;=> true

(get post-traumatic-morris :likes-dogs)
;=> nil
```

The map `post-traumatic-morris` is like the old `morris` in every way except for the fact that he has learned to hate dogs. Thankfully, the Morris tormented by dogs can take solace in his favorite brand of cat food:

```
(get post-traumatic-morris :likes-9lives)
;;=> true
```

Modeling cat and dog societal woes is interesting but far from the only use case for the UDP, as you'll see next.

> **No notion of self**
>
> Our implementation of the UDP contains no notion of self-awareness via an implicit `this` or `self` reference. Although adding such a feature would probably be possible, we've intentionally excluded it in order to draw a clear separation between the prototypes and the functions that work on them (Keene 1989). A better solution, and one that follows in line with a deeper Clojure philosophy, would be to access, use, and manipulate these prototypes using Clojure's multimethods.

9.2.3 *Multimethods to the rescue*

You can easily add behaviors to the UDP using Clojure's multimethod facilities. *Multimethods* provide a way to perform function polymorphism based on the result of an arbitrary dispatch function. Coupled with your earlier UDP implementation, you can implement a prototypal object system with differential inheritance similar to (although not as elegant as) that in the Io language (Dekorte Io). First, you need to define a multimethod `compiler` that dispatches on a key `:os`:

```
(defmulti compiler :os)
(defmethod compiler ::unix [m] (get m :c-compiler))
(defmethod compiler ::osx  [m] (get m :llvm-compiler))
```

The multimethod `compiler` describes a simple scenario: if the function `compiler` is called with a prototype map, then the map is queried for an element `:os`, which has methods defined on the results for either `::unix` or `::osx`. Let's create some prototype maps to exercise `compiler`:

```
(def clone (partial beget {}))
(def unix   {:os ::unix, :c-compiler "cc", :home "/home", :dev "/dev"})
(def osx   (-> (clone unix)
               (put :os ::osx)
               (put :llvm-compiler "clang")
               (put :home "/Users")))

(compiler unix)
;=> "cc"

(compiler osx)
;=> "clang"
```

That's all there is (Foote 2003) to creating behaviors that work against the specific "type" of a prototype map. But a problem of inherited behaviors still persists. Because this implementation of the UDP separates state from behavior, there's seemingly no way to associate inherited behaviors. But as we'll show next, Clojure does provide a way to define ad hoc hierarchies that you can use to simulate inheritance in your model.

9.2.4 *Ad hoc hierarchies for inherited behaviors*

Based on the layout of the `unix` and `osx` prototype maps, the property `:home` is overridden in `osx`. You could again duplicate the use of `get` in each method defined (as in `compiler`), but instead let's say that the lookup of `:home` should be a derived function:

```
(defmulti home :os)
(defmethod home ::unix [m] (get m :home))

(home unix)
;=> "/home"

(home osx)
; java.lang.IllegalArgumentException:
;   No method in multimethod 'home' for dispatch value: :user/osx
```

Clojure allows you to define a relationship stating "`::osx` is a `::unix`" and have the derived function take over the lookup behavior using Clojure's `derive` function:

```
(derive ::osx ::unix)
```

Now the `home` function works:

```
(home osx)
;=> "/Users"
```

You can query the derivation hierarchy using the functions `parents`, `ancestors`, `descendants`, and `isa?`, as shown:

```
(parents ::osx)
;=> #{:user/unix}

(ancestors ::osx)
;=> #{:user/unix}

(descendants ::unix)
;=> #{:user/osx}

(isa? ::osx ::unix)
;=> true

(isa? ::unix ::osx)
;=> false
```

The result of the `isa?` function defines how multimethods dispatch. In the absence of a derivation hierarchy, `isa?` can be likened to pure equality; but when derivations are defined, then a richer check is performed according to the hierarchical relationships constructed.

9.2.5 *Resolving conflict in hierarchies*

What if you interject another ancestor into the hierarchy for `::osx` and want to again call the `home` method? Observe the following:

```
(derive ::osx ::bsd)
(defmethod home ::bsd [m] "/home")

(home osx)
; java.lang.IllegalArgumentException: Multiple methods in multimethod
;   'home' match dispatch value: :user/osx -> :user/unix and
;   :user/bsd, and neither is preferred
```

As shown in figure 9.6, `::osx` derives from both `::bsd` and `::unix`, so there's no way to decide which method to dispatch, because they're both at the same level in the derivation hierarchy. It's worth noting that this situation can't happen in Java due to single implementation inheritance, but it's a common and sometimes painful problem in C++. Fortunately, Clojure provides a way to assign favor to one method over another using the function `prefer-method`:

```
(prefer-method home ::unix ::bsd)
(home osx)                              ⟵  ::unix version is called

;=> "/Users"
```

You can see an illustration of the problem that prefer-method solves in figure 9.6.

In this case, you use prefer-method to explicitly state that for the multimethod home, you prefer the method associated with the dispatch value ::unix over the one for ::bsd. As you'll recall, the home method for ::unix explicitly used get to traverse the prototype chain, which is the preferred behavior.

As you might expect, removing the home method for the ::bsd dispatch value using remove-method removes the preferential lookup for ::osx:

```
(remove-method home ::bsd)
(home osx)
;=> "/Users"
```

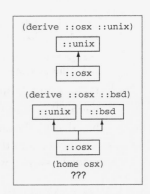

Figure 9.6 Most languages allowing type derivations use a built-in conflict-resolution strategy. In the case of CLOS, it's fully customizable. Clojure requires conflicts to be resolved with prefer-method.

Clojure maintains a global structure that holds the hierarchy information used for multimethod dispatch. By default, all the multimethod functions manipulate and operate off of the global hierarchy map directly. If you prefer to reduce these potentially confusing side effects to the global structure, then you can define a derivation hierarchy using make-hierarchy and derive:

```
(derive (make-hierarchy) ::osx ::unix)
;=> {:parents {:user/osx #{:user/unix}},
     :ancestors {:user/osx #{:user/unix}},
     :descendants {:user/unix #{:user/osx}}}
```

Once you have a separate hierarchy in hand, you can provide it to defmulti to specify the derivation context, thus preserving the global hierarchy map.

9.2.6 Arbitrary dispatch for true maximum power

Until now, you've only exercised multimethods using a single privileged :os property, but this doesn't accentuate their true power. Instead, multimethods are fully open and can dispatch on the result of an arbitrary function, even one that can pull apart and/or combine its inputs into any form:

```
(defmulti  compile-cmd  (juxt :os compiler))        ← juxt builds a vector
                                                       (see sidebar)
(defmethod compile-cmd [::osx "gcc"] [m]            ←
  (str "/usr/bin/" (get m :c-compiler)))            Match the
                                                    vector exactly
(defmethod compile-cmd :default [m]
  (str "Unsure where to locate " (get m :c-compiler)))
```

The dispatch values for the new compile-cmd methods are vectors composed of the results of looking up the :os key and calling the compiler function defined earlier. You can now see what happens when compile-cmd is called:

```
(compile-cmd osx)
;=> "/usr/bin/gcc"

(compile-cmd unix)
;=> "Unsure where to locate cc"
```

Using multimethods and the UDP is an interesting way to build abstractions. Multimethods and ad hoc hierarchies are open systems, allowing for polymorphic dispatch based on arbitrary functions. Clojure also provides a simpler model for creating abstractions and gaining the benefits of polymorphism—types, protocols, and records—which we'll cover next.

The handy-dandy juxt function

The `juxt` function is useful in defining multimethod dispatch functions. In a nutshell, `juxt` takes a bunch of functions and composes them into a function returning a vector of its argument(s) applied to each given function, as shown:

```
(def each-math (juxt + * - /))
(each-math 2 3)
;=> [5 6 -1 2/3]

((juxt take drop) 3 (range 9))
[(0 1 2) (3 4 5 6 7 8)]
```

Having a convenient and succinct way to build vectors of applied functions is powerful for defining understandable multimethods—although that's not the limit of `juxt`'s usefulness.

9.3   *Types, protocols, and records*

We showed in the previous section that Clojure multimethods provide a way to achieve runtime polymorphism based on arbitrary dispatch functions. Although extremely powerful, multimethods are sometimes less than ideal. Interposing a dispatch function into the polymorphism machinery isn't always conducive to raw speed. Likewise, dispatching on an arbitrary function is often overkill. Therefore, Clojure provides facilities for creating logically grouped polymorphic functions that are both simple and performant—types, records, and protocols. We'll delve into these topics in this section and introduce the concept of abstraction-oriented programming, predicated on the creation of logical groupings. But first, we'll discuss the simplest of the three topics, records, which you might recognize.

9.3.1   *Records*

Using maps as data objects is perfectly acceptable and has several lovely features. Chief among these is that maps require no declaration of any sort: you use literal syntax to build them right on the spot. You saw this in section 7.2 when you built an object like this:

```
{:val 5, :l nil, :r nil}
```

This is handy but is missing things that are often desirable, the most significant of which is a type of its own. The object constructed here is some kind of map, but it isn't, as far as Clojure is concerned, a `TreeNode`. That means when it's used in its simple form, as it is here, there's no clean way[2] to determine whether any particular map is a `TreeNode`.

In such circumstances, records become a compelling[3] solution. You define a record type with a `defrecord` form. For example, a `defrecord` for `TreeNode` looks like this:

```
(defrecord TreeNode [val l r])
```

This creates a new Java class with a constructor that takes a value for each of the fields listed. It also imports that class into your current namespace so you can easily use it to create new instances.

Here's how to create an instance of the `TreeNode` record:

```
(TreeNode. 5 nil nil)
;=> #:user.TreeNode{:val 5, :l nil, :r nil}
```

Explicitly importing defrecord and deftype classes

It's important to note that when you define a `defrecord` and a `deftype`, corresponding classes are generated. These classes are automatically imported into the same namespace where the `defrecord` and `deftype` declarations occur, but *not* in any other namespace. Instead, you *must explicitly import* `defrecord` and `deftype` classes using the `import` function or `:import` namespace declaration:

```
(ns my-cool-ns
  (:import joy.udp.TreeNode))
```

Loading a namespace via `:require` or `:use` isn't enough to import `defrecord` and `deftype` classes.

The use of `defrecord` buys you several important benefits. For instance, it provides a simple and specific idiom for documenting the expected fields of the object. But it also delivers several important performance improvements. A record is created more quickly, consumes less memory, and looks up keys in itself more quickly than the equivalent array map or hash map. Record types can also store primitive values (byte, int, long, and so on), which take up considerably less memory than the equivalent class-based object versions (also referred to as *boxed primitives*) like Byte, Integer, Long, and so on.

---

[2] You could test a map for the existence of the keys `:val`, `:l`, and `:r`, a sort of duck-typing but on fields instead of methods. But because there exists a real possibility that some other kind of object may happen to have these keys but use them in a different way, undesirable complexity and/or unexpected behavior is likely. Fortunately, you can mitigate this risk by using namespace-qualified keywords. Despite the general agreement of experts that ducks are Kosher, we'd definitely classify this particular duck as unclean.

[3] There was a pre-Clojure 1.2 convention of attaching `:type` metadata to an object, which can be looked up with the `type` function, but this approach is rarely if ever needed moving forward.

The downfall of defstructs

Clojure provides a `defstruct` mechanism, which can be viewed as a way to define a map that acts as an ad hoc class mechanism. These structs define a set of keys that are required to exist in the map and therefore can't be removed via `dissoc`. With the advent of `defrecord`, the need for structs has been nearly eliminated, and therefore structs aren't covered in this book. But if you have a code base reliant on structs, a record can replace them with minimal code changes, as highlighted here:

```
(defn change-age [p] (assoc p :age 286))

(defstruct person :fname :lname)
(change-age (struct person "Immanuel" "Kant"))
;=> {:fname "Immanuel", :lname "Kant", :age 286}

(defrecord Person [fname lname])
(change-age (Person. "Immanuel" "Kant"))
;=> #:user.Person{:fname "Immanuel", :lname "Kant", :age 286}
```

Note that the `change-age` function works with either structs or records—no change is required. Only the definition and the mechanism of instantiation need to be updated.

Other noteworthy differences between maps and records include the following:

- Records, unlike maps, can't serve as functions.
- Records are never equal to maps with the same key/value mappings.

You still look up values in records by doing (`:keyword obj`); it's just that if `obj` is a record, this code will run dramatically faster. By the way, that means destructuring still works, as well. Records support metadata using `with-meta` and `meta`, just like other Clojure collections, and you can even redefine a record if desired to have different fields giving you the compiled performance of Java dynamically. All of these together mean you can build a lot of code on top of simple hash-map objects and then make minimal changes to switch to using records instead, gaining the performance benefits we already covered.

You should understand records well enough to be able to reimplement the persistent binary tree from chapter 5 using `defrecord` instead of maps. This is shown in the following listing. Note that you have to add the `defrecord` and change the expressions in `xconj` where objects are created, but the `xseq` function is defined identically to how it was before.

Listing 9.1   Persistent binary tree built from records

```
(defrecord TreeNode [val l r])                          ◁— Define a record type

(defn xconj [t v]                        ◁— Add to a tree
  (cond
    (nil? t)        (TreeNode. v nil nil)
    (< v (:val t)) (TreeNode. (:val t) (xconj (:l t) v) (:r t))
    :else           (TreeNode. (:val t) (:l t) (xconj (:r t) v))))
```

```
(defn xseq [t]                                    ← Convert trees to seqs
  (when t
    (concat (xseq (:l t)) [(:val t)] (xseq (:r t)))))
(def sample-
    tree (reduce xconj nil [3 5 2 4 6]))          ← Try it out
  (xseq sample-tree)
;=> (2 3 4 5 6)
```

You can assoc and dissoc any key you want—adding keys that weren't defined in the defrecord works, although they have the performance of a regular map. Perhaps more surprisingly, dissocing a key given in the record works but returns a regular map rather than a record. In this example, note that the return value is printed as a plain map, not with the #:user.TreeNode prefix of a record:

```
(dissoc (TreeNode. 5 nil nil) :l)
;=> {:val 5, :r nil}
```

A final benefit of records is how well they integrate with Clojure protocols. But to fully understand how they relate, we must first explore what protocols are.

9.3.2 Protocols

> *The establishment of protocols … creates an obvious way for two people who are not directly communicating to structure independently developed code so that it works in a manner that remains coherent when such code is later combined.*
>
> —Kent M. Pitman (Pitman 2001)

A *protocol* in Clojure is a set of function signatures, each with at least one parameter, that are given a collective name. Protocols fulfill a role somewhat like Java interfaces or C++ pure virtual classes—a class that claims to implement a particular protocol should provide specialized implementations of each of the functions in that protocol. Then, when any of those functions is called, the appropriate implementation is polymorphic on the type of the first parameter, just like Java. In fact, the first parameter to a protocol function corresponds to the target object (the thing to the left of the dot for a method call used in Java source) of a method in object-oriented parlance.

For example, consider what collections such as stacks (first in, last out: FILO) and queues (first in, first out: FIFO) have in common. Each has a simple function for inserting a thing (call it push), a simple function for removing a thing (pop), and usually a function to see what would be removed if you removed a thing (peek). What we just gave you was an informal description of a protocol; all that's missing is the name. You can replace the changing third item of the acronym with an *X* and call objects that provide these functions FIXO. Note that besides stacks and queues, FIXO could include priority queues, pipes, and other critters.

Let's look at that informal description rewritten as a formal Clojure definition:

```
(defprotocol FIXO
  (fixo-push [fixo value])
  (fixo-pop [fixo])
  (fixo-peek [fixo]))
```

That's it. The only reason we prefixed the function names with *fixo-* is so that they don't conflict with Clojure's built-in functions.[4] Besides that, it's hard to imagine how there could be much less ceremony, isn't it?

But in order for a protocol to do any good, something must implement it. Protocols are implemented using one of the *extend* forms: extend, extend-type,[5] or extend-protocol. Each of these does essentially the same thing, but extend-type and extend-protocol are convenience macros for when you want to provide multiple functions for a given type. For example, the binary TreeNode from listing 9.1 is a record, so if you want to extend it, extend-type is most convenient. Because TreeNode already has a function xconj that works just like push should, let's start by implementing that:

```
(extend-type TreeNode
  FIXO
  (fixo-push [node value]
    (xconj node value)))

(xseq (fixo-push sample-tree 5/2))
;=> (2 5/2 3 4 5 6)
```

The first argument to extend-type is the class or interface that the entire rest of the form will extend. Following the type name are one or more blocks, each starting with the name of the protocol to be extended and followed by one or more functions from that protocol to implement. So, the preceding example implements a single function fixo-push for TreeNode objects and calls the existing xconj function. Got it? This is better than defining a regular function named fixo-push because protocols allow for polymorphism. That same function can have a different implementation for a different kind of object. Clojure vectors can act like stacks by extending FIXO to vectors:

```
(extend-type clojure.lang.IPersistentVector
  FIXO
  (fixo-push [vector value]
    (conj vector value)))

(fixo-push [2 3 4 5 6] 5/2)
;=> [2 3 4 5 6 5/2]
```

Here you're extending FIXO to an interface instead of a concrete class. This means fixo-push is now defined for all classes that inherit from IPersistentVector. Note that you can now call fixo-push with either a vector or a TreeNode, and the appropriate function implementation is invoked.

---

[4] It would be better to fix this problem by defining FIXO in a new namespace and excluding from it the similarly named clojure.core functions, except this would be a distraction from the point of this section. We'll discuss interesting interactions between namespaces and protocols later in this chapter.

[5] Records are a specialized kind of data type, so extend-type is used for both. We'll look at data types later in this section.

Clojure-style mixins

As you proceed through this section, you'll notice that you extend the FIXO protocol's fixo-push function in isolation. This works fine for our purposes, but you might want to take note of the implications of this approach. Consider the following:

```
(use 'clojure.string)

(defprotocol StringOps (rev [s]) (upp [s]))

(extend-type String
  StringOps
  (rev [s] (clojure.string/reverse s)))

(rev "Works")
;=> "skroW"
```

Defining the StringOps protocol and extending its rev function to String seems to work fine. But observe what happens when the protocol is again extended to cover the remaining upp function:

```
(extend-type String
  StringOps
  (upp [s] (clojure.string/upper-case s)))

(upp "Works")
;=> "WORKS"

(rev "Works?")
; IllegalArgumentException No implementation of method: :rev
;    of protocol: #'user/StringOps found for
;       class: java.lang.String
```

The reason for this exception is that for a protocol to be fully populated (all of its functions callable), it must be extended fully, per individual type. Protocol extension is at the granularity of the entire protocol and not at a per-function basis. This behavior seems antithetical to the common notion of a *mixin*—granules of discrete functionality that can be "mixed into" existing classes, modules, and so on. Clojure too has mixins, but it takes a slightly different approach:

```
(def rev-mixin {:rev clojure.string/reverse})

(def upp-mixin {:upp (fn [this] (.toUpperCase this))})

(def fully-mixed (merge upp-mixin rev-mixin))

(extend String StringOps fully-mixed)

(-> "Works" upp rev)
;=> SKROW
```

Mixins in Clojure refer to the creation of discrete maps containing protocol function implementations that are combined in such a way as to create a complete implementation of a protocol. Once mixed together (as in the var fully-mixed), only then are types extended to protocols. As with many of Clojure's features, mixins and protocol extension are fully open.

What we've just done is impossible with Java interfaces or C++ classes, at least in the order we did it. With either of those languages, the concrete type (such as `TreeNode` or vector) must name *at the time it's defined* all the interfaces or classes it's going to implement. Here we went the other way around—both `TreeNode` and vectors were defined before the `FIXO` protocol even existed, and we easily extended `FIXO` to each of them. This matters in the real world because the concrete types and even the protocol could be provided by third-party libraries—possibly even different third-party libraries—and you could still match them up, provide implementations for the appropriate functions, and get back to work. All this without any adapters, wrappers, monkey-patching, or other incidental complexity getting in the way. In fact, *Clojure polymorphism lives in the protocol functions, not in the classes*, as shown in figure 9.7.

You can even extend a protocol to `nil`. You'd be forgiven for not immediately seeing why you'd want to do this, but consider how `TreeNode` implements `fixo-push`; and yet the `sample-tree` you're using was built using `xconj` instead. Trying to build up a tree the same way with `fixo-push` runs into a problem:

```
(reduce fixo-push nil [3 5 2 4 6 0])
; java.lang.IllegalArgumentException:
; No implementation of method: :fixo-push
;   of protocol: #'user/FIXO found for class: nil
```

The `xconj` implementation specifically handled the initial `nil` case, but because protocol methods dispatch on the first argument, you need special support from `extend` to get `fixo-push` to behave similarly. This is done by extending a protocol to the value `nil`, like this:

```
(extend-type nil
  FIXO
  (fixo-push [t v]
    (TreeNode. v nil nil)))

(xseq (reduce fixo-push nil [3 5 2 4 6 0]))
;=> (0 2 3 4 5 6)
```

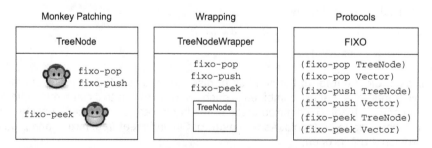

Figure 9.7 As opposed to the notion of monkey-patching and wrapping, the polymorphism in Clojure resides in the functions themselves and not in the classes worked with.

All the options and arrangements of code allowed by extend can be disorienting, but one thing you can keep firmly in mind is that extend is always about a protocol. Each method listed in an extend form is implementing an intersection between a protocol and something else. That something else can be a concrete class, an interface, a record type, or even nil, but it's always being connected to a protocol.

See the following listing for complete implementations of FIXO for TreeNode and vectors. As mentioned in the sidebar, in order for the FIXO protocol to be fully realizable, each of its functions should be mixed in. But you might not always require that a protocol be fully realizable.

Listing 9.2 Complete implementations of FIXO for TreeNode and vector

```
(extend-type TreeNode
  FIXO
  (fixo-push [node value]          <— Delegate to xconj
    (xconj node value))
  (fixo-peek [node]                <— Walk down the left nodes
    (if (:l node)                      to find the smallest
      (recur (:l node))
      (:val node)))
  (fixo-pop [node]                 Build a new path down the
    (if (:l node)                  left to the removed item
      (TreeNode. (:val node) (fixo-pop (:l node)) (:r node))
      (:r node))))

(extend-type clojure.lang.IPersistentVector
  FIXO
  (fixo-push [vector value]        <— fixo-push is vector's conj
    (conj vector value))
  (fixo-peek [vector]              <— fixo-peek is peek
    (peek vector))
  (fixo-pop [vector]              <— fixo-pop is pop
    (pop vector)))
```

If you've done six impossible things this morning, why not round it off with breakfast at Milliways, the Restaurant at the End of the Universe?

—Douglas Adams[6]

Each of the function bodies in the previous example have either had no code in common with each other, or called out to another function such as xconj for implementation details that they have in common. These techniques work well when there's a low level of commonality between the methods being implemented, but sometimes you have many methods of a protocol or even whole protocol implementations that you want to extend to multiple classes. In these cases, some languages would encourage you to create a base class that implements some or all the methods and then inherit from that. Clojure has a different approach.

---

[6] *The Restaurant at the End of the Universe* (Harmony Books, 1981).

SHARING METHOD IMPLEMENTATIONS

Clojure doesn't encourage implementation inheritance, so although it's possible to inherit from concrete classes as needed for Java interoperability,[7] there's no way to use extend to provide a concrete implementation and then build another class on top of that. There are important reasons why Clojure intentionally avoids this, but regardless of the reasons, we're left with the question of how best to avoid repeating code when similar objects implement the same protocol method.

The simplest solution is to write a regular function that builds on the protocol's methods. For example, Clojure's own into takes a collection and uses the conj implementation provided by the collection. You can write a similar function for FIXO objects like this:

```
(defn fixo-into [c1 c2]
  (reduce fixo-push c1 c2))

(xseq (fixo-into (TreeNode. 5 nil nil) [2 4 6 7]))
;=> (2 4 5 6 7)

(seq (fixo-into [5] [2 4 6 7]))
;=> (5 2 4 6 7)
```

But this is only an option when a function can be defined entirely in terms of the protocol's methods. If this isn't the case, you may need the more nuanced solution provided by the extend function. We mentioned it earlier but so far have only given examples of a macro built on top of it, extend-type. Although this and extend-protocol are frequently the most convenient way to implement protocol methods, they don't provide a natural way to mix in method implementations. The extend function takes a map for each protocol you want to implement, and you can build that map however you'd like, including by merging in implementations that are already defined. In the following listing, note how a FIXO implementation can be defined early using a map and extended to a protocol/record type later (while still maintaining every benefit of using the original map).

> **Listing 9.3   Using a map to extend FIXO to TreeNode**

```
(def tree-node-fixo                              ⟵┐  Define a map of
  {:fixo-push (fn [node value]                     │  names to functions
              (xconj node value))
   :fixo-peek (fn [node]
              (if (:l node)
                (recur (:l node))
                (:val node)))
   :fixo-pop (fn [node]
              (if (:l node)
                (TreeNode. (:val node) (fixo-pop (:l node)) (:r node))
                (:r node)))})
```

---

[7] Mechanisms that support something like Java-style implementation inheritance include gen-class, proxy, and extending protocol methods to Java abstract classes and interfaces.

```
(extend TreeNode FIXO tree-node-fixo)
(xseq (fixo-into (TreeNode. 5 nil nil) [2 4 6 7]))
;=> (2 4 5 6 7)
```

◁———┐ **Extend the protocol**
        using the map

These record objects and the way protocols can be extended to them result in rather differently shaped code than the objects built out of closures that we showed in section 7.2. Often this ability to define the data and implementation separately is desirable; but you're likely to find yourself occasionally in a circumstance where closures may feel like a better fit than records, and yet you want to extend a protocol or interface, not just provide ad hoc method names as in section 7.2.

THE REIFY MACRO

The reify macro brings together all the power of function closures and all the performance and protocol participation of extend into a single form. For example, say you want a stack-like FIXO that's constrained to a certain fixed size. Any attempt to push items onto one of these fixed-FIXOs when it's already full will fail, and an unchanged object will be returned. The wrinkle in the requirements that makes reify a reasonable option is that you want this size limit to be configurable. Thus you need a constructor or factory function, shown next, that takes the size limit and returns an object that will obey that limit.

Listing 9.4 Size-limited stack FIXO using reify

```
(defn fixed-fixo
  ([limit] (fixed-fixo limit []))
  ([limit vector]
    (reify FIXO
      (fixo-push [this value]
        (if (< (count vector) limit)
          (fixed-fixo limit (conj vector value))
          this))
      (fixo-peek [_]
        (peek vector))
      (fixo-pop [_]
        (pop vector)))))
```

◁———┐ **Factory to return**
        FIXO instances

◁———┐ **reify can be used to**
        satisfy protocols

Just like the extend forms, reify has method arglists that include the object itself. It's common to name the argument this in methods where you need to use it and _ in methods where you ignore its value. But both these conventions should only be followed where doing so is natural.

NAMESPACED METHODS

A rough analogy can be drawn between protocols and Java interfaces.[8] We've noted some of the differences already, but it can be a useful analogy nonetheless. In such a comparison, where record types are concrete classes, you might see that Java packages and C++ namespaces are like Clojure namespaces. It's normal in all three of these environments for the interface and the class to each be in a namespace, and not

---

[8] Those of you familiar with Haskell might recognize analogies to its typeclasses in our discussion.

necessarily the same one. For example, probably few readers were surprised to see that when the class `IPersistentVector` extended the protocol `user/FIXO`, they were each from a different namespace or package.

One way this analogy breaks down is that methods of the protocol are namespaced in a way that Java and C++ interfaces aren't. In those languages, all methods of a class share the same effective namespace, regardless of interfaces they're implementing. In Clojure, the methods always use the same namespace as the protocol, which means a record or type can extend (via `extend`, `extend-type`, and so on) identically named methods of two different protocols without any ambiguity. This is a subtle feature, but it allows you to avoid a whole category of issues that can come up when trying to combine third-party libraries into a single codebase.

Note that because the methods share the namespace of their protocol, you can't have identically named methods in two different protocols if those protocols are in the same namespace. Because both are under the control of the same person, it's easy to resolve this by moving one of the protocols to a different namespace or using more specific method names.

METHOD IMPLEMENTATIONS IN DEFRECORD

We've already shown how both protocols and interfaces can be extended to record types using the various `extend` forms, but there's another way to achieve similar results. Protocol and interface method implementations can be written directly inside a `defrecord` form, which ends up looking like the following.

Listing 9.5   Method implementations in `defrecord`

```
(defrecord TreeNode [val l r]
  FIXO                                    ◁─┐ Implement FIXO
  (fixo-push [t v]                          │ methods inline
    (if (< v val)
      (TreeNode. val (fixo-push l v) r)
      (TreeNode. val l (fixo-push r v))))) 
  (fixo-peek [t]
    (if l
      (fixo-peek l)                       ◁─┐ Call a method instead
      val))                                 │ of using recur
  (fixo-pop [t]
    (if l
      (TreeNode. val (fixo-pop l) r)
      r)))

(def sample-tree2 (reduce fixo-push (TreeNode. 3 nil nil) [5 2 4 6]))
(xseq sample-tree2)
;=> (2 3 4 5 6)
```

This is more convenient in many cases, and it can also produce dramatically faster code. Calling a protocol method like `fixo-peek` on a record type that implements it inline can be several times faster than calling the same method on an object that implements it via an `extend` form. Also note that the fields of the object are now available as locals—you use `val` instead of `(:val t)`.

Polymorphism and recur

Throughout this section, we've implemented the `fixo-peek` function using different methodologies, but a more subtle difference is worth noting. The first implementation uses `recur` for its recursive call:

```
(fixo-peek [node]
  (if (:l node)
    (recur (:l node))
    (:val node)))
```

Because of the nature of `recur`, the first implementation of `fixo-peek` isn't polymorphic on the recursive call. But the second version of `fixo-peek` uses a different approach:

```
(fixo-peek [t]
  (if l
    (fixo-peek l)
    val))
```

Notice that the recursive call in the second implementation is direct (mundane) and as a result is polymorphic. In the course of writing your own programs, this difference probably won't cause issues, but it's worth storing in the back of your mind.

Putting method definitions inside the `defrecord` form also allows you to implement Java interfaces and extend `java.lang.Object`, which isn't possible using any `extend` form. Because interface methods can accept and return primitive values as well as boxed objects, implementations of these in `defrecord` can also support primitives. This is important for interoperability and can provide ultimate performance parity with Java code.

We do need to note one detail of these inline method definitions in relation to `recur`. Specifically, uses of `recur` in these definitions can't provide a new target object: the initial argument gets the same value as the initial (non-recur) call to the method. For example, `fixo-push` takes args t and v, so if it used `recur`, only a single parameter would be given: the new value for the v arg.

9.3.3 *Building from a more primitive base with deftype*

You may have noticed that we've been using our own function xseq throughout the examples in this section, instead of Clojure's seq. This shouldn't be necessary, because Clojure provides an ISeqable interface that its seq function can use—all you need to do is to have your own type implement ISeqable. But an attempt to do this with defrecord is doomed:

```
(defrecord InfiniteConstant [i]
  clojure.lang.ISeq
  (seq [this]
    (lazy-seq (cons i (seq this)))))
; java.lang.ClassFormatError: Duplicate method
;    name&signature in class file user/InfiniteConstant
```

This is because record types are maps and implement everything maps should—seq along with assoc, dissoc, get, and so forth. Because these are provided for you, you can't implement them again yourself, and thus the preceding exception. For the rare case where you're building your own data structure instead of creating application-level record types, Clojure provides a lower-level deftype construct that's similar to defrecord but doesn't implement anything at all, so implementing seq won't conflict with anything:

```
(deftype InfiniteConstant [i]
  clojure.lang.ISeq
  (seq [this]
    (lazy-seq (cons i (seq this)))))

(take 3 (InfiniteConstant. 5))
;=> (5 5 5)
```

But that also means keyword lookups, assoc, dissoc, and so on will remain unimplemented unless you implement them:

```
(:i (InfiniteConstant. 5))
;=> nil
```

The fields you declare are still public and accessible (although you should try to avoid naming them the same as the methods in java.lang.Object); they just require normal Java interop forms to get at them:

```
(.i (InfiniteConstant. 5))
;=> 5
```

With all that in mind, the following listing is a final implementation of TreeNode using deftype, which lets you implement not only ISeq so that you can use seq instead of xseq, but also IPersistentStack so you can use peek, pop, and conj as well as the fixo- versions.

Listing 9.6   Implementing map interfaces with deftype

```
(deftype TreeNode [val l r]
  FIXO                                    ◁─┐ Implement FIXO
  (fixo-push [_ v]                          │ methods inline
    (if (< v val)
      (TreeNode. val (fixo-push l v) r)
      (TreeNode. val l (fixo-push r v))))
  (fixo-peek [_]
    (if l
      (fixo-peek l)                       ◁─┐ Call a method instead
      val))                                 │ of using recur
  (fixo-pop [_]
    (if l
      (TreeNode. val (fixo-pop l) r)
      r))

  clojure.lang.IPersistentStack           ◁─┐ Implement
  (cons [this v] (fixo-push this v))         │ interfaces
```

```
  (peek [this] (fixo-peek this))
  (pop [this] (fixo-pop this))

  clojure.lang.Seqable
  (seq [t]
    (concat (seq l) [val] (seq r))))
(extend-type nil
  FIXO
  (fixo-push [t v]                          Redefine to use the
    (TreeNode. v nil nil)))                 new TreeNode

(def sample-tree2 (into (TreeNode. 3 nil nil) [5 2 4 6]))
(seq sample-tree2)
;=> (2 3 4 5 6)
```

A final note about `deftype`: it's the one mechanism by which Clojure lets you create classes with volatile and mutable fields. We won't go into it here because using such classes is almost never the right solution. Only when you've learned how Clojure approaches identity and state, how to use reference types, what it means for a field to be volatile, and all the pitfalls related to that, should you even consider creating classes with mutable fields. By then, you'll have no problem understanding the official docs for `deftype`, and you won't need any help from us.

None of the examples we've shown in this section come close to the flexibility of multimethods. All protocol methods dispatch on just the type of the first argument. This is because that's what Java is good at doing quickly, and in many cases it's all the polymorphism that's needed. Clojure once again takes the practical route and makes the highest-performance mechanisms available via protocols, while providing more dynamic behavior than Java does and leaving multimethods on the table for when ultimate flexibility is required.

9.4   *Putting it all together: a fluent builder for chess moves*

People have been known to say that Java is a verbose programming language. This may be true when compared to the Lisp family of languages, but considerable mind share has been devoted to devising ways to mitigate its verbosity. One popular technique is known as the *fluent builder* (Fowler 2005) and can be summed up as the chaining of Java methods to form a more readable and agile instance-construction technique. In this section, we'll show a simple example of a fluent builder supporting the construction of chess move descriptions. We'll then explain how such a technique is unnecessary in Clojure and present an alternative approach that's simpler, concise, and more extensible. We'll use Clojure's records in the final solution, illustrating that Java's class-based paradigm is counter to Clojure's basic principles and often overkill for Java programs.

9.4.1   *Java implementation*

Let's assume that you started by identifying all the component parts of a `Move` class including from and to squares, a flag indicating whether the move is a castling move, and also the desired promotion piece if applicable. (In order to constrain the discussion, we'll limit our idea of a Move to those elements listed.) The next step would be to create a simple class with its properties and a set of constructors, each taking some combination of the expected properties. You'd then generate a set of accessors for the properties, but not their corresponding mutators, because it's probably best for the move instances to be immutable.

Having created this simple class and rolled it out to the customers of the chess move API, you begin to notice that users are sending the to string into the constructor before the from string, which is sometimes placed after the promotion, and so on. After some months of intense design and weeks of development and testing, you release the following elided chess move class:

```java
public class FluentMove {
    private String from, to, promotion = "";
    private boolean castlep;

    public static MoveBuilder desc() { return new MoveBuilder(); }

    public String toString() {
        return "Move " + from +
            " to " + to +
            (castlep ? " castle" : "") +
            (promotion.length() != 0 ? " promote to " + promotion : "");
    }

    public static final class MoveBuilder {
        FluentMove move = new FluentMove();

        public MoveBuilder from(String from) {
            move.from = from; return this;
        }

        public MoveBuilder to(String to) {
            move.to = to; return this;
        }

        public MoveBuilder castle() {
            move.castlep = true; return this;
        }

        public MoveBuilder promoteTo(String promotion) {
            move.promotion = promotion; return this;
        }

        public FluentMove build() { return move; }
    }
}
```

For brevity's sake, this code has a lot of holes, such as missing checks for fence post errors, null, empty strings, assertions, and invariants. It does allow us to illustrate that the code provides a fluent builder given the following main method:

```java
public static void main(String[] args) {
    FluentMove move = FluentMove.desc()
        .from("e2")
```

```
            .to("e4").build();

    System.out.println(move);

    move = FluentMove.desc()
        .from("a1")
        .to("c1")
        .castle().build();

    System.out.println(move);

    move = FluentMove.desc()
        .from("a7")
        .to("a8")
        .promoteTo("Q").build();

    System.out.println(move);
}
//  Move e2 to e4
//  Move a1 to c1 castle
//  Move a7 to a8 promote to Q
```

The original constructor ambiguities have disappeared, with the only trade-off being a slight increase in complexity of the implementation and the breaking of the common Java getter/setter idioms—both of which we're willing to live with. But if you'd started the chess move API as a Clojure project, the code would likely be a very different experience for the end user.

9.4.2 *Clojure implementation*

In lieu of Java's class-based approach, Clojure provides a core set of collection types, and, as you might guess, its map type is a nice candidate for move representation:

```
{:from "e7", :to "e8", :castle? false, :promotion \Q}
```

Simple, no?

In a language like Java, it's common to represent everything as a class—to do otherwise is inefficient, non-idiomatic, or outright taboo. Clojure prefers simplification, providing a set of composite types perfect for representing most categories of problems typically handled by class hierarchies. Using Clojure's composite types makes sense for one simple reason—existing functions, built on a sequence abstraction, *just work*:

```
(defn build-move [& pieces]
  (apply hash-map pieces))

(build-move :from "e7" :to "e8" :promotion \Q)

;=> {:from "e7", :to "e8", :promotion \Q}
```

These two lines effectively replace the Java implementation with an analogous yet more flexible representation. The term *domain-specific language (DSL)* is often thrown around to describe code such as build-move, but to Clojure (and Lisps in general) the line between DSL and API is blurred. The original FluentMove class required a cornucopia of code in order to ensure that the API was agnostic of the ordering of move elements; using a map, you get that for free. Additionally, `FluentMove`, although relatively concise, was still bound by fundamental Java syntactical and semantic constraints.

There's one major problem with this implementation: it doesn't totally replace the Java solution. If you recall, the Java solution used the `toString` method to print its representative form. The existence of a polymorphic print facility in Java is nice, and it allows a class creator to define a default print representation for an object when sent to any Java print stream. This means the same representation is used on the console, in log files, and so on. Using raw maps can't give you this same behavior, so how can you solve this problem?

USING RECORDS

If you instead use a record, then the solution is as simple as this:

```
(defrecord Move [from to castle? promotion]
  Object
  (toString [this]
    (str "Move " (:from this)
         " to " (:to this)
         (if (:castle? this) " castle"
           (if-let [p (:promotion this)]
             (str " promote to " p)
             ""))))))
```

As we mentioned in the previous section, in the body of a record you can take up to two actions: participate in a protocol, or override any of the methods in the `java.lang.Object` class. For the `Move` record, you override `toString` in order to allow it to participate in Java's overarching polymorphic print facility:

```
(str (Move. "e2" "e4" nil nil))
;=> "Move e2 to e4"

(.println System/out (Move. "e7" "e8" nil \Q))
; Move e7 to e8 promote to Q
```

You've once again gone back to positional construction using records, but as we'll show, Clojure even has an answer for this.

SEPARATION OF CONCERNS

Both `FluentMove` and `build-move` make enormous assumptions about the form of the data supplied to them and do no validation of the input. For `FluentMove`, object-oriented principles dictate that the validation of a well-formed move (not a legal move, mind you) should be determined by the class itself. There are a number of problems with this approach, the most obvious being that to determine whether a move is well-formed, the class needs information about the rules of chess. You could rewrite `FluentMove` to throw an exception to prevent illegal moves from being constructed, but the root problem still remains—`FluentMove` instances are too smart. Perhaps you don't see this as a problem, but if you were to extend the API to include other aspects of the game of chess, you'd find that bits of overlapping chess knowledge would be scattered throughout the class hierarchy. By viewing the move structure as a value, Clojure code provides some freedom in the implementation of a total solution:

```
(defn build-move [& {:keys [from to castle? promotion]}]
  {:pre [from to]}
  (Move. from to castle? promotion))

(str (build-move :from "e2" :to "e4"))
;=> "Move e2 to e4"
```

By wrapping the Move constructor in a build-move function, you put the smarts of constructing moves there instead of in the type itself. In addition, using a precondition, you specify the required fields; and by using Clojure's named parameters and argument destructuring, you again ensure argument order independence. As a final added advantage, Clojure's records are maps and as a result can operate in almost every circumstance where a map would. As author Rich Hickey once proclaimed, any new class in general is itself an island, unusable by *any* existing code written by anyone, anywhere. So our point is this: consider throwing the baby out with the bath water.

9.5   *Summary*

Clojure disavows the typical object-oriented model of development. But that's not to say it completely dismisses all that OOP stands for. Instead, Clojure wholeheartedly touts the virtues of interface-oriented programming (or abstraction-oriented programming, as we've called it), in addition to runtime polymorphism. But in both cases, the way that Clojure presents these familiar topics is different from what you may be accustomed to. In almost every circumstance, Clojure's abstraction-oriented facilities will sufficiently represent your problem domain, but there may be times when they can't. We'll preach the virtues of abstractions more throughout the rest of the book, but for now we're compelled to take a side path into an exploration of Clojure's models for managing state.

Mutation and
concurrency

10

Clojure's main tenet isn't the facilitation of concurrency. Instead, Clojure at its core is concerned with the sane management of state, and facilitating concurrent programming naturally falls out of that. Concurrency refers to designing systems using independently executing, logic processes (Pike 2012). A simple concurrent design is a single thread named Tom inserting data into a work queue, as shown in figure 10.1.

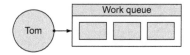

Figure 10.1   Tom, alone

Of course, although this is technically a concurrent design, having Tom work alone doesn't achieve a high degree of concurrency. But if we add another thread to the mix as in figure 10.2, then

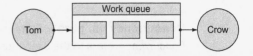

Figure 10.2   Tom inserts data into the work queue

the concurrency in the design begins to become more apparent.

Figure 10.2 is the "Hello World" equivalent for a concurrent message queue such as you might create with something like RabbitMQ (www.rabbitmq.com) or HornetQ (www.jboss.org/hornetq). That is, there is a "producer" named Tom that, whenever he can, inserts some data into the work queue. At the same time (concurrently), there is a "consumer" named Crow that takes available data off the work queue and does something with it. You can ignore the matter of what happens if Tom is slower than Crow or vice versa; the point is, the design illustrates that two entities are operating independently. It's irrelevant whether these two entities actually operate at the same time, because concurrency is more about design than execution details. Sometimes partitioning a system into independent processes is useful regardless of the way that the concurrency is fulfilled at runtime.

In the final illustration of a concurrent design, shown in figure 10.3, you'll notice that we've added another consumer process named Joel. We did this to make one further point: concurrent designs are all about independent processes and not necessarily about operating on related tasks. The details of the tasks are of course domain dependent, but in this design both Crow and Joel could be performing very different tasks on the data fetched from the work queue, or maybe the same task; it doesn't matter. Concurrency is a design strategy only.

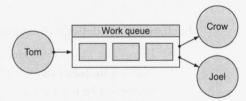

Figure 10.3   Tom inserts data into the work queue while Crow and Joel consume it at their leisure.

Java operates on a shared-state concurrency model built around juggling fine-grained locks that protect access to shared data. Even if you can keep all of your locks in order, rarely does such a strategy scale well, and even less frequently does it foster reusability. But Clojure's state management is simpler to reason about and promotes reusability.

> **CLOJURE APHORISM**   A tangled web of mutation means *any* change to your code potentially occurs in the large.

In this chapter, we'll take the grand tour of Clojure's tools for managing state changes, the so-called *mutation primitives*, and show how Clojure makes concurrent programming not only possible, but fun. Our journey will take us through Clojure's four major mutable references: refs, agents, atoms, and vars. When possible and appropriate, we'll also point out the Java facilities for concurrent programming (including locking) and provide information on the trade-offs involved in choosing them.

> **Concurrency vs. parallelism**
>
> *Concurrency* refers to the execution of disparate tasks at roughly the same time, each sharing a common resource, but not necessarily performing related tasks. The results of concurrent tasks often affect the behavior of other concurrent tasks and therefore contain an element of nondeterminism. *Parallelism* refers to partitioning a task into multiple parts, each run at the same time. Typically, parallel tasks work toward an aggregate goal, and the result of one doesn't affect the behavior of any other parallel task, thus maintaining determinacy. We'll stick to a discussion of concurrency in this chapter, deferring parallelism until chapter 11.

Before we dive into the details of Clojure's reference types, let's start with a high-level overview of Clojure's *software transactional memory (STM)*. A notional definition of STM is that it's a nonblocking way to coordinate concurrent updates between related mutable value cells (Herlihy 1993). We'll discuss the details of Clojure's STM implementation via its ref type in the next section.

10.1   *When to use refs*

> *A faster program that doesn't work right is useless.*
>
> —Simon Peyton-Jones[1]

In chapter 1, we defined three important terms:

- *Time*—The relative moments when events occur
- *State*—A snapshot of an entity's properties at a moment in time
- *Identity*—The logical entity identified by a common stream of states occurring over time

These terms form the foundation for Clojure's model of state management and mutation. In Clojure's model, a program must accommodate the fact that when dealing with identities, it's receiving a snapshot of its properties at a moment in time, not necessarily the most recent. Therefore, all decisions must be made in a continuum. This model is a natural one, because humans and animals alike make decisions based on their current knowledge of an ever-shifting world. Clojure provides some tools for dealing with identity semantics via, among others, its *ref* reference type, the change semantics of which are governed by Clojure's software transactional memory; this ensures state consistency throughout the application timeline, delineated by a *transaction*. A transaction in Clojure is demarked by the dosync form and is used to build a set of the changeable data cells (Shavit 1997) embedded within that should all change together. Similar to a database transaction, the data set in the dosync block changes all together should the transaction succeed and not at all if it fails.

---

[1] In "Beautiful Concurrency," *Beautiful Code* (O'Reilly, 2007).

Clojure currently provides four different reference types to aide in concurrent programming: *refs*, *agents*, *atoms*, and *vars*. All but vars are considered shared references and allow for changes to be seen across threads of execution. The most important point to remember about choosing between reference types is that although their features sometimes overlap, each has an ideal use. The reference types and their primary characteristics are shown in figure 10.4.

The unique feature of refs is that they're *coordinated*. This means reads and writes to multiple refs can be made in a way that guarantees no race conditions. *Asynchronous* means the request to update is queued to happen in another thread some time later,

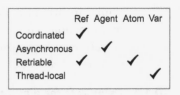

Figure 10.4 Clojure's four reference types are listed across the top, with their features listed down the left. Atoms are for lone synchronous objects. Agents are for asynchronous actions. Vars are for thread-local storage. Refs are for synchronously coordinating multiple objects.

while the thread that made the request continues immediately. *Retriable* indicates that the work done to update a reference's value is speculative and may have to be repeated. Finally, *thread-local* means thread safety is achieved by isolating changes to state to a single thread.

An example dothreads function

To illustrate some major points, we'll use a function `dothreads!` that launches a given number of threads each running a function a number of times:

```
(ns joy.mutation
   (:import java.util.concurrent.Executors))

(def thread-pool                                  Thread pool is
      (Executors/newFixedThreadPool            ◁┘ 2 + available CPUs
         (+ 2 (.availableProcessors (Runtime/getRuntime)))))

(defn dothreads!
   [f & {thread-count :threads       ◁── Number of threads
         exec-count    :times          ◁── Times to run the function
         :or {thread-count 1 exec-count 1}}]    ◁┐
   (dotimes [t thread-count]                       │ Defaults
     (.submit thread-pool
              #(dotimes [_ exec-count] (f)))))   ◁── Call the function
```

The `dothreads!` function is of limited utility—throwing a bunch of threads at a function to see if it breaks:

```
(dothreads! #(.print System/out "Hi ") :threads 2 :times 2)
Hi Hi Hi Hi
```

Value access via the `@` reader feature or the `deref` function provides a uniform client interface, regardless of the reference type used. On the other hand, the write mechanism associated with each reference type is unique by name and specific behavior, but similar in structure. Each referenced value is changed in accordance with the result[2] of a function. The result of this function becomes the new referenced value. Finally, all reference types provide *consistency* by allowing the association of a validator function via `setvalidator` that will be used as the final gatekeeper on any value change.

10.1.1 *Using refs for a mutable game board*

A ref is a reference type allowing synchronous, coordinated change to its contained value. What does this mean? By enforcing that any change to a ref's value occurs in a transaction, Clojure can guarantee that change happens in a way that maintains a consistent view of the referenced value in all threads. But there's a question as to what constitutes coordination. Let's construct a simple vector of refs to represent a 3 x 3 chess board.

Listing 10.1 3 x 3 chess board representation using Clojure refs

```
(def initial-board                      ←──┐ Seed is a vector
     [[:- :k :-]                            │ of vectors
      [:- :- :-]
      [:- :K :-]])

(defn board-map [f board]                   │ Each cell is
  (vec (map #(vec (for [s %] (f s)))        ←─┘ its own ref
           board)))
```

In a change from listing 1.5, the lowercase keyword represents a black king piece and the uppercase a white king piece. We've chosen to represent the mutable board as a 2D vector of refs (returned by `board-map`). There are other ways to represent a board, but we've chosen this because it's nicely illustrative—the act of moving a piece requires a *coordinated* change in two reference squares, or else a change to one square in one thread could lead to another thread observing that square as occupied. Likewise, this problem requires synchronous change, because it would be no good for pieces of the same color to move consecutively. Refs are the only game in town to ensure that the necessary coordinated change occurs synchronously. Before we show refs in action, let's define the auxiliary functions.

Listing 10.2 Setting up the refs example

```
Define          ──▷ (defn reset-board!
mutable             "Resets the board state.  Generally these types of functions are a
state                bad idea, but matters of page count force our hand."
                    []
                    (def board (board-map ref initial-board))
                    (def to-move (ref [[:K [2 1]] [:k [0 1]]]))
                    (def num-moves (ref 0)))                    │ Define legal
                                                                ←─┘ king moves
                    (def king-moves
                      (partial neighbors
```

---

[2] Except for `ref-set` on refs, `reset!` on atoms, and `set!` on vars.

```
       [[-1 -1] [-1 0] [-1 1] [0 -1] [0 1] [1 -1] [1 0] [1 1]] 3))
(defn good-move?
  [to enemy-sq]
  (when (not= to enemy-sq)
    to))
```
> Return nil if "to"
> is occupied

```
(defn choose-move
  "Randomly choose a legal move"
  [[[mover mpos] [_ enemy-pos]]]
  [mover (some #(good-move? % enemy-pos)
               (shuffle (king-moves mpos)))]])
```
> Get first good
> move ...

> ... from shuffled
> list of moves

The `to-move` structure describes the order of moves, so in the base case, it states that the white king `:K` at y=2,x=1 moves before the black king `:k` at y=0,x=1. The example reuses the `neighbors` function from chapter 5 to build a legal-move generator for chess king pieces. You do this by using `partial` supplied with the kingly position deltas and the `board` size. An illustration of how the `king-moves` function calculates the legal moves is shown in figure 10.5.

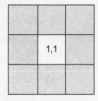

The `good-move?` function states that a move to a square is legal only if the enemy isn't already located there. The function `choose-move` destructures the `to-move` vector and chooses a good move from a shuffled sequence of legal moves. The `choose-move` function can be tested in isolation:

Figure 10.5 The king neighbors of cell 1,1

```
(reset-board!)
(take 5 (repeatedly #(choose-move @to-move)))
;=> ([:K [1 0]] [:K [1 2]] [:K [1 1]] [:K [1 2]] [:K [1 0]])
```

And now let's create a function to make a random move for the piece at the front of `to-move`, shown next.

Listing 10.3 Using `alter` to update refs in a transaction

```
(defn place [[from to] to)

(defn move-piece [[piece dest] [[_ src] _]]
  (alter (get-in board dest) place piece)
  (alter (get-in board src ) place :-)
  (alter num-moves inc))
```
> Place moving
> piece

```
(defn update-to-move [move]
  (alter to-move #(vector (second %) move)))
```
> Swap in new
> move

```
(defn make-move []
  (let [move (choose-move @to-move)]
    (dosync (move-piece move @to-move))
    (dosync (update-to-move move))))
```
> Update board and num-moves
> in one transaction ...

> ... then update to-move in
> another transaction (beware!)

The `make-move` function calls `alter` four different times to update all the refs necessary to represent making a move. You pass the `place` function to `alter` in `move-piece`, which states "given a `to` piece and a `from` piece, always return the `to` piece." With these functions in place, we reset the board and made a couple of moves:

```
(reset-board!)

(make-move)
;=> [[:k [0 1]] [:K [2 0]]]

(board-map deref board)
;=> [[:- :k :-] [:- :- :-] [:K :- :-]]

(make-move)
;=> [[:K [2 0]] [:k [1 1]]]

(board-map deref board)
;=> [[:- :- :-] [:- :k :-] [:K :- :-]]
```

This looks pretty good. The specific moves you see should be different, but as long as the white and black kings are taking turns making valid moves, you're doing well. So why not push it a bit harder? Try running the same `make-move` function from 100 threads simultaneously:

```
(dothreads! make-move :threads 100 :times 100)

(board-map deref board)
;=> [[:- :- :-] [:- :K :-] [:- :- :K]]
```

Clearly something has gone awry. Despite using refs for all of the mutable state, we ended up with two white kings on the board and lost the black king entirely. If you run this code on your own machine, you may see something slightly different (for example, two black kings), but in all likelihood what you see will be wrong. The reason lies in splitting the updates of the `to` and `from` refs into different transactions described by the two separate uses of `dosync` in `make-move`. Judging by its behavior, this is not correct; but to understand why requires an understanding of software transactional memory, starting with what exactly a *transaction* is.

10.1.2 Transactions

Within the first few moments of using Clojure's STM, you'll notice something different than you may be accustomed to: no locks. Because there's no need for ad hoc locking schemes when using STM, there's no chance of deadlock. Likewise, Clojure's STM doesn't require the use of monitors and as a result is free from lost wakeup conditions. Behind the scenes, Clojure's STM uses *multiversion concurrency control (MVCC)* to ensure *snapshot isolation*. In simpler terms, snapshot isolation means each transaction gets its own view of the data it's interested in. This *snapshot* is made up of in-transaction reference values, forming the foundation of MVCC (Ullman 1988). As illustrated in figure 10.5, each transaction merrily chugs along making changes to in-transaction values only, oblivious to and ambivalent about other transactions. At the conclusion of the transaction, the local values are examined against the modification target for conflicts.

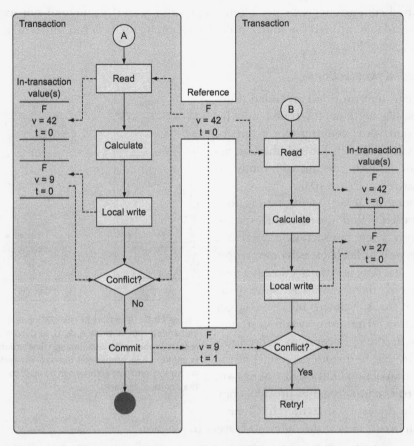

Figure 10.5 Illustrating an STM retry: Clojure's STM works much like a database.

An example of a simple possible conflict is if another transaction B committed a change to a target reference during the time that transaction A was working, thus causing A to retry. If no conflicts are found, then the in-transaction values are *committed* (set as the final value) and the target references are modified with their updated values. Another advantage that STM provides is that in the case of an exception during a transaction, the in-transaction values are thrown away and the exception is propagated outward. In the case of lock-based schemes, exceptions can complicate matters, because in most cases locks need to be released (and in some cases, in the correct order) before an exception can be safely propagated up the call stack.

Because each transaction has its own isolated snapshot, there's no danger in retrying—the data is never modified until a successful commit occurs. STM transactions can easily nest without taking additional measures to facilitate composition. In languages that provide explicit locking for concurrency, matters of composability are often difficult, if not impossible. The reasons for this are far-reaching, and the mitigating forces (Goetz 2006) are complex, but the primary reasons tend to be because lock-based concurrency schemes often hinge on a secret incantation not explicitly understandable through the source itself: for example, the order in which to take and release a set of locks.

10.1.3 *Embedded transactions*

In systems that provide embedded transactions, it's common for transactions to be nested, thus limiting the scope of restarts (Gray 1992). Embedding transactions in Clojure operate differently, as summarized in figure 10.6.

In some database systems, transactions can be used to limit the scope of a restart, as shown when transaction embedded.b restarts only as far back as its own scope. Clojure has only one transaction at a time per thread, thus causing all subtransactions to be subsumed into the larger transaction. Therefore, when a restart occurs in the (conceptual) subtransaction clojure.b, it causes a restart of the larger transaction. Although not shown, some transaction systems provide committal in each subtransaction; in Clojure, commit occurs only at the outermost larger transaction.

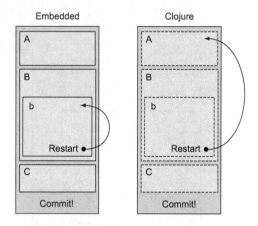

Figure 10.6   A restart in any of Clojure's embedded transactions A, B, b, or C causes a restart in the entire subsuming transaction. This is unlike a fully embedded transaction system, where the subtransactions can be used to restrain the scope of restarts.

10.1.4 *The things that STM makes easy*

The phrase TANSTAAFL, meaning "There ain't no such thing as a free lunch," was popularized in the excellent sci-fi novel *The Moon Is a Harsh Mistress* (Heinlein 1966) and is an apt response to the view that STM is a panacea for concurrency complexities.

As you proceed through this chapter, we urge you to keep this in the back of your mind, because it's important to realize that although Clojure facilitates concurrent programming, it doesn't solve it for you. But there are a few things that Clojure's STM implementation simplifies in solving difficult concurrent problems.

CONSISTENT INFORMATION

The STM allows you to perform arbitrary sets of read/write operations on arbitrary sets of data in a consistent (Papadimitriou 1986) way. By providing these assurances, the STM allows your programs to make decisions given overlapping subsets of information. Likewise, Clojure's STM helps to solve the reporting problem: the problem of getting a consistent view of the world in the face of massive concurrent modification and reading, without manual locking.

No need for locks

In applications of any size, the inclusion of locks for managing concurrent access to shared data adds complexity. Many factors add to this complexity, but chief among them are the following:

- You can't use locks without supplying extensive error handling. This is critical in avoiding orphaned locks (locks held by a thread that has died).
- Every application requires that you reinvent a whole new locking scheme.
- Locking schemes often require that you impose a total ordering that's difficult to enforce in client code, frequently leading to a priority-inversion scenario.

Locking schemes are difficult to design correctly and become increasingly so as the number of locks grows. Clojure's STM eliminates the need for locking and as a result eliminates dreaded deadlock scenarios. Clojure's STM provides a story for managing state consistently. Adhering to this story will go a long way toward helping you solve software problems effectively. This is true even when concurrent programming isn't a factor in your design.

ACI

The verbiage of database transactions includes the well-known acronym ACID, which refers to the properties ensuring transactional reliability. All of Clojure's reference types provide the first three properties: *atomicity*, *consistency*, and *isolation*. The other, *durability*, is missing due to the fact that Clojure's STM resides in memory and is therefore subject to data loss in the face of catastrophic system failure. Clojure relegates the problem of maintaining durability to the application developer instead of supplying common strategies by default: database persistence, external application logs, serialization, and so on.

10.1.5 Potential downsides

There are two potential problems inherent in STMs in general, which we'll only touch on briefly here: write skew and live-lock.

Write skew

For the most part, you can write correct programs by putting all access and changes to references in appropriately scoped transactions. The one exception to this is *write skew*, which occurs in MVCC systems such as Clojure's. Write skew can occur when one transaction uses the value of a reference to regulate its behavior but doesn't write to that reference. At the same time, another transaction updates the value for that same reference. One way to avoid this is to do a "dummy write" in the first transaction, but Clojure provides a less costly solution: the `ensure` function. This scenario is rare in Clojure applications, but possible.

Live-lock

Live-lock refers to a set of transaction(s) that repeatedly restart one another. Clojure combats live-lock in a couple of ways. First, there are transaction-restart limits that raise an error when breached. Generally this occurs when the units of work within some number of transactions are too large. The second way that Clojure combats live-lock is called *barging*. Barging refers to some careful logic in the STM implementation that lets an older transaction continue running while younger transactions retry.

10.1.6 *The things that make STM unhappy*

Certain things can rarely (if ever) be safely performed in a transaction, and in this section we'll talk briefly about each.

I/O

Any I/O operation in the body of a transaction is highly discouraged. Due to restarts, the embedded I/O could at best be rendered useless and could at worst cause great harm . For example, if you choose to embed log messages inside a transaction, then a new log entry will be created for every restart on said transaction. This circumstance is likely to make your log files hard to read and bloated. It's advised that you employ the io! macro whenever performing I/O operations:

```
(io! (.println System/out "Haikeeba!"))
; Haikeeba!
```

When this same statement is used in a transaction, an exception is thrown:

```
(dosync (io! (.println System/out "Haikeeba!")))
; java.lang.IllegalStateException: I/O in transaction
```

Although it may not be feasible to use io! in every circumstance, it's a good idea to do so whenever possible.

CLASS INSTANCE MUTATION

Another thing you should avoid in transactions is object mutation. Unrestrained instance mutation often isn't *idempotent*, meaning that running a set of mutating operations multiple times frequently displays different results.

LARGE TRANSACTIONS

Although the size of transactions is highly subjective, the general rule of thumb when partitioning units of work should always be *get in and get out as quickly as possible.*

It's important to understand that transactions help to simplify the management of state, but you should strive to minimize their footprint in your code. The use of I/O and instance mutation is an essential part of many applications; it's important to work to separate your programs into logical partitions, keeping I/O and its ilk on one side, and transaction processing and mutation on the other.

Fortunately, Clojure provides a powerful toolset for making the management of mutability sane, but none of the tools provide a shortcut to thinking. Multithreaded programming is a difficult problem, independent of specifics, and Clojure's state-management tools won't solve this problem magically. It was relying on this sense of magic that got us in trouble with the misbehaving game board example. Let's see if we can fix the example transactions.

10.2 Refactoring with refs

In this section, we'll discuss some refactorings that are possible for the chess board example. You'll first fix some nagging problems with the example. Next, we'll discuss how you can take advantage of *commutativity* (action order independence) in the design using Clojure's commute function. Finally, we'll talk about how to adjust a ref's default settings to avoid excessive retries.

10.2.1 Fixing the game board example

Take another look at the make-move function that was misbehaving earlier:

```
(defn make-move []
  (let [move (choose-move @to-move)]
    (dosync (move-piece move @to-move))
    (dosync (update-to-move move))))
```

The problem was that the board ended up in a state you wish to be impossible. This implies that the transaction boundaries you provided allow changes to be made independently that you wish to be dependent. Specifically, the two separate dosync forms mean that moving a piece on the board can happen independently of updating whose turn it is.

Being separated into two transactions means they're (potentially) running on different timelines. Because board and to-move are dependent, their states *must* be coordinated into a single transaction, but you've broken that necessity with make-move. Therefore, somewhere along the line board was updated from two subsequent timelines where it was :K's turn to move! As shown in figure 10.7, either transaction can commit or be restarted; but because the two refs were never in the same transaction, the occurrences of these conditions become staggered over time, leading to inconsistent values.

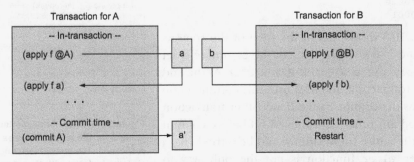

Figure 10.7 If refs A and B should be coordinated, then splitting their updates across different transactions is dangerous. Value a? is eventually committed to A, but the update for B never commits due to retry, and coordination is lost. Another error occurs if B's change depends on A's value and A and B are split across transactions. There are no guarantees that the dependent values refer to the same timeline.

In the following new version, `make-move-v2`, the `alter` function is still called four times, but now in a single `dosync`. Thus the `from` and `to` positions, as well as the `to-move` refs, are updated in a coordinated fashion:

```
(defn make-move-v2 []
  (dosync                                          ⟵── A single transaction
    (let [move (choose-move @to-move)]
      (move-piece move @to-move)
      (update-to-move move))))
```

A single run of `make-move` still looks okay:

```
(reset-board!)
(make-move)
;=> [[:k [0 1]] [:K [2 0]]]

(board-map deref board)
;=> [[:- :k :-] [:- :- :-] [:K :- :-]]

@num-moves
;=> 1
```

You've successfully made a change to two board squares, the `to-move` structure, and `num-moves` using the uniform state-change model. By itself, this model of state change is compelling. The semantics are simple to understand: give a reference a function that determines how the value changes. This is the model of sane state change that Clojure preaches. But you can now throw a bunch of threads at this solution and still maintain consistency:

```
(dothreads! make-move-v2 :threads 100 :times 100)
(board-map #(dosync (deref %)) board)
;=> [[:k :- :-] [:- :- :-] [:K :- :-]]
@to-move
;=> [[:k [0 0]] [:K [2 0]]]
@num-moves
;=> 10001
```

Figure 10.8 shows that at the time of the transaction, the *in-transaction* value of the `to` square is set to (apply place @SQUARE-REF PIECE). At the end of the transaction, the STM uses this in-transaction value as the commit value. If any other transaction updated any other coordinated ref before commit time, the entire transaction would be retried.

The `alter` function is not the only way to update the value stored in a ref. Let's look at a couple others.

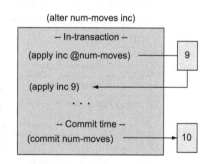

Figure 10.8   The in-transaction value 9 for the ref `num-moves` is retrieved in the body of the transaction and manipulated with the `alter` function `inc`. The resulting value 10 is eventually used for the commit-time value, unless a retry is required.

10.2.2 *Commutative change with commute*

Figure 10.8 showed that using alter can cause a transaction to retry if a ref it depends on is modified and committed while it's running. But there may be circumstances where the value of a ref in a given transaction isn't important to its completion semantics. For example, the num-moves ref is a simple counter, and surely its value at any given time is irrelevant for determining how it should be incremented. To handle these loose dependency circumstances, Clojure offers an operation named commute that takes a function to apply to a ref. Of particular note is that the function you give to commute is run at least twice during the course of a transaction to help increase the level of concurrency around the given reference. Increasing the concurrency in a system is good, right? Well, maybe. What if you were to change the move-piece function to use the commute function instead of alter?

```
(defn move-piece [[piece dest] [[_ src] _]]
  (commute (get-in board dest) place piece)
  (commute (get-in board src ) place :-)
  (commute num-moves inc))

(reset-board!)

(dothreads! make-move-v2 :threads 100 :times 100)

(board-map deref board)
;=> [[:K :- :-] [:- :- :-] [:- :- :k]]

@to-move
;=> [[:K [0 0]] [:k [2 2]]]
```

Everything looks great! But you can't assume the same thing will work for update-to-move:

```
(defn update-to-move [move]
  (commute to-move #(vector (second %) move)))

(dothreads! make-move-v2 :threads 100 :times 100)

(board-map #(dosync (deref %)) board)
;=> [[:- :- :-] [:- :K :-] [:- :- :K]]

@to-move
;=> [[:K [2 2]] [:K [1 1]]]
```

Thanks to your rash decision, you've once again introduced inconsistency into the system. But why? The reason lies in the fact that the new update-to-move isn't amenable to the semantics of the commute function. commute allows for more concurrency in the STM by devaluing in-transaction value disparity resulting from another transaction's commit. In other words, figure 10.9 shows that the in-transaction value of a ref is initially set as when using alter, but the *commit time* value is reset just before commute commits.

By retrieving the most current value for a ref at the time of commit, the values committed might not be those corresponding to the in-transaction state. This leads to a condition of update reordering that the application *must* accommodate. Of course,

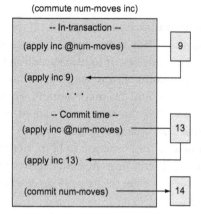

Figure 10.9 The in-transaction value 9 in the num-moves ref is retrieved in the body of the transaction and manipulated with the `commute` function. But the `commute` function `inc` is again run at commit time with the current value 13 contained in the ref. The result of this action serves as the committed value 14.

this new function isn't commutative, because `vector` doesn't give the same answer if its argument order is switched.

Using `commute` is useful as long as the following conditions aren't problematic:

- The value you see in-transaction may not be the value that gets committed at commit time.
- The function you give to `commute` will be run at least twice: once to compute the in-transaction value, and again to compute the commit value. It might be run any number of times.

Although you'll incur a non-zero cost for running the change function twice, this cost is assumed to be small compared to the cost of tracking a changing reference for the duration of a transaction.

10.2.3 *Vulgar change with ref-set*

The function `ref-set` is different from `alter` and `commute` in that instead of changing a ref based on a function of its value, it does so given a raw value:

```
(dosync (ref-set to-move '[[:K [2 1]] [:k [0 1]]]))

;=> [[:K [2 1]] [:k [0 1]]]
```

In general, this sort of vulgar change should be avoided. But because the refs have become out of sync during your experiments with `commute`, you can be forgiven in using `ref-set` to fix it—just this once.

Fixing write skew with ensure

Snapshot isolation means that within a transaction, all enclosed ref states represent the *same* moment in time. Any ref value that you see in a transaction will *never* change unless *you* change it within that transaction. Your algorithms should be devised so that all you care about is that the values of the references haven't changed before commit (unless your change function is commutative, as mentioned previously). If those values have changed, then the transaction retries, and you try again.

Earlier, we talked about write skew, a condition that occurs when you make decisions based on the in-transaction value of a ref that's never written to, which is also changed at the same time. Avoiding write skew is accomplished using Clojure's `ensure` function, which guarantees that a read-only ref isn't modified by another thread. The `make-move` function isn't subject to write skew because it has no invariants on read data and in fact never reads a ref that it doesn't eventually write. This design is ideal because it allows other threads to calculate moves without having to stop them, while any given transaction does the same. But in your own applications, you may be confronted with a true read-invariant scenario, and it's in such a scenario that `ensure` will help.

10.2.4 Refs under stress

After you've created your refs and written your transactions, and simple isolated tests are passing, you may still run into difficulties in larger integration tests because of how refs behave under stress from multiple transactions. As a rule of thumb, it's best to avoid having both short- and long-running transactions interacting with the same ref. Clojure's STM implementation usually compensates eventually regardless, but you'll soon see some less-than-ideal consequences of ignoring this rule.

To demonstrate this problem, listing 10.4 shows a function named `stress-ref` designed specifically to over-stress a ref. It does this by starting a long-running or slow transaction in another thread, where work is simulated by a 200 ms sleep, but all it's really doing is reading the ref in a transaction. This requires the STM to know of a stable value for the ref for the full 200 ms. Meanwhile, the main thread runs quick transactions 500 times in a row, each one incrementing the value in the ref and thereby frustrating the slow transaction's attempts to see a stable value. The STM works to overcome this frustration by growing the history of values kept for the ref. But by default, this history is limited to 10 entries, and the perverse function can easily saturate that.

> **Listing 10.4 How to make a ref squirm**

```
(defn stress-ref [r]
  (let [slow-tries (atom 0)]
    (future
      (dosync                          ⟵┐ One long-running
        (swap! slow-tries inc)            │ transaction
        (Thread/sleep 200)
        @r)
      (println (format "r is: %s, history: %d, after: %d tries"
                       @r (.getHistoryCount r) @slow-tries)))
    (dotimes [i 500]
      (Thread/sleep 10)                 ⟵┐ 500 very quick
      (dosync (alter r inc)))            │ transactions
    :done))
```

What happens when you run the `stress-ref` function? `r` is incremented all the way to 500 without the slow transaction ever succeeding:

```
(stress-ref (ref 0))
;=> :done
; r is: 500, history: 10, after: 26 tries
```

You may see a slightly different number of tries, but the important detail is that the slow transaction is unable to successfully commit and print the value of `r` until the main thread has finished its frantic looping and returned `:done`. The ref's history started at a default of 0 and grew to 10, but this was still insufficient.

Remember that the real problem here is mixing short- and long-running transactions on the same ref. But if this is truly unavoidable, Clojure allows you to create a ref with a more generous cap on the history size:

```
(stress-ref (ref 0 :max-history 30))
; r is: 410, history: 20, after: 21 tries
;=> :done
```

Again, your numbers may be different, but this time the ref's history grew sufficiently (reaching 20 in this run) to allow the slow transaction to finish first and report about `r` before all 500 quick transactions completed. In this run, only 410 had finished when the slow transaction committed.

But the slow transaction still had to be retried 20 times, with the history growing one step larger each time, before it was able to complete. If your slow transactions were doing real work instead of sleeping, this could represent a lot of wasted computing effort. If your tests or production environment reveal this type of situation and the underlying transaction size difference can't be resolved, one final ref option can help. Because you can see that the history will likely need to be 20 anyway, you may as well start it closer to its goal:

```
(stress-ref (ref 0 :min-history 15 :max-history 30))
; r is: 97, history: 19, after: 5 tries
;=> :done
```

This time the slow transaction finished before even 100 of the quick transactions had finished; and even though the history grew to roughly the same size, starting it at 15 meant the slow transaction retried only 4 times before succeeding.

The use of refs to guarantee coordinated change is generally simple for managing state in a synchronous fashion, and tuning with `:min-history` and `:max-history` is rarely required. But not all changes in your applications will require coordination, nor will they need to be synchronous. For these circumstances, Clojure also provides another reference type, the agent, that provides independent asynchronous changes. We'll discuss agents next.

10.3   *When to use agents*

Like all Clojure reference types, an agent represents an *identity*, a specific thing whose value can change over time. Each agent has a queue to hold actions that need to be performed on its value, and each action produces a new value for the agent to hold and pass to the subsequent action. Thus the state of the agent advances through time, action after action, and by their nature only one action at a time can be operating on a given agent. Of course, other actions can be operating on other agents at the same time, each in its own thread.

You can queue an action on any agent by using send or send-off, the minor difference between which we'll discuss later. Agents are integrated with STM transactions, and within a transaction any actions sent are held until the transaction commits or are thrown away if the transaction retries. Thus send and send-off are *not* considered side effects in the context of a dosync, because they handle retries correctly and gracefully.

Agents are created with the agent function:

```
(def joy (agent []))
```

That creates an agent with an initial value of an empty vector. Now you can send an action to it:

```
(send joy conj "First edition")
```

Here is its current value:

```
@joy  ;; read as (deref joy)
;=> ["First edition"]
```

If you slow the action down a little, you can see the old value while the next action is still running. Start by defining a slow version of conj:

```
(defn slow-conj [coll item]
  (Thread/sleep 1000)
  (conj coll item))
```

As soon as you send an action to the agent, the REPL prints the current value of the agent, but slow-conj is still running so the value printed will not yet have changed:

```
(send joy slow-conj "Second edition")
;=> #<Agent@5efefc32: ["First edition"]>
```

But if you wait a second, a final call to deref reveals the consequence of slow-conj:

```
@joy
;=> ["First edition" "Second edition"]
```

10.3.1 *In-process vs. distributed concurrency models*

Both Clojure and Erlang are designed (Armstrong 2007) specifically with concurrent programming in mind, and Erlang's process[3] model is similar in some ways to Clojure agents, so it's fair to briefly compare how they each approach the problem. Erlang takes a distributed, share-nothing (Armstrong 2007b) approach; Clojure instead promotes

---

[3] It's interesting that popular opinion has tagged Erlang processes with the *actor* tag although the language implementers rarely, if ever, uses that term. Because the Erlang elite choose not to use that term, we'll avoid doing so ... almost.

shared, immutable data. The key to Clojure's success is the fact that its composite data structures are immutable, because immutable structures can be freely shared among disparate threads. Erlang's composite data structures are also immutable, but because the communication model is distributed, the underlying theme is always one of dislocation. The implications of this are that all knowledge of the world under consideration is provided via messages. But with Clojure's in-process model, data structures are always accessible directly, as illustrated in figure 10.10, whereas Erlang makes copies of the data sent back and forth between processes. This works well for Erlang and allows it to provide its fault-recovery guarantees, but many application domains can benefit from the shared-memory model provided by Clojure.

The second difference is that Erlang messages block on reception, opening up the possibility for deadlock. On the other hand, when interacting with Clojure agents, both `sends` and `derefs` proceed immediately and never block or wait on the agent. Clojure does have an `await` function that can be used to block a thread until a particular agent has processed a message, but this function is specifically disallowed in agent threads (and also STM transactions) in order to prevent accidentally creating this sort of deadlock.

The final difference lies in the fact that agents allow for arbitrary update functions, whereas Erlang processes are bound to static pattern-matched, message-handling routines. In other words, pattern matching couples the data and update logic, whereas agents decouple them. Erlang is an excellent language for solving the extremely difficult problem of distributed computation, but Clojure's concurrency mechanisms

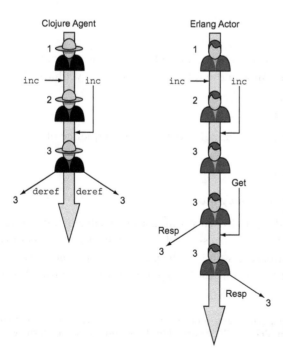

Figure 10.10   Clojure agents versus Erlang processes: each agent and process starts with the value 1. Both receive an `inc` request simultaneously but can process only one at a time, so more are queued. Requests to the process are queued until a response can be delivered, whereas any number of simultaneous `derefs` can be done on an agent. Despite what this illustration may suggest, an agent is not an actor with a hat on.

service the in-process programming model more flexibly than Erlang allows (Clementson 2008).

10.3.2 Controlling I/O with an agent

One handy use for agents is to serialize access to a resource, such as a file or another I/O stream. For example, imagine you want to provide a way for multiple threads to report their progress on various tasks, giving each report a unique incrementing number.

Because the state you want to hold is known, you can go ahead and create the agent:

```
(def log-agent (agent 0))
```

Now you supply an action function to send to log-agent. All action functions take as their first argument the current state of the agent and can take any number of other arguments that are sent:

```
(defn do-log [msg-id message]
  (println msg-id ":" message)
  (inc msg-id))
```

Here msg-id is the state—the first time do-log is sent to the agent, msg-id is 0. The return value of the action function will be the new agent state, incrementing it to 1 after that first action.

Now you need to do some work worth logging about, but for the example in the next listing, let's pretend.

Listing 10.5   Controlling I/O with an agent

```
(defn do-step [channel message]
  (Thread/sleep 1)                         ← Simulate work
  (send-off log-agent do-
    log (str channel message)))            ← Send an action
                                             to log-agent

(defn three-step [channel]                 ← Execute steps,
  (do-step channel " ready to begin (step 0)")   logging as you go
  (do-step channel " warming up (step 1)")
  (do-step channel " really getting going now (step 2)")   ← In real apps,
  (do-step channel " done! (step 3)"))       there's work
                                             between log steps

(defn all-together-now []                  ← Start three threads
  (dothreads! #(three-step "alpha"))
  (dothreads! #(three-step "beta"))        ← Each thread calls
  (dothreads! #(three-step "omega")))        three-step
```

To see how log-agent correctly queues and serializes the messages, you need to start a few threads, each yammering away at the agent. You do this by calling (all-together-now), which generates output like the following:

```
0 : alpha ready to begin (step 0)
1 : omega ready to begin (step 0)
```

```
2  : beta ready to begin (step 0)
3  : alpha warming up (step 1)
4  : alpha really getting going now (step 2)
5  : omega warming up (step 1)
6  : alpha done! (step 3)
7  : omega really getting going now (step 2)
8  : omega done! (step 3)
9  : beta warming up (step 1)
10 : beta really getting going now (step 2)
11 : beta done! (step 3)
```

Your output is likely to look different, but what should be exactly the same are the stable, incrementing IDs assigned by the agent, even while the alpha, beta, and omega threads fight for control.

There are several other possible approaches to solving this problem, and it can be constructive to contrast them. The simplest alternative would be to hold a lock while printing and incrementing. In addition to the general risk of deadlocks when a complex program has multiple locks, there are some specific drawbacks even if this would be the only lock in play. Each client thread would block any time there was contention for the lock, and unless some fairness mechanism were used, there'd be at least a slight possibility of one or more threads being starved and never having an opportunity to print or proceed with their work. Because agent actions are queued and don't block waiting for their action to be processed, neither of these is a concern.

Another option would be to use a queue to hold pending log messages. Client threads would be able to add messages to the queue without blocking and with adequate fairness. But you'd generally need to dedicate a thread to popping messages from the queue and printing them, or write code to handle starting and stopping the printing thread as needed. Why write such code when agents do this for you already? When no actions are queued, the agent in this example has no thread assigned to it.[4]

Agents have other features that may or may not be useful in any given situation. One is that the current state of an agent can be observed cheaply. In the previous example, this would allow you to discover the ID of the next message to be written out, as follows:

```
@log-agent
;=> 11
```

Here the agent is idle—no actions are queued or running, but the same expression would work equally well if the agent were running.

Other features include the `await` and `await-for` functions, which allow a sending thread to block until all the actions it's sent to a given set of agents have completed. This could be useful in this logging example if you wanted to be sure a particular message had been written out before proceeding:

---

[4] Using agents for logging might not be appropriate in all cases. For example, in probing scenarios, the number of log events could be extremely high. Coupling this volume with serialization could make the agent unable to catch its ever-growing queue.

```
(do-step "important: " "this must go out")
(await log-agent)
```

The `await-for` function is similar but allows you to specify a number of milliseconds after which to time out, even if the queued actions still haven't completed.

A final feature agents provide is that the set of actions you can send to an agent is *open*. You can tell an agent to do something that wasn't even conceived of at the time the agent was designed. For example, you could tell the agent to skip ahead several IDs, and this action would be queued up along with all the `log-message` actions and executed by the agent when its turn came:

```
(send log-agent (fn [_] 1000))

(do-step "epsilon " "near miss")
; 1000 : epsilon near miss
```

This is another area in which Clojure allows you to extend your design on the fly instead of requiring recompiling or even restarting your app. If you're paying attention, you might wonder why the last example uses `send` rather than `send-off`.

10.3.3 *The difference between send and send-off*

You can use either `send` or `send-off` with any agent. When you use `send-off`, as in most of the examples so far, only a single action queue is involved: the one managed by the individual agent. Any time the agent has a `send-off` action queued, it has a thread assigned to it, working through the queue. With `send`, there's a second queue: actions still go into the agent's queue, but then the agent itself queues up waiting for a thread from a fixed-sized pool of threads. The size of this fixed pool is based on the number of processors the JVM is running on, so it's a bad idea to use `send` with any actions that might block, tying up one of the limited number of threads. These differences are illustrated in figure 10.11.

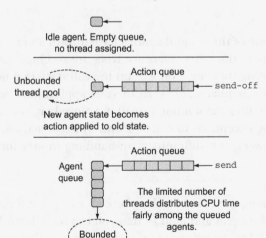

Figure 10.11 **When an agent is idle, no CPU resources are being consumed. Each action is sent to an agent using either send or send-off, which determines which thread pool is used to dequeue and apply the action. Because actions queued with send are applied by a limited thread pool, the agents queue up for access to these threads—a constraint that doesn't apply to actions queued with send-off.**

You can make this scenario play out if you make a gaggle of agents and send them actions that sleep for a moment. Here's a little function that does this, using whichever send function you specify, and then waits for all the actions to complete:

```
(defn exercise-agents [send-fn]
  (let [agents (map #(agent %) (range 10))]
    (doseq [a agents]
      (send-fn a (fn [_] (Thread/sleep 1000))))
    (doseq [a agents]
      (await a))))
```

If you use `send-off`, all the agents begin their one-second wait more or less simultaneously, each in its own thread. The entire sequence of them completes in slightly over one second:

```
(time (exercise-agents send-off))
; "Elapsed time: 1008.771296 msecs"
```

Now we can demonstrate why it's a bad idea to mix send with actions that block:

```
(time (exercise-agents send))
; "Elapsed time: 3001.555086 msecs"
```

The exact elapsed time you see will depend on the number of processors you have; but if you have fewer than eight, this example will take at least two seconds to complete. The threads in the fixed-size pool are clogged up waiting for `sleep` to finish, so the other agents queue up waiting for a free thread. Because clearly the computer could complete all 10 actions in about one second using `send-off`, using `send` is a bad idea.

So that's it: `send` is for actions that stay busy using the processor and not blocking on I/O or other threads, whereas `send-off` is for actions that might block, sleep, or otherwise tie up the thread. This is why the earlier example used `send-off` for the threads that printed log lines and `send` for the one that did no I/O at all.

10.3.4 *Error handling*

You've been fortunate so far—none of these agent actions have thrown an exception. But real life is rarely so kind. Most of the other reference types are synchronous, and so exceptions thrown while updating their state bubble up the call stack in a normal way, to be caught (or not) with a regular `try/catch` in your application. Because agent actions run in other threads after the sending thread has moved on, you need a different mechanism for handling exceptions that are thrown by agent actions. As of Clojure 1.2, you can choose between two different error-handling modes for each agent: `:continue` and `:fail`.

:FAIL MODE

By default, new agents start out using the `:fail` mode, where an exception thrown by an agent's action is captured by the agent and held so that you can see it later. Meanwhile, the agent is considered *failed* or *stopped* and stops processing its action queue— all the queued actions have to wait patiently until someone clears up the agent's error.

One common mistake when dealing with agents is to forget that your action function *must* take at least one argument for the agent's current state. For example, you might try to reset the log-agent's current message ID like this:

```
(send log-agent (fn [] 2000))    ; incorrect

@log-agent
;=> 1001
```

At first glance it looks like the action you sent had no effect or perhaps hasn't been applied yet. But you'd wait in vain for that agent to do anything ever again without intervention, because it's *stopped*. One way to determine this is with the agent-error function:

```
(agent-error log-agent)
;=> #<IllegalArgumentException java.lang.IllegalArgumentException:
;       Wrong number of args passed to: user$eval--509$fn>
```

This returns the error of a stopped agent, or nil if it's still running fine. Another way to see whether an agent is stopped is to try to send another action to it:

```
(send log-agent (fn [_] 3000))
; java.lang.RuntimeException: Agent is failed, needs restart
```

Even though this action would have worked fine, the agent has failed, and so no further sends are allowed. The state of log-agent remains unchanged:

```
@log-agent
;=> 1001
```

In order to get the agent back into working order, you need to restart it:

```
(restart-agent log-agent 2500 :clear-actions true)
;=> 2500
```

This resets the value of log-agent to 2,500 and deletes all those actions patiently waiting in their queue. If you hadn't included the :clear-actions true option, those actions (not including the one that caused the failure) would have survived, and the agent would have continued processing them. Either way, the agent is now in good working order again, and you can again send and send-off to it:

```
(send-off log-agent do-log "The agent, it lives!")
; 2500 : The agent, it lives!
;=> #<Agent@72898540: 2500>
```

Note that restart-agent only makes sense and thus is allowed only when the agent has failed. If it hasn't failed, any attempt to restart it throws an exception in the thread making the attempt, and the agent is left undisturbed:

```
(restart-agent log-agent 2500 :clear-actions true)
;=> java.lang.RuntimeException: Agent does not need a restart
```

This mode is perhaps most appropriate for manual intervention. Agents that normally don't have errors but end up failing in a running system can use :fail mode to keep from doing anything too bad until a human can take things in hand, check to see what happened, choose an appropriate new state for the agent, and restart it as shown here.

:CONTINUE MODE

The other error mode that agents currently support is :continue, where any action that throws an exception is skipped and the agent proceeds to the next queued action (if any). This is most useful when combined with an error handler—if you specify an :error-handler when you create an agent, that agent's error mode defaults to :continue. The agent calls the error handler when an action throws an exception and doesn't proceed to the next action until the handler returns. This gives the handler a chance to report the error in some appropriate way. For example, you could have log-agent handle faulty actions by logging the attempt:

```
(defn handle-log-error [the-agent the-err]
  (println "An action sent to the log-agent threw " the-err))

(set-error-handler! log-agent handle-log-error)

(set-error-mode! log-agent :continue)
```

With the error mode and handler set up, sending faulty actions does cause reports to be printed as you want:

```
(send log-agent (fn [x] (/ x 0)))    ; incorrect
; An action sent to the log-
     agent threw java.lang.ArithmeticException: Divide by zero
;=> #<Agent@66200db9: 2501>

(send log-agent (fn [] 0))           ; also incorrect
; An action sent to the log-agent threw
;    java.lang.IllegalArgumentException:
;    Wrong number of args passed to: user$eval--820$fn
;=> #<Agent@66200db9: 2501>
```

And the agent stays in good shape, always ready for new actions to be sent:

```
(send-off log-agent do-log "Stayin' alive, stayin' alive...")
; 2501 : Stayin' alive, stayin' alive...
```

Note that error handlers can't change the state of the agent (the one in the example keeps its current message ID of 2501 throughout the preceding tests). Error handlers are also supported in the :fail error mode, but handlers can't call restart-agent and so are less often useful for :fail than they are for the :continue error mode.

10.3.5 *When not to use agents*

It can be tempting to repurpose agents for any situation requiring the spawning of new threads. Their succinct syntax and Clojurey feel often make this temptation strong. But although agents perform beautifully when each one is representing a real identity in your application, they start to show weaknesses when used as a sort of "green thread" abstraction. In cases where you need a bunch of worker threads banging away on some work, or you have a specific long-running thread polling or blocking on events, or any other kind of situation where it doesn't seem useful that the agent maintain a value, you can usually find a better mechanism than agents. In these cases, there's every reason to consider using a Java `Thread` directly, or a Java executor (as you did with `dothreads!`) to manage a pool of threads, or in some cases perhaps a Clojure future (discussed in section 11.1).

Another common temptation is to use agents when you need state held but you don't want the sending thread to proceed until the agent action you sent is complete. This can be done by using `await`, but it's another form of abuse that should be avoided. You're not allowed to use `await` in an agent's action, so as you try to use this technique in more and more contexts, you're likely to run into a situation where it won't work. But in general, there's probably a reference type that will do a better job of behaving the way you want. Because this is essentially an attempt to use agents as if they were synchronous, you may have more success with one of the other shared synchronous types. In particular, atoms are shared and uncoordinated like agents, but they're synchronous and so may fit better. Another alternative would be a normal lock, as discussed in section 10.5.

10.4 When to use atoms

Atoms are like refs in that they're synchronous but are like agents in that they're independent (uncoordinated). An atom may seem at first glance similar to a variable, but as we proceed you'll see that any similarities are at best superficial. The use cases for atoms are similar to those of *compare-and-swap (CAS)* spinning operations (keep checking for a value in a loop). Anywhere you might want to atomically compute a value given an existing value and swap in the new value, an atom will suffice. Atom updates occur locally to the calling thread, and execution continues after the atom value has been changed. If another thread B changes the value in an atom before thread A is successful, then A retries. But these retries are spin-loop and don't occur in the STM, and thus atom changes can't be coordinated with changes to other reference types. You should take care when embedding changes to atoms in Clojure's transactions because as you know, transactions can potentially be retried numerous times. Once an atom's value is set, it's set, and it doesn't roll back when a transaction is retried; so in effect, this should be viewed as a side effect. Therefore, use atoms in transactions only when you're certain that an attempt to update its value, performed numerous times, is idempotent.

Aside from the normal use of @ and `deref` to query an atom's value, you can also use the mutating functions `swap!`, `compare-and-set!`, and `reset!`.

10.4.1 Sharing across threads

As we mentioned, atoms are thread-safe and can be used when you require a lightweight mutable reference to be shared across threads. A simple case is one of a globally accessible incrementing timer created using the `atom` function:[5]

---

[5] In this case, the use of a `java.util.concurrent.atomic.AtomicInteger` is a valid choice also.

```
(def ^:dynamic *time* (atom 0))
(defn tick [] (swap! *time* inc))
(dothreads! tick :threads 1000 :times 100)
@*time*
;=> 100000
```

As shown via the use of `dothreads!`, Atoms are safe to use across threads.

10.4.2 Using atoms in transactions

Just because we said that atoms should be used carefully in transactions, that's not to say they can never be used that way. In fact, the use of an atom as the reference holding a function's memoization cache is idempotent on update.

> **NOTE** *Memoization* is a way for a function to store calculated values in a cache so that multiple calls to the function can retrieve previously calculated results from the cache instead of performing potentially expensive calculations every time. Clojure provides a core function `memoize` that can be used on any referentially transparent function.

Individual requirements from memoization are highly specific to the situation, and a generic approach isn't always the appropriate solution for every problem. We'll discuss personalized memoization strategies in section 15.4.1, but for now we'll use an illustrative example appropriate for atom usage.

ATOMIC MEMOIZATION

The core `memoize` function is great for creating simple function caches, but it has some limitations. First, it doesn't allow for custom caching and expiration strategies. Additionally, `memoize` doesn't allow you to manipulate the cache for the purposes of clearing it in part or wholesale. Therefore, let's create a function `manipulable-memoize` that lets you get at the cache and perform operations on it directly. Throughout the book, we've mentioned Clojure's metadata facility, and for this example it will come in handy. As the following listing shows, you can take in the function to be memoized and attach some metadata with an atom containing the cache itself for later manipulation.

Listing 10.6 Resettable `memoize` function

```
(defn manipulable-memoize [function]
  (let [cache (atom {})]              ⟵─ Store the cache in an atom
    (with-meta
      (fn [& args]
        (or (second (find @cache args))     ⟵─ Check the cache first ...
            (let [ret (apply function args)]    ⟵─ ... else calculate
              (swap! cache assoc args ret)
              ret)))
      {:cache cache}))))              ⟵─ Attach metadata
```

Store the result ⟶

Return the result ⟶

This example slightly modifies the core `memoize` function to attach the atom to the function being memoized. You can now observe `manipulable-memoize` in action:

```
(def slowly (fn [x] (Thread/sleep 1000) x))

(time [(slowly 9) (slowly 9)])
; "Elapsed time: 2000.33 msecs"
;=> [9 9]

(def sometimes-slowly (manipulable-memoize slowly))

(time [(sometimes-slowly 108) (sometimes-slowly 108)])
; "Elapsed time: 2000.409 msecs"
;=> [108 108]
```

Slow function twice takes twice as long

Memoized slow function incurs the cost once

The call to slowly is always ... well ... slow, as you'd expect. But the call to sometimes-slowly is only slow on the first call given a certain argument. This too is as you'd expect. Now you can inspect sometimes-slowly's cache and perform some operations on it:

```
(meta sometimes-slowly)
;=> {:cache #<Atom@e4245: {(108) 108}>}

(let [cache (:cache (meta sometimes-slowly))]
  (swap! cache dissoc '(108)))
;=> {}
```

You may wonder why you use swap! to dissoc the cached argument 108 instead of using (reset! cache {}). There are certainly valid use cases for the wholesale reset of an atom's value, and this case is arguably one. But it's good practice to set reference values via the application of a function rather than the in-place value setting. This way, you can be more selective about the value manipulations being performed. Having said that, here are the consequences of your actions:

```
(meta sometimes-slowly)
;=> {:cache #<Atom@e4245: {}>}

(time [(sometimes-slowly 108) (sometimes-slowly 108)])
; "Elapsed time: 1000.3 msecs"
;=> [108 108]
```

And yes, you were able to remove the cached argument value 108 using the metadata map attached to the function sometimes-slowly. There are better ways than this to allow for pointed cache removal, but for now you can take heart in that by using an atom, you've allowed for the local mutation of a reference in a thread-safe way. Additionally, because of the nature of memoization, you can use these memoized functions in a transaction without ill effect. But if you attempt to remove values from a memoization cache, it may not work as you expect. That is, depending on the interleaving of your removal and any restarts, the value(s) you remove might be reinserted the next time through the restart. Even this condition is agreeable, though, if your only concern is reducing total cache size.[6]

---

[6] The discussion of memoization in this section has grown into an official Clojure contrib library, available at https://github.com/clojure/core.memoize.

10.5 *When to use locks*

Clojure's reference types and parallel primitives cover a vast array of use cases. Additionally, Java's rich set of concurrency classes found in the java.util.concurrent package is readily available. But even with this arsenal of tools at your disposal, there still may be circumstances where explicit locking is the only option available, the common case being the modification of arrays concurrently. Let's start with a simple protocol to describe a concurrent, mutable, *safe array* that holds an internal array instance, allowing you to access it or mutate it safely. A naive (and incorrect) implementation is shown in the following listing.

Listing 10.7   Simple `SafeArray` protocol

```
(ns joy.locks
  (:refer-clojure :exclude [aget aset count seq])          ◁─┐ Exclude Clojure core
  (:require [clojure.core :as clj])                            functions to override
  (:use [joy.mutation :only (dothreads!)])))

                                                          ┌ SafeArray features a
(defprotocol SafeArray                                  ◁─┘ small set of functions
  (aset  [this i f])                                                   ◁─┐ Change the standard
  (aget  [this i])                         ◁─┐ aget and aset             semantics of
  (count [this])                              are unguarded             clojure.core/aset and
  (seq   [this]))                                                       clojure.core/aget

(defn make-dumb-array [t sz]
  (let [a (make-array t sz)]
    (reify
      SafeArray
      (count [_]    (clj/count a))
      (seq   [_]    (clj/seq a))                ┌ aget and aset
      (aget  [_ i]  (clj/aget a i))           ◁─┘ are unguarded
      (aset  [this i f]                                       ┌ Delegate to core
        (clj/aset a                                         ◁─┘ for setting
                  i
                  (f (aget this i)))))))        ◁─┐ Implement SafeArray/aset in
                                                  terms of clojure.core/aset
```

You use the :refer-clojure namespace directive to :exclude the array and sequence functions that the SafeArray protocol overrides. You do this not only because it's important to know how to use :refer-clojure, but also because you're changing the semantics of aset to take a mutating function as its last argument instead of a raw value. You then use the :require directive to alias the Clojure namespace as clj, thus avoiding the need to use the fully qualified function names a la clojure.core/aget.

The dumb array created by make-dumb-array is stored in a closure created by reify, and unguarded access is provided without concern for concurrent matters. Using this implementation across threads is disastrous, as you can see:

```
(defn pummel [a]
  (dothreads! #(dotimes [i (count a)] (aset a i inc))       ◁─┐ Increment each array
              :threads 100))                                   slot from 100 threads
```

```
(def D (make-dumb-array Integer/TYPE 8))      ⟵⌐ Start with an unguarded
                                                |  array of 8 slots
(pummel D)
;; wait for pummel to terminate

(seq D)                                       ⌐ Should have 100
;=> (82 84 65 63 83 65 83 87)                 ⟵⌐ in each slot
```

This is very wrong—100 threads incrementing concurrently should result in 100 for each array slot. To add insult to injury, Clojure doesn't throw a Concurrent-ModificationException as you might expect, but instead silently goes along doing bad things. Next, we'll talk a little about locking and provide an alternate implementation for SafeArray using locking primitives.

10.5.1 Safe mutation through locking

Currently, the only way to safely modify and see consistent values for a mutable object (such as an array or a class instance) across threads in Clojure is through locking.

REFERENCES AROUND EVIL MUTABLE THINGS

Wrapping a mutable object in a Clojure reference type provides *absolutely no guarantees for safe concurrent modification*. Doing this will at best explode immediately or, worse, provide inaccurate results.

If at all possible, locking should be avoided; but for those times when it's unavoidable, the locking macro will help. The locking macro takes a single parameter acting as the locking monitor and a body that executes in the monitor context. Any writes and reads to the monitor object are thread safe, and as a bonus the monitor is *always* released at the end of the block.[7] One of the major complexities in concurrent programming using locks is that all errors must be handled fully and appropriately; otherwise you risk orphaned locks, and they spell deadlock. But the locking macro always releases the lock, even in the face of exceptions.

> **Listing 10.8   Implementating `SafeArray` using the `locking` macro**

```
(defn make-safe-array [t sz]
  (let [a (make-array t sz)]          ⟵— Array creation is the same
    (reify
     SafeArray
     (count [_] (clj/count a))
     (seq [_] (clj/seq a))
     (aget [_ i]                      ⟵— aget is locked
        (locking a
          (clj/aget a i)))
     (aset [this i f]                 ⟵— aset is also locked
        (locking a
          (clj/aset a
                    i                             ⌐ Still delegating to
                    (f (aget this i)))))))))      ⟵⌐ core, but now inside
                                                   | of a locked region
```

---

[7] The locking macro works much like a Java synchronized block.

You use the `locking` macro on both the `aget` and `aset` functions so that they can maintain consistency. Because `aset` calls `aget`, the `locking` macro is called twice. This isn't a problem because `locking` is *reentrant*, or able to be called multiple times in the same thread. Typically, you'd have to manage the releasing of a reentrant locking mechanism to match the number of times called, but fortunately `locking` manages that for you. Here is a use of `make-safe-array`:

```
(def A (make-safe-array Integer/TYPE 8))

(pummel A)
;; wait for pummel to terminate

(seq A)
;;=> (100 100 100 100 100 100 100 100)
```

As shown, using locks on the read and write sides of the `SafeArray` protocol implementation ensures consistency in updates across multiple threads. The `locking` macro is the simplest way to perform primitive locking in Clojure. But the implementation of `make-safe-array` is coarse in that the locks used are guarding the entire array. Any readers or writers wishing to access or update any slot in the array *must* wait their turn, a bottleneck known as *contention*. If you need finer-grained locking, the locking facilities provided by Java will help you gain more control, as we discuss next.

10.5.2 Using Java's explicit locks

Java provides a set of explicit locks in the `java.util.concurrent.locks` package. One such lock is provided by the `java.util.concurrent.locks.ReentrantLock` class. You can create a new type of smart array that provides finer-grained locking on a per-slot basis. Rather than using one lock per array element, you can use a small pool of locks to conserve resources. To accomplish this, first let's create a useful function called `lock-i`:

```
(defn lock-i [target-index num-locks]          | Calculation falls within
  (mod target-index num-locks))            ◁─  | 0 and num-locks
```

The `lock-i` function has one purpose: to calculate a lock number based solely on the array index in question and the total size of the target array. A simple way to stripe an array is to use the classic `index modulo array_size` formula. The function that uses `lock-i` is shown next.

Listing 10.9   Implementing `SafeArray` using `ReentrantLock`

```
(import 'java.util.concurrent.locks.ReentrantLock)

(defn make-smart-array [t sz]
  (let [a    (make-array t sz)          ◁─── Array
        Lsz  (/ sz 2)                                      | Locks, one for every
        L    (into-array (take Lsz                     ◁─  | two array slots
                    (repeatedly #(ReentrantLock.))))]
    (reify
      SafeArray
      (count [_] (clj/count a))
```

```
(seq [_] (clj/seq a))
(aget [_ i]
  (let [lk (clj/aget L (lock-i (inc i) Lsz))]
    (.lock lk)                                          <— Explicit locking
    (try
      (clj/aget a i)
      (finally (.unlock lk)))))                         <— Explicit unlocking
(aset [this i f]
  (let [lk (clj/aget L (lock-i (inc i) Lsz))]
    (.lock lk)
    (try
      (clj/aset a
                i
                (f (aget this i)))                      ↵ Reentrant locking
      (finally (.unlock lk))))))))))                      on nested get call
```

The first point of note is that you use a technique (simplified for clarity) called *lock striping* (Herlihy 2008) to reduce the contention of guarding the array as a whole using `locking`. The target array a's slots are guarded by a number of locks equal to half its size, each chosen using the simple formula (`mod target-index num-locks`). This scheme allows readers and writers to (potentially) act independently when accessing different array slots. It's crucial that you close over the lock instance array L, because for explicit locks to work, each access *must* lock and unlock the *same* instance. Additionally, you call the `.unlock` method in the body of a `finally` expression, because failing to do so is a recipe for disaster. Unlike the `locking` macro, the `ReentrantLock` class doesn't manage lock release automatically. Observe the following smart array in action:

```
(def S (make-smart-array Integer/TYPE 8))

(pummel S)
;; wait for pummel to terminate

(seq S)
;;=> (100 100 100 100 100 100 100 100)
```

One flaw of the `make-smart-array` function is that it uses the same locks for readers and writers. But you can allow for more concurrency if you enable some number of readers to access array slots without blocking at all by using the `java.util.concurrent` `.locks.ReentrantReadWriteLock` class. The `ReentrantReadWriteLock` class holds two lock instances, one for reads and one for writes. You won't take advantage of that fact here; but if you choose to do so, you can use the implementation of `make-smart-array` as a guide.

Using the various locking mechanisms, you can guarantee consistency across threads for mutable objects. But as we showed with explicit locks, there's an expected incantation to unlocking that must be strictly observed. Although not necessarily complex in the `SafeArray` implementations, the conceptual baggage incurred in the semantics of the explicit-locking scheme doesn't scale well. The `java.util.concurrent` package contains a cacophony of concurrency primitives above and beyond simple locks, but it's not our goal to provide a comprehensive survey.

10.6 *Vars and dynamic binding*

The last reference type we'll explore is perhaps the most commonly used: the var. Vars are most often used because of two main features:

- Vars can be named and interned in a namespace.
- Dynamic vars can provide thread-local state.

It's through the second feature that vars contribute most usefully to the reference type landscape. The thread-local value of a var by definition can only be read from or written to a single thread, and thus it provides the thread-safe semantics you've come to expect from a Clojure reference type.

But before you can start experimenting with vars at the REPL, we need to address some consequences of the first feature. The other reference objects we've looked at aren't named and so are generally *stored* in something with a name. This means when the name is evaluated, you get the reference object, not the value. To get the object's value, you have to use `deref`. Named vars flip this around—evaluating their name gives the value, so if you want the var object, you need to pass the name to the special operator var.

With this knowledge in hand, let's experiment with an existing var. Clojure provides a var named `*read-eval*`,[8] so you can get its current value by evaluating its name:

```
*read-eval*
;=> true
```

No `deref` needed, because `*read-eval*` is a named var. Now for the var object itself:

```
(var *read-eval*)
;=> #'clojure.core/*read-eval*
```

When a named var object is printed, it starts with `#'` and is then followed by the fully qualified name of the var. The `#'` reader feature expands to the var operator—it means the same thing:

```
#'*read-eval*
;=> #'clojure.core/*read-eval*
```

Now that you've seen how to refer to var objects, you can look at how they behave. The var `*read-eval*` is one of those provided by Clojure that's specifically meant to be given thread-local bindings but by default has only a root binding. You should have seen its root binding when you evaluated it earlier—by default, `*read-eval*` is bound to `true`.

---

[8] `*read-eval*` happens to be a var that has a default configuration useful for this discussion about vars—its actual purpose is unimportant here.

10.6.1 *The binding macro*

The root binding of a var can act as the base of a stack, with each thread's local bindings pushing onto that stack and popping off of it as requested. The most common mechanism for pushing and popping thread-local bindings is the macro binding. It takes one or more var names and a value for each that initializes the new binding when it's pushed. These bindings remain in effect until control passes out of the binding macro, at which point they're popped off the stack.

Here's a simple example of a function that prints the current value of the var *read-eval*, either the root or thread-local value, whichever is currently in effect:

```
(defn print-read-eval []
  (println "*read-eval* is currently" *read-eval*))
```

This function calls print-read-eval three times, the first and last of which print the root binding. The middle time, binding is in effect:

```
(defn binding-play []
  (print-read-eval)
  (binding [*read-eval* false]
    (print-read-eval))
  (print-read-eval))
```

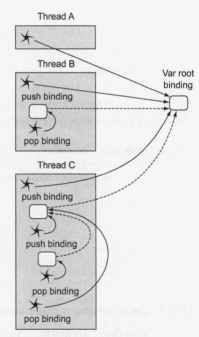

This results in the var temporarily having a thread-local value of false:

```
(binding-play)
; *read-eval* is currently true
; *read-eval* is currently false
; *read-eval* is currently true
```

This is a like thread B in figure 10.12, which also shows a more complex scenario than thread A and a simpler one than thread C.

10.6.2 *Creating a named var*

Vars are most commonly created with the special operator def or one of the many macros that expand to a form that has a def inside:

- defn—Puts a function in a var
- defmacro—Puts a macro in a var
- defonce—Sets the value of an unbound var
- defmulti—Puts a multimethod in a var

There are a few others in clojure.core and many more in contrib. What they have in common is that each of these interns a var in the current namespace. Clojure searches for the named var in the current namespace. If one is found, it's used;

Figure 10.12 Thread-local var bindings. This illustration depicts a single var being used from three different threads. Each rounded box is a var binding, either thread-local or root. Each star is the var being deref'ed, with the solid arrow pointing to the binding used. The dotted lines point from a thread-local binding to the next binding on the stack.

otherwise, a new var is created and added to the namespace, and that one is used.[9] The var (specifically the root binding of the var) is bound to whatever value, function, or macro (and so on) was given. The var itself is returned:

```
(def favorite-color :green)
#'user/favorite-color
```

As you may have noticed at times in this book, when a var is printed, its fully qualified name is given, along with the namespace where the var is interned (user) and the var's name (favorite-color). These are preceded by #' because unlike the other reference types, a named var is automatically dereferenced when its name is evaluated—no explicit @ or call to deref is required:

```
favorite-color
;=> :green
```

So in order to refer to a var instead of the value it's bound to, you need to use #' or the special form var, which are equivalent:

```
(var favorite-color)
;=> #'user/favorite-color
```

A var can exist (or *not* exist) in any of four states. The precise state a var is in can be determined using the functions resolve, bound?, and thread-bound? as shown in table 10.1. The first row of the table shows the results of resolve, bound?, and thread-bound? when a var x is unbound. The remaining rows show how to change x to cause those functions to return the values shown.

Table 10.1 Var states

Initialization mechanism	(resolve 'x)	(bound? #'x)	(thread-bound? #'x)
(def x)	#'user/x	false	false
(def x 5)	#'user/x	true	false
(binding [x 7] ...)	#'user/x	true	true
(with-local-vars [x 9] ...)	nil	true	true

10.6.3 *Creating anonymous vars*

Vars don't always have names, nor do they need to be interned in a namespace. The with-local-vars macro creates dynamic vars and gives them thread-local bindings all at once, but it *doesn't* intern them. Instead, they're bound to locals, which means the associated var isn't implicitly looked up by symbolic name. You need to use deref or var-get to get the current value of the var. Here's an example of a var x created and

---

[9] Not all macros starting with def necessarily create or intern vars. Some that don't: defmethod, defrecord, and deftype.

interned with `def`, and then a local x that shadows it and is bound to a new var via `with-local-vars`:

```
(def x 42)
{:outer-var-value x
 :with-locals (with-local-vars [x 9]
                {:local-var x
                 :local-var-value (var-get x)})}}

;=> {:outer-var-value 42,
     :with-locals {:local-var #<Var: --unnamed-->,
                   :local-var-value 9}}
```

Within the body of the `with-local-vars` macro, you can set the bound value using `(var-set <var> <value>)`, which of course only affects the thread-local value. (Table 10.1 outlines the binding mechanism behind the various ways to create vars in Clojure.) It's almost stunning how rarely `with-local-vars` is useful.

10.6.4 Dynamic scope

Vars have dynamic scope, which contrasts with the lexical scope of `let` locals. The most obvious difference is that with a lexical local, you can easily see where it was initialized by looking at the nested structure of the code. A var, on the other hand, may have been initialized by a `binding` anywhere earlier in the call stack, not necessarily nearby in the code. This difference can create unexpectedly complex interactions and is one of the few areas where Clojure does little to help address such complexity.

An example of this complexity is shown by using the `binding` macro or any macro built on top of it, such as `with-precision` and `with-out-str`. For example, you can use the `with-precision` macro to conveniently set up the built-in `clojure.core/*math-context*` var:

```
(with-precision 4
  (/ 1M 3))
;=> 0.3333M
```

You need to use `with-precision` here because if you don't tell `BigDecimal` you're okay with it rounding off the result, it will refuse to return anything in this case:

```
(/ 1M 3)
; java.lang.ArithmeticException: Non-terminating decimal expansion;
;    no exact representable decimal result.
```

With that in mind, can you see why `with-precision` isn't doing its job in the next snippet? The only thing that makes it different from the example that worked earlier is that it uses `map` to produce a sequence of three numbers instead of just one:

```
(with-precision 4
  (map (fn [x] (/ x 3)) (range 1M 4M)))

; java.lang.ArithmeticException: Non-terminating decimal expansion;
;    no exact representable decimal result.
```

The problem is that `map` is lazy and therefore doesn't call the function given to it immediately. Instead, `map` returns a partially evaluated data structure. The REPL realizes that structure while trying to print it, so the full evaluation technically happens outside of the `with-precision` block. Although the `map` and the function it calls are within the *lexical scope* of `with-precision`, and `with-precision` uses a thread-local binding internally, it doesn't care about lexical scope. When the division operation is performed, you've already left the *dynamic scope* of `with-precision`, and it no longer has any effect. The `BigDecimal` behavior drops back to its default, and it throws an exception.

One way to solve this is to make sure all the division is done before leaving the dynamic scope. Clojure's `doall` function is perfect for this:

```
(with-precision 4
  (doall (map (fn [x] (/ x 3)) (range 1M 4M))))
;=> (0.3333M 0.6667M 1M)
```

One drawback is that it completely defeats `map`'s laziness. An alternate solution is to have the function provided to `map` re-create, when it's run, the dynamic scope in which the function was created. Clojure provides a handy macro `bound-fn` to do exactly that:

```
(with-precision 4
  (map (bound-fn [x] (/ x 3)) (range 1M 4M)))
;=> (0.3333M 0.6667M 1M)
```

Now the sequence being returned is still lazy; but before each item is computed, the dynamic scope of `*math-context*` is re-created, and the exception is avoided.[10]

This kind of mismatch between a function definition that appears lexically in a form like `with-precision` or `binding` and yet has a different dynamic scope when called doesn't cause problems with lazy sequences alone. You may also see problems with functions sent to agents as actions or with the body of a future, because these are executed in other threads outside the dynamic scope where they're set up.

Problems related to dynamic scope aren't even exclusive to vars. The scope of a `try/catch` is also dynamic and can have similarly unexpected behavior. For example, `with-open` uses `try/finally` to close a file automatically when execution leaves its dynamic scope. Failing to account for this can lead to an error when trying to write to a closed file, because the dynamic scope of `with-open` has been left. Although `bound-fn` can help make the dynamic scope of a var borrow from its lexical scope, the only way to deal with `try/catch` is to make sure everything is executed before leaving its dynamic scope.

10.7 Summary

This has been the most complex chapter of the book. State management is a complicated process that can quickly lose all semblance of sanity in the face of concurrent

---

[10] Of course, if the problem called for it, you could also use `(map (fn [x] (with-precision 4 (/ x 3)))` `(range 1M 4M))`, which tightens the dynamic scope to the division itself.

modifications. Clojure's main tenet is not to foster concurrency, but instead to provide the tools for the sane management of state. As a result of this focus, sane concurrency designs follow. The next chapter deals naturally with parallelism and the features that Clojure provides in facilitating it.

Parallelism

Typically, parallel tasks work toward an aggregate goal; and the result of one task doesn't affect the behavior of any other parallel task, thus maintaining determinacy. Whereas in the previous chapter we stated that concurrency was about the design of a system, parallelism is about the execution model. Although concurrency and parallelism aren't quite the same thing, some concurrent designs are parallelizable. Recall that in the previous chapter we showed an illustration of a concurrent work queue design featuring a producer and two consumer threads (see figure 11.1).

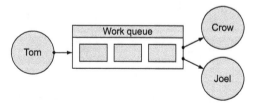

Figure 11.1 The concurrent design with an intermediate work queue from the previous chapter is potentially parallelizable.

In the figure, the independent threads Tom, Crow, and Joel operate independently. For the purposes of this section, assume that Tom, Crow, and Joel are all performing independent, concurrent operations. Yet depending on the type of data placed into the work queue, this design could be parallelized by duplicating it as shown in figure 11.2.

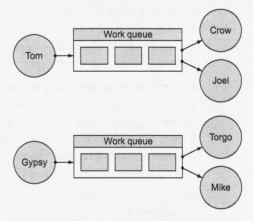

As shown, by duplicating the concurrent design, we can conceive a level of parallelism in the producer/consumer work processing. If we assume that now Tom and Gypsy are feeding subsets of related tasks into their respective queues, then the overall processing of those tasks

Figure 11.2 The concurrent design can be parallelized through the use of another work queue and producer as well as two more consumers.

is done in parallel. Of course, the details of how this might work are entirely application specific, but we hope the intent is clear.

In this chapter, we'll discuss the topic of parallelism in Clojure using futures, promises, and a trio of functions: pmap, pvalues, and pcalls. We'll end the chapter with a discussion of a way to look at parallel computations orthogonal to data structures: reducibles.

11.1 When to use futures

Clojure includes two reference types supporting parallelism: *futures* and *promises*. Futures, the subject of this section, are simple yet elegant constructs that are useful for partitioning a typically sequential operation into discrete parts. These parts can then be asynchronously processed across numerous threads that will block if the enclosed expression hasn't finished. All subsequent dereferencing will return the calculated value. The simplest example of the use of a future that performs a task (sleeping in this case) on a thread and returns a value is shown next:

```
(time (let [x (future (do (Thread/sleep 5000) (+ 41 1)))]
  [@x @x]))
; "Elapsed time: 5001.682 msecs"
;=> [42 42]
```

The processing time of the do block is only experienced on the first dereference of the future x. Futures represent expressions that have yet to be computed.

11.1.1 Futures as callbacks

One nice use case for futures is in the context of a callback mechanism. Normally you might call out to a remote-procedure call (RPC), wait for it to complete, and then proceed with some task depending on the return value. But what happens if you need to make multiple RPC calls? Should you be forced to wait for them all serially? Thanks to futures, the answer is no. In this section, you'll use futures to create an aggregate task that finds the total number of occurrences of a string in a given set of Twitter[1] feeds. This aggregate task will be split into numerous parallel subtasks via futures.

COUNTING WORD OCCURRENCES IN A SET OF RSS/ATOM FEEDS

Like many frequently updated services on the Internet, Twitter provides a feed of status messages in a digest format. One such format provided by services like Twitter is known as the *Rich Site Summary* version 2.0, or *RSS* for short. An RSS 2.0 feed is an XML document used to represent a piece of data that's constantly changing. The layout of a Twitter RSS entry is straightforward:

```
<rss version="2.0">
  <channel>
    <title>Twitter / fogus</title>
    <link>http://twitter.com/fogus</link>
    <item>
      <title>fogus: Thinking about #Clojure futures.</title>
      <link>
        http://twitter.com/fogus/statuses/12180102647/
      </link>
    </item>
  </channel>
</rss>
```

Another format for providing information about site updates is known as the *Atom syndication format*, and it contains similar types of information. Obviously, there's more to the content of a typical RSS or Atom feed than shown in the example Twitter timeline, but for this example you will retrieve only the title of the individual feed elements. To do this, you need to first parse the XML and put it into a convenient format. If you recall from section 8.4, you created a domain DSL to create a tree built on a simple node structure of tables with the keys :tag, :attrs, and :content. As mentioned, that structure is used in many Clojure libraries, and you'll take advantage of this fact. Clojure provides some core functions in the clojure.xml and clojure.zip namespaces to help make sense of the feed.[2]

Listing 11.1   Converting an XML feed to an XML zipper

```
(ns joy.futures
  (:require (clojure [xml :as xml]))
  (:require (clojure [zip :as zip]))
  (:import  (java.util.regex Pattern)))

(defn feed->zipper [uri-str]
  (->> (xml/parse uri-str)          ⬅── Parse XML
       zip/xml-zip))                ⬅── Convert to a zipper
```

---

[1] Twitter is online at http://twitter.com.

[2] Recall from chapter 8 that the ->> macro works like the -> macro, except it inserts the pipelined arguments into the last position.

Using the function clojure.xml/parse, you can retrieve the XML for a Twitter RSS
feed and convert it into the familiar tree format. That tree is then passed into a function clojure.zip/xml-zip that converts that structure into another data structure
called a *zipper*. The form and semantics of the zipper are beyond the scope of this book
(Huet 1997), but using it in this case allows you to easily navigate *down* from the root
rss XML node to the channel node, where you then retrieve its children.

The exact form of a RSS feed versus an Atom feed is slightly different. Therefore,
navigating to the feed elements requires a different sequence of zipper steps to
achieve. But if you take the zipper from the xml/parse step and detect the precise
feed type (RSS or Atom), you can *normalize* the feed elements into a common structure, as shown next.

Listing 11.2   Normalizing RSS and Atom feed entries to a common structure

```
(defn normalize [feed]
  (if (= :feed (:tag (first feed)))          ⟵ Quick and dirty detect
    feed
    (zip/down feed)))                        ⟵ Normalize to a similar XML tree


(defn feed-children [uri-str]
  (->> uri-str
       feed->zipper        ⟵ Zipperfy
       normalize                             ⟵ Normalize
       zip/children
       (filter (comp #{:item :entry} :tag))))) ⟵ Grab entries
```

The child nodes returned from feed-children contain other items besides :item and
:entry nodes; but because you only care about the titles, this example glosses over a
more thorough normalization.

Once you have the normalized child nodes, you then want to retrieve the title text.

Listing 11.3   Retrieving the title text from the normalized feed structure

```
(defn title [entry]
  (some->> entry
           :content                          ⟵ Get the feed content
           (some #(when (= :title (:tag %)) %))   ⟵ Get the title
           :content             ⟵ Get the title content
           first))              ⟵ Assume one
```

Now that you can extract the title content of either an RSS or Atom feed, you'd like a
function to count the number of occurrences of some text (case-insensitive). You can
perform this task using the function count-text-task, defined next.

Listing 11.4   Function to count the number of occurrences of text

```
(defn count-text-task [extractor txt feed]        <--- Take a function to get the text
  (let [items (feed-children feed)
        re    (Pattern/compile (str "(?i)" txt))]
    (->> items
         (map extractor)                  <--- Get children text
         (mapcat #(re-seq re %))                    <--- Match against each
         count)))
```

Although the example focuses on counting text occurrences in the titles of a feed, we couldn't help but make count-text-task a bit more generic. count-text-task doesn't care one bit what the format of a feed is. Instead it works by applying an extractor function to the feed structure to get a sequence of text strings to match over. This indirection will come in handy should you want to extend this code to count text in the body fields, or any other field for that matter.

Here we're using count-text-task to find some text in the titles of the RSS feed for the Elixir language blog:[3]

```
(count-text-task          | Selector function
 title                    | defined earlier
 "Erlang"
 "http://feeds.feedburner.com/ElixirLang")
;=> 0

(count-text-task
  title
  "Elixir"
  "http://feeds.feedburner.com/ElixirLang")
;;=> 14
```

The result you'll see is highly dependent on when you run this function, because blog feeds are ever-changing. This is fine and good, but at the moment, computing the results of count-text-task is a serial operation. What if you wanted to count the occurrences of a pieces of text for multiple feeds? Surely you wouldn't want to wait for each and every feed retrieval/match cycle.

Instead, using the count-text-task function, you can build a set of related tasks to be performed over a sequence of RSS or Atom feeds and spread them over a number of threads for parallel processing using the following code.

Listing 11.5   Manually spreading tasks over a sequence of futures

```
(def feeds #{"http://feeds.feedburner.com/ElixirLang"              <--- Feeds
             "http://blog.fogus.me/feed/"})

(let [results (for [feed feeds]                    <--- for builds the seq
                (future                            <--- Farm the task to a thread
                  (count-text-task title "Elixir" feed)))]
```

---

[3] Elixir (http://elixir-lang.org/) is an exciting new programming language that adds syntax and many Clojure-like features to the Erlang runtime.

```
      (reduce + (map deref results)))            <--- Count via deref

//=> 17
```

You can use this pattern every time to build a seq of futures, each processing a portion of the feed set. *Or* you can create a convenience macro as-futures to build a similar bit of code, as in the following listing.

Listing 11.6 Macro to dispatch a sequence of futures

```
(defmacro as-futures [[a args] & body]
  (let [parts             (partition-by #{'=>} body)      <--|  Parallel actions are separated from the summation by =>
        [acts _ [res]] (partition-by #{:as} (first parts)) <--- Name the results
        [_ _ task]     parts]
    `(let [~res (for [~a ~args] (future  ~@acts))]          <--| Wrap each action in a future
       ~@task)))
```

The as-futures macro implemented here names a binding corresponding to the arguments for a given action, which is then dispatched across a number of futures, after which a task is run against the futures sequence. The body of as-futures is segmented using the partition-by function so that you can clearly specify the needed parts—the action arguments, the action to be performed for each argument, and the tasks to be run against the resulting sequence of futures:

```
(as-futures [<arg-name> <all-args>]
  <actions-using-args>
  :as <results-name>
=>
  <actions-using-results>)
```

To simplify the macro implementation, you use the :as keyword and => symbol to clearly delineate its segments. The as-futures body exits only after the task body finishes—as determined by the execution of the futures. You can use as-futures to perform count-text-task with a new function occurrences, implemented in the following listing.

Listing 11.7 Counting text occurrences in feed titles fetched in parallel

```
(defn occurrences [extractor tag & feeds]
  (as-futures [feed feeds]
    (count-text-task extractor tag feed)
    :as results
  =>
    (reduce + (map deref results)))))     <--| Sum all counts stored in the futures
```

The as-futures macro builds a sequence of futures named results, enclosing the call to count-text-task across the unique set of Twitter feeds provided. You then sum the counts returned from the dereferencing of the individual futures:

```
(occurrences title "released"
  "http://blog.fogus.me/feed/"
  "http://feeds.feedburner.com/ElixirLang"
  "http://www.ruby-lang.org/en/feeds/news.rss")
;=> 11
```

And that's that. Using only a handful of functions and macros, plus using the built-in core facilities for XML parsing and navigation, you've created a simple RSS/Atom text occurrences counter. This implementation has some trade-offs made in the name of page count. First, you blindly dereference the future in occurrences when calculating the sum. If the future's computation freezes, then the dereference will likewise freeze. Using some combination of future-done?, future-cancel, and future-cancelled? in your own programs, you can skip, retry, or eliminate ornery feeds from the calculation. Futures are only one way to perform parallel computation in Clojure, and in the next section we'll talk about another: promises.

11.2 *When to use promises*

Another tool that Clojure provides for parallel computation is the promise and deliver mechanism. Promises are similar to futures, in that they represent a unit of computation to be performed on a separate thread. Likewise, the blocking semantics when dereferencing an unfinished promise are the same. Whereas futures encapsulate an arbitrary expression that caches its value in the future on completion, promises are placeholders for values whose construction is fulfilled by another thread via the deliver function. A simple example is as follows:

```
(def x (promise))
(def y (promise))
(def z (promise))

(dothreads! #(deliver z (+ @x @y)))

(dothreads!
  #(do (Thread/sleep 2000) (deliver x 52)))

(dothreads!
  #(do (Thread/sleep 4000) (deliver y 86)))

(time @z)
; "Elapsed time: 3995.414 msecs"
;=> 138
```

What's not shown is that if you execute @z before executing the two dothreads! calls (defined in the beginning of the previous chapter), the entire REPL will hang. The reason is that @z waits until a value has been delivered, but in our alternate scenario this could never happen because dothreads! would never have the chance to run. Each promise must be delivered once and only once for a dereference to return a value. Promises are write-once; any further attempt to deliver will throw an exception.

11.2.1 *Parallel tasks with promises*

You can create a macro similar to as-futures for handling promises, but because of
the more advanced value semantics, the implementation is more complicated. Let's
again provide a named set of tasks, but additionally let's name the corresponding
promises so that you can then execute over the eventual results.

Listing 11.8   Dispatching a sequence of promises across threads

```
(defmacro with-promises [[n tasks _ as] & body]
  (when as
    `(let [tasks# ~tasks
           n# (count tasks#)
           promises# (take n# (repeatedly promise))]
       (dotimes [i# n#]
         (dothreads!
           (fn []
             (deliver (nth promises# i#)
                      ((nth tasks# i#))))))
       (let [~n tasks#
             ~as promises#]
         ~@body))))
```

You can then build a rudimentary parallel testing facility, dispatching tests across disparate threads and summing the results when all the tests are done.

Listing 11.9   Parallel test runner using `with-promises`

```
(defrecord TestRun [run passed failed])

(defn pass [] true)              <— Fake the results
 (defn fail [] false)

(defn run-tests [& all-tests]                  Spread tests
  (with-promises                              over promises
    [tests all-tests :as results]
    (into (TestRun. 0 0 0)                      Collect the results in a
          (reduce #(merge-with + %1 %2) {}      new summation map
            (for [r results]
              (if @r
                {:run 1 :passed 1}             Depending on the
                {:run 1 :failed 1}))))))       result, increment
                                               the right counter

(run-tests pass fail fail fail pass)
;=> #:user.TestRun{:run 5, :passed 2, :failed 3}
```

This unit-testing model is simplistic by design in order to illustrate parallelization
using promises, not to provide a comprehensive testing framework.

11.2.2 *Callback API to blocking API*

Promises, much like futures, are useful for executing RPCs on separate threads. This can be useful if you need to parallelize a group of calls to an RPC service, but there's also a converse use case. Often, RPC APIs take arguments to the service calls and also a callback function to be executed when the call completes. Using the `feed-children` function from the previous section, you can construct an archetypal RPC function:

```
(defn feed-items [k feed]
  (k
    (for [item (filter (comp #{:entry :item} :tag)
                       (feed-children feed))]
      (-> item :content first :content))))
```

The `feed-items` function is a distillation of the `count-text-task` function from the previous section, as shown:

```
(feed-items
 count
 "http://blog.fogus.me/feed/")
;=> 5
```

The argument `k` to `feed-items` is the callback, or continuation, that's called with the filtered RPC results. This API is fine, but there are times when a blocking call is more appropriate than a callback-based call. You can use a promise to achieve this blocking behavior:

```
(let [p (promise)]
  (feed-items #(deliver p (count %))
              "http://blog.fogus.me/feed/")
  @p)
;=> 5
```

As you see, the call blocks until the `deliver` occurs. This is a fine way to transform the callback into a blocking call, but it would be good to have a way to do so generically. Fortunately, most well-written RPC APIs follow the same form for their callback functions/methods, so the following listing creates a function to wrap this up nicely.

Listing 11.10   Transforming a callback-based function to a blocking call

```
(defn cps->fn [f k]
  (fn [& args]
    (let [p (promise)]
      (apply f (fn [x] (deliver p (k x))) args)
      @p)))

(def count-items (cps->fn feed-items count))

(count-items "http://blog.fogus.me/feed/")
;=> 5
```

This is a simple solution to a common problem that you may have encountered already in your own applications.

11.2.3 *Deterministic deadlocks*

You can cause a deadlock in your applications by never delivering on a promise. One possibly surprising advantage of using promises is that if a promise can deadlock, it will deadlock deterministically. Because only a single thread can ever deliver on a promise, only that thread will ever cause a deadlock. You can use the following code to create a cycle in the dependencies between two promises to observe a deadlock:

```
(def kant (promise))
(def hume (promise))

(dothreads!
  #(do (println "Kant has" @kant) (deliver hume :thinking)))

(dothreads!
  #(do (println "Hume is" @hume) (deliver kant :fork)))
```

The Kant thread is waiting for the delivery of the value for kant from the Hume thread, which in turn is waiting for the value for hume from the Kant thread. Attempting either @kant or @hume in the REPL will cause an immediate deadlock. Furthermore, this deadlock will happen *every* time; it's deterministic rather than dependent on odd thread timings or the like. Deadlocks are never nice, but deterministic deadlocks are better than nondeterministic.[4]

We've only touched the surface of the potential that promises represent. The pieces assembled in this section represent some of the basic building blocks of dataflow (Van Roy 2004) concurrency. But any attempt to do justice to data-flow concurrency in a single section would be a futile effort. At its essence, data flow deals with the process of dynamic changes in values causing dynamic changes in dependent "formulas." This type of processing finds a nice analogy in the way spreadsheet cells operate, some representing values and others dependent formulas that change as the former also change.

Continuing our survey of Clojure's parallelization primitives, we'll next discuss some of the functions provided in the core library.

11.3 *Parallel operations*

In the previous two sections, you built two useful macros, as-futures and with-promises, allowing you to parallelize a set of operations across numerous threads. But Clojure has functions in its core library that provide similar functionality: pvalues, pmap, and pcalls. We'll cover them briefly in this section.

---

[4] There are experts in concurrent programming who say that naïve locking schemes are also deterministic. Our simple example is illustrative, but alas it isn't representative of a scheme that you may devise for your own code. In complex designs where promises are created in one place and delivered in a remote locale, determining deadlock is naturally more complex. Therefore, we'd like to use this space to coin a new phrase: "Determinism is relative."

11.3.1 *The pvalues macro*

The pvalues macro is analogous to the as-futures macro, in that it executes an arbitrary number of expressions in parallel. Where it differs is that it returns a lazy sequence of the results of all the enclosed expressions, as shown:

```
(pvalues 1 2 (+ 1 2))
;=> (1 2 3)
```

The important point to remember when using pvalues is that the return type is a lazy sequence, meaning your access costs might not always present themselves as expected:

```
(defn sleeper [s thing] (Thread/sleep (* 1000 s)) thing)
(defn pvs [] (pvalues
                 (sleeper 2 :1st)
                 (sleeper 3 :2nd)
                 (keyword "3rd")))

(-> (pvs) first time)
;   "Elapsed time: 2000.309 msecs"
;=> :1st
```

The total time cost of accessing the first value in the result of pvs is only the cost of its own calculation. But accessing any subsequent element costs as much as the most expensive element before it, which you can verify by accessing the last element:

```
(-> (pvs) last time)
; "Elapsed time: 2999.435 msecs"
;=> :3rd
```

This may prove a disadvantage if you want to access the result of a relatively cheap expression that happens to be placed after a more costly expression. More accurately, all seq values in a sliding window[5] are forced, so processing time is limited by the most costly element therein.

11.3.2 *The pmap function*

The pmap function is the parallel version of the core map function. Given a function and a set of sequences, the application of the function to each matching element happens in parallel:

```
(->> [1 2 3]
     (pmap (comp inc (partial sleeper 2)))     ◁──┐ pmap attempts to parallelize
     doall                                         the mapping operations,
     time)                                         ideally allowing each sleep to
                                                   occur at the same time.

; "Elapsed time: 2000.811 msecs"
;=> (2 3 4)
```

The total cost of realizing the result of mapping a costly increment function is again limited by the most costly execution time in the aforementioned sliding window.

---

[5] Currently, the window size is $N+2$, where N is the number of CPU cores. But this is an implementation detail, so it's enough to know only that the sliding window exists.

Clearly, in this contrived case, using pmap provides a benefit, so why not replace every call to map in your programs with a call to pmap? Surely this would lead to faster execution times if the map functions were all applied in parallel, correct? The answer is a resounding: it depends. A definite cost is associated with keeping the resulting sequence result coordinated, and to indiscriminately use pmap might incur that cost unnecessarily, leading to a performance penalty. But if you're certain that the cost of the function application outweighs the cost of the coordination, then pmap might help to realize performance gains. Only through experimentation can you determine whether pmap is the right choice.

11.3.3 *The pcalls function*

Finally, Clojure provides a pcalls function that takes an arbitrary number of functions taking no arguments and calls them in parallel, returning a lazy sequence of the results. Its use shouldn't be a surprise by now:

```
(-> (pcalls
       #(sleeper 2 :first)
       #(sleeper 3 :second)
       #(keyword "3rd"))
    doall
    time)
; "Elapsed time: 3001.039 msecs"
;=> (:1st :2nd :3rd)
```

The same benefits and trade-offs associated with pvalues and pmap also apply to pcalls and should be considered before use.

Executing costly operations in parallel can be a great boon when used properly but should by no means be considered a magic potion guaranteeing speed gains. There's currently no magical formula for determining which parts of an application can be parallelized—the onus is on you to determine your application's parallel potential. What Clojure provides is a set of primitives—including futures, promises, pmap, pvalues, and pcalls—that you can use as the building blocks for your own personalized parallelization needs.

In the next section, we'll look briefly at the fold function for processing large collections in parallel.

11.4 *A brief introduction to reducer/fold*

Starting with version 1.5, Clojure ships with a library called clojure.core.reducers. This library was inspired in part by a talk Guy Steele gave at the International Conference on Functional Programming in 2009. In it,[6] Steele pointed out a weakness of data structures that only support sequential access, like Lisp's cons-cell-based lists and Clojure's lazy seq: they're incapable of supporting efficient parallelization because you can't get more input data without walking linearly through the data to get there. Simi-

---

[6] Guy Steele, "Organizing Functional Code for Parallel Execution; or, foldl and foldr Considered Slightly Harmful," http://vimeo.com/6624203.

larly, he called out `foldl` (called `reduce` in Clojure) and `foldr` (which has no native Clojure counterpart) as providing ordering guarantees that thwart parallelization.

Specifically, parallelizing a workload generally involves splitting the work into small parts, doing work on all those parts simultaneously, and then combining the results of those parts to compute the single final result. But `reduce` can't work this way because it promises to call the given reducing function on each input item in order, with the first parameter representing the reduction of everything that has come before it.

But many times when `reduce` is used, these guarantees aren't required by the reducing function being used. For example, addition is associative, which means if you want the sum of three numbers, you'll get the same answer whether you compute it as `(+ (+ a b) c)` or as `(+ a (+ b c))`. Clojure's `reducers` library provides many of the operations you know from the sequence library, but it allows you to choose whether you require sequential processing or whether you'd rather parallelize the work.

Because Clojure's `reduce` function already promises sequential operation, all that's needed is a new function that doesn't. This new function is called `fold`, and you can see its benefit in this contrived micro-benchmark:

```
(require '[clojure.core.reducers :as r])
(def big-vec (vec (range (* 1000 1000))))

(time (reduce + big-vec))
; "Elapsed time: 63.050461 msecs"
;=> 499999500000

(time (r/fold + big-vec))
; "Elapsed time: 27.389584 msecs"
;=> 499999500000
```

The proper use of `fold` in nontrivial cases depends heavily on other aspects of the reducers library that we won't cover until chapter 15. Alas, this means further discussion of `fold` must also wait until then.

11.5 *Summary*

From the expression-centric future; to the function-centric set-once "variable" promise; to the core functions `pcalls`, `pvalues`, and `pmap`, Clojure gives you the raw materials for parallelizing related tasks. These reference types and operations can help to simplify the process of slicing your problem space into simultaneous executions of (possibly) related computations. But truly fostering parallelism in your programs requires a different view of how to build algorithms that can take advantage of `fold`. Although we only touched on this topic in this chapter, we'll dive back into it in chapter 15 when we talk about Clojure's reducers framework. For now, we'll take you on a journey to explore Java interoperability.

Part 5

Host symbiosis

Clojure is a symbiotic programming language, meaning it's intended to run atop a host environment. At the moment, Clojure runs on both the Java Virtual Machine and on any host supporting the execution of JavaScript. In this part of the book, we'll focus on these two hosts and cover topics specific to and motivated by each.

Java.next 12

This chapter covers

- Generating objects on the fly with `proxy`
- Clojure `gen-class` and GUI programming
- Clojure's relationship to Java arrays
- Interfaces that all Clojure functions implement
- Using Clojure data structures in Java APIs
- Using `definterface`
- Exceptions

Regardless of your views on the Java language, it's difficult to deny that the JVM is a stellar piece of software. The confluence of the just-in-time (JIT) compiler, garbage collection, HotSpot, and the flexible bytecode have created an environment in which many programmers have chosen to grow their alternative programming languages. Additionally, the deluge of library options hosted on the JVM further makes the JVM the language target of choice. From Clojure to Groovy to Scala to Fantom to Frink to Rhino to Jess to JRuby to Jython, there seems to be no lack of options for the enthusiastic polyglot programmer. We may soon see job listings for "JVM programmers." But where does that leave Java the programming language?

Java the language isn't dead.

The JVM is optimized for running Java bytecode, and only recently[1] have Java.next languages been a consideration. You may ask yourself whether JVM bytecode is equivalent to Java source code, and the answer is no. Instead, languages such as Clojure and Scala compile directly to bytecode and can access Java compiled libraries as needed. Because of their reliance on the JVM as the runtime environment, Clojure and the other Java.next languages are fundamentally constrained by the limitations of the JVM. The limitations of the JVM as defined by the limitations of the Java language specification set the beat by which the Java.next languages dance. Java isn't dead; it's alive and well, and it runs the show.

> **THE JAVA.NEXT MANTRA**   The apprentice avoids all use of Java classes. The journeyman embraces Java classes. The master knows which classes to embrace and which to avoid.

An expert understanding of the Java Virtual Machine isn't required for writing powerful applications in Clojure, but it will help when issues stemming from host limitations arise. Fortunately, Clojure does a good job of mitigating many of the limitations inherent in its host, but some are too deeply embedded in the fibers of the JVM to avoid. Clojure provides a specific set of interoperability tools: gen-class, proxy, definterface, its exceptions facility, and a host of array functions. We'll touch on each of these in turn, but we'll begin with the creation of anonymous objects using proxy.

12.1   *Generating objects on the fly with proxy*

There's a saying in the Clojure community that Clojure does Java better than Java (Halloway 2009). This is a bold statement, but not one without merit, as we'll show throughout this chapter. Java programmers are accustomed to drawing a severe distinction between development time and runtime. Using Clojure's proxy feature allows you to blur this distinction.

> **CLOJURE APHORISM**   Many software projects require a lot of planning because their implementation languages don't foster change. Clojure makes it a lot easier to plan for change.

Clojure's proxy mechanism is meant strictly for interoperability purposes. In section 9.3, we discuss how reify is intended to realize a single instance of a type, protocol, or interface—in other words, abstractions. But when dealing with Java libraries, you're at times required to extend *concrete classes*, and it's in this circumstance where proxy shines. Be aware that by using proxy, you bring a lot of Java's semantics into your Clojure programs. Although extending concrete classes is seen often in Java, doing so in Clojure is considered poor design,[2] leading to fragility, and should therefore be restricted to those instances where interoperability demands it.

---

[1] You can find more details in JSR-000292, "Supporting Dynamically Typed Languages on the Java Platform," http://mng.bz/174x.

[2] To be fair, it should be noted that many Java programmers think this also.

12.1.1 A simple dynamic web service

Using Clojure breaks the ponderous code/compile/run development cycle by adding an element of dynamism into the fold. Take for example a scenario where you want to develop a web service using an existing Java 1.5+ API.

Listing 12.1   Importing Java classes to create a simple, dynamic web server

```
(ns joy.web
  (:require [clojure.java.io :as io]        <--- Pull in I/O functions
            [clojure.string :as string])
  (:import [com.sun.net.httpserver HttpHandler HttpExchange        <--┐ Pull in
            HttpServer]                                               │ server
           [java.net InetSocketAddress URLDecoder URI]               │ classes
           [java.io File FilterOutputStream]))

(def OK java.net.HttpURLConnection/HTTP_OK)
```

Throughout this book we've mostly glossed over namespace declarations, but this one deserves a moment of reflection. First, Clojure provides a suite of I/O functions in the `clojure.java.io` namespace, of which you'll use a couple. There are various Java-related namespaces under the higher-level `clojure.java` heading, including the aforementioned I/O, web-browser launching, Javadoc viewing, and shell execution functions. Of these, the functions in the `clojure.java.io` namespace are most widely used; and this is where we'll spend some of our focus. For now, here's the kernel of the example dynamic web server:

```
(defn respond
  ([exchange body]                              ┐ Default to return
    (respond identity exchange body))          <-─┘ what's given
  ([around exchange body]                                        ┐ Write bytes to
    (.sendResponseHeaders exchange OK 0)                         │ response, closing
    (with-open [resp (around (.getResponseBody exchange))]       │ automatically
      (.write resp (.getBytes body)))))                        <-─┘ using with-open
```

Always OK └─➤ (line 3)
Wrap response ┌─➤ (line 4)

The `respond` function is the bottom HTTP response mechanism responsible for pushing a bunch of bytes across the wire. For the sake of expediency, in this case you always return the HTTP OK (number 200). If you chose to pursue this code further, you might want a richer return code system. Regardless, let's continue by implementing a function to create a server instance using the `com.sun.net.httpserver.HttpServe` class.

Listing 12.2   Simplest possible web server using Java

```
(defn new-server [port path handler]                 ┐ doto calls methods on
  (doto                                             <-─┘ a common instance ...

    (HttpServer/create (InetSocketAddress. port) 0)      <--┐ ... of an
                                                            │ HttpServer
    (.createContext path handler)          <-─┐            │ instance
    (.setExecutor nil)                        │ Handler to call for
    (.start)))                                │ requests at a path. This
                                              └ is done via delegation.
```

The new-server function takes an HTTP port, the URL path, and a handler, used to build the response strings fed to the client via respond. The HttpServer instance returned from new-server has a handle method that will, for any given path for a request, delegate down to the given handler instance. As a first example, here is a simple handler to build a static message by using Clojure's proxy to extend the HttpHandler class.

> **Listing 12.3   Defining a default web handler using `proxy`**

```
(defn default-handler [txt]
  (proxy [HttpHandler]          <— Extend
    []                          <— No actor args
    (handle [exchange]          <— Override
      (respond exchange txt))))
```

The proxied HttpHandler instance returned by default-handler returns some closed-over text. Just like a function/closure, a Clojure proxy captures the bindings available during its creation. You take advantage of the closure nature of proxies by capturing the text given and returning a handler that uses the text as its response message:

```
(def server
  (new-server
    8123
    "/joy/hello"
    (default-handler "Hello Cleveland")))
```

After entering the code in listing 12.3, you should see the message "Hello Cleveland" in your web browser at address http://localhost:8123/joy/hello. This is only marginally interesting, especially because the source is organized in a way that doesn't take advantage of Clojure's flexibility. So, stop your server and try something a little different:

```
(.stop server 0)
```

Although you can run this code in a Clojure REPL to gain some level of dynamism, having to start and stop the server after each handler change would quickly become cumbersome. If you instead organize the code to bind the return of default-handler, you can manipulate the handler independently and update its behavior at runtime:

```
(def p (default-handler
          "There's no problem that can't be solved
           with another level of indirection"))

(def server (new-server 8123 "/" p))
```

At this point, visiting the URL at http://localhost:8123/ shows the new message. But you can take it one step further by making changes without taking the server instance down in such a clumsy fashion. Clojure provides a function named update-proxy that takes a proxied instance and a map containing method names to functions that implement their new behaviors. The functions supplied in the map must accept as their first argument the this instance that, when called, is the proxied instance. An example will make this clear:

```
(update-proxy p
  {"handle" (fn [this exchange]
              (respond exchange (str "this is " this)))})
```

Revisiting the web address http://localhost:8123/ again shows a new message corresponding to the instance representation of the proxy. The following more interesting handler reflects the request headers back to the client in a Clojure map format.

Listing 12.4   Web handler that echoes the request headers

```
(def echo-handler
  (fn [_ exchange]
    (let [headers (.getRequestHeaders exchange)]
      (respond exchange (prn-str headers)))))
```
Retrieve the headers and stringify them

The interesting part is that by holding on to the proxied handler in the p var, you can manipulate it without taking down the server. You do this by again running the update-proxy call:

```
(update-proxy p {"handle" echo-handler})
```

If you visit the same web address as before, you'll see a map-like representation of the given request headers. Pretty cool, no? For example, ours looks like the following:

```
{"Cache-control" ("max-age=0"),
 "Host" ("localhost:8123"),
 "Connection" ("keep-alive"),
 ...}
```

If you're so inclined, you can also inspect the current proxy mappings using the function proxy-mappings. The question remains—how does update-proxy change the behavior of a previously generated proxy class?

IT'S CALLED PROXY FOR A REASON

Clojure's proxy function generates the bytecode for an actual class on demand, but it does so in such a way as to provide a more dynamic implementation. Instead of inserting the bytecode for the given method bodies directly into the proxy class, Clojure instead generates a proper proxy in which each method looks up the function implementing the method's behavior. That is, based on the method name, the corresponding function is retrieved from a map and invoked with the this reference and the remaining argument(s). This trades highly useful dynamic behavior for some runtime cost, but in many cases this is a fair trade.

PROXIES FOR TRUE POWER DYNAMISM

Working from the abstract model in figure 12.1, observe how Clojure updates the mapped functions within a proxy at runtime. This web service is a humble example, but there's a point to take away from this exercise: to perform this same task in Java wouldn't be impossible but would require an enormous amount of scaffolding to

implement properly, whereas in Clojure it's built
into the language.

PROXIES AS PROPER CITIZENS

In the original `respond` function, you used a hook
named `around` that was intended to take the result
of the call to the `.getResponseBody` method and
do *something* with it. Because the result of this
method call is a `java.io.OutputStream`, you can
use that information to your advantage when creating a filtering function. The use of the `identity`
function as the default filter ensures that the
usage doesn't break in the default case; but if
you're going to use your own filtering function,
you must ensure that you properly wrap the original, which again is a perfect use case for `proxy`. A

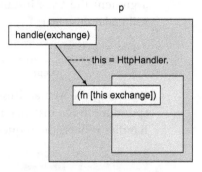

**Figure 12.1   The instance returned by
`proxy` is a proper proxy that does
method dispatch to functions in a
lookup table. These functions can
therefore be swapped out with
replacements as needed.**

simple implementation of an `html-around` filter would be implemented as in the following listing.

Listing 12.5   "Around" filter that wraps an output stream with head and body tags

```
(defn html-around [o]
  (proxy [FilterOutputStream]          ⟵── Extend stream
    [o]                                ⟵── Pass wrapped to ctor
    (write [raw-bytes]
      (proxy-super write               ⟵── Call superclass ...
        (.getBytes (str "<html><body>" ⟵── ... with wrapped bytes
                        (String. raw-bytes)
                        "</body></html>"))))))
```

The proxy returned by `html-around` extends the Java class `java.io.FilterOutput-`
`Stream` to the superclass constructor (via the `[o]` vector). It passes the argument o,
which corresponds to the `OutputStream` obtained from the `.getResponseBody` method
called in the original `respond` function. The call to the `proxy-super` function is similar
to Java's `super.method()` semantics.[3] You could use the HTML filter in the call to echo,
but that would be less than satisfying. Instead, you'll create one more handler that lists
the contents of a directory in HTML and that provides links to navigate a file system.[4]

   At the bottom of the file-system handler named `fs-handler` is a function that takes
a file and attempts to return a sequence of filenames associated with it:

```
(defn listing [file]
  (-> file .list sort))
```

---

[3] Note that in a break from almost every other construct in Clojure, `proxy-super` is *not* thread-safe. If some
    other thread were to call this proxy instance's `write` method while `proxy-super` was still running, the base
    class's method would be called directly, incorrectly skipping the proxy implementation. So be careful using
    `proxy-super` and multiple threads in close proximity to each other.

[4] This new handler operates as a watered-down version of Python's `SimpleHTTPServer` module.

> ### Anaphoric proxy
>
> In section 8.5, we discouraged you from writing *anaphoric* macros (macros with injected forward references), yet you might have noticed that `proxy` contradicts us. The use of the anaphora `this` is subject to the same nesting limitations as previously mentioned and is a good candidate for change in later versions of Clojure. You might notice that the `reify` macro, although similar to `proxy`, doesn't use an anaphoric `this` but instead requires that it be named explicitly—the preferred approach for your own macros, and likely the way forward for all future Clojure core macros.

The `listing` function expects a `File` instance for a directory but returns an empty sequence if given a file:

```
(listing (io/file "."))
;;=> (".gitignore" "README.md" "project.clj" "src" "target" "test")

(listing (io/file "./README.md"))
;;=> ()
```

Now that `listing` is in place, you can use its output to generate some HTML links, as shown next.

Listing 12.6 Quick and dirty function to generate HTML file listings

```
(defn html-links [root filenames]
  (string/join
   (for [file filenames]
     (str "<a href='"
          (str root
               (if (= "/" root)          ⟵— Append directory separator
                 ""
                 File/separator)
               file)
          "'>"
          file "</a><br>"))))
```

The `html-links` function is a quick and dirty way to build a string filled with HTML links. It's fine for the purpose of illustration, but in a production system you'd probably use something like Hiccup instead.[5] In effect, `html` builds a seq of <a> links, as shown next:

```
(html-links "." (listing (io/file ".")))

;;=> "<a href='././.gitignore'>.gitignore</a><br>
;;        <a href='./README.md'>README.md</a><br>
;;        <a href='./project.clj'>project.clj</a><br>
;;        <a href='./src'>src</a><br>
;;        <a href='./target'>target</a><br>
;;        <a href='./test'>test</a><br>"
```

---

[5] Hiccup is a library for representing HTML using Clojure data literals, found at https://github.com/weavejester/hiccup. We've had great success with this little library.

The files listed correspond to the files that happen to be in the directory where you launched your REPL. So far, so good. You have a function in `html` to produce a string for the case of a directory listing, but you'd still like to perform some action in the case where a client requests a file. One thing you could do is to serve the file back to the client, but for simplicity's sake[6] you'll build a string listing the file size.

Listing 12.7   Function to build a string representation of a file-size listing

```
(defn details [file]
  (str (.getName file) " is "
       (.length file)  " bytes."))

(details (io/file "./README.md"))

;;=> "README.md is 330 bytes."
```

To gather the file size, you use the raw `java.io.File` API. You could write a wrapper around the entire `java.io.File` API; but in general, using Java (and JavaScript in the case of ClojureScript) calls directly is perfectly acceptable form in Clojure.[7] You can see `details` in action next.

Listing 12.8   Function to convert a relative-path URI into a file

```
(defn uri->file [root uri]
  (->> uri
       str
       URLDecoder/decode          ⟵ Decode the escaped URL
       (str root)
       io/file))

(uri->file "." (URI. "/project.clj"))      ⟵ Create a file
;;=> #<File ./project.clj>

(details (uri->file "." (URI. "/project.clj")))   ⟵ Feed the file into details
;;=> "project.clj is 289 bytes."
```

Now that you have your pieces together, including `respond`, `html-around`, `html`, and `details`, you can assemble them to build your new handler.

Listing 12.9   Web handler to list and navigate a local file system

```
(def fs-handler
  (fn [_ exchange]
    (let [uri  (.getRequestURI exchange)      ⟵ URI maps to local files
          file (uri->file "." uri)]
      (if (.isDirectory file)                 ⟵ When file is a directory …
        (do (.add (.getResponseHeaders exchange)
```

---

6. The project on which this code is based, named lein-simpleton, does indeed serve the files to the client, as well as some other features not implemented here. The project is located at https://github.com/fogus/lein-simpleton.

7. And as we say that, it's worth noting that Anthony Grimes has create a library named `fs` that puts a nice Clojure face on the `java.io.File` API. It's located at https://github.com/Raynes/fs.

```
                    "Content-Type" "text/html")
              (respond html-around
                      exchange
                      (html-links (str uri) (listing file))))
            (respond exchange (details file)))))))
```

| ... respond with the
    HTML around the filter

| Otherwise just
    return details

The `fs-handler` function uses `respond` to return a string as the response depending on the type of file garnered from the request URI received. In the case of a directory, the HTML links are built and wrapped with the proper HTML blocks via the `html-around` filter. In the case of a file, the string from `details`, without a filter, suffices. Again, to set the new handler you can update the proxy as follows:

```
(update-proxy p {"handle" fs-handler})
```

If you visit the root URL at http://localhost:8123/ in a browser, you'll see the directory listing shown in figure 12.2.

If you click one of the directory links, you'll see the listing of links for that subdirectory. But if you click on one of the file links, you'll see something like figure 12.3.

And that, ladies and gentlemen, is how you can use Clojure to build a dynamic web server using Clojure and `proxy`.

Figure 12.2 A directory listing served by the simple web server

Figure 12.3 File details served by the simple web server

FINAL POINTS ABOUT PROXY

Clojure's proxy capabilities are truly dynamic, allowing you to create fully stubbed proxies using `construct-proxy`, `get-proxy-class`, or `init-proxy`. In all three cases, a partially to fully realized proxy will be constructed, allowing programmatic customization using `update-proxy` and arbitrary mixin maps.

There's a universe of difference between the code outlined in this subsection and systems employing true code hot-loading, but it's a reasonable facsimile. Using `proxy` is powerful, but doing so creates unnamed instances unavailable for later extension. If you instead want to create named classes, you'll need to use Clojure's `gen-class` mechanism, which we'll discuss next.

12.2 *Clojure gen-class and GUI programming*

In section 9.1, we mention that Clojure namespaces can be used as the basis for generating a named class. In this section, we'll address this topic and others related to

Clojure's `gen-class` function and `:gen-class` namespace directive in the context of writing a simple graphical user interface (GUI) library.

12.2.1 Namespaces as class specifications

Similar to the `ns` example in section 9.1, the explanation of `gen-class` begs a declarative approach for a namespace defining a class named `joy.gui.DynaFrame`. Suppose you'd like this class to do two things. First, `joy.gui.DynaFrame` should extend `javax.swing.JFrame` to obtain its behavior (and override where necessary). Second, `joy.gui.DynaFrame` should declare functions that provide its overriding method implementations (to be prefixed[8] by the symbol `df-`). In addition, you'd like the class to implement the `clojure.lang.IMeta` interface. You'd also like a place to store information about instances of this class in `state` and would like the initialization function called on construction to be named `df-init`. You'd like to define a single constructor, taking a string and passing it on to the superclass constructor, which also takes a string. You then want to declare two public methods: `display`, which takes a `java.awt.Container` and returns `void`; and a static method `version` that takes no arguments and returns a string. Finally, you'll declare the required imports needed.

The worded `DynaFrame` class declaration is complex but has the advantage of having a direct code translation, as shown in the following listing.

Listing 12.10 DynaFrame class ns block showing rich `gen-class` usage

```
(ns joy.gui.DynaFrame

    (:gen-class

      :name            joy.gui.DynaFrame

      :extends         javax.swing.JFrame

      :implements      [clojure.lang.IMeta]

      :prefix          df-

      :state           state

      :init            init

      :constructors    {[String] [String]

                        [] [String]}

      :methods         [[display [java.awt.Container] void]
```

:extends flag names the superclass that this namespace extends. Java allows only one superclass.

:implements flag names a vector of interfaces that this namespace implements. Java allows a class to implement the methods of any number of interfaces, but here you only implement one.

Instances can hold some state, and the :state flag names the var that holds the state data.

:init flag names an initializer function that's called after an instance of the class that this namespace implements is instantiated.

:constructors flag expects a mapping of the class constructors to the superclass constructors. You define a mapping for two constructors: one takes a String type and delegates to the constructor for javax.swing.JFrame, which also takes a String; the other takes no arguments and also maps to the superclass String constructor.

:methods flag names the public methods that will be available on the joy.gui.DynaFrame class implemented by this namespace. display takes a java.awt.Container object and returns nothing.

---

[8] If you don't specify a `:prefix`, then the default `-` will be used.

```
                    ^{:static true} [version [] String]])
```

version takes nothing and returns a String object. ^ {:static true} on the vector describing version indicates that the method is static or available on the class itself rather than its instances.

```
(:import (javax.swing JFrame JPanel JComponent)

         (java.awt BorderLayout Container)))
```

You can compile the `joy.gui.DynaFrame` namespace by saving it in a directory joy/gui, located on the classpath, in a file named DynaFrame.clj and executing the function (compile 'joy.gui.DynaFrame) in a fresh REPL. This allows a compiled class to be immediately available. But trying to create an instance in the same REPL will prove fruitless:

```
(joy.gui.DynaFrame. "First try")

; java.lang.UnsupportedOperationException:
;    joy.gui.DynaFrame/df-init not defined
```

Clearly you haven't defined the `df-init` function, so you'll do that now by switching to the `joy.gui.DynaFrame` namespace, defining it outright:

```
(in-ns 'joy.gui.DynaFrame)

(defn df-init [title]
  [[title] (atom {::title title})])
```

Now run the following in your REPL:

```
(joy.gui.DynaFrame. "2nd")

; java.lang.UnsupportedOperationException:
;    meta (joy.gui.DynaFrame/df-meta not defined?)
```

Because you told the Clojure compiler that the class should implement the `IMeta` interface, you should have provided a concrete implementation, which you can do at the REPL:

```
(defn df-meta [this] @(.state this))
(defn version [] "1.0")
```

As an added bonus, you implement the static method version. To see the effects of these functions, execute the following:

```
(meta (joy.gui.DynaFrame. "3rd"))
;=> {:joy.gui.DynaFrame/title "3rd"}

(joy.gui.DynaFrame/version)
;=> "1.0"
```

You've filled in most of the implementation of the `DynaFrame` class except for the `display` function, which you can implement as follows:

```
(defn df-display [this pane]
  (doto this
    (-> .getContentPane .removeAll)
```

```
(.setContentPane (doto (JPanel.)
                       (.add pane BorderLayout/CENTER)))
(.pack)
(.setVisible true)))
```

You can see `df-display` in action in the REPL by running the following:

```
(def gui (joy.gui.DynaFrame. "4th"))

(.display gui (doto (javax.swing.JPanel.)
                    (.add (javax.swing.JLabel. "Charlemagne and Pippin"))))
```

This displays the GUI frame shown in figure 12.4.

And because it's a `DynaFrame`, you should be able to change it on the fly, right? Right:

```
(.display gui (doto (javax.swing.JPanel.)
                    (.add (javax.swing.JLabel. "Mater semper certa est." ))))
```

This changes the view to that shown in figure 12.5.

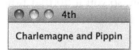

Figure 12.4   Now that you've compiled the DynaFrame class, you can start using it to display simple GUIs.

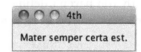

Figure 12.5   You can update the DynaFrame on the fly without restarting.

But now that you have this interesting little frame, what can you do with it? Next, you'll experiment with `DynaFrame` as the foundation for agile GUI prototyping.

12.2.2 *The guts of namespace compilation*

What exactly does the `:gen-class` directive provide in terms of generated class files? With or without `:gen-class`, Clojure generates a set of classes corresponding to each function in a namespace. For the function `joy.gui.DynaFrame/df-display`, a class file is generated on the classpath of `joy.gui.DynaFrame$df_display` containing (at least) a method invoke, at the location CLASSPATH/joy/gui/DynaFrame$df_display .class, as shown:

```
package joy.gui;
public class DynaFrame$df_display extends AFunction {
    . . .
    public Object invoke(Object that, Object container) {
        . . . display actions . . .
    }
}
```

Of course, this describes implementation details and shouldn't be considered fact in future versions of Clojure. As shown earlier, you can add implementations for the parts of the `DynaFrame` class at the REPL because Clojure generates a stub that looks up concrete implementations through vars. But these details are useful for describing the logical product of :gen-class and compile. The :gen-class directive with the argument :name joy.gui.DynaFrame creates a class vaguely resembling the following Java source:

```
package joy.gui;

public class DynaFrame extends javax.swing.JFrame {
    public final Object state;
    public DynaFrame(String title) {
        Object r =  clojure.lang.RT.var("joy.gui.DynaFrame", "df-init")
                            .invoke(title);
        Object cargs = clojure.lang.RT.nth(r, 0);
        state = clojure.lang.RT.nth(r, 1);
        super((String) clojure.lang.RT.nth(cargs, 0));
    }

    public static String version() { return "1.0"; }

    // Delegate to the display function var
    public void display(Object the_this, java.awt.Container c) {
        return clojure.lang.RT.var("joy.gui.DynaFrame", "df-display")
                    .invoke(the_this, c);
    }

    . . .
}
```

The :gen-class directive creates a class that's a delegate for the vars (prefixed as specified with df-) located in the corresponding namespace, contains the state, and also holds any static methods. This is a lot of detail to contend with, but understanding it is important when arranging your Clojure projects to take advantage of code compilation.

One final important point when using gen-class is the semantics surrounding the :impl-ns directive. This example relies on the fact that the gen-class namespace is the same as the implementation namespace (the :impl-ns), meaning the compilation transitively compiles all the implementation functions. On the other hand, when your implementation and gen-class namespaces are distinct, you no longer suffer transitive compilation. This provides the benefit of allowing a mixture of compiled (class files) and uncompiled (.clj files) Clojure products.

12.2.3 *Exploring user interface design and development with Clojure*

Before you begin this example, let's devise a simple model (_why 2007)[9] for exploring user interface design. No need to complicate matters, because the goal is only to get a general idea of how Clojure makes a typically painful task like Java GUI development a joy. To achieve this modest goal, you need the simple containers illustrated in figure 12.6: shelves, stacks, and splitters.

---

[9] The GUI model in this section is based loosely on the Ruby framework Shoes created by _why. Thank you, sir, wherever you are.

Because `DynaFrame` requires a `java.awt` `.Container` as its displayed element, you'll make each container a derivative thereof. This allows the containers to nest, helping to build richer GUIs. Finally, their forms should mirror their graphical layout, within reason. These three containers are implemented in the following listing.

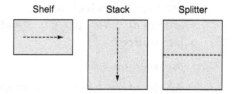

Figure 12.6   Using only a handful of rudimentary containers, you can build neato GUI prototypes.

Listing 12.11   Simple GUI containers

```
(ns joy.gui.socks
  (:import
   (joy.gui DynaFrame)
   (javax.swing Box BoxLayout JTextField JPanel
                JSplitPane JLabel JButton
                JOptionPane)
   (java.awt BorderLayout Component GridLayout FlowLayout)
   (java.awt.event ActionListener)))

(defn shelf [& components]
  (let [shelf (JPanel.)]
    (.setLayout shelf (FlowLayout.))
    (doseq [c components] (.add shelf c))
    shelf))

(defn stack [& components]
  (let [stack (Box. BoxLayout/PAGE_AXIS)]
    (doseq [c components]
      (.setAlignmentX c Component/CENTER_ALIGNMENT)
      (.add stack c))
    stack))

(defn splitter [top bottom]
  (doto (JSplitPane.)
    (.setOrientation JSplitPane/VERTICAL_SPLIT)
    (.setLeftComponent top)
    (.setRightComponent bottom)))
```

These simple GUI elements are built on top of the Java Swing library, where each subwidget in the `components` argument is added to the properly configured `Container`-derived parent. These are good as a starting point, but there's nothing to display unless you dive into the Swing API directly. You can do one better than that by providing a simple base set of widgets: buttons, labels, and text boxes.

Listing 12.12   Set of simple widgets

```
(defn button [text f]
  (doto (JButton. text)
    (.addActionListener
     (proxy [ActionListener] []
       (actionPerformed [_] (f))))))
```

```
(defn txt  [cols t]
  (doto (JTextField.)
    (.setColumns cols)
      (.setText t)))

(defn label [txt] (JLabel. txt))
```

The button element takes a function executed on a mouse click, so you'll next provide a JavaScript-like `alert` function as a simple action:

```
(defn alert
  ([msg] (alert nil msg))
  ([frame msg]
     (javax.swing.JOptionPane/showMessageDialog frame msg)))
```

Having built all these GUI elements, you can describe the first simple GUI, as shown in figure 12.7.

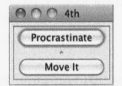

Figure 12.7
`DynaFrame` alerts: you can create slightly more complex GUIs and attach actions on the fly.

It seems simple, if not pointless. But you might be pleasantly surprised by the concise code used to describe this GUI:

```
(.display gui
  (splitter
    (button "Procrastinate" #(alert "Eat Cheetos"))
    (button "Move It" #(alert "Couch to 5k"))))
```

These widgets are adequate enough to create richer user interfaces, and to illustrate let's add one more widget builder for grid-like elements:

```
(defn grid [x y f]
  (let [g (doto (JPanel.)
            (.setLayout (GridLayout. x y)))]
    (dotimes [i x]
      (dotimes [j y]
        (.add g (f))))
    g))
```

With the small amount of code in the following listing, you can build the richer user interface shown in figure 12.8.

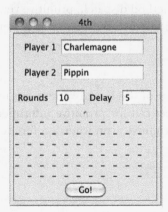

Figure 12.8 A much more elaborate `DynaFrame` GUI. There's no limit to the complexity of this simple GUI model. Go ahead and experiment to your heart's content.

Listing 12.13   A more complex GUI example

```
(.display gui
   (let [g1 (txt 10 "Charlemagne")              ◁—— Define some text boxes
         g2 (txt 10 "Pippin")
         r  (txt 3 "10")
         d  (txt 3 "5")]
      (splitter                                 ◁—— Split view for two stacks ...
        (stack                                  ◁┐
          (shelf (label "Player 1") g1)          │  ... one containing shelves
          (shelf (label "Player 2") g2)          │  of labels and text boxes ...
          (shelf (label "Rounds ") r
                 (label "Delay  ") d))           ┐   ... and another for
        (stack                                   ┘   a grid and a button
          (grid 21 11 #(label "-"))
          (button "Go!" #(alert (str (.getText g1) " vs. "
                                     (.getText g2) " for "
                                     (.getText r)  " rounds, every "
                                     (.getText d)  " seconds.")))))))
```

Although not perfect, it gives you a good idea how to extend these functions to provide a finer level of control over layout and positioning, as well as ways to provide more functionality to create richer interfaces. How would you go about creating an agile environment for incremental GUI development using plain Java? Clojure allows you to start with a powerful set of primitives and incrementally refine them until they suit your exact needs.

This section started as a description of creating a simple dynamic frame using the gen-class facility, but we felt it was worthwhile to expand into the realm of dynamic, incremental development. Sometimes ahead-of-time (AOT) compilation is absolutely necessary (such as with client requirements), but our advice is to avoid it if at all possible. Instead, use the dynamic nature of Clojure to its fullest, designing your system to fit into that model.

12.3   *Clojure's relationship to Java arrays*

In general, the need to delve into arrays should be limited, but such casual dismissal isn't always apropos. In this section, we'll cover some of the uses for Java arrays in Clojure, including but not limited to arrays as multimethod dispatch, primitive versus reference arrays, calling variadic functions and constructors, and multidimensional arrays.

12.3.1 *Types of arrays: primitive and reference*

As mentioned in section 4.1, Clojure numbers are of the boxed variety, but in many cases the Clojure compiler can resolve the correct call for primitive interoperability calls. But it can never resolve the need to pass a primitive array when a reference array is provided instead.

CREATING PRIMITIVE ARRAYS

The Java class `java.lang.StringBuilder` provides[10] a method `.append(char[])` that appends the primitive chars in the passed array to its end. But our first instinct for making this happen in Clojure doesn't bear fruit:

```
(doto (StringBuilder. "abc")
  (.append (into-array [\x \y \z])))

;=> #<StringBuilder abc[Ljava.lang.Character;@65efb4be>
```

The problem is that Clojure's `into-array` function doesn't return a primitive array of `char[]`, but instead returns a reference array of `Character[]`, forcing the Clojure compiler to resolve the call to the `StringBuilder.append(Object)` method instead. That the `Array` class is a subclass of `Object` is a constant cause for headache in Java and clearly can be a problem[11] for Clojure as well. What you really want to do is ensure that a primitive array is used as the argument to `.append`, as shown here:

```
(doto (StringBuilder. "abc")
  (.append (char-array [\x \y \z])))

;=> #<StringBuilder abcxyz>
```

Clojure provides a number of primitive array-building functions that work similarly to `char-array`, as summarized in the following list:

- `boolean-array`
- `byte-array`
- `char-array`
- `double-array`
- `float-array`
- `int-array`
- `long-array`
- `object-array`
- `short-array`

You can also use the `make-array` and `into-array` functions to create primitive arrays:

```
(let [ary (make-array Long/TYPE 3 3)]
  (dotimes [i 3]
    (dotimes [j 3]
      (aset ary i j (+ i j))))
  (map seq ary))

;=> ((0 1 2) (1 2 3) (2 3 4))

(into-array Integer/TYPE [1 2 3])
;=> #<int[] [I@391be9d4>
```

---

[10] When dealing with and manipulating strings, your best options can almost always be found in the core `clojure.string` namespace or the `clojure.contrib.string` namespace in the Clojure contrib library.

[11] In this example, it's preferred that a `java.lang.IllegalArgumentException: No matching method found` exception be thrown, because `StringBuilder` doesn't have a method matching `.append(Character[])` or even `.append(Object[])`.

Populating arrays can often be an iterative affair, as seen in the previous snippet, but there are often more concise ways to do so when creating reference arrays.

CREATING REFERENCE ARRAYS

To intentionally create an array of a particular reference type, or of compatible types, use the into-array function, passing in a sequence of objects:

```
(into-array ["a" "b" "c"])
;=> #<String[] [Ljava.lang.String;@3c3ac93e>

(into-array [(java.util.Date.) (java.sql.Time. 0)])
;=> #<Date[] [Ljava.util.Date;@178aab40>

(into-array ["a" "b" 1M])
; java.lang.IllegalArgumentException: array element type mismatch

(into-array Number [1 2.0 3M 4/5])
;=> #<Number[] [Ljava.lang.Number;@140b6e46>
```

The function into-array determines the type of the resulting array based on the first element of the sequence, and each subsequent element type *must* be compatible (a subclass). To create a heterogeneous array of java.lang.Object, use the to-array or to-array-2d function:

to-array-2d function:

```
(to-array-2d [[1 2 3]
              [4 5 6]])
;=> #<Object[][] [[Ljava.lang.Object;@bdccedd>

(to-array ["a" 1M #(%) (proxy [Object] [])])
;=> #<Object[] [Ljava.lang.Object;@18987a33>

(to-array [1 (int 2)])
;=> #<Object[] [Ljava.lang.Object;@6ad3c65d>
```

Be wary: primitives are autoboxed when using either to-array or to-array-2d.

12.3.2 *Array mutability*

Because JVM arrays are mutable, you need to be aware that their contents can change at any point. For example:

```
(def ary  (into-array [1 2 3]))
(def sary (seq ary))
sary
;=> (1 2 3)
```

What happens to sary if you change the contents of ary?

```
(aset ary 0 42)
sary
;=> (42 2 3)
```

The seq view of an array is that of the live array and therefore subject to concurrent modification. Be cautious when sharing arrays from one function to the next, and especially across threads. This can be especially disastrous if an array changes in the middle of a sequential operation, such as the use of the higher-order array functions amap and areduce, which you might use to define a sum-of-squares function[12] for arrays:

```
(defn asum-sq [xs]
  (let [dbl (amap xs i ret
                  (* (aget xs i)
                     (aget xs i)))]
    (areduce dbl i ret 0
      (+ ret (aget dbl i)))))

(asum-sq (double-array [1 2 3 4 5]))
;=> 55.0
```

At any point during the processing of asum-sq, the underlying array could change, causing inaccurate results or worse. Take great care when using Java's mutable arrays, but note that sharing only the seq of an array (typically created with the seq function) is perfectly safe because there's no way to get at the array when you only have a reference to the seq.

12.3.3 Arrays' unfortunate naming convention

You might have noticed (how could you miss?) the ugly names printed by the Clojure REPL whenever an array is evaluated. There's logic to this madness, because part of the jumble is the legal name of the class corresponding to the array—the part formed as [Ljava.lang.String;. For example, the previous name corresponded to a 1D array of strings. The representation for a 2D array of strings is then [[Ljava.lang.String;, and it therefore follows that [[[Ljava.lang.String; is a 3D array of strings. Are you sensing a pattern here? Table 12.1 lays it out.

Table 12.1 Array type class names and dimensions

Representation	Array type
[Ljava.lang.Object;	Reference array
[B	Primitive byte array
[I	Primitive int array
[C	Primitive char array
[S	Primitive short array
[F	Primitive float array
[D	Primitive double array
[J	Primitive long array
[Z	Primitive boolean array

---

[12] This function is fairly clear but slower than it should be. You'll make it faster in section 15.1.2.

Table 12.1   Array type class names and dimensions *(continued)*

Representation	Array type
Representation	Dimension
[	1D
[[	2D
...	And so on ...

Using what you know about arrays, you can use the class-representation names to do things such as multimethod dispatch:

```
(what-is (into-array ["a" "b"]))
;=> "1d String"

(what-is (to-array-2d [[1 2] [3 4]]))
;=> "2d Object"

(what-is (make-array Integer/TYPE 2 2 2 2))
;=> "Primitive 4d int"
```

You can create methods for identifying arrays and returning a descriptive string using the Class/forName method:

```
(defmulti what-is class)
(defmethod what-is
  (Class/forName "[Ljava.lang.String;")
  [_]
  "1d String")

(defmethod what-is
  (Class/forName "[[Ljava.lang.Object;")
  [_]
  "2d Object")

(defmethod what-is
  (Class/forName "[[[[I")
  [_]
  "Primitive 4d int")
```

Although this isn't the most beautiful task to perform in Clojure, it's easy to understand once you've grasped how the array class names are constructed.

12.3.4   *Multidimensional arrays*

What if you try to construct a 2D array of doubles using into-array? Observe what happens when we try the following call:

```
(what-is (into-array [[1.0] [2.0]]))
; java.lang.IllegalArgumentException: No method in multimethod
;  'what-is' for dispatch value: class [Lclojure.lang.PersistentVector;
```

The problem is that the into-array function builds a 1D array of persistent vectors, but we wanted a 2D array of doubles. In order to do this, the array must be built differently:

```
(defmethod what-is (Class/forName "[[D") [a] "Primitive 2d double")
(defmethod what-is (Class/forName "[Lclojure.lang.PersistentVector;")
[a] "1d Persistent Vector")

(what-is (into-array (map double-array [[1.0] [2.0]])))
;=> "Primitive 2d double"

(what-is (into-array [[1.0] [2.0]]))
;=> "1d Persistent Vector"
```

You have to use the map function with double-array on the inner arrays in order to build the properly typed outer array. When working with multidimensional arrays, be sure you know what your inner elements should be on creation, and create them accordingly.

12.3.5 Variadic method/constructor calls

There's no such thing as a variadic constructor or method at the bytecode level, although Java provides syntactic sugar at the language level. Instead, variadic methods expect an array as their final argument, and this is how they should be accessed in Clojure interop scenarios. Take, for example, this call to the String/format function:

```
(String/format "An int %d and a String %s"
  (to-array [99, "luftballons"]))

;=> "An int 99 and a String luftballons"
```

That covers most of the high points regarding arrays in Clojure interoperability. We'll touch on them briefly when we talk about performance considerations in chapter 15, but for now we'll move on to a more interesting topic: the interoperability underpinnings relating to Clojure's implementation.

12.4 All Clojure functions implement ...

Clojure functions are highly amenable to interoperability. Their underlying classes implement a number of useful interfaces that you can investigate by running (ancestors (class #())). Most of the resulting classes are only applicable to the internals of Clojure, but a few interfaces are useful in interop scenarios: java.util .concurrent.Callable, java.util.Comparator, and java.lang.Runnable. In this section, we'll talk briefly about each and also provide simple examples.

12.4.1 The java.util.Comparator interface

The java.util.Comparator interface defines the signature for a single method .compare that takes two objects l and r and returns < 0 if l < r, 0 if l == r, and > 0 if l > r. Every Clojure function already implements the java.util.Comparator interface, so if a function returns a value in accordance with the comparison protocol, it can be used as a comparator.[13]

---

[13] A function can unintentionally adhere to the comparator protocol and not be a comparator per se, thus causing confusion if used as such. Fortunately, this is a rare occurrence.

The static Java method `Collections/sort` provides an implementation that takes a derivative of `java.util.List` and a `Comparator` and destructively sorts the list provided. Using this knowledge, you can provide some basic infrastructure for the remainder of this subsection:

```
(import '[java.util Comparator Collections ArrayList])

(defn gimme [] (ArrayList. [1 3 4 8 2]))

(doto (gimme)
  (Collections/sort (Collections/reverseOrder)))

;=> [8, 4, 3, 2, 1]
```

In order to write your own version of a comparator (for illustrative purposes) that provides a reverse-sort `Comparator`, you might naively do so:

```
(doto (gimme)
  (Collections/sort
    (reify Comparator
      (compare [this l r]
        (cond
          (> l r) -1
          (= l r) 0
          :else 1)))))
;=> #<ArrayList [8, 4, 3, 2, 1]>
```

Although this works, Clojure provides a better way by allowing the use of potentially *any* function as the `Comparator` directly. You can couple this knowledge with the fact that Clojure already provides numerous functions useful for comparison:

```
(doto (gimme) (Collections/sort #(compare %2 %1)))     ◁— compare function
;;=> #<ArrayList [8, 4, 3, 2, 1]>

(doto (gimme) (Collections/sort >))     ◁— Greater-than function
;;=> #<ArrayList [8, 4, 3, 2, 1]>

(doto (gimme) (Collections/sort <))     ◁— Less-than function
;;=> #<ArrayList [1, 2, 3, 4, 8]>

(doto (gimme) (Collections/sort (complement <)))     ◁— complement function
;;=> #<ArrayList [8, 4, 3, 2, 1]>
```

When presented with numerous possible implementation strategies, often the best one in Clojure is the simplest.

12.4.2 *The java.lang.Runnable interface*

Java threads expect an object implementing the `java.lang.Runnable` interface, meant for computations returning no value. We won't get into the specifics of threaded computation here, but the next two examples are simple enough to require little advance knowledge. If you wish to pass a function to another Java thread, it's as easy as providing it as an argument to the `Thread` constructor, because *every* Clojure function implements the `java.lang.Runnable` interface:

```
(doto (Thread. #(do (Thread/sleep 5000)
                    (println "haikeeba!")))
  .start)
; => #<Thread Thread[Thread-3,5,main]>
; ... 5 seconds later
; haikeeba!
```

This scenario is unlikely to occur often, because Clojure's core concurrency features are sufficient for most needs. But that's not always the case, and therefore it's nice to know that raw Clojure functions can be used seamlessly in the JVM's concurrency API.

12.4.3 *The java.util.concurrent.Callable interface*

The Java interface `java.util.concurrent.Callable` is specifically meant to be used in a threaded context for computations that return a value. You can use a Clojure function using Java's `java.util.concurrentFutureTask` class, representing a "computation to occur later":

```
(import '[java.util.concurrent FutureTask])

(let [f (FutureTask. #(do (Thread/sleep 5000) 42))]
  (.start (Thread. #(.run f)))
  (.get f))
; ... 5 seconds later
;=> 42
```

The call to `FutureTask.get` as the last expression stops execution (a behavior known as *blocking*) until the function passed to the constructor completes. Because the function in question sleeps for five seconds, the call to `.get` must wait.

Clojure's interoperability mechanisms are a two-way street. Not only do they allow Java APIs to work seamlessly in Clojure, but they also provide ways for Clojure functions to work in Java APIs. In the next section, we'll continue on this theme of bidirectional interop with a discussion of the ways you can use Clojure's collection types in traditional Java APIs.

12.5 *Using Clojure data structures in Java APIs*

Clojure functions are ready to use in many Java APIs; and, as it turns out, so are its collection types. Just as the Clojure collections are separated along three distinct equality partitions[14] (maps, sequences, and sets), so too are its levels of Java collection interoperability support. The Java Collections Framework has a nice high-level design philosophy centered around working against interfaces. These interfaces are cognizant of immutability, in that the mutable parts are optional and the immutable parts are clearly demarcated. In this section, we'll give a brief rundown of ways you can use Clojure collections in traditional Java APIs adhering to the immutable collection protocols.

---

[14] You can find a refresher on equality partitions in section 5.1.2 and throughout the remainder of chapter 5.

12.5.1   *The java.util.List interface*

Clojure sequential collections conform to the immutable parts of the `java.util.List` interface, which in turn extends the `java.util.Collection` and `java.lang` `.Iterable` interfaces. You can see this conformance in action in the following listing.

Listing 12.14   `java.util.List` conformance for sequences and seqs

```
(.get '[a b c] 1)              ◁── Vectors
;=> b

(.get (repeat :a) 138)         ◁── Lazy seqs
;=> :a

(.containsAll '[a b c] '[b c])        ◁── Vectors are collections
;=> true

(.add '[a b c] 'd)                  ◁── Sequences aren't mutable
; java.lang.UnsupportedOperationException
```

That Clojure sequences and seqs don't provide the mutable API of typical Java collections is obvious. But the implications are that you can't use them in all Java APIs, such as you might attempt when requiring that a vector be sorted destructively with a Java API call:

```
(java.util.Collections/sort [3 4 2 1])
; java.lang.UnsupportedOperationException
```

A better approach is to either use the method used in the previous section using a Clojure function or, even better, to use the Clojure `sort` function.

12.5.2   *The java.lang.Comparable interface*

The interface `java.lang.Comparable` is the cousin of the `Comparator` interface. `Comparator` refers to objects that can compare two other objects, whereas `Comparable` refers to an object that can *compare itself to* another object:

```
(.compareTo [:a] [:a])
;=> 0

(.compareTo [:a :b] [:a])
;=> 1

(.compareTo [:a :b] [:a :b :c])
;=> -1

(sort [[:a :b :c] [:a] [:a :b]])
;=> ([:a] [:a :b] [:a :b :c])
```

Note that Clojure's vector implementation is currently the only collection type that implements the `java.lang.Comparable` interface providing the `.compareTo` method. As a result, attempting to compare a different collection type to a vector leads to a confusing error message:

```
(.compareTo [1 2 3] '(1 2 3))
; java.lang.ClassCastException: clojure.lang.PersistentList
;     cannot be cast to clojure.lang.IPersistentVector
```

Pay no attention to that class-cast exception behind the curtain.

12.5.3 The java.util.RandomAccess interface

In general, the `java.util.RandomAccess` interface is used to indicate that the data type provides constant-time indexed access to its elements. This allows algorithms to follow optimized paths accordingly. This optimization is generally performed by using the `.get` method for access rather than an iterator:

```
(.get '[a b c] 2)
;=> c
```

Vectors are currently the only Clojure collection type that can make such guarantees.

12.5.4 The java.util.Collection interface

The `java.util.Collection` interface lies at the heart of the Java Collections Framework, and classes implementing it can play in many of Java's core collections APIs. A useful idiom that takes advantage of this fact is the use of a Clojure sequence as a model to build a mutable sequence for use in the Java Collections API:

```
(defn shuffle [coll]
   (seq (doto (java.util.ArrayList. coll)
            java.util.Collections/shuffle)))

(shuffle (range 10))
;=> (3 9 2 5 4 7 8 6 1 0)
```

It's difficult to write a proper sequence-shuffling function, so the `shuffle` function takes full advantage of an existing Java API that has been tested and used extensively for years. As an added bonus, `shuffle` is mostly[15] functional and fast. Clojure favors immutability but doesn't trap you into it when practical solutions are available.

THE JAVA.UTIL.MAP INTERFACE

Like most of the Clojure collections, its maps are analogous to Java maps in that they can be used in nonmutating contexts. But immutable maps have the added advantage of never requiring defensive copies, and they act exactly the same as unmodifiable Java maps:

```
(java.util.Collections/unmodifiableMap
   (doto (java.util.HashMap.) (.put :a 1)))
;=> #<UnmodifiableMap {:a=1}>
(into {} (doto (java.util.HashMap.) (.put :a 1)))
;=> {:a 1}
```

---

[15] `shuffle` isn't referentially transparent. Can you see why?

In both cases, any attempt to modify the map-entry classes of the maps will throw an exception.

12.5.5 *The java.util.Set interface*

In the case of Java and Clojure sets, the use of mutable objects[16] as elements is highly frowned on:

```
(def x (java.awt.Point. 0 0))
(def y (java.awt.Point. 0 42))
(def points #{x y})
points
;=> #{#<Point java.awt.Point[x=0,y=0]>
#<Point java.awt.Point[x=0,y=42]>}
```

Everything looks peachy at this point, but introducing mutability into the equation has devastating costs:

```
(.setLocation y 0 0)
points
;=> #{#<Point java.awt.Point[x=0,y=0]>
#<Point java.awt.Point[x=0,y=0]>}
```

Oh boy. Not only have we confused the set points by modifying its entries out from underneath it, but we've also circumvented Clojure's value-based semantics and the nature of set-ness. Dealing with mutable objects is extremely difficult to reason about, especially when dealing with collections of them. The gates of a mutable class are wide open, and at any point during the execution of your programs this fact can be exploited, willingly or not. But you can't always avoid dealing with mutable nasties in Clojure code because of a strict adherence to fostering interoperability.

We've covered the two-way interop for functions and collection types, but we have one final path to traverse: the use and benefits of Clojure's definterface macro.

12.6   *The definterface macro*

As we mentioned in section 9.3, Clojure was built on abstractions in the host platform Java. Types and protocols help to provide a foundation for defining your own abstractions in Clojure, for use in a Clojure context. But when you're interoperating with Java code, protocols and types won't always suffice. Therefore, you need to be able to generate interfaces in some interop scenarios, and also for performance in cases involving primitive argument and return types. In this section, we'll talk briefly about generating Java interfaces, because the syntax, use cases, and purposes are likely familiar.

12.6.1 *Generating interfaces on the fly*

When you AOT-compile a protocol, you generate a public interface by the same name, with the methods defined. The code in the following listing uses definterface to

---

[16] Clojure's mutable reference types used to represent a logical identity are perfectly safe to use in sets. We explore the reference types in exquisite detail in chapter 11.

define an interface ISliceable. This interface is used to define an abstract thing that has the ability to be sliced using a method slice, which takes start and end indices of type int. Likewise, the interface defines a method sliceCount that returns an int representing the number of possible slices.

Listing 12.15 Interface defining a sliceable object

```
(definterface ISliceable
  (slice [^long s ^long e])
  (^long sliceCount []))
;=> user.ISliceable
```

Notice the inclusion of the type decoration ^long on the arguments to slice and the return type of sliceCount. For now you can assume that they operate the same as a type declaration in most languages. They look similar to type hints discussed in section 12.1, except that only in definterface are primitive hints supported. Now you can create an instance implementing the user.ISliceable interface, as shown next.

Listing 12.16 Dummy reified ISliceable

```
(def dumb
  (reify user.ISliceable
    (slice [_ s e] [:empty])
    (sliceCount [_] 42)))

(.slice dumb 1 2)
;=> [:empty]

(.sliceCount dumb)
;=> 42
```

There's nothing terribly surprising about dumb, but you can instead implement it via deftype, proxy, gen-class, or even a Java class. Note that definterface works even without AOT compilation.

You can take definterface to the next logical step and extend the ISliceable interface to other types using a well-placed protocol.

Listing 12.17 Using a protocol to extend ISliceable

```
(defprotocol Sliceable
  (slice [this s e])
  (sliceCount [this]))

(extend user.ISliceable
  Sliceable
  {:slice (fn [this s e] (.slice this s e))
   :sliceCount (fn [this] (.sliceCount this))})

(sliceCount dumb)
;=> 42

(slice dumb 0 0)
;=> [:empty]
```

By extending the ISliceable interface along Sliceable, ISliceable is able to participate in the protocol, meaning you have the possibility of extending other types—even final types such as String.

```
(defn calc-slice-count [thing]
  "Calculates the number of possible slices using the formula:
     (n + r - 1)!
     ------------
      r!(n - 1)!
   where n is (count thing) and r is 2"
  (let [! #(reduce * (take % (iterate inc 1)))
        n (count thing)]
   (/ (! (- (+ n 2)  1))
      (* (! 2) (! (- n 1))))))

(extend-type String
  Sliceable
  (slice [this s e] (.substring this s (inc e)))
  (sliceCount [this] (calc-slice-count this)))

(slice "abc" 0 1)
;=> "ab"
(sliceCount "abc")
;=> 6
```

The advantages of using definterface over defprotocol are restricted entirely to the fact that the former allows primitive types for arguments and returns. At some point in the future, the same advantages will likely be extended to the interfaces generated, so use definterface sparingly and prefer protocols unless absolutely necessary.

12.7   *Be wary of exceptions*

There's been much debate about the virtues of checked exceptions in Java, so we won't cover that here. Instead, we'll stick to the facts regarding the nuances the JVM imposes on Clojure's error-handling facilities. Before we begin, consider the following view on the use of exceptions in Clojure source:

> When writing Clojure code, use errors to mean can't continue and exceptions to mean can or might continue.

We'll attempt to constrain ourselves to the generalities of exception handling in this section. If you desire information on deciphering exception messages, we talk about that in section 3.4. If you're curious about the effects of exceptions on continuation-passing style, then refer to section 7.3.4. We discuss the behavior of Clojure when it attempts to supplant numerical inaccuracies by throwing exceptions in section 4.1.3. If you want to learn about the interplay between exceptions and Clojure's reference types, such matters can be found throughout chapter 11. Finally, if you have no idea what an exception is, we discuss the basics in section 2.9.

12.7.1 *A bit of background regarding exceptions*

The behavior of Clojure's exception features directly spawns from the JVM enforcing the promulgation of checked exceptions. Virtuous or not in the context of Java development, checked exceptions are antithetical to closures and higher-order functions. Checked exceptions require not only that the thrower and the party responsible for handling them should declare interest, but also that every intermediary is forced to participate. These intermediaries don't have to actively throw or handle exceptions occurring within, but they must declare that they'll be "passing through." Therefore, by including the call to a Java method throwing a checked exception within a closure, Clojure has two possible alternatives:

- Provide a cumbersome exception-declaration mechanism on every single function, including closures.
- By default, declare that all functions throw the root `Exception` or `Runtime-Exception`.

As you can probably guess, Clojure takes the second approach, which leads to a condition of multilevel wrapping of exceptions as they pass back up the call stack. This is why, in almost any (`.printStackTrace *e`) invocation, an error's point of origin is offset by some number of layers of `java.lang.RuntimeException`. Java interfaces and classes get to decide what types of problems potential derivative classes and even callers can have, so Clojure needs to handle the base `java.lang.Exception` at every level, because it has to preserve dynamism in the face of a closed system. Unless you're directly calling something that throws typed exceptions, your best bet is to catch `Exception` and then see what you have in context.

12.7.2 *Runtime vs. compile-time exceptions*

There are two contexts in Clojure where exceptions can be thrown: runtime and compile time. In this section, we'll touch on both, explaining how and when to use them.

RUNTIME EXCEPTIONS

Runtime exceptions may be the most familiar, because you're likely to have encountered and used them in your own code. There are two types of runtime exceptions: errors and exceptions. You can see the difference between the two here:

```
(defn explode [] (explode))
(try (explode) (catch Exception e "Stack is blown"))
; java.lang.StackOverflowError
```

Why can't you catch the `java.lang.StackOverflowError`? The reason lies in Java's exception class hierarchy and the fact that `StackOverflowError` isn't a derivative of the `Exception` class, but instead of the `Error` class:

```
(try (explode) (catch StackOverflowError e "Stack is blown"))
;=> "Stack is blown"
(try (explode) (catch Error e "Stack is blown"))
;=> "Stack is blown"
```

```
(try (explode) (catch Throwable e "Stack is blown"))
;=> "Stack is blown"

(try (throw (RuntimeException.))
  (catch Throwable e "Catching Throwable is Bad"))
;=> "Catching Throwable is Bad"
```

This example starts by catching the most specific exception type StackOverflow-Error and gradually decreases specificity until it's catching Throwable, which you'll notice also catches a RuntimeException. In Java, catching exceptions at the level of Throwable is considered bad form, and it should generally be viewed the same way in Clojure. Therefore, we suggest that you follow the advice stated in the opening to this section and reserve exceptions deriving from Errors for conditions that can't be continued from, and those deriving from Exception for conditions that indicate possible continuation.

COMPILE-TIME EXCEPTIONS

There are a few ways you may come across compile-time exceptions, the most obvious occurring within the body of a macro:

```
(defmacro do-something [x] `(~x))
(do-something 1)
; java.lang.ClassCastException:
;    java.lang.Integer cannot be cast to clojure.lang.IFn
```

Although the type of the exception is a java.lang.ClassCastException, it was thrown by the compiler, which you'd see if you were to trace the stack using something like (for [e (.getStackTrace *e)] (.getClassName e)).[17] It's perfectly acceptable (and even encouraged) to throw exceptions in your own macros, but it's important to make a distinction between compile-time and runtime exceptions.

> **TIP** Why delay until runtime the reporting of an error that at compile time you know exists?

The way to throw a compile-time exception is to make sure your throw doesn't occur in a syntax-quoted form:

```
(defmacro pairs [& args]
  (if (even? (count args))
    `(partition 2 '~args)
    (throw (Exception.
             (str "pairs requires an even number of args")))))

(pairs 1 2 3)
; java.lang.Exception: pairs requires an even number of args

(pairs 1 2 3 4)
;=> ((1 2) (3 4))
```

---

[17] This is a limited analogy to Groovy's .? operator. Clojure also provides convenience functions for displaying and handling stack traces in the clojure.stacktrace namespace.

Nothing is preventing the exception from being thrown at runtime, but because we know pairs requires an even number of arguments, we instead prefer to fail as early as possible—at compilation time. This difference is clearly demonstrated by repeating the preceding test in a function definition:

```
(fn [] (pairs 1 2 3))
; java.lang.Exception: pairs requires an even number of args
```

A runtime exception wouldn't have been thrown until this function was called, but because the pairs macro threw an exception at compile time, users are notified of their error immediately. Although it's powerful, you should always try to balance the benefits of compile-time error checking with macros and the advantages that implementing as a function provides (the use in higher-order functions, apply, and so on).

12.7.3 Handling exceptions

There are two ways to handle exceptions and errors, each defined by the way in which the error-handling mechanisms flow through the source. Imagine that you want a macro that provides a limited[18] null-safe (Koenig 2007) arrow that catches any occurrence of a NullPointerException in a pipeline:

```
(defmacro -?> [& forms]
  `(try (-> ~@forms)
     (catch NullPointerException _# nil)))

(-?> 25 Math/sqrt (+ 100))
;=> 105.0

(-?> 25 Math/sqrt (and nil) (+ 100))
;=> nil
```

The flow of any occurrence of NullPointerException happens from the inner functions of the stitched forms. Conceptually, this flow can be viewed as shown in figure 12.9, which describes the way errors can be caught depending on the direction in which data is moving along the stack.

The typical (try ... (catch ...)) form would therefore be used for the case where the handler catches errors bubbling outward from inner functions and forms, as seen in the -?> macro. But if you want to catch errors at their point of origin, you need a way to pass handlers up the stack. Fortunately, Clojure provides a way to do this via its dynamic var feature, which we'll discuss in section 17.4.1.

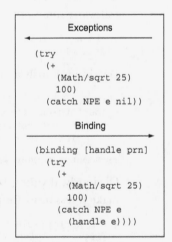

Figure 12.9 There are two ways to handle errors in Clojure. The typical way is to let exceptions flow from the inner forms to the outer. The other way, discussed in section 17.4, uses dynamic bindings to reach into the inner forms to handle errors immediately.

---

[18] You can find much more comprehensive -?> and .?. macros in the clojure.contrib.core namespace, and we recommend those over the one in this section.

12.7.4 *Custom exceptions*

Prior to Clojure 1.4, to write your own exception and error types, you needed to use the gen-class feature described in section 12.2, thus requiring that your code be compiled. JVM exceptions are a closed system, and it might be a good idea to explore other possibilities [19] for enhanced error reporting and handling. But, should you wish to ignore this advice, bear in mind that it's rare for Clojure core functions to throw exceptions, and even more rarely are they checked exceptions. The idiom is for Clojure to throw derivatives of RuntimeException or Error, and thus your code should also strive for this when appropriate.

At a lower level of operation, Clojure 1.4 introduced two new core functions ex-data and ex-info, used to attach information to load-bearing runtime exceptions. Java exceptions have always been load bearing in that they allow an arbitrary message string accessible via the Throwable#getMessage method. But to encode a finer level of detail than an error message requires extending a class from Java's exception/error hierarchy or, even worse, encoding some data type as a message string.

Clojure provides a new exception type ExceptionInfo that holds both a message string and a map. The function ex-info is a convenience function to construct instances of the ExceptionInfo type for throwing. Before you do that, consider the following function:

```
(defn perform-unclean-act [x y]
  (/ x y))
```

Division is hardly an unclean act; it's how you abuse it that corrupts:

```
(try
  (perform-unclean-act 42 0)
  (catch RuntimeException ex
    (println (str "Something went wrong."))))

;; Something went wrong.
```

Obviously, dividing by zero is an unclean act, but with the use of ex-info you can make it less nasty for potential callers:

```
(defn perform-cleaner-act [x y]
  (try
    (/ x y)
    (catch ArithmeticException ex
      (throw (ex-info "You attempted an unclean act"
                      {:args [x y]})))))
```

By catching a runtime exception like ArithmeticException you can rethrow a load-bearing exception with more contextual information. With this additional information, the caller can perhaps recover more appropriately by extracting the error context information using ex-data, as shown next:

---

[19] One library offering enhanced exception definition and handling is Slingshot, located at http://github.com/scgilardi/slingshot.

```
(try
  (perform-cleaner-act 108 0)
  (catch RuntimeException ex
    (println (str "Received error: "    (.getMessage ex)))
    (when-let [ctx (ex-data ex)]
      (println (str "More information: " ctx)))))
;; Received error: You attempted an unclean act
;; More information: {:args [108 0]}
```

The beauty of ex-data is that it can be called on any exception type, but it returns a map only if presented with a Clojure load-bearing kind. This nicely decouples the throw side from the catch side and doesn't force either to throw or catch any given concrete type.

12.8 Summary

Clojure provides an extensive set of data abstractions via its types and protocols. It also provides an extensive interoperability facility through proxy, gen-class, definterface, exception handling, and the implementation of core Java collection interfaces. Although we stress that types and protocols provide the performant abstractions needed for solving most problems, we realize that not all interop scenarios are solved this way. In these circumstances, you should use the features listed in this chapter to push you the remainder of the way toward your solution. Clojure embraces Java interoperability, but it does so in specific ways and with a specific set of tools.

In the next chapter, we move on to discuss an exciting entry in the Clojure language ecosystem: ClojureScript, a version of Clojure that runs on top of JavaScript..

Why ClojureScript?

ClojureScript is a redesign and reimplementation of Clojure and its compiler, written in a combination of Clojure and ClojureScript itself. Although the original purpose of the ClojureScript compiler was primarily to generate JavaScript to target runtimes and devices supporting it, in the long term this may be the least important feature of its design. After all, Clojure's own compiler, which currently generates JVM bytecode, could have been altered to produce JavaScript as well.

In this chapter, we'll examine the major design differences between Clojure and ClojureScript, and explore the implications of these differences. Even though ClojureScript is newer and designed with all the knowledge gleaned from the development of Clojure, Clojure is by no means abandoned. Instead, ClojureScript is an alternative implementation of Clojure that targets any platform that runs

JavaScript. ClojureScript cleverly reuses parts of Clojure such as the reader and macro-expansion machinery. This implies ClojureScript's design isn't superior to Clojure's in every context, so we'll discuss that as well.

The differences between Clojure and ClojureScript are listed on the GitHub wiki (http://mng.bz/kKZK), but many of them result from the differences between JavaScript and the JVM. They may be important details when writing programs, but they don't speak to the motivations that drove the redesign and thus are perhaps a less rich topic. Although some of these more trivial differences will come up naturally in this chapter, our focus will be on design decisions that separate concepts into simpler parts or take better advantage of parts Clojure has already separated:

- Clojure's protocols provide good separation of interfaces from implementations. In the next section, we'll look at how ClojureScript makes more use of protocols than Clojure does.
- In section 13.2, we'll look at how the ClojureScript compiler has analyze and emit phases separated by regular data values.
- Finally, in section 13.3, we'll examine how ClojureScript clarifies the distinction between compile time and runtime.

Let's begin by comparing the approaches taken by Clojure and ClojureScript in both implementing and defining the interface to count.

13.1 Implementation vs. interface

Many of the core abstractions provided by Clojure are defined using Java interfaces, whereas ClojureScript uses protocols for the same purposes. ClojureScript's approach provides much more power to programmers, as you'll see in this section. One such abstraction is Clojure's count function, which returns the number of items in a collection. Although it's defined in core.clj, the definition calls the static method clojure .lang.RT/count. Following is the implementation of this method in Clojure 1.5.1:

```
;; Clojure 1.5.1 clojure/src/jvm/clojure/lang/RT.java line 527
public static int count(Object o){
    if(o instanceof Counted)                          ◄─❶ Preferred type dispatch
        return ((Counted) o).count();
    return countFrom(Util.ret1(o, o = null));         ◄─❷ Fallback to countFrom
}

static int countFrom(Object o){                       ◄─❸ Fallback type dispatches
    if(o == null)
        return 0;
        /* ...some else-if's elided for brevity... */
    else if(o instanceof Collection)
        return ((Collection) o).size();
    else if(o instanceof Map)
        return ((Map) o).size();
    else if(o.getClass().isArray())
        return Array.getLength(o);

    throw new UnsupportedOperationException(
```

```
      "count not supported on this type: "
      + o.getClass().getSimpleName());
}
```

The methods `count` and `countFrom` form a hand-coded type-based dispatch, where the type of the collection indicates which specific behavior `count` exhibits. The first type checked is `clojure.lang.Counted` **❶**, an interface provided by Clojure specifically to indicate that a collection knows its size so `count` can return in constant or near-constant time; a map is an example. Many of Clojure's collection types implement `Counted` directly, and you are free to do so in any appropriate collection types you create. But many other types existed before Clojure's `Counted` interface was created, and although they provide methods for computing their size, they do so using different methods. Thus you have the fallback option **❷** and the various `else if` clauses of `countFrom` **❸** to dispatch to the appropriate functionality for these other types. Handling all cases in a single chain of `else if` works, of course, and is relatively fast at runtime. In particular, `count` delegates to `countFrom` so `count` can remain small enough that the JVM sees it as a good candidate for inlining.

But despite being sufficient, the design is closed—if you discover another type (either in Java or in a third-party library) that would be a good candidate to implement `count`, you have a limited and rather poor set of options. These may include wrapping the object in a new object of your own that implements `Counted` and delegates at runtime, patching Clojure to add the type to `countFrom`, and giving up and not using `count`. The first of these is a popular option, but it has several drawbacks. Wrapped objects aren't equal to their unwrapped counterparts. Also, consider what happens if another programmer wraps your object again to implement a different interface. This is another example of the expression problem we mentioned back in section 1.4.3.[1]

The solution ClojureScript uses, not surprisingly, is its protocol facility, which if you'll recall is a feature that allows you to describe interfaces for related functions (discussed more deeply in section 9.3.2). But whereas protocols allow you to solve the expression problem in your own code, they can't help Clojure itself because the code that implements protocols is built on top of a good deal of Clojure. This is where ClojureScript comes in. As you'll see in a moment, when given the opportunity to design ClojureScript, Rich and his team chose to put protocols at the bottom, building the other abstractions on top rather than the other way around as they did with Clojure. Thus the definition of `count` in ClojureScript looks a bit different:

```
;; ClojureScript r1835 src/cljs/cljs/core.cljs line 195
(defprotocol ICounted                              ◁──❶ Define the protocol
  (-count [coll] "constant time count"))

;; ClojureScript r1835 src/cljs/cljs/core.cljs line 492
(extend-type nil
```

---

[1] You can learn more about the expression problem in the description by Philip Wadler at http://mng.bz/sRul.

```
    ICounted                          ◄─❷ Define -count for nil
    (-count [_] 0))

;; ClojureScript r1835 src/cljs/cljs/core.cljs line 730
(extend-type array
    ICounted                          ◄─❸ Define -count for arrays
    (-count [a] (alength a))

;; ClojureScript r1835 src/cljs/cljs/core.cljs line 840
(defn count
    "Returns the number of items in the collection. (count nil) returns
    0.  Also works on strings, arrays, and Maps"
    [coll]
    (if (counted? coll)
        (-count coll)                 ◄─❹ Define count in terms of -count
        (accumulating-seq-count coll)))
```

The function count in ClojureScript delegates ❹ directly to the -count method of
the ICounted protocol ❶. This is then extended to JavaScript nil ❷ and arrays ❸.
The primary benefit of this approach is that you can make Clojure's count function
work with any existing JavaScript type. For example, listing 13.1 shows how you can
make count work on Google's rather interesting LinkedMap objects, without monkey
patching or risking name collisions even if an object gets a method named count or
-count. This is a substantial benefit, and ClojureScript does this in a way that has very
good runtime performance, which is why it was deemed appropriate to build Clojure-
Script's internal behavior on top of protocols. Protocol implementations can be dis-
persed to places in the code that may be far from each other, as you see in the large
variation in line numbers in the previous listing.

Listing 13.1 Extending `ICounted` to `LinkedMap`

```
(ns cljs.user
    (:require [goog.structs.LinkedMap]))

(extend-type goog.structs.LinkedMap        ❶ Delegate to
    cljs.core.ICounted                          LinkedMap's
    (-count [m] (.getCount m)))                 getCount

                                           ❷ Create an instance
(def m (goog.structs.LinkedMap.))             of LinkedMap

(count m)
;=> 0                          ❸ Unfortunately,
                                  LinkedMap is
(.set m :foo :bar)                mutable      ❹ Fortunately, you
(.set m :baz :qux)                               can still count
                                                 its elements
(count m)
;=> 2
```

The important work of telling count how to count LinkedMap is done by extend-
type ❶. In this example, the instance is created ❷ *after* the type is extended, but
reversing the order of these would work fine. This listing demonstrates that it works

by putting a couple entries in the `LinkedMap` ❸ and then using ClojureScript's normal `count` method on it ❹.

Another example of the flexibility provided by ClojureScript's deep use of protocols is the `IFn` protocol, which takes the place of the `IFn` interface in Clojure: any object that satisfies `IFn` can be called as a function. In Clojure and ClojureScript, persistent maps can be called as functions taking one argument as a key to look up within themselves:

```
(def pm {:answer 42})

(pm :answer)
;=> 42
```

But Clojure doesn't allow you to use Java's `Map` objects in this way; and, similarly, ClojureScript doesn't let you use Google's `Map` objects as functions. This is probably for good reasons, perhaps having to do with functions being immutable, whereas while those host-provided collection objects aren't. And in Clojure, nothing can be done but accept the wisdom of this decision: in Clojure, `IFn` is a Java interface and thus can't be extended to the existing Java classes, a victim of Java's unsolved expression problem.

In ClojureScript, you can ignore the value of keeping functions immutable, throw caution to the wind, and extend `IFn` to Google's `LinkedMap`.

Listing 13.2 Extending `IFn` to `LinkedMap`

```
(.set m 43 :odd)                    ◁─── Add another entry to the LinkedMap

(m 43)                              ◁─── Calling a LinkedMap as a fn doesn't work yet
;; "Error evaluating:" (m 43) :as "cljs.user.m.call(null,43)"

(extend-type goog.structs.LinkedMap
  cljs.core/IFn
  (-invoke                         ◁─── Define invoke for LinkedMaps
    ([m k] (.get m k nil))
    ([m k not-found] (.get m k not-found))))

(m 43)                             ◁─── Calling m now works
;=> :odd
```

Regardless of whether this particular extension of `IFn` is a good idea, the separation of interface from implementation provided by protocols—and ClojureScript's use of these as its most basic abstraction—hands a great deal of power to users of ClojureScript.

Another way ClojureScript grants power to its users is by separating the phases of the compiler. Let's look at that next.

13.2 Compiler internals: analysis vs. emission

In this section, we'll present an overview of the ClojureScript compiler by taking a small example expression through all the stages normally applied by the compiler. Then we'll present a much more substantial ClojureScript program, which we'll use to discuss compilation details you wouldn't normally see in tiny programs, including advanced compilation and externs files.

13.2.1 Stages of compilation

When compiling Clojure code, there's no official way[2] to see anything between the source code going in one end and the bytecode coming out the other end. Clojure-Script, on the other hand, somewhat more officially separates the compiler's analysis phase (where the input code becomes *understood*) from the emission phase (where the target language is specified). The data format between these phases is the output of the analysis phase, known as the *abstract syntax tree (AST)*.

A common misconception perpetuated about Lisp languages (and Clojure, of course) is that because source code is data, this data is an AST. But although AST is a fuzzy term whose specific meaning may vary depending on context, we think it's not an accurate way to describe Clojure source code in either its textual or its read form. For example, the forms passed into a macro aren't yet macroexpanded, and even after macroexpansion there is more analysis to be done.

Although there is no comprehensive documentation for either Clojure or Clojure-Script's AST, the ClojureScript version is just a tree of immutable data. We'll show you how to examine the AST of a given ClojureScript form, and then you'll do something useful with that information. We'll begin with an initial tour of the compilation process and the AST. Next we'll introduce a more substantial body of input code to work on, specifically some functions that use the Web Audio API to play music. Then you'll use what you've learned about the AST to examine the audio example code to help you produce more compact JavaScript output.

Let's begin by looking at the stages of compilation leading up to analysis, starting with reading, which converts text into Clojure data. This requires the ClojureScript compiler, which is packed by default in the ClojureScript distribution. Run `lein repl` in a directory that contains a project.clj file, like this:

```
(defproject joy/music "1.0.0"
  :dependencies [[org.clojure/clojure "1.5.1"]
                 [org.clojure/clojurescript "0.0-1835"]])
```

Start with a string containing the textual code for a `defn`:

```
(require '[cljs.compiler :as comp]
         '[cljs.analyzer :as ana])

(def code-string "(defn hello [x] (js/alert (pr-str 'greetings x)))")
```

To convert the `code-string` into Clojure data, read it with `read-string`:

```
(def code-data (read-string code-string))
code-data
;=> (defn hello [x] (js/alert (pr-str (quote greetings) x)))
```

---

[2] Although an exciting unofficial way is provided by Ambrose Bonnaire-Sergeant's https://github.com/clojure/jvm.tools.analyzer contrib library.

The stark difference between text and data becomes clear when you begin to interact with it:

```
(first code-string)  ;; A Character:
;=> \(
(first code-data) ;; A Symbol:
;=> defn
```

As with all LISPs, Clojure and ClojureScript both separate the reading done here from the following compilation stages. But ClojureScript separates the compilation itself into *analysis* and *emission* more clearly than Clojure does. So the next step is to analyze the read code, generating an AST:

```
(def ast (ana/analyze (ana/empty-env) code-data))
```

The AST generated even from this small snippet is dauntingly large, so although you may choose to print it, we're not going to include it verbatim in this book. Instead, we handle it gently and with respect. The AST is, as its name indicates, a tree, and each node of the tree is a persistent map. You can see the keys of the root node like this:

```
(keys ast)
;=> (:children :env :op :form :name :var :doc :init)
```

Because each node has so many keys, you can write a function, shown in the following listing, that summarizes the tree.

Listing 13.3 Definition of the `print-ast` function

```
(require '[clojure.walk :refer [prewalk]]
         '[clojure.pprint :refer [pprint]])

(defn print-ast [ast]
  (pprint                          ⟵── Print nicely indented
    (prewalk
      (fn [x]                      ⟵── Rewrite each node of the AST
        (if (map? x)
          (select-
       keys x [:children :name :form :op])   ⟵──❶ Return some entries
          x))                      ⟵┐
        ast)))                       │  Non-map nodes are
                                   ❷ left unchanged
```

The specific keys in each node depend on the node type, which is primarily indicated by its `:op`. Some other common keys are `:form` and `:name` ❶. Every non-leaf node has a `:children` key, and although the components of its value are often available under more specific keys of the node, the existence of the `:children` entry eases generic navigation of the tree. The leaves of the tree are left alone ❷, and the entire tree is printed with pleasant indentation via `pprint`. The output of calling `(print-ast ast)` is as follows:

```
{:op :def,                              ⟵──❶ def node, expanded from defn
 :form (def hello (clojure.core/fn ([x]
                   (js/alert (pr-str 'greetings x)))))),
```

```
:name cljs.user/hello,
:children
[{:op :fn,                                ◁──❷ fn* node, also expanded from defn
  :form (fn* ([x] (js/alert (pr-str 'greetings x)))),
  :name hello,
  :children
  [{:op :do,
    :form (do (js/alert (pr-str 'greetings x))),
    :children
    [{:op :invoke,
      :form (js/alert (pr-str 'greetings x)),
      :children
      [{:op :var, :form js/alert}
       {:op :invoke,
        :form (pr-str 'greetings x),
        :children
        [{:op :var, :form pr-str}
         {:op :constant, :form greetings}
         {:op :var, :form x}]}]}]}]}]}
```

Note how each node's :form value is the result of fully macroexpanding the outermost form at that point, whereas inner forms are left alone until deeper into the tree. For example, defn became def at the root node ❶, but its fn doesn't become fn* until the next level deeper ❷. We'll come back to macroexpansion in the next section.

What's important is that at this point, almost all the heavy lifting of the compilation process has been done, and most of it is unrelated to JavaScript. This AST can be used for a variety of things. Of course, it's meant primarily to be used in emitting JavaScript:

```
(comp/emit ast)
; cljs.user.hello = (function hello(x){
; return alert(cljs.user.pr_str.call(null,
;    new cljs.core.Symbol(null,"greetings","greetings",
;                   432603411,null),x));
; });
;=> nil
```

It can also be used to generate other outputs or to identify patterns that can be optimized. We have another use in mind, but first we need a more substantial example.

13.2.2 Web Audio

"Ah, music," he said, wiping his eyes. "A magic far beyond all we do here!"
—Professor Albus Dumbledore[3]

Web Audio is a W3C Working Draft (W3C 2013) for synthesizing real-time audio streams in the browser. Currently, only WebKit browsers like Chrome and Safari support the draft as written, but despite it being at the cutting edge of browser support, ClojureScript can use it just fine. Bear in mind that we don't plan to cover the Web Audio API in depth.

---

[3] *Harry Potter and the Sorcerer's Stone*, by J. K. Rowling (Scholastic, 1999).

To easily get your ClojureScript compiled and loaded into the browser, update project.clj (refer to the preface for what this file does and means) as shown in the following listing to include the `cljsbuild` plug-in and related configuration options.

Listing 13.4   project.clj for music

```clojure
(defproject joy/music "1.0.0"
  :dependencies [[org.clojure/clojure "1.5.1"]
                 [org.clojure/clojurescript "0.0-1835"]]
  :plugins [[lein-cljsbuild "0.3.2"]]          ← cljsbuild requirement
  :cljsbuild
  {:builds                     ← cljsbuild options
   [{:source-paths ["src/cljs"]
     :compiler
     {:output-to "dev-target/all.js"
      :optimizations :whitespace
      :pretty-print true}}]})
```

You also need a small amount of HTML to load the JavaScript that the ClojureScript compiler will produce. Put the following HTML in a file named music.html in the same directory as project.clj.

Listing 13.5   HTML contents of music.html

```html
<!DOCTYPE html>
<html lang="en">
  <head><title>Web Audio with ClojureScript</title></head>
  <body>
    <button onclick="joy.music.go()">Play</button>
    <script src="dev-target/all.js"></script>
  </body>
</html>
```

Now all you need is the ClojureScript that this HTML is expecting. Begin with the functions in the next listing, which use host interop to manipulate Web Audio. These functions belong in a file named src/cljs/joy/music.cljs. The src directory belongs in the project root, next to project.clj and music.html.

Listing 13.6   Web Audio functions in ClojureScript

```clojure
(ns joy.music)
                                        ❶ Create and configure
(defn soft-attack                          a gain node
  "Return a gain node that goes from silent at time <delay>
  up to <volume> in 50 milliseconds, then ramps back down
  to silent after <duration>"
  [ctx {:keys [volume delay duration]}]
  (let [node (.createGainNode ctx)]
    (doto (.-gain node)
      (.linearRampToValueAtTime 0 delay)        ❷ Set the max volume
      (.linearRampToValueAtTime volume (+ delay 0.05))  ←  of the gain node
      (.linearRampToValueAtTime 0 (+ delay duration)))
    node))
```

```
(defn sine-tone
  "Return an oscillator that plays starting at
  <delay> for <duration> seconds"
  [ctx {:keys [cent delay duration]}]
  (let [node (.createOscillator ctx)]
    (set! (-> node .-frequency .-value) 440)
    (set! (-> node .-detune .-value) (- cent 900))
    (.noteOn node delay)
    (.noteOff node (+ delay duration))
    node))
```

❸ Create and configure an oscillator node

❹ Set the cent of the oscillator

```
(defn connect-to
  "Connect the output of node1 to the input of node2,
  returning node2"
  [node1 node2]
  (.connect node1 node2)
  node2)
```

❺ Connect two nodes

```
(defn woo
  "Play a 'woo' sound; sounds a bit like a glass harp."
  [ctx note]
  (let [linger 1.5
        note (update-in note [:duration] * linger)]
    (-> (sine-tone ctx note)
        (connect-to (soft-attack ctx note)))))

(def make-once (memoize (fn [ctor] (new ctor))))
```

❻ Create and connect nodes to play a note

```
(defn play!
  "Kick off playing a sequence of notes. note-fn must take
  two arguments, an AudioContext object and a map
  representing one note to play. It must return an AudioNode
  object that will play that note."
  [note-fn notes]
  (if-let [ctor (or (.-AudioContext js/window)
                    (.-webkitAudioContext js/window))]
    (let [ctx (make-once ctor)
          compressor (.createDynamicsCompressor ctx)]
      (let [now (.-currentTime ctx)]
        (doseq [note notes]
          (->
            (note-fn ctx (update-in note [:delay] + now))
            (connect-to compressor))))
      (connect-to compressor (.-destination ctx)))
    (js/alert "Sorry, this browser doesn't support AudioContext")))
```

❼ Play notes using a note fn

❽ Protect your speakers and ears

Many of these functions take ctx and an AudioContext argument. This is an object the browser uses to track real mutable resources, so unfortunately none of these functions are pure. The functions soft-attack ❶ and sine-tone ❸ each construct and return a specific kind of AudioNode. Each AudioNode in the Web Audio API can have inputs and outputs, and the connect-to ❺ function supports hooking these together conveniently. The woo function ❻ does exactly this, creating and connecting Audio-Nodes to produce an output that sounds something like a glass harp, lingering for a bit longer than the specified note's duration. One more node is created at ❽: a compressor that prevents you from accidentally over-driving your speakers.

The final function in this listing, play! ❼, plays an entire tune based on its two parameters. The first, note-fn, should be a function like woo that takes a single note and returns an AudioNode that plays that note at the appropriate time. The second parameter to play! is a sequence of notes, each of which is a map with keys :cent, :duration, :delay, and :volume. A *cent* is a number that describes the pitch of a note relative to a chromatic scale, where the distance from one note on the scale to the next is 100 cents. The cent is used by sine-tone ❹. The duration and delay here are given in seconds and are used in soft-attack and sine-tone. The volume is on a scale from 0 to 1 as used at ❷. The delay indicates how long to wait from the beginning of the tune until this note is played. Thus to play a single note that lasts a little longer than a second, you can call play! like this:

```
(play! woo [{:cent 1100, :duration 1, :delay 0, :volume 0.4}])
```

To try that, add it to the end of your music.cljs file, compile it by running lein cljsbuild once, and then open music.html in your WebKit-based web browser. When the page has finished loading, you should be greeted by a tone. Make sure your volume is turned up!

You can change the tone to an arpeggio chord like this:

```
(play! woo [{:cent 1100, :duration 1, :delay 0.0, :volume 0.4}
            {:cent 1400, :duration 1, :delay 0.2, :volume 0.4}
            {:cent 1800, :duration 1, :delay 0.4, :volume 0.4}])
```

But these notes aren't as pleasant as a tune, so next let's build up some pure functions to help construct melodies. Add the following functions to your music.cljs file.

Listing 13.7 Tune-construction functions

```
(defn pair-to-note                                    ←──❶ Convert a pair to a map
  "Return a note map for the given tone and duration"
  [[tone duration]]
  {:cent (* 100 tone)
   :duration duration
   :volume 0.4})

(defn consecutive-notes                               ←──❷ Put the notes in order
  "Take a sequence of note maps that have no :delay, and return them
  with correct :delay's so that they will play in the order given."
  [notes]
  (reductions (fn [{:keys [delay duration]} note]
                (assoc note
                   :delay (+ delay duration)))         ←──❸ Compute the delay
              notes))

(defn notes [tone-pairs]                              ←──┐
  "Returns a sequence of note maps at moderate tempo for      Convert pairs to
  the given sequence of tone-pairs."                    ❹  maps in order
  (let [bpm 360
        bps (/ bpm 60)]
    (->> tone-pairs
         (map pair-to-note)
```

```
          consecutive-notes
          (map #(update-in % [:delay] / bps))
          (map #(update-in % [:duration] / bps)))))
(defn magical-theme                          ⟵ 5  Define a melody
  "A sequence of notes for a magical theme"
  []
  (notes
    (concat
      [[11 2] [16 3] [19 1] [18 2] [16 4] [23 2]]
      [[21 6] [18 6] [16 3] [19 1] [18 2] [14 4] [17 2] [11 10]]
      [[11 2] [16 3] [19 1] [18 2] [16 4] [23 2]]
      [[26 4] [25 2] [24 4] [20 2] [24 3] [23 1] [22 2] [10 4]
       [19 2] [16 10]]])))
(defn go []                                  ⟵ 6  Play a melody
  (play! woo (magical-theme)))
```

Starting with `magical-theme` ❺ near the bottom of the listing, you can see a tune described somewhat conveniently as a sequence of pairs, where each pair is a vector of tone and duration. This time, each tone is given in hundreds of cents so you don't have to type as many zeros, and the duration is given in beats so you can speed up or slow down the playback later.

Although these pairs are succinct for defining a tune, they're not the format expected by `play!` and thus need to be transformed. The `pair-to-note` function ❶ does the first part of this, returning a map for a pair, computing a cent, and setting the volume. The `consecutive-notes` function ❷ takes a sequence of these notes and adds a `:delay` field ❸ to each of them such that they will play one after another. This is no good for generating chords, but it's handy for melodies. Finally, `notes` ❹ takes the entire sequence of pairs, uses the other functions just described, and converts the beat-based duration and delay values to seconds as needed by `play!`. With all these together, the `go` function ❻ has what it needs to call `play!` and play your tune.

If you compile this with `lein cljsbuild once` and reload music.html in your browser, the tune shouldn't play right away. Nothing has called the `go` function yet. To play the tune, click the Play button on the web page. The `onclick` handler of that button calls the JavaScript function `joy.music.go`, which is generated from the `go` function in the `joy.music` ClojureScript namespace. Voilà, music!

This `go` function, as well as all the other ClojureScript functions you've written, plus all the other functions provided by ClojureScript to support the entire language runtime, are compiled into your dev-target/all.js file. Would you be surprised to learn that this file is well over 700 KB, at least on our computer? Although this may not be a lot for the runtime system of an entire language, you can do better.

13.2.3 *Advanced compilation*

By itself, the ClojureScript compiler generates JavaScript code that, simply speaking, is bulky. The reason for the size of the generated JavaScript code is that the ClojureScript compiler is naive (by design) about the structure and content of the code it compiles.

Rather than attempt to create a compiler that was smart about the code that it produces, the ClojureScript creators decided to defer the smarts of code compression and elision to another tool developed by Google, which we'll discuss in brief shortly.

An optional (but on by default) part of the ClojureScript build process is the Google tool called the Closure compiler (note the *s*)—we'll call it GClosure for clarity. This compiler reads in JavaScript, groks it quite deeply, and writes new JavaScript back out. If you look at the dev-target/all.js file, you'll see one style of JavaScript it can produce, as specified in project.clj: `{:output-to "dev-target/all.js", :optimizations :whitespace, :pretty-print true}`. In this mode, GClosure pulls in all the files it's asked to, removes whitespace and comments, fixes the indentation, and concatenates the files into a single output file, 700 KB worth in this case.

But GClosure also has an advanced optimization mode in which functions and variables, both local and global, are renamed to shorter names and dead code is eliminated. You can try this mode by adding another item to the `:builds` value of project.clj:

```
{:source-paths ["src/cljs"]
 :compiler
 {:output-to "prod-target/all.js"
  :optimizations :advanced
  :pretty-print false}}
```

Now, when you run `lein cljsbuild once`, in addition to an updated dev-target/all.js file you'll also get a new prod-target/all.js file. This file is about 54 KB—dramatically less than the 700 KB produced by whitespace-optimization mode. To try it, update the HTML to point at it:

```
<script src="prod-target/all.js"></script>
```

Reload the HTML in your browser, click the Play button, and … nothing happens. If you check your JavaScript console, you may see an error like this:

```
Uncaught ReferenceError: joy is not defined
```

What a dismal world, where there is no definition of *joy*. This is where GClosure's function renaming gets you into trouble. The problem is that the `joy.music` namespace and the `go` function in it have been renamed; but because GClosure never sees the HTML file, it doesn't know that the call to `joy.music.go()` in the `onclick` handler needs to be renamed. So instead of renaming `go` in the HTML file, you can use export to tell GClosure to skip renaming the `go` function everywhere. Any time you have ClojureScript that wants to expose a specific var name to other code, you need to mark it as export, like this:

```
(defn ^:export go []
  (play! woo (notes magical-theme)))
```

Now, after rebuilding and reloading, you'll get a different error. The code trips your browser's missing-feature detectors, and an alert pops up saying, "Sorry, this browser doesn't seem to support AudioContext." You know this to be a lie, because the music was working fine in the previous section. What's actually going on is more trouble with renaming. In this case, it's the mirror image of the problem with go. The code is attempting to use public names from the AudioContext API, but when GClosure processes the code, it renames calls to that API. To prevent this, you need to use an externs file to tell GClosure which names to leave alone. Specify the externs file to use by adding it to the :compiler section of project.clj from listing 13.4 so it looks like this:

```
{:output-to "prod-target/all.js"
 :optimizations :advanced
 :externs ["externs.js"]
 :pretty-print false}
```

Then provide an externs.js file in your project root directory. The first thing this example tries to do is detect whether the browser has an AudioContext or webkit-AudioContext property in its window object. To make sure these aren't renamed by GClosure, add references to them in the externs.js file:

```
var window = {};
window.AudioContext = function(){};
window.webkitAudioContext = function(){};
```

This tells GClosure about three names that it should leave alone. The first the ubiquitous JavaScript global, window. This isn't strictly necessary because GClosure already knows not to rename references to window, but we include it for completeness. The next two lines name the properties AudioContext and webkitAudioContext. Globals and properties are the two kinds of entries GClosure understands in an externs file.

With the project.clj and externs.js files updated, you can try rebuilding and reloading the program. The cljsbuild plug-in doesn't generally notice changes to externs files, so you need to touch the music.cljs file, perhaps by forcing your editor to write it to disk again, before rebuilding and reloading. This time the browser should get past the feature sniffing, but then it fails again this time with

```
Uncaught TypeError: Object #<AudioContext> has no method 'ub'
```

Your error may have something other than ub, but it's no doubt just as meaningless. So you've found a couple names that must be in the externs file, but apparently more are needed. How can you find all the entries needed for this ClojureScript example to run? One solution would be to go through the Web Audio API documentation and hand-write an externs.js file, updating it in the future as new versions of the API come out.

Another solution would be to carefully analyze your code by hand, identify public globals and properties used, and continue to add them manually to the externs file. If the program still didn't work, you could assume you missed one and repeat the process. But we already showed how to use the ClojureScript compiler to analyze source code, so let's see if you can use that to automate the creation of externs.js.

13.2.4 Generating an externs.js file

In the previous example of using the ClojureScript analyzer, you were analyzing a single form. To analyze the music example, you need to read an entire file and analyze each of the forms in it. Functions for doing this are shown in the following listing.

Listing 13.8   Using `analyze` to generate an AST for a ClojureScript file

```
(ns joy.externs-for-cljs
  (:require [cljs.compiler :as comp]
            [cljs.analyzer :as ana]
            [clojure.walk :refer [prewalk]]
            [clojure.pprint :refer [pprint]]
            [clojure.java.io :as io])
  (:import (clojure.lang LineNumberingPushbackReader)))

(defn read-file
  "Read the contents of filename as a sequence of Clojure values."
  [filename]
  (let [eof (Object.)]
    (with-open [reader (LineNumberingPushbackReader.
                         (io/reader filename))]
      (doall
        (take-while #(not= % eof)
                    (repeatedly #(read reader false eof)))))))
```

Force an entire seq so it doesn't escape the with-open

```
(defn file-ast
  "Return the ClojureScript AST for the contents of filename. Tends to
  be large and to contain cycles -- be careful printing at the REPL."
  [filename]
  (binding [ana/*cljs-ns* 'cljs.user
            ana/*cljs-file* filename]
    (mapv #(ana/analyze (ana/empty-env) %)
          (read-file filename))))
```

Use cljs.user as the default namespace

You already saw how large the AST is even for a small piece of code, so it's wise to handle the return value of `file-ast` with care:

```
(count (file-ast "src/cljs/joy/music.cljs"))
;=> 11

(first (file-ast "src/cljs/joy/music.cljs"))
;=> {:requires nil, :form (ns joy.music) ...}
```

When finding specific uses of JavaScript interop that may need to have their names protected, you want to find all uses of interop, but you don't really care about the nested forms in which they're found. So you can define a function that turns the entire AST into a single flat sequence of nodes:

```
(defn flatten-ast [ast]
  (mapcat #(tree-seq :children :children %) ast))

(def flat-ast (flatten-ast (file-ast "src/cljs/joy/music.cljs")))

(count flat-ast)
;=> 473
```

By exploring the AST yourself, you could no doubt find the interop forms you're seeking. There's not currently any comprehensive documentation for the ClojureScript AST, so exploring examples and reading the compiler source code are generally the only options for gaining that kind of knowledge. Or we can tell you: interop nodes in the AST use :dot in their :opentry, and a name in either a :method or :field entry. You can find these names with a get-interop-used function:

```
(defn get-interop-used
  "Return a set of symbols representing the method and field names
  used in interop forms in the given sequence of AST nodes."
  [flat-ast]
  (set (keep #(some % [:method :field]) flat-ast)))

(get-interop-used flat-ast)
;=> #{noteOn value webkitAudioContext AudioContext gain
 createDynamicsCompressor frequency detune linearRampToValueAtTime
 destination currentTime createOscillator createGainNode connect
 noteOff}
```

The symbols returned by get-interop-used look like names from the Web Audio API that must remain unmodified in the final JavaScript, which is encouraging. Aren't you glad you didn't have to find them all by squinting at code and using trial and error? Now you just need to use these to generate the appropriate lines of JavaScript to populate the externs file.

Fortunately, GClosure isn't currently smart enough to determine the actual class used in your application's source code at each method call or field usage, so it ignores the class name in the externs file. This means you can use a dummy name for the class when defining method and field externs:

```
(defn externs-for-interop [syms]
  (apply str
        "var DummyClass={};\n"
        (map #(str "DummyClass." % "=function(){};\n")
            syms)))
```

It's time to try this and see if the music will live again. First generate the externs.js file for the music project:

```
(spit "externs.js" (externs-for-interop (get-interop-used flat-ast)))
```

As mentioned earlier, changes to externs files aren't enough to trigger a rebuild, so you need to touch your music.cljs file. With that done, regenerate the optimized JavaScript:

```
lein cljsbuild once
```

Reload in the browser, click the Play button, and you should once again hear your little melody.

A quick check of the latest prod-target/all.js shows a working file that weighs in at just 60 KB, down from the first working dev-target/all.js file that was over 700 KB: an order of magnitude improvement. But it did take a lot of effort to get GClosure's advanced mode to generate working code. You'll have to decide for yourself which situations call for advanced mode and which don't.

We showed you how to examine the AST to find the methods and fields that were used, but there is another category of names that must sometimes be protected via externs files: class names. Extracting a useful set of class names from the AST is a bit trickier because they can look to the ClojureScript compiler like namespace names instead. The mechanisms required to do this are beyond the scope of this section, but the necessary code is provided in the joyofclojure github repository.

This may be a good time to step back for a moment to note the benefits and costs generated by the ClojureScript AST being made of regular Clojure data types. One cost is that you have to put extra thought into dealing with lazy sequences when used in proximity to side effects like reading from a mutable input stream. On the other hand, you can take advantage of familiar and powerful functions like take-while, keep, and some and techniques like using hash maps as functions to succinctly compute the results you want. Contrast this with the work that would be required if each node of the AST were a different class with its data tucked behind type-specific accessors. ClojureScript provides interesting options by giving you access to the workings of the compiler and providing an AST made up of normal data.

All this analysis, emission, and GClosure work is done at compile time. Next we'll look at the separation of compile time from runtime.

13.3   *Compile vs. run*

> *LISP programmers know the value of everything and the cost of nothing.*
>
> —Alan Perlis[4]

One of the defining characteristics of all but the most minimal LISPs is that you can execute arbitrary code at compile time via macros. In Clojure, this blurs and interleaves the lines between runtime and compile environments. The compiler evaluates user functions, which may in turn be defined in terms of macros. The runtime environment provides eval, which in turn invokes the compiler. ClojureScript draws sharper lines between these pieces, resulting in interesting implications.

A runtime without eval or a compiler has no need for all the mechanics of analysis, optimization, and emission. Part of analysis is macroexpansion, so that isn't needed either. Without macroexpansion, there is no need for the runtime environment to even be aware of the concept of macros, let alone specific macros and the namespaces where they live. Without macros, there is no need for any functions that are used exclusively by those macros.

You can see one aspect of this separation in ClojureScript's ns operator, which has two different *requires* directives: :requires and :require-macros. The former declares which namespaces must be made available at runtime in order for the cur-

---

[4] "Epigrams on Programming," *SIGPLAN Notices* 17, no. 9 (1982): 7-13.

rent namespace to run, and the latter declares which namespaces must be made available at compile time in order for the current namespace to compile.

The separation is solidified even more by the differences between the JVM and JavaScript. Everything ClojureScript does at compile time, including macroexpansion and calling the functions used by macros, uses Clojure and runs in the JVM; whereas everything named by `:requires` is compiled to JavaScript and is run in the browser or other JavaScript environment.

This can be easily explored using the earlier music example. Although the Web Audio functions `soft-attack`, `sine-tone`, and so on (shown in listing 13.6) use the Web Audio API and thus *must* run in the browser, the functions `pair-to-note`, `consecutive-notes`, and `notes` (listing 13.7) purely manipulate Clojure data and thus could be run at compile time so the browser would see only the results, not the functions for computing them. To do this, you need to port these functions from ClojureScript to Clojure and make your project aware of them. This requires a few steps:

1 Add a line to project.clj to add a new Clojure source directory: `:source-paths` `["src/clj"]`.
2 Copy the functions from listing 13.7 into a new file, src/clj/joy/macro_tunes.clj.
3 Add a header to the top of the file: `(ns joy.macro-tunes)`.
4 Add a macro definition to the bottom of the file:

    `(defmacro magical-theme-macro [] (vec (magical-theme)))`.

At this point the port is complete except for a couple of bugs we'll track down later, but the existing ClojureScript code isn't using this new macro. Fix that next:

1 In src/cljs/joy/music.cljs, add a `:require-macros` line so your header looks like this: `(ns joy.music (:require-macros [joy.macro-tunes :as mtunes]))`.
2 Make the `go` function use the new macro by replacing the call to `(magical-theme)` with one to `(mtunes/magical-theme-macro)`.

You're now in a position to try the new arrangement of the code. But a couple of bugs are lurking—code that was correct ClojureScript but is incorrect Clojure. Over the next few paragraphs, we'll show the error messages, explain the differences between Clojure and ClojureScript that cause the messages, and describe how to fix these issues.

The first problem can be discovered by running `lein cljsbuild once`, which generates a rather inscrutable message having to do with a null pointer. The mistake is in the `consecutive-notes` function, in listing 13.7, where you call `reductions` with only two arguments, causing it to seed the parameters to the anonymous function with a `nil`. The function destructures, assigning `nil` to both `delay` and `duration`. These are then added together. This was happening all along in ClojureScript, but that meant it was JavaScript's semantics for addition that were in play; and in JavaScript, adding null to null is perfectly legal and returns zero such that subsequent additions work fine.

But this code is now running at compile time in Clojure, where adding `nil`s is a throwable offense. Fix this by adding a seed value to the `reductions` call, shown in the following listing.

```
(defn consecutive-notes
  "Take a sequences of note maps that have no :delay, and return them
  with correct :delay's so that they will play in the order given."
  [notes]
  (reductions (fn [{:keys [delay duration]} note]
                (assoc note
                  :delay (+ delay duration)))
              {:delay 0 :duration 0}          ⟵— New seed value
              notes))
```

You may need to touch or resave the music.cljs file to make `cljsbuild` recognize that anything needs to be rebuilt. Another attempt to build then uncovers the next (and final) bug in the Clojure port:

```
No method in multimethod 'emit-constant'
for dispatch value: class clojure.lang.Ratio
```

This is because you're doing division on integers. Because JavaScript only has floating-point numbers, dividing any two things results in a float. But in Clojure, dividing two integers returns a ratio. Note the subtle but real difference between the environment in which the compiler and macros are running and the one in which the compiled code runs. ClojureScript doesn't know how to take the ratios your macros create and emit them as JavaScript, so you have to help it. In `notes` of listing 13.7, replace the last two uses of `/` with `(comp double /)` so that it looks as shown next.

```
(defn notes [tone-pairs]
  "Returns a sequence of note maps at moderate tempo for the given
  sequence of tone-pairs."
  (let [bpm 360
        bps (/ bpm 60)]
    (->> tone-pairs
         (map pair-to-note)
         consecutive-notes
         (map #(update-in % [:delay] (comp double /) bps))     ⟵——┐ Emit doubles
         (map #(update-in % [:duration] (comp double /) bps))))))    instead of
                                                                     ratios
```

Touch music.cljs, and your next rebuild should produce clean results. Reload the browser, and the Play button should work once again. The runtime behavior is identical to what it was before you ported half the code to Clojure, but the compiled results are different in an important way. If you compare prod-target/all.js before and after the port to Clojure, you'll see that where there used to be JavaScript literals for vector pairs and functions for processing them, now there is instead JavaScript that expresses the sequence of note maps directly. There could be use cases for doing this kind of port in order to reduce the size of the final .js file or to hide proprietary algorithmic code from being sent to browsers over the network.

But although there may be such use cases, our main point here is more general. ClojureScript makes the distinction between compile time and runtime a good deal sharper than it is in Clojure. But they're distinct even in Clojure. One kind of distinction is demonstrated by how you use build tools like Leiningen and Maven to resolve dependencies at compile time. Although an uber jar[5] built by such tools has all the current dependencies and can even eval new Clojure code at runtime, there is no guarantee the runtime system will be able to add new dependencies the way you do all the time during development. The systems where you develop and build generally have access to servers that provide dependencies for download, but the systems running the deployed application may not. Hopefully the fact that ClojureScript's build and runtime environments are so clearly distinct can help you think more clearly about the distinctions in Clojure.

ClojureScript's clearer separation has other practical benefits. You could add a top-level call to (go) at the end of music.cljs without any fear that the ClojureScript compiler would attempt to play music at compile time. It wouldn't make any sense, because no Web Audio API is available in the JVM where the compiler is executing. Yet the compiled JavaScript would have the equivalent call so that as soon as the all.js file was done loading in the browser, the tune would start playing. Contrast this with Clojure, where each top-level form is evaluated immediately after it's compiled, even when ahead of time (AOT) compilation is being used. This is sometimes described as the compiler "launching missiles," although in our example it would be more likely to launch music.

Another benefit is that separation of the sort ClojureScript provides allows for cross-compilation without an emulator. You've been doing this all along in this chapter, compiling to JavaScript but only needing a JavaScript interpreter to test the results. Imagine if you had this ability for compiling to other runtimes such as the CLR. Right now, in order to compile a Clojure project for CLR, you either need to use ClojureCLR, where the compiler itself is running the CLR runtime, or you need to use a JVM emulator running inside the CLR.

These circumstances are inherent to the behavior promised by Clojure, where each top level form is evaluated immediately upon compilation and the very next top-level form can use the results. As is often the case, a layer of software restricts its flexibility by promising specific behavior to the next layer. By changing this promise, ClojureScript brings within reach interesting possibilities such as the ones we've just discussed.

This separation is similar to that of many classic compiled languages, where cross-compilers are common and REPLs aren't. The most obvious cost of this approach has already been mentioned: no eval at runtime. This has direct consequences on tools

---

[5] A jar file containing all of an application's relevant class files, resources, and dependencies.

like the REPL. A Clojure REPL is easy to write because each of the parts named happens in the same environment. A ClojureScript REPL can do the read, print, and loop parts in the JVM, but eval needs special treatment. The easiest solution is to use a JavaScript interpreter like Rhino, which runs inside the JVM. You can experiment with this easily by running

```
lein trampoline cljsbuild repl-rhino
```

This is often insufficient, because a runtime environment is more than just the language interpreter. Rhino provides neither a DOM nor a Web Audio API. To address this, the cljsbuild tool also provides a couple ways of setting up communication between the compilation environment in the JVM and the runtime environment in a browser. But however you solve this, it's unlikely to ever be as convenient as sharing exactly the same runtime as Clojure.

Another cost of separating the environments can be seen in the amount of code you had to move when moving some of the music example to compile time. In order for magical-theme-macro to work without failure, all the functions it used had to be explicitly defined at compile time by moving them into a .clj file. Contrast this with Clojure, where it's easy to define a macro that uses functions at compile time that were previously only used at runtime, without having to change those functions in any way. It's a significant benefit that despite being technically separate, the compile-time environment is similar to the runtime, because this allows many functions to be ported by copying. It's even likely that in the future there will be an officially supported way to make a single namespace available to both the runtime and compile-time environments.

13.4   *Summary*

ClojureScript's design is another example of how teasing apart things that were previously tangled together results in powerful new capabilities. Using protocols to define the abstractions provided by the language and opening access to the analysis phase both provide additional power with little or no cost. In fact, you were able to use the AST to construct the externs file needed to use advanced Closure compilation in the Web Audio example. Finally, separating runtime more fully from compile time provides benefits that are critical especially for JavaScript, and ClojureScript's tooling goes a long way to mitigate the costs that incurs.

You've seen several examples already of treating code as data, such as when looking at the stages of compilation in this chapter. We'll explore this topic more thoroughly in the next chapter.

Part 6

Tangential considerations

Some topics are so interesting and important that we must include them, even if they don't fit well in another chapter or warrant a chapter to themselves. In this part of the book, we'll cover several such topics, including transient collections, domain-specific languages, and testing.

Data-oriented
programming

14

This chapter covers

- Code as code, and data as data
- Data as data
- Data as code
- Code as data
- Code as data as code

Of primary importance to functional programming languages, and Clojure is no exception, is the relationship between an application's data elements and the code manipulating it. Some programming languages, in support of their paradigms, view the code/data relationship differently. In this chapter, we'll talk about the data/code split in *some* modern languages and the way effective Clojure programs are constructed to blur that line. We'll discuss how elevating data to the level of information can enable interesting simulation and testing solutions by being explicit about data in terms of time. We'll touch on some representations of data and dig into the power achieved by having code that is data. But to start, we'll talk about data on its own terms.

14.1   Code as code, and data as data

In a typical application, perhaps created in Java, the way we think of data is summarized in the following table:

Product ID	Product name	Supplier ID	Price	Unit sales	Total
0	Pumpkin spice	0	0.99	400,000	396,000.00
1	Dung spice	1	1.99	null	null

Another way of viewing this same data is at the level of the definition language used to describe it. For the purpose of illustration, we'll use a rectangle definition language (RDL) that is a variant of SQL:[1]

```
create table COFFEE
  (COF_ID int NOT NULL AUTO_INCREMENT,
   COF_NAME varchar(64) NOT NULL,
   SUP_ID int NOT NULL,
   PRICE numeric(10,2) NOT NULL,
   UNIT_SALES integer,
   TOTAL numeric(10,2),
   PRIMARY KEY (COF_ID),
   FOREIGN KEY (SUP_ID) REFERENCES SUPPLIERS (SUP_ID));
```

Compared to the earlier table, the definition language used to describe our data is far more opaque. For those of you accustomed to viewing SQL, the definition may appear clear (regardless of your opinion on its structure). But we hope you agree that the definition is a step removed from the purity of the table-based layout. We can tolerate a conceptual gap between data and its schema because their purposes are related, yet different. What about accessing the data via query? A simple example is as follows:

```
select COF_NAME from COFFEE
  where COFFEE.UNIT_SALES is NULL;

--> COF_NAME
--> --------
--> Dung spice
```

This query deals in the language of the rectangle and is fairly straightforward in its intent: find all product names without a sale. But as we'll explore in the next section, the distance between data and the way we access it in a language like Java is widened further.

14.1.1   A strict line betwixt

To access the data discussed so far in Java, the following snippet suffices:

```
// ... some details elided

public static void viewTable(Connection con) throws SQLException {
```

---

[1] We ran and tested our SQL code on the SQL Fiddle site at http://sqlfiddle.com.

```
            Statement stmt = null;
            String query = "select COF_NAME, SUP_ID, " +
                              "PRICE, UNIT_SALES, TOTAL from " +
                              "COFFEE_DB.COFFEE";
            try {
                stmt = con.createStatement();
                ResultSet rs = stmt.executeQuery(query);
                while (rs.next()) {
                    String coffeeName = rs.getString("COF_NAME");
                    int supplierID = rs.getInt("SUP_ID");
                    float price = rs.getFloat("PRICE");
                    int sales = rs.getInt("UNIT_SALES");
                    float total = rs.getFloat("TOTAL");
                    doPrint(coffeeName, supplierID, price, sales, total);
                }
            } catch (SQLException e ) {
                JDBCTutorialUtilities.printSQLException(e);
            } finally {
                if (stmt != null) { stmt.close(); }
            }
        }
```

Where did the data go? It's certainly in there, as shown by the creation of variables like coffeeName and price; but the data and its method of access in Java are obfuscated by the baggage required for query construction, database connection, data unwrapping, and exception handling. If the data is likened to a meal, then this approach to access is a recipe or even a menu for data access. Data manipulation in Java via this obfuscation sadly mistakes the menu for the meal.[2] In fact, the obfuscation works to draw a severe line between the data in question and the code used to access it, as illustrated in figure 14.1.

Figure 14.1 Accessing rectangular data in Java is often a chore, highlighting the vast differences in the data model and the code to access it.

By default, there is a fundamental disparity between Java code and the rectangle model of data modeling. But as we'll show in the next section, there have been efforts, some with millions of person-hours behind them, to shorten the gap between the pure rectangle model of data and Java's class-based paradigm.

14.1.2 ORMG

Perhaps it would be nice if Java allowed data rectangles to be directly expressed in terms of the language, with a transparent mapping between the two worlds. As it turns out, many[3] such tools and libraries exist to facilitate this condition; they're typically known as object-relational mappers (ORMs). Without getting into the specifics of implementation, figure 14.2 gives a good summary of the ORM modus operandi.

---

[2] With apologies to Alan Watts for our use of the menu analogy.
[3] Both authors are independently guilty of creating ORM frameworks in the past.

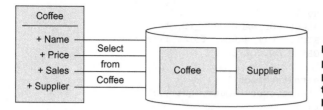

Figure 14.2 **Via various programming magicks, an ORM provides a class-instance interface that maps to database tables on the back end for its property values.**

In short, an ORM such as the popular Hibernate[4] allows a Java programmer to work in the idiom they're familiar with—that of classes and instances—instead of the more foreign and seemingly disconnected[5] world of the database. In concrete terms, defining an ORM-able Java class in a fictional ORM for the coffee model might look like the following:

```
@Entity
@Table(name="COFFEE")
public class Coffee implements Ormish {
    @Id
    Long id;

    @Column(name="COF_NAME")
    String name;

    @Reference(via="SUPPLIERS")
    Supplier supp;

    ... more elided
}
```

Through some compile-time bytecode hacking, the fictional ORM would write the needed database-access code and exception handling automatically, allowing the following familiar interactions:

```
Supplier supp = new Supplier("Quarks Coffee");
supp.save();

Coffee   coff = new Coffee();
coff.setName("Pumpkin spice");
coff.setSupplier(supp);
coff.setPrice(1.99);
coff.save();
```

Although this certainly narrows the gap between the class-based model of Java and the underlying rectangles, the use of an ORM is deficient in a wholly different way: its model, while preserving data, lacks information.

---

[4] Hibernate, a JBoss project, is available at www.hibernate.org.

[5] The authors are aware that there is a mountain of past and present research into the use and development of object databases, but for various reasons such databases haven't caught on in the greater OO world. The late Daniel Weinreb wrote frequently on object databases at http://danweinreb.org/blog/category/objectstore.

14.1.3 *Common ways to derive information from data*

Hearkening back to our original data model, a fundamental problem is highlighted by the way that the `price` field is handled. Zeroing in on the price column for the data predicates the problem, as shown at right.

Product name	Price
Pumpkin spice	0.99
Dung spice	1.99

Based on this data, you can answer only a single question: *what is the price of coffee X right now?* But what if you wanted to know what the price was last week? That information isn't available! This condition illustrates the difference between data and information. That is, although this model provides a mechanism for storing data[6] such as names and prices, it's insufficient for providing information because, as we mentioned way back in section 1.4.1 (recall the runner whose leg was being erased), this type of mutable model has no notion of time. Therefore, when you see a piece of data that says "The price of pumpkin spice is 0.99," no robust information is provided. A couple questions immediately spring to mind when looking at the data:

- Has the price always been 0.99?
- What is the price unit? Dollars? Pounds? Bitcoins?[7]

This model is a common approach to relational and object-oriented data modeling in general that views data as a "place" to modify as conditions in a program's manifest. We'll talk further about the limitations of a place-modification data scheme presently.[8]

14.1.4 *PLOP*

A *pl*ace *o*riented *p*rogramming (Hickey 2012) model is one where data representing entity state is updated in place over the data that existed previously, thus obliterating any notion of time and seriously subverting object equality. As it stands, the PLOP model is prevalent in many popular programming languages. But functional languages in general, and Clojure in particular, eschew the widespread use of PLOPing and instead advocate a purer model where values take center stage. Before we discuss the relative virtues of PLOP versus data-oriented programming (DOP), let's recap what we've covered in this section.

A STRICT LINE BETWEEN DATA AND CODE

Many programming languages make a stark distinction between program data and the code that operates on it. That is, accessing raw data in a language like Java has an alien feel: the code is here, and the data is over there.

---

[6] Yes, we realize this particular model can supply more information with added historical tables and foreign keys, but it's meant to convey the general failings of place-oriented programming (PLOP).

[7] You might also want to know about quantities, IDs, and so on, but we're intentionally keeping things small for the sake of discussion.

[8] That's not to say that PLOP is necessarily bad. As a model for data, it's severely limited. There will always be programming domains where in-place data modification is needed for speed or abstraction (for example, many systems development problems).

ORMs ARE A BANDAGE OVER A GAPING WOUND

Although an ORM can close the gap between the conceptual models of the relational (rectangular or table-based) and an object-oriented language like Java, its use only exacerbates a problem inherent in popular implementations. Rampant mutation as a foundational model of data representation is inherently problematic.

PLACE-ORIENTED PROGRAMMING OBLITERATES INFORMATION

The problems of a data model built on PLOP manifest themselves in the obliteration of both time and, subsequently, information. This occurs because when data is updated in place, the previous value is lost by default, and special care is needed to maintain it. But if we instead view data as unchangeable values, as Clojure advocates, then the information problem brought about by PLOP disappears. In the next section, we'll explore one of the facets of data-oriented programming: dealing with data on its own terms—as values.

14.2   *Data as data*

Data can take various roles in your applications, but more often than not it takes the role of, well, data. In other words, data is represented as an unchanging value. If you'll recall from section 1.4.1, our definition of *value* is an object's constant representative amount, magnitude, epoch, or worth. No one is surprised when we claim that the number 108 is a value; but as we've mentioned, Clojure's approach of treating even composite types as values is somewhat surprising for those accustomed to the PLOP model.

In this section, we'll discuss in detail Clojure's value-based data support and benefits. We'll cover the recent addition of tagged literals and their general usage and role in an extensible data notation. Before we dig into that, we'll first discuss some of the benefits of viewing any given datum strictly as a value.

14.2.1   *The benefits of value*

There are numerous benefits to centering your programs around values rather than mutable places. But as we discussed in section 6.1, the immutability of values provides some abstract benefits outright:

- *Reasonable*—You don't need to worry about change over time.
- *Equality*—Equal values are always equal, forever.
- *Inexpensive*—Reference sharing is cheaper than defensive copying.
- *Flatness*—All subcomponents of a value are also values.
- *Sharing*—Sharing values across threads or in a cache is stress-free.

These points are wonderful in the abstract, but it would be nice to see some tangible benefit also. In the next section, we'll walk through a few such benefits and provide some motivating examples along the way.

VALUES CAN BE REPRODUCED

One huge advantage of Clojure values is that they are what they look like. That is, the textual form `{:a 1, :b 2}` is a map with two entries in it. No magic or high-wire balancing act is required to reproduce this map. It is what it looks like it is. This seems fundamental, but a similar map in Java, although close, isn't precisely the same syntactically as it is in itself:

```
Map<String,Integer> stuff = new HashMap<String,Integer>() {{
    put("a", 1);
    put("b", 2);
}};
```

This is relatively compact as far as Java goes, but there is a problem: this code is code—it's not data. The creation of the data occurs as a result of executing the code. To build a Java map requires the execution of code, whereas in Clojure a map is a literal `{:a 1, :b 2}` away.

VALUES CAN BE REPRODUCED AND FABRICATED

Because a data value in Clojure is immutable, creating one occurs via straightforward data manipulation. Likewise, fabricating values is simple, as shown using Clojure's built-in `rand-int` function:

```
(rand-int 1024)
;;=> 524

(+ (rand-int 100) (rand-int 100))
;;=> 114
```

Sure, that's pretty fun for rolling during Dungeons and Dragons games, but how much harder would it be to generate a more complex structure?[9] As it turns out, not too difficult:

```
(ns joy.generators)

(def ascii (map char (range 65 (+ 65 26))))      <─── Uppercase characters
                                                       start at ASCII code 65
```

To begin, you defined a restricted sequence of characters for the generation of strings:

```
(defn rand-str [sz alphabet]
  (apply str (repeatedly sz #(rand-nth alphabet))))

(rand-str 10 ascii)
;;=> "OMCIBULTOB"
```

You can generate strings from your alphabet by choosing a certain number of random characters and joining them together in the end. This function also forms the basis for symbol and keyword generation:

---

9 Although it's fun to create a random data generator in a few minutes, we advise the use of a Clojure-contrib library called `clojure.data.generators` that is more feature-rich and robust. It's located at http://github.com/clojure/data.generators.

```
(def rand-sym #(symbol  (rand-str %1 %2)))
(def rand-key #(keyword (rand-str %1 %2)))

(rand-key 10 ascii)
;;=> :JRFTYTUYQA

(rand-sym 10 ascii)
;;=> DDHRWLOVME
```

Now you can use these generators to build composite structures like vectors:

```
(defn rand-vec [& generators]
  (into [] (map #(%) generators)))

(rand-vec #(rand-sym 5  ascii)
          #(rand-key 10 ascii)
          #(rand-int 1024))
;;=> [EGALM :FXTDTCMGRO 703]
```

And even maps:

```
(defn rand-map [sz kgen vgen]
  (into {}
        (repeatedly sz #(rand-vec kgen vgen))))

(rand-map 3 #(rand-key 5 ascii) #(rand-int 100))
;;=> {:RBBLD 94, :CQXLR 71, :LJQYL 72}
```

And that's all there is to creating a useful little library of data fabricators. What does the same look like in Java?

VALUES FACILITATE TESTING

Extrapolating from the previous section, perhaps you can imagine how to use the random data for testing purposes. The basic unit of reproducible testing is aptly named *unit testing*. Unit tests are meant to determine if some base-level unit of source, usually a function, adheres to a known behavior given known input conditions. Utilizing values as input to pure functions couldn't be easier. Take the following small example:

```
(assert (= [1 2 3] (conj [1 2] 3)))
```

This code says that the conj of a vector [1 2] and 3 is the vector [1 2 3]. The advantage of using values directly in the unit test is that a value speaks for itself. It's clear what is being tested in this unit test. Sticking with value testing allows for easy differential checking should something go wrong. In a good unit-testing framework, failing tests should show the differences between the expected and actual values. We can show what this looks like using Clojure's packaged tools:

```
(use 'clojure.data)

(diff [1 2 3] [1 2 4])
;;=> [[nil nil 3] [nil nil 4] [1 2]]
```

The result shows that the first item has a 3 in its last position, whereas the second has a 4; and both items have the values [1 2]. Values and their difference views are valuable for facilitating unit testing.

We've already shown that fabricating values is straightforward. But we can extend the idea of fabrication to the notion of generative testing. Clojure's contrib community has a generative testing library named `clojure.test.generative`[10] that provides a set of tools for describing the operational bounds of functions. This mini-language of operational bounds then executes a specifications checker fed by randomly generated data adhering to the data-specification bounds for the functions under test. Take the following specification example as illustration:

```
(defspec slope-rules
  (fn [p1 p2] (slope :p1 p1 :p2 p2))
  [^{:tag (vec long 2)} p1, ^{:tag (vec long 2)} p2]
    (assert (float? %)))
```

This specification says that for any two vectors, each containing two long integers, the `slope` function returns a floating-point number.[11] The machinery behind `clojure.test.generative` will generate millions of random long integers and run them all against `slope` to ensure that at no point does the specification fail. Of course, this isn't a full specification of `slope`, but a full treatment of generative testing is outside the scope of this book.[12]

Simulation testing is a technique that feeds representational actions into a system to simulate interactions, stimulate (and simulate) subsystems, and model load. If your systems are driven by data values instead of entirely by the execution of source code, then simulation testing becomes a reasonably straightforward approach to augmenting your existing testing strategies. We'll run through an example of a simulation test in the next section, but for now we'll continue with our discussion.

VALUES FACILITATE DEBUGGING

Like most world-weary programmers, we've created our share of systems that dump out mountains of log data in hopes of helping to debug errors that might occur at runtime. In a PLOP-centric system, it's often difficult to get a handle on the state of a system at any given point of failure. But in a value-centric system, a well-placed log statement may make all the difference. Imagine you have a function in your system of the following form:

```
(defn filter-rising [segments]
  (clojure.set/select
    (fn [{:keys [p1 p2]}]
      (> 0
         (/ (- (p2 0) (p1 0))
            (- (p2 1) (p1 1)))))
    segments))
```

---

[10] You can find more information about `clojure.test.generative` at https://github.com/clojure/test.generative.

[11] Note that a fully conformant `slope` function might also return the constant `Double.POSITIVE_INFINITY` when given a vertical line. We intentionally avoid doing so, to focus the discussion rather than diverging into a discussion about Java numerics and the like.

[12] Another emerging option in this space is simple-check by Reid Draper, available at https://github.com/reiddraper/simple-check.

You can use this function to (presumably) pull out line segments in a set with a rising slope, like so:

```
(filter-rising #{{:p1 [0 0]   :p2 [1 1]}
                 {:p1 [4 15] :p2 [3 21]}})

;;=> #{{:p1 [4 15], :p2 [3 21]}}
```

But when the system runs, the line segments drawn have a downward-sloping descent. Fortunately, in the universe where you've placed log statements perfectly, you have a snapshot of the full set of line segments. You can use that set directly by feeding it textually into the filter-rising function for debugging purposes, finding that the vector indexes were reversed.[13] There was no need to set up a brittle system state to find this problem. Instead, the values in play were logged and used as is to debug the problem at hand.[14]

VALUES ARE LANGUAGE INDEPENDENT

The final benefit of programming with values is the idea that values transcend programming languages. Think of all the systems on the internet connected by a stream of JSON packets flowing back and forth. JSON is by nature a pure data structure composed of maps, arrays, strings, numbers, and the constants, true, false, and null. This ubiquity and simplicity of JSON's primitives facilitates the current explosion in polyglot systems.

But these basic primitives, although basic as can be, are insufficient for modeling some types of data. For example, a mathematical set of data where there are no repeated elements can be simulated via a JSON array and strict API convention. In the chaotic world of the net, though, there are seldom guarantees that the sender believes in mathematical sets, thus potentially wreaking havoc on your server.

It would be nice if JSON had sets as a primitive data type instead of foisting the guarantees of set-ness onto the receiver. Do you see where this is leading? Clojure has a set type, and its literal data structures are compact, semantic, and easy to describe and therefore parse. Why can't we use Clojure data literals instead of JSON? As it turns out, we can, and many Clojure applications do that very thing.

JSON vs. Clojure data literals

Both JSON and Clojure share a subset of similar data elements, including array-likes (vectors in Clojure), maps, strings, floats, truthiness, and nullity. But Clojure literal data provides a richer superset, including the following:

- *More data types*—These include characters, lists, sets, larger precision numbers, symbols, and keywords.
- *Namespacing*—Symbols and keywords allow prefixes.

---

[13] The division line should be (/ (- (p2 1) (p1 1)) (- (p2 0) (p1 0)))))) instead.

[14] Although if you were simulation testing and/or using pre- and postconditions, you probably would have caught the problem before now.

- *Nonstring keys*—Any of Clojure's types can serve as map keys.
- *Extensibility*—Clojure provides a way to extend the reader to accept user-defined data literals. A simple example is that in JSON, a date is encoded as a string, with the knowledge that it's in fact a date encoded out of band or via some sort of project-specific convention. In Clojure, a date literal is encoded via the tagged-literal capability and read by the proper tag reader.

Clojure programmers already use Clojure data over the wire because of these advantages. Others can as well—see the section "Extensible Data Notation (EDN)."

In the next two sections, we'll talk about using and extending Clojure's core data literals via a recently added feature: tagged literals.

14.2.2 Tagged literals

In Clojure 1.4, a capability was added that provides a way to programmatically extend the reader. The syntax of the readable forms allowed via this new functionality looks like the following:

```
#a-ns/tag some-legal-clojure-form
```

For example, Clojure now includes numerous tagged literals, including universally unique identifiers (UUIDs) and a time-instance form that can be used as follows:

```
#inst "1969-08-18"
;;=> #inst "1969-08-18T00:00:00.000-00:00"
```

The instance literal starts with a # followed by the tag `inst` and ends with a legal Clojure string `"1969-08-18"`. We used a simplified date in the string, but the instance reader allows a richer time specification adhering to the RFC-3339[15] time-stamp specification.

GENERIC SYNTAX, DEFERRED TYPE

An interesting facet of this new capability is that the thing generated by the `inst` tag parser is specific to the host (JVM, JavaScript, and so on) of the Clojure implementation. That is, for Clojure, the type is by default a `java.util.Date` instance, whereas in ClojureScript it's an instance of the built-in `Date` type. The implication of this fact is important: using the same tagged syntactic form, the precise runtime types are left up to the language reading the form.

EXTENSIBLE DATA NOTATION (EDN)

Although JSON has an advantage in that it's a minimal data-exchange format directly representable as JavaScript, it's a bit too spartan. That is, there are classes of data types and usages that can't be easily represented in JSON but that nonetheless are legitimate for the purposes of exchange.

In addition, JSON is a fixed format and doesn't support extensibility of the base literal types as XML does. With the addition of the tagged-literal feature, Clojure also

---

[15] You can find the murderous details at www.ietf.org/rfc/rfc3339.txt.

allows extension of its literal notation. An informal standardization effort is underway to formalize the use of Clojure data literals and its tagged extensions as *Extensible Data Notation* (EDN, pronounced "Eden").

DEFINING NEW TAGGED-DATA SOURCE-CODE LITERALS

Imagine that you wanted to create a data literal of the form #unit/length [1 :km] that provided a way to describe a unit of measure corresponding to length. The value of the syntactic tag #unit/length would be a numeric value relative to some base unit. The benefit of a literal form for such a thing is that the literal itself is self-explanatory (as the redundancy of the previous sentence shows).

You may recall from chapter 7 that we showed a way to recursively define units of measure using a map, and likewise derive their values in terms of a base unit. As it turns out, you can use the derivation function convert directly to implement the #unit/length tag parser. The problem, of course, is that tag-reader functions expect one argument, but convert takes two. This is an easy fix because you can use partial to define a new function as shown in the following listing.

Listing 14.1   Function to read distance units

```
(in-ns 'joy.unit)

(def distance-reader
  (partial convert
           {:m  1
            :km 1000,
            :cm 1/100,
            :mm [1/10 :cm]}))
```

But before you can start using distance-reader, you need to tell Clojure to use the function whenever it encounters the #unit/length tag. To do that, you need only create a file called data_readers.clj at the root of your classpath (for example, in our-project-directory/src/) with a simple map of symbol to symbol, like so:

```
{unit/length joy.unit/distance-reader}
```

The data_readers.clj map keys define the literal tags, and their associated values name a fully qualified var containing a function that will receive the tagged data packet to parse. The type of the return value of the data parser is relative to the use case in general, but in this example it will be a number.

With the data_readers.clj file properly populated, you can start a REPL and test the results:

```
#unit/length [1 :km]
;;=> 1000
```

If you'll recall, the length parser used meters as its base unit, so the value of the tagged type is legitimate. You can also manipulate the data readers used to read Clojure types at runtime by dynamically binding a var named *data-readers* with a map in the same shape as you've created. To set this up, define a new reader called time-reader:

```
(in-ns 'joy.unit)

(def time-reader
     (partial convert
              {:sec 1
               :min 60,
               :hr  [60 :min],
               :day [24 :hr]}))
```

You use the time-reader function as a data reader dynamically as follows:

```
(binding [*data-readers* {'unit/time #'joy.units/time-reader}]
  (read-string "#unit/time [1 :min 30 :sec]"))

;;=> 90
```

And indeed, 1 minute and 30 seconds is 90 seconds.

One important feature added before the 1.5 release was the inclusion of a *default-data-reader-fn* var accessible to user code. This var, when bound to a function, serves as a catch-all for literal tags that don't have any associated readers. Observe the following:

```
(binding [*default-data-reader-fn* #(-> {:tag %1 :payload %2})]
  (read-string "#nope [:doesnt-exist]"))

;;=> {:tag nope, :payload [:doesnt-exist]}
```

default-data-reader-fn is useful when you encounter tags in a source file that you're not prepared to handle. But as a general-purpose data-exchange mechanism, the use of *data-readers*, *default-data-reader-fn*, read-string, and the data_readers.clj file are less than ideal. The reason is that these mechanisms work at the level of the Clojure language-read mechanism. Therefore, using them to handle data from untrusted sources (from an HTTP POST, perhaps) opens up Clojure's privileged runtime mechanisms to potential exploitation—via arbitrary constructor execution, for example. Therefore, *the use of* *data-readers*, *default-data-reader-fn*, *and* read-string *is not recommended for processing data from untrusted sources.* Instead, we *highly* recommend you use the utilities in the clojure.edn namespace for handling Clojure data sources, as we'll discuss next.

HANDLING CLOJURE'S EDN DATA USING CLOJURE.EDN

The potential of using Clojure data literals, or EDN, as an extensible data-exchange format is extremely promising. Many Clojure programmers already use the EDN data formats as wire-transfer formats for things such as web-service data exchange in addition to general-purpose formats for configuration files and the like. But until version 1.5, we were forced to use privileged built-in mechanisms like read-string to process data. Fortunately, the version 1.5 release included a new namespace clojure.edn that provides the safe EDN data-read functions clojure.edn/read and clojure.edn/read-string. Recall that in our discussion of tagged literals, we mentioned that Clojure has a built-in UUID form that looks like this:

```
#uuid "dae78a90-d491-11e2-8b8b-0800200c9a66"
```

The UUID tagged literal resolves to a relevant UUID type in either Clojure or Clojure-Script, but for the former you can expect the following type resolution:

```
(class #uuid "dae78a90-d491-11e2-8b8b-0800200c9a66")
;;=> java.util.UUID
```

We won't go into the details of why and where you might wish to use a UUID, but we can show you how to use `clojure.edn/read-string` to read one:

```
(require '[clojure.edn :as edn])

(edn/read-string "#uuid \"dae78a90-d491-11e2-8b8b-0800200c9a66\"")
;;=> #uuid "dae78a90-d491-11e2-8b8b-0800200c9a66"
```

This example requires the `clojure.edn` namespace and uses its version of read-string to process a UUID tagged literal. Of course, EDN readers work on other Clojure forms:

```
(edn/read-string "42")
;;=> 42

(edn/read-string "{:a 42, \"b\" 36, [:c] 9}")
;;=> {:a 42, "b" 36, [:c] 9}
```

But you'll run into issues if you try to process a tagged literal that you've defined yourself:

```
(edn/read-string "#unit/time [1 :min 30 :sec]")

;; java.lang.RuntimeException: No reader function for tag unit/time
```

The "limitation" is that the `clojure.edn` functions, by design, make no assumptions about how to parse an unknown tag and require that you tell them how to handle tags in place. Therefore, the `clojure.edn/read-string` function accepts an options map that lets you specify the tag readers to use on the string processed:

```
(def T {'unit/time #'joy.units/time-reader})

(edn/read-string {:readers T} "#unit/time [1 :min 30 :sec]")
;;=> 90
```

As shown, the options map `T` passed into `clojure.edn/read-string` specifies the `:readers` to use on the input string. You can also specify a default reader function using the `:default` mapping:

```
(edn/read-string {:readers T, :default vector} "#what/the :huh?")
```

```
;;=> [what/the :huh?]
```

We can't emphasize enough that for processing untrusted EDN data, we *highly* recommend you use the utilities in the `clojure.edn` namespace. We think you'll enjoy using Clojure at every level of your architecture, including as the data format passing between its components.

14.3 Data as code

Sure, you say, data is data. There's nothing terribly groundbreaking in that statement, right? Perhaps so, but as it stands, many programming languages seem to get data wrong. Fortunately, a respectable trend is taking root in the way applications and services are constructed: *the data-programmable engine.* In this section, we'll talk about the ways data can be viewed as programming elements and the implications of that view on how we can develop more robust systems.

14.3.1 The data-programmable engine

Imagine a generic model of computation representing some sort of behavior called an Engine. The Engine might take some data as input, perform some action, and then perhaps return some more data. A block model of the Engine looks like figure 14.3.

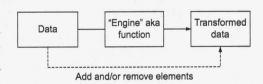

Figure 14.3 Many programs can be viewed as an Engine of computation, taking an input and performing some action.

If you've been paying attention, this figure could be used numerous times throughout this book, including in the introduction to functional programming. When we view functions as models for a computation Engine, the idea of data as code begins to reveal itself, as shown in the modified image in figure 14.4.

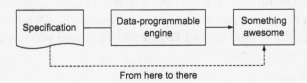

Figure 14.4 The data-programmable model is composed of an Engine taking a specification, performing some actions, and eventually returning or materializing a result.

In the next section, we'll cover a few well-known examples of data-programmable engines, including one of our own design.

14.3.2 Examples of data-programmable engines

The data-programmable engine isn't a new concept. In fact, if you look deeply enough, you'll find that systems built this way have existed since the dawn of computation. In an attempt to give a flavor of how this model might benefit you, we'll start by discussing a few well-known engines before you create one of your own.

ANT

One famous example of the data-programmable engine model is the famous Ant system, used for building Java source projects. Ant as a data-programmable engine is shown in figure 14.5. The specification for Ant is[16] an XML document containing build, maintenance, and testing directives in a form that Ant is able to interpret.

---

[16] In the early days of Ant history, the XML files were fairly limited and straightforward in their effects. But as Java projects go, Ant became much more complex, allowing all sorts of wild directives including XML-ified conditionals!

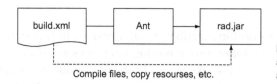

Figure 14.5   **The Ant engine: Ant takes a build specification and returns a build artifact.**

An easy example of a specification is as follows:

```
<project name="EngineSummer" basedir="." default="compile">
    <property name="src" value="src"/>
    <property name="output" value="classes"/>
    <target name="compile" depends="create">
      <javac destdir="${output}">
        <src path="${src}"/>
        <classpath refid="java"/>
      </javac>
    </target>
</project>
```

This XML snippet tells the Ant engine to compile all the sources in the src directory into the output destination. Bear in mind that this is a naive script, but we think the intent is clear. One advantage you'll find when using data this way is that the input data is declarative in form.

CLOJURE

It behooves us in covering data-programmable engines to mention the quintessential example, the Lisp compiler. Because this is a book about Lisp, we'll talk a bit about Clojure's compiler. Viewing the compiler as an Engine fits the model we've outlined throughout this section, as shown in figure 14.6.

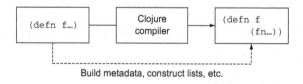

Figure 14.6   **The Lisp compiler as the ultimate computation engine. The Clojure compiler is a data-programmable engine taking Clojure data as input and returning Clojure data as a result.**

We'll talk more about Clojure's compiler as a programmable device in section 14.5, but for now we'll wrap up by exploring a synthesized example: a simple event-sourced engine.

14.3.3 *Case study: simple event sourcing*

Event sourcing is an interesting architectural model that defines system state solely in terms of system events (Fowler 2005). For example, imagine a system that models a baseball player's statistical achievements. One way to model such a system is to store a table of the player's statistics, such as how many times he's batted and the number of hits:

At-bats	Hits	Average
5	2	0.400

But an equally good model, and one that has interesting properties, is an event-sourced model. In an event-sourced model, the state is derived from a sequence (a strict sequence isn't always required) of events pertaining to the domain in question. In the case of the baseball player, an example is shown in table 14.1.

At the end of the events, the state of the player in question is exactly the same: five at-bats with two hits. But with event sourcing, it's derived from the events themselves.

Table 14.1   Baseball events

Event number	Result
1	:out
2	:hit
3	:out
4	:hit
5	:out

EVENTS AS DATA

Before we explore the implementation of a simple event sourcing engine, we'll take a moment to make a point that should ring true based on the trajectory of this chapter. As we mentioned in section 14.2, recent advances in system design have taken advantage of a client-server model exchanging data in a regular format (such as JSON). But we can extend this idea further by exchanging event data between disparate, polyglot systems (written in different programming languages). Although the codebases can take any form in such systems, their behaviors are driven via events toward a common goal (see figure 14.7).

Systems built this way are made possible by observing that the events forming the unit of currency in an event-sourced model are themselves data! This is a powerful idea (did you notice the exclamation mark?) because if your events are data, then they can be persisted in a database and served in a straightforward way to re-create a system's state at any time in the future. This is the model that we'll sketch.

A SIMPLE EVENT-SOURCED MODEL

The example event-sourced model starts with a snapshot of some state. In the case of the baseball world, it's a map like the following:

```
{:ab   5
 :h    2
 :avg 0.400}
```

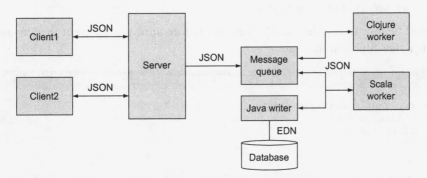

Figure 14.7   Integrating polyglot systems using events as data

This is similar to a data table except that this state is never directly modified, but instead is derived from events, which themselves are maps:

```
{:result :hit}
```

To get from an event or a sequence[17] of events requires a few auxiliary functions. First is a function called valid? that checks the form of an event.

Listing 14.2 Checking the form of an event

```
(ns joy.event-sourcing)

(defn valid? [event]
  (boolean (:result event)))

(valid? {})
;;=> false

(valid? {:result 42})
;;=> true
```

Next you need an effect function that takes a state and event and applies the event to the state in the proper way.

Listing 14.3 Event-sourcing function that affects state

```
(defn effect [{:keys [ab h] :or {ab 0, h 0}}    ◄─┐ Set default fields
               event]                               │ if not present
  (let [ab  (inc ab)
        h   (if (= :hit (:result event))         ◄─┐ Handle a subset
               (inc h)                              │ of possibilities
               h)
        avg (double (/ h ab))]
    {:ab ab :h h :avg avg}))                     ◄─ Return the new state
```

Running effect through a few tests validates your thinking:

```
(effect {} {:result :hit})
;;=> {:ab 1 :h 1 :avg 1.0}

(effect {:ab 599 :h 180}
        {:result :out})
;;=> {:ab 600 :h 180 :avg 0.3}
```

It would be nice to use the valid? function before applying an event to your state, so define a new function that uses it:

Listing 14.4 Function that applies an effect only when the event is valid

```
(defn apply-effect [state event]
  (if (valid? event)
    (effect state event)
    state))
```

---

[17] For the sake of simplicity, we've decided to ignore explicit sequence values in the event maps. But if you take this path, you may need them.

You can test `apply-effect` in place like so:

```
(apply-effect {:ab 600 :h 180 :avg 0.3}
              {:result :hit})

;;=> {:ab 601, :h 181, :avg 0.3011647254575707}
```

Finally, you can define another function `effect-all` that takes a state and a sequence of events and returns a final state.

Listing 14.5   Event-sourcing, mass-effect function

```
(def effect-all #(reduce apply-effect %1 %2))
```

Again, you can test `effect-all` in isolation:

```
(effect-all {:ab 0, :h 0}
            [{:result :hit}
             {:result :out}
             {:result :hit}
             {:result :out}])

;;=> {:ab 4, :h 2, :avg 0.5}
```

Taking `effect-all` for a spin proves the model:

```
(def events (repeatedly 100               <--- Create 100 random ...
              (fn []
                (rand-map 1               <--- ... event maps ...
                  #(-> :result)
                  #(if (< (rand-int 10) 3) <--- ... each with a 3/10 chance of :hit
                    :hit
                    :out)))))
```

You can now feed these 100 random events into the `effect-all` function to see what happens:

```
(effect-all {} events)
;;=> {:ab 100 :h 32 :avg 0.32}
```

What you have at the end of the call to `effect-all` is a snapshot of the state at the time of the hundredth event. Rewinding is as simple as applying only a subset of the events:

```
(effect-all {} (take 50 events))
;;=> {:ab 50 :h 14 :avg 0.28}
```

The events can be sliced and diced in any conceivable way to garner information about the states at any given moment along the event stream. In addition, you can change the way states are saved to gather a historical timeline:

```
(def fx-timeline #(reductions apply-effect %1 %2))

(fx-timeline {} (take 3 events))
;;=> ({}
;     {:ab 1, :h 0, :avg 0.0}
;     {:ab 2, :h 0, :avg 0.0}
;     {:ab 3, :h 1, :avg 0.3333333})
```

You could use `fx-timeline` to infer trends, build histograms, and many other useful actions. With an event-sourced model, the possibilities are seemingly endless.

SIMULATION TESTING

Throughout this chapter, we've highlighted ways that building programs around values facilitates certain ways of constructing solutions. One particularly interesting technique that arises from data orientation is the idea of *simulation testing*. As we hinted earlier, simulation testing is the act of feeding actions, represented as data, into a system or library to simulate interactions, stimulate subsystems, and model load. In this section, we'll run through an example library used to process a simple model of baseball ability and generate possible statistical sets. The first part of the library, shown in the following listing, sets up the data model for ability representation.

Listing 14.6   Data model for representing baseball player abilities

```
(ns joy.sim-test
  (:require [joy.event-sourcing :as es]
            [joy.generators :refer (rand-map)]    <──  Pull in data-centric libs
            [clojure.set :as sql]))

(def PLAYERS #{{:player "Nick", :ability 32}    <──  Simple ability model
               {:player "Matt", :ability 26}
               {:player "Ryan", :ability 19}})
(defn lookup [db name]
  (first (sql/select
           #(= name (:player %))    <──  Pretend SQL data source
           db)))
```

The baseball library is built on a simple ability model: a ratio of player's ability over total possible ability. You store the set of abilities as a set of maps so you can access the data in a way similar to how you might access a relational data store, but with an abstract `lookup` function.[18]

Listing 14.7   `lookup` function

```
(lookup PLAYERS "Nick")

;;=> {:ability 8/25, :player "Nick"}
```

There's nothing stunning about the `lookup` function, but it serves nicely as a cornerstone of an update function.

Listing 14.8   Applying a baseball result event to a database

```
(defn update-stats [db event]
  (let [player    (lookup db (:player event))
        less-db   (sql/difference db #{player})]    <──  Remove old player stats
```

---

[18] If you wanted to, you could create a data-source abstraction based on protocols that would include a `lookup` function. Because that isn't the focus of this section, we leave this as an exercise for you.

```
    (conj less-db                                        ⟵── Add updated player stats
           (merge player (es/effect player event)))))
```

The update-stats function takes a database value[19] and an event (:hit or :miss) and returns a new database with the updated player statistics:

```
(update-stats PLAYERS {:player "Nick", :result :hit})

;;=> #{{:ability 19/100, :player "Ryan"}
;;     {:ability 8/25,   :player "Nick", :h 1, :avg 1.0, :ab 1}
;;     {:ability 13/50,  :player "Matt"}}
```

As shown, when given a single event denoting a :hit by Nick, the database value returned shows the updated player stats for a single at-bat. You can make this more like a database write by creating another function named commit-event that assumes it gets a ref and updates its value using update-stats.

Listing 14.9 Transactionally applying result events to a data store

```
(defn commit-event [db event]
  (dosync (alter db update-stats event)))

(commit-event (ref PLAYERS) {:player "Nick", :result :hit})

//=> #<Ref@658ba666: #{...}>
```

This is all fine and good, but we still haven't shown the tenets of simulation testing. To move toward that discussion, let's create a way to generate random at-bat events.

Listing 14.10 Generating a random baseball event based on player ability

```
(defn rand-event [{ability :ability}]
  (let [able (numerator ability)            ⟵── Extract the ability components
        max  (denominator ability)]
    (rand-map 1
              #(-> :result)
              #(if (< (rand-            ┃    Message is generated
   int max) able)                      ┃    from a simple
                   :hit                 ⟵──┛ percentage formula
                   :out))))
```

As shown, rand-event takes advantage of the strength of values to build random at-bat events. Specifically, using the ability components, you build a proper event map based on the probability of either a :hit or :miss occurring.[20] Now that you have a way to create a single random event, it would be nice to create a function to build many random events.

---

[19] Clojure favors values over mutable places, including at the database layer. Viewing the database as a value resulting from a function application is an extremely powerful paradigm (Hickey 2012).

[20] We intentionally simplified the baseball ability model so as not to distract from the main point, but we can't help but hope that Bill James never reads this section.

Listing 14.11   Generating a number of random baseball events

```
(defn rand-events [total player]
  (take total                              <--- Limit to a certain number
        (repeatedly #(assoc (rand-event player)
                            :player
                            (:player player))))))   <--- Associate the event
                                                          with a certain player
```

We decided to limit the `rand-events` function to accept a count of events that it creates. We could have written it to return an infinite seq of events but saw no reason to do so at the moment. In general, when creating APIs, if you're unsure about the capabilities a given function should have, it's a good idea to start with the most limited ability. It's always easier to widen a function's capabilities than to restrict them after creation. Regardless, you can see the `rand-events` function in action:

```
(rand-events 3 {:player "Nick", :ability 32/100})

;;=> ({:player "Nick", :result :out}
;;    {:player "Nick", :result :hit}
;;    {:player "Nick", :result :out})
```

Now that you have the event-generation component in place, it's high time we explained a little about the kernel of a simulation-testing framework.[21] The domain of this library is, by design, amenable to simulation testing. That is, the players and the results of their abilities map nicely onto the notion of autonomous actors operating asynchronously within and on a system or library. Therefore, you can implement each player as a unique agent that stores its total event stream. The function that creates a unique agent per player is shown next.

Listing 14.12   Creating or retrieving a unique agent for a given player name

```
(def agent-for-player                      ❶ Memoize to ensure
  (memoize                                    uniqueness of the agent
    (fn [player-name]
      (-> (agent [])                       <--❷ New agent
          (set-error-
      handler! #(println "ERROR: " %1 %2))  <--❸ ... with base error
          (set-error-mode! :fail)))))           handling ...
                                           <--❹ ... and failure mode
```

`agent-for-player` is a bit subtle, so we'll explain it in depth. First, the function that takes a player name and returns a new agent instance is memoized ❶. This technique allows you to use the player name as an index to a table of agents without having to explicitly manage and look up agents in a table. Clojure's memoization machinery manages that entire process for you. Next, the agent that's created ❷ is given a fairly dumb error handler ❸ and put into failure mode on creation ❹. Although we don't

---

[21] The framework described in this section is motivated by the vastly superior Simulant library, located at https://github.com/Datomic/simulant. We highly recommend that you use that library rather than the one shown here.

anticipate errors in this section, we felt it worth showing this neat memoization pattern, because we've found it useful on occasion.

The next function in the simulation-testing framework takes a "database" (that is, a ref) and an event and updates the contained players stats. It returns the agent that will perform the update.

Listing 14.13 Feeding an event into the data store and player event store

```
(defn feed [db event]
  (let [a (agent-for-player (:player event))]     <—— Grab a unique player agent
    (send a
          (fn [state]
            (commit-event db event)      <—— Update the DB
            (conj state event)))))       <—— Add the event to the agent's vector
```

On its own, the feed function isn't terribly interesting. Instead, a more useful function is one that operates on a sequence of events.

Listing 14.14 Feeding all events into a data store and player event stores

```
(defn feed-all [db events]
  (doseq [event events]        ⟵⎤ Loop through all events, and
    (feed db event))               ⎦ update the DB each time
  db)
```

This listing is fairly straightforward. That is, it loops over a sequence of events and feeds each into the database and agent event vector. You can see feed-all operate over a sequence of 100 random events as follows:

```
(let [db (ref PLAYERS)]
  (feed-all db (rand-events 100 {:player "Nick", :ability 32/100}))
    db)

;;=> #<Ref@321881a2: #{{:ability 19/100,  :player "Ryan"}
;;                     {:ability 13/50,   :player "Matt"}
;;                     {:player "Nick",  :h 27,  :avg 0.27,  :ab 100,...}}
```

The 100 random events for Nick appear to have been applied to the ref database. If you run this code yourself, you may occasionally see an :ab count slightly less than 100. This happens because agents are dispatched in a thread pool (as we talked about in section 11.2), and by the time the function returns its ref, all agents may not have been dispatched. We'll handle this inconsistency later, but for now you can check the agent events vector manually to see if it looks sane:

```
(count @(agent-for-player "Nick"))

;;=> 100
```

The agent for Nick has 100 stored events, which is exactly what you expected. You can also use the effect-all function created earlier in this chapter to see if the stats match your expectations:

```
(es/effect-all {} @(agent-for-player "Nick"))
;;=> {:ab 100, :h 27, :avg 0.27}
```

This multisource verification of behavior is where simulation testing can shine. Coupled with the proliferation of data-oriented programming, verification of a simulation test can be a matter of data comparisons. Even in the face of stochastic processes, simulation testing can work to exercise a system along expected usage patterns.

The final function in this discussion of simulation testing is a driver named simulate, shown in the next listing.

Listing 14.15   Simulation driver

```
(defn simulate [total players]                          ① Interleave events
  (let [events    (apply interleave  ←─┘                   for all players
                    (for [player players]
                      (rand-events total player)))       ② Apply all events
        results (feed-all (ref players) events)]  ←─┘
    (apply await (map #(agent-for-player (:player %)) players))  ←─┐
    @results))                                                     │
                                  **Wait for all agents to complete ③**
```

The simulate function is a fairly standard driver routine with a few points worth noting. First, all the messages are generated for every player and interleaved into a single event stream ①. You do this to gain a modicum of parallelization among different agents that are fed events serially ②. As hinted at earlier, you use the await function ③ to ensure that every agent has run its course before returning a snapshot of the resulting database value. If you were returning the database reference, this use of await probably wouldn't be necessary. Here's simulate in action:

```
(simulate 2 PLAYERS)
```

```
;;=> #{{:ability 8/25,    :player "Nick", :h 2, :avg 1.0, :ab 2}
;;     {:ability 19/100, :player "Ryan", :h 1, :avg 0.5, :ab 2}
;;     {:ability 13/50 , :player "Matt", :h 0, :avg 0.0, :ab 2}}
```

As a start, we asked simulate to run through only two events per player, and the database snapshot seems reasonable on return. Running simulate again with a higher event count should work similarly:

```
(simulate 400 PLAYERS)
```

```
;;=> #{{:ability 13/50,   :player "Matt", :h 95, :avg 0.2375, :ab 400}
;;     {:ability 8/25,    :player "Nick", :h 138, :avg 0.345, :ab 400}
;;     {:ability 19/100, :player "Ryan", :h 66, :avg 0.165, :ab 400}}
```

As before, you can use the effect-all function to process the raw event stream for a given player to see if it matches up with the database snapshots returned thus far:

```
(es/effect-all {} @(agent-for-player "Nick"))
```

```
;;=> {:ab 402, :h 140, :avg 0.3482587064676617}
```

And indeed, the small simulation of two events, plus the results of the large simulation results for 400 events, sum to the amount given by the raw event stream! Simulation testing is facilitated by data orientation and data collection on multiple facets of the same simulation executions. By collecting multiple sources of event data—the aggregate in the database and the raw event stream—you can derive one from the other to ensure that they match, even in the face of stochastic processes. This is powerful stuff.

ESSENTIAL STATE AND DERIVED STATE

One particularly sharp (as the double-edged sword goes) aspect of the event-sourcing model is the differentiation between essential and derived state. The *essential state* is the state created from direct mappings in the event model, namely :ab (from the event count) and :h (from the :result type). The *derived state* is the data that exists only in code, derived from specific rules and conditions therein. In the baseball model, the :avg state element is derived from the mathematical relation between two essential elements.

By virtue of storing the events, you can easily make changes to live systems. That is, if a system's state is the product of the event stream, then you should be able to re-create it at any time by re-running the events into a fresh system (Fowler 2011). But if the code generating the derived state changes in the interim, re-running the events may not result in the expected state. Using a language like Clojure that is built with data processing in mind helps to soften the pain of deep code changes affecting the generation of derived state.

Likewise, complications may arise if the form of the events in the system changes from one version to another. That you've used maps as the basis for your events provides agility in alleviating this particular complication; see section 5.6 for a deeper discussion of this matter. Providing the ability to rewind and fast-forward a system is extremely powerful, but it's not without caveats.

By implementing an event-sourcing model, you can apply the data-programmable engine paradigm to state calculation. This is a powerful approach to constructing software, and we've only scratched the surface of its benefits. Alas, we now need to take a few pages to discuss the decidedly Lispian notion of code as data.

14.4 *Code as data as code*

In this final section of our exploration into data-oriented programming, we come full circle and explore the possibilities of viewing Clojure itself as the ultimate data-programmable engine. We'll tie up the loose ends on a codebase to convert units of measure, and we'll explore an approach to create domain-specific languages by viewing a practical domain specification as data and metaprogramming it into submission.

In most members of the Lisp family, the code syntax is a data representation, and Clojure is no different. Some interesting metaprogramming techniques come directly from this capability, as we'll show next.

14.4.1 Hart's discovery and homoiconicity

In October 1963, Timothy Hart, one of the original creators of Lisp, released a memo entitled "MACRO Definitions for LISP" (Hart 1963). In the memo, he discussed the observation that special operators called *macros* could operate on a data structure representing Lisp code, transforming it into another data structure prior to final evaluation. This was an elegant solution and an important conceptual leap in the development of Lisp. Most modern Lisps have a different mechanism for handling macros, but the general principle discovered by Hart holds true.

14.4.2 Clojure code is data

As you already discovered in chapter 8, Clojure code is composed of data elements. This condition of Lisp is known as *homoiconicity*, and it's nicely summarized in figure 14.8.

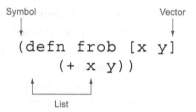

Figure 14.8   **Clojure code is a data structure that Clojure can manipulate.**

Clojure (and most Lisp) code is a data structure that Clojure can manipulate. If a Clojure program is a data structure, then the code can be transformed by Clojure prior to execution. This, of course, is the condition that gives Clojure macros their power.

We won't reiterate the fundamental dictums of macrology that we covered in chapter 8. But it bears noting that the Clojure compiler is essentially the ultimate data-programmable engine. In effect, it's a meta-data-programmable engine. In the next section, we'll go a bit further down this meta rabbit hole and see what comes out.

14.4.3 Putting parentheses around the specification

Many applications deal in measurements of differing units. For example, it's widely known that the United States works almost exclusively in English units of measure, whereas most of the rest of the planet works in SI, or metric units. To convert[22] from one to the other isn't an arduous task and can be handled easily with a set of functions of this general form:

```
(defn meters->feet [m] (* m 3.28083989501312)))
(defn meters->miles [m] (* m 0.000621)))

(meters->feet 1609.344)
;;=> 5279.9999999999945

(meters->miles 1609.344)
;;=> 0.999402624
```

---

[22] There is a spectacular general-purpose JVM language named Frink that excels at conversions of many different units. We highly advocate exploring Frink at your next available opportunity: http://futureboy .homeip.net/frinkdocs/.

This approach certainly works if only a few functions define the extent of your conversion needs. But if your applications are like ours, then you probably need to convert to and from differing units of measure of many different magnitudes. You may need to convert back and forth between units of time, dimension, orientation, and a host of others. Therefore, it would be nice to be able to write a specification of unit conversions (Hoyte 2008) as a Clojure DSL and use its results as a low-level layer for high-layer application specifics. This is precisely the nature of Lisp development in general: each level in an application provides the primitive abstractions for the levels above it.

In this section, you'll create a small specification and then convert it into a Clojure DSL using a technique that Rainer Joswig (Joswig 2005) called "putting parentheses around the specification."

An ideal representation for a unit-conversion specification language would be simple:

> *The base unit of distance is the meter. There are 1,000 meters in a kilometer. There are 100 centimeters in a meter. There are 10 millimeters in a centimeter. There are 3.28083 feet in a meter. And finally, there are 5,280 feet in a mile.*

Of course, to make sense of free text is a huge task in any language, so it would behoove us to change it so it's easier to reason about programmatically but not so much that it's cumbersome for someone attempting to describe unit conversions. As a first pass, let's try to group the most obvious parts using some Clojure syntactical elements:

```
(Our base unit of distance is the :meter
  [There are 1000 :meters in a :kilometer]
  [There are 100 :centimeters in a :meter]
  [There are 10 :millimeters in a :centimeter]
  [There are 3.28083 :feet in a :meter]
  [There are 5280 :feet in a :mile])
```

This specification is starting to look a little like Clojure code, but it would still be difficult to parse into a usable form. Likewise, it would be difficult for the person writing the specification to use the correct terms, avoid spelling mistakes, properly punctuate, and so on. This form is still not *useful*. It would be ideal if we could make this into a form that was recognizable to both Clojure *and* a conversion expert. Let's try one more time:

```
(define unit of distance
  {:m 1,
   :km 1000,
   :cm 1/100,
   :mm [1/10 of a :cm],
   :ft 0.3048,
   :mile [is 5280 :ft]})
```

This *almost* looks like the units map from chapter 7, except for a few minor details. We'll eventually zero in on a specification that matches the form expected by the convert function from chapter 7, but there is a more pressing matter at hand. That is, although you can use the convert function directly, it assumes a well-formed unit conversion map. This is problematic for use in a DSL because the details of covert will leak out to users in the form of nasty exceptions or errors. Instead, let's create a driver function that checks input values and reports more sensible errors.

Listing 14.16 Driving the calculation of compositional units of measure

```
(in-ns 'joy.units)

(defn relative-units [context unit]
  (if-let [spec (get context unit)]
    (if (vector? spec)
      (convert context spec)
      spec)
    (throw (RuntimeException. (str "Undefined unit " unit)))))
```

The function `relative-units` uses the same unit-conversion map form as `convert` but does an existential check and error report on problematic input:

```
(relative-units {:m 1, :cm 1/100, :mm [1/10 :cm]} :m)
;;=> 1

(relative-units {:m 1, :cm 1/100, :mm [1/10 :cm]} :mm)
;;=> 1/1000

(relative-units {:m 1, :cm 1/100, :mm [1/10 :cm]} :ramsden-chain)
;; RuntimeException Undefined unit :ramsden-chain
```

We decided to avoid the natural language phrase "in a" because English isn't good for a DSL. Natural language often lacks the precision of a simple yet regular form. Having said that, let's now create a macro to interpret a unit specification:

```
(defunits-of distance :m
  :km 1000
  :cm 1/100
  :mm [1/10 :cm]
  :ft 0.3048
  :mile [5280 :ft])
```

This is a simplification of the original verbal form of the conversion specification, but this final form is more conducive to parsing without appreciably sacrificing readability. The implementation of the `defunits-of` macro is presented in the next listing.

Listing 14.17 `defunits-of` macro

```
(defmacro defunits-of [name base-unit & conversions]
  (let [magnitude (gensym)
        unit (gensym)                                              Create the
        units-map (into `{~base-unit 1}                   ◁─────┐  units map
                        (map vec (partition 2 conversions)))]
    `(defmacro ~(symbol (str "unit-of-" name))      ┐
       [~magnitude ~unit]                           │  Define the    Multiply the magnitude
       `(* ~~magnitude                           ◁──┘  unit-of macro  by the target unit
          ~(case ~unit
             ~@(mapcat
                 (fn [[u# & r#]]                              ◁───┐  Unroll the unit
                   `[~u# ~(relative-units units-map u#)])         │  conversions into
                 units-map))))))                                  │  a case lookup
```

The macro `defunits-of` is different from any macro you've seen thus far, but it's typical for macros that expand into another macro definition. In this book, you've yet to see a macro that builds another macro and uses multiple levels of nested syntax-quotes. You won't likely see macros of this complexity often; but this example uses nested syntax-quotes in order to feed structures from the inner to the outer layers of the nested macros, processing each fully before proceeding. At this point you can run a call to `defunits-of` with the simplified metric-to-English units conversion specification, to define a new macro named `unit-of-distance`:

```
(unit-of-distance 1 :m)
;;=> 1

(unit-of-distance 1 :mm)
;;=> 1/1000

(unit-of-distance 1 :ft)
;;=> 0.3048

(unit-of-distance 1 :mile)
;;=> 1609.344
```

Perfect! Everything is relative to the base unit `:m`, just as you would like (read as "How many meters are in a _"). The generated macro `unit-of-distance` allows you to work in your given system of measures relative to a standard system without loss of precision or the need for a bevy of awkward conversion functions. To calculate the distance a home-run hit by the Orioles' Matt Wieters travels in Canada requires a simple call to `(unit-of-distance 441 :ft)`. The expansion of the `distance` specification given as `(defunits-of distance :m ...)` looks like this:

```
(defmacro unit-of-distance [G__43 G__44]
  (* G__43
     (case G__44
       :mile 1609.344
       :km 1000
       :cm 1/100
       :m 1
       :mm 1/1000
       :ft 0.3048)))
```

That is, the `defunits-of` macro is an interpreter of the unit-conversion DSL that generates another macro `unit-of-distance` that performs a straightforward lookup of relative unit values. Amazingly, the expansion given by `(macroexpand '(unit-of-distance 1 :cm))` is that of a simple multiplication `(* 1 1/100)`. This is an awe-inspiring revelation. We've fused the notions of compilation and evaluation by writing a relative units of measure mini-language that is interpreted into a simple multiplication at compile time!

This is nothing new, of course; Lisp programmers have known about this technique for decades, but it never ceases to amaze us. There is one downside to this implementation: it allows for circular conversion specifications (for example, seconds defined in terms of minutes, which are then defined in terms of seconds), but this can be identified and handled in `relative-units` if you're so inclined.

14.5 *Summary*

This chapter has been a whirlwind tour of data-oriented programming. Clojure is particularly adept at data manipulation and handling values, and it should motivate you to find ways to make all your programs data-centric. Whether it's viewing data as data or viewing data as the code for a programmable engine like Ant or Overtone, Clojure is agile enough to handle varying program architecture models.

Likewise, an idea prevalent in functional programming—state manipulation as the result of pure functions—maps nicely onto a promising architecture pattern called event sourcing. Finally, we couldn't help showing you that by viewing Clojure and its compiler as programmable engines, you can, via macros, reach infinitely deep into the dark recesses of the metaprogramming vortex.

In the next chapter, we'll put our feet firmly on the ground again and deal with important techniques and approaches to squeezing maximum performance from Clojure and ClojureScript.

15 *Performance*

Now that you've spent a book's worth of material learning the why and how of Clojure, it's high time we turned our attention to the subject of performance. There's a meme in programming that can be summarized as follows: make it work first, and then make it fast. Throughout this book, we've taught you the ways Clojure allows you to "make it work," and now we're going to tell you how to "make it fast."

In many cases, Clojure's compiler can highly optimize idiomatic Clojure source code. But there are times when the form of your functions, especially in interoperability scenarios, will prove to be ambiguous or even counter to compiler optimizations. Therefore, we'll lead you through optimization techniques such as type hints, transients, chunked sequences, memoization, and coercion. Using a combination of these techniques will help you approach, and sometimes exceed, the performance of Java.

The most obvious place to start, and the one you're most likely to encounter, is type hinting—so this is where we'll begin.

15.1 Type hints

The path of least resistance in Clojure often produces the fastest and most efficient compiled code, but not always. The beauty of Clojure is that this path of least resistance allows you to use simple techniques to gain speed via type hints. The first thing to know about type hints is that they're used to indicate that an object is an instance of some class—never a primitive.

> **THE RULE OF TYPE HINTING**   Write your code so it's first and foremost correct; then add type-hint adornment to gain speed. Don't trade the efficiency of the program for the efficiency of the programmer.

15.1.1 Advantages of type adornment

There are epic debates about the virtues of static versus dynamic type systems; we won't engage in those arguments here. Instead we'll note that Clojure provides the advantages of a dynamic type system but also allows type hinting after development, to mitigate some of the performance drawbacks of a dynamic type system. In the case of Clojure, when its compiler can't infer the type of a method's target object, it generates inefficient code that relies on Java reflection. Type adornments work to eliminate the slow reflective calls with minimal fuss (even after the bulk of the code has been written). Another advantage is that unlike a static type system, where the cost of changing types in argument lists is extended to all the callers, Clojure instead defers the cost of updating type hints until adornment time or even avoids it outright.[1] This contrast isn't limited to function arguments but applies to any typed element. This dynamic type system provides an agile experience in general to Clojure, which can later be optimized when needed.

15.1.2 Type-hinting arguments and returns

In section 12.3, you created a function asum-sq that took an array of floats and performed a sum of squares on its contents. Unfortunately, asum-sq wasn't as fast as it could have been. You can see the cause of its inefficiency using a REPL flag named *warn-on-reflection*, which by default is set to false:

```
(set! *warn-on-reflection* true)
;=> true
```

What this seemingly innocuous statement does is signal the REPL to report when the compiler encounters a condition in which it can't infer the type of an object and must

---

[1] Aside from the case where type hints don't require client changes, the use of keyword arguments as discussed in section 7.1 can help to localize additional function requirements to only the callers needing them.

use reflection to garner it at runtime. You can see a reflection warning by entering asum-sq into the REPL:

```
(defn asum-sq [xs]
  (let [dbl (amap xs i ret
                  (* (aget xs i)
                     (aget xs i)))]
    (areduce dbl i ret 0
      (+ ret (aget dbl i)))))

; Reflection warning - call to aclone can't be resolved.
; ...
```

Although this isn't terribly informative in and of itself, the fact that a reflection warning occurs is portentous. Running the call to asum-sq in a tight loop verifies that something is amiss:

```
(time (dotimes [_ 10000] (asum-sq (float-array [1 2 3 4 5]))))
; "Elapsed time: 410.539 msecs"
;=> nil
```

The reflection warning doesn't point to the precise inefficiency, but you can infer where it is, given that Clojure deals with the java.lang.Object class across function boundaries. Therefore, you can assume that the problem lies in the argument xs coming into the function as something unexpected. Adding two type hints to xs and dbl (because it's built from xs) may do the trick:

```
(defn asum-sq [ ^floats xs]
  (let [^floats dbl (amap xs i ret
    ...
```

Rerunning the tight loop verifies that the assumption was correct:

```
(time (dotimes [_ 10000] (asum-sq (float-array [1 2 3 4 5]))))
; "Elapsed time: 17.087 msecs"
;=> nil
```

This is a dramatic increase in speed using a simple type hint that casts the incoming array xs to one containing primitive floats. The whole range of array type hints is shown next:

- objects
- ints
- longs
- floats
- doubles
- chars
- shorts
- bytes
- booleans

The problems still may not be solved, especially if you want to do something with the return value of asum-sq, as shown:

```
(.intValue (asum-sq (float-array [1 2 3 4 5])))
; Reflection warning, reference to field intValue can't be resolved.
;=> 55
```

This is because the compiler can't garner the type of the return value and must therefore use reflection to do so. If you hint the return type of asum-sq, the problem goes away:

```
(defn ^Float asum-sq [ ^floats xs]
  ...

(.intValue (asum-sq (float-array [1 2 3 4 5])))
;=> 55
```

With minor decoration on the asum-sq function, you've managed to increase its speed as well as potentially increasing the speed of expressions downstream.

15.1.3 *Type-hinting objects*

In addition to hinting function arguments and return values, you can also hint arbitrary objects. If you didn't have control over the source to asum-sq, then the reflection problems would be insurmountable when executing (.intValue (asum-sq (float-array [1 2 3 4 5]))). But you can instead hint at the point of usage and gain the same advantage as if asum-sq had been hinted all along:

```
(.intValue ^Float (asum-sq (float-array [1 2 3 4 5])))
;=> 55
```

All isn't lost when you don't own a piece of code that is causing performance problems, because Clojure is flexible in the placement of type hints.

15.2 *Transients*

Throughout this book, we've harped about the virtues of persistent data structures. In this section, we'll present a Clojure optimization technique that uses something called *transients*, which offer a mutable view of a collection. This seems like blasphemy, but we assure you there's a good reason for their existence, as we'll discuss.

15.2.1 *Ephemeral garbage*

The design of Clojure is such that it presumes the JVM is extremely efficient at garbage collection of ephemeral (short-lived) objects, and in fact this is the case. But as you can imagine based on what you've learned so far, Clojure creates a lot of young objects that are never again accessed, as shown (in spirit) here:

```
(reduce merge [{1 3} {1 2} {3 4} {3 5}])
;=> {1 2, 3 5}
```

A naive implementation[2] of reduce would build intermediate maps corresponding to the different phases of accumulation. Creating all this garbage can bog down the JVM or JavaScript host.

> **THE RULE OF TRANSIENTS** Write your code so it's first and foremost correct using the immutable collections and operations; then make changes to use transients in order to gain speed. You may be better served by writing idiomatic and correct code and letting the natural progression of speed enhancements introduced in new versions of Clojure take over. Spot optimizations often become counter-optimizations by preventing the language/libraries from doing something better.

We'll explore how you can use transients in the next section.

15.2.2 *Transients compare in efficiency to mutable collections*

Mutable objects generally don't make new allocations during intermediate phases of an operation on a single collection type, and comparing persistent data structures against that measure assumes a lesser memory efficiency. But you can use transients to provide efficiency not only of allocation, but often of execution as well. Take a function zencat, intended to work similarly to Clojure's concat, but with vectors exclusively:

```
(defn zencat1 [x y]
  (loop [src y, ret x]
    (if (seq src)
      (recur (next src) (conj ret (first src)))
      ret)))

(zencat1 [1 2 3] [4 5 6])
;=> [1 2 3 4 5 6]

(time (dotimes [_ 1000000] (zencat1 [1 2 3] [4 5 6])))
; "Elapsed time: 486.408 msecs"
;=> nil
```

The implementation is simple enough, but it's not all that it could be. The effects of using transients is shown next:

```
(defn zencat2 [x y]
  (loop [src y, ret (transient x)]          ← Create a transient

    (if src
      (recur (next src) (conj! ret (first src)))   ← Use the transient conj!

      (persistent! ret))))                  ← Return a persistent


(zencat2 [1 2 3] [4 5 6])
;=> [1 2 3 4 5 6]
```

---

[2] The actual implementation of reduce follows a reduce protocol that delegates to a smart "internal reduce" mechanism that's meant for data structures that know the most efficient way to reduce themselves.

```
(time (dotimes [_ 1000000] (zencat2 [1 2 3] [4 5 6])))
; "Elapsed time: 846.258 msecs"
;=> nil
```

Wait, what? It seems that by using transients, you've made things worse—but have you? The answer lies in the question, "What am I actually measuring?" The timing code is executing zencat2 in a tight loop. This type of timing isn't likely representative of actual use and instead highlights an important consideration: the use of persistent! and transient, although constant time in their performance characteristics, isn't free. By measuring the use of transients in a tight loop, you introduce a confounding measure, with the disparate cost of using transients compared to the cost of concatenating two small vectors. A better benchmark is instead to measure the concatenation of larger vectors, therefore minimizing the size-relative cost of transients:

```
(def bv (vec (range 1e6)))

(first (time (zencat1 bv bv)))
; "Elapsed time: 181.988 msecs"
;=> 0

(first (time (zencat2 bv bv)))
; "Elapsed time: 39.353 msecs"
;=> 0
```

In the case of concatenating large vectors, the use of transients is ~4.5 times faster than the purely functional approach. Be careful how you use transients in your applications, because as you've seen, they're an incredible boon in some cases and the opposite in others. Likewise, be careful designing performance measurements, because they may not always measure what you think.

Because transients are a mutable view of a collection, you should take care when exposing them outside of localized contexts. Fortunately, Clojure doesn't allow a transient to be modified across threads[3] and will throw an exception if you attempt to do so. But it's easy to forget you're dealing with a transient and return it from a function. That's not to say you couldn't return a transient from a function—it can be useful to build a pipeline of functions that work in concert against a transient structure. Rather, we ask that you remain mindful when doing so.

Using transients can help you gain speed in many circumstances. But remember the trade-offs when using them, because they're not cost-free operations.

15.3 *Chunked sequences*

With the release of Clojure 1.1, the granularity of Clojure's laziness was changed from a one-at-a-time model to a chunk-at-a-time model. Instead of walking through a sequence one node at a time, chunked sequences provide a windowed view (Boncz 2005) of sequences some number of elements wide, as illustrated here:

---

[3] On the JVM, checking for the current thread is computationally inexpensive.

```
(def gimme #(do (print \.) %))

(take 1 (map gimme (range 32)))
```

You might expect this snippet to print (.0) because you're only grabbing the first element; and if you're running Clojure 1.0, that's exactly what you see. But in later versions, the picture is different:

```
;=> (................................0)
```

If you count the dots, you'll find there are 32, which is what you'd expect given the statement from the first paragraph. Expanding a bit further, if you increase the argument to range to 33, you'll see the following:

```
(take 1 (map gimme (range 33)))
;=> (................................0)
```

Again you can count 32 dots. Moving the chunky window to the right is as simple as obtaining the 33rd element:

```
(take 1 (drop 32 (map gimme (range 64))))
;=> (....................................................................32)
```

As we showed in chapter 5, Clojure's sequences are implemented as trees fanning out at increments of 32 elements per node. Therefore, chunks of size 32 are a natural fit, allowing for the garbage collection of larger chunks of memory as shown in figure 15.1.

You might be worried that chunked sequences have squashed the entire point of lazy sequences, and for small sequences this is correct. But the benefits of lazy sequences are striking when dealing with cyclopean magnitudes or sequences larger than memory. Chunked sequences in extreme cases are an incredible boon because not only do they make sequence functions more efficient overall, but they also fulfill the promise of lazy sequences: avoiding full realization of interim results.

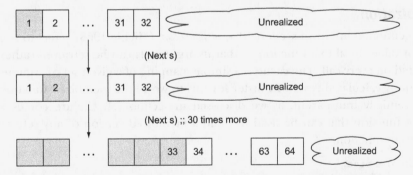

Figure 15.1 Clojure's chunked sequences allow a windowed view of a sequence. This model is more efficient, in that it allows for larger swaths of memory to be reclaimed by the garbage collector and better cache locality in general. There's a cost to total laziness, but often the benefit gained is worth the cost.

15.3.1 *Regaining one-at-a-time laziness*

There are legitimate concerns about this chunked model, and one such concern is the desire for a one-at-a-time model to avoid exploding computations. Assuming you have such a requirement, one counterpoint against chunked sequences is that of building an infinite sequence of Mersenne primes.[4] Implicit realization of the first 32 Mersenne primes through chunked sequences will finish long after the Sun has died.

But you can use lazy-seq to create a function seq1 that can be used to restrict (or dechunkify, if you will) a lazy sequence and enforce the one-at-a-time model:

```
(defn seq1 [s]
  (lazy-seq
    (when-let [[x] (seq s)]
      (cons x (seq1 (rest s))))))

(take 1 (map gimme (seq1 (range 32))))
;=> (.0)

(take 1 (drop 32 (map gimme (seq1 (range 64)))))
;=> (...............................32)
```

You can again safely generate a lazy, infinite sequence of Mersenne primes. The world rejoices. But seq1 eliminates the garbage-collection efficiencies of the chunked model and again regresses back to that shown in figure 15.2.

Clojure may one day provide an official API for one-at-a-time lazy sequence granularity, but for now seq1 will suffice. We advise that you instead stick to the chunked model, because you'll probably never notice its effects during normal usage.

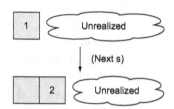

Figure 15.2 Using seq1, you can reclaim the one-at-a-time sequence model. Although not as efficient as the chunked model, it does provide total sequence laziness.

15.4 *Memoization*

As we mentioned briefly in section 10.4, *memoization* (Michie 1968) refers to storing a cache of values local to a function so that its arguments can be retrieved rather than calculated on every call. The cache is a simple mapping of a given set of arguments to a previously calculated result. In order for this to work, the memoized function *must* be referentially transparent, as we discussed in section 7.1. Clojure comes with a memoize function that can be used to build a memoized version of any referentially transparent function:

```
(def gcd (memoize
           (fn [x y]
             (cond
               (> x y) (recur (- x y) y)
               (< x y) (recur x (- y x))
               :else x))))
```

---

4 See http://en.wikipedia.org/wiki/Mersenne_Primes.

```
(gcd 1000645475 56130776629010010)
;=> 215
```

Defining a "greatest common denominator" function using `memoize` helps to speed subsequent calculations using the arguments `1000645475` and `56130776629010010`. The function `memoize` wraps another function[5] in a cache lookup pass-through function and returns it. This allows you to use `memoize` on literally any referentially transparent function. The operation of `memoize` is analogous to, but not exactly the same as, the operation of Clojure's lazy sequences that cache the results of their realized portions. This general technique can be useful, but the indiscriminate storage provided by `memoize` may not always be appropriate. Therefore, let's take a step back and devise a way to generalize the operation of memoization into useful abstractions and build a framework for employing caching strategies more appropriate to the domain at hand.

Similar to Haskell's typeclasses, Clojure's protocols define a set of signatures that provide a framework of adherence to a given set of features. This section serves a threefold goal:

- Discussion of memoization
- Discussion of protocol design
- Discussion of abstraction-oriented programming

15.4.1 *Reexamining memoization*

As mentioned in section 10.4, memoization is a personal affair, requiring certain domain knowledge to perform efficiently and correctly. That's not to say the core `memoize` function is useless, only that the base case doesn't cover all cases. In this section, you'll define a memoization protocol in terms of these primitive operations: `lookup`, `has?`, `hit`, and `miss`. Instead of providing a memoization facility that allows the removal of individual cache items, it's a better idea to provide one that allows for dynamic cache-handling strategies.[6]

15.4.2 *A memoization protocol*

The protocol for a general-purpose cache feature is provided in the following listing.

> **Listing 15.1 Protocol for caching**

```
(defprotocol CacheProtocol
  (lookup  [cache e])
  (has?    [cache e] )
  (hit     [cache e])
  (miss    [cache e ret]))
```

---

[5] You might have noticed that we explicitly bound the var `gcd` to the memoization of an anonymous function but then used `recur` to implement the function body. This approach suffers from the inability to cache the intermediate results (Norvig 1991) of `gcd`. We leave the solution to this shortcoming as an exercise for you.

[6] This section is motivated by the fantastic work of the brilliant Clojurians Meikel Brandmeyer, Christophe Grand, and Eugen Dück, summarized in Brandmeyer's "Memoize Done Right," http://mng.bz/0xIX.

The function `lookup` retrieves the item in the cache if it exists. The function `has?` checks for a cached value. The function `hit` is called when an item is found in the cache, and `miss` is called when it's *not* found. Moving on, you next implement the core `memoize` functionality.

```
(deftype BasicCache [cache]
  CacheProtocol
  (lookup [_ item]
    (get cache item))
  (has? [_ item]
    (contains? cache item))
  (hit [this item] this)
  (miss [_ item result]
    (BasicCache. (assoc cache item result))))
```

`BasicCache` takes a cache on construction used for its internal operations. Testing the basic caching protocol in isolation shows the following:

```
(def cache (BasicCache. {}))

(lookup (miss cache '(servo) :robot) '(servo))
;=> :robot
```

In the case of a miss, the item to be cached is added and a new instance of `BasicCache` (with the cached entry added) is returned for retrieval using `lookup`. This is a simple model for a basic caching protocol but not terribly useful in isolation. You can go further by creating an auxiliary function `through`, meaning in effect, "Pass an element through the cache and return its value":

```
(defn through [cache f item]
  (if (has? cache item)
    (hit cache item)
    (miss cache item (delay (apply f item)))))
```

With `through`, the value corresponding to a cache `item` (function arguments, in this case) is either retrieved from the cache via the `hit` function or calculated and stored via `miss`. Notice that the calculation `(apply f item)` is wrapped in a `delay` call instead of performed outright or lazily through an ad hoc initialization mechanism. The use of an explicit delay in this way helps to ensure that the value is calculated only on first retrieval. With these pieces in place, you can create a `PluggableMemoization` type, as shown next.

```
(deftype PluggableMemoization [f cache]
  CacheProtocol
  (has? [_ item] (has? cache item))
  (hit  [this item] this)
  (miss [_ item result]
    (PluggableMemoization. f (miss cache item result))))
```

```
(lookup [_ item]
    (lookup cache item)))
```

The purpose of the `PluggableMemoization` type is to act as a delegate to an underlying implementation of a `CacheProtocol` occurring in the implementations for `hit`, `miss`, and `lookup`. Likewise, the `PluggableMemoization` delegation is interposed at the protocol points to ensure that when using the `CacheProtocol`, the `Pluggable-Memoization` type is used and not `BasicCache`. This example makes a clear distinction between a caching protocol fulfilled by `BasicCache` and a concretized memoization fulfilled by `PluggableMemoization` and `through`. With the creation of separate abstractions, you can use the appropriate concrete realization in its proper context.

15.4.3 Abstraction-oriented programming

Clojure programs are composed of various abstractions. In fact, the term *abstraction-oriented programming* is used to describe Clojure's specific philosophy of design.

The original `manipulable-memoize` function from section 10.4 is modified in the following listing to conform to the memoization cache realization.

> **Listing 15.4   Applying pluggable memoization to a function**

```
(defn memoization-impl [cache-impl]
  (let [cache (atom cache-impl)]
    (with-meta
      (fn [& args]
        (let [cs (swap! cache through (.f cache-impl) args)]
          @(lookup cs args)))
      {:cache cache})))
```

If you'll recall from the implementation of the `through` function, you store delay objects in the cache, thus requiring that they be deferenced when looked up. Returning to our old friend the `slowly` function, you can exercise the new memoization technique as shown:

```
(def slowly (fn [x] (Thread/sleep 3000) x))
(def sometimes-slowly (memoization-impl
                        (PluggableMemoization.
                          slowly
                          (BasicCache. {})))))

(time [(sometimes-slowly 108) (sometimes-slowly 108)])
; "Elapsed time: 3001.611 msecs"
;=> [108 108]

(time [(sometimes-slowly 108) (sometimes-slowly 108)])
; "Elapsed time: 0.049 msecs"
;=> [108 108]
```

You can now fulfill your personalized memoization needs by implementing pointed realizations of `CacheProtocol`, plugging them into instances of `PluggableMemoization`, and applying them as needed via function redefinition, higher-order functions, or dynamic binding. Countless caching strategies can be used to better support your needs, each displaying different characteristics; or, if necessary, your problem may call for something new.

We've only scratched the surface of memoization in this section, in favor of providing a more generic substrate on which to build your own memoization strategies. Using Clojure's abstraction-oriented programming techniques, your own programs will likewise be more generic and be built largely from reusable parts.

15.5 *Understanding coercion*

As a dynamic language, Clojure is designed to postpone until as late as possible decisions about how to handle specific types of values. As a practical language, Clojure allows you to specify types at compile time in some cases where doing so may significantly improve the runtime speed of your program. One way to do this is with type hints on symbols used with interop, as covered in section 15.1. Another way is through the Java primitive types that Clojure supports, which is the subject of this section.

Java primitives include variously sized numbers (byte, short, int, long, float, and double) as well as boolean and char types. Each of these has a counterpart that is a normal class spelled with a capital first letter: for example, an int value can be boxed up and stored in an instance of Int. Java primitives can improve performance a lot because they use less memory, generate less memory garbage, and require fewer memory dereferences than their boxed counterparts. These primitives are useful both with interop and with Clojure functions that have been defined specifically to support primitives, although Clojure functions only support primitive arguments of type long and double.

To see the value of primitives, consider this factorial function, which is a favorite of micro-benchmarkers everywhere.

Listing 15.5 Tail-recursive factorial, with no type declarations

```
(defn factorial-a [original-x]
  (loop [x original-x, acc 1]      ←—❶ Set a recur target
    (if (>= 1 x)
      acc                                    ←—❷ Terminate now?
      (recur (dec x) (* x acc)))))     ←—❸ Next iteration
```

This may not be the most natural way to define factorial, because instead of using nesting recursion, it uses the recur operator in the tail position (see section 2.6.3). You do this so the recursion consumes no stack. Try it, and observe how quickly the result of factorial grows very large:

```
(factorial-a 10)
;=> 3628800

(factorial-a 20)
;=> 2432902008176640000
```

This chapter is about performance, so you should measure the function's speed. Be sure to run this a few times to give the JVM a chance to optimize it:

```
(time (dotimes [_ 1e5] (factorial-a 20)))
; "Elapsed time: 172.914384 msecs"
```

This is the baseline: 100,000 calls of (factorial 20) in under 200 milliseconds. To see how coercion can help, you need to think about what the Clojure compiler knows about the type of each expression.

15.5.1 Using primitive longs

Starting with Clojure 1.3, literal numbers compile as primitives. Look back at listing 15.5 to see the primitive literals at ❶ and ❷. This means Clojure knows that acc is a long, so the use of dec at ❸ should be taking advantage of that. But the type of x is unknown to the compiler, which means the comparison and the multiplication must be compiled in a way that it will work regardless of the actual numeric type encountered at runtime. If you want x to be a primitive long, you can coerce it where it's defined in loop as shown in the next listing. This kind of coercion also works in let forms.

Listing 15.6 Factorial with a coerced local

```
(defn factorial-b [original-x]
  (loop [x (long original-x), acc 1]          ⟵── Coerce the value so x will be long
    (if (>= 1 x)
      acc
      (recur (dec x) (* x acc)))))

(time (dotimes [_ 1e5] (factorial-b 20)))
; "Elapsed time: 44.687297 msecs"
```

Another way to get similar results is to declare the type of the function parameter, as shown in listing 15.7. This looks like type hinting but isn't. Whereas type hints can only refer to class names and only influence the compilation of interop forms, functions with primitive arguments are compiled to code that coerces inputs to the declared types so that interop and math functions can assume the primitive type.

Listing 15.7 Factorial with a primitive long argument

```
(defn factorial-c [^long original-x]          ⟵── Declare arg as long
  (loop [x original-x, acc 1]                  ⟵┐
    (if (>= 1 x)                                 │ No coercion is needed here
      acc
      (recur (dec x) (* x acc)))))

(time (dotimes [_ 1e5] (factorial-b 20)))
; "Elapsed time: 43.797143 msecs"
```

By avoiding the boxing and unboxing of x in both these listings, you have a function that runs around four times faster for this test. But you can avoid even more work. Specifically, every time a number is computed, it's checked to make sure it falls within the range of the type it's using (in this case, long). And longs are huge, so surely you don't need to worry about out-of-range values. The following listing shows how to turn off the overflow checking.

Listing 15.8 Factorial without overflow checking

```
(set! *unchecked-math* true)                    ⟵ Turn off overflow checking

(defn factorial-d [^long original-x]            ⟵ Still use a primitive argument
  (loop [x original-x, acc 1]
    (if (>= 1 x)
      acc
      (recur (dec x) (* x acc)))))

(set! *unchecked-math* false)                   ⟵ Turn unchecked-math back off
```

Timing this shows impressive results:

```
(time (dotimes [_ 1e5] (factorial-d 20)))
; "Elapsed time: 15.674197 msecs"
```

This is another doubling or more of the function's speed. Unfortunately, you've introduced an error that can be extremely difficult to find:

```
(factorial-d 21)
;=> -4249290049419214848
```

A factorial should never produce a negative number, and yet there it is. By turning off overflow checking, you can generate incorrect results without even noticing, and you have no easy way to find the source of the problem. This is in stark contrast to the default behavior, which you can observe by trying the original factorial-a version:

```
(factorial-a 21)
; ArithmeticException integer overflow
```

The stack trace generated by this exception shows not only the use of multiplication that sent the accumulator outside the range of long, but also the entire call chain that led to it. This is much more helpful than a silently incorrect result. You might consider using unchecked math, but only very carefully—perhaps by manually including checks at larger-grained places for inputs that will cause out-of-bounds results. Most of the time, it's best to leave overflow checking on and accept the performance hit, which in most real-world situations isn't as dramatic as shown in this example.

Although the primitive long type turned out to be a poor choice for factorial, in many situations a long is perfectly acceptable. In these cases, using primitive longs with overflow checking on may be an ideal compromise between safety and performance.

But what if you have an application somewhat like factorial, and you want neither an incorrect answer nor an overflow exception for small input values like 21? We'll explore two different solutions, each with its trade-offs. The first sacrifices only accuracy, and the second sacrifices only performance.

15.5.2 *Using primitive doubles*

One way to avoid overflow is to use a floating-point representation. Because Clojure has broad support for primitive doubles, it's reasonable to try replacing long with double in your function definition. Let's try this in the next listing, updating the literals to be doubles as well for better performance.

Listing 15.9 Factorial with a primitive double argument

```
(defn factorial-e [^double original-x]        ⟵ Use double, not long
  (loop [x original-x, acc 1.0]
    (if (>= 1.0 x)                             ⟵ ❶ Use double literals, too
      acc
      (recur (dec x) (* x acc)))))

(factorial-e 10.0)
;=> 3628800.0

(factorial-e 20.0)                             ❷ Double is less
;=> 2.43290200817664E18         ⟵ accurate than long

(factorial-e 30.0)                             ❸ Double doesn't overflow
;=> 2.652528598121911E32        ⟵ as early as long

(factorial-e 171.0)
;=> Double/POSITIVE_INFINITY    ⟵ Double does overflow eventually

(time (dotimes [_ 1e5] (factorial-e 20.0)))
; "Elapsed time: 15.678149 msecs"   ⟵ ❹ Primitive doubles are fast
```

As promised, doubles give up accuracy, as shown at ❷ and ❸; but they deliver excellent performance, as shown at ❹. Note that the literals at ❶ and the previous line are written as 1.0 instead of 1 so they will be compiled as literal doubles instead of longs. Using longs would have meant mixed types for the multiplication, which would hurt performance (but only slightly).

Again, this seems to be a poor choice for factorial, but there are domains where the inaccuracy of floating-points isn't a problem and their range is sufficient for the domain. In these domains, the performance provided by primitive doubles can be fantastic.

Let's examine one more solution, giving up some performance in order to maintain perfect accuracy.

15.5.3 *Using auto-promotion*

Prior to Clojure 1.3, math operations auto-promoted to number objects that could handle arbitrary precision when necessary. Although this behavior is no longer the default, sometimes it's exactly what you want, and so it's provided in the prime math operators: +', -', *', inc', and dec'. These are spelled just like their non-promoting counterparts, but with trailing single-quote character. The following listing uses *' to allow acc to be promoted but continues to use a primitive long for x on the assumption that nobody wants to wait for this factorial function to iterate Long/MAX_VALUE times.

Listing 15.10 Factorial with auto-promotion

```
(defn factorial-f [^long original-x]          ⟵ ❶ Still a primitive long argument
  (loop [x original-x, acc 1]
    (if (>= 1 x)
      acc                                      ❷ Use auto-promoting
      (recur (dec x) (*' x acc)))))   ⟵ multiplication
```

```
(factorial-f 20)
;=> 2432902008176640000
```
❸ **No rounding as
   with double**
```
(factorial-f 30)
;=> 265252859812191058636308480000000N
```

```
(factorial-f 171)
;=> 124101... this goes on a while ...0000N
```

```
(time (dotimes [_ 1e5] (factorial-f 20)))
; "Elapsed time: 101.7621 msecs"
```
◁— **Faster than the original baseline**

Using a primitive long for original-x as declared at ❶ allows Clojure to assume x is also a primitive long. Together this gives performance that beats the baseline back in listing 15.5.

The use of auto-promoting multiplication at ❷ produces an arbitrary-precision BigInt object when needed, which is visible in the trailing N in the result of ❸. Clojure uses its own BigInt for arbitrary-precision integers like this and Java's Big-Decimal for arbitrary-precision decimal reals. Literals for BigDecimal can be written with a trailing M, but don't forget about the option of using rationals when dealing with non-integers (see section 2.7.2).

This finally seems like a good compromise for the implementation of factorial, but let's review the coercion options we considered. We showed that numbers can be represented as either primitive or boxed. Primitives are prone to overflow but provide the best performance and can even be used in dangerous unchecked ways. Boxed numbers are slower but can be used with auto-promoting math operations to maintain arbitrary precision. And, of course, you can choose the most appropriate type for each local to achieve the desired trade-off between behavior and performance.

15.6 *Reducibles*

Modern languages often provide a common interface for all their collection types, such as some kind of iterator interface. In Clojure, this is naturally supplied by the seq abstraction. Much of the power of these interfaces derives from their minimalism—their requirements are so humble that it's easy for a new collection type to comply. This leads to a ubiquity that allows users of the abstraction to work across a powerfully wide range of collections.

Clojure's seq abstraction is indeed minimal, requiring the implementation of essentially just first and rest. But Clojure 1.5 provides even more minimal [7] collection interfaces, CollReduce and CollFold, each of which requires a single method to be implemented. We'll come to the justification for these interfaces later, but for now try to be satisfied with the proposition that a more minimal interface *may be* more powerful and possibly lead to better performance.

---

[7] You'll see later why the good ol' seq abstraction continues to be useful as well.

15.6.1 *An example reducible collection*

In some programming languages (Ruby springs to mind), a *range* is an object that denotes a start value, an end value, and the steps in between. Although Clojure has a range function that builds a sequence of numbers based on these criteria, a range isn't a first-class object in Clojure. But you can think of a range as a collection that is traversed and built according to the dictates of the start, end, and step values. The following listing implements a version of range that requires these three elements and returns a lazy sequence of numbers. It follows the lazy-seq recipe set out earlier by starting with the lazy-seq macro, then checking for the termination case, and finally constructing a cons cell of the current and remaining values.

Listing 15.11   Reimplementing Clojure's `range` function using `lazy-seq`

```
(defn empty-range? [start end step]
  (or (and (pos? step) (>= start end))
      (and (neg? step) (<= start end))))

(defn lazy-range [i end step]
  (lazy-seq
    (if (empty-range? i end step)        ◁── Termination case
      nil                                       ◁── nil terminates lazy seq
      (cons i
            (lazy-range (+ i step)
                        end               ◁── Construct first and rest values
                        step)))))
```

Although interesting (maybe), the lazy sequence returned from lazy-range is nothing special, but it probably behaves as you expect:

```
(lazy-range 5 10 2)
;=> (5 7 9)

(lazy-range 6 0 -1)
;=> (6 5 4 3 2 1)
```

Given the lazy sequences returned here, it's easy to produce another collection such as a vector, or compute some other reduced value such as a sum:

```
(reduce conj [] (lazy-range 6 0 -1))
;=> [6 5 4 3 2 1]

(reduce + 0 (lazy-range 6 0 -1))
;=> 21
```

Both of these are perfectly reasonable things to do with a lazy sequence, but neither takes advantage of the signature feature of a lazy sequence: *laziness*. Even though they don't need laziness, they're still paying for it by allocating a couple objects on the heap for each element of the range. So instead of returning a lazy seq, what if you were to return a function that acted like reduce? Let's call this function a *reducible*.

```
(fn [reducing-fn initial-value]
  ;; ...
```

```
;; returns the reduced value
)
```

Rather than pass the reducible to reduce as you did with the lazy seq, in order to execute the reduction and produce the final reduced value, you call the reducible. If you had a version of lazy-range that built collections following the minimal collection interface named reducible-range, you could use it as follows:

```
(def countdown-reducable (reducible-range 6 0 -1))

(countdown-reducible conj [])
;=> [6 5 4 3 2 1]

(countdown-reducible + 0)
;=> 21
```

This is the more minimal collection interface—a function that can be used to extract the contents of the collection, as you did with conj and [], or to produce some other derived value. The definition of reducible-range demonstrated here is given in the following listing. This is different from lazy-range primarily in that it drives the reduction loop itself, using loop and recur, and finally returns the reduced value instead of terminating with nil.

Listing 15.12   Reimplementation of `range` that returns a reducible

```
(defn reducible-range [start end step]
  (fn [reducing-fn init]
    (loop [result init, i start]
      (if (empty-range? i end step)        ⟵— Termination case
        result
        (recur (reducing-
      fn result i)
              (+ i step)))))))
```

Reduce this step and continue to the next

Return the result and terminate the loop

15.6.2   *Deriving your first reducing function transformer*

You may be wondering how this reducible, a mere function, can possibly support anything like the wide range of manipulations that lazy seqs support. How can a reducible be filtered or mapped when all you can do with it is call it? This is a troubling question, and to help answer it we'll take a step back and look at what exactly it means to map a sequence. Then we'll examine how well the answer extends to filtering and concatenating.

Let's begin with an easy-to-grasp function that you'd like to map across a collection. That function is half:

```
(defn half [x]
  (/ x 2))

(half 4)
;=> 2

(half 7)
;=> 7/2
```

In the context of using reduce, the easiest way to use half is to combine it with a reducing function like + to make a new reducing function. Let's call this one sum-half, because it sums up the halves of the inputs:

```
(defn sum-half [result input]
  (+ result (half input)))

(reduce sum-half 0 (lazy-range 0 10 2))
;=> 10

((reducible-range 0 10 2) sum-half 0)
;=> 10
```

You can map across the input values, halving them as you go, but so far only by hard-coding the mapping function half and the reducing function + into a new function. This is the essence of mapping only as much as Paul McGann's Doctor is the essence of The Doctor[8] or margarine is the essence of butter. To get where you want to be, you need to change these hard-coded functions into parameters. Begin by wrapping sum-half in another function that takes the + function (or any other reducing function) as a parameter:

```
(defn half-transformer [f1]
  (fn f1-half [result input]
    (f1 result (half input))))
```

First notice how f1-half is nearly identical to sum-half. Then notice how many of the functions here are reducing functions in that they take two arguments, a previous result or seed and an input, and return a new result: sum-half and f1-half are reducing functions, as are f1 and +. This is why you can describe the previous function as a transformer, specifically a *reducing function transformer*, because it takes one reducing function (f1) and returns another (f1-half).

You can of course use this directly, just as you did sum-half:

```
((reducible-range 0 10 2) (half-transformer +) 0)
;=> 10

((reducible-range 0 10 2) (half-transformer conj) [])
;=> [0 1 2 3 4]
```

But you're not done yet, because half is still hard-coded. So you repeat the same pattern as last time by wrapping half-transformer in another function that takes half (or any other mapping function) as a parameter, and derive mapping as shown next.

Listing 15.13 Essence of mapping, bundled to be used with a reducible

```
(defn mapping [map-fn]          ◁— Transformer constructor
  (fn map-transformer [f1]      ◁— Transformer
    (fn [result input]          ◁— Reducing function
      (f1 result (map-fn input)))))
```

---

[8] An argument can be made for Tom Baker, but we digress.

Compare `mapping` with `half-transformer`, and note that you again replace a specific function with a parameter. But this time, neither the parameter `map-fn` nor what it returns (`map-transformer`) is a reducing function. They're two different sorts altogether. `map-fn` takes a single input and returns a single result (making it a *mapping function*), whereas `map-transformer`, as we said, is a transformer. So `mapping` isn't any kind of transformer; it's a *transformer constructor*. Functions of this variety take whatever parameters they need but always return reducing function transformers. Feel free to consult table 15.1 if you're starting to feel flustered by all the different kinds of functions.

Table 15.1   The various kinds of reducer-related functions

Name	Parameters	Return value	Example
Mapping function	Input	Mapped output	`half`
Reducing function	Previous result, next input	Reduced value	`sum-half`
Reducible	Reducing function, init value	Reduced value	`(reducible-range 0 5 1)`
Reducible constructor	Various	Reducible	`reducible-range`
Reducing function transformer	Reducing function	Reducing function	`half-transformer`
Transformer constructor	Various	Reducing transformer	`mapping`

You now have a function in which everything has been abstracted away except the core idea of what it means to map a value, and that idea is bundled into a form that can be applied to reducibles. With these two abstractions, reducibles and mapping, you can do quite a bit:

```
((reducible-range 0 10 2) ((mapping half) +) 0)
;=> 10

((reducible-range 0 10 2) ((mapping half) conj) [])
;=> [0 1 2 3 4]

((reducible-range 0 10 2) ((mapping list) conj) [])
;=> [(0) (2) (4) (6) (8)]
```

The syntax falls short of what you might hope for, and it certainly doesn't look like a drop-in replacement for lazy seqs yet. We'll see what we can do about the syntax a little later. For now, we should explore more deeply the power available with reducibles and also what we're giving up compared to lazy seqs.

15.6.3 *More reducing function transformers*

Mapping allows a broad range of transformations to collections, as long as the output collection is the same size as the input. One way to produce a smaller collection is with filter, which can be implemented as shown in the following listing.

Listing 15.14 Essence of `filtering`, bundled to be used with a reducible

```
(defn filtering [filter-pred]
  (fn [f1]
    (fn [result input]
      (if (filter-pred input)
        (f1 result input)

        result)))))
```

Test the predicate

1 If true, reduce the input untouched …

2 … else ignore this input

There are exactly three important differences between the filtering and mapping functions:

- Unsurprisingly, filtering has an if where mapping had none. The given predicate is tested against the input and either included **1** or ignored **2**.
- The reducing call to f1[9] is almost identical, except the input is passed through untouched instead of being passed through a mapping function. We could certainly imagine a different form of the filtering function that supported a mapping function as well, but we'll show in a moment why that's unnecessary.
- When the predicate returns false, this iteration of the filter must have no impact on the accumulating result, so the result passed in is returned unchanged.

Using filtering with a reducible is just like using mapping:

```
((reducible-range 0 10 2) ((filtering #(not= % 2)) +) 0)
;=> 18

((reducible-range 0 10 2) ((filtering #(not= % 2)) conj) [])
;=> [0 4 6 8]
```

If you wish to map the values with a mapping function either before or after filtering, you can do so by combining calls to mapping and filtering. Remember that conj and + in the previous example are reducing functions, which is the same kind of function that transformers take and return. And because (mapping half) and (filtering #(not= % 2)) are both transformers, they can be chained together like so:

```
((reducible-range 0 10 2)
  ((filtering #(not= % 2))
   ((mapping half) conj))
  [])

;=> [0 2 3 4]
```

---

[9] Clojure's implementation of reducers in `clojure.core.reducers` frequently uses the name "f1"" for a reducing function passed in to a transformer.

That is, the reducible calls the function returned by filtering for each value of the sequence. The filtering function calls the function returned by mapping only for those values that pass the predicate supplied as filtering's argument. It's left up to the mapping function to use conj to add only those values to the resulting sequence.

In the previous code, you replaced conj with ((mapping half) conj), so after filtering the values they were divided in half before being conjed onto the resulting vector. Because the use of filtering left out the number 2, it's the number 1 that is missing from the final vector. You can map *before* filtering, if you'd rather, by nesting them in reverse:

```
((reducible-range 0 10 2)
  ((mapping half)
   ((filtering #(not= % 2)) conj))
  [])

;=> [0 1 3 4]
```

Here you do the mapping first: only after 4 has been divided by 2 does filtering exclude the resulting 2 from the final vector.

Now that you've seen reducibles adjusted in ways that remove some elements (filtering) and leave the number of elements alone (mapping), look at the next listing to see how to construct a transformer that adds elements in the same way mapcat does for lazy seqs.

Listing 15.15   Essence of `mapcatting`, bundled to be used with a reducible

```
(defn mapcatting [map-fn]
  (fn [f1]
    (fn [result input]
      (let [reducible (map-fn input)]
        (reducible f1 result)))))
```

New reducible →

Return the result of applying the previous result to a new reducible

The interesting difference here is that mapcatting expects map-fn to return a reducible, which then must be merged into the result. So the returned reducible is called with the previous result as its starting point, passing f1 on through.

To demonstrate this, you need a little helper function for map-fn that takes a number from reducible-range and returns a new reducible:

```
(defn and-plus-ten [x]
  (reducible-range x (+ 11 x) 10))

((and-plus-ten 5) conj [])
;=> [5 15]
```

Now you can pass that to mapcatting and see how the resulting reducibles are all concatenated:

```
((reducible-range 0 10 2) ((mapcatting and-plus-ten) conj) [])
;=> [0 10 2 12 4 14 6 16 8 18]
```

We've shown a nice range of composable functionality on top of reducibles, but the syntax leaves quite a bit to be desired. Fortunately, this can be fixed.

15.6.4   Reducible transformers

One key difference between the way sequence functions are composed and what you've been doing with reducibles is that the examples have been piling on to the reducing function instead of the collection. That is, you're used to modifying the collection and getting a new collection that can be reduced later:

```
(filter #(not= % 2)
  (map half
       (lazy-range 0 10 2)))
;=> (0 1 3 4)
```

In order to compose *reducing function* transformers in a similar way, you need to turn them into *reducible* transformers instead. The new reducible transformers must take as parameters not just the reducing function that the transformer constructors took, but also a reducible that acts as input. These two parameters correspond to the half and lazy-range that map is given in the previous snippet. Here's how these reducible transformers are written for map and filter.

Listing 15.16   A couple of reducible transformers

```
(defn r-map [mapping-fn reducible]        <— Transformer
  (fn new-reducible [reducing-fn init]    <— Resulting reducible
    (reducible ((mapping mapping-fn) reducing-fn) init)))

(defn r-filter [filter-pred reducible]
  (fn new-reducible [reducing-fn init]
    (reducible ((filtering filter-pred) reducing-fn) init)))
```

Both these functions take the two parameters we just described and return a new reducible. Remember, a reducible is just a function that takes a reducing function and a starting value, and returns the result of running that reducing function across the entire collection. In this case, the collection is described by the passed-in reducible. But between that and the init, you interject your own reducing function, wrapping the user's reducing-fn by passing it to the reducing function transformer created by calling either mapping or filtering.

With r-map and r-filter defined, you can now write reducible pipelines of the same shape as the equivalent lazy sequence pipeline:

```
(def our-final-reducible
  (r-filter #(not= % 2)
            (r-map half
                   (reducible-range 0 10 2))))

(our-final-reducible conj [])
;=> [0 1 3 4]
```

The similarities between the implementations of r-map and r-filter are obvious and suggest the repeated code could be factored out. Clojure's clojure.core.reducers namespace does exactly this, using the function reducer, which we'll look at in a moment.

15.6.5 *Performance of reducibles*

Having achieved a code shape nearly identical to that of a lazy sequence, you might be wondering what the benefit is of this new collection abstraction. Although you'll see some side benefits later, the primary win is performance. You can use criterium, a third-party Clojure library (https://github.com/hugoduncan/criterium),[10] to measure the performance of Clojure expressions. We measured a reduction across a two-step pipeline on our own lazy-range:

```
(require '[criterium.core :as crit])
(crit/bench
   (reduce + 0 (filter even? (map half (lazy-range 0
             (* 10 1000 1000) 2)))))
; Execution time mean : 1.593855 sec
```

That is 10 million numbers mapped, filtered, and added in just over 1.5 seconds, which gives us a baseline to improve on. Since version 1.1, Clojure itself has improved on this with chunked sequences, which we discussed in section 15.3. Clojure's lazy range function returns a chunked sequence that can be reduced more efficiently than lazy-range:

```
(crit/bench
 (reduce + 0 (filter even? (map half (range 0 (* 10 1000 1000) 2)))))
; Execution time mean : 603.006967 ms
```

This helps a lot. By allocating and processing chunks of the lazy sequence at a time, instead of individual cons cells, the work gets done more than 60% faster. How do reducibles fare?

```
(crit/bench
 ((r-filter even? (r-map half
     (reducible-range 0 (* 10 1000 1000) 2))) + 0))
; Execution time mean : 385.042958 ms
```

In this case, we get another 35% improvement beyond what chunked seqs provided. But again, a critical difference is that this difference was achieved via a *simpler* interface and naive implementations rather than the more complex interface and implementations demanded by chunked sequences. Reducers seem to be a win.

The range of expressions that can be built out of this reducible abstraction is remarkable. Many of the composable processing functions you're familiar with from lazy seqs can be brought over, and all this with nothing but closures and function calls—not a cons cell or deftype in sight. But there are a few trade-offs, as you might expect.

---

[10] Our project.clj file includes :dependencies [[criterium "0.3.0"]].

15.6.6 *Drawbacks of reducibles*

The primary drawback of reducibles is that you give up laziness. Because the reducible collection is responsible for reducing its entire contents, there's no way, short of she-nanigans with threads or continuations, to suspend its operation in the way we regularly do with lazy seqs. This gets in the way of reducibles efficiently consuming multiple collections at once, the way map and interleave do for lazy seqs.

The closest Clojure's implementation comes to supporting suspension is early termination. You can use reduced to mark that a reduction loop should be terminated early, and reduced? to test for this case.

15.6.7 *Integrating reducibles with Clojure reduce*

So far you've worked with reducibles that are functions. This is fine as long as reducing is the only thing you need to do with them. But real collections have to support being built up such as with conj or assoc and may want to support other interfaces such as Seqable for getting lazy seqs or ILookup for random access. In short, they must implement many interfaces, not just the most minimal and ubiquitous interface.

This is why Clojure provides the clojure.core.protocols.CollReduce protocol instead of using function-based reducibles as we introduced earlier. To make the previous work integrate with Clojure's reducers framework, we need to address this protocol. As is usual with protocols, two sides must be addressed: the implementation of the protocol (making reducible-range available by calling coll-reduce) and the use of the protocol (making mapping and friends call coll-reduce). From now on, when we refer to *core* reducibles, transformers, and so on, we mean those made to work with Clojure's CollReduce and related protocols, in contrast to the function-based ones we discussed in previous sections.

Let's begin by making reducing function transformers work with Clojure collections. Clojure makes this easy with the reducer function, which automates the kind of transformation you did to define r-map and r-filter back in listing 15.16. But reducer returns a core reducible (that is, an object that implements CollReduce), so you can use it to define a couple new functions as in this listing.

Listing 15.17 Converting transformers to core reducibles

```
(require '[clojure.core.reducers :as r])     ←— Load the reducers namespace
(defn core-r-map [mapping-fn core-reducible]
  (r/reducer core-reducible (mapping mapping-fn)))     ←— Call mapping

(defn core-r-filter [filter-pred core-reducible]
  (r/reducer core-reducible (filtering filter-pred)))     ←— Call filtering
```

Now you can use the functions like this:

```
(reduce conj []
        (core-r-filter #(not= % 2)
                       (core-r-map half [0 2 4 6 8]))))
;=> [0 1 3 4]
```

You use a vector as input to the pipeline because vectors already implement Coll-Reduce, which makes them core reducibles themselves. The new transformers, `core-r-map` and `core-r-filter`, also return core reducibles. Finally, the `reduce` function in Clojure 1.5 knows how to work not only with sequences but also with core reducibles, so the entire pipeline is executed the same way as the function-based reducibles were earlier.

If you want to provide your own reducible-range as a core reducible, the second side of the protocol implementation, you have to do a bit more work. Specifically, you need to implement it via a protocol instead of a function.

Listing 15.18 Implementing a reducible-range via the CollReduce protocol

```
(defn reduce-range [reducing-fn init, start end step]     ◁─── Factor out the
  (loop [result init, i start]                                 range loop
    (if (empty-range? i end step)
      result
      (recur (reducing-fn result i)
             (+ i step)))))

(defn core-reducible-range [start end step]
  (reify protos/CollReduce
    (coll-reduce [this reducing-fn init]                  ◁─── Implement the
      (reduce-range reducing-fn init, start end step))         familiar 3-arg case
    (coll-reduce [this reducing-fn]                        ◁─── Implement the
      (if (empty-range? start end step)                        2-arg case
        (reducing-fn)
        (reduce-range reducing-fn start, (+ start step) end step)))))
```

You need to run the main range-reducing loop from a couple different contexts, so here you abstract it out and have it take all five parameters (separating the reduce args from the range args with a comma). This is nearly identical to the definition of reducible-range back in listing 15.12, but it's defined here with no closure and thus less memory allocation when run.

Now that `reduce-range` is factored out, implementing the three-argument form of `coll-reduce` is easy. The two-argument form of `coll-reduce` corresponds to the two-argument form of `reduce`. That is, the first item of the collection is used as the seed or init value of the reduction. You do this by peeling off the `start` value and calling reduce-range with that as the `init` and shorter-by-one remainder of the range.

This form also means you must deal with the possibility of an empty collection with no init value to return. In this case, Clojure's definition of `reduce` requires you to return the result of calling the reducing function with no arguments.

Together, this allows you to use `core-reducible-range` with Clojure's `reduce` function in all the normal ways:

```
(reduce conj []
        (core-r-filter #(not= % 2)
                       (core-r-map half
                                   (core-reducible-range 0 10 2)))))
;=> [0 1 3 4]
```

```
(reduce + (core-reducible-range 10 12 1))
;=> 21

(reduce + (core-reducible-range 10 11 1))
;=> 10

(reduce + (core-reducible-range 10 10 1))
;=> 0
```

You've now seen the simplicity of the reducibles interface and how it can improve performance while providing syntax nearly identical to Clojure's seq library. By using protocols, you can even use some of the same functions and collections you already know, like reduce and vectors. But it's possible to get results even faster by giving up more guarantees. If you don't care about the order in which your reducing functions are called, several of them can be run in parallel.

15.6.8 *The fold function: reducing in parallel*

We briefly mentioned fold back in chapter 11, but now we have covered enough background to look more closely at how it works. All the reduce and reduce-like operations we've discussed so far have worked in a linear fashion, starting at the beginning of a collection and proceeding in order. But as we pointed out in chapter 11, in many situations the reducer we want to use is associative and doesn't need to proceed in order. So just as with lazy seqs versus reducibles, our abstraction is too specific, promises too much, and as a consequence isn't useful in some situations where it could be.

The alternative to reduce that supports parallel instead of sequential operation is called fold. The clojure.core.reducers/fold function is similar to reduce. In its shortest form, it can take exactly the same parameters as reduce and return the same result:

```
(reduce + [1 2 3 4 5])
;=> 15

(r/fold + [1 2 3 4 5])
;=> 15
```

The primary difference is that it doesn't make any promises about order of execution and requires that your reducing function be associative.[11] This gives fold the freedom it needs to do the divide-and-conquer work for you.

This ties in to the reducibles abstraction, because all the reducing function transformers we've presented (mapping, filtering, and mapcatting), as well as many others, if given a pure associative reducing function, will return another pure associative reducing function. In other words, they're as compatible with the requirements of fold as they are with reduce, and as a result they can be made similarly available with a conversion function provided in the reducers namespace.

---

[11] Actually, if your reducing function is different than your combining function, only the combining function must be associative. We'll get to combining functions soon.

Listing 15.19   Converting transformers to core foldables

```
(defn core-f-map [mapping-fn core-reducible]
  (r/folder core-reducible (mapping mapping-fn)))        <— Call mapping

(defn core-f-filter [filter-pred core-reducible]
  (r/folder core-reducible (filtering filter-pred)))     <— Call filtering
```

These new foldable transformers can now be used with `fold`:

```
(r/fold +
        (core-f-filter #(not= % 2)
                       (core-f-map half
                                   [0 2 4 6 8])))
;=> 8
```

Alas, they're unnecessary, because Clojure's reducers library provides them already, under the names `map` and `filter`:

```
(r/fold +
        (r/filter #(not= % 2)
                  (r/map half
                         [0 2 4 6 8])))
;=> 8
```

Also provided are a few other functions whose names and behavior will be familiar to anyone who knows the seq library. These currently include `drop`, `filter`, `flatten`, `map`, `mapcat`, `remove`, `take`, and `take-while`.

So far we've only looked at the two-argument form of `fold`. Like `reduce`, `fold` has more complex forms, but they're different than `reduce`'s. One of the optional parameters that `fold` takes is a *combining* function. We'll look at that in more detail in a moment, but for now keep in mind that if you don't specify one, `fold` will use your reducing function for combining as well.

Another difference is that `fold` doesn't take an initial or seed value as a parameter. Instead, it calls the combining function with no arguments to determine an initial value. For example, if you wanted to sum up some values but start with an initial value of 100, you could do it like this:

```
(r/fold (fn ([] 100) ([a b] (+ a b))) (range 10))
;=> 145
```

Here you supply a reducing function that takes either no parameters, in which case it returns 100, or two parameters a and b and returns their sum. You didn't need this in the earlier example of `fold` because the + function returns zero when called with no arguments, which is often exactly what you want.

But when you do want to provide an initial value, the two-body function syntax just demonstrated is a bit awkward, so Clojure provides a tool to build such functions for you. This tool is a function called `monoid` that takes an operator (+ in this example) and a constructor that returns the initial value. You could write the previous example like this:

```
(r/fold (r/monoid + (constantly 100)) (range 10))
;=> 145
```

Now on to the combining function. As mentioned previously, fold divides the work to be done into smaller pieces and reduces all the elements in each piece. By default, each piece has approximately 512 elements, but this number can be specified as an optional parameter to fold. When two pieces of work have been done and need to be combined, this is done by calling the combining function, another optional parameter to fold. With all default arguments given, the previous example is equivalent to

```
(r/fold 512                              ⟵ Elements per piece of work
         (r/monoid + (constantly 100))
         +                               ⟵ Reducing function
         (range 10))
;=> 145
```

Combining function →

If you don't specify a combining function, the reducing function will be used. This makes sense when the reducing function accepts two parameters of the same type it returns, such as when using + for summing up the numbers in a collection as we showed previously. But for some operations this isn't the case, such as when conjing elements into a vector. In this case, when fold is reducing the small pieces of work, it's conjing individual elements into a vector. But when combining these pieces of work, it has two vectors—combining this with conj won't achieve the desired results:

```
(r/fold 4 (r/monoid conj (constantly [])) conj (vec (range 10)))
;=> [0 1 [2 3 4] [5 6 [7 8 9]]]
```

Using conj on two vectors puts the second *inside* the first, instead of joining them into a single vector, which is what produces the mess of nested vectors shown here.

The combining function we're looking for is into, which, when given two vectors, joins them into a single vector in the natural order, like this:

```
(r/fold 4 (r/monoid into (constantly [])) conj (vec (range 10)))
;=> [0 1 2 3 4 5 6 7 8 9]
```

It's interesting to consider how the reducing and combining steps together give us the tools we need to solve the same kinds of problems that map/reduce frameworks do, and with fold we can run them in a similarly parallel way. And just as with map/reduce jobs, we often need to provide custom functions for the reducing and combining steps, as well as transformers for the input collection. But our specific example of combining all the elements from a foldable into a collection is common enough that Clojure provides a high-performance function to do exactly that: foldcat. It doesn't build a vector, but it does internally call fold using reducing and combining functions that efficiently build a collection that is reducible, foldable, sequable, and counted. You can use it like this:

```
(r/foldcat (r/filter even? (vec (range 1000))))
;=> #<Cat clojure.core.reducers.Cat@209bc0df>

>(seq (r/foldcat (r/filter even? (vec (range 10)))))
;=> (0 2 4 6 8)
```

What has all this splitting up of work and recombining bought us in terms of performance? If you recall, the fastest our benchmark ran using reducers was 385 milliseconds. Let's see what `fold` can do:

```
(def big-vector (vec (range 0 (* 10 1000 1000) 2)))

(crit/bench
 (r/fold + (core-f-filter even? (core-f-map half big-vector))))
;; Execution time mean : 126.756586 ms
```

We used a vector here because none of the range functions currently available return a foldable collection. But even accounting for that difference, `fold` still gets the job done at least 55% faster on our test machine. Of course, many factors may cause you to see different results, not the least of these being the number of processor cores used for the test; but nevertheless it's clearly a marked improvement.

In this section, you've seen how a minimal abstraction can be built up from simple functions and used as a basis for higher-performance collection processing. You've also seen how that can be combined with weaker promises about order of operation to provide parallelism and even higher performance.

15.7 *Summary*

Clojure provides numerous ways to gain speed in your applications. Using some combination of type hints, transients, chunked sequences, memoization, and coercion, you should be able to achieve noticeable performance gains. Like any powerful tool, these performance techniques should be used cautiously and thoughtfully. But once you've determined that performance can be gained, the use of these techniques is minimally intrusive and often natural to the unadorned implementation.

In the next chapter, we'll cover a topic that has captured the imagination of a growing number of Clojure programmers: logic. Clojure is an excellent programming language for exploring new ways of thinking, and although logic programming isn't new, it leads to different ways of thinking about solving problems.

Thinking programs

16

This chapter covers
- Searching
- Thinking data via unification
- Logic programming
- Constraint programming

Functional programming is an attempt to reach a declarative ideal in program composition. Functional techniques can lead to code that mirrors the form of the solution, but sometimes levels of expressiveness come at a cost in terms of speed. In problems of search, for example, matters related to the "how" of search intermingle with the "what" of the solution. In this chapter, we'll explore matters of search and querying using functional approaches compared to logical techniques.

We'll start by discussing search and building a Sudoku solver that uses a brute-force functional approach that strives to solve the problem declaratively. Next we'll explore the idea of *thinking data* using a special kind of pattern matching called *unification*. Our exploration of unification will transition into a discussion of a promising Clojure contrib library called core.logic. The core.logic library provides a logic-programming system allowing declarative descriptions of problem spaces that actually run. We'll conclude this chapter by exploring ways to constrain the search space involved in solving logic problems to speed up execution times.

16.1   *A problem of search*

Logic programming is largely a matter of search. To solve a problem requiring logic requires you to explore the sea of possibilities available. Many logic programming languages (such as Prolog) are abstractions over the act of searching trees of possible solutions to a query. This isn't a book about Prolog, but often you'll find yourself needing to search a vast space to solve a tricky problem. For example, Prolog is often used to implement systems containing many business rules that can interact and counteract in a huge number of ways.

When we think of searching, the subject of games and puzzles often comes to mind. Game and puzzle searches provide a nice Petri-dish environment for exploring logic programming and search-space culling. In this section, we'll talk about a simple type of puzzle called Sudoku and explore an inefficient approach to searching for solutions to puzzles.

16.1.1   *A brute-force Sudoku solver*

The game Sudoku is a vaguely mathematical puzzle with a few advantages for the purpose of exploration. First, the rules of Sudoku are simple to describe and are therefore easy to encode in code. Second, a naive Sudoku solver can be created in a few lines of code. We'll show you how to create such a solver for the purpose of introducing some logic programming concepts.

Here's a description of what a Sudoku game looks like:

- You start with a 9 x 9 square.
- The square is subdivided into nine 3 x 3 sections.
- Some of the spaces in the square contain numbers.

The objective is to fill the empty spaces so that the following puzzle constraints are satisfied:

- Each column must contain one occurrence of each digit from 1–9.
- Each row must contain one occurrence of each digit from 1–9.
- Each 3 x 3 subsection must contain one occurrence of each digit from 1–9.

Figure 16.1 shows the Sudoku board you'll use for the example in this chapter.

```
-----------------------------
|3 - -|- - 5|- 1 -|
|- 7 -|- - 6|- 3 -|
|1 - -|- 9 -|- - -|
-----------------------------
|7 - 8|- - -|- 9 -|
|9 - -|4 - 8|- - 2|
|- 6 -|- - -|5 - 1|
-----------------------------
|- - -|- 4 -|- - 6|
|- 4 -|7 - -|- 2 -|
|- 2 -|6 - -|- - 3|
-----------------------------
```

Figure 16.1   Starting position of the example Sudoku board

You can create a bare-bones representation of this board using a Clojure vector like the following:

```
(def b1 '[3 - - - - 5 - 1 -
          - 7 - - - 6 - 3 -
          1 - - - 9 - - - -
          7 - 8 - - - - 9 -
          9 - - 4 - 8 - - 2
          - 6 - - - - 5 - 1
          - - - - 4 - - - 6
          - 4 - 7 - - - 2 -
          - 2 - 6 - - - - 3])
```

Although it's convenient for entry, this board doesn't look anything like a Sudoku board, so let's define a function prep that makes it more accurate:

```
(defn prep [board]
  (map #(partition 3 %)
       (partition 9 board)))
```

This function does what you might expect: it segments the board into the divisions expected for a 9 x 9 Sudoku board. Now you can write a simple, imperative board printer to print the textual board shown in figure 16.1; the function print-board is given next.

> **Listing 16.1   Printing the starting position of a Sudoku board**

```
(defn print-board [board]
  (let [row-sep (apply str (repeat 37 "-"))]
    (println row-sep)
    (dotimes [row (count board)]
      (print "| ")
      (doseq [subrow (nth board row)]
        (doseq [cell (butlast subrow)]
          (print (str cell "   ")))
        (print (str (last subrow) " | ")))
      (println)
      (when (zero? (mod (inc row) 3))
        (println row-sep)))))
```

As is often the case when printing, the structure of print-board is highly declarative. All you're doing is looping through each row and printing each entry, with a special character to denote subgrid sections. The function print-board is used as follows:

```
(-> b1 prep print-board)
```

Now that the technicalities are out of the way, we can move on to the mechanics of implementing a solver.

THE REGIONS OF A SUDOKU BOARD

As we explained earlier, the objective of Sudoku is to complete the square such that each column, each row, and each 3 x 3 subsection contains one occurrence of every digit from 1–9. As it turns out, making the board into a more reasonable representation works well for printing, but it's nicer to keep it flat for calculating groupings. This means for any cell on the board, you'll calculate three things:

- The row containing the cell
- The column containing the cell
- The 3 x 3 subgrid containing the cell

To get these pieces of information, you'll write three auxiliary functions: `row-for`, `column-for`, and `subgrid-for`. The implementation of `row-for` is as follows:

```
(defn rows [board sz]
  (partition sz board))

(defn row-for [board index sz]
  (nth (rows board sz) (/ index 9)))
```

This is similar to the implementation of the `rank-component` shown way back in listing 1.6. Its entire purpose is to take a one-dimensional coordinate in a vector and map it onto the logical two-dimensional space of the Sudoku board. It does this by using the helper function `rows` to slice the board into rows and taking the one containing the adjusted (by 9) index. Testing the implementation for the first empty cell at index 1 gives the following result:

```
(row-for b1 1 9)
;=> (3 - - - - 5 - 1 -)
```

This matches the first row for board b1. Moving on, the `column-for` implementation is somewhat similar:

```
(defn column-for [board index sz]
  (let [col (mod index sz)]
    (map #(nth % col)
         (rows board sz))))
```

The difference is that you don't preprocess the board into columns, but instead grab the precise column you need. You can do this because you provide a specific size for the columns and go to the correct place with some `mod` math. Testing the function quickly for the column at index 2 gives this result:

```
(column-for b1 2 9)
;=> (- - - 8 - - - - -)
```

The explicit-size approach is useful. You need the same behavior when you grab the columns of the subgrids using `subgrid-for`:

```
(defn subgrid-for [board i]
  (let [rows (rows board 9)                          ⟵ Calculate the subgrid's
        sgcol (/ (mod i 9) 3)                           row index
        sgrow (/ (/ i 9) 3)                          ⟵ Calculate the subgrid's
        grp-col (column-for (mapcat #(partition 3 %) rows) sgcol 3)   column index
        grp (take 3 (drop (* 3 (int sgrow)) grp-col))]   ⟵
    (flatten grp)))
```

Group all entries by column ⟶

Pull out only the elements in the subgrid

The `subgrid-for` function is unfortunately a complex beast. Due to the board representation, you're forced to massage and extract relevant subdata elements so that you can deal with the board in a first-class way. In the case of `subgrid-for`, the logical representation, a 3 x 3 square, diverges from the actual representation of a 1D vector of data and also from the logical 9 x 9 Sudoku board. `subgrid-for` attempts to rectify the disparity between three data representations and returns a flattened representation of the logical 3 x 3 subgrid. Testing `subgrid-for` yields the following:

```
(subgrid-for b1 0)
;=> (3 - - - 7 - 1 - -)
```

If you recall the top-left subgrid from figure 16.1, you'll see that the result matches:

```
-------------
| 3   -   - |
| -   7   - |
| 1   -   - |
-------------
```

That is all that you need to start encoding the rules of Sudoku.

THE RULES OF SUDOKU

As is often the case in problems like Sudoku, the rules are incredibly simple to describe, but this simplicity is deceptive. For some starting configurations, a Sudoku solution is simple; but for others, the solution may be non-existent. Here's some pseudocode to find any solution:

```
* Place a number into the first empty square
* Check if the constraints hold
  - If so, then start this algorithm again
  - If not, then remove the number and start this algorithm again
* repeat
```

Eventually, using this process, you'll come to a solution—or the process will run forever (if a solution doesn't exist). In the parlance of searching, this method is called *brute-force searching*. There is nothing particularly smart about this algorithm, but it will exhaustively search the tree of possibilities until it runs out of choices or finds a solution. Brute-force searching, given enough time, will always find a solution if one exists.

Fortunately, the implementation of a brute-force Sudoku solver can be reasonably translated into Clojure based on the rules we listed and the helper and region functions you already created. First, let's create a function to gather all the numbers present in the set containing the row, column, and subgrid for a given cell:

```
(defn numbers-present-for [board i]
  (set
   (concat (row-for board i 9)
           (column-for board i 9)
           (subgrid-for board i)))))
```

The function `numbers-present-for` is straightforward in its implementation. It gets all the elements for a cell's row, column, and subgrid and removes all the duplicates. So the possible numbers at the index of the first occurrence of - on the example board are given as follows:

```
(numbers-present-for b1 1)
;=> #{1 2 3 4 5 6 7 -}
```

This result says that at that cell, you have representatives for all the necessary numbers by the rules of Sudoku except 8 and 9, plus some number of unfilled slots. You can now use this function to great effect. First, as we mentioned, you want the brute-force algorithm to enter a value in the first empty cell it finds and check the constraints against that value. Because the board is a vector, and vectors are associative, the placement function is as simple as `assoc`. Here's what happens when you place a value and check the same cell:

```
(numbers-present-for (assoc b1 1 8) 1)
;=> #{1 2 3 4 5 6 7 8 -}
```

As you might have expected, the set returned grew by one number because you placed a number that you happened to know was needed. But how might you tell the solver to place a number that is needed? Using set operations, you can build a set of possible values that would fit into the cell in question:

```
(set/difference #{1 2 3 4 5 6 7 8 9}
                (numbers-present-for b1 1))
;=> #{8 9}
```

If you recall from section 5.5.4, the `difference` function returns the values that differ between one set and another. Placing this behavior into an appropriately named function will prove useful in a moment:

```
(defn possible-placements [board index]
  (set/difference #{1 2 3 4 5 6 7 8 9}
                  (numbers-present-for board index)))
```

Now, to solve the board, you can encode the rest of the rules in Clojure, as shown in the following listing.[1]

---

[1] The pos function was implemented back in chapter 5. As a quick reference, its implementation is `(defn pos [pred coll] (for [[i v] (index coll) :when (pred v)] i))`.

Listing 16.2 Brute-force Sudoku solver

```
(defn solve [board]
  (if-let [[i & _]                               | Find first
          (and (some '#{-} board)              <--| occurrence of -
               (pos  '#{-} board))]
    (flatten (map #(solve (assoc board i %))    <--- Solve the new board ...
                  (possible-placements board i)))   <--| ... with a possible
    board))                                          | replacement for -
```

The encoded solver is a recursive solution that maps over every possible legitimate placement of a number in an empty position. By "legitimate" we mean placements that adhere to the legal rules of Sudoku as encoded in the interplay between possible-placements and numbers-present-for.

You can see the solution by running the following:

```
(-> b1
    solve
    prep
    print-board)
```

After running for a few seconds, this square should be printed:

```
-------------------------------------
| 3   8   6 | 2   7   5 | 4   1   9 |
| 4   7   9 | 8   1   6 | 2   3   5 |
| 1   5   2 | 3   9   4 | 8   6   7 |
-------------------------------------
| 7   3   8 | 5   2   1 | 6   9   4 |
| 9   1   5 | 4   6   8 | 3   7   2 |
| 2   6   4 | 9   3   7 | 5   8   1 |
-------------------------------------
| 8   9   3 | 1   4   2 | 7   5   6 |
| 6   4   1 | 7   5   3 | 9   2   8 |
| 5   2   7 | 6   8   9 | 1   4   3 |
-------------------------------------
```

The solver should work for most Sudoku starting positions, but some may take longer than others. Although you haven't used the most efficient algorithm, you've composed a solution that involves a functional approach that is fairly declarative. And that's the goal, right?

16.1.2 *Declarative is the goal*

We've mentioned throughout this book that we like to write our programs in such a way that the code looks like a description of the solution; and to a large extent, we accomplished that goal with the Sudoku solver. Even in this simple implementation, we were forced to add a number of tangential concerns, especially in subgrid-for, in order to calculate the proper indices into the puzzle board. What if we could eliminate most, if not all, of the noise in the implementation? We would be that much closer to a declarative ideal.

Throughout this chapter, we'll describe ways to achieve varying levels of declarativeness beyond what is possible via functional techniques. We'll address logic programming in sections 16.3 and 16.4 by working through an example related to the solar system and revisiting the Sudoku puzzle from a new angle. First, let's take a step back and try to combine the world of functional declarativeness and data declarativeness via *unification*.

16.2 *Thinking data via unification*

If we summarize chapter 14 as "thinking with data in mind," then this section can be summarized as "data that thinks." This might be a bit too spectacular, but it's not far from reality. The real problem at hand is that although we've talked about the declarative nature of data and the declarative nature of functional techniques, we haven't yet bridged the gap between the two ideas. In this section, we'll talk about unification, which is a technique for determining whether two pieces of data are *potentially equal*. This is a loose term, but we'll explain it soon.

16.2.1 *Potential equality, or satisfiability*

What is the result of the following expression?

```
(= ?something 2)
```

The correct answer is—it depends on what the value of ?something is. That is, the equality check (= ?something 2) is said to be *potentially equal*, depending on the value of ?something. In the case where this expression is preceded by (def ?something 2), the equality check results in true. The symbol ?something in this case is a variable. Although we've been careful in our use of the word *variable* throughout this book, here it's applicable.

Further, we can say that one possible map[2] representing the bindings used to satisfy the equality is {?something 2}. What we would like is a function named satisfy1 that, when given two arguments, returns a map of the bindings that would make the two items equal, if possible. You'll implement satisfy1 presently.

SATISFYING VARIABLES

We need to define a word that we'll use throughout this section: *term*. In logic programming, *term* has the same sense as *value* in functional programming. A term can contain variables, but it's still a value rather than an expression needing evaluation. Terms without variables are called *ground terms*. Here are some examples:

```
1       ;; constant term
?x      ;; variable term
(1 2)   ;; ground term
(1 ?x)  ;; term
```

---

[2] Another is {?something 20/10} and yet another is {?something (length [4 5])}—the possibilities are endless—but we'll keep things simple.

In the previous subsection, we mentioned that a bindings map describes the values needing assignment to logic variables to make two terms equal. In this section, we'll show you a simple algorithm for deriving a bindings map for two terms, each of which is either a variable or a constant. First, you need to create a function that identifies symbols that represent logic variables. An implementation of the function lvar? is shown next.

Listing 16.3 Identifying logic variables

```
(defn lvar?
  "Determines if a value represents a logic variable"
  [x]
  (boolean
   (when (symbol? x)
     (re-matches #"^\?.*" (name x)))))
```

The operation of lvar? states that only symbols starting with \? are considered logic variables. You can demonstrate its operation as follows:

```
(lvar? '?x)
;;=> true

(lvar? 'a)
;;=> false

(lvar? 2)
;;=> false
```

These results shouldn't be too surprising. Now that you have a way to identify logic variables, the next listing shows an implementation of satisfy1. Of particular note is how small it is.

Listing 16.4 Simplified satisfiability function

```
(defn satisfy1
  [l r knowledge]
  (let [L (get knowledge l l)
        R (get knowledge r r)]          ← ❶ Look up terms
    (cond
     (= L R)    knowledge               ← ❷ No new knowledge
     (lvar? L) (assoc knowledge L R)    ←   Bind the variable to
     (lvar? R) (assoc knowledge R L)    ❸ the other term
     :default  nil)))
```

The function satisfy1 starts by attempting to build knowledge about the potential equality of two terms. It does this by first using the existing knowledge about the terms (or the terms themselves, if no existing knowledge is found in the lookup) ❶. You require a Clojure map as the final argument for the sake of simplicity, but that requirement will need adjustment in the next section.

Moving on, you assume that if the terms are equal, you want to return the existing knowledge ❷. By not adding any binding to the map, you effectively say that the terms are already equal. For example, how do you satisfy the equality of 1 and 1?

Equality between the terms is already satisfied. Returning the existing knowledge allows you to chain `satisfy1` calls for the purpose of gradually satisfying high-order relationships (shown in a moment).

If either term is a variable, the way to satisfy it is to set the binding from the variable term to the other term ❸. This flip-flop action on the variable binding is a simple yet elegant solution to satisfying variable terms. Although returning `nil` at the end of the `cond` isn't strictly necessary, it helps to clarify that by default, two terms aren't satisfiable.

Here are two calls:

```
(satisfy1 '?something 2 {})
;;=> {?something 2}

(satisfy1 2 '?something {})
;;=> {?something 2}
```

In both cases, the results say that in order to satisfy equality of the number 2 and the variable ?something, the latter must equal 2. This is so intuitive that it hardly bears mentioning; but the subtlety of unification in general is shown with the following call:[3]

```
(satisfy1 '?x '?y {})
;;=> {?x ?y}
```

This is more subtle. The result of `satisfy1` in this case states that to achieve the equality of two variables, one variable must equal the other. This condition is what makes unification different than something like destructuring or even pattern matching.[4] By allowing variables to occupy the solution, you can defer satisfying the equality until further knowledge becomes available. For example, if you know that satisfying equality of two variables requires that one equal the other, whatever their value, then you can fully satisfy the terms by supplying a value:

```
(->> {}
     (satisfy1 '?x '?y)
     (satisfy1 '?x 1))

;;=> {?y 1, ?x ?y}
```

You can see that if ?x equals ?y and ?y equals 1, then ?x equals 1 also. Your first attempt at solving satisfiability can't make this kind of inference, but with a few modifications you can make it do so.

SATISFYING SEQS

Observe the following:

```
(= '(1 2 3) '(1 2 3))
```

---

[3] Unification is a surprisingly rich topic of exploration, and we've barely begun to scratch the surface. Our introduction should be enough to get you through this chapter. If you'd like to learn more, feel free to petition Manning for a book on logic programming.

[4] Although unification can be thought of as two-way pattern matching.

You would expect this expression to evaluate to `true`, and your expectation would be met. Likewise, the expression (= '(1 2 3) '(100 200 300)) results in `false`. (1 2 3) and (100 200 300) aren't equal to each other, nor could they ever be. But conceptualize the following:

```
(= '(1 2 3) '(1 ?something 3))
```

You might say that, as in the previous section, the equality check will pass or fail depending on the value of ?something. In some books on functional or logic programming, the authors try to draw a connection between programming logic and mathematical logic. The reason is that there is a connection: one only hinted at by our use of the word *variable* to represent an unknown value in a vector.[5] In algebra class, you might have seen problems of this form:

```
What is the value of x in the term:

38 - (x + 2) = 5x
```

We won't make you break out your paper and pencil—the answer to this formula is x = 6. The variable x is in effect the same as our notion of a variable ?something.

To *satisfy* the equality of the two seqs (1 2 3) and (1 ?something 3), the binding of ?something would have to be equal to the number 2. But satisfy1 from the previous section won't help you derive that information. Instead, you need to modify the algorithm as shown next, to account for nested variables and recursive definitions.[6]

Listing 16.5 Function that satisfies seqs

```
(defn satisfy
  [l r knowledge]
  (let [L (get knowledge l l)
        R (get knowledge r r)]
    (cond
     (not knowledge)      nil           ← ❶ Knowledge required
     (= L R)              knowledge
     (lvar? L)            (assoc knowledge L R)
     (lvar? R)            (assoc knowledge R L)
     (every? seq? [L R])                ← ❷ Seqs detected
       (satisfy (rest L)
                (rest R)               ← ❸ Remainder of the seq ...
                (satisfy (first L)
                         (first R)        ← ┐ ... satisfied to the
                         knowledge))    ❹ first part of the seq
     :default nil)))
```

Although basically the same shape as satisfy1, the new function satisfy has two additions that extend it. First, because the definition is recursive, you can no longer

---

[5] Usually, first-order (or maybe higher-order) logic with universal or existential quantifiers is considered the philosophical motivation for logic programming. Although our algebra example isn't of the same nature, it can be encoded in first-order logic.

[6] In most of the literature on logic programming, our function satisfy is called unify.

assume knowledge is given. Because the default case returns `nil`, you can use that fact as the terminating condition for failure ❶. But this is a minor change compared to the recursive calls themselves. The point is easy to elucidate: when both terms are seqs, you want to attempt to satisfy them as deeply as they go ❷. This is accomplished by building the knowledge of the first elements in each seq ❸ and using that as a seed for then satisfying the rest of the seqs ❹. This is where the advantage of adding to the knowledge comes in handy: `satisfy` uses knowledge it learned earlier to resolve bindings later in the process. Observe the following:

```
(satisfy '(1 2 3) '(1 ?something 3) {})
;;=> {?something 2}
```

This, as we discussed earlier, is the binding that makes the two seqs equal. It doesn't matter how deeply nested the variables are:

```
(satisfy '((((?something)))) '((((2)))) {})
;;=> {?something 2}
```

Nor does it matter how scattered the variables happen to be:

```
(satisfy '(?x 2 3 (4 5 ?z))
         '(1 2 ?y (4 5 6))
         {})

;;=> {?z 6, ?y 3, ?x 1}

(satisfy '?x '(?y) {})
;;=> {?x (?y)}
```

The new function satisfies the terms when possible:

```
(satisfy '(?x 10000 3) '(1 2 ?y) {})
;;=> nil
```

Using a simple recursive algorithm (let's call it a data-programmable engine), you can derive a specific kind of knowledge from two pieces of data: the variable bindings required to make them equal. There is a hard limit to how far this knowledge takes you, though. On its own, deriving bindings is of limited use. But you can take that knowledge and build on it to form more complex functions.

16.2.2 *Substitution*

The `satisfy` function can return a map representing variable bindings. You can view those bindings as an environment providing a context for substituting holes in a template for actual values. The function that fulfills this substitution, named `subst`, is defined in the following listing.

> **Listing 16.6 Walking a data structure and substituting logic variables for bound values**

```
(require '[clojure.walk :as walk])

(defn subst [term binds]
  (walk/prewalk
```

```
(fn [expr]
  (if (lvar? expr)
    (or (binds expr) expr)
    expr))
term))
```

The function `subst` uses Clojure's tree-traversal library `clojure.walk` to examine each element in turn, attempting to replace it with its value binding if it's a logic variable. You can see `subst` in action here:

```
(subst '(1 ?x 3) '{?x 2})
;;=> (1 2 3)
(subst '((((?x)))) '{?x 2})
;;=> ((((2))))
(subst '[1 ?x 3] '{?x 2})
;;=> [1 2 3]
(subst '{:a ?x, :b [1 ?x 3]} '{?x 2})
;;=> {:a 2, :b [1 2 3]}
```

And here's how `subst` acts when given incomplete knowledge (bindings):

```
(subst '(1 ?x 3) '{})
;;=> (1 ?x 3)
(subst '(1 ?x 3) '{?x ?y})
;;=> (1 ?y 3)
```

The beauty of using the `clojure.walk` library is that it preserves the original type of the target, as shown. You could imagine a web-templating system built on something like subst:

```
(def page
  '[:html
    [:head [:title ?title]]
    [:body [:h1 ?title]]])

(subst page '{?title "Hi!"})
;;=> [:html [:head [:title "Hi!"]] [:body [:h1 "Hi!"]]]
```

But the reason we mention it is that it serves as the basis for the unification of two terms.

16.2.3 *Unification*

The term *unification* is defined as a function that takes two terms and unifies them in the empty context, finally returning a new substitution. For practical purposes, unification is composed of three separate and orthogonal functions:

- Deriving a binding as defined in `satisfy`
- Substitution as defined in `subst`
- Melding two structures together as defined shortly in `meld`

Based on what we've shown so far, you've created two of the tools needed to perform the unification suite. The missing tool, meld, takes two seqs and melds them together, taking into account all embedded logic variables.

Listing 16.7   Melding two seqs, substituting logic variables

```
(defn meld [term1 term2]
  (->> {}
       (satisfy term1 term2)
       (subst term1)))
```

meld derives the bindings in play between two seqs and then uses those bindings to perform a substitution on either one. Although it's not a comprehensive solution, it can handle a fair amount of melds, including many with relative bindings:

```
(meld '(1 ?x 3) '(1 2 ?y))
;;=> (1 2 3)

(meld '(1 ?x) '(?y (?y 2)))
;;=> (1 (1 2))
```

Throughout this chapter, you've built up gradually more complex, yet declarative functions using nothing but data and the bare minimum of program logic. In every case, from satisfy to subst to meld, you've implemented tiny data-programmable engines and supplied them with data to see how they worked. Likewise, you built one on the other to create higher-level functionality; each in turn its own data-programmable engine. But although unification is interesting and useful for various problems, as a model for declarative computation it's left wanting.

A powerful feature of unification that nevertheless causes issue is shown next:

```
(satisfy '?x 1 (satisfy '?x '?y {}))
;;=> {?y 1, ?x ?y}

(satisfy '(1 ?x) '(?y (?y 2)) {})
;;=> {?x (?y 2), ?y 1}
```

In these examples, variables are retained in the answer (there are non-ground terms). Although you can probably see that in both cases, ?y is 1, the algorithm can't. Therefore, you need to take this process a step further.

Simple unification unfortunately only gets you so far. On its own, it's not enough to solve even a simple algebraic expression:

```
What is the value of x in the term:

5x - 2(x - 5) = 4x
```

Instead, you need some kind of operational logic to solve general-purpose problems in a declarative fashion. Fortunately, the Clojure contrib library provides a tool called core.logic that builds on the principles of unification to move us closer to a declarative ideal.

16.3 An introduction to core.logic

In this book, we've tried hard to maintain a strict policy of highlighting core Clojure functions and features. But one Clojure-contrib library has grabbed not only our attention and imagination but also those of the Clojure community as a whole. The library, called core.logic, provides a system of operational logic for making general inferences using the principles of unification. This section covers the basics of core.logic including some examples.

First, to use core.logic, you need to include it in your project dependencies (or see the example in the preface) in your preferred way and add the following declaration to a namespace for use:

```
(ns joy.logic.cl
  (require [clojure.core.logic :as logic]))
```

From here, you have access to core.logic's features.

16.3.1 It's all about unification

Previously in this chapter, you created a simplified unification system out of three functions: `satisfy`, `subst`, and `meld`. Of particular importance is the `satisfy` function. Recall how `satisfy` works:

```
(satisfy '?answer 5 {})
;;=> {answer 5}
```

The `satisfy` function attempts to answer this question: How can two terms be made equal? Surprisingly, this simple question forms the basis for much of what is commonly known as *logic programming*. Before diving deeper into that particular point, it's worth noting that the core.logic library contains a *goal constructor* named == that isn't the same as `clojure.core/==`. Mimicking the action of `satisfy` using core.logic's == is as follows:

```
(logic/run* [answer]
  (logic/== answer 5))
;;=> (5)
```

The `run*` form provides a lexical binding [answer] that declares the logic variables in context for the forms nested within. Likewise, the answer logic variable, because it's bound by the `run*` form, represents the final result. The == unifier looks similar to the `satisfy` call, except that the context map is implicit rather than supplied as an argument. The return value (5) maps one for one with the established binding [answer]. To see how multiple bindings are established, observe the following:

```
(logic/run* [val1 val2]
  (logic/== {:a val1, :b 2}
            {:a 1,    :b val2}))
;;=> ([1 2])
```

This is already more powerful than satisfy: although satisfy only unifies with scalars and lists, core.logic unifies against all Clojure's data types.[7] This ability obviates the need to continue with satisfy. Like satisfy, logic/== can leave logic variables in its wake:

```
(logic/run* [x y]
  (logic/== x y))

;;=> ([_0 _0])
```

The binding represented by _0 is a logic variable (like ?x in satisfy), and core.logic represents logic variables using an underscore followed by unique numbers. In the previous case, the dual-variable binding states: in order for x and y to be equal, they must both be the same unknown value.

Another example of unification in core.logic is the case where unification fails:

```
(logic/run* [q]
  (logic/== q 1)
  (logic/== q 2))

;;=> ()
```

Two attempted unifications against the same logic variable q fail unification because the logic variable's binding can't be both 1 and 2 at the same time. But core.logic provides another form called conde that attempts to unify terms in multiple universes:

```
(logic/run* [george]
  (logic/conde
    [(logic/== george :born)]
    [(logic/== george :unborn)]))

;;=> (:born :unborn)
```

The conde form takes any number of forms inside the [], and it can contain multiples. In the previous example, the bindings represent the value of george in two different universes, one where he is born and another where he isn't born.[8]

An interesting aspect of core.logic is that, although it utilizes unification, it provides an operational system of logic called miniKanren[9] (Friedman 2006) embedded right inside Clojure. With the inclusion of conde, core.logic provides a way of reasoning about unification along different parameters aside from attempting to make two terms equal. Before diving into solving problems with core.logic, let's take a few moments to cover the information model core.logic uses: relational data.

16.3.2 *Relations*

In common database terminology, a *relation* is a group of related properties (often called *tuples*). The best way to explain a tuple is to think about things in reality that are

---

[7] Additionally, core.logic provides mechanisms for unifying against arbitrary types including Java objects! This capability is sadly outside the scope of this chapter.

[8] As in the Frank Capra film *It's a Wonderful Life*, starring Jimmy Stewart.

[9] MiniKanren is a system of logic classified as relational logic programming.

related. For example, planets are related to stars in that they often orbit around them. Therefore, a useful relation for describing orbits could be aptly named `orbits`. The core.logic library has a macro `defrel` that you use to define the structure of relations:

```
(ns joy.logic.planets
  (require [clojure.core.logic :as logic]))

(logic/defrel orbits orbital body)
```

The relation `orbits` contains two attributes: `orbital` (the thing that orbits: Earth) and `body` (the thing that is orbited around: Sun). Defining data for the `orbits` relation is done via the `fact` macro:

```
(logic/fact orbits :mercury :sun)
(logic/fact orbits :venus   :sun)
(logic/fact orbits :earth   :sun)
(logic/fact orbits :mars    :sun)
(logic/fact orbits :jupiter :sun)
(logic/fact orbits :saturn  :sun)
(logic/fact orbits :uranus  :sun)
(logic/fact orbits :neptune :sun)
```

Each of these `logic/fact` calls describes a single *tuple* in the relation `orbits`. A tuple is a grouping of named properties. In the case of the `orbits` relation, the tuples can be imagined logically laid out as vectors of the following form:

```
'[orbits :mercury :sun]

; ...

'[orbits :neptune :sun]
```

In these vectors, the entries can be said to align with the property names:

- The relation tag `orbits`
- The `orbital` tag (`:mercury`)
- The `body` tag (`:sun`)

Seems pretty simple right? Table 16.1 presents this information in a tabular way.

Table 16.1 Planets table

ID	Planet	Orbits
1	Mercury	Stars[1]
2	Venus	Stars[1]
3	Earth	Stars[1]
4	Mars	Stars[1]
5	Jupiter	Stars[1]
6	Saturn	Stars[1]
7	Uranus	Stars[1]
8	Neptune	Stars[1]

This table is laid out in a way that hearkens to something you might see describing a relational database table. Specifically, the ID fields and especially the Stars[1] entries refer to the way keys relate one set of properties to another. In the case of the Orbits link, it might logically point to an entry in table 16.2.

Table 16.2   Stars table

ID	Star
1	Sun
2	Alpha Centauri

In the case of the orbits core.logic relation, a planet is related to a star because the same name :sun is used to refer to the same star in all the tuples forming the orbits relation. This is subtly different from the way traditional relational databases link entries together explicitly via ID chains. In a relational scheme like that used in core.logic, links between relations are derived via symbolic matching. We'll show what this means in the next section.

QUERYING THE ORBITS RELATION

Now that we've explained relations in excruciating detail, we'll turn our attention to how core.logic is used to form queries over relations. If you'll recall, you initiate a call to core.logic using the run* command. In the body of the run* call, you use the unification operator == to satisfy variable bindings and retrieve answers. In the case of querying the orbits relation, you'll do likewise, but you'll rearrange things a bit and use a new core.logic operator: fresh. Without further ado, a query to find all the planets that orbit anything is shown in the following listing.

Listing 16.8   Querying planetary bodies

```
(logic/run* [q]                          ←—❶ Define the query lvar
  (logic/fresh [orbital body]            ←—❷ Define local lvars
    (orbits orbital body)
    (logic/== q orbital)))               ←—❸ Unify the query

;;=> (:earth :saturn :jupiter :mars
;;    :mercury :neptune :uranus :venus)
```

The form of this query looks similar to what you've seen so far, except for a few significant differences. The first major difference is that you bind a single name in the run* call q. You'll see this a lot in core.logic programs. Using q at the outermost level basically states that q is the overall query result ❶. To isolate the logic variables used to perform the query, you use the fresh macro, which works similarly to Clojure's let form. The fresh macro declares scoped logic variable names for use in enclosed goals ❷. Additionally, any goals aggregated within fresh are grouped together to form a logical conjunction (logical and). In other words, both the fact (orbits orbital body) *and* the unification (logic/== q orbital) should be satisfied for the entire body of fresh to be considered satisfied. If either fails, then the conjunction as a whole fails.

This example uses the names orbital and body, which happen to correspond to the orbits property tags, but you could just as easily use o and p instead. The purpose of fresh is to declare logic variable names used as holes to be satisfied via unification within the subgoals (nested goals grouped together to form larger goals) and to logically group those goals via conjunction. Finally, unifying the orbital logic variable with the query variable q ❸ returns all bindings with a value in the orbital property—which of course are all the planets in our solar system.[10]

16.3.3 Subgoals

A *subgoal* in core.logic is a way to aggregate common matches under a common name for the purposes of drawing logical data connections, without needing to lift connections into data explicitly. Imagine if you wanted to rewrite the original query that listed all the planets. The original query uses the idea that anything that orbits anything else is a planet. You can encapsulate that idea in a subgoal planeto, or a function that takes a relation and returns a relation:

```
(logic/defrel stars star)

(logic/fact stars :sun)

(defn planeto [body]
  (logic/fresh [star]
    (stars star)
    (orbits body star)))
```

> **NOTE** By convention, functions that take a core.logic relation as input end with the letter o, as in the definition we just presented.[11]

The planeto subgoal provides a way to jack in to the core.logic inference engine to offer discrete chunks of inferencing, often referred to as *rules* or *axioms*. In the case of planeto, the rule states that something is a planet if it orbits a star. You facilitate this subgoal by creating a new relation defining stars. We know that not everything that orbits a star is a planet, but for the sake of illustration we'll make that assumption here. Now, if you plug the use of planeto into run*, you should get some interesting results:

```
(logic/run* [q]
  (planeto :earth))

;;=> (_0)
```

Attempting to ask the query, "Is :earth a planet?" returns a logic variable. If you recall from our previous discussion, the return of a logic variable means the query is sound but there was no unification. In this case, you can unify q with a value to see a different result:

```
(logic/run* [q]
  (planeto :earth)
  (logic/== q true))

;;=> (true)
```

---

[10] We're not really Pluto haters—please don't judge us.

[11] If you cross your eyes, the o looks like a degree symbol: the traditional ending to relational functions in mini-Kanren. If you cross your eyes a little more, the degree symbol looks like a question mark, just as Dr. Friedman would like it.

So the answer to "Is :earth a planet?" according to the rule defined by planeto is true. You can attempt to ask the same question of :sun:

```
(logic/run* [q]
  (planeto :sun)
  (logic/== q true))
```

```
;;=> ()
```

As shown, the query states that indeed, :sun isn't a planet. To show one more example of planeto, you can use it to show all the planets in your fact-base:

```
(logic/run* [q]
  (logic/fresh [orbital]
    (planeto orbital)
    (logic/== q orbital)))
```

```
;;=> (:earth :saturn :jupiter :mars
;;    :mercury :neptune :uranus :venus)
```

You can augment the current fact-bases by adding new facts and running the same queries to see how the answers change:

```
(logic/fact stars :alpha-centauri)
(logic/fact orbits :Bb :alpha-centauri)
```

```
(logic/run* [q]
  (planeto :Bb))
```

```
;;=> (_0)
```

The good news is that adding a new star and one of its orbitals resolves exactly the way you expect. And of course, running the original query again does too:

```
(logic/run* [q]
  (logic/fresh [orbital]
    (planeto orbital)
    (logic/== q orbital)))
```

```
;;=> (:earth :saturn :jupiter :mars :Bb
;;    :mercury :neptune :uranus :venus)
```

As shown, the idea of planet-ness exists nowhere in either of your fact-bases. But the notion of planet-ness can be derived from the data as a result of the relationships between relations and their properties.

THE SATELLITEO SUBGOAL

It turns out that planets can orbit things other than stars. But when a planet orbits another planet, it's called a *satellite* rather than a planet. You can add the notion of satellite-ness to the example relational model via table 16.3.

Table 16.3 Satellites table

ID	Satellite	Planet
1	Moon	Planet[3]
2	Phobos	Planet[4]

But now you've separated the idea of *satellite* from *planet*; and although there is a *logical* difference, they aren't really different because satellites are still planets. Therefore, you could jam the satellites into the `Planets` table and instead implement the `Satellites` table to contain links only, as shown in table 16.4.

Table 16.4 Satellites table implemented as links

Satellite	Planet
Planet[9]	Planet[3]
Planet[10]	Planet[4]

The problem with this scheme is that the idea of satellite-ness has been lifted into the realm of data, where it's just a logical distinction. Where symbolic logical programming shines is that logical distinctions can be expressed in terms of subgoals.

A subgoal similar to, but slightly more complicated than, `planeto` is `satelliteo`:

```
(defn satelliteo [body]
  (logic/fresh [p]
    (orbits body p)
    (planeto p)))
```

The subgoal `satelliteo` uses the existing subgoal `planeto` to state that a planet is a satellite if: 1) it orbits something and 2) the thing it orbits is a planet.

The interesting aspect of informally stating the behavior of `satelliteo` in words is that you impose an ordering of clauses. But core.logic is under no such constraints. You could swap the check of `(orbits body p)` and `(planeto p)`, and the subgoal would work the same. Here it is in action:

```
(logic/run* [q]
  (satelliteo :sun))

;;=> ()

(logic/run* [q]
  (satelliteo :earth))

;;=> ()
```

As you might expect, neither `:sun` nor `:earth` is a satellite according to the rules of `satelliteo`. In fact, none of the facts in your fact-bases constitute logical satellites, so you need to add one:

```
(logic/fact orbits :moon :earth)
```

Now the check of `satelliteo` should pass:

```
(logic/run* [q]
  (satelliteo :moon))

;;=> (_0)
```

We've shown you how to use `run*`, `fresh`, `==`, and subgoals. You're ready to begin forming your own inferences using core.logic.

CLOSED-WORLD PRINCIPLE

Let's add a few more data points:

```
(logic/fact orbits :phobos :mars)
(logic/fact orbits :deimos :mars)
(logic/fact orbits :io :jupiter)
(logic/fact orbits :europa :jupiter)
(logic/fact orbits :ganymede :jupiter)
(logic/fact orbits :callisto :jupiter)

(logic/run* [q]
  (satelliteo :io))
;;=> (_0)
```

Adding a smattering of new orbitals allows you to infer more data for your existing goals. But imagine if you attempted to ask the following perfectly legitimate query:

```
(logic/run* [q]
  (orbits :leda :jupiter))
;;=> ()
```

Perhaps this is no surprise, because you created facts about only 4 of Jupiter's 67 moons, not including Leda. But this result points to the *closed-world* nature of core.logic inferencing. A closed-world system is one that makes inferences under the assumption that every fact available to it represents the entire set of knowledge in the "world." Even though Leda is in reality a satellite of Jupiter, it isn't, according to this query, because in the closed world of the core.logic fact-base there is no such fact nor any way to derive that information. The converse to the closed-world principle is the *open-world* principle, which states that any query is assumed to be unknown if it can't be derived.

In the next section, we'll talk about the idea that although core.logic is a powerful logic-programming system, it's a little too open-ended.

16.4 *Constraints*

In this final section on logic programming, we'll explore the way that, by itself, the core.logic search facilities are too open-ended. Even though core.logic's search is still more directed than a brute-force solver, it could be more directed given a finer-grained degree of specification. We'll talk first about the notion of constraint programming and core.logic's capabilities supporting it.

16.4.1 *An introduction to constraint programming*

When we begin to discuss constraint logic programming, it's worth taking a step back and drawing analogies. Take the following definition of a function called `doubler`:

```
(defn doubler [n] (* n 2))
```

Because of the dynamic nature of Clojure's type system, the `doubler` function isn't constrained in any way in the types of arguments it takes:

```
(doubler 2)
;;=> 4

(doubler Math/E)
;;=> 5.43656365691809

(doubler 38781787272072020703083739N)
;;=> 77563574544144041406167478N

(doubler 1/8)
;;=> 1/4
```

But with the good comes the bad. The doubler function will happily take absolutely any value:

```
(doubler [])
;; ClassCastException ...

(doubler #(%))
;; ClassCastException ...

(doubler "")
;; ClassCastException ...
```

You get the idea. Although a Clojure function *can* take any value as an argument, doing so may not make logical sense. Therefore, in chapter 8 you created a defcontract form that allowed you to define input and output constraints on functions, which were checked at runtime:

```
(def doubling
  (defcontract c [x]
    (require (number? x))
    (ensure  (= % (* 2 x)))))
```

This contract states that as long as a function receives a number, it will return that number doubled. Otherwise an AssertionError will occur:

```
(def checked-doubler (partial doubling doubler))

(checked-doubler "")
;; AssertionError: Assert failed: (number? x)
```

The doubling contract constrains the legal input types taken on by the argument to the doubler function.

In much the same way, you can view the unification of a logic variable with a function parameter. Observe the following:

```
(logic/run* [q]
  (logic/fresh [x y]
    (logic/== q [x y])))

;;=> ([_0 _1])
```

The result ([_0 _1]) states that the query variable q will unify with the vector [x y] as long as x and y are, well, anything:

```
(logic/run* [q]
  (logic/fresh [x y]
```

```
    (logic/== [:pizza "Java"] [x y])
    (logic/== q [x y]))))

;;=> ([:pizza "Java"])
```

But core.logic provides a simple operator != that allows you to define "dis-equality" constraints on a logic variable. Plugging the use of != into the previous simple query yields this:

```
(logic/run* [q]
  (logic/fresh [x y]
    (logic/== q [x y])
    (logic/!= y "Java")))

;;=> (([_0 _1] :- (!= (_1 "Java")))))
```

This is certainly an odd-looking result, but it makes sense once you know how it's constructed. The first part, [_0 _1], states the same thing as before: x and y can be anything. But the next segment describes the constraint that the variable _1 can't equal "Java". In other words, x and y can be anything, as long as y isn't "Java". You can prove this by plugging the constraint into this larger query:

```
(logic/run* [q]
  (logic/fresh [x y]
    (logic/== [:pizza "Java"] [x y])
    (logic/== q [x y])
    (logic/!= y "Java")))

;;=> ()
```

Because y is constrained to never take on the value "Java", attempting to unify a term where such a value is present causes the unification to fail. You can make unification succeed by attempting a different value instead:

```
(logic/run* [q]
  (logic/fresh [x y]
    (logic/== [:pizza "Scala"] [x y])
    (logic/== q [x y])
    (logic/!= y "Java")))

;;=> ([:pizza "Scala"])
```

Although it's useful to limit the values a logic variable can take on via the dis-equality operator !=, its use only works to slightly limit a near-limitless range of values. There are further ways to constrain the values by defining the bounds of possible values, called *finite domains*.

16.4.2 *Limiting binding via finite domains*

Similar to the way the doubler function takes any possible value, the following query allows any possible value unification:

```
(logic/run* [q]
  (logic/fresh [n]
    (logic/== q n)))

;;=> (_0)
```

As shown in the previous section, you can constrain such queries using the dis-equality constraint !=:

```
(logic/run* [q]
  (logic/fresh [n]
    (logic/!= 0 n)
    (logic/== q n)))

;;=> ((_0 :- (!= (_0 0))))
```

But how can you instead constrain the unification to exclude negative numbers? The core.logic library provides a way to express such a constraint using its *finite-domain* constraint system, which is located in the clojure.core.logic.fd namespace:

```
(require '[clojure.core.logic.fd :as fd])
```

The finite-domain namespace provides a number of functions to constrain logic binding, including +, -, *, quot, ==, !=, <, <=, >, >=, in, interval, domain, and distinct. Among these options, the in and interval constraints seem promising for realizing the aforementioned constraint:

```
;; CAUTION: RUN THIS AT YOUR OWN RISK
(logic/run* [q]
  (logic/fresh [n]
    (fd/in n (fd/interval 1 Integer/MAX_VALUE))
    (logic/== q n)))

;;=> (1 2 3 ... many more numbers follow)
```

The fd/in macro states that the logic variable n is constrained to fall within certain values or intervals. For example, you can tighten the range using the fd/domain macro as follows:

```
(logic/run* [q]
  (logic/fresh [n]
    (fd/in n (fd/domain 0 1))
    (logic/== q n)))

;;=> (0 1)
```

The fd/in macro always takes a domain as the last argument, with possible values within that domain preceding it. Here's a way to enumerate all the possible combinations for tossing two consecutive coins:

```
(logic/run* [q]
  (let [coin (fd/domain 0 1)]
    (logic/fresh [heads tails]
      (fd/in heads 0 coin)
      (fd/in tails 1 coin)
      (logic/== q [heads tails]))))

;;=> ([0 0] [0 1] [1 0] [1 1])
```

The result matches our intuition: heads/heads, heads/tails, tails/heads, or tails/tails. But we can go deeper than this; as it happens, the use of a finite domain matches closely with the problem that started this chapter, Sudoku solving.

16.4.3 *Solving Sudoku with finite domains*

As we said earlier in the chapter, when we enumerated the rules of Sudoku, the following constraints are imposed on the solutions to a puzzle:

- Each column must contain one occurrence of each digit from 1–9.
- Each row must contain one occurrence of each digit from 1–9.
- Each 3 x 3 subsection must contain one occurrence of each digit from 1–9.

Something that should jump out in those descriptions is the range 1–9. That a range is involved points to a finite domain. Indeed, any given cell must fall within (domain 1 9). But before we dive in to solving Sudoku with core.logic, some parts could be simplified from the previous attempt using the brute-force solver.

For example, the brute-force solver worked by placing mostly random, yet legal, values on the board one square at a time. Although a core.logic solver will operate somewhat the same way, the placement is internal and driven by the constraint rules. Therefore, you need to adjust the new solver to operate over three different structures: row, column, and subgrid sequences. To start, the following function implements the logic to create a sequence of all the rows on a Sudoku board:

```
(defn rowify [board]
  (->> board
       (partition 9)
       (map vec)
       vec))
```

Observe how rowify works on the original puzzle b1:

```
(rowify b1)

;;=> [[3 - - - - 5 - 1 -]
     [- 7 - - - 6 - 3 -]
     [1 - - - 9 - - - -]
     [7 - 8 - - - - 9 -]
     [9 - - 4 - 8 - - 2]
     [- 6 - - - - 5 - 1]
     [- - - - 4 - - - 6]
     [- 4 - 7 - - - 2 -]
     [- 2 - 6 - - - - 3]]
```

The row view is multipurpose, serving as a structure for further processing. Another function colify operates on the row view to build the columns:

```
(defn colify [rows]
  (apply map vector rows))
```

The use of colify is as follows:

```
(colify (rowify b1))
;;=> ([3 - 1 7 9 - - - -] [- 7 - - - 6 - 4 2] ... )
```

Finally, creating a subgrid view is trickier, but it can be solved with nested `for` comprehensions:

```
(defn subgrid [rows]
  (partition 9
    (for [row (range 0 9 3)
          col (range 0 9 3)
          x (range row (+ row 3))
          y (range col (+ col 3))]
      (get-in rows [x y])))))
```

The `subgrid` function is an indexer that walks the rows structure: it plucks out each element in every subgrid, starting from the top-left and moving down from left to right. The result of a call to `subgrid` is as follows:

```
(subgrid (rowify b1))

;;=> ((3 - - - 7 - 1 - -) (- - 5 - - 6 - 9 -) ... )
```

These subgrid views align with the subgrids shown back in figure 16.1. But in order to work with a Sudoku board within the confines of the core.logic system, you won't work directly on the numbers and empty slots. Instead, you'll preprocess the board so the cells are logic variables. You can create a function `logic-board` that initializes a completely empty Sudoku-sized board filled with logic variables:

```
(def logic-board #(repeatedly 81 logic/lvar))
```

The `logic-board` function yields an 81-cell (9 x 9) flat Sudoku board filled with uninitialized logic variables. A logic variable can take on any value via unification, as we've shown throughout this chapter. But you need a way to initialize the cells containing logic variables with corresponding number hints in the initialization board. The natural way to perform this initialization is to unify the number hint with the corresponding logic variable. You can do this recursively, as shown in the following listing.

Listing 16.9   Recursively initializing a Sudoku board filled with logic variables

```
(defn init [[lv & lvs] [cell & cells]]
  (if lv
    (logic/fresh []
      (if (= '- cell)                  ❶ Always pass empty
        logic/succeed
        (logic/== lv cell))            ❷ Unify the number and lvar
      (init lvs cells))
    logic/succeed))
```

On the surface, the `init` function looks like a normal recursive walk of two sequences. Although this is true, the reality of its action is subtle and bears explanation. To start, the use of `fresh` with no bindings serves only to aggregate subgoals. The first subgoal is one of two choices. First, if the value in a given board cell is the symbol -, the goal is considered successful by default ❶. On the other hand, if the cell contains any other value, then the corresponding logic variable is unified with that value ❷. The purpose of init is to bind known number values to certain logic variables, as shown here:

```
-------------------------------------
| 3    ?    ? | ?    ?    5 | ?    1    ? |
| ?    7    ? | ?    ?    6 | ?    3    ? |
| 1    ?    ? | ?    9    ? | ?    ?    ? |
-------------------------------------
| 7    ?    8 | ?    ?    ? | ?    9    ? |
| 9    ?    ? | 4    ?    8 | ?    ?    2 |
| ?    6    ? | ?    ?    ? | 5    ?    1 |
-------------------------------------
| ?    ?    ? | ?    4    ? | ?    ?    6 |
| ?    4    ? | 7    ?    ? | ?    2    ? |
| ?    2    ? | 6    ?    ? | ?    ?    3 |
-------------------------------------
```

The initialized board becomes important when you reuse the same logic variables to form the row-, column-, and subgoal-view sequences in the following listing.

Listing 16.10   A core.logic Sudoku solver

```
(defn solve-logically [board]
  (let [legal-nums (fd/interval 1 9)      ←❶ Set the domain
        lvars (logic-board)
        rows  (rowify lvars)              ←❷ Set up views
        cols  (colify rows)
        grids (subgrid rows)]
    (logic/run 1 [q]
      (init lvars board)                  ←❸ Propagate bindings
      (logic/everyg #(fd/in % legal-nums) lvars)
      (logic/everyg fd/distinct rows)         ↖
      (logic/everyg fd/distinct cols)          Check each view
      (logic/everyg fd/distinct grids)       ❺ for distinctness
      (logic/== q lvars))))
```

Check each lvar ❹

We're not sure about you, but we find it breathtaking that a Sudoku solver can be described in 12 lines of Clojure code. The key to its functionality lies in a few interrelated factors. First, establishing the domain of each logic variable to fall within the range (fd/interval 1 9) is a direct transcription of the constraints described in the rules of Sudoku ❶. The rowify, colify, and subgrid functions are used to build different views of the Sudoku cells while sharing common logic variables ❷. Because the logic variables are shared, initializing certain logic variables with the number hints propagates the bindings to all shared views ❸. The core.logic everyg function takes a function containing a subgoal and checks that each element succeeds that goal. The first case where everyg is used checks that the lvar bindings fall within the legal range ❹. This check not only ensures that you're given a legal seed board but also constrains every logic variable binding to fall within the domain. The fd/distinct function is applied across each logical view (rows, columns, and subgrids) to check that the domain is adhered to and that each grouping contains unique values ❺.

Striving for distinctness in each view's components drives the core.logic search to an eventual solution:

```
(-> b1
    solve-logically
    first
    prep
    print-board)

;; -------------------------------------
;; | 3   8   6 | 2   7   5 | 4   1   9 |
;; | 4   7   9 | 8   1   6 | 2   3   5 |
;; | 1   5   2 | 3   9   4 | 8   6   7 |
;; -------------------------------------
;; | 7   3   8 | 5   2   1 | 6   9   4 |
;; | 9   1   5 | 4   6   8 | 3   7   2 |
;; | 2   6   4 | 9   3   7 | 5   8   1 |
;; -------------------------------------
;; | 8   9   3 | 1   4   2 | 7   5   6 |
;; | 6   4   1 | 7   5   3 | 9   2   8 |
;; | 5   2   7 | 6   8   9 | 1   4   3 |
;; -------------------------------------
```

You use `logic/run 1` to perform the logic query and find only one solution.[12] Well-designed Sudoku boards have only one solution, but many starting boards have more than one (Norvig 2011). We leave as an exercise for you an exploration of the vagaries of Sudoku. And core.logic is a wonderful vehicle for such an exploration.

The core.logic rabbit hole runs much deeper than we're able to show in a single chapter, but we hope that, given a taste, you'll further explore the wonders of logic programming.

16.5 Summary

This concludes our chapter on thinking code using logical programming techniques and the core.logic library. Although there are other ways to write a Sudoku solver more efficient than our brute-force solver, we attempted to draw a balance between functional and declarative techniques. Leading up to our discussion of the core.logic contributor library, we took a detour into a discussion of unification that provides a way to pattern-match structures containing variables. As a building block of the core.logic system, unification was a natural way to transition into the workings of the system, including facts, goals, subgoals, and the various functions and macros that provide those. Although core.logic can provide a convenient and powerful in-memory database query language, as shown with the planets example, you also saw how to use it to perform calculations. Along these lines, we explained how such calculations can be made more efficient by using constraints and finite domains to reduce the search space.

---

[12] Whereas the brute-force solver takes on the order of seconds to calculate the same board position, the constraint-logic solution takes on the order of milliseconds.

If you're unaccustomed to writing logic programs with systems like core.logic, this chapter has likely exposed you to a different way of thinking about programs. We've found that Clojure has motivated us to think differently about building programs via its internal "why" and "how" and libraries like core.logic. In the next and final chapter of the book, we'll share some of the ways Clojure has helped us look at problems and their solutions in new ways.

Clojure changes
the way you think

This chapter covers

- Thinking in the domain
- Testing
- Invisible design patterns
- Error handling and debugging

In this final chapter, we'll cover some tangential topics that you might already be familiar with, but perhaps not from a Clojure perspective. Our discussion will start with domain-specific languages (DSLs) and the unique way Clojure applications are built from a layering of unique application-specific DSLs. Next, you're unlikely to be ignorant of the general push toward a test-driven development (TDD) philosophy with a special focus on unit testing. We'll explore why Clojure is especially conducive to unit testing and why it's often unnecessary. Next, whether you agree with the cult of design patterns or not, it's inarguable that patterns have changed the way object-oriented software is designed and developed. The classical design patterns are often invisible and at times are outright nonexistent in Clojure code, as we'll discuss. As we'll then show, error handling in Clojure flows in two directions:

423

from inner functions to outer via exceptions, and from outer functions inward via dynamic bindings. Finally, we'll explore how having the entire language at your disposal can help change the way your debugging occurs. We hope that by the time you've finished this chapter, you'll agree—Clojure changes the way you think about programming.

17.1 Thinking in the domain

> *Lisp is not the right language for any particular problem. Rather, Lisp encourages one to attack a new problem by implementing new languages tailored to that problem.*
>
> —Harold Abelson and
> Gerald Jay Sussman[1]

In chapter 8, we explored the notion of a domain-specific language for describing domains with the man-versus-monster example, and the `domain` macro in particular. This meta-circularity, although playful, was meant to make a subtle point: Clojure blurs, and often obliterates, the line between DSL and API. When a language is built from the same data structures that the language itself manipulates, it's known as *homoiconic* (Mooers 1965). When a programming language is homoiconic, it's simple to mold the language into a form that bridges the gap between the problem and solution domains. We hinted at this point in chapter 14 during the discussion of the `defunits-of` macro; the best language for solving a problem is the language of the domain itself. But with DSLs, a caveat always applies:

> *Just because you can create a DSL, doesn't mean you should.*
>
> —This book, right now

Creating DSLs introduces new syntax, and with new syntax comes some level of complexity, in implementation and (potentially) in use. You should think through each chance for a DSL and weigh the complexities. When designing DSLs in Clojure, it's important to determine when the existing language facilities will suffice (Raymond 2003) and when it's appropriate to create one from whole cloth (Ghosh 2010). In this section, we'll do both and provide a little discussion about each.

17.1.1 A ubiquitous DSL

The declarative language SQL is among the most widespread DSLs in use today. Interestingly, Clojure provides a comprehensive library for relational algebra, on which SQL is based (Date 2009). Imagine the following dataset:

```
(def artists
  #{{:artist "Burial"  :genre-id 1}
    {:artist "Magma"   :genre-id 2}
    {:artist "Can"     :genre-id 3}
    {:artist "Faust"   :genre-id 3}
    {:artist "Ikonika" :genre-id 1}
    {:artist "Grouper"}})
```

---

[1] "Lisp: A Language for Stratified Design" (Abelson 1988).

```
(def genres
  #{{:genre-id 1 :genre-name "Dubstep"}
    {:genre-id 2 :genre-name "Zeuhl"}
    {:genre-id 3 :genre-name "Prog"}
    {:genre-id 4 :genre-name "Drone"}})
```

The vars artists and genres are sets of maps and can conceptually stand in for a couple of database tables. The artists data is shown in table 17.1. The genres data is laid out as in table 17.2.

Table 17.1 Artists

:artist	:genre-id
Burial	1
Magma	2
Can	3
Faust	3
Ikonika	1
Grouper	4

Table 17.2 Genres

:genre-id	:genre-name
1	Dubstep
2	Zeuhl
3	Prog
4	Drone

Laying out the data this way allows you to view the data relationally, similarly to SQL relations. You can try Clojure's relational functions by entering the example shown in the following listing to return all the data in a table, emulating a SQL select * clause on the genres table.

Listing 17.1 select * example using Clojure's relational algebra functions

```
(require '[clojure.set :as ra])

(def ALL identity)

(ra/select ALL genres)

;;=> #{{:genre-id 4, :genre-name "Drone"}
       {:genre-id 3, :genre-name "Prog"}
       {:genre-id 2, :genre-name "Zeuhl"}
       {:genre-id 1, :genre-name "Dubstep"}}
```

The clojure.set/select function works by taking a function and collecting every map that, when supplied to that function, returns a truthy value. Because the ALL function is identity, all maps are collected in the result set. To filter on a given genre ID, you can use a custom function as follows:

```
(ra/select (fn [m] (#{1 3} (:genre-id m))) genres)

;;=> #{{:genre-id 3, :genre-name "Prog"}
       {:genre-id 1, :genre-name "Dubstep"}}
```

You can make that code a bit more fluent by currying[2] a function named `ids`:

```
(defn ids [& ids]
  (fn [m] ((set ids) (:genre-id m))))
```

Now the query reads more nicely:

```
(ra/select (ids 1 3) genres)

;;=> #{{:genre-id 3, :genre-name "Prog"}
       {:genre-id 1, :genre-name "Dubstep"}}
```

SQL supports natural joins, combining tables by finding a field in one table's rows that matches a field in a second table's rows. When the fields that are matched have the same name in both tables, this is called a *natural* join.

The `clojure.set` namespace also provides a function named `join` that performs a SQL-like natural join and is used as follows:

```
(take 2 (ra/select ALL (ra/join artists genres)))

;;=> #{{:artist "Burial", :genre-id 1, :genre-name "Dubstep"}
       {:artist "Magma", :genre-id 2, :genre-name "Zeuhl"}}
```

The relational functions in `clojure.set` are a perfect example of the way Clojure blurs the line between API and DSL. No macro tricks are involved, but through the process of functional composition, the library provides a highly expressive syntax that closely matches (Abiteboul 1995) that of SQL. You can create queries as complex as your imagination can dream up using the `clojure.set` offerings.

You might be tempted to create a custom query language for your own application(s), but there are times when the relational functions are exactly what you need. Although querying small datasets in Clojure sets might be appropriate for some tasks, it's not likely to scale to meet your enterprise needs. Instead, any significantly large data will likely be stored in a database, and chances are good that it will be relational.

17.1.2   *Implementing a SQL-like DSL to generate queries*

The relational algebra functions in the `core.set` namespace are useful for ad hoc data queries on small data sets, but in reality you would probably want to use a real database coupled with a real database query language. If we were to sketch an embedded variant of SQL in a hypothetical Clojure library, it might look as follows:

```
(defn fantasy-query [max]
  (SELECT [a b c]
    (FROM X
      (LEFT-JOIN Y :ON (= X.a Y.b)))
    (WHERE (< a 5) AND (< b max))))
```

We hope some of those words look familiar to you, because this isn't a book on SQL. Regardless, our point is that Clojure doesn't have SQL support built in. The words

---

[2] A *curried* function is one that returns a function for each of its logical arguments, executing the function logic only after each logical argument is exhausted.

SELECT, FROM, and so forth aren't built-in forms. They also can't be implemented as regular functions: if SELECT were, then the use of a, b, and c would be an error because they hadn't been defined yet.

What does it take to define a DSL like this in Clojure? Well, if you've been paying attention so far, the answer should be readily available: macros.

The following code isn't production-ready and doesn't tie in to any real database servers; but with just one macro and three functions, the preceding fantasy-query function should return something like this:

```
(fantasy-query 5)

;;=> {:query "SELECT a, b, c FROM X LEFT JOIN Y ON (X.a = Y.b)
             WHERE ((a < 5) AND (b < ?))"
     :bindings [5]}
```

Note that some words such as FROM and ON are taken directly from the input expression, whereas others such as max and AND are treated specially. The max argument that was given the value 5 when the query was called is extracted from the literal SQL string and provided in a separate vector, perfect for use in a prepared query in a way that guards against SQL-injection attacks. To keep thing simpler in the implementation, we won't require that the AND symbol be used as an infix operator in the macro body; but for posterity's sake we'll make sure it becomes infix in the generated query.

The DSL you're creating must do three things: extract bindings, convert prefix to infix, and generate each of the more complex SQL clauses supported. These are all pieces of infrastructure the DSL implementation will need, which you'll combine and provide access to using a nice sugary syntax.

The first thing you need is a helper named shuffle-expr that walks a Clojure-like expression and converts it from prefix notation into infix notation, building a string from the new form. You'd also like it to handle references to locals in a special way so you can supply their values later in a substitution structure. The implementation of shuffle-expr is shown next.

Listing 17.2 Shuffling SQL-like operators into infix position

```
(ns joy.sql
  (:use [clojure.string :as str :only []]))

(defn shuffle-expr [expr]
  (if (coll? expr)
    (if (= (first expr) `unquote)           ← ❶ Identify local
      "?"
      (let [[op & args] expr]
        (str "("
          (str/join (str " " op " ")        ← ❷ Infixify operator
                    (map shuffle-expr args)) ")")))
    expr))
```
Recurse ❸ →

The shuffle-expr function works off clojure collections and indeed returns the expression outright when not given one:

```
(shuffle-expr 42)
;;=> 42
```

But `shuffle-expr` treats collections that start with `clojure.core/unquote` specially ❶.
You can see what happens when `shuffle-expr` encounters this special condition:

```
(shuffle-expr `(unquote max))
;;=> "?"
```

When an expression starts with the `clojure.core/unquote` function, `shuffle-expr`
returns a simple string `"?"` to stand in for the value that is meant to fill its place. By
using the unquote operator ~, you can build this special expression at read-time:

```
(read-string "~max")

;;=> (clojure.core/unquote max)
```

Marking value slots like this is a common technique for guarding against common
SQL attacks, and we'll show how it works soon. First, it's worth following through with
our explanation of `shuffle-expr` and mentioning that when a regular collection type
is encountered, its head, referring to its function, is switched into an infix position ❷,
as shown:

```
(shuffle-expr '(= X.a Y.b))
;;=> "(X.a = Y.b)"
```

The infix alignment is proper SQL, but you need to traverse the collection recursively
in order to "infixify" the nested expressions ❸:

```
(shuffle-expr '(AND (< a 5) (< b ~max)))
;;=> "((a < 5) AND (b < ?))"
```

This nested expansion will work up to an arbitrary depth:

```
(shuffle-expr '(AND (< a 5) (OR (> b 0) (< b ~max))))
;;=> "((a < 5) AND ((b > 0) OR (b < ?)))"
```

You maintain the same number of parentheses, but you change them so they work to
group sub-expressions.

Now that `shuffle-expr` is in place, you can use it to complete the last category of
your DSL infrastructure: the clause-specific portions of the SQL-like DSL. Start with a
function to process a `WHERE` clause:

```
(defn process-where-clause [processor expr]
  (str " WHERE " (processor expr)))
```

The implementation of `process-where-clause` effectively delegates down to the
behavior of `shuffle-expr` and concatenates a `"WHERE"` string onto the front:

```
(process-where-clause shuffle-expr '(AND (< a 5) (< b ~max)))

;;=> " WHERE (((a < 5) AND (b < ?)))"
```

A similarly implemented clause processor `process-left-join-clause` does a little
more work, but not much:

```
(defn process-left-join-clause [processor table _ expr]
  (str " LEFT JOIN " table
       " ON " (processor expr)))
```

Where `process-left-join-clause` differs is in the fact that it takes three arguments rather than a single expression meant for shuffling. You can see how `process-left-join-clause` might work, given a list of its expected features:

```
(apply process-left-join-clause
       shuffle-expr
       '(Y :ON (= X.a Y.b)))

;;=> " LEFT JOIN Y ON (X.a = Y.b)"
```

Providing a more fluent `LEFT-JOIN` clause is a simple alias away:

```
(let [LEFT-JOIN (partial process-left-join-clause shuffle-expr)]
  (LEFT-JOIN 'Y :ON '(= X.a Y.b)))

;;=> " LEFT JOIN Y ON (X.a = Y.b)"
```

Your SQL-like DSL is starting to shape up, but we'll defer the topic of a fluent DSL for now and focus instead on what you've accomplished so far. If you'll recall from chapter 14, we discussed the notion of "putting parentheses around the specification." The purpose of that pithy phrase was to invoke the spirit of data and function-orientation in the development of DSLs. Clojure is especially suited to DSLs because of its inherent flexibility and default rich data types. In this section, you've so far built a subset of a SQL-like DSL on lists and a few simple data-processing functions. This is a surprisingly powerful way to build DSLs in general:

- Start with core data types and their syntax as the base for your DSL.
- Gradually build up to the DSL by filling in the constituent data processors.

You won't implement a full SQL-like DSL, but we can show how you might continue building out the remaining features by implementing a few more data processors. The `FROM` clause meant to name a target table in a `SELECT` clause is fairly straightforward:

```
(defn process-from-clause [processor table & joins]
  (apply str " FROM " table
         (map processor joins)))
```

And now you can stitch the use of `process-from-clause` (with an alias) to the use of `LEFT-JOIN` to see how they compose:

```
(process-from-clause shuffle-expr 'X
  (process-left-join-clause shuffle-expr 'Y :ON '(= X.a Y.b)))

;;=> " FROM X LEFT JOIN Y ON (X.a = Y.b)"
```

You can also round off the data processors by implementing the `SELECT` clause as follows:

```
(defn process-select-clause [processor fields & clauses]
  (apply str "SELECT " (str/join ", " fields)
         (map processor clauses)))
```

Notice that the data processors have a similar form. If you *really* wanted to be fancy, you could build a DSL to help build the SQL-like DSL; we'll leave that as an exercise for you. Instead, observe how the use of SELECT works to compose with the existing data processors:

```
(process-select-clause shuffle-expr
  '[a b c]
  (process-from-clause shuffle-expr 'X
    (process-left-join-clause shuffle-expr 'Y :ON '(= X.a Y.b)))
  (process-where-clause shuffle-expr '(AND (< a 5) (< b ~max))))

;;=> "SELECT a, b, c FROM X
;;     LEFT JOIN Y ON (X.a = Y.b)
;;     WHERE ((a < 5) AND (b < ?))"
```

Now that you have the data processors in place and operating as you expect, you can start to think about cleaning up the DSL so your users don't need to explicitly quote the clause elements but can instead write queries in a more natural way. This is where macros come into play: now that you've built your DSL infrastructure on data and processors, you can use macros to provide some syntactic sugar. First, it's not a terribly compelling DSL if it requires you to use long clauses with names of the form process-*-clause. Instead, it would be fun to define a mapping from more relevant names like SELECT and FROM. You can describe this name mapping directly to the functions that provide the data processing:

```
(declare apply-syntax)

(def ^:dynamic *clause-map*
  {'SELECT    (partial process-select-clause apply-syntax)
   'FROM      (partial process-from-clause apply-syntax)
   'LEFT-JOIN (partial process-left-join-clause shuffle-expr)
   'WHERE     (partial process-where-clause shuffle-expr)})
```

Adding a level of indirection in the way a DSL syntax maps to the underlying processors is a powerful technique. By making such a split, we're viewing *DSLs as a way to define a language to decouple the problem from the strategies for solving it.* That is, you can swap out the data-processing functions for other, more powerful and robust functions at any time to enhance the effect of the DSL while maintaining a consistent SQL-like syntax.

Because the process-select-clause and process-from-clause functions allow nested clauses, they're partially applied with a function to look up the mapped function for their subclauses from clause-map. The function that performs the lookup is named apply-syntax.

Listing 17.3   Looking up syntax processors in the processor table

```
(defn apply-syntax [[op & args]]
  (apply (get *clause-map* op) args))      ◁── Look up the data processor
```

The apply-syntax function takes the first word of a clause, looks it up in *clause-map*, and calls the appropriate function to do the actual conversion from Clojure s-expression to SQL string. `*clause-map*` provides the specific functionality needed for each part of the SQL expression: inserting commas or other SQL syntax, and sometimes recursively calling `apply-syntax` when subclauses need to be converted. One of these is the WHERE clause, which handles the general conversion of prefix expressions to the infix form required by SQL by delegating to the `shuffle-expr` function.

Because the DSL triggers on a SELECT clause, you can implement it as a macro in the next listing so that its nested elements don't explicitly require quoting.

Listing 17.4 Building a SQL-like SELECT statement DSL

```
(defmacro SELECT [& args]
  {:query (apply-syntax (cons 'SELECT args))      <— Generate a SQL string
   :bindings (vec (for [n (tree-seq coll? seq args)
                    :when (and (coll? n)
                                (= (first n) `unquote))]   <— Generate bindings
                (second n)))})
```

The `:query` element in the returned map is generated by calling `apply-syntax`, which generates the converted query string; the `:bindings` entry is a vector of expressions marked by ~ (read-time expanded to `unquote`) in the input. But one interesting point is that by taking advantage of the split between the read-time and compile-time phases, you can effectively grab the values of locals for use as bindings.

The point here isn't that this is a particularly good SQL DSL—more complete ones are available.[3] Our point is that once you have the skill to easily create a DSL like this, you'll recognize opportunities to define your own DSLs that solve much narrower, application-specific problems than SQL does. Whether it's a query language for a non-SQL data-store, a way to express functions in some obscure math discipline, or another application we as authors can't imagine, having the flexibility to extend the base language like this, without losing access to any of the language's features, is a game-changer:

```
(defn example-query [max]
  (SELECT [a b c]
    (FROM X
          (LEFT-JOIN Y :ON (= X.a Y.b)))
    (WHERE (AND (< a 5) (< b ~max)))))

(example-query 9)
;;=> {:query "SELECT a, b, c
;;            FROM X LEFT JOIN Y ON (X.a = Y.b)
;;            WHERE ((a < 5) AND (b < ?))"
;;     :bindings [9]}
```

Overall, the flexibility of Clojure demonstrated in this section comes largely from the fact that macros accept code forms, such as the SQL DSL example we showed, and can treat them as data—walking trees, converting values, and more. This works not

---

[3] One of note is Korma (http://sqlkorma.com).

only because code can be treated as data, but also because in a Clojure program, code *is* data.

17.1.3   *A note about Clojure's approach to DSLs*

DSLs and control structures implemented as macros in Common Lisp tend to be written in a style more conducive to macro writers. But Clojure macros such as SELECT, cond, and case are idiomatic in their minimalism; their component parts are paired and meant to be grouped through proper spacing, as shown in this example of cond:

```
(cond
  (keyword? x) "x is a keyword"
  :else "x is not a keyword")
```

This is in contrast to some LISPs, which prefer to group pairs of related clauses in another set of parentheses. Clojure macro writers should understand that the proliferation and placement of parentheses are legitimate concerns for some, and as a result you should strive to reduce the number whenever possible. Why would you explicitly group your expressions when their groupings are only a call to partition away?

> **CLOJURE APHORISM**   If a project elicits a sense of being lost, begin from the bottom up.

DSLs are an important part of a Clojure programmer's tool-set and stem from a long Lisp tradition. When Paul Graham talks about "bottom-up programming" in his perennial work *On Lisp* (Prentice Hall, 1993), this is what he's referring to. In Clojure, it's common practice to start by defining and implementing a low-level language specifically for the levels above. Creating complex software systems is hard, but using this approach, you can build the complicated parts out of smaller, simpler pieces.

Clojure changes the way that you think.

17.2   Testing

Object-oriented programs can be highly complicated beasts to test properly when they're built on mutating state and deep class hierarchies. Programs are a vast tapestry of interweaving execution paths, and to test each path comprehensively is difficult, if not impossible. In the face of unrestrained mutation, the execution paths are overlaid with mutation paths, further adding to the chaos. Conversely, Clojure programs tend to be compositions of pure functions with isolated pools of mutation. The result of this approach helps to foster an environment conducive to unit testing. But although the layers of an application are composed of numerous functions, each individually and compositionally tested, the layers themselves and the wiring between them must also be tested.

Test-driven development (Beck 2002) has conquered the software world, and at its core it preaches that test development should drive the architecture of the overall application. Certainly TDD presents one way of writing and testing software, but it's far from the only way. We already showed in chapter 14 how a data-driven approach to software design can facilitate powerful testing techniques like simulation and generative (property-based) testing; in this section, we'll cover a few more interesting ways that Clojure programs are validated using contracts-programming and unit testing.

17.2.1 Some useful unit-testing techniques

We don't want to disparage TDD, because its goals are virtuous and testing in general is essential. Clojure programs are organized using namespaces, and they're themselves aggregations of functions, often pure, so the act of devising a unit-test suite at the namespace boundary is frequently mechanical in its directness. From a larger perspective, devising comprehensive test strategies is the subject of numerous volumes and therefore outside the scope of this book; but there are a few Clojure-specific techniques that we wish to discuss.

USING WITH-REDEFS

Stubbing (Fowler 2007) is the act of supplying an imitation implementation of a function for testing purposes. One mechanism that can perform this stubbing is the with-redefs macro introduced in Clojure 1.3.

The function feed-children from listing 11.2 parses a Twitter RSS2 feed, returning a sequence of the top-level feed elements. Testing functions that rely on feed-children is futile against live Twitter feeds, so a stubbed implementation returning a known sequence is more prudent, as shown in the following listing.

Listing 17.5 Using with-redefs to create stubs

```
(ns joy.unit-testing
  (:require [joy.futures :as joy]))

(def stubbed-feed-children
  (constantly [{:content [{:tag :title
                           :content ["Stub"]}]}]))      <─ Create the stub

(defn count-feed-entries [url]
  (count (joy/feed-children url)))

(count-feed-entries "http://blog.fogus.me/feed/")       <─ Call without the stub
;;=> 5

(with-redefs [joy/feed-children stubbed-feed-children]
  (count-feed-entries "dummy url"))                     <─ Temporarily use the stub

;;=> 1
```

The stubbed-feed-children function returns a sequence of canned data. Therefore, when testing the count-feed-entries function, you temporarily change the value of feed-children so that it resolves to stubbed-feed-children instead. This change is made at the root of the feed-children var and so is visible to all threads. As long as all the test calls to it are made before control leaves the with-redefs form, the stub will be invoked every time. Because occurrences doesn't return until it collects results from all the futures it creates, it uses the redef given by with-redefs:

```
(with-redefs [feed-children stubbed-feed-children]
  (joy/occurrences joy/title "Stub" "a" "b" "c"))
```

```
;=> 3
```

As shown, the joy/occurrences function attempts to fetch the feeds at the (clearly nonconforming) URLs "a", "b", and "c". Even though those URLs couldn't possibly resolve to a feed, the fact that the feed-children function is stubbed out means joy/occurrences *thinks* each feed has a single element, each with the title "Stub".

Another option that is sometimes suggested is to use binding in place of with-redefs. This would push a thread-local binding for feed-children, which might seem attractive in that it could allow other threads to bind the same var to a different stub function, potentially for simultaneously running different tests. Because occurrences uses futures, the bindings are conveyed to the used threads. But using binding requires that the function under test be defined as ^:dynamic. Therefore, because future isn't the only way to spawn threads, with-redefs is still recommended for mocking out functions during tests.

CLOJURE.TEST AS A SPECIFICATION

Clojure ships with a testing library in the clojure.test namespace that you can use to create test suites that can further serve as partial system specifications. We won't provide a comprehensive survey of the clojure.test functionality, but you should get a feel for how it works. Unit-test specifications in Clojure are declarative in nature, as shown next.

Listing 17.6 clojure.test as a partial specification

```
(require '[clojure.test :refer (deftest testing is)])

(deftest feed-tests                                       ❶ Set up the
  (with-redefs [joy/feed-children stubbed-feed-children]  ←┘   stub(s)
    (testing "Child Counting"                             ←┐
      (is (= 1000 (count-feed-entries "Dummy URL"))))     ❷ Aggregate the
    (testing "Occurrence Counting"                          related tests
      (is (= 0 (joy/count-text-task   ←─❸ Use "is" for checks
                joy/title
                "ZOMG"
                "Dummy URL"))))))))
```

Clojure's test library provides a DSL for describing unit test cases that interacts as you would expect with the stubbing code we showed earlier ❶. The testing form ❷ is useful for aggregating related tests, each checked by the is macro ❸. Notice that we added a failing test to the "Child Counting" test so that when run, the test fails as expected:

```
(clojure.test/run-tests 'joy.unit-testing)
; Testing joy.unit-testing
;
;   FAIL in (feed-tests)
;   Child Counting
;   expected: (= 1000 (count-feed-entries "Dummy URL"))
;     actual: (not (= 1000 1))
```

```
;
;  Ran 1 tests containing 2 assertions.
;  1 failures, 0 errors.
;;=> {:type :summary, :pass 1, :test 1, :error 0, :fail 1}
```

The tools for unit testing contained in clojure.test are more extensive than we've outlined here and provide support for fixtures, different assertion macros, test ordering, and customized test reports. It will be a wise investment to explore the unit-testing tools available in the core Clojure distribution; and we love the wide variety of excellent documentation available in the public domain and in existing Clojure books (Emerick 2012). Regardless of your views on software development, tests work to help ensure your software's quality, and Clojure provides a usable and ubiquitous testing tool by default.

Although tests are a good way to find *some* errors, they make few guarantees that the system works properly. Planning, interaction with domain experts and potential users, and deep thinking *must* come before testing begins. No amount of testing can substitute for thoroughly thinking through the implications of potential designs. One interesting way to tease out the requirements and shape of a solution is to explore its fundamental expectations, as we'll discuss next.

17.2.2 Contracts programming

Test-driven development is in many ways a heuristic affair. People tend to only test the error conditions and expectations they can conceptualize. Surely there's no such thing as an exhaustive test suite, but in many cases test suites tend toward a local maxima. There's a better way to define semantic expectations in applications: using Clojure pre- and postconditions.

REVISITING PRE- AND POSTCONDITIONS

In section 7.1, we explored Clojure's pre- and postcondition facility. Function-constraint specification is a conceptually simple model for declaring the expectations for any given function. Function constraints can cover the full range of expected conditions imposed on the function's inputs, its outputs, and their relative natures. The beauty of specifying constraints is that they can augment a testing regimen with the application of random values. This works because you can effectively throw out the values that fail the preconditions and instead focus on the values that cause errors in the postconditions. Let's try this approach for a simple function to square a number:

```
(def sqr (partial
  (contract sqr-contract
    [n]
    (require (number? n))
    (ensure (pos? %)))
  #(* % %)))

[(sqr 10) (sqr -9)]
;=> [100 81]
```

The contract for sqr is as follows: require a number, and ensure that its return is positive. Now let's create a simple test driver[4] that throws many random values at it to see if it breaks:

```
(doseq [n (range Short/MIN_VALUE Short/MAX_VALUE)]
  (try
    (sqr n)
    (catch AssertionError e
      (println "Error on input" n)
      (throw e))))
; Error on input 0
;=> java.lang.AssertionError: Assert failed: (pos? %)
```

Even when adhering to the tenets of the preconditions, we've uncovered an error in the sqr function at the postcondition end. Postconditions should be viewed as the guarantee of the return value given that the preconditions are met. Errors like this are an indication of a disagreement between the precondition, the implementation, and the postcondition. One way to resolve the disagreement and eliminate the postcondition error is to decide that the function's contract should specify that the number n should not be zero. By adding a check for zero (not= 0 n) in the preconditions, we can guarantee that the sqr function acts as expected. To perform this same verification using unit testing is trivial in this case, but what if the edge condition wasn't as obvious? In such a case, the error might not be caught until it was too late. Of course, there's no guarantee that contracts are comprehensive, but that's why domain expertise is often critical when defining them.

ADVANTAGES OF PRE- AND POSTCONDITIONS

Function constraints aren't code. They take the form of code, but that is only a matter of representation. Instead, constraints should be viewed as a specification language describing expectations and result assurances. On the other hand, unit tests are code, and code has bugs. Contracts are essential semantic coupling, independent of any particular test case.

Another potential advantage of contracts over tests is that in some cases, tests can be generated from the contracts. Also, pre- and postconditions are amenable to being expressed as an overall description of the system, which can thus be fed into a rule base for query and verification. Both of these cases are outside the scope of this book, but you shouldn't be surprised if they make their way into future versions of Clojure.[5] There's tremendous potential in Clojure's pre- and postconditions. Although they're currently low-level constructs, they can be used to express full-blown design by contract facilities for your own applications.

Clojure changes the way that you think.

---

[4] For the sake of highlighting this technique, we've simplified the test driver. Testing a limited range of input values might not be an appropriate approach in all circumstances.

[5] A contrib library named core.contracts hopes to fulfill this role: www.github.com/clojure/core.contracts.

17.3 Invisible design patterns

> *Any sufficiently complicated C or Fortran program contains an ad hoc, informally-specified, bug-ridden, slow implementation of half of Common Lisp.*
>
> —Greenspun's Tenth Rule[6]

The book *Design Patterns: Elements of Reusable Object-Oriented Software* (Gamma et al. 1995) was a seminal work of software design and development. You'd be hard pressed to find a software programmer in this day and age who's not familiar with this work. The book describes 23 software practices encountered throughout the course of experience in developing software projects of varying sizes.

Design patterns have obtained a bad reputation in some circles, whereas in others they're considered indispensable. From our perspective, design patterns are a way to express *certain* architectural elements found in programs written in *some* object-oriented programming languages, and of course to name these elements. But where design patterns fall short is that they don't represent pure abstraction. Instead, design patterns have come to be viewed as goals in and of themselves, which is likely the source of the antagonism aimed at them. Simultaneously, they're most often employed in languages that can't express the patterns, so programs must repeat much or all of a pattern each time it's used. The ability to think in abstractions is an invaluable skill for a software programmer to strengthen, and the ability to name and reuse these abstractions is an invaluable quality in a language. In this section, we'll survey some classic design patterns (Norvig 1998) and address how in many cases Clojure provides a component that implements the pattern, and in others such a component is unnecessary because of inherent qualities of Clojure.

17.3.1 Clojure's first-class design patterns

Most, if not all, of the patterns listed in the *Design Patterns* book are applicable to functional programming languages in general and to Clojure in particular. But at the book's most pragmatic, the patterns described are aimed at patching deficiencies in popular object-oriented programming languages. This practical view of design patterns isn't directly relevant to Clojure, because in many ways the patterns are ever present and are first-class citizens of the language. We won't provide a comprehensive survey of the ways Clojure implements or eliminates popular design patterns but will provide enough information to make our point.

OBSERVER PATTERN

Clojure's `add-watch` and `remove-watch` functions provide the underpinnings of an observer (publisher/subscriber) capability based on reference types. You can see this through the implementation of the simple `defformula` macro shown in the following listing.

---

[6] http://philip.greenspun.com/research/.

Listing 17.7   Creating formulas that are like spreadsheet cells

```
(ns joy.cells)

(defmacro defformula [nm bindings & formula]
  `(let ~bindings                                    ❶ Create a formula
     (let [formula#    (agent ~@formula)               as an Agent
           update-fn# (fn [key# ref# o# n#]
                        (send formula# (fn [_#] ~@formula)))]
       (doseq [r# ~(vec (map bindings                 ❷ Iterate over bindings
                     (range 0 (count bindings) 2)))]
         (add-watch r# :update-formula update-fn#))    ❸ Add a watch to
       (def ~nm formula#)))))                            each reference
```

The `defformula` macro defines a syntactic form that builds a reference type (in this case, an agent) ❶ that depends on the value of other reference types. These constituent references on which the formula depends are given in a binding structure as the bindings argument. This `bindings` vector is iterated over ❷, and for each reference found, a watch is added ❸. An example of `defformula` in action is as follows.

Listing 17.8   `defformula` to track baseball averages

```
(def h (ref 25)                      Define constituent refs
(def ab (ref 100))

(defformula avg                      Define the formula,
  [at-bats ab, hits h]               dependent on two refs
  (float (/ @hits @at-bats)))
```

Now that you have the constituent refs h and ab and the dependent formula avg in place, you can see the initial formula value:

```
@avg
;;=> 0.25
```

That avg equals 0.25 is a good sign, given that the value of 25/100 converted to a float is the same. To see a change in the formula, you can enter something like the following to trigger an automatic calculation:

```
(dosync (ref-set h 33))

@avg
;;=> 0.33
```

Changing one of the constituent refs, h, triggers a recalculation of the formula, resulting in a new value given by 33/100: 0.33. By now we hope it's clear that the Observer pattern is satisfied by the way reference types and watchers operate in Clojure and ClojureScript. By using watchers on references, you can use `defformula` to provide an abstract value that changes when any of its parts change. This style of programming hints at a more general, spreadsheet-like style of operation. If you look at figure 17.1, perhaps you'll see how the analogy applies.

Using watchers allows for a reactive style of programming triggered on value changes in references. A more traditional Lisp approach is to provide predefined hooks (Glickstein 1997) that are called at certain times in the execution cycle. To participate in a classical Observer pattern in a Java codebase, you can of course use `proxy` or `gen-class` to extend the `java.util.Observable` class.

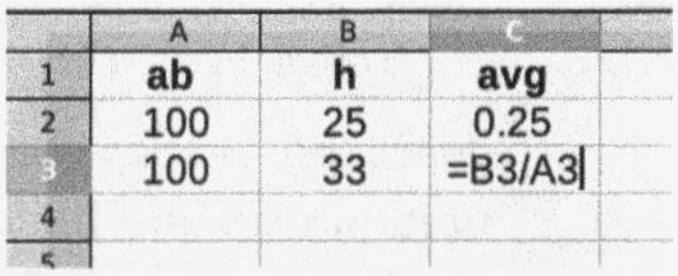

	A	B	C
1	ab	h	avg
2	100	25	0.25
3	100	33	=B3/A3
4			
5			

Figure 17.1 Using `defformula` is akin to programming a spreadsheet.

STRATEGY PATTERN

Algorithm strategies selected at runtime are common practice in Clojure, and there are a number of ways to implement them. One way is via continuation-passing style, as we explored in section 7.3. A more general solution is to pass the desired function as an argument to a higher-order function, such as you'd see in the ubiquitous `map`, `reduce`, and `filter` functions. Further, we'll provide a case of dynamic error functions in the next section, illustrating how Clojure's multimethods are a more powerful substitute for the classic Strategy pattern.

VISITOR PATTERN

The Visitor pattern is designed to describe a way to decouple operations on a structure from the structure itself. Even casual observers will see the parallel to Clojure's multimethods, protocols, types, proxies, and reify features.

ABSTRACT FACTORY PATTERN

The Abstract Factory pattern is used to describe a way to create related objects without having to name explicit types at the point of creation. Clojure's types avoid the creation of explicit hierarchies (although ad hoc hierarchies can be created, as seen in section 9.2). Therefore, in Clojure this particular usage scenario is relegated to use in Java interoperability contexts. But the use of factory functions to abstract the call to the constructors of types and records is actively promoted, even in the presence of the auto-generated factory functions. For example, imagine you're building a system that allows the creation of subsystems based on a configuration file structured as a Clojure map. Ignoring the file I/O for reading, you can create an example map corresponding to a configuration:

```
(ns joy.patterns.abstract-factory)

(def config
  '{:systems {:pump {:type :feeder, :descr "Feeder system"}
              :sim1 {:type :sim,    :fidelity :low}
              :sim2 {:type :sim,    :fidelity :high, :threads 2}}})
```

The `config` var holds a fragment of a plausible system configuration, specifically the portion dealing with subsystem types and parameters. Before we show you how to dynamically initialize the systems described, you can create a function that creates something like a system descriptor:

```
(defn describe-system [name cfg]
  [(:type cfg) (:fidelity cfg)])
```

describe-system is a simple function that takes a name (that it ignores) and a configuration map and builds a vector of the :type and :fidelity values. Here's an example descriptor:

```
(describe-system :pump {:type :feeder, :descr "Feeder system"})

;;=> [:feeder nil]
```

These kinds of descriptors can form the basis for a baseline subsystem-initialization multimethod named construct. That is, you can associate methods with construct that dispatch to specific system builders based on the descriptors. First, let's provide a default that builds a map of a couple of key values.

> **Listing 17.9 Basis for an abstract factory implementation using multimethods**

```
(defmulti construct describe-system)        ←—  Abstract factory multimethod

(defmethod construct :default [name cfg]     ←—  Default factory
  {:name name
   :type (:type cfg)})

(defn construct-subsystems [sys-map]         ←—  Constructor driver
  (for [[name cfg] sys-map]
    (construct name cfg)))
```

The multimethod construct dispatches based on the system descriptor returned from describe-system and starts with a simple default that returns a map. The function construct-subsystems builds a seq of system objects based on the return values given by calls to construct. A quick run with the defaults in place should give you a seq of three generic system maps:

```
(construct-subsystems (:systems config))

;;=> ({:name :pump, :type :feeder}
;;    {:name :sim1, :type :sim}
;;    {:name :sim2, :type :sim})
```

You've put in place a simple system for dynamically constructing a map that describes in brief a subsystem in the hypothetical system. But in reality, you would probably want more specific types for certain subsystems. To see how you can do that, start with the simple case of building a type of object other than a map for the :pump subsystem:

```
(defmethod construct [:feeder nil]
  [_ cfg]
  (:descr cfg))

(construct-subsystems (:systems config))
;;=> ("Feeder system"
;;    {:name :sim1, :type :sim}
;;    {:name :sim2, :type :sim})
```

You create another method on the `construct` multimethod that deals with the descriptor `[:feeder null]`. Although in a real system you'd probably want a more agreeable type than a string to return, this exercise shows how you can extend your abstract factory function to build instances for the two `:sim` types:

```
(defrecord LowFiSim [name])
(defrecord HiFiSim  [name threads])
```

A complete program built using this abstract factory type of layout would probably have richer types adhering to system-like protocols, but because our goal is to show construction only, we've decided to keep things simple. Having said that, you can dispatch on a descriptor for each of the records to see the complete implementation.

Listing 17.10   Defining concrete factories using multimethods

```
(defmethod construct [:sim :low]        ◁── Factory for the LoFi type
  [name cfg]
  (->LowFiSim name))

(defmethod construct [:sim :high]       ◁── Factory for the HiFi type
  [name cfg]
  (->HiFiSim name (:threads cfg)))
```

The new concrete constructors dispatching from the low- and high-fidelity simulation systems work to build the precise implementations:

```
(construct-subsystems (:systems config))

;;=> ("Feeder system"
;;     #joy.patterns.abstract_factory.LowFiSim{:name :sim1}
;;     #joy.patterns.abstract_factory.HiFiSim {:name :sim2, :threads 2})
```

We could have used a simple `case` statement to implement a similar construction program, but we chose to use a multimethod-based approach because it's more open for extension. An added advantage of a multimethod-based factory is that it allows you to add project-specific functionality to the constructor, including, but not limited to, keyword arguments, default values, and validations.

BUILDER PATTERN

The creation of complex structures from representations is central to Clojure programming, although it's viewed differently from a similar object-oriented approach: the Builder pattern. In section 8.4, you used a simple data representation as the input to Clojure's `clojure.xml/emit` function to produce an analogous XML representation. If you prefer a different output representation, you can write another conversion function. If you prefer finer control over the constituent parts, you can write functions or multimethods for each, and specialize at runtime.

FAÇADE PATTERN

The use of Clojure namespaces, as discussed in section 9.1, is the most obvious way to provide a simplified façade for a more complex API. You can also use the varying levels of encapsulation (as outlined in section 2.4) for more localized façades.

ITERATOR PATTERN

Iteration in Clojure is defined through an adherence to the seq protocol, as outlined in section 5.1 and later elaborated on in section 9.3 about types and protocols.

DEPENDENCY INJECTION IN CLOJURE

Although not a classical pattern in the *Design Patterns* sense, dependency injection has become a de facto pattern for object-oriented languages that don't allow overridable class constructors. This condition requires that separate factory methods and/or classes create concrete instances conforming to a given interface. We sowed the seeds for this discussion in the previous section about how the Abstract Factory pattern is absorbed by multimethods. Recall the following distillations of the high- and low-fidelity simulation configurations:

```
(ns joy.patterns.di
  (:require [joy.patterns.abstract-factory :as factory]))

(def lofi {:type :sim, :descr "Lowfi sim", :fidelity :low})

(def hifi {:type :sim, :descr "Hifi sim", :fidelity :high, :threads 2})
```

As shown, the configurations are the focused simulation construction arguments and are useful in building instances of specific records:

```
(factory/construct :lofi lofi)

;;=> #joy.patterns.abstract_factory.LowFiSim{:name :lofi, ...}
```

Based on this code, we're effectively right back where we were in our discussion of abstract factories. But we can extend this idea into a discussion of dependency injection and how Clojure's core features subsume its paradigm. To start, let's define a set of protocols used to describe system-level and simulation capabilities.

Listing 17.11 Protocols describing system-level and simulation capabilities

```
(defprotocol Sys        ←— System is stopped and started
  (start! [sys])
  (stop!  [sys]))

(defprotocol Sim
  (handle [sim msg]))    ←— Sim handles messages
```

The protocols defined, Sys and Sim, define the set of capabilities available to higher-level system objects and specific simulation systems, respectively. If you were putting together an application to take advantage of these abstractions, you might start with a function build-system that uses the existing factory constructors to instantiate a system object and get it started.

Listing 17.12 Using abstract system construction and a system-level protocol

```
(defn build-system [name config]
  (let [sys (factory/construct name config)]
    (start! sys)
    sys))
```

Although it's nice that you have a system-builder function in place, you currently have nothing that adheres to the Sys protocol. You can take care of that by extending the joy.patterns.abstract_factory.LowFiSim record type to that protocol, as shown in the next listing.

Listing 17.13 Extending an existing type to the Sys and Sim protocols

```
(extend-type joy.patterns.abstract_factory.LowFiSim
  Sys
  (start! [this]
    (println "Started a lofi simulator."))      ◁— Sys behaviors are printouts
  (stop!  [this]
    (println "Stopped a lofi simulator."))

  Sim
  (handle [this msg]
    (* (:weight msg) 3.14)))      ◁— Sim behavior is an approximation
```

As shown, the Sys protocol is implemented for the LowFiSim type as simple printouts. You also extend the LowFiSim type to Sim, for good measure. To capture the spirit of what it means to be low fidelity, you perform a calculation using a weak approximation of pi. Now, observe what happens when you call the start! function with a new instance of the LowFiSim type:

```
(start! (factory/construct :lofi lofi))
;; Started a lofi simulator.
```

As you might have guessed, the implementation of the LowFiSim type's start! function was called, as evinced by the proper printout. Now, if you run the proper configuration parameters through the build-system function, you should see the same thing:

```
(build-system :sim1 lofi)
;; Started a lofi simulator.
;;=> #joy.patterns.abstract_factory.LowFiSim{:name :sim1, ...}
```

And if you ask an instance of a LowFiSim type to handle a message, you should see the low-fidelity behavior:

```
(handle (build-system :sim1 lofi) {:weight 42})
;;=> 131.88
```

This is interesting because it demonstrates that you can instantiate a specific type, adhering to a specific protocol, and based solely on configuration parameters.[7] The Dependency Injection pattern is usually more interesting when more than one type is involved. So, let's monkey with the HiFiSim type as well.

---

[7] Not only that, but you extend an existing type to a protocol of your design, without ever changing the original type.

Listing 17.14   Extending the existing `HiFiSim` type to `Sys` and `Sim`

```
(extend-type joy.patterns.abstract_factory.HiFiSim
  Sys
  (start! [this] (println "Started a hifi simulator."))
  (stop!  [this] (println "Stopped a hifi simulator."))

  Sim
  (handle [this msg]
    (Thread/sleep 5000)
    (* (:weight msg) 3.1415926535897932384626M)))
```

◁┐ **Sys implementations
  │ are printouts**

│ **High-fidelity calculation uses a**
◁┘ **more precise pi and takes longer**

Based on the extension shown, you'll see different behavior occurring if you change the system configuration:

```
(build-system :sim2 hifi)
;; Started a lofi simulator.
;;=> #joy.patterns.abstract_factory.HiFiSim{:name :sim2,...}

(handle (build-system :sim2 hifi) {:weight 42})
;; wait 5 seconds...
;;=> 131.9468914507713160154292M
```

Not only is the printout different from that of the previously instantiated, low-fidelity sim, but the message handler for the `HiFiSim` takes longer and is more precise in the number of decimal places. In simulation, you often instantiate low-fidelity and high-fidelity models for the purposes of speed, fallback, and the like. A useful pattern using both a high- and a low-fidelity model is to use the low-fidelity model as the immediate answer and then hope a high-fidelity answer eventually replaces it. The following listing shows a function that realizes this kind of usage pattern.

Listing 17.15   Calculating both a low- and a high-fidelity answer

```
(def excellent (promise))

(defn simulate [answer fast slow opts]
  (future (deliver answer (handle slow opts)))

  (handle fast opts))
```

│ **Calculate hifi on**
◁┘ **another thread**

◁── **Calculate lofi now**

The `excellent` promise is meant to store the high-fidelity answer, should it ever be delivered. In any case, the `simulate` function always returns a low-fidelity answer:

```
(simulate excellent
          (build-system :sim1 lofi)
          (build-system :sim2 hifi)
          {:weight 42})

;;=> 131.88
```

The answer 131.88 is the same as before when you ran the low-fidelity calculation. Because you passed in the `excellent` promise, you can check to see if you have a better answer:

```
(realized? excellent)
;;=> false
```

Clojure's `realize?` function is used to check whether *realizable* objects have a graspable representation. In the case of promises, they're realized if a value has been delivered. Additionally, you can use `realized?` to check whether all the slots in a lazy seq have been calculated or whether futures and delays have calculated values inside. It's been a few moments, so check the promise again:

```
;; wait a few seconds

(realized? excellent)
;;=> true

@excellent
;;=> 131.9468914507713160154292M
```

Because the `excellent` promise contains a high-fidelity answer, you could use it instead of the less-precise value.

Before we conclude our discussion of dependency injection, we'll provide one more example to hammer the point home. Imagine that, for the purposes of testing, you want to create a new kind of simulation that returns canned answers and tracks certain call conditions. In testing parlance, this type of object is known as a *mock*, which by virtue of its tracking behavior differentiates itself from a stub. Following a similar pattern of protocol extension in listings 17.16 and 17.17, you can create a mock simulation that will stand in for either the low- or high-fidelity models.

Listing 17.16   Creating a mock of a system

```
(ns joy.patterns.mock
  (:require [joy.patterns.abstract-factory :as factory]
            [joy.patterns.di :as di]))

(defrecord MockSim [name])

(def starts (atom 0))
```

The `starts` atom is meant to contain the number of times that the `times!` function is called overall.[8] Extending the `MockSim` record type to the relevant protocols is shown.

Listing 17.17   Extending a mock system to existing protocols.

```
(extend-type MockSim
  di/Sys
  (start! [this]                              Check that start! is
    (if (= 1 (swap! starts inc))         ◁┘  only called once
      (println "Started a mock simulator.")
      (throw (RuntimeException. "Called start! more than once."))))
  (stop!  [this] (println "Stopped a mock simulator.")))

  di/Sim
  (handle [_ _] 42))          ◁—  Return a canned answer
```

---

8 If you wanted to track these calls on a per-instance basis, then you would have to structure this differently—do you see how?

Whereas the LoFiSim and HiFiSim record types had default construction functions, MockSim has no such function. Instead, you can wire into the construct multimethod from afar.

Listing 17.18 Construction function for the mock system

```
(defmethod factory/construct [:mock nil]
  [nom _]
  (MockSim. nom))
```

That Clojure allows all the mock concerns to live in a single location is a powerful way to build and compose systems. We've often used this technique in our own code to build up applications from components adhering to well-defined protocols in a generic way. A simple system to pull this together is shown in the following listing.

Listing 17.19 Tying together a system via configuration

```
(ns joy.patterns.app
  (require [joy.patterns.di :as di]))

(def config {:type :mock, :lib 'joy.patterns.mock})
```

The configuration to describe mock instances is similar to that of the high- and low-fidelity simulations, except for something new: the :lib key is mapped to a symbol corresponding to the namespace where the mock simulation code exists. This symbol helps to fully realize a system built with Clojure that allows the injection of dependencies, as shown next.

Listing 17.20 Injecting dependencies

```
(defn initialize [name cfg]
  (let [lib (:lib cfg)]
    (require lib)
    (di/build-system name cfg)))
```

The initialize function knows nothing about the type of object being built. But by extracting the symbol held at :lib, it can dynamically require the correct namespace and therefore trigger the correct multimethod overload and protocol extensions:

```
(di/handle (initialize :mock-sim config) {})
;; Started a mock simulator.
;;=> 42
```

As shown, the initialization routine creates the correct type of object (MockSim) and delegates the start logic to the underlying machinery. Additionally, the call to handle resolves to the correct canned implementation. Now you can check to see whether the mock simulation checks for the number of calls to start!:

```
(initialize :mock-sim config)

;; java.lang.RuntimeException: Called start! more than once.
```

The mock simulation indeed checks that the correct call structure is observed. You can use this approach as the basis for a test suite and as a general-purpose way to build systems—and you have.[9]

We could go further with this survey of design patterns, but to do so would belabor the point: most of what are known as design patterns are either invisible or trivial to implement in Clojure. But what about the Prototype pattern, you ask? You implemented the UDP in section 9.2. Decorators or chain of responsibility? Why not use a macro that returns a function built from a list of forms spliced into the -> or ->> macro? Proxies would likely be implemented as closures, and so would commands. The list goes on and on, and in the end you must face the inevitable: Clojure changes the way that you think.

17.4 Error handling and debugging

Our goal throughout this book has been to show the proper way to write Clojure code, with mostly deferral and hand-waving regarding error handling and debugging. In this section, we'll cover these topics with what you might view as a unique twist, depending on your programming background.

17.4.1 Error handling

As we showed in figure 10.7, there are two directions for handling errors. The first, and likely most familiar, refers to the passive handling of exceptions bubbling outward from inner functions. But when using Clojure's dynamic var binding, you can achieve a more active mode of error handling, where handlers are pushed into inner functions. In section 10.6.1, we mentioned that the `binding` form is used to create thread-local bindings, but its utility isn't limited to this use case. In its purest form, dynamic scope is a structured form of a side effect (Steele 1978). You can use it to push vars down a call stack from the outer layers of a function, nesting into the inner layers: a technique that we'll demonstrate next.

DYNAMIC TREE TRAVERSAL

In section 8.4, you built a simple tree structure for a domain model where each node was of this form:

```
{:tag <node form>, :attrs {}, :content [<nodes>]}
```

As it turns out, the traversal of a tree built from such nodes is straightforward using mundane recursion:

```
(defn traverse [node f]
  (when node
    (f node)
    (doseq [child (:content node)]
      (traverse child f))))
```

---

[9] Many of the principles described in this section are explored by Stuart Sierra in various talks and especially in his Component library at https://github.com/stuartsierra/component.

For each node in the tree, the function f is called with the node, and then each of the node's children is traversed in turn. Observe how traverse works for a single root node:

```
(traverse {:tag :flower :attrs {:name "Tanpopo"} :content []}
          println)

; {:tag :flower, :attrs {:name Tanpopo}, :content []}
```

But it's much more interesting if you traverse trees larger than a single node. Let's build a quick tree from an XML representation using Clojure's clojure.:

xml/parse function:

```
(use '[clojure.xml :as xml])

(def DB
  (-> "<zoo>
         <pongo>
           <animal>orangutan</animal>
         </pongo>
         <panthera>
           <animal>Spot</animal>
           <animal>lion</animal>
           <animal>Lopshire</animal>
         </panthera>
       </zoo>"
      .getBytes
      (java.io.ByteArrayInputStream.)
      xml/parse))
```

The DB var contains an animal listing for a small zoo. Note that two of the animals listed have the elements Spot and Lopshire; both are seemingly out of order for a zoo. Therefore, you can write a function to handle these nefarious intruders.

Listing 17.21   Handling nefarious tree nodes with exceptions

```
(defn ^:dynamic handle-weird-animal        ⟵── Define the default handler
  [{[name] :content}]
  (throw (Exception. (str name " must be 'dealt with'"))))
```

The default handler handle-weird-animal is set as ^:dynamic to foster something we like to call *dynamic delegation.* By setting up the default function this way, you can dynamically bind specialized handlers, as we'll show soon. First, though, you need a function to make the actual delegation.

Listing 17.22   Example of dynamic delegation

```
(defmulti visit :tag)

(defmethod visit :animal [{[name] :content :as animal}]
  (case name
    "Spot"     (handle-weird-animal animal)
    "Lopshire" (handle-weird-animal animal)
    (println name)))
```
Dynamic delegation

The multimethod `visit` can be used as the input function to the `traverse` function; it triggers only when a node with the `:tag` attribute of `:animal` is encountered. When the method triggered on `:animal` is executed, the node `:content` is destructured and checked against the offending `Spot` and `Lopshire` values. When found, the devious node is then passed along to an error handler `handle-weird-animal` for reporting. By default, the handler `handle-weird-animal` throws an exception. This model of error reporting and handling is the inside-out model of exceptions and stops processing cold:

```
(traverse DB visit)
; orangutan
; java.lang.Exception: Spot must be 'dealt with'
```

You've managed to identify `Spot`, but the equally repugnant `Lopshire` escapes your grasp. It would be nice to instead use a different version of `handle-weird-animal` that allows you to both identify and deal with every such weird creature. You could pass `handle-weird-animal` along as an argument to be used as an error continuation,[10] but that would pollute the argument list of every function along the way. Likewise, you could inject `catch` blocks at a point further down the call chain, say in `visit`, but you might not be able to change the source; and if you could, it would make for more insidious pollution. Instead, using a dynamic binding is a perfect solution, because it lets you attach specific error handlers at any depth in the stack according to their appropriate context:

```
(defmulti handle-weird  (fn [{[name] :content}] name))

(defmethod handle-weird "Spot" [_]
  (println "Transporting Spot to the circus."))

(defmethod handle-weird "Lopshire" [_]
  (println "Signing Lopshire to a book deal."))

(binding [handle-weird-animal handle-weird]
  (traverse DB visit))

; orangutan
; Transporting Spot to the circus.
; lion
; Signing Lopshire to a book deal.
```

As you might expect, this approach works across threads to allow for thread-specific handlers:

```
(def _ (future
         (binding [handle-weird-animal #(println (:content %))]
           (traverse DB visit))))
; orangutan
; [Spot]
; lion
; [Lopshire]
```

---

[10] See section 7.3 for more on continuation-passing style.

What we've outlined here is a simplistic model for a grander error-handling scheme. Using dynamic scope via `binding` is the preferred way to handle recoverable errors in a context-sensitive manner.

17.4.2 Debugging

The natural progression of debugging techniques as discovered by a newcomer to Clojure follows a fairly standard progression:

1 `(println)`
2 A macro to make `(println)` inclusion simpler
3 Some variation on debugging as discussed in this section
4 IDEs, monitoring, and profiling tools

Many Clojure programmers stay at step 1, because it's simple to understand and also highly useful, but there are better ways. After all, you're dealing with Clojure—a highly dynamic programming environment. Observe the following function:

```
(defn div [n d] (int (/ n d)))
```

The function `div` divides two numbers and returns an integer value. You can break `div` in a number of ways, but the most obvious is to call it with zero as the denominator: `(div 10 0)`. Such an example probably wouldn't give you cause for concern if it failed, because the conditions under which it fails are limited, well known, and easily identified. But not all errors are this simple, and the use of `println` is fairly limited. Instead, a better tool would likely be a generic breakpoint[11] that could be inserted at will and used to provide a debug console for the current valid execution context. It would work as follows:

```
(defn div [n d] (break) (int (/ n d)))
(div 10 0)
debug=>
```

At this prompt, you can query the current lexical environment, experiment with different code, and then resume the previous execution. As it turns out, such a tool is within your grasp. Most of the behavior desired at this prompt is already provided by the standard Clojure REPL, so you can reuse that and extend it from inside a macro expansion to satisfy your particular requirements.

A BREAKPOINT MACRO

We hope that by the end of this section, you'll understand that Lisps in general, and Clojure in particular, provide an environment where the entire language truly is "always available" (Graham 1993). First, it's interesting to note that the Clojure REPL is available and extensible via the Clojure REPL itself, via the `clojure.main/repl` function. By accessing the REPL implementation directly, you can customize it as you see fit for application-specific tasks.

---

[11] The code in this section is based on `debug-repl`, which was created by the amazing George Jahad, extended by Alex Osborne, and integrated into Swank-Clojure by Hugo Duncan.

Typing (clojure.main/repl) at the REPL seemingly does nothing, but rest assured you've started a sub-REPL. What use is this? To start, the repl function takes a number of named parameters, each used to customize the launched REPL in different ways. Let's use three such hooks—:prompt, :eval, and :read—to fulfill a breakpoint functionality.

OVERRIDING THE REPL'S READER

The repl function's :read hook takes a function of two arguments: one corresponding to a desired display prompt, and one to a desired exit form. You want the debug console to provide convenience functions—you'd like it to show all the available lexical bindings and to resume execution. It also needs to be able to read valid Clojure forms, but because that's too complex a task, you'll instead farm that functionality out to Clojure's default REPL reader.

Listing 17.23   A modest debug console reader

```
(defn readr [prompt exit-code]
  (let [input (clojure.main/repl-read prompt exit-code)]    ◁─┐ Delegate to
    (if (= input ::tl)      ◁─┐                                │ core read
      exit-code               │ Check for a top-level flag
      input)))
```

You can begin testing the reader immediately:

```
(readr #(print "invisible=> ") ::exit)
[1 2 3]   ;; this is what you type

;=> [1 2 3]

(readr #(print "invisible=> ") ::exit)
::tl   ;; this is what you type

;=> :user/exit
```

The prompt you specified isn't printed, and typing ::tl at the prompt does nothing because the readr function isn't yet provided to the repl as its :read hook. But before you do that, you need to provide a function for the :eval hook. Needless to say, this is a more complex task.

OVERRIDING THE REPL'S EVALUATOR

In order to evaluate things in context, you first need to garner the bindings in the current context. Fortunately, Clojure macros provide an implicit argument &env that's a map of the local bindings available at macro-expansion time. You can extract from &env the values associated with the bindings and zip them up with their names into a map for the local context, as shown next.

Listing 17.24   Creating a map of the local context using &env

```
(defmacro local-context []              │ Use the special &env
  (let [symbols (keys &env)]    ◁─┘
    (zipmap (map (fn [sym] `(quote ~sym))    ◁─┐ Zip up the local names
                 symbols)                       │ with local values
            symbols)))
```

One interesting point is the use of the `&env` symbol. This special symbol holds the value of the bindings available to the macro in which it occurs. The bindings are of a special type that is opaque to your direct inspection, but by putting them into the return map you can build a Clojure data structure from them for direct use and manipulation. Observe `local-context` in action:

```
(local-context)
;=> {}

(let [a 1, b 2, c 3]
  (let [b 200]
    (local-context)))
;=> {a 1, b 200, c 3}
```

The `local-context` macro provides a map to the most immediate lexical bindings, which is what you want. But you want to provide a way to evaluate expressions with this contextual bindings map. Wouldn't you know it, the `contextual-eval` function from section 8.1 fits the bill. Now that you have the bulk of the implementation complete, you can hook into the `repl` function to provide a breakpoint facility.

PUTTING IT ALL TOGETHER

The hard parts are done, and wiring them into a usable debugging console is relatively easy.

> Listing 17.25   Implementation of a breakpoint macro

```
(defmacro break []
  `(clojure.main/repl
     :prompt #(print "debug=> ")
     :read readr
     :eval (partial contextual-eval (local-context))))
```

Using this macro, you can debug the original `div` function:

```
(defn div [n d] (break) (int (/ n d)))
(div 10 0)
debug=>
```

Querying locals to find the "problem" is simple:

```
debug=> n
;=> 10

debug=> d
;=> 0

debug=> (local-context)
;=> {n 10, d 0}

debug=> ::tl
; java.lang.ArithmeticException: Divide by zero
```

There's the problem! You passed in a zero as the denominator. You should fix that.

MULTIPLE BREAKPOINTS, AND BREAKPOINTS IN MACROS

What would be the point if you couldn't set multiple breakpoints? Fortunately, you can, as shown in the following listing.

Listing 17.26   Using multiple breakpoints in the `keys-apply` function

```
(defn keys-apply [f ks m]
  (break)
  (let [only (select-keys m ks)]
    (break)
    (zipmap (keys only) (map f (vals only)))))

(keys-apply inc [:a :b] {:a 1, :b 2, :c 3})

debug=> only
; java.lang.Exception: Unable to resolve symbol: only in this context
debug=> ks
;=> [:a :b]
debug=> m
;=> {:a 1, :b 2, :c 3}
debug=> ::tl
debug=> only
;=> {:b 2, :a 1}
debug=> ::tl
;=> {:a 2, :b 3}
```

And you can also use breakpoints in the body of a macro (in its expansion, not its logic), as shown next.

Listing 17.27   Using a breakpoint in the `awhen` macro

```
(defmacro awhen [expr & body]
  (break)
  `(let [~'it ~expr]
     (if ~'it
       (do (break) ~@body))))

(awhen [1 2 3] (it 2))
debug=> it
; java.lang.Exception: Unable to resolve symbol: it in this context
debug=> expr
;=> [1 2 3]
debug=> body
;=> ((it 2))
debug=> ::tl
debug=> it
;=> [1 2 3]
debug=> (it 1)
;=> 2
debug=> ::tl
;=> 3
```

There's much room for improvement, but we believe our point has been made. Having access to the underpinnings of the language allows you to create a powerful debugging environment with little code. We've run out of ideas, so we'll say our credo only once more, and we hope by now you believe us: Clojure changes the way that you think.

17.5   *Fare thee well*

This book possesses many lacunae, but it's this way by design. In many cases, we've skipped approaches to solving problems via a certain route to avoid presenting non-idiomatic code. In many examples, we've left exposed wiring. For example, the defcontract macro requires that you partially apply the contract to the function under constraint instead of providing a comprehensive contract-overlay façade. It was our goal to leave wiring exposed, because exposed wiring can be explored, tampered with, and ultimately enhanced—which we hope you'll find the motivation to do. We've worked hard to provide a vast array of relevant references, should you choose to further enhance your understanding of the workings and motivations for Clojure. But it's likely that we've missed some excellent resources, and we hope you can uncover them in time. Finally, this wasn't a survey of Clojure, and many of the functions available to you weren't used in this book. We provide some pointers in the resource list, but there's no way we could do justice to the libraries and applications mentioned and those unmentioned. We implore you to look deeper into the functionality of not only Clojure, but also the rich ecology of libraries and applications that have sprung up in its relatively short life span.

Thank you for taking the time to read this book; we hope it was as much a pleasure to read as it was for us to write. Likewise, we hope you'll continue your journey with Clojure. Should you choose to diverge from this path, then we hope some of what you've learned has helped you to view the art of programming in a new light. Clojure is an opinionated language, but it and most of its community believe these opinions can work to enhance the overall state of affairs in our software industry. The onus is on us to make our software robust, performant, and extensible. We believe the path toward these goals lies with Clojure.

Do you?

—FOGUS AND HOUSER 2014

resources

Miscellaneous resources

Abadi, Martin, and Luca Cardelli. 1996. *A Theory of Objects.* New York: Springer. Although not a mathematical concept, object-oriented programming has obtained rigor with this gem.

Abelson, Harold, and Gerald Jay Sussman. 1988. "Lisp: A Language for Stratified Design." MIT, *AI Memo* 986.

———. 1996. *Structure and Interpretation of Computer Programs.* Cambridge, MA: MIT Press. There is no better book for learning Scheme and the fine art of programming.

Abiteboul, Serge, Richard Hull, and Victor Vianu. 1995. *Foundations of Databases.* Boston: Addison-Wesley. Clojure's `clojure.set` namespace is actually modeled more on the named conjunctive algebra, for which this book provides a great reference.

Armstrong, Joe. 2007. *Programming Erlang.* Raleigh, NC: Pragmatic Bookshelf.

———. 2007. "A History of Erlang." *Proceedings of the Third ACM SIGPLAN Conference on History of Programming Languages.*

Bagwell, Phil. 2001. *Ideal Hash Trees.* Technical report. Clojure's persistent data structures owe a lot to Phil Bagwell's paper.

Baker, Henry. 1993. "Equal Rights for Functional Objects or, The More Things Change, The More They Are the Same." ACM SIGPLAN OOPS *Messenger* 4, no. 4.

Beck, Kent. 2002. *Test Driven Development: By Example.* Boston: Addison-Wesley.

Bloch, Joshua. 2008. *Effective Java.* Upper Saddle River, NJ: Addison-Wesley.

Boncz, Peter, Zukowski Marcin, and Niels Nes. 2005. "MonetDB/X100: Hyper-Pipelining Query Execution." *Proceedings of the CIDR Conference.* This paper motivated the implementation of chunked sequences.

Bratko, Ivan. 2000. *PROLOG: Programming for Artificial Intelligence.* New York: Addison Wesley.

Budd, Timothy. 1995. *Multiparadigm Programming in Leda.* Reading, MA: Addison-Wesley. This is an expanded discussion of the complexities wrought from a mono-paradigm approach to software development.

Clinger, William. 1998. "Proper Tail Recursion and Space Efficiency." *Proceedings of the ACM SIGPLAN 1998 Conference on Programming Language Design and Implementation.*

Cormen, Thomas, Charles Leiserson, Ronald Rivest, and Clifford Stein. 2009. *Introduction to Algorithms.* Cambridge, MA: MIT Press. This is a great reference on algorithmic complexity and Big-O, and as an added bonus, you could use it to stop a charging rhinoceros.

Crockford, Douglas. 2008. *JavaScript: The Good Parts.* Yahoo Press.

Date, C.J. 2009. *SQL and Relational Theory: How to Write Accurate SQL Code.* Sebastopol, CA: O'Reilly.

Dijkstra, Edsger Wijbe. 1959. "A Note on Two Problems in Connexion with Graphs." *Numerische Mathematik* 1, no. 1. You could change the h function in listing 7.3 to (defn dijkstra-estimate-cost [step-cost-est sz y x] 0) to conform to the ideal presented in this paper.

Flanagan, David. 2006. *JavaScript: The Definitive Guide.* Sebastopol, CA: O'Reilly.

Forman, Ira, and Nate Forman. 2004. *Java Reflection in Action*. Greenwich, CT: Manning. Although reflection provides some meta-level manipulation, it's quite apart from the notion of functions as data.

Friedl, Jeffrey. 1997. *Mastering Regular Expressions*. Sebastopol, CA: O'Reilly.

Friedman, Daniel, Mitchell Wand, and Christopher T. Haynes. 2001. *Essentials of Programming Languages*. Cambridge, MA: MIT Press.

Friedman, Daniel, Oleg Kiselyov, and William Byrd. 2006. *The Reasoned Schemer*. Cambridge, MA: MIT Press. A beautiful book that describes, in detail, a logic engine in less than 100 lines of code.

Gabriel, Richard, and Kent Pitman. 2001. "Technical Issues of Separation in Function Cells and Value Cells." Originally published in *Lisp and Symbolic Computation* 1, no. 1 (1988). This is a more thorough examination of the differences between Lisp-1 and Lisp-2.

Gamma, Erich, Richard Helm, Ralph Johnson, and John Vlissides. 1995. *Design Patterns: Elements of Reusable Object-Oriented Software*. Reading, MA: Addison-Wesley.

Ghosh, Debasish. 2010. *DSLs in Action*. Greenwich, CT: Manning. There is a much finer level of distinction determining what constitutes whole cloth, including that between internal and external DSLs. In this book, we focus on the classical Lisp model of internal DSLs, but *DSLs in Action* provides a survey of many DSL-creation techniques.

Glickstein, Bob. 1997. *Writing GNU Emacs Extensions*. Sebastopol, CA: O'Reilly.

Goetz, Brian. 2006. *Java Concurrency in Practice*. Upper Saddle River, NJ: Addison-Wesley. Why haven't you read this yet?

Goldberg, David. 1991. "What Every Computer Scientist Should Know About Floating-Point Arithmetic." *Computing Surveys* (March).

Graham, Paul. 1993. *On Lisp*. Englewood Cliffs, NJ: Prentice Hall. Is there any book or any author more influential to the current generation of dynamic programmers than Graham and *On Lisp*?

———. 1995. *ANSI Common Lisp*. Englewood Cliffs, NJ: Prentice Hall.

Gray, Jim, and Andreas Reuter. 1992. *Transaction Processing: Concepts and Techniques*. San Mateo, CA: Morgan Kaufmann Publishers.

Halloway, Stuart. 2009. "Clojure Is a Better Java Than Java." Presented at the Greater Atlanta Software Symposium. The origin of the phrase "Java.next" most likely stems from this talk by Halloway.

Hart, Peter, Nils Nilsson, and Bertram Raphael. 1968. "A Formal Basis for the Heuristic Determination of Minimum Cost Paths." *IEEE Transactions on Systems Science and Cybernetics in Systems Science and Cybernetics* 4, no. 2.

Hart, Timothy. 1963. *MACRO Definitions for LISP*. MIT *AI Memo* AIM-57 (October). Existing copies of this amazing three-page memo are blurred to the point of near incomprehensibility. But if you take the time to digest its contents, you'll understand how macros are facilitated by a pre-evaluation-evaluation step! That is, the new algorithm for evaluation in Lisp could be: 1) read; 2) eval macros; 3) eval what comes out of the macros.

Heinlein, Robert. 1966. *The Moon Is a Harsh Mistress*. New York: Putnam. We had considered offering an implementation of Mike as an appendix, but we ran over our page count.

Herlihy, Maurice, and Eliot Moss. 1993. "Transactional Memory: Architectural Support for Lock-Free Data Structures." *Proceedings of the 20th Annual International Symposium on Computer Architecture* 21, no. 2 (May). In our opinion, a very lucid description of transactional memory.

Herlihy, Maurice, and Nir Shavit. 2008. *The Art of Multiprocessor Programming*. Amsterdam; Boston: Elsevier/Morgan Kaufmann.

Hewitt, Carl, Peter Bishop, and Richard Steiger. 1973. "A Universal Modular ACTOR Formalism for Artificial Intelligence." *Proceedings of the Third International Joint Conference on Artificial Intelligence*.

Hickey, Rich. 2009. "Are We There Yet?" Presented at the JVM Languages Summit. This wonderful presentation made firm the popular view of Rich as Philosopher Programmer.

Hofstadter, Douglas. 1979. *Gödel, Escher, Bach: An Eternal Golden Braid.* New York: Basic Books. See the sections "Classes and Instances," "The Prototype Principle," and "The Splitting-off of Instances from Classes" for more detail of the topics in section 9.2.

Hoyte, Doug. 2008. *Let Over Lambda.* Lulu.com. This is an amazing look into the mind-bending power of Common Lisp macros that provided the motivation for the DSLs section of this book. It will blow your mind—in a good way.

Hudak, Paul. 2000. *The Haskell School of Expression: Learning Functional Programming Through Multimedia.* New York: Cambridge University Press.

Huet, Gerard. 1997. "Functional Pearl: The Zipper." *Journal of Functional Programming* 7, no. 5.

Hutton, Graham. 1999. "A Tutorial on the Universality and Expressiveness of fold." *Journal of Functional Programming* 9, no. 4.

Iverson, Kenneth. 1962. *A Programming Language.* New York: Wiley. A beautifully written book that strives to find a universal notation of computation that eventually became the APL programming language.

Kahan, William, and Joseph Darcy. 1998. "How Java's Floating-Point Hurts Everyone Everywhere." Presented at the ACM Workshop on Java for High-Performance Network Computing. This paper provides more information on the cyclopean nightmares awaiting you in Java floating point.

Keene, Sonya. 1989. *Object-Oriented Programming in Common Lisp: A Programmer's Guide to CLOS.* Boston: Addison-Wesley. The best book on CLOS ever written.

Knuth, Donald. 1997. *The Art of Computer Programming: Volume 1 - Fundamental Algorithms.* Reading, MA: Addison-Wesley. This book goes into exquisite detail about the primary characteristics of FIFO queues and is highly recommended reading.

———. 1998. *The Art of Computer Programming, Vol. 3: Sorting and Searching.* Reading, MA: Addison-Wesley. Running quick-sort on a sorted sequence is an $O(n^2)$ operation, which for our implementation in chapter 6 completely defeats its laziness.

Koenig, Dierk, Andrew Glover, Paul King, Guilaume LaForge, and Jon Skeet. 2007. *Groovy in Action.* Greenwich, CT: Manning.

Kuki, Hirondo, and William James Cody. 1973. "A Statistical Study of the Accuracy of Floating Point Number Systems." *Communications of the ACM* 16, no. 4.

Laddad, Ramnivas. 2003. *AspectJ in Action: Practical Aspect-Oriented Programming.* Greenwich, CT: Manning. We don't do justice to the notion of aspects—so read this instead.

Levin, Mike. 1963. LISP 1.5 Library, November 1963. Computer History Museum, Herbert Stoyan Collection on LISP Programming (lot X5687.2010). Available on Paul McJones's Lisp history archive at http://mng.bz/5CAa. This archive is pure gold.

Martin, Robert. 2002. *Agile Software Development: Principles, Patterns, and Practices.* Upper Saddle River, NJ: Prentice Hall.

McCarthy, John. 1960. "Recursive Functions of Symbolic Expressions and Their Computation by Machine, Part I." *Communications of the ACM* 3, no. 4. This is the essay that started it all.

———. 1962. *LISP 1.5 Programmer's Manual.* Cambridge, MA: MIT Press. Lisp had an array type at least as early as 1962. Sadly, this fact is little known.

McConnell, Steve. 2004. *Code Complete: A Practical Handbook of Software Construction.* Redmond, WA: Microsoft Press.

Meyer, Bertrand. 1991. *Eiffel: The Language.* New York: Prentice Hall. The programming language Eiffel relies heavily on contract-based programming methodologies, a cornerstone element of Fogus's philosophy of Apperception-Driven Development.

———. 2000. *Object-Oriented Software Construction.* Upper Saddle River, NJ: Prentice Hall.

Michie, Donald. 1968. "Memo Functions and Machine Learning." *Nature* 218.

Mooers, Calvin, and Peter Deutsch. 1965. "TRAC, A Text-Handling Language." ACM, *Proceedings of the 1965 20th National Conference.*

Moseley, Ben, and Peter Marks. 2006. "Out of the Tar Pit." Presented at SPA2006.

Mozgovoy, Maxim. 2009. *Algorithms, Languages, Automata, and Compilers: A Practical Approach.* Sudbury, MA: Jones and Bartlett Publishers.

Noble, James, and Brian Foote. 2003. "Attack of the Clones." *Proceedings of the 2002 Conference on Pattern Languages of Programs 13.* The clone function is inspired by this paper.

Norvig, Peter. 1991. *Paradigms of Artificial Intelligence Programming: Case Studies in Common Lisp.* San Francisco: Morgan Kaufman Publishers.

Odersky, Martin, Lex Spoon, and Bill Venners. 2008. *Programming in Scala: A Comprehensive Step-by-Step Guide.* Mountain View, CA: Artima.

Okasaki, Chris. 1996. "The Role of Lazy Evaluation in Amortized Data Structures." Presented at the International Conference on Functional Programming. This is a much more thorough discussion of incremental versus monolithic computation.

———. 1999. *Purely Functional Datastructures.* Cambridge University Press. Chris Okasaki to the rescue again! Clojure's persistent queue implementation is based on Okasaki's batched queue from this seminal work.

Olsen, Russ. 2007. *Design Patterns in Ruby.* Upper Saddle River, NJ: Addison-Wesley.

Papadimitriou, Christos. 1986. *Theory of Database Concurrency Control.* New York: Computer Science Press, Inc.

Pierce, Benjamin. 2002. *Types and Programming Languages.* Cambridge, MA: MIT Press. Fun fact: representing numbers using lambda calculus is known as *church encoding.* The church-encoded number 9 would be represented as (fn [f] (fn [x] (f (f (f (f (f (f (f (f (f x))))))))))) in Clojure.

Raymond, Eric. 2003. *The Art of Unix Programming.* Reading, MA: Addison-Wesley Professional.

Rosenberg, Doug, Mark Collins-Cope, and Matt Stephens. 2005. *Agile Development with ICONIX Process: People, Process, and Pragmatism.* Berkeley, CA: Apress.

Shavit, Nir, and Dan Touitou. 1997. "Software Transactional Memory." *Distributed Computing* 10, no. 2 (February). This paper introduced the first software model of transactional memory.

Skeel, Robert. 1992. "Roundoff Error and the Patriot Missile." *SIAM News* 25, no. 4.

Steele, Guy L. 1977. "Lambda: the Ultimate GOTO." ACM, *Proceedings of the 1977 Annual Conference.*

———. 1990. *Common LISP: The Language.* Bedford, MA: Digital Press. This is a very witty book in addition to being packed with information.

Steele, Guy L., and Gerald Sussman. 1978. "The Art of the Interpreter." MIT, *AI Memo* 453.

Stewart, Ian. 1995. *Concepts of Modern Mathematics.* New York: Dover. These Dover math books are often true gems. It would be great to see an adventurous publisher print a similar series revolving around C.S.-relevant topics—monads, category theory, lambda calculus, and so on.

Sussman, Gerald, and Guy L. Steele. 1975. "Scheme: An Interpreter for the Extended Lambda Calculus." *Higher-Order and Symbolic Computation* 11, no. 4. This is a discussion of Scheme's early implementation of lexical closures.

Symbolics Inc. 1986. *Reference Guide to Symbolics Common Lisp: Language Concepts.* Symbolics Release 7 Document Set.

Thompson, Simon. 1999. *Haskell: The Craft of Functional Programming.* Reading, MA: Addison-Wesley.

Ullman, Jeffrey. 1988. *Principles of Database & Knowledge-Base Systems Vol. 1: Classical Database Systems.* Rockville, MD: Computer Science Press.

Ungar, David, and Randal Smith. 1987. "SELF: The Power of Simplicity." Presented at the Conference on Object-Oriented Programming Systems, Languages, and Applications (OOPSLA), Orlando. The Self programming language is likely the greatest influence on prototypal inheritance.

Van Roy, Peter, and Seif Haridi. 2004. *Concepts, Techniques, and Models of Computer Programming.* Cambridge, MA: MIT Press.

Wadler, Philip. 1989. "Theorems for Free!" Presented at the Fourth International Conference on Functional Programming and Computer Architecture.

Wampler, Dean, and Alex Payne. 2009. *Programming Scala.* Sebastopol, CA: O'Reilly.

Whitehead, Alfred North. 1929. *Process and Reality: An Essay in Cosmology.* Cambridge University Press. For a general overview of Whitehead, see *The Wit And Wisdom of Alfred North Whitehead* by A.H. Johnson (Boston: Beacon Press, 1947).

Williams, Laurie. 2002. *Pair Programming Illuminated.* Boston: Addison-Wesley Professional. The limitations of the book format only shadow the idealistic model of pair programming.

Online resources

Braithwaite, Reginald. 2007. "Why Why Functional Programming Matters Matters." http://mng.bz/2pZP. This column discusses a language-level separation of concerns.

Clementson, Bill. 2008. "Clojure Could Be to Concurrency-Oriented Programming What Java Was to OOP." http://mng.bz/6S95. A much deeper discussion concerning Erlang actors and Clojure agents.

Dekorte, Steve. Io. http://iolanguage.com.

Fogus, Michael. 2009. Lithp. http://github.com/fogus/lithp.

Fowler, Martin. 2005. "Event Sourcing." http://mng.bz/5q9A. A very nice article about the motivations, history, and implementation of event sourcing. At least one of the authors of this book has studied this page intently.

———. 2005. "Fluent Interface." http://mng.bz/e2r5.

———. 2007. "Mocks Aren't Stubs." http://mng.bz/mq95.

———. 2011. "Memory Image." http://mng.bz/6s59. Boils an event-sourcing model down to the basic idea of state as a result of stored events. As always, Fowler presents a lucid explanation.

Graham, Paul. Arc. www.paulgraham.com/arc.html.

———. 2001. "What Made Lisp Different." www.paulgraham.com/diff.html. As Graham states, "The whole language always available" appears as a theme throughout this book.

Hickey, Rich. 2012. "The Database as a Value." Presented at QCon NY. www.infoq.com/presentations/Datomic-Database-Value. This presentation describes the architecture and design motivations behind the Datomic database.

Joswig, Rainer. 2005. "DSLs in Lisp, an Example for an Advanced DSL Development Technique in Lisp." http://archive.is/KKCLp. Rainer Joswig is a fount of Lisp (especially Common Lisp) wisdom, anecdotes, and technical guidance.

Krukow, Karl. 2009. "Understanding Clojure's PersistentVector Implementation." http://mng.bz/0Fjo.

Lindholm, Tim, and Frank Yellin. 1999. Java Language and Virtual Machine Specifications. http://java.sun.com/docs/books/jvms/.

Norvig, Peter. 1998. "Design Patterns in Dynamic Programming." http://norvig.com/design-patterns/. The section in this book on design patterns was inspired by this presentation.

———. 2011. "Solving Every Sudoku Puzzle." http://norvig.com/sudoku.html. Norvig's Python solver uses search and constraint propagation explicitly rather than using a logic library such as core.logic that provides these features as part of the operational logic. It's a great article and well worth reading, especially if you wish to learn more about constraints or Sudoku in general. Included in this post are numerous boards with multiple solutions, a few of which send our solver into spasms.

Pike, Rob. 2012. "Concurrency Is Not Parallelism." http://vimeo.com/49718712. Presented at Heroku's Waza conference. Contains nice visualizations of concurrent designs and a quick introduction to the Go programming language.

Tarver, Mark. 2008. "Functional Programming in Qi." http://mng.bz/Jmi0. Some programming languages perform partial application automatically when a function is supplied with fewer than the expected number of arguments. One such language is Qi.

————. 2009. "The Next Lisp: Back to the Future." http://mng.bz/qVfz. The notion of Lisp as a programming language genotype is explored.

W3C. 2013. Web Audio API. W3C Working Draft 10 (October). www.w3.org/TR/webaudio/. A nice reference to the Web Audio API that will serve as the basis for an upcoming talk entitled "The Sound of Functional Programming."

_why. Shoes. http://github.com/shoes/shoes.

Yegge, Steve. 2006. "Execution in the Kingdom of Nouns." http://mng.bz/E4MB.

————. 2008. "The Universal Design Pattern." http://mng.bz/6531. Like many programmers of our generation, we were in many ways inspired and influenced by Steve Yegge's work—which is why we asked him to write the foreword to the first edition of this book.

index

MORE TITLES FROM MANNING

Clojure in Action, Second Edition
by Amit Rathore

    ISBN: 9781617291524
    400 pages
    $49.99
    September 2014

Big Data
Principles and best practices of scalable realtime data systems
by Nathan Marz and James Warren

    ISBN: 9781617290343
    425 pages
    $49.99
    October 2014

For ordering information go to www.manning.com